CONTRACT LAW

LONGMAN LAW SERIES

GENERAL EDITORS
PROFESSOR I. H. DENNIS, *University College London*
PROFESSOR R. W. RIDEOUT, *University College London*
PROFESSOR J. A. USHER, *University of Edinburgh*

PUBLISHED TITLES
PETER STONE, *The Conflict of Laws*
CHRISTOPHER HARDING AND ANN SHERLOCK,
European Community Law: Text and Materials
ANDREW LE SUEUR AND MAURICE SUNKIN, *Public Law*
ANDREW CHOO, *Evidence: Text and Materials*
ROGER J. SMITH, *Property Law*
ROGER J. SMITH, *Property Law – Cases and Materials*

CONTRACT LAW

ROGER HALSON

University of Hull

Longman

An imprint of **Pearson Education**

Harlow, England · London · New York · Reading, Massachusetts · San Francisco
Toronto · Don Mills, Ontario · Sydney · Tokyo · Singapore · Hong Kong · Seoul
Taipei · Cape Town · Madrid · Mexico City · Amsterdam · Munich · Paris · Milan

Pearson Education Limited
Edinburgh Gate
Harlow
Essex CM20 2JE
England

and Associated Companies throughout the world

Visit us on the World Wide Web at:
www.pearsoneduc.com

First published in Great Britain 2001

© Pearson Education Limited 2001

The right of Roger Halson to be identified as author of
this work has been asserted by him in accordance with
the Copyright, Designs and Patents Act 1988.

ISBN 0-582-08647-7

British Library Cataloguing-in-Publication Data
A CIP catalogue record for this book can be obtained
from the British Library.

1   3   5   7   9   10   8   6   4   2

Set by 7 in 10/12 pt Plantin.
Printed in Great Britain by Henry Ling Ltd.,
at the Dorset Press, Dorchester, Dorset.

CONTENTS

Preface   xv
Bibliographical note   xiii
Table of cases   xvii
Table of statutes   1
Table of statutory instruments   liv

1 Introduction   1
  Explanation of the scheme of the book   1
  History of contract law   3
  The basis of contract   5
  The law of contract or contracts   8
  The law of obligations   9
  The real world   10
  Europe and beyond   11

Part I
THE NEGOTIATION STAGE

2 Negotiating the contract   15
  Introduction   15
  Estoppel by convention   16
  The objective test of agreement and the 'snapping up' of mistaken
    offers   20
  Mistake of identity   22
  Misrepresentation   26
  General principles   27
    Representations of fact   27
    Silence as misrepresentation   31
    Inducement   34
  The actions for misrepresentation   40
    Rescission   40
    The recovery of damages   54
    Misrepresentation in overview   73
  Proprietary estoppel   73
  Restitution: failed contract cases   80
    Advantages and disadvantages of a restitutionary analysis   85
  Collateral contracts   87
  A duty to disclose?   94
    Disclosure of terms   96
    Contracts *uberrimae fidei*   98

Undue influence 99
Fiduciary relationships 101
Inequality of bargaining power 101
Statutory disclosure requirements 104
Quasi exceptions: conduct, half-truths, and *With* v *O'Flanagan* 104
Other encouragements to disclosure: Sale of Goods Act 1979 105
A wider duty to disclose 106
A duty to negotiate in good faith 109
What is it? 109
Do we have it? 112
Do we need it? 113
Conclusion 116

Part II
THE BIRTH OF THE CONTRACT

A Formation of a contract: the positive requirements 119

3 Agreement: offer and acceptance 119
Introduction 119
Offers and invitations to treat 120
Two caveats 122
Advertisements 123
Displays of goods 125
Auctions 127
Tenders 128
Standing offers 133
Tickets and machines 133
The termination of an offer 134
Revocation – bilateral contracts 134
Revocation – unilateral contracts 136
Rejection 139
Lapse of time 144
Death of offeror and offeree 145
Acceptance 145
Acceptance in bilateral contracts 146
The postal rule of acceptance 148
Silence as acceptance 152
Acceptance in unilateral contracts 155
Conclusion 157

4 Consideration and its substitutes 159
The traditional definition 161
Consideration and gift 161
Consideration need not be adequate 162
Past consideration 164
Moral and economic consideration 165

Compromise agreements   166
Pre-existing duties   168
  The pre-existing duty arises from a contract with a third party   169
  The pre-existing duty arises from the law generally   171
The substitutes   173

5 **Form, intention and certainty**   176
Form   176
  Cautionary formal requirements   178
  Informational formal requirements   179
  Transferable formal requirements   180
Intention   180
  Domestic and social arrangements   182
  Business agreements between strangers   184
Certainty   187
  Vagueness   188
  Incompleteness   188

B **Formation: negative factors**   191

6 **Illegality in formation**   191
Introduction   191
Policy objectives   193
Statutory illegality   197
Illegality at common law   199
  Contracts to commit a crime or a tort   201
  Contracts promoting sexual indecency   202
  Contracts prejudicial to the administration of justice   203
  Contracts injurious to the institution of marriage or
    prejudicial to family life   206
  Contracts liable to affect adversely the state's relations with
    other states   209
  Contracts inconsistent with good government   209
  Contracts in restraint of trade   209
  Employment contracts   210
  Contracts for the sale of a business   211
  Other anti-competitive practices   212
Statutory control of anti-competitive practices   214
Gambling contracts   216
  The effects of a gambling contract   219
The consequences of illegality   220
  Enforcement of the contract   220
  The recovery of money and property   221
  Recovery without reliance upon the illegal contract   226
The non-reliance principle and the law of trusts   228
  Critique of the non-reliance exception   228

Severance 230
Reform of the law 231

7 Non-agreement mistakes 233
Common mistake as to the existence of the subject matter of the
    contract 234
Common mistake as to quality 237
Mistake as to ownership of property 240
Conclusion 241

C Personnel 242

8 Capacity 242
Minors 242
    Contracts for necessaries 242
    Beneficial employment contracts 243
    Ratification 244
    Voidable contracts 244
    Restitution by a minor 244
Mental incapacity 245
Companies 246
Conclusion 246

9 Third parties 247
Introduction 247
The first rule: strangers cannot enforce contracts 249
Exceptions to non-enforceability 252
    Contracts (Rights of Third Parties) Act 1999 252
    Other statutory exceptions 259
    The trusts exception 261
    Agency 264
    Collateral contracts 265
    Assignment 268
    The law of tort 269
Action by the promisee 271
    Specific performance 271
    Stay of action 272
    Damages 275
The second rule: contracts cannot impose obligations upon
    strangers 278
    Land law 279
    The tort of interference with contractual rights 279
    Bailment 281

Part III
THE LIFE OF THE CONTRACT

10 The content of the contract: express and implied terms   285
Express terms   285
  Term or representation?   286
Implied terms   290
  Statute   290
  Custom   296
  The common law   296

11 The content of the contract: exclusion clauses   300
Exemption clauses   300
Incorporation   302
Construction   304
The Unfair Contract Terms Act 1977   307
  Scope, concepts and definitions   308
  Liability for negligence   310
  Contractual liability   311
  Statutory implied terms   312
The Misrepresentation Act 1967, s 3   314
The Unfair Terms in Consumer Contracts Regulations 1999   314
Overview   316

12 The modification of contracts   318
Introduction   318
Contractual flexibility   320
Opportunism   321
  Where a rule of non-enforcement works   322
  Where a rule of non-enforcement fails   322
The pre-existing duty doctrine   325
  Rescission and new contract   328
  A finding of new consideration   330
Duress   337
  Introduction   337
  The present approach   339
  The legitimacy of the threat   340
  The requirement of 'compulsion'   346
  The law provides a remedy for the damage which would result
    if the threat were carried out   350
  The law provides a remedy for the damage which would result
    if the threat were carried out which in all the circumstances
    of the case is an adequate one   351
  Either the law provides a remedy for the damage which would
    result if the threat were carried out which in all the
    circumstances is an adequate one, or there exists an

extra-legal alternative which in all the circumstances of
the case is an adequate one 353
Independent advice 354
Subsequent affirmation 355
The ability to pass on costs 355
The non-enforcement rule 356
Waiver 357
Introduction 357
Waiver as forbearance 358
Promissory estoppel 363
Introduction 363
Unambiguous representations 365
Reliance 365
Promisee must have acted equitably 367
Is promissory estoppel suspensory or extinctive? 368
The offensive limits of promissory estoppel 370
The estoppel spectrum operationalised 380
Should promissory estoppel create a new cause of action? 383
Frustration 385
Introduction 385
Frustration and the allocation of risk 387
Increases in performance costs 395
Imposed modifications 400
Mitigation 402
Conclusion 404

13 Performance 407
Withholding performance 407
Incomplete performance 409
Illegality in performance 411

Part IV
THE DEATH OF THE CONTRACT

14 Frustration 417
Introduction 417
The juristic basis of frustration 421
The implied term theory 421
Total failure of consideration 423
The just and reasonable solution 423
Frustration of the adventure 424
The 'radical difference' approach 424
The main applications 425
Impossibility 425
Illegality 426
Frustration of objective 426

The effects of frustration 427

15 Termination for breach 431
Anticipatory breach 432
Conditions and warranties 434
  By statute 434
  By the parties' own classification 435
  The courts' classification 436
  Innominate terms 436

Part V
THE AFTERMATH

16 Literal performance 441
Introduction 441
Specific performance 441
  Should specific performance be more widely available? 442
  What the parties want 444
  History 444
  Restrictions 444
  Damages are an adequate remedy 444
  Constant supervision 449
  Contracts of personal service 450
  Severe hardship 451
  Conduct and inaction of the claimant 452
  Absence of mutuality 452
  Expectation longstop 453
Injunction 453
Action in debt 455

17 Damages for breach of contract 461
Introduction 461
The general compensatory aim 461
  The three types of award 462
  Loss, proof and opportunity 464
  The net loss principle 466
Extra compensatory damages 470
  Exemplary and aggravated damages 470
  The requirement of a property interest 471
  Restitution measure damages: enrichment by wrongdoing 474
  The rule in *Cory* v *Thames Ironworks Co* 476
Unliquidated damages 477
  The time of assessment 477
  The expectation measure: pecuniary loss 478
  The expectation measure: non-pecuniary loss 483
  The reliance measure: pecuniary loss 486

The reliance measure: non-pecuniary loss 488
The restitution measure 490
The relationship between the measures of damage 492
Limits upon recovery 494
Causation 494
Contributory negligence 495
Remoteness 497
Recovery for ordinary losses 502
Recovery for unusual losses 503
Mitigation 504
Liquidated damages and penalties 506
Policy 506
Lord Dunedin's guidelines 508
The effect of liquidated damages clauses and penalties 516
Liquidated damages clause 516
Penalty clauses 516
Evasion of the jurisdiction 518
Sum made payable on an event other than breach of contract
by the payer 518
Creation of a present debt and an acceleration clause 519
Termination clause in *Lombard North Central* v *Butterworth* 519
The forfeiture of deposits and advance payments 519
Deposits 520
Advance payments 522

Index 525

PREFACE

Writing a book is a humbling experience. It is far easier to comment on the efforts of others than it is to provide an alternative. For a number of years now I have begun my contract seminars with a joke that the perfect book on the law of contract has not yet been written but that I am working on it. I have now finished working on it but realise that it has still not yet been written. What I hope I have achieved is a book from which students can learn the living and developing law of contract, understand important inter-relationships within it and gain some understanding of its position and status in the wider law of obligations.

The writing of this book has occupied me for more years than my publisher will care to remember and thinking about it for more years than I like to admit to. During this prolonged gestation period I have incurred many debts. The book was written while I was a lecturer at University College London and so benefited from the research culture of that institution and the challenges of the students who followed a course of seminars based upon the book's themes. A number of colleagues and former colleagues have been generous enough to comment upon draft chapters or articles from which their themes are derived. I would like to thank especially Thomas Krebs, Professor Ewan McKendrick, Richard O'Dair, Professor Roger Rideout, Professor J C Smith and Jim Stephens. Their help was invaluable, but for what remains they, of course, bear no blame. I would also like to acknowledge the assistance I have received from Pat Bond and Liz Tarrant, who have worked hard on behalf of Pearson Education to bring the project to press despite my continued attempts to subvert their timetable. I have also received valuable research assistance from a number of former students including Luke Harris, Stephen Kempner and Devi Shah.

The scheme of arrangement followed in this book is novel and is explained in the first chapter. This departure would not have been possible were it not for the efforts of others who have brought doctrinal order to the subject. I would like especially to acknowledge the work of Sir Guenter Treitel. The American jurist and 'father' of the United States' Uniform Commercial Code, Karl Llewellyn, is reported to have said that he did not understand the law of contract until he discovered Lloyd's Law Reports. I think many contract lawyers might add that they did not understand the contents of Lloyd's Law Reports until they read Professor Treitel's *Law of Contract*. His authoritative textbook is an invaluable resource for others who seek to write about the subject.

My greatest debt is owed to my partner Jane and my three-year-old son Marcus who respectively encouraged and distracted me, together ensuring that I completed the book and retained a sense of humour. The publishers have been careful to curb some of the jarring excesses of my sense of humour but it is hoped that what remains will make the account of the law more readable.

I have tried to state the law on the basis of the materials available to me at the end of August 2000, though in some cases it has been possible to include later references at proof stage.

The book is dedicated to my loving parents David and Jean Halson.

Roger Halson

BIBLIOGRAPHICAL NOTE

The following abbreviations (shown here in **bold**) are used in the text:

Birks (1989) *An Introduction to the Law of Restitution*. Clarendon.

Cheshire, Fifoot and Furmston (1996) *The Law of Contract* (13th edn). Butterworths.

Treitel (1999) *The Law of Contract* (10th edn). Sweet and Maxwell.

Burrows (*Restitution*) (1993) *The Law of Restitution*. Butterworths.

Burrows (*Remedies*) (1994) *Remedies for Torts and Breach of Contract* (3rd edn). Butterworths.

Spencer-Bower and Turner (1977) *Estoppel by Representation* (3rd edn). Butterworths.

TABLE OF CASES

A to Z Bazaars (Pty) Ltd v Minister of Agriculture (1974)(4) SA 392 (c) 152
Abery v Chandler (1948) 64 TLR 394 219
Abrahams v Herbert Reiach [1922] 1 KB 477 . . . . .468, 469
Abrahams v Performing Rights Society [1995] ICR 1028 516
Adams v Lindsell (1818) 1 B & Ald 681 . . . . .148, 149
Adderley v Dixon (1824) 1 Sim & St 607 445
Addis v Gramophone Co Ltd [1909] AC 488 . . . . .472, 483, 486, 490
Adler v Dickson and Another [1955] 1 QB 158 266
AEG (UK) Ltd v Logic Resource Ltd [1996] CLR 265 304
Aerial Advertising v Bachelors Peas Ltd [1938] 2 All ER 788 . . . . .486, 489
Aiken v Stewart Wrightson Members' Agency Ltd [1995] 1 WLR 1281 174
Ailsa Craig Fishing Co Ltd v Malvern Fishing Co Ltd [1983] 1 WLR 964
. . . . .307, 518
Airways Corporation of New Zealand v Geyserland Airways Ltd [1996]
    1 NZLR 116 163
Ajax Cooke Pty Ltd t/a Ajax Spurway Fasteners v Nugent (unreported)
    Victoria SC 335
Ajayi (Emmanuel Ayodej) v R T Briscoe [1964] 3 All ER 556 . . . . . . .366, 368, 369
Alan & Co v El Nasr Export [1972] 2 QB 189 . . . . .361, 362, 365, 368
Alaskan Trader, The [1984] 1 All ER 129 . . . . .459, 460
Albazero, The [1977] AC 774 . . . . .276–7, 471, 472, 473
Albert v MIB [1972] AC 301 183
Albert (L) and Son v Armstrong Rubber Co (1949) 178 F 2d 182 493
Alcoa Co of America v Essex Group Inc (1980) 499 F Supp 53
. . . . .324, 393, 400–2, 405
Alder v Moore [1961] 2 QB 57 . . . . .510, 514
Alderslade v Hendon Laundry Ltd [1945] 1 KB 189 305
Alec Lobb (Garages) Ltd v Total Oil (Great Britain) Ltd [1983] 1 WLR 87, and
    reversed in part [1985] 1 WLR 173 . . . . .213, 214, 344, 346, 352
Alev, The [1989] 1 Lloyd's Rep 138 . . . . .326, 330, 337, 340, 343, 344, 351
Alexander v Ragson [1936] 1 KB 169 223
Alexander v Standard Telephones & Cables plc [1990] IRLR 55 450
Allcard v Skinner (1887) 36 Ch D 145 100
Allen v Bloomsbury Health Authority [1993] 1 All ER 651 243
Allen v Pink (1838) 4 M & W 140 289
Allen v Rescous (1676) 2 Lev 174 . . . . .191, 201, 202
Alliance & Leicester v Edgestop [1993] 1 WLR 1463 . . . . .60, 66
Allied Marples v Simmons & Simmons [1994] 4 All ER 907 465
Alloy Products Corporation v United States (1962) 302 F 2d 528 354
Aluminum Co of America v Essex Group (1980) 499 F Supp 53 . . . . .391, 394
Amalgamated Investment & Property Co Ltd v John Walker & Sons Ltd [1977]
    1 WLR 164 . . . . .417, 427
Amalgamated Investment & Property Co Ltd v Texas Commerce International Bank
    Ltd [1982] QB 84 . . . . .17, 76, 77, 373

Amar Singh v Kulubya [1964] AC 142 226
American Trading and Production Corporation v Shell International Marine (1972)
 453 F 2d 139 398
AMEV-UDC Finance Ltd v Austin (1986) 162 CLR 170 . . . . .511, 517
Amos v Citibank Ltd [1996] QCA 129 336
Anand v Geraghty & Co [2000] 3 WLR 1041 206
Anangel Atlas Compania Naviera SA v Ishikawajima-Harima Heavy Industries Co
 Ltd (No 2) [1990] 2 Lloyd's Rep 526 335
Anderson v Daniel [1924] 1 KB 138 411
Anderson v Equitable Life Assurance Society (1926) 42 TLR 302 400
Andrews v Parker [1973] Qd R 93 . . . . .203, 225
Angel v Murray (1974) 322 A 2d 630 344
Angelic Star, The [1988] 1 Lloyd's Rep 122 514
Anglia Television Ltd v Reed [1972] 1 QB 60 . . . . .463, 464, 487, 488
Antclizo, The [1992] 1 Lloyd's Rep 558 90
Appleby v Myers (1867) LR 2 CP 651 429
Applegarth v Colley (1842) 10 M & W 723 219
Appleson v H Littlewood Ltd [1939] 1 All ER 464 185
Appleton v Campbell (1826) 2 C & P 347 202
Archbolds v Spanglett [1961] 1 All ER 47 412
Arcos Ltd v EA Ronaasen & Son [1933] AC 470 292
Argy Trading v Lapid Developments [1977] 3 All ER 785; [1977] 1 WLR 444
 . . . . .18, 28, 370
Aristoc Industries Pty Ltd v R A Wenham (Builders) Pty Ltd [1965]
 NSWR 581 447
Ariston SRL v Charly Records Ltd [1990] Financial Times, 21 May 515, 516
Armstrong v Jackson [1917] 2 KB 822 . . . . .45, 46, 101
Aronson v Meloga (1927) 32 Com Cas 276 506
Arpad, The [1934] P 189 502
Ashburn Anstalt v Arnold [1989] Ch 1 188
Ashbury Railway Carriage and Iron Co Ltd v Riche (1875) LR 7 HL 653 246
Ashington Piggeries Ltd v Christopher Hill Ltd [1972] AC 441 292
Ashmole v Wainwright (1842) 2 QB 837 338
Ashmore v Corporation of Lloyd's [1992] Lloyd's Rep 620 . . . . .296, 297, 298
Ashton v Turner [1981] QB 137 191
Associated Distributors Ltd v Hall [1938] 2 KB 83 510
Associated Japanese Bank (International) Ltd v Crédit du Nord SA [1989] 3 All ER
 902 . . . . .236, 238
Astley v Reynolds (1731) 2 Str 915 . . . . .338, 351, 447
Astley v Weldon (1801) 2 B & P 346 . . . . .508, 515
Aswan Engineering Establishment Co v Lupdine Ltd [1987] 1 WLR 1 295
Atkins (G W) Ltd v Scott (1980) 7 Const LJ 215 486
Atkinson v Ritchie (1809) 10 East 530 425
Atlantic Baron, The [1979] 1 QB 705 . . .160, 321, 326, 330, 331, 334, 344, 355, 356
Atlantic Computers plc, Re [1995] BCC 696 187
Atlas Express Ltd v Kafco (Importers and Distributors) Ltd [1989] QB 833; [1989]
 1 All ER 641 . . . . .326, 340, 349
Attorney-General v Barker [1990] 3 All ER 257 211
Attorney-General v Blake [1998] 1 All ER 833; [2000] 3 WLR 625 (HL)
 . . . . .201, 211, 462, 464, 475–6

Attorney-General v Guardian Newspapers (No 2) [1988] 3 All ER 545 211
Attorney-General for Canada v Vancouver (1943) 1 DLR 510 349
Attorney-General of Commonwealth of Australia v Adelaide Steamship Co [1913]
    AC 781 211
Attorney-General of Hong Kong v Humphrey's Estate (Queen's Gardens) [1987]
    AC 114 . . . . .75, 488
Attwood v Lamont [1920] 3 KB 571 210
Attwood v Small (1838) 6 Cl & F 232 . . . . .36, 37
Auckland Electric Power Board v Electricity Corporation of New Zealand Ltd
    [1994] 1 NZLR 551 163
Augiėr v Secretary of State for the Environment (1978) 38 P & CR 219 366
August P Leonhardt, The [1985] 2 Lloyd's Rep 28 17
Austin Co v United States (1963) 314 F 2d 518 392
Austin Instrument Inc v Loral Corporation (1971) 272 NE 2d 533 353
Austotel Pty Ltd v Franklins Selfserve Pty Ltd (1989) 16 NSWLR 582 378
Avery v Bowden (1855) 5 E & B 714 434

B & S Contracts and Design Ltd v Victor Green Publications Ltd [1984] 1 CR 419
    . . . . .343, 344, 346, 348, 353
Bacon & Cooper (Metals) Ltd [1982] 1 All ER 397 . . . . .504, 505
Bailey v Bullock (1950) 66 TLR (Pt 2) 791 488
Bailey v De Crespigny (1869) LR 4 QB 180 390
Bainbridge v Furmston (1838) 8 Ad & El 743 163
Bal v Van Staden [1902] TS 128 150
Baleares, The [1993] 1 Lloyd's Rep 215 502
Balfour v Balfour [1919] 2 KB 571 . . . . .181, 183, 184
Balfour Beatty Civil Engineering v Docklands Light Railway [1996] 78 BLR 42
    . . . . .110, 113
Balfour Beatty Construction Ltd v Scottish Power plc 1994 SLT 807 500
Banco de Portugal v Waterlon [1932] AC 452 506
Bank Line v Arthur Capel & Co [1919] AC 435 . . . . .387, 388, 390, 421, 424
Bank Negara Indonesia v Phillip Haolim [1973] 2 Malagan LJ 3 366
Bank of New South Wales v Milvain (1884) 10 VLR 3 489
Bank of New Zealand v Ginivan [1991] 1 NZLR 178 186
Bannerman v White (1861) 10 CB (NS) 844 286
Banning v Wright [1922] 1 WLR 972 359
Banque Brussels Lambert SA v Australian National Industries (1989) NSWLR 502
   186
Banque Bruxelles v Eagle Star [1995] 2 All ER 769 73
Banque Financière de la Cité SA v Westgate Insurance Co Ltd [1989] 2 All ER 952
    . . . . .71, 95, 98
Banque Keyser Ullmann SA v Skandia (UK) Insurance Co Ltd. *See* Banque
    Financière de la Cité SA v Westgate Insurance Co Ltd
Barber v Vincent (1860) Freem KB 497 243
Barclays Bank plc v Coleman [2000] 3 WLR 405 100
Barclays Bank plc v Fairclough Building Ltd [1995] 1 All ER 289 496
Barclays Bank v Fairclough (No 2) [1998] IRLR 605 .496
Barclays Bank plc v O'Brien [1994] 1 AC 180; [1993] 4 All ER 417 . . . . . .100, 202
Barns v Queensland National Bank (1906) 3 CLR 925 364
Baron v Armstrong [1976] AC 104 347

Barrow *v* Cappell & Co [1976] RPC 355 450
Barry *v* Davies [2000] 1 WLR 1962 . . . . .128, 161
Basham (deceased), *Re* [1987] 1 All ER 405; [1986] 1 WLR 1498 . . . . .74, 77, 79, 374
Basischo Co Ltd, *Re* [1921] 2 Ch 331 390
BCCI *v* Aboody [1992] 4 All ER 955 100
Beach *v* Reed Corrugated Cases [1956] 2 All ER 652 468
Beale *v* Taylor [1967] 1 WLR 1193 . . . . .288, 289
Beesley *v* Hallwood Estates Ltd [1960] 2 All ER 324, affd [1961] Ch 549 370
Behnke *v* Bede [1927] 1KB 649 446
Bell *v* Lever Bros [1932] AC 161 . . . . .220, 237, 238, 324, 386, 389
Bellgrove *v* Eldridge (1954) 90 CLR 613 479
Bentsen *v* Taylor [1883] 2 QB 274 435
Berg *v* Sadler & Moore [1937] 2 KB 158 . . . . .201, 223
Bernstein *v* Pamson Motors (Golders Green) Ltd [1987] 2 All ER 220 . . .295, 485
Best Cleaners and Contractors Ltd *v* Canada [1985] 2 FC 293 130
Beswick *v* Beswick [1968] AC 58 . . . . .247, 251, 253, 271–2, 444
Bevan, *Re* [1912] 1 Ch 196 245
Bevan Ashford *v* Geoff Leandle (Contractors) Ltd (in liquidation) [1998] 3 WLR
   173 206
Bigg *v* Boyd Gibbons Ltd [1971] 2 All ER 183 122
Bigos *v* Boustead [1951] 1 All ER 92 224
Biotechnology Australia Pty Ltd *v* Pace (1988) 15 NSWLR 130 468
Birkmyr *v* Darnell (1805) 1 Salk 27 179
Birmingham and District Land Co *v* London and Northwestern Railway Co (1888)
   40 ChD 268 . . . . .361, 362, 363, 364
Biss *v* Howard Son & Gooch [1990] 1 EGLR 173 . . . . .488, 489
Bisset *v* Wilkinson [1927] AC 177 . . . . .29, 30
Blackett *v* Bates (1865) 1 Ch App 117 448–50
Blacklock and Macarthur *v* George G Kirk 1919 SC 57 395
Blackpool and Fylde Aero Club Ltd *v* Blackpool Borough Council [1990]
   1 WLR 1195 . . . . .91, 93, 110, 129, 130
Blake *v* Concannon (1870) IR 4 CL 323 244
Bliss *v* South East Thames Regional Health Authority [1987] 1CR 700
   . . . . .434, 485
Bloom *v* American Swish Watch Co [1915] AppD 100 155
Bolton *v* Mahadeva [1972] 1 WLR 1009 410
Boomer *v* Muir (1933) 24 P 2d 570 492
Boresford *v* Royal Insurance Co Ltd [1938] AC 386 . . . . .196, 201
Borthwick (Thomas) & Sons (Australasia) Ltd *v* South Otago Freezing Co Ltd
   [1978] 1 NZLR 538 454
Bowerman *v* Association of British Travel Agents Ltd [1996] CLC 451 186
Bowlay Logging Ltd *v* Demtar Ltd (1978) 87 DLR (3d) 325 . . . . . . .464, 492, 493
Bowmaker Ltd *v* Barnet Instruments Ltd [1945] KB 65 227
BP Exploration (Libya) Ltd *v* Hunt [1979] 1 WLR 783 429
BP Refinery (Westernport) Pty Ltd *v* President, Councillors and Ratepayers
   of Shire of Hastings (1978) 52 AJLR 20
Bradbury *v* Morgan (1862) 1 H & C 249 145
Bradley *v* Walsh (1903) 88 LT 737 515
Brandt *v* Liverpool Steam Navigation Co [1924] 1 KB 575 261
Brauer & Co *v* James Clark [1952] 2 All ER 497 397

Bremer Handelsgesellschaft MbH *v* Vanden Avenue Izegem PVBA [1978] 2 Lloyd's
  Rep 109 . . . . .17, 360, 361
Brett *v* East India Shipping Co (1864) 2 H & C 404 .450
Brett *v* JS (1600) Cro Eliz 756 165
Brewer Street Investments Ltd *v* Barclays Woollen Co Ltd [1954] 1 QB 428 83
Brewster *v* Kitchell (1691) 1 Salk 198 425
Brickwoods *v* Butler and Walker (1970) 21 PCR 256 .365
Bridge *v* Campbell Discount Co Ltd [1962] AC 600 . . . . .510–13, 515
Bridger *v* Savage (1884) 15 QBD 363 220
Brikom Investments *v* Carr [1979] 1 QB 467 . . . . .357, 365, 366, 368, 376–7, 380
Brikom Investments *v* Seaford [1981] 1 WLR 863 19
Brimnes, The [1975] QB 929 . . . . .135, 147
Brinkibon Ltd *v* Stahag Stahl [1983] 2 AC 34 . . . . .146, 147
Bristol Airport plc *v* Powdrill [1990] Ch 744 446
Bristol & West Building Society *v* Mathew [1997] 2 WLR 436 71
Bristol & West Building Society *v* May, Mayo & Merrimans (No 2) [1998] 1 WLR
  336 460
British Bank for Foreign Trade *v* Novinex [1949] 1 KB 623 189
British Benningtons *v* NW Cachar Tea [1923] AC 48 .329
British Columbia Saw Mill Co Ltd *v* Nettleship (1868) LR 3 CP 499 . . . . .497, 503
British Fermentation Products Ltd *v* Compair Reavell Ltd [1999] BLR 352 311
British Guiana Credit Corporation *v* Da Silva [1965] 1 WLR 248 468
British Movietonews *v* London and District Cinemas Ltd [1951] 1 KB 190
  . . . . .386, 389, 395, 397, 400, 401, 423, 425
British Steel Corporation *v* Cleveland Bridge and Engineering Co Ltd [1984]
  1 All ER 504 . . . . .84, 86, 187
British Westinghouse Electric & Manufacturing Co Ltd *v* Underground Electric
  Railway Co of London Ltd [1912] AC 673 . . . . .402, 461, 462
Brocklehurst (deceased), *Re* [1978] Ch 14 101
Brodie *v* Brodie [1917] P 271 208
Brogden *v* Metropolitan Railway Co (1877) 2 App Cas 666 . . . . .142, 147, 148
Bromage *v* Genning (1616) 1 Roll Rep 368 . . . . .441, 443
Brown *v* KMR Services Ltd [1995] 4 All ER 598 502
Brownlie *v* Campbell (1880) 5 App Cas 925 . . . . .33, 63
Bruner *v* Moore [1904] 1 Ch 305 . . . . .148, 149, 151, 363, 372, 382
BSC *v* Cleveland Bridge & Engineering Co Ltd [1984] 1 All ER 504 . . . . .143, 491
Buckpitt *v* Oates [1968] 1 All ER 1145 183
Budget Rent-A-Car Ltd *v* Goodman [1991] 2 NZLR 715 380
Bugler *v* McManaway [1963] NZLR 427 451
Bunge Corporation *v* Tradax Export SA [1981] 1 WLR 711 436
Burberry Mortgage & Savings Ltd *v* Hindsbank Holdings Ltd [1989]
  · 1 NZLR 356 379
Burrows (John) Ltd *v* Subsurface Surveys Ltd (1968) 68 DLR 21 354 365
Burton *v* Birches Timeshare [1991] 2 NZLR 641 29
Burton *v* Pinkerton (1867) LR 2 Exch 340 488
Bush *v* Canfield (1818) 2 Conn 485 494
Bush *v* Whitehaven Port and Town Trustees (*Hudson's Building Contracts*,
  14th edn, Vol. 2) 396
Butler *v* Countrywide Finance Ltd [1993] 3 NZLR 623 . . . . . . .380, 442, 446, 451
Butler Machine Tool Co *v* Ex-Cell-O Corporation [1979] 1 WLR 401 141–3

Buttery *v* Pickard [1946] WN 25 364
Buxton *v* Lister (1746) 3 Atk 383 443
Byle *v* Byle (1990) 65 DLR (4th) 641 355
Byrne *v* Australian Airlines Ltd (1995) 131 ALR 422 450
Byrne *v* Van Tienhoven (1880) 5 CPD 344 ....133, 135, 148

C & P Haulage (a firm) *v* Middleton [1983] 3 All ER 94 .....464–6, 493
Calabar Properties *v* Stitcher [1984] 1 WLR 287 480
Caledonia, The [1903] P 104 163
Camdex International Ltd *v* Bank of Zambia [1996] 3 All ER 431; [1996] 3 WLR
   759 ....205, 269
Canada Steamship Co *v* The King [1952] AC 192 305
Canadian Industrial Alcohol Co *v* Dunbar Molasses (1932) 179 NE 383 393
Candler *v* Crane, Christmas & Co [1959] 2 QB 164 69
Caparo *v* Dickman [1990] 2 AC 617 ....68, 69, 73
Capps *v* Georgia Pacific Corporation (1969) 453 P 2d 935 351
Captain Gregos (No. 2), *The* [1990] 2 Lloyd's Rep 395 ....17, 282
Car & Universal Finance Co Ltd *v* Caldwell [1965] 1 QB 525 ....43, 44
Carapanayoti & Co Ltd *v* ET Green Ltd [1959] 1 QB 131 395
Carlill *v* The Carbolic Smoke Ball Co [1892] 2 QB 484; [1893] 1 QB
   256 ....121, 123, 124, 136, 156, 217
Carnfoot *v* Fowke (1840) 6 M&W 359 60
Carpenter Paper Co *v* Kearney Hub Publishing Co (1956) 78 NW 2d 80 341
Carr-Glynn *v* Frearsons [1998] 4 All ER 225 270
Carter *v* Boehm (1766) 3 Burr 1905 112
Casey's Patents, *Re* [1892] 1 Ch 104 164
Cavalier Insurance Co Ltd, *Re* [1989] 2 Lloyd's Rep 430 225
CCC Film (London) Ltd *v* Impact Quadrant Films Ltd [1984] 3 All ER 298
   ....487, 493–4
Cellulose Acetate Silk Co *v* Widnes Foundry Ltd [1933] AC 20 517
Cemp Properties (UK) Ltd *v* Dentsply Research and Development Corporation
   [1991] EG 62 64
Central Estates (Belgravia) Ltd *v* Woolgar [1971] 3 All ER 647 110
Central London Property Trust Ltd *v* High Trees House Ltd [1956]
   1 All ER 256 ....332, 359, 365, 366, 368–70
Centrex Homes Corporation *v* Boag (1974) 320 A 2d 194 445
Centrovincial Estates plc *v* Merchant Investors Assurance Co Ltd [1983]
   Com LR 158 ....20, 123
Century 21 Campbell Munro Ltd *v* S & G Estates (1992) 89 DLR (4th) 413
  346
Chai Sau Yin *v* Liew Kwee Sam [1962] AC 304 198
Chandler Bros Ltd *v* Boswell [1936] 3 All ER 179 491
Chandler *v* East African Airways Corporation [1960] EA 78 484
Chandler *v* Webster [1904] 1 KB 493 ....392, 427
Chapelton *v* Barry Urban District Council [1940] 1 KB 532 .....125, 127, 303
Chaplin *v* Hicks [1911] 2 KB 786 465
Chappell & Co Ltd *v* Nestlé Co Ltd [1960] AC 87 163
Charrington *v* Simons & Co Ltd [1970] 1 WLR 725 452
Charter *v* Sullivan [1957] 2 QB 117 481
Chaudhry *v* Pradhaker [1988] 3 All ER 718 69

Cheall *v* Association of Professional, Executive, Clerical and Computer Staff [1983] 2 AC 180 418

Chelini *v* Nieri 196 P 21 915 (1948) 470

Chesneau *v* Interhome [1983] 134 NLJ 341 64

Chester Grosvenor Hotel Co Ltd *v* Alfred McAlpine Ltd (1991) 56 BLR 115 . .309

Chevalier Rose, The [1983] 2 Lloyd's Rep 438 275

Chicago Coliseum Club *v* Dempsey (1932) 265 Ill App 542 487

Chichester *v* Cobb (1866) 14 LT 433 169

Chillingworth *v* Esche [1924] 1 Ch 976 185

Chinook Aggregates Ltd *v* Abbotsford (Mun Dist) (1989) 40 BCLR (2d) 345 130

CIBC Mortgages *v* Pitt [1993] 4 All ER 433 100

Citizens Bank of Louisiana *v* First National Bank of New Orleans (1873) LR 6 HL 352 28

Citra Constructions Ltd *v* Allied Asphalt Co Pty Ltd (unreported) NSW Supreme Court 321

City of London *v* Nash (1747) 3 Atk 512 447

City of Moncton *v* Stephen (1956) 5 DLR (2d) 722 341

City of Westminster Properties *v* Mudd [1959] Ch 129 290

Clarion Ltd *v* National Provident Institution [2000] 1 WLR 1888 240

Clark *v* Marsiglia [1845] Denio 317 458

Clark *v* Price (1819) 2 Wils Ch 157 450

Clarke *v* Dickson (1858) EB & E 148 45–7

Clay *v* Yates (1856) 1 H&N 73 202

Clayton (Herbert) *v* Oliver [1930] AC 209 486

Clayton Green *v* De Courville (1920) 36 TLR 790 404

Clef Aquitaine SARL v Laporte Materials Ltd [2000] 3 WLR 1760 58

Clements *v* London & North Western Railway [1894] 2 QB 482 243

Clifford Davies Management *v* WEA Records [1975] 1 WLR 61 212

Clifton *v* Palumbo [1944] 2 All ER 497 122

Clippens Oil Co *v* Edinburgh and District Water Trustees [1907] AC 291 506

Clydebank Engineering and Shipbuilding Co *v* Don Jose Ramos Yzquierdo y Castanada [1905] AC 6 . . . . .509, 513, 515, 516

Cobb *v* Great Western Railway [1984] AC 499 497

Cochrane (Decorators) Ltd *v* Sarabandi (1983) 133 NLJ 558 503

Cockburn *v* Alexander (1818) 6 CB 791 467

Cockerton *v* Naviera Aznar SA [1960] 2 Lloyd's Rep 450 133

Collins *v* Blanton (1767) 2 Wilson 341 222

Collins *v* Godefroy (1831) 1 B & Ad 950 172

Colt *v* Nettervill (1725) 2 P Wms 301 443

Combe & Combe [1951] 2 KB 215 . . . .18, 132, 163, 215, 332, 365, 370, 372, 373

Commercial Plastics Ltd *v* Vincent [1965] 1 QB 623 210

Commission for New Towns *v* Cooper (GB) Ltd [1995] Ch 259 178

Commonwealth of Australia *v* Amman Aviation Pty Ltd (1992) 66 AJLR 123 . . . . .465, 468, 470, 493

Commonwealth of Australia *v* Verwayen (1990) 170 CLR 395 . .376, 377, 378, 380

Connell *v* MIB [1972] AC 301 183

Constantine (J) Steamship Line *v* Imperial Smelting Corporation Ltd [1942] AC 154 . . . . .408, 418, 419, 423

Consten and Grundig *v* Commission of the European Communities (Cases 56/64, 58/64) [1966] ECR 299 215
Conwest Exploration *v* Letain (1964) 41 DLR 2d 198 382
Cooden Engineering Co Ltd *v* Stanford [1953] 1 QB 86 515
Cook *v* Lister (1983) 132 CB (NS) 543 336
Cook *v* S [1967] 1 All ER 299 485
Cook *v* Wright (1861) 1 B & S 559 . . . . .167, 168, 204, 336
Cook Island Shipping Co Ltd *v* Colson Buildings Ltd [1975] 1 NZLR
   422 . . . . .326, 317
Cooper *v* Phibbs (1867) LR 2 HL 149 240
Co-operative Insurance Society Ltd *v* Argyll Stores (Holdings) Ltd [1998] AC 1;
   [1997] 2 WLR 898 . . . . .272, 442–3, 448–9
Cope *v* Rowlands (1836) 2 MAW 149 199
Coral Leisure Group Ltd *v* Barnett [1981] 1 CR 503 .202
Cory *v* Thames Ironworks Co (1868) LR 3 QB 181 .476
Cottrill *v* Steyning and Littlehampton Building Society [1966] 1 WLR 543 503
Couchman *v* Hill [1947] KB 554 287
Coulls *v* Bagot's Executor and Trustee Co Ltd [1907] ALR 385 250
County and Metropolitan Homes (Surrey) Ltd *v* Topelcim Ltd [1997]
   1 All ER 254 521
County NatWest *v* Barton [1999] *The Times*, 29 July 39
Couturier *v* Hastie (1856) 5 HLC 673 . . . . .234, 237, 241
Coward *v* MIB [1963] 1 QB 259 183
CRA Ltd *v* NZ Goldfields Investments (1989) VR 870 512
Crabb *v* Arun District Council [1976] 1 Ch 179 . . . . .18, 74, 76, 78, 79, 373
Craig, *Re* [1971] Ch 95 100
Crédit Lyonnais Bank Nederland NV *v* Burch [1997] 1 All ER 144 . . . . . .100, 103
Crescendo Management Pty Ltd *v* Westpac Banking Corporation [1988] 19
   NSWLR 46 347
Creswell & Potter [1978] 1 WLR 255 103
Cricklewood Property and Investment Trust *v* Leightons Trust [1945]
   AC 221 390
Crisp *v* Churchill, cited in Lloyd *v* Johnson (1798) 1 Bos & P 340 202
Crocker *v* Sundance Northwest Resorts Ltd (1989) 51 DLR (4th) 321
Cross *v* David Martin & Mortimer [1989] 1 EGLR 154 489
Crown House *v* Amec [1980] 48 Build LR 37 86
CTN Cash and Carry Ltd *v* Gallagher Ltd [1994] 4 All ER 714 341
Cubitt *v* Smith (1864) 11 LT 298 448
Cuff *v* Penn (1813) 1 M&S 21 360
Cundy *v* Lindsay (1878) 3 App Cas 459 24
Currie *v* Misa (1875) LR 10 Ex 153 . . . . .84, 159, 333
Curtis *v* Chemical Cleaning & Dyeing Co Ltd [1951] 1 KB 805 302
Cutter *v* Powell (1795) 6 Term Rep 320 407–10

D & C Builders *v* Rees [1966] 2 QB 617 . . . . .336, 339, 351, 365–8
D & F Estates Ltd *v* Church Commissioners [1989] AC 177 270
Dagenham (Thames) Dock, *ex p* Hulse, *Re* (1873) 8 Ch App 1022 522
Dahl *v* Nelson (1881) 6 App Cas 38 422
Dale *v* Government of Manitoba (1997) 147 DLR (4th) 605 137
Danforth Heights *v* McDermid Bros (1922) 52 OLR 412 . . . . .17, 73, 357, 361

Darlington Borough Council *v* Wiltshier Northern Ltd [1995] 3 All ER
  895 . . . . .250, 251, 263, 277–8, 473–4, 479
Daulia Ltd *v* Four Millbank Nominees Ltd [1978] Ch 231 . . . . .136, 138
Davidson *v* Barclays Bank Ltd [1940] 1 All ER 316 489
Davidson *v* Norstant (1921) 61 SCR 493 . . . . .363, 372
Davies *v* London and Provincial Marine Insurance Co (1878) 8 ChD 469 225
Davies *v* Sumner [1984] 1 WLR 1301 294
Davies *v* Taylor [1974] AC 207 464
Davis Contractors Ltd *v* Fareham Urban District Council [1956] AC
  696 . . . . .390, 395, 396, 401, 420–2, 424–5
Day *v* Mead [1987] 2 NZLR 443 443
Day *v* United States (1917) 245 US 159 387
De Bernardy *v* Harding (1853) 8 Exch 822 491
De Francesco *v* Barnum (1890) 45 ChD 430 450
De la Bere *v* Pearson [1908] 1 KB 280 495
De Mattos *v* Gibson (1858) 4 D & J 276 449
De Wutz *v* Hendricks (1824) 2 Bing 314 209
Dean *v* Ainley [1987] 1 WLR 1729 . . . . .478, 483
Deane *v* Attorney-General [1997] 2 NZLR 180 376
Debenham *v* Sawbridge [1901] 2 Ch 98 241
Debtors (Nos 4449 and 4450 of 1998), *Re* [1999] 1 All ER (Comm) 149 91
Deeny *v* Gooda Walker (in liquidation) [1995] 4 All ER 289 467
Deepak *v* ICI [1998] 2 Lloyd's Rep 139 274
Denmark Productions Ltd *v* Boscobel Productions Ltd [1969] 1 QB 699 390
Denny, Mott and Dickson *v* James B Fraser & Co [1944] AC 265 . . .422, 423, 426
Denton *v* GN Railway (1856) 5 E & B 860 . . . . .125, 133
Derry *v* Peek (1889) 14 App Cas 337 . . . . .26, 54, 55, 68
Derry *v* Sidney Phillips & Son [1982] 1 WLR 1297 479
Diamond *v* Campbell-Jones [1961] Ch 22 503
Dianna Prosperity, The [1976] 1 WLR 989 292
Dick Bentley Productions Ltd *v* Harold Smith (Motors) Ltd [1965] 1 WLR
  623 288
Dickinson *v* Dodds (1876) 2 ChD 463 . . . . .133, 135, 145
Dickson *v* James B Fraser [1944] AC 265 423
Dies *v* British and International Mining and Finance Corporation Ltd [1939] 1 KB
  724 523–4
Diesen *v* Sampson [1971] SLT 49 485
Diestal *v* Stevenson [1906] 2 KB 345 . . . . .507, 514, 516
Diggle *v* Higgs (1877) 2 Ex D 422 220
Dillwyn *v* Llewelyn (1862) 4 De GF & J 517 . . . . .75, 76, 77, 79
Dimmock *v* Hallett (1866) 2 Ch App 21 31
Dimond *v* Lovell [2000] 2 WLR 1121 466
Dimsdale Developments (South East) *v* De Haan (1983) 47 P&CR 1 522
Director-General of Fair Trading *v* First National Bank plc [2000] 2 WLR
  1353 . . . . .315, 316
Doe (deceased), Morgan *v* Boyer (1854) 9 UCQB 318 349
Dominion Court Co Ltd *v* Dominion Wolverhampton Corporation [1971] 1 WLR
  204 449
Don King Productions *v* Warren [1998] 2 Lloyd's Rep 176 268
Donaldson *v* Gray [1920] VLR 379 349

Donoghue *v* Stevenson [1932] AC 562 . . . . .114, 281
Dorset County Council *v* Southern Felt Roofing Co Ltd (1989) 48 BLR 96 . . .305
Dowager Marchioness of Annondale *v* Ann Harris (1727) 2 P Wms,
    affd 1 Bro PC 250 202
Downs *v* Chappell [1996] 3 All ER 344 . . . . .39, 40, 59, 65
Doyle *v* Olby (Ironmongers) Ltd [1969] 2 QB 158 58
Doyle *v* White City Stadium Ltd [1935] 1 KB 110 243
DPP for Northern Ireland *v* Lynch [1975] AC 653 347
Drane *v* Evangelou [1978] 1 WLR 455 471
Drennan *v* Star Paving Co (1958) 333 P 2d 757 132
Drexel Burnham Lambert International NV *v* El Nasr [1986] 1 Lloyd's Rep
    356 361
Drive Yourself Hire Co (London) Ltd *v* Strutt [1954] 1 QB 250 251
Drowling *v* White's Lumber & Supply Co 170 Mis (1934) 458
Drummond *v* SU Stores (1980) 258 EG 1293 478
Dudley, Clarke and Hall *v* Cooper Ewing & Co (unreported) 359
Duke of Westminster *v* Guild [1985] QB 688 299
Dunbar *v* A & B Painters Ltd [1986] 2 Lloyd's Rep 38 460
Dunbar Bank plc *v* Nadeem (1998) 31 HLR 402 100
Dunk *v* George Waller & Sons Ltd [1970] 2 QB 163 486
Dunlop *v* Lambert (1839) 6 Cl & F 600 . . . . .260, 263, 276–7, 471–4
Dunlop Pneumatic Tyre Co *v* New Garage & Motor Co Ltd [1915] AC
    79 . . . . .508, 509, 512–15
Dunlop Pneumatic Tyre Co Ltd *v* Selfridge & Co Ltd [1915] AC 847 249
Dunmore *v* Alexander (1830) 9 Shaw 190 152
Dunn *v* Disc Jockey Unlimited Co Ltd (1978) 87 DLKR (3d) 408 484
Durham Fancy Goods Ltd *v* Michael Jackson (Fancy Goods) Ltd [1968] 2
    QB 839 376

Eadie *v* Township of Brantford (1967) 63 DLR (2d) 561 . . . . . .349, 352, 354, 447
East *v* Maurer [1991] 1 WLR 461 . . . . .57, 58, 221
East Ham Borough Council *v* Bernard Sunley & Sons Ltd [1966] AC 406
    . . . . .478, 480
Eastern Airlines Inc *v* Gulf Oil Corporation (1975) 415 F Supp 429;
    19 VCC Rep 721 . . . . .399, 447
Eastern Counties Railway Co *v* Hawkes (1955) 5 HLC 331 445
Eastham *v* Newcastle United Football Club Ltd [1964] Ch 413 210
Eastwood *v* Kenyon (1840) 11 A & E 438 . . . . .164, 165
Ecay *v* Godfrey (1947) 80 Lloyd's LR 286 286
Edgington *v* Fitzmaurice (1885) 8 App Cas 467 . . . . .28, 32, 34, 37, 76
Edwards *v* Carter [1893] AC 360 244
Edwards *v* Skyways Ltd [1964] 1 All ER 494 185
EE Caledonia Ltd *v* Orbit Valve Co Europe [1993] 4 All ER 165 307
Eggleston *v* Humble Pipe Line Co (1972) 482 SW 2d 905 341
Ehrman *v* Bartholomew [1898] 1 Ch 671 454
Elbe Maru, The [1978] 1 Lloyd's Rep 206 275
Elder Dempster & Co Ltd *v* Patherson Zochonis & Co Ltd [1924] AC 522 282
Eliason *v* Henshaw (1819) Wheat 225 150
Ellesmere *v* Wallace [1929] 2 Ch 1 219
Elphinstone *v* Monkland (1886) 11 App Cas 332 509

Elsey *v* J G Collins Insurance Agencies Ltd (1978) 83 DLR (3d) 1 517
Emerald Resources Ltd *v* Sterling Oil Properties Management Ltd (1969) 3 DLR
    (3d) 630 450
Employment (SS) *v* Globe Elastic Thread Co [1980] AC 506; [1979] 2 All ER
    1007 . . . . .18, 270
Empresa Exportadora de Azúcar *v* Industrie Azucarera Nacional SA [1985] 2
    Lloyd's Rep 171 291
Enderby Town Football Club Ltd *v* The Football Association [1971] Ch 591 . . .200
Entores Ltd *v* Miles Far East Corporation [1955] 2 QB 327 146
Equitable Life Assurance Society *v* Hyman [2000] 3 WLR 529 296
Equity Funding Corporation *v* Coral Management (1971) 322 NYS 2d 965 . . .352
Erlanger *v* New Sombrero Phosphate Co (1878) 3 App Cas 1218 . . . . .45, 46
Errington *v* Errington & Woods [1952] 1 KB 290 .136, 138
Ertel Beiber & Co *v* Rio Tinto Co Ltd [1918] AC 260 .426
Esso Petroleum Co Ltd *v* Harper's Garage (Stourport) Ltd [1968] AC
    269 . . . . .192, 209, 213
Esso Petroleum Co Ltd *v* Kingswood Motors (Addlestone) Ltd [1974] 1 QB
    142 280
Esso Petroleum Co Ltd *v* Mardon [1976] QB 801; [1976] 2 WLR
    583 . . . . .29, 69, 70, 290, 505
Eugenia, The [1964] 2 QB 226 395
Eurocopy *v* Teesdale [1992] BCLC 1067 35
European Asian Bank *v* Punjab and Sind Bank [1982] 2 Lloyd's Rep 356 274
Eurymedon, The [1975] AC 154 . . . . .170, 171, 253, 264, 266–8, 271
Evening Standard *v* Henderson [1987] ICR 588 454
Everet *v* Williams (1725) reported at (1893) 9 LQR 197 . . . . .191, 220
Eves *v* Eves [1975] 1 WLR 1338; [1975] 3 All ER 768 182
Evia Luck (No. 2), *The* [1992] 2 AC 152 . . . . .279, 340, 346, 347
Export Credits Guarantee Department *v* Universal Oil Products Co [1983]
    1 WLR 399 511
Exportelisa SA *v* Rocco Giuseppe & Figli Soc Cell [1978] 1 Lloyd's Rep 433 . . .395
Express Newspapers *v* Silverstone Circuits Ltd [1989] *Independent*, 16 June 297
Ezekiel *v* McDade [1995] 2 EGLR 107 491

Fairbanks *v* Snow (1887) 13 NE 2d 596 346
Fairclough Building *v* Port Talbot Borough Council (1990) 62 BLR 82 131
Falcke *v* Gray (1859) 4 Drew 651 445
Fanning *v* Wicklow County Council (unreported, 30 April 1984) 83
Fells *v* Read (1796) 3 Ves 70 446
Felthouse *v* Bindley (1862) 11 CB (NS) 869 . . . . .148, 153
Fenner *v* Blake [1900] 1 QB 426 364
Fibrosa Spolka Akcyjna *v* Fairbairn Lawson Combe Barbour Ltd [1943]
    AC 32 . . . . .84, 426–8
Finagrain *v* Kruse [1976] 2 Lloyd's Rep 508 302
Financings Ltd *v* Baldock [1963] 2 QB 104 519
Financings Ltd *v* Stimson [1963] 1 WLR 1184 145
Finland Steamship Co *v* Felixstowe Dock & Railway Co [1980] 2 Lloyd's
    Rep 287, 396
First Energy *v* HIB [1993] 2 Lloyd's Rep 194 143
First National Commercial Bank plc *v* Humberts [1995] 2 All ER 673 71

Fisher *v* Bell [1961] 1 QB 394 125
Fisher & Co *v* Apollinaris [1875] LR 10 Ch App 297 204
Fitch *v* Dewes [1921] 2 AC 158 . . . . .210, 211
Fitch *v* Snedaker (1868) 38 NY 248 155
Fitzgerald *v* F J Leonhardt (1997) 189 CLR 215 199
Fletcher *v* Tayleur (1855) 17 CB 21 502
Flint *v* Brandon (1808) 3 Ves 159 448
Floods of Queensferry Ltd *v* Shand Construction Ltd [2000] BLR 81 51
Foakes *v* Beer (1884) 9 App Cas 605 . . . . .335, 336, 337, 363, 368
Foaminol Laboratories *v* British Artid Plastics [1941] 2 All ER 393 476
Foley *v* Classique Coaches [1934] 2 KB 1 189
Ford Motor Co *v* AUEW [1969] 2 QB 303 181
Fordy *v* Harwood [1999] Lloyd's Law Reports Alert Service (August) 31
Forsjkringsaktieselskapet Vesta *v* Butcher [1986] 2 All ER 488; [1988] 2 All ER 43;
    affd [1989] AC 880 . . . . .66, 67, 495
Forster *v* Outred & Co [1982] 1 WLR 86 71
Forster *v* Silvermere Golf and Equestrian Centre Ltd (1981)125 SJ 397 247
Forum Craftsman, The [1985] 1 Lloyd's Rep 291 282
Foster *v* Charles (1830) 7 Bing 105 54
Foster *v* Driscoll [1929] 1 KB 470 209
Francis *v* Cowcliffe (1976) 33 P & CR 368 452
Freeman *v* Niroomand (1997) 52 Con LR 116 462
Frost *v* Aylesbury Dairy Co [1905] 1 KB 608 295
Frost *v* Knight (1872) LR 7 Exch 111 432
Fuller *v* Richmond (1850) 2 Gr 24 447

Gallagher *v* Pioneer Concrete (NSW) Pty Ltd (1993) 113 ALR 159 378
Gallie *v* Lee. *See* Saunders *v* Anglia Building Society [1971] AC 1004 302
Galloway *v* Galloway (1914) 30 TLR 531 236
Galoo *v* Bright Grahame Murray [1995] 1 All ER 16 . . . . .69, 73, 494
Gamerco SA *v* ICM/Fair Warning (Agency) Ltd [1995] 1 WLR 1226 . . . . .426, 428
Garden Neptune Shipping *v* Occidental Worldwide Investment Corporation
    [1990] 1 Lloyd's Rep 330 62
Gardner *v* Ford (1863) 13 UCCP 446 160
Gardner *v* Marsh & Parsons [1997] 1 WLR 489 466
Gebr. Van Weelde Scheepvaart-Kantor VB *v* Compania Naviera Sea Orient SA
    [1985] 2 Lloyd's Rep 496 154
Getreide-Import Gesellschaft *v* Contimar [1953] 207 .152
Gibbons *v* Proctor (1891) 64 LT 594 156
Gibson *v* Manchester City Council [1979] 2 WLR 294 121
Gilbert-Ash (Northern) Ltd *v* Modern Engineering (Bristol) Ltd [1974] AC 689
   512
Gilbert Steel *v* University Construction Ltd (1973) 36 DLR (3d) 496;
    affd (1976) 67 DLR (3d) 606 . . . . .330, 379
Giles (C H) & Co *v* Morris [1972] 1 WLR 307 .449, 450
Giles *v* Thompson [1994] 1 AC 142 205
Gillespie *v* Great Atlantic & Pacific Stores (1972) 187 SE 2d 441 127
Gillies *v* Keogh [1989] 2 NZLR 327 . . . . .379, 380
GKN Centrax Gears *v* Matbro Ltd [1976] 2 Lloyd's Rep 555 . . . . .489, 503
Glasbrook Bros Ltd *v* Glamorgan County Council [1925] 2 AC 270 172

Glidden Co *v* Hellenic Lines [1960] 275 F 2d 253 390
Gnapp (Eric) *v* Petroleum Board [1949] WN 180 341
Goldcorp Exchange Ltd, *Re* [1994] 3 WLR 199 380
Goldsoll *v* Goldman [1915] 1 Ch 292 230
Gollin & Co Ltd *v* Consolidated Fertilizer Sales Pty Ltd [1982] Qd R 435 375
Gomez *v* Olds Discount (TCC) Ltd (1964) 7 WIR 98 . . . . .409, 469
Gordon *v* Gordon (1821) 3 Swan 400 99
Gordon *v* Roebuck (1989) 64 DLR (4th) 568 346
Gordon *v* Selico Co Ltd [1986] 1 EGLR 71; [1986] 11 HLR 219; [1987]
    Conv 121 . . . . .38, 104
Gore *v* Van der Lann [1967] 2 QB 31 . . . . .273, 274
Gosling *v* Anderson (1972) 223 EG 1743 . . . . .62, 63, 65
Goss *v* Nugent (1833) 5 B & Ad 58 358
Grainger & Son *v* Gough [1896] AC 325 125
Gran Gelato Ltd *v* Richcliff (Group) Ltd [1992] 1 All ER 865 . . . . .65, 67
Grant *v* Australian Knitting Mills Ltd [1936] AC 85 .127
Grant *v* Edwards [1986] Ch 638 76
Gray *v* Southouse [1949] 2 All ER 1019 226
Greaseley *v* Cooke [1986] 1 WLR 1306 76
Great Northern Railway Co *v* Witham (1873) LR 9 CP 16 133
Green *v* Symons [1897] 13 TLR 301 286
Greer *v* Kettle [1938] AC 156 17
Gregory *v* Rangitikei District Council [1995] 2 NZLR 208 129
Greig *v* Insole [1978] 1 WLR 302 214
Griffith *v* Brymer (1903) 19 TLR 434 239
Griffiths *v* Peter Conway [1939] 1 All ER 685 295
Grimsby Steel Furniture Co *v* Columbia Gramophone Records (1922)
    23 OWN 188 . . . . .364, 365
Grist *v* Bailey [1967] Ch 532 240
Grogan *v* Robert Meredith Plant Hire (1996) 15 Tr LR 371 302
Grundt *v* Great Boulder Pty Gold Mines Ltd (1938) 59 CLR 641 366

H *v* W (1857) 3 K & J 282 208
Habib Bank Ltd *v* Habib Bank Ltd [1981] 1 WLR 1264 . . . . .74, 373
Hackley *v* Headley (1881) 8 NW 511 . . . . .350, 351
Hadley *v* Baxendale (1854) 9 Exch 341 .356, 498, 502–3
Haggar *v* de Placide [1969] 1 WLR 328 184
Haigh *v* Town Council of Sheffield (1874) LR 10 QB 102 217
Halifax Building Society *v* Thomas [1996] WLR 63 .463
Hall (Arthur J S) & Co *v* Simons [2000] 3 All ER 673 69
Hall (R & H) and W H Pim Jnr, *Re* (1928) 139 LT 50 . . . . .482, 500, 502
Hamer *v* Sidaway (1891) 27 NE 256 166
Hamlin *v* Great Northern Railway Co (1856) 1 H & N 408 484
Hands *v* Slaney (1800) 8 TR 578 243
Hannah Blumenthal, The [1983] AC 854 154
Hansa Nord, The [1976] QB 44 437
Harbutt's Plasticine Ltd *v* Wayne Tank and Pump Co Ltd [1970] 1 QB 447;
    [1970] 1 All ER 225 306
Hardman *v* Booth (1863) 1 H&C 803 22
Hardwick *v* Johnson [1978] 1 WLR 683 182

Hardwick Game Farm *v* Suffolk Agricultural Poultry Producers Association [1969]
AC 31 304
Hardy *v* Losner Formals [1997] Current Law Digest 60 484
Harlingdon and Leinster Enterprises Ltd *v* Christopher Hull Fine Art Ltd [1991] 1
QB 564; [1990] 3 WLR 13 . . . . .288, 293
Harlow & Jones Ltd *v* Panex (International) Ltd (1967) 2 Lloyd's Rep 509 404
Harries *v* Edmonds (1845) 1 Car & K 686 403
Harris *v* Carter (1854) 3 E&B 559 326
Harris *v* Nickerson (1873) LR 8 QB 286 128
Harris *v* Sheffield United Football Club [1988] QB 77 172
Harris *v* Watson (1791) Peake 102 326
Harris, *Ex parte* (1872) LR 7 Ch App 567 148
Hart *v* O'Connor [1985] AC 1000 244
Hartlepool Gas & Water Co *v* West Hartlepool Harbour & Railway Co (1865) 12 LT
366 451
Hartley *v* Hymans [1920] 3 KB 475 . . . . .358, 359, 360
Hartley *v* Ponsonby [1857] 7 E&B 872 . . . . .326, 363
Hartog *v* Colin and Shields [1939] 3 All ER 566 . . . . .21, 22, 97, 157
Harvela Investments Ltd *v* Royal Trust Co of Canada Ltd [1985] 2 All ER 966;
[1986] AC 207 . . . . .128, 129, 131, 136, 145, 453
Harvey *v* Farey [1893] AC 552 122
Harvey *v* Graham (1836) 5 Ad & E 61 358
Hayes *v* James & Charles Dodd [1990] 2 All ER 815 . . . . .463, 485
Hebb's Case (1867) LR 4 Eq 9 122
Hedley Byrne & Co Ltd *v* Heller & Partners [1964] AC 465 . .26, 61, 69–71, 73, 81
Heglibiston Establishment *v* Heyman (1978) 36 P & CR 351 . . . . .196, 202
Heine Bros (Aust) Pty Ltd *v* Forrest [1963] VR 383 .454
Hellenic Lines Ltd *v* Louis Dreyfus Corporation (1966) 249 F Supp 526 338
Henderson *v* Merrett Syndicates Ltd [1995] 2 AC 145; [1994] 3 WLR 761
. . . . .69, 70, 102, 106, 174, 497, 501
Hennessy *v* Craigmyle & Co Ltd [1986] ICR 461 . . . . .344, 346, 348
Henryk Sif, The [1980] 2 Lloyd's Rep 245; [1982] 1 Lloyd's Rep
456 . . . . .77, 365, 369, 372, 376, 380
Henthorn *v* Fraser [1892] 2 Ch 27 . . . . .148, 150
Hermann *v* Charlesworth [1905] 2 KB 123 207
Hermosa, The [1982] 1 Lloyd's Rep 570 437
Herne Bay Steamboat Co *v* Hutton [1903] 2 KB 683 . . . . .426, 427
Heron II, The [1969] 1 AC 350 . . . . .462, 499, 503
Heskell *v* Continental Express [1950] 1 All ER 1033 .494
Hewett *v* Court (1983) 149 CLR 639 452
Heywood *v* Wellers [1976] QB 446 485
Hickman *v* Haynes (1875) LR 10 CP 598 . . . . .358, 360, 477
High Trees Case. *See* Central London Property Trust Co v High Trees House [1947]
KB 130 . . . . .364, 371
Highland and Universal Properties Ltd *v* Safeway Properties Ltd [2000] SLT 414
. 448
Hill *v* Barclays (1810) 16 Ves 402 447
Hill *v* C A Parsons Ltd [1972] Ch 305 451
Hill *v* William Hill [1949] AC 530 219
Hillas & Co Ltd *v* Arcos Ltd (1932) 147 LT 503 . . . . .188, 189

Hills *v* Street (1929) 5 Bing 37 338

Hirachand Punamchand *v* Temple [1911] 2 KB 330 .336

Hirji Muliji *v* CheongYue Steamship Co [1926] AC 497 . . . . .385, 397, 418, 421–4

HL Motorworks *v* Alwatibi [1977] RTR 276 505

Hobbs *v* London and South Western Railway Co (1875) LR 10 QB 111 . . .484, 488

Hochman *v* Zigler's Inc (1946) 50 A 2d 97 342

Hochster *v* De La Tour (1853) 2 E&B 678 432

Hodges *v* Earl of Lichfield (1835) 1 Bing NC 492 487

Hodgson *v* Richardson 1 W Blac 463 112

Hoenig *v* Isaacs [1952] 2 All ER 176; [1952] 12 TLR 1360 . . . . .331, 410, 479

Hoffberger *v* Ascot International Bloodstock Bureau Ltd [1976] *The Times*,
    29 January 505

Hoffman *v* Red Owl Stores (1967) 133 NW 2d 267 374

Hoffman *v* Sportsman Yachts Inc (1992) 89 DLR (4th) 600 302

Holiday Inns Inc *v* Broadhead [1974] 232 EG 951 .77, 80

Hollier *v* Rambler Motors (AMC) Ltd [1972] 2 QB 71 . . . . .304, 306

Holman *v* Johnson (1775) 1 Comp 341 195

Holwell Securities *v* Hughes [1974] 1 WLR 155; [1974] 1 All ER 161 . . . .150, 151

Home Office *v* Dorset Yacht Co Ltd [1970] AC 1004 95

Homsy *v* Murphy (1997) 73 P & CR 26 502

Hong Kong and Whampoa Dock Co *v* Netherton Shipping Co (1909) SC 34 . .395

Hong Kong Fir Shipping Co Ltd *v* Kawasaki Kisen Kaisha Ltd
    [1962] 2 QB 26 436

Hooper and Grass' Contract, *Re* [1949] VLR 269 . . . . .343, 352

Hopkins *v* Tanqueray (1854) 15 CB 130 287

Horne *v* Midland Railway (1873) LR 8 CP 503

Horsfall *v* Thomas (1862) 1 H & C 90 . . . . .38, 105

Hounslow London Borough Council *v* Twickenham Garden Developments Ltd
    [1971] Ch 233 . . . . .448, 457, 459

Household Fire etc Insurance Co *v* Grant (1879) 4 ExD 216 . . . . . . .148, 150, 151

Howard Marine & Dredging Co Ltd *v* Ogden & Sons (Excavations) Ltd [1978] QB
    574 . . . . .62, 65, 69, 70

Howe *v* Teefy (1927) 27 SR (NSW) 301 465

Hughes *v* Kingston-upon-Hull City Council [1999] 2 All ER 49 206

Hughes *v* Metropolitan Railway (1877) 2 App Cas 439 . . . . .359–64, 370, 372

Hughes Aircraft Systems International *v* Air Services Australia (1997) 146
    ALR 1 . . . . .110, 130

Humphreys *v* Polak [1901] 2 KB 385 208

Hunt *v* Severs [1994] 2 AC 350 467

Hunter (Ian), Bowman *v* Durham Holdings Pty Ltd (1973) 47 ALJR 606
    . . . . .363, 373

Hurlbert *v* Thomas (1847) 3 UCQB 258 379

Hurst *v* Bryk [2000] 2 All ER 193 431

Hurst *v* Ustorre (1856) 18 CB 144 387

Hussey *v* Eels [1990] 2 QB 227 466

Hutton *v* Warren (1836) 1 M & W 466 296

Huyton *v* Cremer [1999] 1 Lloyd's Rep 620 . . . . .340, 347

Hyde *v* Wrench (1840) 3 Beav 334 . . . . .139, 140

Hydraulic Engineering Co *v* McHaffie (1878) 4 QBD 670 . . . . .487, 499, 503

Hylton *v* Hylton (1754) 2 Ves Sen 547 100

Hyundai Heavy Industries Co Ltd *v* Papadoulos [1980] 2 All ER 29 524

Imperial Loan Co *v* Stone [1892] 1 QB 599 245
Indian Endurance, The (No 2). Republic of India *v* India Steamship Co Ltd [1997] 4
    All ER 380 . . . . .74, 385
Ingram *v* Little [1961] 1 QB 31 . . . . .21, 23, 25, 42–4
Interfoto Picture Library *v* Stiletto Visual Programme [1989] QB
    433 . . . . .15, 97, 112, 303, 518
International Paper Co *v* Rockefeller Corp (1914) 146 NYS 371 399
International Scholarship Foundation and National Trust Co, *Re* (1992) DLR (4th)
    267 299
Inwards *v* Baker [1965] 2 QB 29 78
Ion, The [1980] 2 Lloyd's Rep 245 . . . . .368, 381
Ionides *v* Pender (1874) LR 9 QB 531 98
Iowa Electric Light Co *v* Atlas Corporation (1978) 467 F Supp 129 399
Irani *v* S W Hamps AHA [1985] IRLR 302 451
Iron Trade Mutual Insurance Co Ltd *v* J F Buckenham Ltd [1990] 1 All ER 808 . .174
Ironmonger & Co *v* Dyre (1928) 44 TLR 497 218

Jackson *v* Chrysler Acceptance [1978] RTR 474 484
Jackson *v* Horizon Holidays Ltd [1975] 1 WLR 1468 275
Jackson *v* Turquand (1869) LR 4 HL 305 122
Jackson *v* Union Marine Insurance (1874) LR 10 CP 125
    . . . . .385, 387, 389, 417, 424–5
Jacob *v* Bills [1967] NZLR 249 451
Jacob & Youngs Inc *v* Kent (1921) 230 NY 239 479
Jacobs *v* Batavia & General Plantations Trust Ltd [1924] 1 Ch 287 289
Jacobs (George Porky) Enterprises Ltd *v* City of Regina (1964) 44 DLR
    (2d) 179 352
Jaggard *v* Sawyer [1995] 1 WLR 269 . . . . .452, 464, 466, 475
Jamaica Telephone *v* Robinson [1970] 1 WLR 174 366
James *v* Heim Gallery (1980) 256 EG 819 . . . . .365, 366, 377
James *v* Hutton [1950] 1 KB 9 479
Jarvis *v* Swans Tours Ltd [1973] 1 QB 233; [1978] RTR 474 . . . . .63, 484
Je Maintiendra Pty Ltd *v* Queglia (1980) 26 SASR 101 . . . . .369, 375
Jenkins *v* Livsey [1985] AC 424 99
Jervis *v* Harris [1996] 1 All ER 303 455
Jeune *v* Queen's Cross Properties Ltd [1974] Ch 97 .447
Jobson *v* Johnson [1989] 1 All ER 621 . . . . .511, 516
Joel *v* Law Union & Crown Insurance Co Ltd [1908] 2 KB 863 99
Johnson *v* Agnew [1980] AC 367 .64, 461, 477, 492
Johnson *v* Driefontein Consolidated Mines Ltd [1902] AC 484 200
Johnson *v* Shrewsbury and Birmingham Railway Co (1853) 22 LJ Ch 921
    . . . . .448, 450
Johnson *v* Unisys [1999] 1 All ER 854 . . . . .483, 490
Johnson Matthey *v* Constantine Terminals Ltd [1976] 2 Lloyd's Rep 215 282
Johnstone *v* Bloomsbury Health Authority [1991] 2 All ER 293 299
Jones *v* Padavatton [1969] 1 WLR 328 . . . . .170, 181, 183, 184
Jones *v* Vernon's Pools Ltd [1938] 2 All ER 626 185
Jones *v* Waite (1839) 5 Bing NC 341 171

Jorden *v* Money (1854) 5 HL Cas 185 . . . . .28, 174, 364
Joseph *v* National Magazine Co [1959] Ch 14 486
Junior Books Ltd *v* Veitchi & Co Ltd [1983] 1 AC 520 . . . . .254, 255
Junior K, The [1988] 2 Lloyd's Rep 583 185

K, Re [1988] Ch 310 245
Kanchenjunga, The [1990] 1 Lloyd's Rep 391 . . . . .40, 369
Karsales (Harrow) Ltd *v* Wallis [1956] 1 WLR 936 306
Keates *v* Earl of Cadogan (1851) 10 CB 591 . . . . .96, 104, 109
Keeley *v* Guy MacDonald (1984) 134 NLJ 522 478
Kelly *v* Cruise Catering Ltd [1994] 2 IRLM 394 151
Kemp *v* Intasun Holidays Ltd [1988] 6 T & L 161 . . . . .503, 504
Kendall (Henry) & Sons *v* William Lillico & Sons Ltd [1969] 2 AC 31 295
Kennedy *v* Panama etc. Royal Mail Co (1867) LR 1 QB 580 238
Keteley's Case (1613) 1 Brown 120 244
Ketley *v* Gooden (1997) 73 PCR 305 471
Kilbuck Coal *v* Turner and Robinson (1915) 7 OWN 673 330
Kindlace *v* Murphy (NI) (unreported) 316
King *v* Michael Faraday & Partners Ltd [1939] 2 KB 753 269
King Construction Co *v* W M Smith Electric Co (1961) 350 SW (2d) 940 353
Kingalock, The (1854) 1 Sp Ecc & Ad 263 . . . . .112, 163
Kings Norton Metal Co Ltd *v* Edridge Merrett & Co Ltd (1897) 14 TLR 98
. 24
Kiriri Cotton Co Ltd *v* Dewani [1960] AC 192 . . . . .225, 226
Kirton *v* Eliot (1613) Roll Abr 731 244
Kitchen *v* Royal Air Forces Association [1958] 1 WLR 563 465
Kleinwort Benson Ltd *v* Lincoln CC [1998] 4 All ER 513 27
Kleinwort Benson Ltd *v* Malaysia Mining Corporation Bhd [1988] 1 All ER
    714 . . . . .86, 186–7
Knutson *v* Bourkes Syndicate (1941) 3 DLR 593 .352
Kores Manufacturing Co Ltd *v* Kolak Manufacturing Co Ltd [1959] Ch
    108 214
Koufos *v* C Czarnikow Ltd. *See The Heron II.*
Kpohraror *v* Woolwich Building Society [1996] 4 All ER 119 . . . . 464, 489
Kralj *v* McGrath [1986] 1 All ER 54 471
Krell *v* Henry [1903] 2 KB 740 . . . . .392, 426, 427
Kriti Rex, The [1996] 2 Lloyd's Rep 171 500
Kuenigl *v* Donnersmarck [1955] 1 QB 515 209

Lacey (William) (Hounslow) Ltd *v* Davis [1957] 1 WLR 932 . . . . .83, 129, 492
Lafayette *v* Ferent (1934) 29 NW 2d 57 342
Laguna Nitrate *v* Lagunas Syndicate [1899] 2 Ch 392 46
Lake *v* Simmons [1927] AC 487 22
Lamare *v* Dixon (1873) LR 6 HL 414 444
Lambert *v* HTV Cymru (Wales) Ltd [1998] *The Times*, 13 March; [1998]
    Current Law Digest, April, para 106 90
Lamm *v* Shingleton (1949) 55 SE 2d 810 486
Lampleigh *v* Brathwait (1615) Hob 105 164
Langden *v* Stokes (1634) Cro Car 383 328
Lark *v* Outhwaite [1991] 2 Lloyd's Rep 132 156

Larringa *v* Société France-Américaine des Phosphates de Medulla (1923) 245 US
159; (1923) 92 LJ KB 455; (1923) 39 TLR 316 . . . . .387, 393, 424
Lasky *v* Economy Grocery Stores (1946) 65 NE (2d) 305 127
Laurence *v* Lexcourt Holdings [1978] 2 All ER 810 .240
Lavarack *v* Woods of Colchester [1967] 1 QB 278 . . . . .466, 468
Law Debenture Trust Corporation *v* Ural Caspian Oil Corporation [1993] 1 WLR
138 280
Lawrence *v* Fox (1859) 20 NY 268 (New York Court of Appeals) 248
Lazenby Garages *v* Wright [1976] 1 WLR 459 481
Leaf *v* International Galleries [1950] 2 KB 86 . . . . .44, 47–9
Leather Cloth Co *v* Hieronimus (1875) LR 10 QB 140 . . . . .359, 360
Lee *v* GEC Plessey Telecommunications [1993] IRLR 383 335
Lee (Paula) Ltd *v* Robert Zehil & Co Ltd [1983] 2 All ER 390 468
Lefkowitz *v* Great Minneapolis Surplus Store (1957) 86 NW 2d 689
. . . . .123, 124, 136
Legione *v* Hateley (1983) 52 CLR 406 375
Leigh and Sillivan Ltd *v* Aliakmon Shipping Co Ltd (*The Aliakmon*) [1986] AC 785;
[1986] 2 All ER 145 . . . . .144, 216, 447
Lens *v* Devonshire Club [1914] *The Times*, 4 December 184
Les Affréteurs Réunis Société Anonyme *v* Leopold Walford (London) Ltd [1919] AC
801 262
Lesters Leather and Skin Co Ltd *v* Home and Overseas Brokers Ltd (1948) 64 TLR
569 . . . . .481, 506
L'Estrange *v* Graucob [1934] 2 KB 394 302
Levey & Co *v* Goldberg [1922] 1 KB 688 358
Levi *v* Gordon (1992) 12 November (unreported) 471
Lewis *v* Averay [1972] 1 QB 198 . . . . .23, 25
Liesbosch, The. Dredger *Liesbosch* (Owners) *v* Owners of *SS Edison* [1933]
AC 449 504
Lim Teng Huan *v* Ang Swee Chuan [1992] 1 WLR 113 . . . . 78, 79
Linden Gardens Trust Ltd *v* Lenesta Sledge [1994] 1 AC 85; [1993] 3 All
ER 417 . . . . .253, 260, 263, 268, 276–8, 472–4
Lindon *v* Hooper (1776) 1 Cowp 414 350
Lingen *v* Simpson (1824) 1 Sim & St 600 446
Lingenfelder *v* Wainwright Brewery Co (1891) 15 SW 844 327
Linz *v* Schuck (1907) 67 A 286 . . . . .320, 344, 357
Lipkin Forman *v* Karpnale [1991] 2 AC 548 . . . . .10, 81, 143, 162, 163, 220
Littler *v* Holland (1799) 3 TR 590 360
Littlewoods Organisation *v* Harris [1978] 1 All ER 1026 210
Livingstone *v* Raywards (1880) 5 App Cas 25 463
Livingstone *v* Roskilly [1992] 3 NZLR 230 110
Lloyd *v* Johnson (1798) 1 Bos & P 340 202
Lloyd *v* Stanbury [1971] 1 WLR 1461; [1971] 2 All ER 267 . . . . .464, 487, 503
Lloyd's *v* Harper (1880) 16 ChD 290 276
Lloyds and Scottish Finance Ltd *v* Modern Cars and Caravans (Kingston) Ltd
[1966] 1 QB 764 505
Lloyds Bank Ltd *v* Bundy [1975] QB 326; [1974] 3 All ER 757 . . . . . .99, 100, 102
Lloyds Bank plc *v* Waterhouse [1993] 2 FLR 97 22
Load *v* Green (1846) 15 M&W 216 45
Lodder *v* Slowey [1904] AC 442 492

Lombard North Central plc *v* Butterworth [1987] QB 527 . . . . .435, 519
Lombard Tricity Ltd *v* Paton [1989] 1 All ER 918 189
London & North Western Railway *v* M'Michael (1850) 5 Ex 114 244
London & Northern Bank, *Re* [1900] 1 Ch 220 151
London and South of England Building Society *v* Stone [1983] 1 WLR 1242 . . .506
London Assurance *v* Mansel (1879) 11 ChD 363 98
London Drugs Ltd *v* Kuchne & Nagel International Ltd (1992) 97 DLR
   (4th) 261 248
London Wine Co (Shippers), *Re* [1986] PCC 121 . . . . .443, 447
Long *v* Lloyd [1958] 1 WLR 753 . . . . .44, 47
Low *v* Bouverie [1891] 3 Ch 82 17
Lowther *v* Lowther (1806) 13 Ves 95 445
Lucas (T) & Co Ltd *v* Mitchell [1974] Ch 129 231
Lucy, The [1983] 1 Lloyd's Rep 188 . . . . .38, 46
Lumley *v* Wagner (1852) 1 De GF & J 604 454
Lutor *v* Cooper [1941] AC 108 296
Luxor (Eastbourne) Ltd *v* Cooper [1941] AC 108 . . . . .139, 297
Lynn *v* Bamber [1930] 2 KB 72 174

M & S Drapers *v* Reynolds [1957] 1 WLR 9 212
McAlpine (Alfred) Construction Ltd *v* Panatown Ltd (1998) 88 BLR 67; [2000] 3
   WLR 946 . . . . .260, 277, 278, 472, 473, 474
McAlpine *v* Property and Land Contractors [1995] 76 BLR 59 466
McCausland *v* Duncan Lawrie Ltd [1996] 4 All ER 995 329
McCullagh *v* Lane Fox & Partners Ltd [1994] 1 EGLR 48 76
McDowell *v* Fraser (1779) 1 Douglas 247 39
McEvoy *v* Belfast Banking Co Ltd [1935] AC 24 250
McGregor *v* McGregor (1888) 21 QBD 424 204
Mac-Jordan Construction Ltd *v* Brockmount Erostin Ltd [1992] BCLC 350 . . .280
McLeish *v* Amoo-Gottfreid & Co (1993) 137 Sd Jo LB 204 485
MacLeod *v* Ker 1965 SC 253 43
McLoughlin *v* O'Brien [1983] 1 AC 410 204
McManus *v* Fortescue [1907] 2 KB 1 127
McRae *v* Commonwealth Disposals Commission (1951) 84 CLR
   377 . . . . .235, 237, 464, 465, 487, 493
Macclesfield (Earl of) *v* Davies (1814) 3 Ves & B 16 445
Magee *v* Pennine Insurance Co Ltd [1969] 2 QB 507 . . . . .99, 240
Mahkutai, The [1996] AC 650 . . . . .170, 267, 268
Mahmoud and Ispahani, *Re* [1921] 2 KB 716 . . . . .192, 193, 198, 411
Mahraj *v* Chand [1986] AC 898 374
Malcolm *v* Chancellor, Masters and Scholars of the University of Oxford [1990]
   The Times, 19 December 187
Malik *v* Bank of Credit & Commerce International SA (in liquidation) [1997]
   3 All ER 1 . . . . .483, 485, 489, 490
Malins *v* Freeman (1837) 2 Keen 25 245
Mallet *v* McMonagle [1970] AC 166 464
Manches *v* Trimborn (1946) 115 LJKB 305 245
Manchester Homoeopathic Clinic Trustees *v* Manchester Corporation (1970)
   22 P & CR 241 366
Mansukhani *v* Sharkey [1992] 2 EGLR 105 165

Manubens *v* Leon [1919] 1 KB 208 . . . . .464, 465, 468

Maple Farms *v* City Schools District (1974) 352 NYS 784 399

Maori Trustee *v* Rogross Farm Ltd [1991] 3 NZLR 369 479

Marbe *v* George Edwardes (Daley's Theatre) Ltd [1928] 1 KB 269 486

Marcus *v* Myers and Davis [1895] 11 TLR 327 486

Maritime National Fish Ltd *v* Ocean Trawlers Ltd [1935] AC 524 418

Markholm Construction Ltd *v* Wellington City Council [1985] 2 NZLR
  520 . . . . .124, 452

Marles *v* Philip Trent & Son Ltd [1954] 1 QB 29 412

Marshall *v* Lynn (1840) 6 M&W 109 358

Marston Construction Co Ltd *v* Kigass [1989] 15 Con LR 116 . . . . .81, 83, 84

Martell *v* Consett Iron & Steel Co Ltd [1955] Ch 363 269

Maskell *v* Horner [1915] 3 KB 106 . . . . .338, 349

Mason *v* Provident Clothing and Supply Co Ltd [1913] AC 724 211

Mason *v* State of New South Wales (1959) 102 CLR 108 . . . . .349, 355

Mason *v* Westside Cemeteries (1996) 135 DLR (4th) 361 485

Massalia, The [1961] 2 QB 278 395

Matharu *v* Matharu [1994] 2 FLR 597 . . . . .75, 76, 77, 79

Mathieson Gee (Ayrshire) Ltd *v* Quigley 1952 SLT 239 86

Matthews *v* Baxter (1873) LR 8 Ex 132 245

Mavro Vetranic, The [1985] 1 Lloyd's Rep 586 436

May and Butcher Ltd *v* R [1934] 2 KB 17 188

Mayfield Holdings Ltd *v* Moana Reef Ltd [1973] 1 NZLR 309 448

Merchant's Trading Co *v* Banner (1871) LR 12 Eq 18 448

Merritt *v* Merritt [1970] 1 WLR 1211; [1970] 2 All ER 760 182

Mersey Steel & Iron Co *v* Naylor Benzon & Co (1882) 9 QBD 648 40

Metropolitan Water Board *v* Dick Kerr & Co Ltd [1918] AC 119 396

Meudell *v* Mayor etc. of Bendigo (1900) 26 VLR 158 129

Midland Bank Trust Co Ltd *v* Hett, Stubbs & Kemp [1979] Ch 384 496

Midland Silicones Ltd *v* Scruttons Ltd [1962] AC 446 . .250, 264, 266, 267, 281, 282

Mihalis Angelos, The [1971] 1 QB 164 . . . . .436, 469

Milburn Services Ltd *v* United Trading Group (1997) 52 Con LR 130 493

Miljus (t/a A & Z Engineering) *v* Yamazaki Machinery UK Ltd [1997] Current
  Law Digest, July, 125 87

Millar's Machinery Co Ltd *v* David Way & Son (1935) 40 Com Cas 204 492

Miller *v* Korinsk (1945) 62 TLR 85 230

Mineral Park Land Co *v* Howard [1916] 156 P 458 .398

Minories Finance Ltd *v* Afribank Nigeria Ltd [1995] 1 Lloyd's Rep 134 154

Missowi Public Service Co *v* Peabody Coal Co (1979) 583 SW 2d 655 393

Mitchell (George) (Chesterhall) Ltd *v* Finney Lock Seeds Ltd [1983] 2 AC 803;
  [1983] 2 All ER 737 . . . . .307, 309

MJB Enterprises *v* Defence Corporation Ltd [1999] 1 SCR 619 . . . . .129, 130

Mohamed *v* Alaya & Co [1998] 2 All ER 720; [2000] 1 WLR 1815 . . . . . .206, 220

Mohammad Habib Ullah (Sheikh) *v* Bird & Co (1921) 37 TLR 405 481

Mok *v* Mao [1995] DCR 845 452

Molyneux *v* Richard [1906] 1 Ch 43 448

Monarch Steamship Co *v* Karlshamns Oljefabriker (A/B) [1949] AC 196
  . . . . .494, 499, 502

Montevideo Gas *v* Clan Line Steamers (1921) 37 TLR 544 504

Moorcock, The (1889) 14 PD 64 297

Moore & Co and Landauer & Co, *Re* [1921] 2 KB 519 292
Moral *v* Northern Steamship Co [1922] NZLR 966 133
Morgan Crucible Co plc *v* Hill Samuel & Co Ltd [1991] Ch 259 . . . . . . .27, 69, 73
Morgan Grenfell *v* Welwyn Hatfield District Council [1995] 1 All ER 1 218
Morris *v* Baron [1918] AC 1 329
Morris *v* Britannia Hotels Ltd [1997] Current Law Digest 63 484
Morris *v* McCulloch (1763) Amb 432 207
Morris (Herbert) Ltd *v* Saxelby [1916] 1 AC 688 210
Morrison *v* Thoelke (1963) 155 So 2d 889 152
Morrow *v* Carty [1975] N1 174 366
Morton Construction *v* City of Hamilton (1961) 31 DLR (2d) 323 341
Morton-Jones *v* R B and J R Knight Ltd [1992] 3 NZLR 582 379
Moschi *v* Lep Air Services [1973] AC 331 179
Mountford *v* Scott [1975] Ch 258; [1975] 2 WLR 114 . . . . .135, 452
Moyes and Groves Ltd *v* Radiation (NZ) Ltd [1982] 1 NZLR 368 330
Muhammad Issa El Sheikh Ahmed *v* Ali [1947] AC 414 504
Municipality of St John *v* Fraser-Brace Overseas Corporation (1958)
    13 DLR (2d) 352
Munro *v* Wivenhoe and Brightlingsea Railway Co (1864) 12 LT 654 448
Murphy *v* Brentwood District Council [1991] 1 AC 398 270
Murray (Edmund) Ltd *v* SP International Foundations Ltd (1992)
    33 Con LR 1 309
Museprime Properties Ltd *v* Adhill Properties Ltd [1990] 2 EGLR 196 . . . . .39, 40
Musumieci *v* Winadell (1994) 34 NSWLR 723 . . . . . .327, 328, 330, 334, 335, 337
Mutual Finance Ltd *v* John Wetton & Sons Ltd [1937] 2 KB 389 342
Mutual Life & Citizens Assurance Co *v* Evatt [1971] AC 793 69

Nagle *v* Fielden [1966] 2 QB 633 . . . . .209, 216
Nash *v* Inman [1908] 2 KB 1 . . . . .243, 245
National Carriers Ltd *v* Panalpina (Northern) Ltd [1981] 1 AC 675
    . . . . .386, 395, 400, 421, 423–5
National Guardian Mortgage Co *v* Wilkes [1993] CCLR 1 179
National Presto *v* United States (1964) 338 F 2d 99 .401
National Westminster Bank plc *v* IRC [1940] 3 All ER 1 122
National Westminster Bank plc *v* Morgan [1983] 3 All ER 85 100
National Westminster Finance NZ Ltd *v* National Bank of New Zealand Ltd
    [1996] 1 NZLR 548 380
Naughton *v* O'Callaghan [1990] 3 All ER 191 . . . . .65, 478, 492
Naxos, The [1990] 1 WLR 1337 435
Neal Cooper Gain Co *v* Texas Gulf Sulphur Co (1974) 508 F 2d 283 398
Nelson *v* Nelson [1995] 70 ALJR 47 229
Nema, The [1982] AC 724 . . . . .420, 425
Neville *v* Dominion of Canada News Co Ltd [1915] 3 KB 556 200
Neville *v* Kelly (1862) 32 LJCP 118 155
New York Star, The [1981] 1 WLR 139 . . . . .170, 218
Newbigging *v* Adam (1886) 34 ChD 582 . . . . .52, 53
Newborne *v* Sensolid (Great Britain) Ltd [1954] 1 QB 45 24
Newmans Tours Ltd *v* Ranier Investments Ltd [1992] 2 NZLR 68 . . . . . . .335, 443
Niblett Ltd *v* Confectioners' Materials Co Ltd [1921] 3 KB 387 291
Nicholson & Venn *v* Smith-Marritt [1947] LT 189 239

Nicolene Ltd *v* Simmonds [1953] 1 QB 543 185
Nissan Finance UK *v* Lockhart [1993] CCLR 39 179
Nixon *v* Murphy (1925) 25 SR (NSW) 151 343
Nocton *v* Lord Ashburton [1914] AC 932 68
Noma, The [1982] AC 724 205
Nordenfelt *v* The Maxim Nordenfelt Guns and Ammunition Co Ltd [1894] AC
   535 . . . . .210, 212
North Ocean Shipping Co Ltd *v* Hyundai Construction Co Ltd. *See The Atlantic
   Baron.*
North Sea Energy Holdings NV *v* Petroleum Authority of Thailand [1997]
   2 Lloyd's Rep 418 . . . . .476, 502
Northland Airliners Ltd *v* Dennis Ferranti Meters (1970) 114 SJ 845 141
Northumberland and Durham District Banking Co, *Re, ex p* Bigge (1859)
   28 LJ Ch 50 38
Norwich City Council *v* Harvey [1981] 1 WLR 828 .271
Notcutt *v* Universal Equipment Co (London) Ltd [1986] 1 WLR 641 424
Nottinghamshire Patent Brick and Tile Co *v* Butler (1866) 16 QBD 778 . . .33, 105
Nutbrown *v* Thornton (1804) 10 Ves 159 446
Nykredit plc *v* Edward Erdman Group Ltd [1997] 1 WLR 1627 . . . . .71, 463

Oakes *v* Turquand and Harding (1867) LR 2 HL 325 45
Obde *v* Schlemeyer (1960) 353 P 2d 672 104
O'Dea *v* Allstates Leasing System (WA) Pty Ltd (1983) 152 CLR 359 510
Odenfeld, The [1978] 2 Lloyd's Rep 357 . . . . .459, 460
Official Trustee in Bankruptcy *v* Tooheys Ltd (1993) 29 NSWLR 641 378
Offord *v* Davies (1862) 12 CB (NS) 748 133
Offredy Developments *v* Steinbeck (1972) 221 EG 963 365
Ogle *v* Earl Vane (1867) LR 2 QB 275, affd (1868) LR 3 QB 272 . . . . .357–60, 477
Olib, The [1992] 2 AC 1; [1991] 2 Lloyd's Rep 108 .344
Olley *v* Marlborough Court Ltd [1949] 1 KB 532 303
Olsson *v* Dyson (1969) 120 CLR 365 248
O'Neil *v* Arnew (1976) 78 DLR (3d) 671 452
Ontario *v* Ron Engineering Construction Eastern Ltd (1981) 119 DLR (3d) 267
  132
Oom *v* Bruce (1880) 12 East 225 225
Oremus *v* Wynhoff (1963) 123 NW 2d 441 354
Orgee *v* Orgee [1997] EGCS 152 . . . . .75, 80
Ormes *v* Beadel (1860) 2 Giff 166; rvsd on other grounds 2 De GF & J 333 . .339, 351
Oro Chief, The [1983] 2 Lloyd's Rep 509 447
Osborne *v* Amalgamated Society of Railway Servants [1910] AC 87 209
Oscar Chess Ltd *v* Williams [1957] 1 WLR 370 . . . . .238, 287–9
Oswald *v* Countryside Surveyors Ltd (1994) 47 Con LR 50;
   (1996) 50 Con LR 1 (CA); [1996] 2 EGLR 104 . . . . .479, 489
Overseas Medical Supplies Ltd *v* Orient Transport Services [1999]
   2 Lloyd's Rep 273 . . . . .309, 310

P (Minors) (Wardship: Surrogacy) [1987] 2 FLR 42 .208
Pacific Associates Inc *v* Baxter [1990] 1 QB 993 271
Page *v* Combined Shipping and Trading Co Ltd [1997] 3 All ER 656 47
Page One (Records) Ltd *v* Britton [1968] 1 WLR 157 . . . . .450, 454

Pagnan (R) & Fratelli *v* Corbisa Industrial Agropacuaria Lda [1970] 2 Lloyd's
    Rep 14 . . . . .481, 482
Palmco Shipping Co *v* Continental Ore Corporation [1970] 2 Lloyd's Rep 21 . .395
Pan Atlantic Co Ltd *v* Pine Top Insurance Co Ltd [1994] 3 All ER 581 . . .39, 98, 112
Panoutsos *v* Raymond Hadley Corpn [1917] 2 KB 473 359
Pao On *v* Lau Yiu Long [1980] AC 614
    . . . . .164, 170, 171, 339–40, 343, 346, 348–9, 352–4
Paradine *v* Jane (1647) Aleyn 26 417
Parker *v* Clark [1960] 1 All ER 93 183
Parker (Harry) Ltd *v* Mason [1940] 2 KB 590 223
Parkinson *v* The College of Ambulance Ltd and Harrison [1925] 2 KB 1
    . . . . .209, 223, 224
Parsons Bros Ltd *v* Shea (1966) 53 DLR (2d) 86 429
Parsons (H) (Livestock) Ltd *v* Uttley Ingham & Co Ltd [1978] QB 791;
    [1978] 1 All ER 525 500
Partridge *v* Crittenden [1968] 2 All ER 421 . . . . .123, 124, 125
Pascoe *v* Turner [1979] 1 WLR 431 . . . . .79, 94
Pasley *v* Freeman (1789) 3 TR 51 54
Patel *v* Ali [1984] Ch 283 452
Patrick *v* Russo-British Grain Exports [1927] 2 KB 535 503
Payne *v* Cave (1789) 3 Term Rep 148 127
Payzu *v* Saunders [1919] 2 KB 581 . . . . .353, 403, 404, 504
Pearce *v* Brain [1929] 2 KB 310 . . . . .242, 492
Pearce *v* Brooks (1866) LR 1 Exch 213 . . . . .192, 202, 222
Pearson (S) & Son Ltd *v* Lord Mayor of Dublin [1907] AC 354 . . . . .37, 54, 60
Peck *v* Lateu [1973] SJ 185 217
Peco Arts Inc *v* Haslitt Gallery Ltd [1983] 1 WLR 1315 48
Pegase, The [1981] 1 Lloyd's Rep 175 503
Pepper (Inspector of Taxes) *v* Hart [1993] AC 593 51
Percival *v* London County Council Asylum etc Committee (1918) 87 LJKB 677
   133
Perestrello & Compania Limitada *v* United Paint Co Ltd [1969] *The Times*,
    16 April 487
Perpetual Executors and Trustees Association of Australia Ltd *v* Wright (1917)
    23 CLR 185 223
Perry (Howard E) & Co *v* British Railways Board [1980] 1 WLR 1375 447
Perry *v* Sidney Phillips & Son [1982] 1 WLR 1297 . . . . .489, 504
Peters *v* Fleming (1860) 6 M&W 42 243
Pettit *v* Pettit [1970] AC 806 183
Peyman *v* Lanjani [1985] QB 428 . . . . .47, 48
Pfizer Corporation *v* Paton [1965] AC 512 169
Pharmaceutical Society of Great Britain *v* Boots Cash Chemists (Southern) Ltd
    [1952] 2 QB 795; [1952] 2 All ER 456; [1953] 1 All ER 482 . . . . .126, 127
Pharmaceutical Society of Great Britain *v* Dickson [1970] AC 403 216
Philips Electronique Grand Publique SA *v* British Sky Broadcasting Ltd [1995]
    EMLR 472 . . . . .113, 298
Philips Hong Kong Ltd *v* Attorney-General of Hong Kong (1993) 61 BLR
    41 . . . . .507, 508, 513, 515, 520–1
Phillips *v* Brooks [1919] 2 KB 243 25
Phillips *v* Lamdin [1949] 2 KB 33 446

Phillips Petroleum Co UK Ltd *v* Enron Europe Ltd (unreported) (CA)
  10 October 1996 90
Phillips Products *v* Hyland [1987] 2 All ER 620 .310, 311
Phoenix Insurance Co *v* De Monchy of Hartford (1929) 141 LTR 439 . . . .15, 389
Photo Production Ltd *v* Securicor Transport Ltd [1980] AC 827
  . . . . .306, 403, 431, 468
Pierce *v* Empey (1939) 4 DLR 672 . . . . .363, 373
Pilkington *v* Wood [1953] Ch 770 503
Pillans *v* Van Mierop (1782) 1 Cowp 289 165
Pilmore *v* Hood (1838) 5 Bing NC 97 38
Pillsworth *v* Cobourg [1930] 4 DLR 757 352
Pinnel's Case (1602) 5 Co Rep 117a .335, 336, 367, 368
Pioneer Container, The [1994] 2 AC 207; [1994] 2 All ER 250 . . . . .247, 282
Pitcaithly & Co *v* Thacker (1903) 23 NZLR 783 .133
Pits *v* Hung [1991] 1 QB 24 191
Pitt *v* PHH Asset Management Ltd [1994] 1 WLR 327 . . . . .92, 166, 168, 185
Planché *v* Colburn (1831) 8 Bing 14 409
Playa Larga, The [1983] 2 Lloyd's Rep 171 .291, 292
Plevins *v* Downing (1876) 1 CPD 220 359
Pollard *v* Clayton (1855) 1 K & J 462 449
Port Caledonia, The [1903] P 184 112
Port Line *v* Ben Line Steamers [1958] 2 QB 146 . . . . .279, 280, 423
Porter (William) & Co, *Re* [1937] 2 All ER 361 .364
Posner *v* Scott-Lewis [1987] Ch 25 449
Post Chaser, The [1981] 2 Lloyd's Rep 695 . . . . .17, 256, 361, 362, 365, 368
Potts *v* Bell (1800) 8 Term Rep 548 209
Pratt *v* Vizard (1833) 5 B & Ad 808 348
Pratt Contractors Ltd *v* Palmerston North City Council [1995] 1 NZLR 469
 129–31
Price *v* Hartwell [1998] GCS 98 77
Price *v* Strange [1978] Ch 337 453
Prior *v* McNab (1976) 78 DLR (3d) 319 460
Proodos C, The [1980] 1 Lloyd's Rep 390 . . . . .344, 346, 370
Prudential Assurance Co Ltd *v* London Residuary Body [1992] AC 386 188
Prudential Building Investment Society *v* Hankins [1997] 1 NZLR 114
  . . . . .381, 382
Public Works Commissioner *v* Hills [1906] AC 368 513
Publicator Industries *v* Union Carbide (1975) 17 UCC Rep 989 399
Puerto Buitrago, The [1976] 1 Lloyd's Rep 250 . . . . .455, 459, 460
Pusey *v* Pusey (1684) 1 Vern 273 445

Quadrant Visual Communications Ltd *v* Hutchinson Telephone (UK) Ltd [1993]
  BCLC 442 . . . . .444, 452
Quantum Claims Compensation Specialists Ltd *v* Powell 1998 SC 316 206
Queensland Electricity Generating Board *v* New Hope Collieries Pty Ltd [1989]
  1 Lloyd's Rep 205 89
Quenerduaine *v* Cole (1883) 32 WR 185 . . . . .145, 150
Quinn *v* Burch Bros (Builders) Ltd [1966] 2 QB 370 495

R *v* Clarke (1927) 40 CLR 227 . . . . .136, 155, 156

R *v* Disciplinary Committee of the Jockey Club, *ex p* Aga Khan [1993] 1 WLR
   909 216
R *v* Morris [1984] AC 320 126
R *v* Panayiotou [1973] 3 All ER 112 203
R *v* Warwickshire County Council, *ex p* Johnson [1993] AC 583 125
R & B Customs Brokers Ltd *v* United Dominions Trust Ltd [1988] 1 WLR
   321 . . . . .294, 309
Radford *v* De Froberville [1978] 1 All ER 33 . . . . .477, 479, 505
Raflatac *v* Eade [1999] 1 Lloyd's Rep 506 497
Rafsanjan Pistachio Producers Co-operative *v* Bank Leumi (UK) plc [1992]
   1 Lloyd's Rep 514 40
Raggow *v* Scougall (1915) 31 TLR 564 . . . . .329, 363
Ramsden *v* Dyson (1866) LR 1 HL 129 75
Rann *v* Hughes (1778) 7 Term Rep 350 165
Raphael, The [1982] 2 Lloyd's Rep 42 305
Ratcliffe *v* Evans [1892] 2 QB 524 465
Rattrays Wholesale *v* Meredyth-Young & A'Court [1997] 2 NZLR 363 380
Reardon Smith Line Ltd *v* Yngvar Hansen-Tangen [1976] 1 WLR 989 292
Record *v* Bell [1991] 1 WLR 863 . . . . .178, 446
Redgrave *v* Hurd (1881) 20 Ch D 1 . . . . .35, 36, 39, 60, 67
Redhead *v* Midland Railway Co (1866–67) LR 2 QB 412 326
Redpath *v* Belfast Railway [1947] NI 167 467
Reed *v* Madon [1989] Ch 408 470
Reese Silver Mining Co *v* Smith (1869) LR 4 HL 64 42
Regalgrand Ltd *v* Dickerson and Wade (1997) 74 P & CR 312 474
Regalian Properties plc *v* London Docklands Development Corporation
   [1995] 1 All ER 1005; [1995] 1 WLR 212 .83, 87, 493
Reigate *v* Union Manufacturing Co (Ramsbottom) Ltd [1918] 1 KB 592 297
Revell *v* Litwin Construction (1973) Ltd (1991) 86 DLR (4th) 169 379
Reynolds *v* Atherton (1922) 127 LT 189 145
Richardson *v* Davis (1931) 2 P 2d 860 458
Richardson *v* Mellish [1824] 2 Bing 229 200
Rickards (Charles) Ltd *v* Oppenheim [1950] 1 KB 611 . . . . .359, 365
Rijn, The [1981] 2 Lloyd's Rep 267 468
Rio Sun, The [1981] 2 Lloyd's Rep 489; [1982] 1 Lloyd's Rep 404 205
Robb *v* London Borough of Hammersmith and Fulham [1991] 1 RLR 72 451
Robbins of Putney *v* Meek [1971] RTR 345 506
Roberts *v* Gray [1913] 1 KB 520 243
Roberts (Graham H) Pty Ltd *v* Maurbeth Investments Pty Ltd [1974]
   1 NSWLR 93 448
Robertson *v* Minister of Pensions [1949] 1 KB 227 . . . . .365, 372, 376
Robinson *v* Harman (1848) 1 Exch 850 . . . . .56, 462, 478
Robinson (William) & Co Ltd *v* Heuer [1898] 2 Ch 217 454
Robophone Facilities *v* Blank [1996] 1 WLR 1428 508
Rock *v* Vandive (1920) 189 P 157 504
Rodocanachi, Sons & Co *v* Milburn Bros (1886) 18 QBD 67 481
Rogers *v* Parish (Scarborough) Ltd [1987] QB 933 295
Rolin *v* Stewart (1854) 14 CB 595 491
Ronald Elwyn Lister *v* Dunlop of Canada Ltd (1978) 19 OR (2d) 380 354
Rondel *v* Worsley [1969] 1 AC 465 69

Rookes *v* Barnard [1964] AC 1129 339
Rookes *v* Dawson [1895] 1 Ch 480 . . . . .128, 471
Roscorla *v* Thomas (1842) 3 QB 234 164
Rose (Frederick E) (London) Ltd *v* Wiliam H Pim Jnr & Co Ltd [1953]
    2 QB 450 297
Rose *v* Vulcan Materials Co (1973) 194 SE 2d 521 353
Rose and Frank Co *v* Crompton & Bros Ltd [1923] 2 KB 261 184
Ross *v* Caunters [1980] Ch 297 . . . . .69, 255, 270
Ross Systems *v* Linden Dari Delite Co (1961) 173 A 2d 258 351
Routledge *v* McKay [1954] 1 All ER 855 287
Rowland *v* Divall [1923] 2 KB 500 84
Royal Bank of Scotland *v* Etridge (No 2) [1998] 4 All ER 705 99
Royscot Trust Ltd *v* Rogerson [1991] 2 QB 297; [1991] 3 WLR 57
    . . . . .62, 63, 66, 71, 288
Rozanes *v* Bowen (1928) 32 Lloyd's LR 98 98
Rural Municipality of St James *v* Bailey and Driscoll (1975) 7 DLR 2d 179 . .363, 373
Rust *v* Abbey Life [1979] 2 Lloyd's Rep 334 154
Ruxley Electronics and Construction Ltd *v* Forsyth [1995] 3 All ER 268;
    [1996] 1 AC 344 . . . . .462, 470, 470–1, 484, 487
Ryan *v* Mutual Tontine Westminster Chambers Association [1893] 1 Ch
    116 . . . . .448, 450

St Albans City and District Council *v* International Computers Ltd [1996]
    4 All ER 481 . . . . .311, 467
St John Shipping Co *v* Spanglett Joseph Bank Ltd [1957] 1 QB 267 412
Sainsbury (J) plc *v* O'Connor (Inspector of Taxes) [1991] 1 WLR 963 446
Salisbury (Marquess) *v* Gilmore [1942] 2 KB 38 . . . . .28, 364
Saint Line *v* Richardson [1940] 2 KB 99 502
Sancho-Lopez *v* Fedor Food Corporation (1961) 211 NYS (2d) 953 . . . . .126, 127
Sanderson *v* Cockermouth and Workington Railway Co (1842) 2 Y & C Ch
    Cas 48 449
Sanix Ace, The [1987] 1 Lloyd's Rep 465 472
Sasso *v* KK & G Realty Construction Co (1923) 120 A 158 344
Saunders *v* Anglia Building Society [1971] AC 1004 .302
Saunders *v* Edwards [1987] 1 WLR 1116 221
Saunt *v* Belcher (1920) 26 Com Cas 115 478
Savage *v* Peter Kiewit Sons Co (1967) 432 P 2d 519 . . . . .390, 391
Scally *v* Southern Health and Social Services Board [1992] 1 AC 294;
    [1991] 4 All ER 563 . . . . .296, 299, 465
Scammell (G) & Nephew Ltd *v* Ouston [1941] AC 251 188
Scaptrade, The [1983] 1 All ER 301; affd [1983] 2 All ER 763 . . .361, 365, 449, 524
Schawel *v* Reade [1913] 2 Ir Rep 81 287
Schebsman, *Re* [1944] Ch 83 262
Schenkers Ltd *v* Overland Shoes Ltd [1998] 1 Lloyd's Rep 498 310
Schering Agrochemicals Ltd *v* Resibel NV SA (1992) 26 November
    (unreported) 497
Schuler *v* Wickham [1974] AC 239 435
Schwabacher, *Re* (1908) 98 LT 127 443
Schwartzreich *v* Bauman-Basch (1921) 131 NE 887 .329
Scot *v* Haughton and Fuller (1706) 2 Vern 560 162

Scotson v Pegg (1861) 30 LJ Ex 225 169
Scott v Brown [1892] 2 QB 724 222
Scott v Coulson [1903] 2 Ch 249 239
Scott v Hanson (1829) 1 Russ & M 128 31
Scott v Sebright (1886) 12 PD 21 ....337, 350
Scott (James) & Sons v Del Sol 1922 SC 592; 1923 SC 37 422
Scriven Bros and Co v Hindley & Co [1913] 3 KB 504 ....21, 22, 97
Scruttons Ltd v Midland Silicones Ltd. *See* Midland Silicones Ltd v
  Scruttons Ltd
Security Stone and Manufacturing Co v American Railway Express Co
  (1932) 51 SW 2d 572 487
Selectmove Ltd, *Re* [1995] 1 WLR 474 ....154, 368
Senator Hanseatische Verwaltungsgesellschaft GmbH, *Re* [1997] 1 WLR 515
  ....192, 217
Service Station Association Ltd v Bennett & Associates Pty Ltd (1993)
  117 ALR 393 15
Shadwell v Shadwell (1860) 9 CB (NS) 159 ....169, 170, 184
Shanklin Pier Ltd v Detel Products Ltd [1951] 2 KB 854 ....220, 265
Shaw v Applegate [1978] 1 All ER 123 373
Shaw v Fitzgerald [1992] 1 FLB 357 208
Shaw v Groom [1970] 2 QB 501 198
Shaw v Woodcock (1827) 7 B & C 73 338
Shearman v Polland [1950] 2 KB 43 467
Shearson Lehman Hutton Inc v MacLaine Watson & Co Ltd [1989]
  2 Lloyd's Rep 570 ....77, 216, 372
Shearson Lehman Hutton Inc v MacLaine Watson & Co Ltd (No 2) [1990]
  3 All ER 723 482
Sheeskin v Giant Food Inc (1974) 318 A 2d 874 127
Shell Chemicals Ltd v P & O Roadtanks Ltd [1995] 1 Lloyd's Rep 297 305
Shelley v Paddock [1980] QB 348 221
Shepherd (FC) & Co Ltd v Jerrom [1987] 1 QB 301 422
Shindle v Northern Raincoat Co Ltd [1960] 1 WLR 1038 403
Shine v General Guarantee Corpn Ltd [1988] 1 All ER 911 296
Shipton Anderson & Co v Weil Bros [1912] 1 KB 574 410
Shirlaw v Southern Foundries Ltd [1939] 2 KB 206 298
Shroeder Music Publishing Co Ltd v Macaulay [1974] 3 All ER 616;
  [1974] 1 WLR 1308 ....212, 213
Shuey v United States (1875) 92 US 73 136–7
Siben, The [1996] 1 Lloyd's Rep 35 ....57, 58, 94, 196
Siboen (The) and *The Sibotre* [1976] 1 Lloyd's Rep 293
  ....60, 338, 343, 345, 349, 475
Silliman v United States (1879) 101 US 465 350
Silver Sky, The [1981] 2 Lloyd's Rep 95 495
Silverstone Records v Mountfield [1993] EMLR 152 213
Simaan General Contracting Co v Pilkington Glass (No 2) [1988] QB 758 255
Simon Container Machinery Ltd v Emba Mchinery MB [1998] 2 Lloyd's
  Rep 429 335
Simon v Metivier (or Motivis) (1766) 1 Wm B1 599 177
Simpkins v Pays [1955] 1 WLR 975 184
Simpson v L & NW Railway (1876) 1 QBD 274 504

Sindall (William) plc *v* Cambridge County Council [1994] 3 All ER
  932 . . . . .33, 50, 51, 239
Singer Co (UK) Ltd *v* Tees and Hartlepool Port Authority [1988] 2 Lloyd's Rep
  164 310
Singh *v* Ali [1960] AC 167 227
Sistrom *v* Anderson (1942) 124 P 2d 372 343
Skeate *v* Beale (1840) 11 Ad & El 983 . . . . .338, 339
Skopas, The [1983] 2 All ER 1 . . . . .62, 65
Sky Petroleum *v* VIP Petrol Ltd [1974] 1 WLR 576 447
Slater *v* Finning [1996] 3 All ER 398 295
Sledmore *v* Dalby [1996] 72 P & CR 204 .74, 77, 79
Sloan *v* Union Oil Co (1955) 4 DLR 664 . . . . .18, 370
Slot *v* Haughton & F Fuller (1706) 2 Vern 560 .217
Smith *v* Chadwick (1884) App Cas 187 . . . . .35, 36
Smith *v* Eric S Bush [1990] 1 AC 831 . . . . .66, 68, 70, 310, 311
Smith *v* Hughes (1871) LR 6 QB 597 . . . . .20, 22, 38, 96, 123
Smith *v* Kay (1859) 7 HLC 750 40
Smith *v* Lenchner (1964) 205 A 2d 626 354
Smith *v* Littlewoods Organisation Ltd [1987] AC 241 95
Smith *v* Mawhood (1845) 14 MAW 452 199
Smith *v* UMB Chrysler (Scotland) Ltd 1978 SC (HL) 1 305
Smith *v* William Charlick Ltd (1924) 34 CLR 38 341
Smith and Snipers Hall Farm Ltd *v* River Douglas Catchment Board
  [1949] 2 KB 500 251
Smith New Court Securities Ltd *v* Scrimgeour Vickers Ltd [1992]
  BCLC 1104 59
Snelling *v* John G Snelling [1973] QB 87; [1972] 2 WLR 588 . . .184, 272, 273, 275
Soames *v* British Empire Shipping Co (1860) 8 HLC 338 338
Société Commerciale de Réassurance *v* ERAS (International) Ltd [1992]
  1 Lloyd's Rep 570 174
Société des Industries Métallurgiques SA *v* Bronx Engineering Co Ltd [1975]
  1 Lloyd's Rep 464 446
Solle *v* Butcher [1950] 1 KB 671 240
Solholt, The [1983] 1 Lloyd's Rep 605 . . . . .353, 403, 504
Somerset *v* Cookson (1735) 3 P Wms 390 445
Soper *v* Arnold (1889) 14 App Cas 429 520
South Australia Asset Management Corporation *v* York Montague Ltd
  [1997] AC 191; [1996] 3 All ER 365 . . . . .59, 71, 462, 479
Southern Water Authority *v* Carey [1985] 2 All ER 1077 263
Southwark London Borough Council *v* Logan [1995] Times LR 565 . . . . . .76, 162
Sowler *v* Potter [1939] 4 All ER 478 24
Spencer *v* Harding (1870) LR 5 CP 561 . . . . .122, 130
Spartan Steel & Alloys Ltd *v* Martin & Co (Contractors) Ltd [1973] QB 27
  . . . . .204, 501
Spiers *v* Hunt [1908] 1 KB 720 207
Spring *v* Guardian Assurance plc [1995] 2 AC 296 . . . . .67, 70
Spurling (J) Ltd *v* Bradshaw [1956] 1 WLR 461 303
Stackhome *v* Barnston (1805) 10 Ver 453 . . . . .73, 357
Staffordshire Area Health Authority *v* South Staffordshire Waterworks Co
  [1978] 3 All ER 769 . . . . .396, 397, 400

Standard Chartered Bank *v* Pakistan National Shipping Corp (No 1)
 [2000] 3 WLR 1692 60
Stead *v* Dawber (1839) 10 A & E 57 358–60
Steadman *v* Steadman [1976] AC 536 177
Stees *v* Leonard (1874) 20 Minn 448 387
Steinberg *v* Scala (Leeds) Ltd [1923] 2 Ch 452 244
Stena Nautica (No 2), *The*, CN Marine Inc *v* Stena Line A/B and Rege voor
 Maritem Transport [1982] 2 Lloyd's Rep 336 446
Stevenson *v* Clarke (1853) 4 Gr 540 447
Stevenson, Jacques & Co *v* McLean (1880) 5 QBD 346 . . . . .140, 151
Stevenson *v* Rogers [1999] 2 WLR 1064 . . . . .294, 309
Stewart Gill Ltd *v* Horatio Myer & Co Ltd [1992] 2 WLR 721 309
Stilk *v* Myrick (1809) 2 Camp 317 . . . . .327, 336, 343
Stockloser *v* Johnson [1954] 1 QB 476 522–3
Stocks *v* Wilson [1913] 2 KB 235 245
Stoczia Gdanska SA *v* Latvian Shipping [1998] 1 All ER 883 524
Stoneleigh Finance Ltd *v* Phillips [1965] 2 QB 537 197
Storer *v* Manchester City Council [1974] 3 All ER 824 122
Stovin *v* Wise [1996] AC 923 95
Stowell *v* Robinson (1837) 3 Bing NC 928 358
Strathcona (Lord) Steamship Co Ltd *v* Dominion Coal Co Ltd
 [1926] AC 108 279
Strongman (1945) *v* Sincock [1955] 2 QB 528 220
Strutt *v* Whitnell [1975] 1 WLR 870 404
Sudbrook Trading Estate Ltd *v* Eggleton [1983] 1 AC 448; [1982] 3 All
 ER 1 . . . . .188, 189, 445
Suisse Atlantique Société d'Armement Maritime SA *v* Rotherdamashe Kolen
 Centrale [1967] 1 AC 361 . . . . .306, 507, 517
Suleyman Stalskiy, The [1976] 2 Lloyd's Rep 609 268
Sumnall *v* Statt (1984) P & CR 367 418
Sumpter *v* Hedges [1898] 1 QB 673 . . . . .408, 409
Sundell & Sons *v* Emm Yannoulatos (Overseas) Pty Ltd (1956) 56 SR (NSW)
 323 343
Super Servant Two, The [1990] 1 Lloyd's Rep 1 418
Surrey County Council *v* Bredero Homes Ltd [1993] 3 All ER 705
 . . . . .462, 464, 475
Swain *v* Law Society [1982] 1 AC 598 263
Swingcastle Ltd *v* Alistair Gibson (a firm) [1991] 2 AC 233 71
Swiss Bank Corporation *v* Lloyds Bank Ltd [1978] Ch 581 280
Sydenham (JT) & Co Ltd *v* Enichem Elastomers [1989] 1 EGLR 257 369

Tailby *v* Official Receiver (1888) 13 App Cas 523 443
Tak & Co Inc *v* AEL Corporation Ltd (1995) 5 NZBLC 99, 357, 471
Tamplin (FA) Steamship Co *v* Anglo-Mexican Petroleum Products Co
 [1916] 2 AC 397 . . . . .390, 401, 421, 425
Tanner *v* Tanner [1975] 1 WLR 1346 182
Tappenden *v* Randall (1801) 2 BOS 2 Pul 467 191
Target Holding *v* Priestley (unreported) 330
Tatem *v* Gamboa [1939] 1 KB 132 . . . . .387, 392, 423
Taylor *v* Allen [1965] 1 All ER 557 155

Taylor v Bank of Athens (1922) 27 Com Cas 142 466
Taylor v Bhail [1996] CLC 377 194
Taylor v Bowes (1876) 1 QBD 291 226
Taylor v Caldwell (1863) 3 B & S 826 . . . . .385, 421, 422, 425
Taylor v Dickens [1997] *The Times*, 24 November 74
Taylor v Neville, cited in Buxton v Lister (1746) 3 Ark 383 447
Taylor v NUS [1967] 1 WLR 532 450
Taylor Fashions Ltd v Liverpool Victoria Trustees Co Ltd [1981] 1 QB 133;
   [1981] 1 All ER 897 . . . . .74, 373
Tengku Abdullah Sultan Abu Bakan v Mohd Latiff bin Shah [1996] 2 MLJ 265 . . .203
Texaco Melbourne, The [1994] 1 Lloyd's Rep 473 477
Thacker v Hardy [1878] 4 QBD 685 218
Thackwell v Barclays Bank plc [1986] 1 All ER 676 231
Thai Trading Co (a firm) v Taylor [1998] 3 All ER 65 206
Thomas v Brown (1876) 1 QBD 714 244
Thomas v Dering (1837) 1 Keen 729 451
Thomas v Thomas (1842) 2 QB 851 . . . . .162, 163
Thompson v London, Midland & Scottish Railway Co [1930] 1 KB 41 . . .134, 304
Thompson (WL) v Robinson (Gunmakers) Ltd [1955] Ch 177 481
Thompson Crane and Trucking v Eyman (1954) 267 P 2d 1043 352
Thorensen Car Ferries Ltd v Weymouth Portland Borough Council [1977]
   2 Lloyd's Rep 614 160
Thorn v Public Works Commission (1863) 32 Beav 490 445
Thorne v Motor Trade Association [1937] AC 797 342
Thornton v Shoe Lane Parking Ltd [1971] 2 QB 163 . . . . .133, 134, 303
Thoroughgood's Case (1584) 2 Co Rep 9a 302
Tilden Rent-a-Car Co v Glendenning (1978) 83 DLR (3d) 400 302
Timeload v British Telecommunications [1995] EMLR 459 . . . . .113, 311, 312
Tinn v Hoffman & Co (1873) 29 LT 271 . . . . .150, 156
Tinsley v Milligan [1994] 1 AC 340 . . . . .194–5, 227, 228, 229, 230, 232
Tito v Waddell (No 2) [1977] Ch 106 . . . . .188, 409, 448–9, 452, 462, 474–5, 479
Tolnay v Criterion Film Productions Ltd [1936] 2 All ER 1625 486
Tool Metal Manufacturing v Tungsten Electric Co Ltd [1955] 1 WLR 761
   . . . . .365, 366, 368, 369
Total Liban SA v Vitol Energy SA [2000] 3 WLR 1142 462
Trans Trust SPRL v Danubian Trading Co Ltd [1952] 2 QB 297 504
Transatlantic Financing Corporation v United States (1966) 363 F 2d 312
   . . . . .391, 398
Trendtex Trading Corporation v Crédit Suisse [1982] AC 679 206
Trent and Humber Co, ex p Cambrian Steam Packet Co (1868) LR 6 Eq 396 . .502
Trentharm (G Percy) v Architral Luxfer Ltd [1993] 1 Lloyd's Rep 25 . . . .141, 142
Tribe v Tribe [1990] Ch 107 . . . . .194, 223, 224
Trident General Insurance v McNeice Bros (1988) 165 CLR 107; 62 AJLR
   508 . . . . .248, 261, 263
Trigg v M1 Movers International Transport Services Ltd (1991) 84 DLR (4th)
   504 302
Tristake Roofing Co v Uniontown (1958) 142 A (2d) 333 353
Trustees of the Manchester Homoeopathic Clinic v Manchester Corp. *See*
   Manchester Homoeopathic Clinc Trustees v Manchester Corporation.
Tsakiroglou & Co v Noblee Thorl GmbH [1962] AC 93 395

Tudale Explorations Ltd, *Re* (1978) 20 OR 2d 593 ....18, 365, 366, 370, 381, 382
Tulk *v* Moxhay (1848) 2 Ph 774 279
Tweddle *v* Atkinson (1861) 1 B & S 393 ....249, 250
Twyford *v* Manchester Corporation [1946] Ch 236 ....349, 350
Tymshare Inc *v* Covell 727 F 2d 1145 113

UBAF Ltd *v* European American Banking Corporation [1984] QB 713 71
Unchained Growth III plc *v* Granby Village Management Co Ltd
   [2000] 1 WLR 739 317
Union Eagle Ltd *v* Golden Achievements Ltd [1997] 2 All ER 215 ....520, 523
Union Pacific Ry Co *v* Public Service Commission of Missouri (1918) 248
   US 67 346
United Dominions Corporation (Jamaica) Ltd *v* Shoucair [1969] 1 AC 340 329
United Dominions Trust (Commercial) Ltd *v* Ennis [1968] QB 54 511
United Food and Chemical Workers Union of New Zealand *v* Talley [1993] 2 ERNZ
   360 335
United States *v* Bethlehem Steel Corporation (1942) 315 US 289 341
United States *v* Stamp Home Specialities Manufacturing Inc (1990) 905 F 2d
   1117 327
Universe Sentinel, The [1983] 1 AC 366; [1982] 2 All ER 67
   ....339, 341, 345, 348, 349
Upfill *v* Wright [1911] 1 KB 506 ....195, 196, 202
Upper Lakes Shipping Ltd *v* St Lawrence Cement Inc (1992) 89 DLR (4th) 722 ..305
Upton Rural District Council *v* Powell [1942] 1 All ER 220 ....156, 157

Vachon Construction *v* Cariboo (Regional District) (1996) 136 DLR (4th)
   307 ....129, 130
Valpy *v* Manley (1945) 1 CB 594 348
Vanbergen *v* St Edmund Properties [1933] 2 KB 223 336
Van Camp Chocolates Ltd *v* Auslebrooks Ltd [1984] 1 NZLR 354 443
Van den Hurk *v* Martens & Co Ltd [1920] 1 KB 850 478
Vandepitte *v* Preferred Accident Insurance Corporation of New York [1933]
   AC 70 262
Vaswani *v* Italian Motors Ltd [1996] 1 WLR 270 433
Vaughan (AIS) & Co Ltd *v* Royscot Trust plc [1999] 1 All ER (Comm) 856 ...341
Victoria Laundry (Windsor) Ltd *v* Newman Industries Ltd [1949] 2 KB 528
   ....351, 476, 499, 501–3, 506
Victorian Daylesford Syndicate Ltd *v* Dott [1905] 2 Ch 624 199
Vitol SA *v* Norelf Ltd [1996] 3 WLR 105 ....155, 431, 470
Vorvis *v* Insurance Corporation of British Columbia (1989) 58 DLR (4th) 193
  470

W & R Sack Ltd *v* Fifield [1996] 2 NZLR 105 361
Wade *v* Simeon (1846) 2 CB 548 ....160, 167, 168, 204
Wadham Stringer Finance Ltd *v* Meaney [1981] 1 WLR 39 514
Wagon Mound, The (No 1) [1961] AC 388 ....58, 66, 500
Wait, *Re* [1927] 1 Ch 606 44
Wales *v* Wadham [1977] 1 WLR 199 ....32, 99
Walford *v* Miles [1992] 2 AC 128; [1992] 2 WLR 174 ....88–93, 114, 130
Walford's Case [1919] AC 801 296

Walker, *Re* [1905] 1 Ch 60 246
Wallems Rederij *v* Muller [1927] 2 KB 99 504
Wallis *v* Smith (1882) 21 Ch D 243 . . . . .508, 509
Wall's Case [1915] 3 KB 66 . . . . .514, 517
Walters *v* Roberts (1980) 41 P & CR 210 451
Walton Harvey Ltd *v* Walker Homfrays Ltd [1931] 1 Ch 274 390
Walton's Stores (Interstate) Ltd *v* Maher (1988) 64 CLR 387
. . . . .74, 175, 374–7, 380, 383
Ward *v* Byham [1956] 1 WLR 496 . . . . .166, 172, 332
Warlow *v* Harrison (1859) 1 E & E 309 128
Warner Bros Pictures Inc *v* Nelson [1937] 1 KB 209 . . . . .444, 454
Warren *v* Mendy [1989] IRLR 210; [1989] 1 WLR 853 450
Warren *v* Stagg (1787), cited in Littler *v* Holland (1799) 3 TR 590 360
Warrington *v* Great West Life Assurance Co (1996) 139 DLR (4th) 18 485
Warwick (Countess of) *v* Le Nickel SA [1918] 1 KB 372 . . . . .388, 424, 425
Wates *v* GLC (1983) 25 BLR 1 425
Wathes (Western) Ltd *v* Austins (Menswear) Ltd [1976] 1 Lloyd's Rep 14 306
Watkins *v* Watkins [1896] P 222 269
Watkins & Son *v* Craig (1941) 21 A 2d 591 . . . . .320, 344
Watson *v* Canada Permanent Trust Co (1972) 27 DLR (3d) 735 382
Watson *v* Prager [1991] 1 WLR 726 213
Watts *v* Morrow [1991] 4 All ER 302; [1991] 1 WLR 1421` 479, 485, 489
Watts *v* Spence [1976] Ch 165 63
Watts, Watts & Co Ltd *v* Mitsui & Co Ltd [1917] AC 227 . . . . .514, 517
Wauchope *v* Maida (1972) 22 DLR 142 . . . . .365, 368
Way *v* Lotilla [1937] 3 All ER 759 86
Wayling *v* James (1995) 69 P & CR 170 76–8
Webster *v* Cecil (1861) 30 Beav 62 21
Welch *v* O'Brian Financial Corporation (1991) 86 DLR (4th) 155 379
Wells *v* Cooper [1958] 2 QB 265 31
Westcoast Transmission Co *v* Cullen Detroit Diesel Allison Ltd (1990) 70 DLR
  (4th) 503 307
Western Advertising Co *v* Mid-West Laundries (1933) 61 SW 2d 251 458
Western Fish Products *v* Penrith District Council [1981] 2 All ER 204 77
Westinghouse Electric Corporation Uranium-Contracts Litigation, *Re*
  (1975) 405 F Supp 316 . . . . .394, 399
Wham-O Mfg Co *v* Lincoln Industries [1984] 1 NZLR 641 380
Whincup *v* Hughes (1871) LR 6 CP 78 . . . . .428, 429
Whitall *v* Kaur (1970) 8 DLR 3d 163 361
White *v* Bluett (1853) 23 LJ Ex 36 . . . . .165, 166, 172
White & Carter (Councils) Ltd *v* McGregor [1962] AC 413; [1961] 3 All ER
  1178 . . . . .112, 443, 456–9, 513
White *v* Jones [1995] 2 AC 207 . . . . .69, 247, 255, 269–71
Whittington *v* Seale-Hayne (1900) 82 LT 49 52
Wigsell *v* School for the Indigent Blind (1882) 8 QBD 357 479
Wilkie *v* Belhame (1848) 11 D 132 395
Wilkie *v* London Transport Board [1947] 1 All ER 258 . . . . .133, 134, 273
Wilkinson *v* Clements (1872) 8 Ch App 96 448
Wilkinson *v* Lloyd (1845) 7 QB 27 494
Williams *v* Bayley (1866) LR 1 HL 200 102

Williams *v* Carwardine (1833) 5 C & P 566 . . . . .155, 156
Williams *v* Moor (1843) 11 M & W 256 244
Williams *v* Moss Empires [1915] 3 KB 242 329
Williams *v* Reynolds (1865) 6 B & S 495 481
Williams *v* Roffey Bros & Nicholls (Contractors) Ltd [1991] 1 QB 1;
    [1990] 1 All ER 512 . . . . .323, 331–7, 344, 411
Williams *v* Williams [1957] 1 WLR 148 . . . . .172, 204, 230, 332
Williams Bros Ltd *v* Edward T Agius Ltd [1914] AC 510 481
Wilmott *v* Barber (1880) 15 Ch D 96 75
Wilson *v* Best Travel Ltd [1993] 1 All ER 353 296
Wilson *v* Darling Island Stevedoring and Lighterage Co Ltd (1956) 95 CLR 43;
    [1956] 1 Lloyd's Rep 346 . . . . .263, 267
Wilson *v* General Ironscrew Company (1878) 47 LJQB 23 502
Wilson *v* Sooter Studios (1989) 55 DLR (4th) 484
Wilson *v* United Counties Bank Ltd [1920] AC 102 . . . . .464, 489
Wilson *v* Wilson [1848] 1 HLC 538 208
Windle, *Re* [1975] 1 WLR 1628 182
Winn *v* Bull (1877) 7 ChD 29 185
Winter *v* Trimmer (1762) 1 Wm Bl 395 517
With *v* O'Flanagan [1934] 1 Ch 575 . . . . .27, 31, 32, 33, 98, 105
Wither *v* TBP Industries [1996] 2 All ER 573 .50, 51, 56
Withers *v* General Theatre Corporation Ltd [1933] 2 KB 536 . . . . .468, 489
Wolverhampton Corporation *v* Emmons [1901] 1 QB 515 448
Wood *v* Roberts (1818) 1 Stark 417 336
Woodar Investment Development Ltd *v* Wimpey Construction UK Ltd [1980]
    1 WLR 277 . . . . .112, 247, 254, 275, 432, 433
Woodhouse AC Israel Cocoa Ltd SA *v* Nigerian Produce Marketing Co Ltd [1972]
    AC 741 . . . . .17, 330, 365
Workers Trust and Merchant Bank Ltd *v* Dojap Investments Ltd [1993] 2 All ER
    370 . . . . .520–1, 523
World Beauty, The [1970] P 144 505
World Navigator, The [1991] 2 Lloyd's Rep 23 468
Wormell *v* RHM Agriculture (East) Ltd [1987] 1 WLR 1091 295
Wroth *v* Tyler [1974] Ch 30 . . . . .451, 478, 505, 506
Wrotham Park Estate Co *v* Parkside Homes Ltd [1974] 1 WLR 798 . . . . . .464, 475
Wyatt *v* Kreglinger and Fernau [1933] 1 KB 793 . . . . .161, 211, 214
Wyvern Development Ltd, *Re* [1974] 1 WLR 1097 . . . . .18, 370

Yango Pastoral Company Pty Ltd *v* First Chicago Australia Ltd (1979) 139 CLR
    410 199
Yates *v* Whyte (1838) 4 Bing (NC) 272 467
Yaxley *v* Gotts [1999] 2 FLR 941 80
Yorbrook Investments Ltd *v* Aylesford [1986] P & CR 51 409
Youell *v* Bland Welch & Co Ltd [1992] 2 Lloyd's Rep 127 289

Zealander *v* Laing (unreported) 316
Zhi Jiang Kow, The [1991] 1 Lloyd's Rep 491 . . . . .371, 378
Zoan *v* Rouamba [2000] 1 WLR 1509 179
Zockoll Group Ltd *v* Mercury Communications Ltd [1998] FSR 354 . . . .113, 312

TABLE OF STATUTES

Australia
Victoria Goods Act 1928
  s 11 235

New Zealand
Contracts (Privity) Act 1982 254
Illegal Contracts Act 1970 . . . .231, 232
  s 8(1) .231

United Kingdom
Access to Justice Act 1999 206
Apportionment Act 1870
  s 2 409
  s 5 409
  s 7 409
Administration of Justice Act 1970
  s 11 443
Arbitration Act 1950
  s 27 371
Arbitration Act 1979 205
Arbitration Act 1996 205
  s 1(2) .205
  s 41(3) 154
Bills of Exchange Act 1882
  s 3(1) .180
Bills of Lading Act 1855 . . . . .260, 261
  s 1 473
Carriage of Goods by Sea Act 1992 . . . .
  . . . . .261, 473
Charities Act 1993
  ss 50, 60 173
Child Support Act 1991
  s 9 204
Children Act 1989
  s 2 208
Companies Act 1985 68
  s 14 259
  s 35 246
  s 36A(4) 173
Competition Act 1998 215
  s 2 215
  s 18 215
  s 25 215

  s 26 215
  s 44 215
Consumer Credit Act 1974 . . . .97, 194
  s 8 179
  s 16 . . . . .179, 523
  s 62 . . . . .97, 179
  s 63 . . . . .97, 179
  s 65 179
  s 67 . . . . .97, 179
  ss 67–73 158
  s 127(4) 179
  ss 137–140 522
Consumer Protection Act 1987 127
Contract (Scotland) Act 1997
  s 1 289
Contracts (Rights of Third Parties) Act
  1999 . . . . . . .252–9, 263, 278, 301–2
  s 1 . . . . .249, 253, 259
    (1)(a) 253, 255
    (2) .254
    (3) .254
    (5) .257
  s 2 (1) .255
    (2)(a)–(b) 256, 257
    (3) .255
    (4)(a)–(b) 255
    (5) .255
  s 3 (2)–(4)(b) 258
  s 4 . . . . .249, 258
  s 5 258
  s 6 (3) .259
    (5) .259
    (6) .259
  s 7 (1) 249, 263
    (2) .258
Copyright Act 1956
  s 8 163
Courts and Legal Services Act 1990
  s 28 206
  s 58 206
  s 58A .206
Criminal Justice Act 1988
  Pt VI .201

Criminal Law Act 1967
s 1 203
s 5(1) 173
s 13(1) 206
s 14(1)–(2) 206
s 501 .203
Debtors Act 1869
ss 4–5 443
Directors Liability Act 1890 . . . .55, 68
Employers' Liability Act 1880 243
Employment Protection (Consolidation)
Act 1978 451
Employment Rights Act 1996
s 1 .98, 180
ss 113–117 451
Fair Employment (Northern Ireland)
Act 1989
s 49 201
Fair Trading (Northern Ireland) Act
1976
s 16 201
Financial Services Act 1986 . . .104, 219
s 47(1) 104
s 63 218
s 146 . . . . .104, 111
s 150 . . . . .55, 104
s 163 .104
s 166 . . . . .55, 104
Sch 1, para 12 219
Fire Prevention (Metropolis) Act 1774
s 11 259
Gaming Act 1845 . . . . . . .216, 218, 219
s 18 . . . . .217, 219
Gaming Act 1968
s 52(1) 219
Hallmarking Act 1973 104
Housing Act 1988
ss 27–28 474
Human Fertilisation and Embryology
Act 1990
s 36 208
Human Organs Transplants Act 1989
s 1 197
Human Rights Act 1998 . . . . .200, 201
Land Clauses Consolidation Act 1845
. 363
Landlord and Tenant Act 1985
s 4 180
Law of Property Act 1925
s 40 . . . . .177, 178, 329

(1) .80
(2) .177
s 47 259
s 49(2) 521
s 52 . . . . .120, 180
s 54(2) 120, 180
s 174 .104
Law of Property (Miscellaneous
Provisions) Act 1989
s 1(2) 173
s 2 . . . . .119, 180, 329
(1) .80
(8) .80
Law Reform (Contributory Negligence)
Act 1945 . . . . .495, 496
s 1(1) 60, 495
s 4 60
Law Reform (Enforcement of
Contracts) Act 1954 177
s 2 329
Law Reform (Frustrated Contracts) Act
1943 . . . . .385, 386, 429
s 1 (2) 400, 428, 430
(3) 428–30
s 2(5)(a) 428
(b) 400, 428
Law Reform (Married Women and
Tortfeasors) Act 1935 183
Law Reform (Miscellaneous Provisions)
Act 1970
s 1 207
(1) 170, 432, 484
(3) .173
(4) .173
s 2 . . . . .177, 207
(8) .177
Life Assurance Act 1774
s 1 217
Limitation Act 1980
s 5 . . . . .120, 173
s 8(1) 120, 173
s 11 .120
s 14 .173
s 14A .174
s 33 .120
Marine Insurance Act 1906
s 4 217
s 14(2) 259
Married Women's Property Act 1882
s 11 259

Matrimonial Causes Act 1973
s 34 204
Mental Health Act 1983
Pt VII 246
Minors' Contracts Act 1987
s 3(1) 245
Misrepresentation Act 1967 68
s 1 285
s 2(1)
...26, 50, 51, 55, 61–8, 70–2, 94, 98
(2) 49–53, 56, 61, 72
(3) 49
s 3 ....313, 314, 317
National Assistance Act 1948
s 42 ....166, 172
Official Secrets Act 1911
s 1(1)(a) 201
Police Act 1964
s 15(1) 172
Proceeds of Crime Act 1995 201
Protection of Birds Act 1954 123
Public Passenger Vehicles Act 1981
s 29 273
Race Relations Act 1976 201
Restriction of Offensive Weapons Act
1959
s 1(1)(a) 197
Restrictive Practices Act 1956 215
Road Traffic Act 1960
s 151.....................273
Road Traffic Act 1988
s 148(7) 257
Sale and Supply of Goods Act 1994
........................294
Sale of Goods Act 1893
s 4 329
s 6 235
s 52 ....446, 447
Sale of Goods Act 1979
.......44, 48, 296, 455, 477, 482
s 3 242
(2) 246
s 6 235–7
s 8(2) 189, 491
ss 12–15 290
s 12 ....202, 291, 313
(1) 290, 291, 434
(2) 291
(4) 434
(5) 434

s 13 ....265, 292–3, 313, 434
(1) 290, 434
s 14 ......105, 294, 295, 309, 313
(1) 500
(2)   105, 290,
295, 296, 305, 313, 434, 496
(2A) 294
(2B) 294
(2C) 294
(3) .105, 290, 295, 313, 434, 500
s 15 ....313, 434
(2) 290, 296, 434
s 15A 434
s 28 408
s 35 48
s 49 484
(1)–(2) 455
s 50(3) 477, 482, 505
s 51 477
(1) 481
(3) 481, 482, 505
s 52 446
s 55 236
s 53(3) 480, 481, 487, 492
s 57(2)–(4) 127
s 61(2)(b) 434
Sale of Land by Auction Act 1875
s 5 127
Sex Discrimination Act 1986 200
Sexual Offences Act 1956
s 1(1)–(2) 56
Statute of Frauds 1677 ......153, 177
s 4 ....176, 177
s 17 176
Suicide Act 1961
s 1 201
Supply of Goods and Services Act 1982
ss 2–5 296
ss 7–10 296
s 13 ...290, 293, 296, 305, 437, 496
s 15(1) 189, 491
s 61(1) 293
Supply of Goods (Implied Terms) Act
1973
ss 8–11 296
Supreme Court Act 1981
s 50 477
Theft Act 1968
s 15 201
s 16 201

s 21(1) .341
Third Parties (Rights Against Insurers)
  Act 1930
  s 1 259
Trade Descriptions Act 1968 293
Trade Union and Labour Relations Act
  1974 345
Trade Union and Labour Relations
  (Consolidation) Act 1992
  s 11 214
  s 236 450
Unfair Contract Terms Act 1977
        68, 258, 291, 293, 294, 301,
    302, 304, 306–14, 316, 317, 518
  s 1 (3) 308, 310, 313
    (4) .310
  s 2 . . . . .257, 305, 307, 310, 311
    (1) 308, 314, 317
    (2) 258, 314, 317
  s 3 . . . .257, 305, 310, 311, 314, 317
    (1) .257
    (2)(a) 311, 312
    (b) 311, 312
  s 4 308
  s 5 . . . . .308, 317

s 6   106, 236, 291, 305, 310, 312,
  . . . . .314, 317
    (1) .314
    (2)(a) 314
    (3) .314
s 7 . . . . .236, 310, 312
s 8 317
s 11 . . . . .313, 314
    (1) 309, 314
    (2) .310
    (4) .310
    (5) .309
s 12 . . . . .106, 308, 309, 313
    (1) .308
    (2) .309
    (3) .309
s 13 . . . . .308, 313, 317
s 14 309
s 26 308
Sch 1 . . . . .99, 308
    para 1 317
Sch 2 . . . . .310, 313, 317
Unsolicited Goods and Services Act
  1971 153
Commercial Agents (Council Directive)

TABLE OF STATUTORY INSTRUMENTS

Regulations 1993
(S1 1993/3053) 470
Consumer Credit (Agreements)
Regulations 1983
(SI 1983/1553) 97, 111
General Product Safety Regulations
1994 (SI 1994/2328) 104
Licensed Dealers (Conduct of Business
Rules 1983 (SI 1983/585)
r 18(2) 218
Package Travel, Package Holidays and
Package Tours Regulations 1992
(SI 1992/3288) . . .11, 104, 180, 259
reg 2 180
(1) 259
regs 7–9 104
reg 9 (1)(a)(c) 180
reg 15 259
Sch 2 . . . . .104, 180
Public Services Contracts Regulations
1993
(SI 1993/3228) 11, 132
Public Supply Contracts Regulations
1991 (SI 1991/2679) 130
Public Supply Contracts Regulations
1995 (SI 1995/201) 11, 132
Public Works Contracts Regulations
1991 (S1 1991/2680) 11, 132
Unfair Terms in Consumer Contract

Regulations 1994
(SI 1994/3159) 11, 115, 314
Unfair Terms in Consumer Contract
Regulations 1999
(SI 1999/2083) 11, 97, 99, 113,
301, 302, 304, 314, 317, 512, 518
reg 2(1) 512, 518, 522
reg 3 . . . . .97, 317
(1) 315, 512, 518, 522
reg 4 317
(1) 97, 315
(4) 512, 518, 522
reg 5(1) 113, 315, 317, 512, 518, 522
(2) 315
(3) 315
(5) 97, 316, 409
reg 6(2)(a)–(b) 316
reg 7(2) 304
reg 8 315
(1) 97
Sch 1 .518
paras 1(a)–(b)(i) 316
Sch 2 . . . . .316, 409
para 1 . . . . .97, 317
Sch 3 . . . . .512, 522
para 1(1) 113

1

INTRODUCTION

EXPLANATION OF THE SCHEME OF THE BOOK

When I set out to write this book, more years ago than my publisher cares to remember, I looked at the structure of the popular student textbooks. Their scheme of arrangement differed little from that adopted in their first edition, which in some cases was half a century or even a century before. In order to find the origin of that structure, I traced a first edition of *Anson's Law of Contract* in the Depository of The Institute for Advanced Legal Studies.[1] Interleaved in it I found some old correspondence between Sir William Anson and Theseiger LJ. After enquiring about Mrs Theseiger's health, Anson wrote of his new work:

> ... writing as I have done, for students and beginners, I have assumed a definiteness of statement as to the results of the cases which would have been presumptuous in a book of practice. I took a good deal of trouble to arrange the various parts of the subject in due proportion and order but it wasn't until I began to fill in my outline that I realised how much labour was needed and how much more learning than I possessed.

Like Anson I have written this book primarily for students. Like Anson I have tried to achieve a definiteness of statement to aid those seeking a knowledge of the subject for the first time. Like Anson I have taken a 'deal of trouble' with the arrangement of the book. However, much has happened to the law of contract since the first edition of Anson appeared in 1879. The structure adopted in this book seeks to accommodate and reflect the intervening doctrinal changes as well as some of the insights offered by academic writers.

The book's arrangement is premised upon a view of a contract as a transaction with distinct phases. *Part I* examines the negotiation phase when parties 'negotiate' the terms of their exchange. In some contracts the 'negotiation' may be one-sided and conducted on a 'take it or leave it' basis. Have you ever tried to ask London Underground for a discount? None the less, there are several legal doctrines which collectively police pre-contractual negotiations and which may even sometimes be called in aid by travellers against monopoly suppliers of travel services! *Part II* considers the next

---

[1] Originally the book appears to have been presented by Anson to his former pupil master, who by that time was a Lord Justice of Appeal. I suspect the book had come from G.C. Cheshire's private collection as it bore his initials.

phase in the life of a contract: contract formation. This examines the positive requirements for a valid contract, negative factors that might affect an otherwise enforceable contract and the legal personnel who may be parties to, or acquire rights or obligations under, the contract. *Part III* takes as its subject the life of a contract and examines the middle age of contract when contracts are often modified in order to reflect the changing preferences of the parties or external events which affect the contract. This part also contains chapters examining the contents of a contract and its performance. Accompanied by violins, *Part IV* records the passing of our subject: the death of a contract. A post-mortem then follows, when the remedies available for a breach of contract are examined.

This approach has allowed me to bring together material that would other-wise be dispersed throughout a doctrinally-arranged textbook. In particular, I have been able to emphasise two important episodes in the life of a con-tract: pre-contractual negotiation and contract modification. To take contract modification, the issues raised are not the same as those raised by contract formation. Having entered a contract with another and relied upon his or her assurance of performance, there is a unique potential for one party to act opportunistically and seek to extort a concession from the other in the knowledge that the other now has no practical option but to submit. This opportunity for extortion was explicitly recognised in a number of nineteenth-century cases concerning demands by sailors for extra wages.[2] For the next century and a half the courts appeared to forget this problem, or at least refused to address it directly. In the last quarter-century the courts redis-covered the issue and fashioned a doctrine, economic duress, to deal with it. However, there is a tension in the law relating to contractual modifications between the desire to attenuate opportunism and the need to promote contractual flexibility. Contractors are not omniscient or, as an economist would say, they exhibit 'bounded rationality'. They cannot provide in advance for every situation. Nor if they could would it be desirable to encourage them to do so. Rather they should be able to adapt their relationship to reflect their changing circumstances and preferences. Such non-opportunistic adaptive behaviour should not be frustrated by technical doctrines, such as consideration, which in this context appear to serve little useful purpose[3] and elsewhere were dispensed with long ago.[4] This, I believe, explains the rise of promissory estoppel (see Chapter 2).

It can be seen that two of the most important doctrinal developments in the law of contract in the past 50 years concern contractual modifications. Yet the traditional doctrinal arrangement of a textbook would separate these two developments by a few hundred pages. Economic duress would be considered as one of a list of morbid defects that might afflict the infant contract and estoppel would be digested as an uncomfortable postscript to the doctrine of consideration in a chapter dealing with contract formation.

---

[2] See Chapter 12.
[3] Below, p. 168.
[4] Below, p. 331.

By putting these and other doctrines together, I believe that I have been able to offer a coherent account of the law relating to contractual modifications which is both theoretically satisfying and practically useful. It emphasises disguised relationships between distinct doctrines and enables one to answer real-world problems. I believe that a similar case could be made for the better orchestration of the law relating to pre-contractual negotiations, but I will not do so in this introductory section.

On a lighter note, you will see that I often cannot refrain from using a biological analogy for my approach: the birth, life and death of a contract. In my seminars at UCL I have always found it useful, if indelicate, to describe the remedy of rescission for breach as the 'morning-after pill' of the law of contract and to use the menopause to convey the idea of a time of change in the period between contract formation and termination.

HISTORY OF CONTRACT LAW

In a magisterial survey of the relationship between socio-economic changes and the prevailing principles of contract law, Patrick Atiyah charts the rise and fall of classical contract law.[5] He describes its rise in these terms:[6]

Although much of the English law of contract has roots going back to the Middle Ages, most of the general principles of the modern law were developed and elaborated in the eighteenth and nineteenth centuries. These principles and, perhaps even more so the general approach of the courts to contractual questions may not improperly be referred to as the traditional, or classical theory of contract ... [J]udges of the eighteenth century ... [thought] that men had an inalienable right to own property, and therefore to make their own arrangements to buy or sell or otherwise deal with that property, and hence to make their own contracts for themselves. At the same time the law was still influenced by the paternalism which was one of the characteristics of eighteenth-century ideology. So, during this period some of the harshness of a strict regime of freedom of contract was mitigated by paternalist doctrines and rules, which enabled the judges to protect those less capable people of standing up for themselves in the free market. During the nineteenth century, paternalist ideas waned, as the philosophy of *laissez-faire*[7] took root. To the judges, the function of the civil law came to be seen as largely a negative one. Its main object was to enable people to 'realise their wills', or, in more prosaic language, to leave them to get on with their business ... unhampered by government interference. By and large this meant that the law of contract was designed to provide for the enforcement of the private arrangements which the contracting parties had agreed upon. In general, the law was not concerned with the fairness or justice of the outcome, and paternalistic ideas came to be thought of as old fashioned. The judges were not even greatly concerned with the possibility that a contract might not be in the public interest. So the function of contract law was merely to assist one of the contracting parties when the other broke the rules of the game and defaulted in the performance of his contractual obligations.

---

[5] (1979) *The Rise and Fall of the Freedom of Contract*. More manageable is Atiyah's own distillation of this work in (1995) *Introduction to the Law of Contract*. 5th edn, pp. 7–26.

[6] (1995) *Introduction to the Law of Contract*. 5th edn, pp. 7–8 (paragraph breaks removed).

[7] Literally 'leave to do', meaning non-intervention.

Atiyah dates the apogee of the classical law of contract at about 1870. After this date political, social and economic changes led to the 'hands off' approach of classical contract law appearing to be inappropriate to more modern conditions. Atiyah[8] attributes this decline to three factors: the widespread use of standard-form contracts rather than individually-negotiated contracts, the declining importance attached to free choice and intention as justifying legal liability, and the emergence of the consumer as contractor and litigant.[9]

Atiyah's account of the recent history[10] of the law of contract in this country and particularly its connection with prevailing socio-economic conditions and intellectual traditions has been anticipated and reflected in America.[11] None the less, both elements of Atiyah's work have attracted criticism.[12] A very different and broader account of the historical origins of modern contract law is offered by James Gordley.

Gordley's account begins earlier than that of Atiyah in the sixteenth and early seventeenth centuries when:[13]

> A fairly small group of theologians and jurists [the 'late scholastics'] ... attempted to synthesise the Roman legal Texts with the moral theology of Thomas Aquinas. The fundamental concepts and doctrines of private law with which we are familiar are a simplification of the synthesis they achieved ... [T]his is the origin of modern contract law.

Gordley traces the influence upon the late scholastics of the work of Aquinas which itself sought to reconcile the philosophy of Aristotle with Christian teaching. What is surprising according to Gordley is that the legal doctrines based upon this philosophy endured long beyond the philosophical ideas which justified them.[14]

> ... doctrines which in a modified form, now govern most of the world were founded on philosophical ideas that fell from favour centuries ago ... [which] depended directly on Aristotelian and Thomistic moral conceptions about virtue and metaphysical conceptions about the nature or essence of things. Making a contract, for example, was an exercise of the virtue of liberality by which one enriched another, or of the virtue of commutative justice by which one exchanged things of equal value.

Perhaps with Atiyah in mind, Gordley admits that '[t]his account of the

---

[8] As per note 6 above, pp. 15–26.

[9] In an interesting postscript to this analysis, Atiyah observes a Phoenix-like re-emergence since 1980 of the values and solutions of the supposedly discredited and superseded classical principles of contract law. *Ibid.* at pp. 27–34 and Atiyah 'Freedom of Contract and the New Right' reprinted as ch. 12 in Atiyah (1986) *Essays on Contract.*

[10] For the earlier origins of contract law, see Ibbetson (1999) *A Historical Introduction to the Law of Obligations*, pp.1–10 and 24–30, as well as the work of Gordley considered below.

[11] See Friedman (1965) *Contract Law in America*; Horwitz (1977) *The Transformation of American Law, 1780–1860*; Horwitz (1992) *The Transformation of American Law, 1870–1960*; Gilmore (1974) *The Death of Contract.*

[12] For example, Mensch, 'Freedom of Contract as Ideology' (1981) 33 Stan L Rev 733.

[13] (1991) *The Philosophical Foundations of Modern Contract Law*, p. 3.

[14] *Ibid.*, pp. 6–7.

origins of modern legal doctrine will seem odd to those who are used to economic explanations of legal change'.[15] The content and breadth of these two accounts is obviously different, but so are the conclusions. For Atiyah the insistence of classical contract law that the legal consequences of a contract are simply an emanation of the parties' own preferences expressed the ideological needs of the industrial revolution. For Gordley this insistence was puzzling because the philosophical tradition that inspired it was long forgotten at the time of its greatest influence.

THE BASIS OF CONTRACT

Modern contract law has been described as 'a body of law whose underlying theories are inadequate and inconsistent'.[16] Slightly more optimistically, Patrick Atiyah has commented that it probably works well enough in most situations but that its theory is in a 'mess'.[17] Writings have variously asserted that contract law is about indeterminacy and legitimation, promises, reliance, efficiency, relations and nothing of great relevance to transactors.[18] It is not possible in a work of this kind to engage comprehensively with the competing claims of these different theoretical perspectives. Rather, this section will try to give a flavour of these approaches, supported by a few key references. None the less, this section, and the theoretical matters discussed at the end of the next chapter, might be found difficult. If so, it is suggested that you return to these pages when you are more familiar with the 'substantive' law.

Critical legal studies build on the insight that the law is not a value-free enterprise.[19] Legal rules, including those of the law of contract, are indeterminate. This indeterminacy results from the fact that for each principle that might be appealed to in order to resolve a dispute there exists an opposite counter principle. Courts will sometimes apply an objective test of agreement and sometimes a subjective one. Courts will sometimes only enforce agreements when supported by consideration but at other times will 'waive' the requirement either by 'inventing' consideration or using the doctrine of promissory estoppel. At a more general level, critical legal scholars emphasise the contradiction between individualism and collectivism – between the freedom of individuals to pursue their own ends and the need to live as interdependent members of a community.[20] Further, the effect of law is seen to be the legitimation of a certain social ordering. It reinforces a particular

---

[15] *Ibid.*, p. 4.

[16] Feinman, 'Critical Approaches to Contract Law' [1983] UCLA Law Rev 829 at 830.

[17] (1986) *Pragmatism and Theory in English Law*, p. 173.

[18] The references are to, respectively: critical legal studies, Fried, Atiyah and others, the law and economics movement, institutional or transaction cost economics and Macauley. For an overview, see Hillman (1997) *The Richness of Contract Law*, which expands and updates his 'The Crisis in Modern Contract Theory' (1988) 67 Texas Law Rev 103.

[19] See generally Feinman, 'Critical Approaches to Contract Law' [1983] UCLA Law Rev 829 and Dalton, 'An Essay on the Deconstruction of Contract Doctrine' (1985) 94 Yale LJ at 1010–11.

[20] See generally Kennedy, 'Form and Substance in Private Law Adjudication' (1976) 89 Harv L Rev 1685.

set of values and priorities. Critical legal studies are hostile to theories that seek to capture the essence of law in simple formulae As a result, the literature emphasises the inadequacy of classical contract theory and its modern descendants, rather than constructing a viable alternative.

Charles Fried is the author of *Contract as Promise*,[21] which is an elegant and accessible elaboration of a theory of contract based upon the morality of promise making. According to Fried: 'By promising we transform a choice that was morally neutral into one that is morally compelled.'[22] He explains this transformation in the following way:[23]

> An individual is morally bound to keep his promises because he has intentionally invoked a convention whose function is to give grounds – moral grounds – for another to expect the promised performance. To renege is to abuse a confidence he was free to invite or not, and which he intentionally did invite.

Fried then uses this promise principle to explain the operation of parts of the modern law of contract. When the promise principle encounters doctrines which it cannot accommodate, these are either dismissed as incoherent, e.g. the doctrine of consideration,[24] or explained on the basis of another competing principle, such as the tort principle of compensation for harm, the restitution principle for benefits conferred or the sharing principle. As Fried explains, the appeal to other principles to explain aspects of the law of contract does not in any way invalidate the promise principle. However, it does raise the question of whether the promise principle rather than, say, the tort principle should be regarded as the dominant principle justifying the modern law of contract. Further, Fried's account of the law of contractual remedies might be questioned. If fidelity to promise is the guiding principle, why should parties not be required to do the very thing they promised? Why pay damages rather than complete the contract? In other words, why is the expectation measure of damages regarded as the primary contractual remedy rather than an order of specific performance?

Patrick Atiyah builds upon his historical analysis of the law of contract to present an account of the law of obligations based upon three principles of recompense for benefit, protection of reasonable reliance, and the voluntary creation and extinction of rights and liabilities. The law of contract is only a part of the law of obligations and according to Atiyah the role of the third principle has been over-emphasised in discussions of the law of contract by the adoption of a misleading paradigm and the persistence of will theories of contract. He challenges the view that an executory (unperformed) contract should be regarded as typical. He points out that conduct frequently gives rise to responsibility in the law of contract and that several doctrines, such as misrepresentation and estoppel, explicitly protect the reasonable reliance of parties.[25] This leads him to conclude that it is no longer appropriate to

[21] 1981.
[22] *Ibid.*, p. 8.
[23] *Ibid.*, p. 16.
[24] *Ibid.*, ch. 3.
[25] See especially ch. 2 in (1986) *Essays on Contract*.

conceive of a 'great divide between duties which are voluntarily assumed' (contract) and 'duties which are imposed by law' (tort).[26]

Whereas critical legal studies emphasise the complexity, the value-laden nature and ultimate indeterminacy of the law, the economic analysis of law is often characterised as an attempt to state simple, value-free formulae to help develop a clear and predictable law. However, like critical legal studies, the law and economics movement is a broad alliance of scholarship with many different approaches, and there is a regrettable tendency to attack the boldest claims and then conclude that any scholar in that tradition has nothing valuable to say.

The dominant school of economic analysis, sometimes called neo-classical law and economics, emphasises the efficiency of legal rules.[27] It makes a claim to be able to explain much of the law we have and also suggest ways that the law should be developed.[28] In other words, it has both a positive or descriptive element as well as a normative one. Legal economists see contracting as a valuable activity that maximises societal welfare by moving resources to their most highly valued uses. Under certain assumptions, such as adequate access to information, individuals will trade only when the exchange at least makes one of them better off.[29] The role of the law of contract is to encourage, protect and reduce the cost of this process. Exchanges are encouraged by the provision of contractual remedies, such as the expectation measure of damages, which discourage inefficient breaches of contract.[30] Exchange is protected by doctrines such as fraud, duress, etc., which discourage attempts to abuse the process. Finally, the law of contract reduces the cost of transactions by supplying a set of 'default' terms so that the parties do not have to renegotiate certain matters every time they contract.[31]

The criticisms of this approach are numerous. Some critics point out the unreality of some of the assumptions upon which the model is based, e.g. that contractors have full information,[32] the difficulty of defining the volun-

---

[26] *Ibid.*, p. 42. A view which is unchanged despite the declared satisfaction of others with the *status quo*. See Burrows, 'Contract, Tort and Restitution – A Satisfactory Division or Not?' (1983) 99 LQR 216 and Atiyah (1986) *Essays on Contract*, Postscript: Reply to My Critics in Essays on Contract, 43 at pp. 52–6. See also the very readable book by Grant Gilmore cited in n. 11 above.

[27] Accessible overviews are: Posner (1992) *The Economic Analysis of Law*. 4th edn; Polinsky (1989) *An Introduction to Law and Economics*. 2nd edn; Cooter and Ulen (1989) *Law and Economics*. 2nd edn. There are three valuable collections of materials relating to contract: Kronman and Posner (1979) *The Economics of Contract Law*; Goldberg (1989) *Readings in the Economics of Contract Law*; Craswell and Schwartz (1994) *Foundations of Contract Law*.

[28] Polinsky, *ibid.*, preface.

[29] This is described as being Pareto efficient.

[30] Economists also claim that the law should encourage the breach of a contract where it is efficient, i.e. where the breach rather than the performance of a contract will cause goods or services to end up in the hands of the party who places the highest value on them. To give an example, A agrees to sell a car to B for £10,000. B was prepared to pay up to £15,000 for it. C offers A £20,000 for it. If A breached the contract with B and sold the car to C, all parties would be better off even after A has compensated B for the breach by paying him £5,000 (£15,000 – £10,000). Breach would be Pareto optimal.

[31] See the materials books above in n. 27 for articles pursuing these themes.

[32] Trebilcock (1993) *The Limits of Freedom of Contract*, p. 103.

tariness of the parties[33] and that the approach simply assumes the present distribution of wealth and so can say nothing about distributional issues.[34]

A different tradition of law and economics scholarship emphasises the importance of the costs that attend any transaction and particularly how these can be minimised by the adoption of different governance structures.[35] These governance structures are selected because of their ability to harmonise the otherwise contrary interests of the parties. The ultimate harmonisation would be represented by the amalgamation of the two contractors, e.g. a supermarket running its own farms. The literature describes the spectrum of arrangements which exist between the paradigm 'discrete' contract of neo-classical contract law and the vertical integration just described. This work builds upon empirical studies of contract law which reveal the general irrelevance of the formal law[36] and the writing of Ian MacNeil[37] which emphasises the failure of modern contract law to address the problems posed by 'relational' contracts. These are contracts which are characterised by factors such as long duration, intimate personal relations, anticipated co-operative behaviour and sharing and imprecise identification of subject matter.

THE LAW OF CONTRACT OR CONTRACTS

The classical law of contract has been described by Friedman in these terms:[38]

> 'Pure' contract doctrine is blind to details of subject matter and person. It does not ask who buys and who sells, and what is bought and sold ... Contract law is abstraction – what is left in the law relating to agreements when all particularities of person and subject matter are removed.

To what extent can the modern law of contract live up to this claim to generality? Not easily, it seems. Vast tracts of law which were once thought to fall within the general law of contract have now started lives of their own. Like grown-up children embarrassed by their parents, they left, formed new relationships and rarely communicated with home. Employment law, landlord and tenant law, insurance law and the law relating to mortgages are

---

[33] *Ibid.*, pp. 19–20.

[34] Polinsky, *op. cit.*, pp. 7–10 expresses this graphically by saying that economic analysis of law is concerned with maximising the size of the pie rather than advising how it should be cut up.

[35] See Goldberg, 'Towards an Expanded Theory of Contract' (1976) 10 J Econ Issues 45; Klein, 'Transaction Cost Determinants of "Unfair" Contractual Arrangements' (1980) Am Econ Rev (P & P) 356; Williamson, 'Transaction–Cost Economics: The Governance of Contractual Relations' (1979) 22 J Law & Econ 233 and 'The Economics of Organisation: The Transaction Cost Approach' (1981) 87 Am J Sociol 548.

[36] *Infra.*

[37] 'The Many Futures of Contracts' (1974) 47 S Cal L Rev 691; 'Contracts: Adjustments of Long Term Economic Relations under Classical, Neo-Classical and Relational Contract Law' (1978) 72 NWULR 854; (1980) *The New Social Contract*. For an overview, see Campbell, 'The Social Theory of Relational Contract: MacNeil as the Modern Proudhon' (1990) 18 Int J Soc Law 75.

[38] Friedman (1965) *Contract Law in America*, p. 20.

examples. The traffic is not all one way. Occasionally the vacated rooms in the family home are let to a lodger. There is evidence of an increasing contractualisation of several aspects of the relationship between the individual and the state, perhaps evidenced by the introduction of a 'quasi-market' for healthcare whereby health authorities and fundholding practices 'purchase' healthcare from NHS trust hospitals.[39]

The general part of the law of contract is undoubtedly less pervasive than it once was. Indeed, for some time[40] it has been apparent that, in the general part that remains, there has been a further split between commercial and consumer transactions. It is as if the deserted parents have 'sold up', 'down-sized' and are now themselves not getting on too well.

None the less, what remains is still a large corpus of law which may on its own regulate fewer contracts than in the past but which still regulates parts of the contracts that have 'left home'. The principles of contract formation are still recognisable in many of the areas which have started lives of their own even if the rules relating to content and remedy are situation specific. Perhaps one could say that the fleeing children still send their dirty laundry home. And there, thankfully, this tortured analogy will end.

THE LAW OF OBLIGATIONS

The law of obligations has three branches: contract, tort and restitution. We have already encountered Atiyah's objections to defining the law of contract only in terms of voluntarily assumed obligations. The modern law of contract is a blend of voluntarily assumed obligations and externally imposed ones, the relative proportions depending upon the type of contract under consideration. However, we now need a definition of contract's near neighbours in the law of obligations, tort and restitution:

> A tort is a civil wrong recognised by the common law, or (possibly) equity (but not being merely a breach of contract or breach of trust), the remedy for which is an action for damages.[41]

If you carelessly drive your car in a way that causes me to fall off my motor-cycle, I can sue you in the tort of negligence. Negligence is the main tort we will encounter in this book, particularly in those exceptional circumstances when it allows the recovery of economic, rather than (as in my example), physical and consequential losses.

---

[39] These contracts are not legally enforceable according to the NHS and Community Care Act 1990, s 4. See Allen, 'Contracts in the National Health Service Internal Market' [1995] 58 MLR 321.

[40] See Karl Llewellyn, 'The Rule of Law in Our Case Law of Contract' (1938) 47 Yale LJ 1243:

... it is not safe to reason about business cases from cases in which an uncle became interested in having his nephew see Europe, go to Yale, abstain from nicotine, or christen an infant heir 'Alvardus Torrington III'. And it may even be urged that safe conclusions as to business cases of the more ordinary variety cannot be derived from what courts or scholars rule about the idiosyncratic desires of one A to see one B climb a fifty foot greased flagpole or push a peanut across the Brooklyn Bridge.

[41] Hepple and Williams (1984) *Foundations of the Law of Tort*. 2nd edn. p. 27.

Restitution is the response which consists in causing one person to give up to another an unjust enrichment received at his expense or its value in money.[42]

At several points we will discuss the law of restitution. The first occasion will be where the law of restitution provides an action when contractual negotiations fail. Such examples may give the impression that the law of restitution is a supplement to the law of contract. However, the law of restitution arguably gives expression to a more primitive and basic instinct than the law of contract. It is a large subject in its own right but in this country has only recently been recognised as such.[43]

THE REAL WORLD[44]

It is perhaps surprising that little has been written about the effect upon transactors of the formal law which is described in the rest of this book. The more so when the few empirical studies that have been conducted reveal unexpected and surprising things about contractors in the real world. A pioneering study in the United States by Stewart Macaulay[45] examined the attitudes of a number of manufacturing companies in Wisconsin. This study revealed that some of the assumptions commonly made about the effects of legal rules 'are just wrong or so greatly overstated as to be seriously misleading'.[46] Contractors do not plan their dealing in the light of legal requirements and the possibility of non-performance. Neither do they have immediate recourse to legal remedies when things go wrong. In MacNeil's memorable phrase, they do not 'go for the jugular when trouble arises'.[47] A similar picture emerged from a study in this country of engineering businesses in the Bristol area.[48] Another survey in this country considered the attitude of general contractors and sub-contractors in the building industry towards the question of whether a sub-contractor's tender should bind him once acted upon by the main contractor in computing the price for the job. It might have been expected that general contractors would welcome any moves towards making the sub-contractor's bid binding on him, but this was not the case. General contractors preferred to rely upon extra-legal pressure to hold sub-contractors to their tender price.[49]

---

[42] Birks (1989) *An Introduction to the Law of Restitution*, p. 11.

[43] By the House of Lords in *Lipkin Gorman v Karpnale* [1987] 1 WLR 987.

[44] See generally Wightman (1996) *Contract: A Critical Commentary*, ch. 4; and Harris, Campbell and Halson (forthcoming) *Remedies in Contract and Tort*, ch. 2.

[45] 'Non-Contractual Relations in Business: A Preliminary Study' (1963) 28 Am Soc Rev 45. See also 'The Use and Non-Use of Contracts in the Manufacturing Industry' (1963) 9 Practical Lawyer 13, and 'Elegant Models, Empirical Pictures and the Complexities of Contract' (1976) 11 J Law and Soc Rev 507.

[46] This is Macaulay's own assessment of his earlier work. See 'An Empirical View of Contract' [1985] Wis L Rev 465.

[47] 'Economic Analysis of Contractual Relations: Its Shortfalls and the Need for a Rich Classificatory Apparatus' (1981) 75 NWULR 1018 at 1048.

[48] Beale and Dugdale, 'Contracts between Businessmen: Planning and the Use of Contractual Remedies' (1975) 2 Brit J Law and Soc 18.

[49] Lewis, 'Contracts between Businessmen: Reform of the Law of Firm Offers and an Empirical Study of Tendering Practices in the Building Industry' (1982) 12 J L&S 153.

EUROPE AND BEYOND

Membership of the European Union has had an undoubted effect upon the law of contract. Several European Directives have resulted in new domestic regulations. Some of these are commercial in nature, such as the public procurement regulations,[50] while others are directed to consumers, such as the Package Travel, Package Holidays and Package Tours Regulations 1992.[51] However, the broadest measure has undoubtedly been the Unfair Terms in Consumer Contract Regulations 1994 and 1999.[52] These regulations were introduced to further the economic aims of the single market by providing a minimum level of consumer protection in member countries. However, the manner of their implementation, by simply copying out the Directive in a statutory instrument, with no attempt to relate the new measure to existing protection, is not a precedent to follow.

Another way of promoting a uniform approach to contracting in Europe is by the publication of model codes. Such a code has been published by a Commission on European Contract Law[53] with the hope that the principles contained therein will be used by contractors when making contracts, by the courts when adjudicating disputes and by legislators when enacting new legislation.

A similar enterprise has been commenced by the International Institute for the Unification of Private Law (Unidroit) which has published a Statement of Principles for International Commercial Contracts. Again, it is hoped that contractors as a predictable basis for their dealing will voluntarily adopt these principles.[54]

A very different European influence may soon be felt by our domestic law of contract. The Human Rights Act 1998 has legal effect from October 2000 and incorporates into English law the European Convention on Human Rights. The Act creates Convention Rights which are enforceable under domestic law.[55] Both the nature and, to a lesser extent, the content of these Convention Rights are unsettled. There is disagreement as to whether Convention Rights apply between two non-public entities (i.e. individuals or companies) as opposed to between public bodies and non-public ones.[56] Even if this jurisdictional question is settled, the content of Convention

---

[50] For instance, the Public Works Contracts Regulations 1991, SI 1991 No. 2680; Public Services Contracts Regulations 1993, SI 1993 No. 3228; Public Supply Contracts Regulations 1995, SI 1995 No. 201. These measures seek to create a fair European market for government and utility procurement contracts.

[51] SI 1992 No. 3288.

[52] SI 1994 No. 3159 and SI 1999 No. 2083.

[53] This is helpfully reproduced in Rose (ed.) *Blackstone's Statutes on Contract, Tort and Restitution 1999–2000.*

[54] *Ibid.*

[55] The main rights under the Act are: protection of property; right to life; prohibition of torture, inhuman or degrading treatment; prohibition of slavery or forced labour; the right to liberty/security, a fair and public hearing, and no punishment without lawful authority; respect for private/family life, home and correspondence; freedom of thought, conscience and religion; freedom of expression, freedom of assembly/association; freedom to marry; and prohibition of discrimination in enjoyment of Convention Rights.

[56] See, e.g., Buxton, 'The Human Rights Act and Private Law' (2000) 116 LQR 48.

Rights will remain unclear. On this issue it will be necessary to refer to non-domestic law to clarify their content.

Such measures are to be welcomed as aids to European integration and encouragements to cross-border trade. However, as voluntary arrangements, it will take a long time for their influence to permeate and displace more imperfect and familiar domestic measures.

It should not unreflectively be assumed that uniformity is either achievable or that it is a good thing. National forums may apply the same code in different ways perhaps in the light of their own practices and customs. Many would suggest that such differentiation is to be encouraged rather than stifled.[57] Perhaps this explains the United Kingdom's failure to ratify the United Nations Convention on Contracts for the International Sale of Goods, commonly known as the Vienna Convention. This convention applies to international trade contracts on an opt-out basis, i.e. once ratified it is to apply unless the parties provide otherwise.

One area of business where uniformity would seem desirable is in 'computer contracting' or, as it is popularly known, e-commerce. This poses many challenges for traditional concepts of the law of contract. The European Commission has proposed a Directive on Electronic Commerce which would operate to protect consumers. The United Nations Commission on International Trade Law has adopted a model law on electronic commerce. The model law has no binding force and is aimed at business-to-business transactions. Both of these measures are considered by way of comparison with orthodox principle in Part II of this book.

---

[57] See generally Hobhouse, 'International Conventions and Commercial Law: the Pursuit of Uniformity' (1990) 106 LQR 530.

PART I

THE NEGOTIATION STAGE

2

NEGOTIATING THE CONTRACT

INTRODUCTION

Lord Atkin once remarked that: 'Businessmen habitually ... trust to luck or the good faith of the other party ...'.[1] This comment[2] provides more than an insight into the motivations of businessmen. It also implicitly acknowledges a limitation of the common law in policing the activities of contractors: the law no more ensures the good faith of your contractual partner than it guarantees your good fortune in business dealings. However, this might not be an accurate description of the law relating to pre-contractual negotiations. In a recent interesting Court of Appeal judgment Bingham LJ observed that:[3]

> In many civil law systems, and perhaps in most legal systems outside the common law world, the law of obligations recognises and enforces an overriding principle that in making and carrying out contracts parties should act in good faith ... It is in essence a principle of fair and open dealing ... English law has, characteristically, committed itself to no such overriding principle but has developed piecemeal solutions to demonstrated problems of unfairness.

This judgment makes it clear that the gap between civil and common-law jurisdictions is exaggerated by observations at too high a level of generality. While it is true to say that the common law does not explicitly adopt a principle of good faith, it is as obviously untrue to say that the common law encourages bad faith. Rather the jurisdictional difference is one of control technique. The common law takes a more fragmented approach with several doctrines providing redress in respect of narrowly defined examples of bad faith between contractors, frequently without any acknowledgement of the shared purpose of the different doctrines.[4]

The transaction-based approach adopted in this book serves to bring into clearer focus the common threads running through the principles of law which are considered in this part of the book. In any doctrinal rather than

---

[1] *Phoenix Ins Co* v *DeMonchy* (1929) 141 LTR 439 at 445.
[2] Which is confirmed by several empirical studies. See Macauley, 'Non-contractual Relations in Business: A Preliminary Study' (1963) 28 Am Soc Rev 55; Beale and Dugdale, 'Contracts between Businessmen: Planning and the Use of Contractual Remedies' (1975) 2 Brit J. Law & Soc 45.
[3] *Interfoto Library Ltd* v *Stiletto Ltd* [1989] 1 QB 433.
[4] 'Anglo-Australian contract law ... has developed ... with greater emphasis upon specifics rather than the identification of a genus expressed in wide terms': *Service Station Association Ltd* v *Bennett & Associates Pty Ltd* (1993) 117 ALR 393 at 406 *per* Gummow J.

functional exposition of the law of contract, these links are often obscured. However, the problem is not simply one of unperceived interrelationships *within* the traditional conception of the law of contract. Rather there are problems deriving from the definition of the boundaries of contract itself. A proper account of how the law regulates the bargaining process cannot respect the borders of a rigid map of the law of civil obligations. To do so would be to ignore the important role of contiguous areas of civil liability, such as the law of tort or restitution.

The identification of common purpose in disparate doctrines may help to refine a consistent approach to the policing of contractual negotiations in a way which avoids some of the difficulties attending an approach based upon a requirement of good faith. One of the most pressing of these difficulties is that of definition: what is good faith? Some commentators deny that the phrase can be given any sensible meaning[5] other than as excluding[6] from its ambit particular behaviour that can be characterised as bad faith. Others have pointed out that the meaning of the phrase in common parlance would only extend to cover deliberate deception, whereas, for example, the law of misrepresentation seeks to control both intentional, careless and wholly innocent misdescription.[7] The problem of definition is made worse by the breadth of work expected of the idea of good faith, for it is a principle used to regulate all episodes in the life of a contract from negotiation to termination. The structure of this book, by examining these episodes separately and sequentially, exposes such over-ambition and is sensitive to the differing policy objectives which influence the law relating to the distinct phases in the life of a contract.

As Bingham LJ observed, the approach of the common law to the control of so-called bad faith has been piecemeal and fragmented. This is certainly true in relation to the policing of contractual negotiations. However, the lack of orchestration in this area should not be allowed to obscure the considerable breadth of the legal control exercised under various rubrics. This regulation is effected via several distinct doctrines, the most obvious of which is the law of misrepresentation, but which also include estoppel by convention, the objective test of agreement and the 'snapping up' principle, mistaken identity, proprietary estoppel, the law of restitution as applied to 'failed contracts', collateral contracts and the duties to disclose and negotiate in good faith. We will first consider estoppel by convention, where the parties to the contract are stopped from questioning what they have already 'agreed'.

ESTOPPEL BY CONVENTION

This is said to arise:

> when the parties have acted in their transaction on the agreed assumption that a given state of facts is to be accepted between them as true then as regards the

---

[5] See e.g. Summers (1968) 54 Virg Law Rev 195.
[6] *Ibid.*, p. 196. See generally Hall (1959) Analysis 1.
[7] See Collins (1997) *The Law of Contract*. 3rd edn, p. 204.

transaction each will be estopped against the other from questioning the truth of the state of facts so assumed.[8]

The party alleged to be estopped must have acquiesced in the mistaken assumption of the party claiming the benefit of the estoppel, and both parties must have proceeded on the basis of the shared assumption. It is not necessary that the assumption was induced by any unambiguous representation[9] or promise[10] made by any party. However, both parties must have conducted themselves on the basis of such a shared assumption which has been said to require communications to pass between the parties.[11] To the extent that such communication is a requisite of the doctrine, estoppel by convention represents a powerful tool to protect the reasonable expectations of negotiating parties. It has been applied in this way in a number of recent decisions after a considerable period of doctrinal obsolescence.[12] A good illustration of its use is provided by *Amalgamated Investment & Property Co Ltd* v *Texas Commerce International Bank Ltd*.[13]

The facts of the case are as follows. The claimants received a loan from the defendant bank. When a further loan was sought by a foreign subsidiary owned by the claimants, a guarantee was executed in respect of all monies which might be owing to the bank by the subsidiary. To avoid Bahamian banking regulations, the advance was made to the claimants' subsidiary via a subsidiary of the defendant. The claimants went into liquidation and the defendant bank sought to apply money, which it owed to the claimants, to discharge the claimants' alleged obligations, owed under the guarantee.

The claimants sought a declaration that the defendant bank was wrong to apply in this way the monies owed to the claimants, because the guarantee given by the claimants was effective only to cover money advanced by the defendant itself and did not extend to sums advanced by the defendant's own subsidiary, as in fact occurred. The Court of Appeal held that the guarantee should not be interpreted literally but rather should be construed in the context of the total transaction and, therefore, the guarantee did cover the loan between the two subsidiaries. Further, since at the relevant time the parties had acted upon the common assumption that the claimants were liable under the guarantee in respect of the advance which was now in dispute, the claimants were estopped by convention from denying their liability under the guarantee.

The Court of Appeal also discussed a possible limit on the use that could be made of this doctrine, for it is often said that estoppel, other than a

---

[8] Spencer, Bower and Turner, p.157.

[9] *Cf.* estoppel by representation. *Low* v *Bouverie* [1891] 3 Ch 82.

[10] *Cf.* promissory estoppel. *Woodhouse AC Israel Cocoa Ltd* v *Nigerian Produce Marketing Co* [1972] AC 741; *Danforth Heights* v *McDermid Bros* (1922) 52 OLR 412, 416 *per* Sutherland J; *Bremer Handelsgesellschaft MBH* v *Vanden Avenne-Izegem PVBA* [1978] 2 Lloyd's Rep 109, 126 *per* Lord Salmon; *The Post Chaser* [1981] 2 Lloyd's Rep 701.

[11] *The August P Leonhardt* [1985] 2 Lloyd's Rep 28, 35. *The Captain Gregos* (No. 2) [1990] 2 Lloyd's Rep 395, 405.

[12] Perhaps since the last major consideration in *Greer* v *Kettle* [1938] AC 156.

[13] [1982] QB 84.

proprietary estoppel,[14] does not of itself create a new cause of action. Cases have undoubtedly foundered when it was realised that one party was basing his cause of action on an estoppel.[15] Many commentators[16] and judges[17] have said that this cannot be done. A typical statement is:[18]

> Our consistent and uncontroversial approach in this work has been that estoppel (with the exception of proprietary estoppel) is an evidentiary doctrine that does not create substantive rights.

Yet, confusion persists regarding the proper limits of the offensive use that can be made of estoppel by convention. This may be attributable to the relative paucity of case law or, perhaps more likely, is caused by the lack of terminological clarity[19] in the area, because the courts frequently try to summarise the offensive limits of estoppel doctrines by reference to misleading metaphors. The best known of which is probably the 'vivid' phrase used by counsel,[20] and approved by Birkett LJ,[21] in *Combe v Combe* which described the doctrine of promissory estoppel as one to be used as a shield and not as a sword.[22] The confusion that such phrases create is perhaps evident from the judgments in the Court of Appeal. For example, Everleigh LJ speculated what the result would have been if an action had been brought by the defendant bank to enforce the guarantee.[23] The reason for such speculation is hard to understand. Surely it should not matter to the operation of the doctrine who brings the action; the formal position of the parties (who is the claimant, who is the defendant) may simply be a matter of litigation tactics. To hold otherwise would be to encourage any party seeking to rely upon an estoppel to try to manoeuvre his opponent into bringing the action so that the estoppel is being used defensively or vice versa.

It is sometimes really little more than a matter of chance who formally brings an action. For example, in *Re Tudale Exploration and Bruce*[24] the respondent (Tudale) had granted the appellant (Teck) an option for three years to develop some mining claims. During this period the claims were held by an escrow agent. If the claims were not taken up by Teck, they were

---

[14] *Crabb v Arun* DC [1976] 1 Ch 179, 187 E *per* Lord Denning.
[15] *Combe v Combe* [1951] 2 KB 215; *Sloan v Union Oil Co* [1955] 4 DLR 664; *Argy Trading v Lapid Developments* [1977] 3 All ER 785; *SS Employment v Globe Elastic Thread Co* [1979] 2 All ER 1007.
[16] Cheshire, Fifoot and Furmston, p. 87; Spencer, Bower and Turner, p. 387.
[17] See but *contra Re Wyvern Developments Ltd* [1974] 1 WLR 1097 at 1104 F–1105 A.
[18] Wilken and Villiers (1998) *Waiver, Variation and Estoppel*, pp. 204–5.
[19] This appears to be acknowledged and perpetrated by Wilken and Villiers (*op. cit.*) who say that 'an estoppel by convention cannot create, *in the proper sense of the word*, a cause of action' (p. 205, emphasis added) but who persist in questioning whether estoppel can operate 'as a sword' (e.g. pp. 204–5).
[20] [1951] 2 KB 215 at 218.
[21] *Ibid.*, p. 224. *Cf. Re Tudale Exploration* (1978) 20 OR 593, considered below.
[22] In the introduction to the classic work on estoppel, Spencer, Bower and Turner, the editor writes: 'To use the language of naval warfare, estoppel must always be either a mine layer or a mine sweeper: it can never be a capital unit.'
[23] At p. 126 E.
[24] (1978) 20 OR 593. See also *Conwest v Letain* [1964] 41 DLR 2d 198.

to revert to Tudale. Two extensions of time were granted but the third one was disputed. Before its expiry, Teck purported to exercise the option.

In this case, because the shares were held by a third party who received contrary instructions from the parties as to what to do with the shares, it was necessary for one party to commence proceedings. The litigation arose from a successful application to the Mining and Lands Commissioner, by Tudale, to have the claims vested in it. It was simply fortuitous that Tudale rather than Teck made the application.

The careful judgment of Brandon LJ in *Texas Commerce* holds the key to a better understanding of this issue. He observes that 'much of the language used in connection with these concepts is no more than a question of semantics'.[25] When considering the same hypothetical action by the bank which was addressed by Everleigh LJ, he stated what he took to be the true proposition of law:

> ... while a party cannot in terms found a cause of action on an estoppel, he may, as a result of being able to rely on an estoppel, succeed on a cause of action ...[26]

It is suggested that the approach of Brandon LJ is to be preferred. It avoids the myriad uncertainties that would have to be resolved if estoppel by convention was considered to create a new cause of action to sit beside tort, contract and restitution: e.g. what is the appropriate measure of damages, principle of remoteness, etc.? Also, if estoppel by convention were regarded as creating a new cause of action, the sensible further development of the doctrine might be hampered by a confusion of purpose, for it would then cease to function solely as a doctrine concerned with the process of contract negotiation but rather would also regulate the formation of promissory liability – processes as different as conception and birth.

Implicit in the approach of Brandon LJ is the fact that estoppel by convention is not concerned with the legal effect of the common assumption made. Rather that legal effect is specified by some principle of substantive law. So if the estoppel takes effect in relation to a promise, i.e. it is assumed between two parties that a promise has been made, it will be the law of contract which determines the enforceability of the promise, so consideration will be required,[27] and the usual contractual remedies will be available. That the estoppel may result in the enforcement of a contractual obligation must not be allowed to obscure what is being protected, the reasonable expectations of negotiating parties. Understood in this way, as a means of upholding a norm of fair dealing in the process of contract negotiation, the parallel between the doctrine of estoppel by convention and the objective theory of contractual formation is immediately obvious, as the objective

---

[25] At p. 131 E. See also Ormrod LJ delivering the judgment of the Court of Appeal in *Brikom Investments* v *Seaford* [1981] 1 WLR 863 at 869 B: 'These dichotomies are dangerously neat and apt to mislead.'

[26] Lord Denning seems to endorse a similar principle at p. 122 A.

[27] If there is no consideration present, the estoppel by convention may establish the existence of a promise and the doctrine of promissory estoppel may give limited legal effect to it. See Treitel (8th edn) p. 113.

theory (explained below) seeks to hold a party to a reasonable interpretation of his or her words rather than to give legal effect to any secret uncommunicated subjective intention.

THE OBJECTIVE TEST OF AGREEMENT AND THE 'SNAPPING UP' OF MISTAKEN OFFERS

In Chapters 3, 4 and 5 we will see that a contract is formed when there is agreement, consideration and an intention to create legal relations. Agreement consists of corresponding offer and acceptance and is determined *objectively*. In a celebrated statement Blackburn J said:[28]

> If, whatever a man's real intention may be, he so conducts himself that a reasonable man would believe that he was assenting to the terms proposed by the other party, and that other party upon that belief enters into the contract with him, the man thus conducting himself would be equally bound as if he had intended to agree to the other party's terms.

An example will help to clarify this objective test of agreement.

While standing beside and looking at a new sports car, I ask you whether you would like to buy 'my car' for £10,000. You agree. Thereupon, I walk down the street and return with an old jalopy worth £500 which I say is the car I intended to sell to you.

If on the above facts you had obliged yourself to pay £10,000 for the old jalopy, the law would indeed be an ass. You have not, and it is not (usually). The contractual offer I am considered to be making is not the one which I secretly, subjectively intend but the one that a reasonable onlooker would think I was making, i.e. to sell the new sports car.

This principle was applied in *Centrovincial Estates plc* v *Merchant Investors Assurance Co Ltd*[29] where the claimants purchased commercial property let to the defendants at a rent of £68,320 p.a. subject to review. The claimants erroneously suggested a new rent of £65,000 p.a. when they actually intended £126,000 p.a. Unsurprisingly, the defendants quickly accepted the mistaken offer. The Court of Appeal allowed the appeal from the judge's declaration that there was no binding agreement to let the premises for £65,000. Due to the nature of the proceedings, this does not amount to a holding by the court that there *existed* a contract to re-let at the lower rent, but rather that it was reasonably *arguable* that this was so. Slade LJ applied the:[30]

> well-established principle of the English Law of contract that an offer falls to be interpreted not subjectively by reference to what has actually passed through the

---

[28] *Smith* v *Hughes* (1871) LR 6 QB 597.
[29] [1983] Com LR 158.
[30] At p. 158.

mind of the offeror, but objectively, by reference to the interpretation which a reasonable man[31] ... would place on the offer.

The claimants argued that no reasonable person would expect the rent to be reduced. However, the defendants countered that they reasonably anticipated some concessions due to their dissatisfaction with the conduct of the previous term. The Court of Appeal thought that this was at least an arguable position.

Therefore, the objective test of agreement, like the doctrine of estoppel by convention, will prevent a party to negotiations from denying the reasonable expectations he has excited in another. In this way it operates to impose a standard of fair dealing upon the negotiation process. However, exceptionally the courts are prepared to depart from the objective test of agreement and take account of the subjective intentions of the parties. The occasions on which the courts do so to prevent a contractor from 'snapping up' a mistaken contractual offer also represent the enforcement by the courts of a standard of fair dealing in negotiations where one party is restrained from consciously taking advantage of the other. In other words, both the rule (the general objective test) and the exception (the 'snapping up' cases) enforce a different standard to be observed by negotiations. Both operate to restrain a party to negotiations from taking advantage of another's mistake, the former to prevent an offeror from denying the reasonable expectations of the offeree, the latter to restrain the offeree from denying the reasonable belief of the offeror.

In *Hartog* v *Colin & Shields*[32] the defendants offered to sell 30,000 rabbit skins to the claimant at a price 'per pound' when, following trade practice and previous negotiations between these parties, he meant to do so at a price 'per piece'. As there were three skins to the pound, this mistake had the effect of substantially undervaluing the pelts. The buyer was not permitted to 'snap up' the mistaken offer. In another case[33] the defendant, who had previously declined to sell certain property to the claimant for £2,000, mistakenly offered it to him for £1,250. The claimant's action for specific performance of the contract of sale at the lower price was refused.

In both of these cases the court prevented the offeree from taking advantage of an offer which he knew was mistaken. However, the principle extends further and is applied whenever the offeree *should* have known of the offeror's mistake, perhaps because he induced it. In *Scriven Bros & Co* v *Hindley & Co*[34] the claimant auctioneers offered for sale two lots for which the defendant successfully bid in the belief that both were hemp. In fact, only one was hemp and the other was tow, a less valuable commodity. The claimants' action for the price failed and so they were not permitted to take

---

[31] It has been suggested that the test of the reasonable man disguises a number of different personas. See Howarth (1984) 100 LQR 265; Vorster (1987) 103 LQR 274.

[32] [1939] 3 All ER 566.

[33] *Webster* v *Cecil* (1861) 30 Beav 62. Although specific performance (an action to literally compel performance) was refused, damages may have been available at common law. Romilly MR said that the claimant 'might bring such action at law as he might be advised'.

[34] [1913] 3 KB 504.

advantage of the defendant's mistake. Contrary to the usual practice, the auctioneer had put the same shipping mark on different commodities landed from the same ship, so the defendant's mistake had been induced by the claimant's own careless action. The same principle has been applied[35] when an illiterate farmer was negligently induced by a bank manager to sign a written guarantee in respect of his son's indebtedness to the bank. The bank was prevented from accepting the farmer's offer because it was based upon the mistaken belief that it only extended to the purchase of land by the son and did not cover other debts to the bank and this mistake was induced by the bank's own negligence.

It is important to stress a limitation upon this principle. It only applies where the offeree is aware (*Hartog*) or should be aware (*Scriven*) that the offeror is mistaken as to the *terms* of his offer. Where the mistake relates to another matter, perhaps some quality which the goods are supposed to have but which is not being contractually guaranteed, different principles apply. In *Smith* v *Hughes* oats were sold which the buyer thought were old oats (more suitable for his purpose than new oats). If the buyer mistakenly believed that the oats were 'old' there was a valid contract even though the seller was aware of this. However, if, to the seller's knowledge, the buyer thought he was purchasing oats contractually guaranteed to be old, on the principles we have just discussed there would be no contract.

MISTAKE OF IDENTITY[36]

A different type of mistake to the one considered above is where one party to a contract is mistaken as to the identity of the person he is contracting with. In all of the cases we will examine, the mistake is one which was deliberately induced by one party.[37] The cases all follow a similar pattern with an innocent party being induced to enter a contract by a rogue who deliberately misrepresents his identity.[38] In such circumstances the innocent party would

---

[35] *Lloyds Bank plc* v *Waterhouse* [1993] 2 FLR 97.

[36] See Goodhart, 'Mistake as to Identity in the Law of Contract' (1941) 57 LQR 228 and Williams, 'Mistake as to Party in the Law of Contract' 23 Canadian Bar Review 271.

[37] Where one party is aware of the other party's mistake, the case is sometimes said to involve a 'unilateral' mistake (e.g. Cheshire, Fifoot and Furmston at pp. 234–7). In this sense the cases discussed in this section and the 'snapping up' cases discussed in the previous one may be said to involve unilateral mistakes. For a case involving mistaken identity where the knowledge of the party who induced the mistake was not clear, see *Boulton* v *Jones* (1857) 2 H & N 564 (purchaser of goods claimed he intended to deal with the former owner of a business who owed him money rather than the new owner – unclear whether latter was aware of purchaser's mistake).

[38] See also, in addition to the cases discussed below, *Hardman* v *Booth* (1863) 1 H & C 803 (clerk of business who had same surname as proprietor ordered and intercepted goods intended to be sold to proprietor – held: no contract between supplier and clerk) and the difficult case of *Lake* v *Simmons* [1927] AC 487 (jeweller gave necklaces on approval to woman who represented herself to be wife of a wealthy man). The case involved a claim by the jeweller on his insurance policy when she disappeared with the items. The case might involve no more than the proper interpretation of the insurance policy (*per* Devlin LJ in *Ingram* v *Little* [1961] 1 QB 31 at 73–4); a wide interpretation is that giving the jewels to her was not outside the terms of the policy because no property was transferred to her because of the jeweller's mistake.

be able to bring an action against the rogue in the tort of deceit. In this action the innocent party could claim damages and ask the court to rescind (set aside) the contract for misrepresentation. Unfortunately for the innocent party, these two remedies are usually of little practical value. The action for damages is worthless because such rogues do not usually leave a forwarding address and if they can be traced, would struggle to pay the damages out of their prison wages! The action for rescission is also of little use to the party duped. The nature of the rogue's 'sting' is usually to obtain possession of the innocent party's property and then sell it for cash as soon as possible thereafter. If the sale or pledge by the rogue takes place before the innocent party tries to set aside the ostensible contract with the rogue, it is said that the third-party purchaser's rights bar (i.e. prevent) the contract from being rescinded. Remedies for misrepresentation are examined in detail later in this chapter. The point we need to note here is that they are of little practical value to the victim of a fraudulent misrepresentation who, as a result, has parted with valuable property. For this reason, many such victims seek to claim that no contract with the rogue ever came into existence[39] because of the mistake as to the identity made by the original owner. The consequence of this would be that the rogue never obtained any title to the goods from the original owner and so could not pass any on[40] to the third-party purchaser. As the property (often a motor car), as opposed to the rogue himself, can usually be traced, the original owner can bring an action to recover his property.[41] In practical terms, the only 'help'[42] offered by the law to the victim of such a fraud is if he can bring himself within the narrow doctrine of mistake. The law relating to mistake as to the identity of the contracting parties, therefore, forms part of the general legal control of the negotiating process, even though in the main it is directed to a particular and narrow abuse of that process.

---

[39] Usually but confusingly described as a claim that the contract was void. Is it meaningful to describe a contract which never comes into existence as a contract at all?

[40] Under the so-called *nemo dat* rule (*nemo dat quod non habet* – you cannot give what you do not have, i.e. title to the goods).

[41] Usually an action in the tort of conversion. Conversion is the wrongful usurpation of the rights of the owner of property.

[42] A different solution has been proposed by Devlin LJ in *Ingram* v *Little* [1961] 1 QB 31. He suggested that the loss should be shared between the two innocent parties (i.e. the original owner and the purchaser from the rogue) in proportion to their respective fault. This would avoid the all-or-nothing approach of the present law (either the contract is void and the loss effectively falls on the third-party purchaser or it is voidable and falls on the original owner). It would also allow the courts to fine-tune the outcome to reflect the relative culpability of the 'innocent' parties. Perhaps the original owner should bear most of the responsibility as it is he who has foolishly given up possession of his property. However, the third party sometimes appears to buy the goods at undervalue (but not sufficiently to deprive him/her of the status of an 'innocent' purchaser for value) and so perhaps should be on notice that there might be some doubt as to the provenance of the goods (e.g. *Lewis* v *Averay* [1972] 1 QB 198 original sale £450, sale by rogue £200). The matter was examined by the Law Reform Committee in its *Twelfth Report Transfer of Title to Chattels*, Cmnd 2958 of 1966, which declined to act on Devlin LJ's suggestion on the basis that such apportionment would introduce considerable complexity into the law particularly where there is a series of sub-purchasers, one or more of whom might themselves become insolvent.

A distinction is sometimes drawn between a mistake as to identity and a mistake as to attributes. Only the former is capable of rendering the contract void. In *Kings Norton Metal Co v Edridge Merrett & Co Ltd*[43] the claimant received an order for goods which purported to come from 'Hallam & Co, Soho Hackle Pin and Wire Works, Sheffield' with depots in Belfast, Lille and Ghent. In fact, there was no such business. The letter had been sent by a fraudster named Wallis, who never paid for the goods. Wallis sold the goods to the defendant who bought them in good faith. The claimant's action to recover their goods from the defendant failed because the claimant intended to contract with the writer of the letter. That contract was voidable (i.e. liable to be set aside) for misrepresentation but was not set aside before the defendant's rights intervened. The contract with Wallis was not void for mistake because the claimant was merely mistaken as to the attributes of the party who placed the order; the claimant thought that it was a respectable creditworthy business when it was not. In fact, there were not two entities in existence.[44] Hallam & Co, was just an alias for Wallis. If there had been a business called Hallam & Co, which was known to the claimant, there would have been a mistake as to identity, and the result would have been different.

In *Cundy v Lindsay*[45] a rogue called Blenkarn, who lived at 37 Wood Street, Cheapside, ordered linen from the claimant. He signed his name to look like Blenkiron & Co, a respectable business at 123 Wood Street, Cheapside. The goods were despatched to Blenkiron & Co, 37 Wood Street, Cheapside, where Blenkarn received them and subsequently sold them to the defendant. When the mistake came to light, the claimant sought the return of its goods from the defendant. Blackburn J held that the claimant intended to deal with the entity that did business at 37 Wood Street, Cheapside and so dismissed the claimant's action. This judgment was reversed by the Court of Appeal whose decision was affirmed by the House of Lords. The appellate courts took the view that the claimant intended to deal with Blenkiron & Co, but made a mistake as to identity, which meant that no contract at all came into existence between the claimant and Blenkarn.[46] Blenkarn did not receive any title to the goods and so could not pass one on. Therefore, the claimant's action against the defendant succeeded.

Greater problems arise when the parties deal face-to-face rather than through the medium of the post. These are well illustrated by a famous

---

[43] (1897) 14 TLR 98.

[44] See also *Newborne v Sensolid* [1954] 1 QB 45 (no contract formed when contract purportedly made on behalf of a company which at that time had not yet been registered and so was not yet in existence); *contra: Sowler v Potter* [1939] 4 All ER 478 (lease void when tenant who had previously been convicted of permitting disorderly conduct negotiated for the lease under a different name). The latter case is open to question because when the lease was negotiated the possibility that the tenant was the convicted person was not in the mind of the landlord's agent. Therefore, how could there be said to be a mistake between two entities?

[45] (1878) 3 App Cas 459.

[46] 'Of him they knew nothing, and of him they never thought. With him they never intended to deal.' *Ibid.* at p. 465 *per* Lord Cairns LC.

trilogy of cases starting with *Phillips* v *Brooks*.[47] A polished con man called North went to the claimant jeweller and selected a ring priced at £450 and a pearl necklace priced at £2,250. When he produced his chequebook he said, 'You see who I am, I am Sir George Bullough'. This person was known to the claimant who also checked that Sir George Bullough lived at the address given by North. When asked if he would like to take the jewellery with him, the rogue suggested that the claimant should get the cheque cleared first but that he would like to take the ring because it was his wife's birthday the following day. North left with the ring which he pledged to the defendant for £350. The cheque was, of course, dishonoured. Horridge J held that the claimant '... in fact contracted to sell and deliver [the ring] to the person who came into the shop'. The consequence was that the claimant could not maintain an action against the defendant.

The second case was *Ingram* v *Little*[48] where two elderly sisters and a friend (Elsie, Hilda and Mrs Badger) were tricked into selling their car by a rogue. The rogue visited their house and agreed to buy their car. When he produced a chequebook to pay for it, the ladies made it clear that they would not accept a cheque. The rogue then said that he was 'P.G.M. Hutchinson of Stanstead House, Caterham'. One of the ladies went to the Post Office and checked that there was a man of that name living at the address given. When this was confirmed, they accepted his cheque. The rogue quickly sold the car to an innocent third party. The Court of Appeal held that no contract came into existence between the three old ladies and the rogue. They considered that there was a prima facie presumption in cases of face-to-face dealings that the owner intends to deal with the actual person in front of him, but that this presumption was rebutted by the facts of this case. The crucial point of distinction between this case and *Phillips* v *Brooks* appears to be that in this case the ladies initially refused to accept a cheque. It was only after the rogue's assertion as to who he was that the deal was 'on' again. At no time in *Phillips* v *Brooks* was the deal ever called off by the jeweller. This shows the greater importance attached to the identity of their contractual partner by the three old ladies than the jeweller sufficient to justify the conclusion, in conflict with the usual presumption, that they had made a mistake as to the identity of the other party.

The final case in the trilogy is *Lewis* v *Averay*[49] where a rogue impersonated a famous actor called Richard Greene.[50] He offered a cheque for the claimant's car and produced a (false) Pinewood Studio's pass to support his identity. The cheque 'bounced' and the claimant sought the return of the car from the party who technically had bought it in good faith from the rogue. In this case the Court of Appeal held that the usual presumption applied. There was nothing to justify its displacement. The original owner, therefore,

---

[47] [1919] 2 KB 243.
[48] [1961] 1 QB 31.
[49] [1972] 1 QB 198.
[50] Whom mature students might remember as 'Robin Hood, Robin Hood riding through the glen, Robin Hood, Robin Hood with his band of men ...'.

entered a contract with the rogue which was voidable (but not avoided in time) for misrepresentation, but was not void for mistake. The claimant's mistake was characterised as one as to attributes only. The claimant assumed that the person he was contracting with was creditworthy when he was not.

MISREPRESENTATION

We have seen that if a party makes an assumption during contractual negotiations, the doctrine of estoppel by convention will sometimes protect a party from the adverse consequences resulting from reliance upon that assumption. The objective theory of agreement offers a similar protection to negotiating parties by holding parties to a reasonable interpretation of their words and actions. The protection offered by the latter differs in that it requires an unequivocal statement or conduct directed from one to the other, whereas the former can be based upon a common assumption, provided that there is present a background of communications between the parties. Both doctrines are often not recognised as examples of the law regulating the process of contract negotiation. This is attributable in part to the nature of the sanction which is applied if the norm of fair negotiation endorsed by the doctrines is violated. The sanction is that a party is held to a particular inter-pretation of a contract. Hence, there is a tendency to ignore the 'wrong' which the law is seeking to address and simply classify the doctrines as an aspect of contract formation. Such an approach simply fails to recognise the functional role of the doctrines. The same may be said of the law relating to the mistaken identity of contracting parties.

This has not been the case with the set of principles collectively known as the law of misrepresentation. It has always been recognised that these prin-ciples seek to give relief to parties who suffer loss as a result of reliance upon a misleading statement made during contractual negotiations. However, the law of misrepresentation is still classified as a 'vitiating' factor, i.e. as a defect in the process of contract formation, and so is not examined until after contract formation has been discussed. This is curious: misrepresentation is about controlling the bargaining process, but is best considered after that process is complete. Such a view seems to involve simultaneously acknowledging the functional significance of the doctrine and then disguising it by examining it out of context. This is more surprising when one considers the recent origins of the actions to recover damages in respect of negligent misrepresentations. It is only since the 1960s that damages have been available in the tort of negligent misrepresentation[51] and under the Misrepresentation Act 1967, s 2(1) in respect of negligent, as opposed to deliberate,[52] misrepresentations. Indeed, damages in tort may be claimed in circumstances where other claims to damages (e.g. under the Misrepresen-tation Act 1967, s 2(1)) are not available. An example would be where the

[51] See *Hedley Byrne* v *Heller* [1964] AC 465.
[52] On the tort of deceit, see *Derry* v *Peek* (1889) 14 App Cas 337, considered below.

representee relies upon the misrepresentation and suffers loss other than by entering a contract with the representor, e.g. by entering a contract with a third party,[53] and could extend to cases where the representee makes a gift to a third party.

This functional confusion is all the more regrettable because of the broad sweep of the law of misrepresentation and the variety of remedies available. Redress is available under these principles in respect of false representations, half-truths and, exceptionally, on the basis of a simple failure to disclose information. The law of misrepresentation also exhibits considerable remedial richness with subtle distinctions between methods of damage assessment. For these reasons Table 2.1 (see p. 72) has been compiled which should be examined by way of summary of, and later contrast between, the various avenues of redress and available remedies which collectively comprise the law of misrepresentation.

GENERAL PRINCIPLES

There are certain principles which are common to the different actions for misrepresentation. These common principles are discussed below and can be assumed to apply to each of the substantive actions unless specifically excepted.

Representations of fact

A representation differs fundamentally from a promise. In this context a representation is understood to mean a *statement of existing fact*, whereas a promise has an element of futurity: it expresses a willingness to do something in the future. As Fried[54] puts it, 'A promise invokes trust in my future actions, not merely in my present sincerity.' However, the conceptual distinction should not disguise the difficulty of distinguishing the two in practice. We will see that it is sometimes possible to raise an implied statement of existing fact from a statement as to the future.[55] Indeed, with a little ingenuity it is often possible to see in many promises as to the future a statement as to the present.[56]

A statement of fact is usually contrasted with a statement of intention and a statement of opinion.[57] A statement of intention is a representation as to

---

[53] See *Morgan Crucible Co plc v Hill Samuel & Co Ltd* (profit forecasts prepared by accountants with the express purpose of persuading an interested party to increase a takeover bid may give rise to liability in negligence). Here the representee (interested party) would be relying upon the representor (accountant's) statement when entering contracts to purchase shares from third parties.

[54] (1981) *Contract as Promise*, p. 11.

[55] See *With v O'Flanagan* [1934] 1 Ch 575.

[56] See Thompson 'From Representation to Expectation: Estoppel as a Cause of Action' [1983] 42 Comb LJ 257 at 259–60.

[57] And sometimes with a statement of law – see Allen (1988) *Misrepresentation*, pp. 14–15 and Treitel, pp. 307–8, who says that this distinction is 'ripe for reconsideration' in the light of *Kleinwort Benson Ltd v Lincoln CC* [1998] 4 All ER 513 (HL) (payment made under a mistake of law may be claimed back in restitutionary damages).

the future and does not give rise to an action for misrepresentation. The most important type of representation as to the future is a promise but the category is wider than that. Of course, a promise may be enforceable as a contract if further formalities are fulfilled,[58] but the point here is that any element of futurity excludes an action for misrepresentation.

The difference between a statement of fact and a statement of intention is illustrated in a different context by the case of *Jorden* v *Money*[59] which concerned the enforceability of a debt where the creditor had said that *he would not enforce it*. The question of whether the creditor's statement was one of fact or not arose because the debtor declined to pay asserting that the creditor was prevented from enforcing the debt by the doctrine of estoppel by representation. This variety of estoppel can only be founded upon a representation of existing fact.[60] The House of Lords held that the doctrine does not apply where 'the representation is not a representation of fact but a statement of something which the party intends or does not intend to do'. Therefore, the doctrine of estoppel by representation did not prevent the creditor from enforcing the debt.

If a statement appears to be one of intention, it may none the less conceal an implied statement of fact. In this sense the law of misrepresentation as much as the doctrine of estoppel by representation looks to the substance and not the form of what was said. In *Salisbury (Marquess)* v *Gilmore*,[61] a tenant, in breach of covenant, failed to leave the leased premises in a satisfactory state of repair because the landlord had earlier indicated his intention to demolish the premises. It was argued that the principle of estoppel by representation could not apply to the landlord's statement. MacKinnon LJ expressed the view that:[62]

> ... the question must be what is the substance of the intimation by the man concerned, not what is the form or language of it ... In substance the communication stated facts ...'

The exact process as to how a statement of intention can be reduced to one of fact is revealed by *Edgington* v *Fitzmaurice*.[63] In this case the directors of a company issued a prospectus inviting investors to purchase debentures[64] in the company. The prospectus stated that the objects of the issue of debentures were to complete alterations in the company's buildings, to purchase horses and vans, and to develop the trade of the company. However, the real object of the loan was to allow the directors to pay off existing debts. It was held that the statements in the prospectus were misrepresentations, in this

---

[58] Or it may be given more limited legal effect as a modification to an already existing contract under the doctrine of promissory estoppel.

[59] (1854) 5 HL Cas 185.

[60] *Citizens Bank of Louisiana* v *First National Bank of New Orleans* (1873) LR 6 HL 352, 360. See more recently *Argy* v *Lapid Developments* [1977] 1 WLR 444. Cf. promissory estoppel.

[61] [1942] 2 KB 38.

[62] *Ibid.*, pp. 51–2.

[63] (1885) 8 App Cas 467.

[64] A type of loan to the company.

case fraudulent ones.[65] Although the statements looked like statements of intention, they contained an implied statement of fact: that, at the time of making the statements, the directors *in fact* had the represented intention. For, as Bowen LJ pithily remarked,[66] 'the state of a man's mind is as much a fact as the state of his digestion'.[67]

This technique is of wide application but limited practical use. It is likely that all statements of intention can be treated as concealing an implied statement of fact that the representor actually held the intention at the time he made the statement. However, this offers no protection to someone who relies on the statement of intention when the intention is genuinely stated at the time of the representation but where the representor *subsequently* changes his mind. In the absence of a duty to disclose the change of mind or some other method of extending the effect of the representation into the future,[68] the representee is left without a remedy.

There is another way in which a statement of intention may be held to disclose an implied statement of fact. This is where the representor may be taken to be impliedly asserting his ability to do something. For example, if while negotiating the sale of my car I state my intention of fixing the slipping clutch before delivery, such a statement may be considered sufficient to imply a statement of present existing fact about my skill as a mechanic, i.e. that I am possessed of sufficient skill to do the job properly.

A statement of opinion is also distinguished from a statement of fact and so will not of itself give rise to remedies for misrepresentation. So in *Bisset* v *Wilkinson* when a New Zealand farmer made a statement that an area of land 'would carry 2,000 sheep', the Privy Council held that the statement was only one of opinion and so did not give rise to liability for misrepresentation. However, someone who proffers an opinion, like someone who states an intention, will be taken to be making a statement about his present state of mind. If at the time of proffering the opinion it is not genuinely held, the representor has misrepresented a present existing fact, the then state of his mind. Like the statement of intention, this principle of itself gives the representee no protection against any subsequent change of mind on the part of the representor.

Perhaps more important is the second way in which a statement of opinion may be considered to conceal an implied statement of fact. When the representor has specialist skill and knowledge in relation to the matter stated, this will be sufficient to raise an implied statement that the representor is aware of facts sufficient to reasonably justify the opinion. Such was the approach taken by Lord Denning MR in *Esso Petroleum Co Ltd* v *Mardon*[69] when Esso's experienced representative told a future franchisee that the estimated annual throughput of petrol on a certain site would reach 200,000

[65] *Infra.*
[66] *Ibid.*, p. 483.
[67] See also *Burton* v *Birches Timeshare* [1991] 2 NZLR 641.
[68] See *infra.*
[69] [1976] 2 WLR 583.

gallons in the third year of operation. In fact, the site was not good enough to achieve a throughput in excess of 60,000–70,000 gallons. Lord Denning MR said:[70]

> ... it was a forecast made by a party, Esso, who had special knowledge and skill. It was the yardstick ... by which they measured the worth of a filling station. They knew the facts. They knew the traffic in the town. They knew the throughput of comparable stations. They had much expertise and experience at their disposal. They were in a much better position than Mr Mardon to make a forecast ... it can well be interpreted as a warranty that the forecast is sound and reliable.

In this case Lord Denning held that the statement gave rise to a warranty (i.e. a term of a contract) but there is no reason why, if it stated facts, the term could not give rise to liability for misrepresentation as well as an action for breach of contract. This reveals two important points: first a contract consists of a number of terms which if broken give rise to an action for breach of contract. However, not all things said in pre-contractual negotiations become terms of the contract;[71] some do not and are termed 'mere' representations. If these mere representations prove to be untrue, the only redress available to the innocent party is provided by the law of misrepresentation. Whereas if a statement becomes a term of the parties' contract, the innocent party has a choice of two sets of remedies: those available for misrepresentation and those available for breach. Second, while any representation *may* be incorporated into the contract as a term, not all terms may be actionable as misrepresentations, e.g. because they are statements as to the future which disclose no untrue statements of present existing fact.

Therefore, if the representor in *Bisset* v *Wilkinson*[72] had himself been a sheep farmer, it would have been possible to find an implied representation of fact, to the effect that the estimated carrying capacity of the land in question was founded upon past experience or possessed knowledge. However, the principle should perhaps extend beyond those who possess specialist skills and knowledge to encompass those who simply hold themselves out as possessing that skill and knowledge, e.g. I am selling privately my second-hand car and I assure a prospective purchaser that the clutch is in good condition as I replaced it myself. Even though I do not have any particular mechanical know-how, it seems fair that the mere act of taking upon myself such a technical job should justify the imposition of some responsibility for the consequences of doing so. This is achieved by regarding the statement that I undertook the work as implying that I am possessed of reasonable mechanical skill, i.e. I held myself out as expert enough to perform the task. Problems may arise as to what precise standard of expertise I can be taken to profess to have. Reference to tort cases dealing with the appropriate standard of care to be achieved by home handymen may be useful here. In the law of tort such persons are not usually held to the standard of a time-

---

[70] At p. 593.
[71] See below for the relevant principles for distinguishing terms from 'mere' representations.
[72] *Supra.*

served professional unless the work is of such a nature that a reasonable person would only entrust it to such a person. In all other cases, the appropriate standard of care is that of the reasonable home handyman.[73]

There is further category of statement which is sometimes distinguished from an actionable misrepresentation, that of vague and usually laudatory sales talk which is sometimes referred to as 'mere puffery'. Therefore, descriptions of land as 'fertile' or 'uncommonly rich'[74] have been held not to disclose statements of fact. In contrast, an advertisement which described a car as 'Absolutely mint. All the right bits ... and does it go. Probably cost a fortune to build' was sufficiently ascertained to amount to a representation of fact.[75]

Silence as misrepresentation

When contractual negotiations are taking place, each party may be aware of facts which, if disclosed, would affect the willingness of their prospective contractual partner to deal with them or, at least the terms on which they would be prepared to deal with them. However, as a general principle, it is said that the common law does not recognise a duty to disclose valuable information. In the law of misrepresentation this finds expression in the rule that silence cannot constitute a misrepresentation. This is really no more than an application of the more general disinclination on the part of the common law to recognise a duty to negotiate in good faith. We have already stated[76] that the denial of an obligation to negotiate in good faith is often overstated in a way which disguises the extent of the piecemeal regulation of the bargaining process which does take place. Therefore, it should not occasion surprise to learn that the rule that silence cannot amount to misrepresentation is itself subject to a number of exceptions. It is these exceptions that we will now examine.

Change of circumstances

When a representation of fact has been made and, before any contract is entered, there is a change of circumstances which affects the truth of the thing asserted a responsibility may be cast on the representor to correct the statement when he becomes aware of its untruth. The case of *With* v *O'Flanagan*[77] involved negotiations for the sale of a medical practice. At the beginning of negotiations the vendor stated truthfully that the takings of the practice were £2,000 per annum. However, due to the illness of the vendor, the figure was considerably less by the time the contract was entered. The disappointed purchaser succeeded in his action for rescission but the precise basis of the Court of Appeal's decision is not clear. Statements in the case appear to support two different explanations of the result. The first can be

---

[73] *Wells* v *Cooper* [1958] 2 QB 265.
[74] *Dimmock* v *Hallet* (1866) 2 Ch App 21 and *Scott* v *Hanson* (1829) 1 Russ & M 128.
[75] *Fordy* v *Harwood* [1999] Lloyd's Law Reports Alert Service (August)
[76] See Introduction to this chapter.
[77] [1934] 1 Ch 575.

termed 'the fiction of the continuing representation'. When a representation of fact is made in order to induce another to enter a contract, by a legal fiction, the representor is regarded as continually remaking that statement from moment to moment.[78] This has the result that when there is a change in circumstances which renders the original statement untrue the representor is by the fiction held to be making not only a statement of fact but an *untrue* statement of fact which may give rise to the right to rescind. The alternative explanation is that the right to rescind derives from the breach of a duty to communicate the change of circumstances.[79] Although the result of this particular case is independent of the choice of juristic bases, that choice may be important, since if the latter explanation is preferred, the case might stand as an exception to the general duty of non-disclosure rather than the narrower rule that silence cannot amount to a misrepresentation. The conclusion could then more easily be reached that where there was a breach of such a duty the victim might be entitled to redress if he suffered loss even though no contract with the representor ensued, e.g. if the untruth of the statement was discovered when the representee commissioned a report by an accountant which was costly to obtain and which dissuaded the representee from purchasing the practice.[80]

The case of *With v O'Flanagan* was distinguished at first instance by Tudor Evans J in *Wales v Wadham*[81] in relation to the statement of a separated wife that she had no intention of remarrying. It seems that this statement was true when made but had become untrue by the time an agreement was entered between the husband and wife to the effect that the latter should receive £13,000 from the sale of their former home. The judge stated that, unlike *With v O'Flanagan*, in *Wales v Wadham* there was no representation of existing fact; rather there was only:

> a statement of intention [which] is not a representation of existing fact, unless the person making it does not honestly hold the intention he is expressing

In the judge's view, this conclusion follows from *Edgington v Fitzmaurice*, where we have seen that a statement of intention may be held to conceal an implied statement of fact about the present disposition of the representor's mind.

Unfortunately, the judge failed to properly apply the principles associated with *Edgington v Fitzmaurice* and *With v O'Flanagan* to the facts of *Wales v Wadham*. The judge's error lay in his starting point. It is simply wrong to say that a statement of intention is not a statement of fact unless the person making it does not honestly hold that intention. *Edgington v Fitzmaurice* tells us that a statement of intention *always* conceals a statement of fact about the present disposition of the representor's mind. If at the time the statement was made the representor actually holds that intention, the reason it is not actionable is because it is a *true* statement of fact *not* because it is not a

---

[78] *Ibid., per* Lord Wright MR at p. 584 and *per* Romer LJ intervening in the argument of counsel at p. 579.
[79] *Ibid., per* Lord Wright MR at p. 583.
[80] See below on the tort of negligent misrepresentation.
[81] [1977] 1 WLR 199.

statement of fact. When this is appreciated, it can be seen that even according to the narrow view of *With* v *O'Flanagan*, this statement of existing fact as to the present disposition of the representor's mind is to be regarded as being remade continually.[82] Therefore, when Mrs Wadham subsequently formed the intention to remarry, it became an *untrue* statement of fact and was, therefore, actionable.

Half-truths

Sometimes a statement is made which is true in a literal sense but which is none the less misleading. *Nottinghamshire Patent Brick and Tile Co* v *Butler*[83] was such a case where the solicitor acting for the vendors of land was asked by the purchaser whether the land was affected by any restrictive covenants. The solicitor replied that he was not aware of any. This was literally true, he was not aware of any but this was because he had not troubled to look! The statement was held to be a misrepresentation. Similarly, in *Dimmock* v *Hallet*[84] a statement by the vendor of land to the effect that the land in question was let was held to be a misrepresentation when the representor was aware that the tenants had already given notice to quit. The principle amounts to a requirement to correct any statements which are literally true but which convey a different meaning to the reasonable man. Failure to correct may give rise to the right to rescind.

An amusing case (though not for the couple involved) was recently reported in a newspaper not usually noted for its law reports.[85] A man and wife booked a holiday at a resort which the vendor represented to be flat.[86] This was important for the couple, both of whom had health problems. In fact, their villa was located half a mile from the sea 300 yards up a one-in-three slope known locally as 'Cardiac Hill'! The salesman claimed that the resort was flat at the seafront. The judge awarded the couple damages saying: 'You have said the resort was flat by which you meant the promenade and sea front. Nobody needs to be told the seafront is flat.' In other words, at best, the salesman's statement was a half-truth, which should have been corrected.

The principle was applied recently by the Court of Appeal in *William Sindall plc* v *Cambs CC*.[87] The defendant sold a development site to the claimant. The contract of sale was entered after the prospective purchaser had received satisfactory replies to a number of questions (called 'pre-contract enquiries'). These included the following question:

---

[82] See also the older authority of *Brownlie* v *Campbell* (1880) 5 App Cas 925 at 950 *per* Lord Blackburn: 'I further agree in this: that when a statement or representation has been made in the bona fide belief that it is true, and the party who has made it afterwards comes to find out that it is untrue, and discovers what he should have said, he can no longer honestly keep up that silence on the subject after that has come to his knowledge, thereby allowing the other party to go on, and still more, inducing him to go on, upon a statement which was honestly made at the time when it was made ...'.

[83] (1866) 16 QBD 778.

[84] (1866) 2 Ch App 21.

[85] Not worthy of citation.

[86] The holiday was booked at a car-boot sale, but nothing turned on this.

[87] [1994] 3 All ER 932.

Is the vendor aware of any rights ... specifically affecting the property ... which are exercisable by virtue of an easement ... or which are in the nature of public ... rights?

The vendor responded: 'Not so far as the vendor is aware.' The Court of Appeal applied the 'well-established' principle that this reply carries with it an implied assurance that he has taken reasonable steps to ascertain whether any exist. The vendor was able to show that such steps had been taken and did not reveal the existence of a sewer running under the land. In this case the Court of Appeal thought that the reply carried with it a further implied assurance that the vendor's records were not in such a state that a reasonable conveyancer would realise that they were inadequate for the purpose of enabling him to answer the question. The Council was able to show that its records satisfied this requirement and so the claimant's action failed.

Continuing representations and half-truths provide two examples of situations where the law of misrepresentation permits a representee to escape from a contractual obligation because the party he was negotiating with has induced him to enter that contract in reliance upon a misrepresentation. The relief is granted because of a representation made which becomes a misrepresentation as a result of things that were left unsaid. Therefore, these situations should be distinguished from those where the only complaint of the party seeking relief is that the other party has failed to disclose something. These 'true' cases of non-disclosure are considered later because, though they are obviously related to the foregoing discussion, they more obviously raise wider issues and may involve redress which extends beyond the law of misrepresentation.

Inducement

In addition to proving that a misrepresentation of fact has been made, the representee must show that this misrepresentation induced him to an act of reliance in respect of which he now seeks recompense. However, this is a less demanding requirement than might at first be thought, for the law is sensitive to the danger that a misrepresentor should not be able to escape liability because the representee relied upon other motivations in addition to the effect of the actionable misrepresentation. In *Edgington* v *Fitzmaurice*[88] the representee made advances to the company in reliance upon two factors: first the express representation that the monies raised would be applied to expand the business and second the (self-induced) mistaken belief that the advance was secured by a charge upon the company's property. It was held that it was not necessary for the representee to show that the representation was the sole cause of him acting as he did. If he acted on the statement, even though he was also influenced by another or several other factors, the representor remained liable. In other words, the presence of contributory causes does nothing to break the causal link between the actionable misrepre-

[88] *Supra.*

sentation and the reliance of its subject. The burden of proof has shifted. Rather than the representee having to prove his reliance on the representation for the representor to avoid liability, it would be necessary to demonstrate that the representee had not relied upon the misrepresentation *at all*.[89]

There are four circumstances when a misrepresentor will be able to demonstrate that the representee did not rely upon the misrepresentation in any way. These are: (i) when the representee was aware of the untruth of the statement; (ii) where the representee relied only upon some other inducement; (iii) where the representee was simply not aware of the misrepresentation; and (iv) where the representee would have entered into the transaction even if aware of the untruth.

Awareness of the untruth of the statement[90]

The representee's awareness of the untruth of the statement must be proved strictly. It will not be a bar to relief for a representee if the representor shows that the representee failed to avail himself of an opportunity to find out the truth; nothing short of actual full knowledge will suffice. According to established authority, this is so even if a reasonable person in the position of the representee would have taken the opportunity to verify the statement. This is sometimes explained on causal grounds: 'nothing can be plainer ... the effect of false representation is not got rid of on the ground that the person to whom it was made is guilty of negligence'.[91] The interposition of the unused opportunity to verify does nothing to break the causal link between the misrepresentation and the reliance for which the representee now seeks relief. In *Redgrave* v *Hurd*[92] a solicitor placed an advertisement offering to take a new partner who was prepared to buy the solicitor's house. The defendant agreed to buy the house after he had been assured at an interview that the profits from the claimant's practice amounted to '£300 a year, or from £300 to £400 a year'. At another interview the claimant produced summaries of business transacted which showed gross receipts of about £200 a year. When asked how the difference was made up, the claimant produced a quantity of papers which related to other business. The defendant did not examine these papers, other than cursorily, but, if he had, they would have revealed business of only £5–6 a year. When the defendant discovered the true worth of the practice, he refused to complete the purchase of the house and so the claimant brought an action for specific performance.[93] The defendant counterclaimed successfully for the rescission of the contract on the ground of misrepresentation. The failure to inspect the papers simply did not affect the defendant's rights.

The policy behind the strict application of this exception is clear. If a representee could easily evade liability by the assertion that the party with

---

[89] *Smith* v *Chadwick* (1884) App Cas 187, 196.
[90] *Eurocopy* v *Teesdale* [1992] BCLC 1067.
[91] *Redgrave* v *Hurd* (1881) 20 Ch D 1.
[92] *Ibid.*
[93] An order that the defendant perform his contract as promised. See below.

whom he dealt should have taken more care, then careless representees would find their action barred by the actions of opportunistic representors.

Redgrave v *Hurd* reveals another interesting point which is that it is not only a claimant who might seek relief for misrepresentation. In *Redgrave* it was the defendant who was pleading misrepresentation as a defence to the claimant's action to specifically enforce the contract to purchase the claimant's property.

Representee relied upon some other inducement

Where a representee who was not aware of the untruth of the statement relies completely upon some other inducement for which the representor is not legally accountable, there is no causal link between the misrepresentation and the representee's loss. Such would be the case where the representee simply did not allow the misrepresentation to affect his judgment. In the absence of further facts, such an assertion by a representor would be unlikely to be believed. However, in *Smith* v *Chadwick*,[94] where a party suffered a loss in reliance upon a claim in a prospectus to the effect that a particular eminent person would be on a board of directors, in cross-examination the representee admitted that he had not been in the least affected by the untrue claim. This admission was fatal to his claim to have the contract set aside.

The frankness of the claimant in *Smith* v *Chadwick* is probably as laudable as it is uncommon. Therefore, it will be necessary for the representee to adduce sufficient evidence to support his assertion that the misrepresentation did not act on the mind of the representee. The most usual evidence would be where the representee has actually taken the opportunity to verify the truth of the statement, rather than, as in *Redgrave* v *Hurd* considered above, having merely been furnished with the opportunity to verify which opportunity was not taken. If the survey or inspection revealed the untruth of the statement and the representor continued with the transaction, the case would fall within (i) above. If the inspection or survey failed to reveal the falsity of the statement, the representee may be considered to have entirely relied upon the results of his own investigations and, again, be unable to claim relief from the representor.

In *Atwood* v *Small*[95] the claimant contracted to sell his mine. In the negotiations he made misleading statements about the available deposits in it. The purchaser arranged to have a survey of the mine to verify the statements and erroneously the surveyors reported that the vendor's statements were true. Some time later the purchaser discovered the truth and sought to have the contract rescinded for misrepresentation. It was held that the contract could not be set aside because the purchaser relied upon his own judgment based on the findings of his own agents and did not rely upon the misrepresentation. Of course, in such circumstances the disappointed purchaser would

[94] *Supra.*
[95] (1838) 6 Cl & F 232.

probably have an action for negligence in contract or tort against his surveyors.

An interesting problem would be posed if it was concluded that the representee relied upon both the erroneous results of a false survey or inspection *and* the continuing effect of the misrepresentation. In such circumstances the principle in *Edgington* v *Fitzmaurice* (where there are several causes of the representee's reliance, only one of which is an actionable misrepresentation, then the presence of the 'innocent' causes does not affect the actionability of the misrepresentation) would require that the rights of the innocent party should be the same as if there was only one cause, the misrepresentation.

If the actionable misrepresentation was made fraudulently, that is the representor knew it was untrue, had no belief in its truth or was reckless as to whether it was true, it is thought that then the presence of the inadequate inspection would be irrelevant to the liability of the representor. In *S. Pearson & Son* v *Lord Mayor of Dublin*[96] the claimant agreed to do certain work for the defendant in reliance upon plans supplied by the claimant. The contract required the claimant to satisfy itself as to the accuracy of the plans. Lord Loreburn LC stated that:[97]

> ... no one can escape liability for his own fraudulent statements by inserting in a contract a clause that the other party shall not rely upon them.

It is unclear from the facts of the case what steps, if any, the claimant had taken to verify the plans but this is probably irrelevant. Here, as elsewhere in the law of misrepresentation,[98] it seems that the technical rules will always be applied or admit of exceptions in a way that offers no refuge to fraudsters. However, the principle of *Atwood* v *Small* will dictate a different result where the non-actionable cause (i.e. against the misrepresentor) is reliance upon an inspection or survey and the misrepresentation was not fraudulent.[99]

The following propositions emerge from this discussion:

Where there are two or more reasons for entering a contract, if one of these reasons is reliance upon a misrepresentation, the representee's remedies for misrepresentation are unaffected by the multiple causes (*Edgington* v *Fitzmaurice*). However, this is subject to the following:

(a) if the misrepresentation was not fraudulent, and one of the other reasons is reliance by the representor upon his own survey, the representor will lose his remedies for misrepresentation (*Atwood* v *Small*);

---

[96] [1907] AC 351.
[97] *Ibid.*, pp. 353–4.
[98] *Infra*.
[99] It could be argued that the *Atwood* v *Small* principle does not stand as an exception to this facet of *Edgington* v *Fitzmaurice*. Rather the two cases may be considered compatible because the former case is premised upon a finding that the survey conducted was the *only* factor upon which the purchaser relied. However, as this seems to be a conclusion of *law* rather than one of fact, the proposition stated in the text must be the correct one.

(b) if the misrepresentation was fraudulent, reliance by the representee upon his own survey is irrelevant (*Pearson* v *The Lord Mayor of Dublin*).

Representee not aware of the misrepresentation

In this situation the representee is simply not aware of the misrepresentation at all at the relevant time, i.e. prior to suffering the loss for which he now seeks redress. In *Re Northumberland and Durham District Banking Co, ex parte Bigge*[100] the claimant failed in his action when he was unable to demonstrate either that he had read the false statements about the financial state of a company in which he bought shares or that anyone had communicated the contents to him. This case illustrates the further point that it is not necessary that a misrepresentation be addressed to the party who was misled in the sense of being communicated directly from representor to representee. Rather it would be sufficient if the communication was via a third party if the original representor intended the information ultimately to be communicated to the representee.[101]

The strange case of *Horsfall* v *Thomas*[102] further illustrates this principle. The claimant sold a gun to the defendant which was paid for with a bill of exchange.[103] When fired, the gun exploded, which the buyer alleged was caused by a metal plug that had been used to cover up a defective part of the gun's breach. As the buyer had in fact never examined the gun in any way, the Court of Exchequer Chamber held that the concealment of the fault could not have affected the purchaser's decision to buy.[104] The representation which was made but not communicated was an unusual one because it was a representation by conduct. The representation resided in the act of concealing the defective breach with the plug of metal. The case is also a rare illustration of the principle that a representation may be made by conduct alone without any accompanying words.

Representee would have entered the transaction even if aware of the untruth

The Lucy[105] concerned a dispute between the charterers of a ship and sub-charterers. The latter claimed that they had been induced to enter the sub-charter by the former's misrepresentation that the terms of the sub-charter were the same as those in the head charter (i.e. between the shipowner and the charterers).[106] Mustill J held that the misrepresentation

---

[100] (1859) 28 LJ Ch 50.
[101] *Pilmore* v *Hood* (1838) 5 Bing NC 97.
[102] (1862) 1 H & C 90 *dicta* in *Gordon* v *Selico Co Ltd* [1986] 1 EGLR 71 at 74 and 77.
[103] A type of negotiable instrument.
[104] Baron Bramwell suggests that there is a general duty on the seller of goods to disclose latent defects. This aspect of the case is no longer good law. See *Smith* v *Hughes* (1871) LR 6 QB 597 *per* Cockburn CJ at 605 and Cheshire, Fifoot and Furmston. 12th edn, p. 275, n. 6.
[105] [1983] 1 Lloyd's Rep 188.
[106] The dispute concerned the 'trading limits' imposed, i.e. the geographical restrictions upon where the ship may carry cargo.

was made but that no remedies were available to the sub-charterer because he would have entered the sub-charter even if he had been aware of the representation's untruth. It is perhaps significant that the terms of the sub-charter were actually *more* generous than those of the head charter, i.e. the terms of the sub-charter were more favourable to the sub-charterer than they were represented to be.[107]

Must the representation be a 'material' one?

In *Redgrave* v *Hurd* the Master of the Rolls referred to a 'material false representation'. This and other statements[108] have led many commentators[109] to state a further requirement of all actions for misrepresentation, that the representation be a material one. This means that to be actionable, the misrepresentation must be such that it would have affected the judgement of the hypothetical reasonable man or perhaps have dissuaded him from making further enquiries. The matter has been the subject of some debate[110] but appears to have been resolved by the case of *Museprime Properties Ltd* v *Adhill Properties Ltd*.[111] This held that any misrepresentation which in fact induced a person to enter into a contract entitled him to rescind it; the question of whether or not it would have induced a reasonable man to enter the contract related only to the onus of proof. This means that if the misrepresentation would have induced a reasonable person to enter into a contract, the court will presume that the representee was so induced and the representor bears the burden of showing that the representee did not in fact rely on the representation. However, if the misrepresentation was such that it would not have induced a reasonable person to enter a contract, the onus will be on the representee to show that the representation induced him to act as he did.[112] In *Museprime* the action was one to set aside a contract entered in reliance upon a misrepresentation made by a party to that contract but the principle should extend to cover any other forms of reliance which occasion loss to the representee, e.g. entering a contract with a third party. Of course, no question of rescission can arise when A relies upon a misrepresentation made by B in order to enter a contract with C. A's remedy must be a claim for damages against B. The misrepresentation is irrelevant to the validity of the contract between A and B.

The explanation offered in *Museprime* of the requirement of materiality may not have finally settled on the issue. In *Downs* v *Chappell*[113] Hobhouse

---

[107] The sub-charterer claimed that this was still disadvantageous to him because a situation may arise where he orders the ship to go to an area within the territorial limits of the sub-charter but which order is refused by the ship's captain because it is outside the limits of the head charter.

[108] See *McDowell* v *Fraser* (1779) 1 Douglas 247, 248 *per* Lord Mansfield. It is suggested that the more recent decisions said to support this principle in insurance cases, e.g. *Pan Atlantic Co Ltd* v *Pine Top Insurance Co Ltd* [1994] 3 All ER 581 should be confined to that context.

[109] See, e.g., Treitel, p. 301.

[110] *Cf.* Goff and Jones (1998) *The Law of Restitution*. 5th edn, pp. 272–3.

[111] [1990] 2 EGLR 196. See also *County NatWest* v *Barton* (1999) *The Times*, 29 July.

[112] Approving passages in Goff and Jones, *op. cit.*

[113] [1996] 3 All ER 344.

LJ, with whose judgment Roche and Butler-Sloss LJJ agreed, stated that it was a requirement of an action for deceit that the representation was a material one. It is submitted that for two reasons the view expressed in *Museprime* should be preferred. First, the statement of Hobhouse LJ may have been made *obiter dicta* as in *Downs* v *Chappel*, as indeed in most cases, the issue of materiality was not addressed. Second, the statement was made *per incuriam*[114] as, whatever the position with regard to other types of misrepresentation, it has always been thought that any requirement of materiality did not extend to cases of fraud and *Downs* was a case of fraud.[115]

All the general principles we have examined in this section can be considered to apply to the various actions for representation which are outlined in the following section save to the extent that, as with the question of materiality in the tort of deceit, the text indicates that a particular avenue of redress is an exception to the general rule. The tort of deceit seems often to stand as an exception to the general rule and so be governed by its own sub-rules.

THE ACTIONS FOR MISREPRESENTATION
Rescission

Rescission is a term that is used (some would say abused) to refer both to a right possessed by a party who is the victim of a wrong which precedes the process of contractual formation and to a right possessed by a party who receives a defective performance under a pre-existing contract. The former is sometimes called rescission for misrepresentation and the latter rescission for breach. Throughout this book we will act upon a warning issued by Bowen LJ that, 'A fallacy may possibly lurk in the use of the word "rescission".'[116] Therefore, the word termination will be used to refer to the right of an innocent party to treat himself as discharged from any future obligation to perform because of the breach of his contractual partner and rescission will be used to refer to the claim of a party who was induced to enter a contract in reliance upon an untruth to have that contract set aside. A fundamental distinction between these two rights should now be apparent. Termination refers to the right of an innocent party to treat himself as free from all future obligations to perform. Rescission, as we have defined it, refers to the setting aside of the contract for all purposes, in the language used in a decision by the House of Lords, *The Kanchenjunga*,[117] it is wiped out altogether. In other words, the right to terminate is *prospective* while the right to rescind is *retrospective*. This difference in effect follows from the location of the objectionable conduct. Where the objectionable conduct

---

[114] That is, in ignorance of a contrary authority.
[115] *Smith* v *Kay* (1859) 7 HLC 750, *Rafsanjan Pistachio Producers Co-operative* v *Bank Leumi (UK) plc* [1992] 1 Lloyd's Rep 514 at 542.
[116] *Mersey Steel and Iron Co* v *Naylor Benzon & Co* (1882) 9 QBD 648 at 671.
[117] [1990] 1 Lloyd's Rep 391 at 398.

preceded the formation of the contract, the law should seek to restore the innocent party to the position he was in before he relied on the misrepresentation. In contrast, where it is the performance of a contractual obligation which is defective this should only affect the contract from the time when the innocent party elects to 'accept' the breach. This rule alone may appear to work harshly in the case of an innocent party who was required under the terms of the contract to tender his performance substantially, or totally before, that of the party in breach. However, in this situation the innocent party's rights are protected by an award of damages which may include an element to reflect the 'unjust enrichment' of the defendant at the cost of the claimant; the defendant who has given no performance is said to have tendered a consideration which totally failed and which justifies an action for restitution of benefit thereby conferred.

When a contract is entered in reliance upon a misrepresentation, the contract is said to be voidable, that is liable to be set aside at the option of the innocent party. In contrast, certain kinds of mistake are said to render a contract void. The concept of a so-called void contract is something of a contradiction because when a contract is said to be void, in fact what is meant is that no contract ever came into existence. Thus, we have so far seen three different consequences which are said to flow from three different wrongs associated with contracts and purported contracts. They are:

1. a contract which is void for mistake – a contract never came into existence;
2. a contract which is voidable for misrepresentation – a contract came into existence but is liable to be set aside both prospectively and retrospectively at the option of the innocent party;
3. a contract which is terminated for breach – a contract came into existence but is liable to be set aside prospectively at the option of the innocent party.

Considering these three different consequences like this serves to emphasise the points of similarity and contrast between them. Although the courts' aim when they set aside a voidable contract is to put the parties in the position they were in before they entered the contract, they may not be able to do this because of events which have occurred before the party who has the option to have the contract set aside takes steps to exercise that option. Such a circumstance would be where the property which was the subject of the contract has passed into the hands of an innocent third party. Common sense tells us that such a person should not be dispossessed of his property because the person that he acquired it from had obtained it as a result of a misrepresentation; a statement made by A to B should not generally affect contractual relations between B and C. This kind of consideration finds expression in the factors which are said to bar rescission, which are considered in detail below.

Viewed from the perspective of the party seeking relief, the common law may be said to have a generous doctrine of misrepresentation and an ungenerous doctrine of mistake. As the same set of facts often raises both issues of mistake and misrepresentation, the larger ambit of one may be said to compensate for the reduced scope of the other. However, where one of the so-called bars to rescission has arisen, the innocent party may be forced to try to bring himself within the narrow confines of the doctrine of mistake. Occasionally the claimant is successful, as was the case with Elsie, Hilda and Mrs Badger in *Ingram* v *Little*, considered above.[118]

Any misrepresentation of fact which induces a party to enter a contract will give rise to a claim for rescission. However, this simple statement needs some clarification. To give rise to such a right, the statement must be one of fact and must cause the representee to enter a contract with the representor within the principles discussed above. Therefore, if the statement is not one of fact, although the representee may be able to recover damages by a different avenue of redress, e.g. in the tort of negligent misrepresentation if the statement was one of opinion and the requirements of the tort are satisfied, no action for rescission will lie. Perhaps self-evidently, if B enters a contract with C in reliance upon a misrepresentation made by A, then even if the statement is one of fact and the necessary causal link is established, this cannot give rise to a claim for rescission of the contract between B and C. Again, an action for damages in the tort of negligent misrepresentation may lie; indeed, this would seem to be one of the main attractions of such an action.

However, in a different sense, the claim to rescind is the most widely available form of redress for misrepresentation. This is because its availability is independent of any consideration of the mental state of the representor. It is available in respect of misrepresentations made by representors who are aware of the untruth of the statement made as well as those made by representors who should have been aware of a statement's falsity and even when the representor has a reasonable belief in the truth of the statement made.

The requirement of communication to the representor

Misrepresentation makes a contract voidable. The contract is valid until the victim of the misrepresentation exercises his election to have the contract set aside; rescission does not take place automatically. Rescission, therefore, requires notice to be given by the representee to the representor. The court's assistance may be required to give effect to the representee's intention, e.g. where the representor refuses to return or pay money due to the representee. Even if the assistance of the court is required to order the return of money or property, the date from which rescission is effective is the date of notice to the representor.[119] However, if there has been no other communication between the parties, it is possible that rescission is effective when notice of commencement of proceedings is communicated.

A problem may arise where the representee has deliberately absented himself and so is unavailable to receive the representor's notice of rescission.

---

[118] [1961] 1 QB 31.
[119] *Reese Silver Mining Co* v *Smith* (1869) LR 4 HL 64.

Such was the case in *Car & Universal Finance Co Ltd* v *Caldwell*[120] where the defendant 'sold' his car to a rogue who took delivery of the car in exchange for a cheque which was subsequently dishonoured. The rogue and the car then promptly disappeared. The defendant notified the police and a motoring organisation of what had happened. Eventually the car was purchased in good faith by the claimants. It was held that the notification to the police and the motoring organisation was sufficient to avoid the contract. This would seem to be a sensible principle for how can the representee give direct notice of his intention to rescind to someone who has absconded? Yet, the effect of this case should not be lost sight of, for the defendant was not the rogue but an innocent third party who was being sued for the return of the car in the tort of conversion.[121] The court was, therefore, faced with the difficult task of deciding which of two innocent parties should bear a loss, the original representee who was duped by the rogue into parting with his property or the innocent third party purchaser from the rogue or in this case from an intermediate purchaser from the rogue. The court's decision favoured the interests of the representee. However, the unfortunate position of the innocent third party has provoked criticism[122] and the contrary pertains in Scotland.[123] However, the rule remains and it seems that the effect of the criticism may be to confine the principle to the facts of *Caldwell*. It will only apply where the representor cannot be contacted and will probably only apply where the representor is fraudulent. In *Caldwell* the Court of Appeal deliberately reserved its view as to whether the principle would apply if the representor was merely negligent.

The bars to rescission

Events[124] may occur subsequent to the entering of the voidable contract which prevent the representee from exercising the right to have the contract set aside for misrepresentation. In such circumstances the representee's right to rescind is said to be barred. The facts of *Ingram* v *Little*[125] provide an excellent example of this.

A rogue persuaded three elderly ladies – Elsie, Hilda and Mrs Badger – to sell their car to him for £717. When he proposed to pay by cheque, the ladies withdrew their offer to sell. Following repeated assertions by the rogue that he was Phillip Gerald Morpeth Hutchinson of Stanstead House Caterham with business interests in Guildford and a check that there was such a person listed in the telephone directory, the ladies again agreed to sell the car. The

---

[120] [1965] 1 QB 525.

[121] The action was one in tort for conversion: 'The gist of conversion ... is any dealing with another's property in a way which amounts to a denial of his right over it, or an assertion of a right inconsistent with his right, by wrongfully taking, detaining or disposing of it.' Markessinis and Deakin (1999) *Tort Law*. 4th edn, p. 408.

[122] *Law Reform Committee 12th Report* (1966) Cmnd 2958, para 16.

[123] *Macleod* v *Ker* 1965 SC 253 quoted by Treitel (10th edn) p. 345, n. 5.

[124] 'Events' here are interpreted broadly to refer in some circumstances to the simple passage of time. See below.

[125] [1961] 1 QB 31.

rogue drove away in the car and the cheque he left with the claimants was subsequently dishonoured. The rogue then sold the car to the defendant who acted in good faith.

The ladies were undoubtedly prima facie entitled to rescind the contract with the rogue; they had been induced to enter the contract by a mis-representation of fact. It has been questioned whether rescission for mis-representation is available in relation to a contract of sale of goods. This doubt arises because the remedy is not included in the Sale of Goods Act 1979 and the view expressed in *Re Wait*[126] that the Act[127] provided a complete code of legal remedies available in respect of contracts within its ambit. However, the better view now is that the Act does not deal exhaustively with every topic associated with contracts of sale of goods. Indeed it cannot even be said that the Act provides a complete list of remedies available in respect of the *breach* of such contracts (e.g. injunctions are not mentioned) let alone their inducement by misrepresentation.[128] This preferred view is supported by more recent authorities. In a number of cases considered below[129] rescission of contracts for the sale of goods has been refused not because it is unavailable in respect of a contract of sale of goods but because the remedy which was prima facie available was subsequently barred.

In *Ingram* v *Little*, as I have said, the claimants were also undoubtedly prima facie entitled to rescind their contract with the rogue. Indeed, the ladies could effect rescission by informing the appropriate authorities (the *Caldwell* principle discussed above). The reason they did not seek to do so was that it would be to no avail because an effective bar to rescission had already arisen: the intervention of innocent third-party rights. In order to 'defeat' the claim of the innocent third party, the ladies needed to show that the rogue had not even obtained a voidable title to the goods so that he could not pass on any title to the third party under the principle that you cannot transfer a better title than you yourself possess.[130] Therefore, they sought to show that the contract with the rogue was *void* for mistake rather than *voidable* for misrepresentation. In this they were successful and so their action against the third party in the tort of conversion[131] succeeded.

The intervention of third-party rights

A common illustration of third-party rights intervening to bar rescission arises where, as in *Ingram* v *Little* above, the owner of goods has been per-suaded to part with them in reliance upon a fraudulent representation. It is the usual practice of the perpetrators of such frauds that they try to liquidate

---

[126] [1927] 1 Ch 606 at 635.
[127] Then the 1893 Sale of Goods Act.
[128] See Treitel, p. 347.
[129] *Long* v *Lloyd* [1958] 1 WLR 753 and *Leaf* v *International Galleries* [1950] 2 KB 86.
[130] This is the *nemo dat* principle: *nemo dat quod non habet* (you cannot give what you do not have).
[131] See n. 41 above for a definition of conversion.

the goods they obtained by selling them on to an innocent third party as soon as possible.

Another illustration is provided by the rule that rescission is not available in respect of an allocation of shares in a company after the company has gone into receivership.[132] It seems that the commencement of winding-up proceedings signals the intervention of the rights of innocent third parties, the creditors of the company. Strangely, an equivalent rule does not apply to personal bankruptcy where the trustee in bankruptcy is said to take subject to any pre-existing claims to rescission.[133]

Restitution is impossible

At common law a rule pertained that the remedy of rescission was not available where the innocent party was himself unable to return to the other party what he had received from that party. This limit upon the right to rescind was said to be applicable both to a claim to 'rescission' for breach as well as one for misrepresentation.[134] Whether this is an accurate statement of common law principle is not free from doubt. However, in view of the more liberal approach taken by courts of equity, it is not necessary to consider the matter further because, since the fusion of common law and equity by the Judicature Acts 1873–5, where there is a conflict between the two jurisdictions, it is equity that must prevail. It is to avoid this very confusion that we have used a different phrase, termination, to describe the right of an innocent party to be discharged from his outstanding obligations because of the breach of his contractual partner.

The approach of equity is illustrated by *Erlanger* v *New Sombrero Phosphate Co*[135] which involved the purchase of a phosphate mine. Despite the fact that the representee took possession of the mine and extracted some phosphate before he exercised his right to rescind on the basis of untrue statements about the extent of the recoverable deposits, the inability of the representee to return the mine in precisely the state in which he received it was not a bar to rescission. Any injustice towards the representor who does not receive back exactly what he gave is compensated for by an account of profits by the representee in respect of the sale of phosphate he extracted.

This principle, which may require the representee to account for interim profits, should not be thought of as a way of compensating the representee for any decrease in the value of the property returned where the property is less valuable because of exogenous factors e.g. changes in market prices. In *Armstrong* v *Jackson*[136] a broker was instructed to buy shares for a client. In

---

[132] *Oakes* v *Turquand and Harding* (1867) LR 2 HL 325.
[133] *Load* v *Green* (1846) 15 M & W 216. Treitel, p. 355 points out that the different approaches are based on the assumption that third parties are likely to place greater reliance upon a company's nominal share capital than on the appearance of wealth of an individual.
[134] *Clarke* v *Dickson* (1858) EB & E 148.
[135] (1878) 3 App Cas 1218.
[136] [1917] 2 KB 822.

fact, the broker sold to the client shares which the broker owned. Rescission was obtained several years later despite a considerable decrease in the value of the shares subject to an order requiring the representee to account for all dividends received. The diminution in the market value of the shares was itself neither a bar to rescission nor a justification for an account of profits.

In order to appraise the law in this area rather than simply explain its historical origin, it is necessary to ask: why should the inability to make restitution ever act as a bar to rescission? The justifying principle here is that of avoiding unjust enrichment, the very principle which justifies the initial act of rescission. How is it that the reversal or avoidance of unjust enrichment can justify both the remedy of rescission and also its limitation? The answer is that while the representor should not be unjustly enriched by the retention of an advantage he secured as a result of his misrepresentation, so also the reversal of that unjust enrichment should not itself result in the unjust enrichment of the representee by permitting him to retain benefits for which, following rescission, he has not paid. However, the justification for the bar on rescission is only convincing where it is not appropriate for some reason to protect by a financial order the representor's interest in receiving counter-restitution. If such an order, e.g. an account of interim profits as in *Erlanger* and *Armstrong* above, is sufficient to protect the representee, there is nothing to justify the operation of a bar to rescission.[137] Such an approach would lend considerable support to the approach taken in *Erlanger* and would support the calls for the abolition of this bar to rescission.[138]

However, there are some cases which seem to conflict with this statement of principle and with the approach taken in *Erlanger*. These are cases where the misrepresentation was made by the seller of property and the representee subsequently altered substantially the property transferred. So the purchaser of a mine will not be permitted to rescind once he has exhausted its reserves.[139] This principle is inconsistent with the approach of *Erlanger* and the argument of principle described above which suggest that rescission should always be available where an accompanying monetary order is regarded as sufficient to protect the legitimate interests of the representee. A judgment of degree seems to be in operation here: where the order requiring the representee to pay sums to the representor is small compared to the value of the property being returned the inability to make perfect restitution is not a bar to rescission. However, where the former exceeds the latter, the bar should operate. In the first case the law is imposing a rough-and-ready justice on the parties; in the second it is acting upon the lack of equivalence to the benefit of the representor. Like all judgments of degree, it is hard to predict its operation in every circumstance, i.e. to ascertain the precise point

---

[137] 'It is not a bar to rescission that the contract has been partially performed, although the imposition of some order for the payment of money as an adjunct to the order for rescission will often be required to bring about a full adjustment of the rights of the parties,' *per* Mustill J in *The Lucy* [1983] 2 Lloyd's Rep 188 at 202.

[138] See e.g. Burrows (*Restitution*), pp. 134–5.

[139] *Clarke v Dickson* (1858) EB & E 215; *Laguna Nitrate v Lagunas Syndicate* [1899] 2 Ch 392.

at which the right to rescind yields to the bar to rescission. Polar cases are easy: the extraction of a shovel full of anthracite should no more justifiably bar the rescission of a contract for the sale of a coal mine than the buyer of an animal should be permitted to return its corpse after it has been slaughtered.[140] However, in the area between the poles it is difficult with certainty to advise parties of their rights.

Affirmation

The right to rescind is lost if, at a time when he is aware of both the circumstances that give rise to the right and also the existence of that right, the representee makes clear his intention to continue with the contract. This 'dual knowledge test' was laid down by the Court of Appeal in *Peyman* v *Lanjani*[141] where an Iranian who spoke little English was induced by a misrepresentation to buy the lease of a restaurant. The claimant was held to be entitled to the remedy of rescission notwithstanding the fact that he had indicated a willingness to continue with the contract at a time when he was aware of the facts that gave rise to the right to rescind because at that time he was not actually aware of the existence of the right itself. This extra requirement does seem to give an advantage to victims of misrepresentations who are not fully aware of their legal rights and thereby conflict with the general principle that ignorance of the law is no defence (*ignorantia lex haud excusat*).

Affirmation may, of course, be express but it may also be implied from the conduct of the representee. In *Long* v *Lloyd*[142] the claimant lost his right to rescind for misrepresentation when he retained the defective lorry for a period following the second attempt by the representor to effect repairs to it. An intention to affirm was inferred from this retention.

A more difficult problem is the relationship between the circumstances when the right to rescind for misrepresentation may be lost by affirmation and the circumstances when the right to reject goods sold under a contract for the sale of goods is lost by 'acceptance'.[143] Both of these rights were considered in *Leaf* v *International Galleries*[144] where Denning LJ put forward the view that the right to rescind for misrepresentation must be barred in any circumstance when the right to reject has been lost through acceptance. This approach appears to be based upon the idea that there exist a hierarchy of remedies in which the remedies available for breach of contract occupy a superior position to those available in respect of misrepresentation. This in turn reflects the view that breach of contract is more serious than mis-

---

[140] *Clarke* v *Dickson* (1858) EB & E 148, 155.
[141] [1985] QB 428.
[142] [1958] 1 WLR 753.
[143] The right to reject non-conforming goods under a sale of goods contract is very similar to the right to terminate for breach of condition which is available irrespective of the type of contract. However, they are not identical because the seller could re-tender conforming goods within the period allowed under the contract for delivery.
[144] [1950] 2 KB 86.

representation. In Denning LJ's words,[145] 'misrepresentation is much less potent than a breach of condition'. On this view it becomes necessary to know when the right to reject is lost through acceptance. Acceptance may take place in three ways: by express intimation, by an act inconsistent with the ownership of the seller and by the buyer's retention beyond a reasonable time.[146] Before 1994 this operated very harshly against the buyer who might find that he lost the right to reject before he could reasonably have known that had arisen. The rules were amended by the Sale and Supply of Goods Act 1994 to provide that in the first two circumstances the buyer must first have been given a reasonable opportunity to inspect the goods[147] and the determination of a reasonable time for the third circumstance must now take account of whether a sufficient time has elapsed to permit a reasonable inspection.[148] Despite these improvements in the rights of buyers, it is still the case that when considering whether the right to reject goods has been lost through acceptance, the focus is upon the opportunity to inspect rather than the exercise of it. Exceptionally the right to reject may still be lost before it is known to exist. If the right to rescind is not available where the right to reject is lost, the right to rescind also could be lost before it is known to exist. Such an approach would be counter to the trend of developments in the law of misrepresentation as well as the law of sale of goods. In the former, as we saw in *Peyman* v *Lanjani*, there has been evident a disinclination to deprive the victim of a misrepresentation of the remedy of rescission when he is not aware of its existence. In the latter the changes to the principles of acceptance introduced in the Sale and Supply of Goods Act 1994 to a limited extent ameliorated the harshness of the old law.

A further objection to a broad interpretation of Denning LJ's approach in *Leaf* points to the anomalies it would produce if contracts for the sale of goods were treated differently to other contracts. The law applicable to actions in respect of a misrepresentation as to the amount of coal available which induced a contract for the sale of a mine would be different to the law applicable to the same misrepresentation which induced a contract for the sale of the contents of a coal yard. The Sale of Goods Act 1979 (as amended) would not apply to the former because it is a sale of real property. However, such difficulties could be avoided if Denning LJ's comments were interpreted narrowly[149] as only applying to the facts of *Leaf*. In *Leaf* the possibility of rescission being available in circumstances where the right to reject had been lost was avoided by introducing a new bar to rescission, lapse of time. Therefore, if Denning LJ's principle of acceptance limiting rescission

---

[145] *Ibid.*, p. 90.
[146] Sale of Goods Act 1979, s 35.
[147] Section 35(2).
[148] Section 35(5).
[149] Some support for a narrow implementation of Denning LJ's judgment in *Leaf* can be derived from *Peco Arts Inc* v *Haslitt Gallery Ltd* [1983] 1 WLR 1315 where the judgment was interpreted as being solely concerned with bars to rescission and so irrelevant to the question of limitation which arose in that case on facts very similar to those in *Leaf*.

was considered only to apply to cases where rescission is resisted on the basis of lapse of time the discontinuity is reduced.[150] The bar of lapse of time will now be considered.

Lapse of time

In *Leaf* v *International Galleries*[151] the claimant purchased a painting in reliance upon the representation that the painter was 'Constable'. It was five years before the purchaser discovered the untruth of this statement and tried to rescind the contract of purchase. The claimant's claim failed for reasons we have already examined concerning the interrelationship between the law of sale of goods and that of misrepresentation. In this case there was no evidence of affirmation as the claimant tried to pursue the remedy of rescission as soon as he discovered the falsity of the misrepresentation. The policy behind this bar to rescission appears to be that of encouraging purchasers to examine the pedigree of their purchases as soon after they receive possession as is reasonable[152] in order to promote finality in dealings.[153] The pursuit of these policy objectives would presumably yield to the more important policy of discouraging parties from deliberately telling 'lies'[154] and so the bar of lapse of time would not apply where the misrepresentation was a fraudulent one.

Misrepresentation Act 1967, s 2(2)

This section of the statute introduces a restriction upon the availability of the remedy of rescission which is different in operation and origin to the common law bars we have already considered. Section 2(2) provides:

> Where a person has entered into a contract after a misrepresentation has been made to him otherwise than fraudulently, and he would be entitled, by reason of the misrepresentation, to rescind the contract, then, if it is claimed ... that the contract ought to be or has been rescinded, the court or arbitrator may declare the contract subsisting and award damages in lieu of rescission where it is equitable to do so, having regard to the nature of the representation and the loss that would be caused if the contract were upheld, as well as the loss that rescission would cause to the other party.

The section does not apply to fraudulent misrepresentations, mirroring the assumed position as regards the bar of lapse of time. Although the section specifies the factors which a court may take into account when considering whether to exercise its discretion, these are described in very broad terms.

---

[150] This is the suggestion of Treitel, pp. 356–7.
[151] [1950] 2 KB 86.
[152] '[The purchaser] had ample opportunity for examination in the first few days after he had bought it', *per* Denning LJ at p. 91.
[153] *Per* Jenkins LJ at p. 92.
[154] *Infra.*

The breadth of the section was illustrated by *obiter dicta* of the Court of Appeal in *William Sindall plc v Cambridgeshire County Council*.[155] In *Sindall* an action for rescission was brought by a builder who purchased some playing fields from the council for just over £5,000,000. It was subsequently discovered that there was a small sewer running under the land which had not been disclosed by the council but of which it was unaware. The Court of Appeal held that there had been no operative mistake because the contract[156] allocated to the purchaser the risk of the existence of easements and encumbrances, other than those of which the vendor has knowledge or means of knowledge, which might affect the land. This conclusion was also fatal to the claimant's assertion that he was entitled to rescind for misrepresentation. However, the Court of Appeal went on to consider, *obiter dicta*, the correct application of Misrepresentation Act 1967, s 2(2) and concluded that if there had been a misrepresentation this would be a suitable case for the exercise of the discretion conferred by s 2(2) to award damages in lieu of rescission. In exercising this discretion, the court had to take account of the nature of the misrepresentation, the loss it would cause if the contract were upheld and the loss that would be caused to the vendor by rescission. If rescission was granted, the purchaser would be able to escape the consequences of a bad bargain, as the land had halved in value[157] due to the general fall in property values when the only loss attributable to the misrepresentation would be the cost of re-routing the sewer, which was assessed at £18,000. Furthermore, the council would be deprived of the benefit of a contract of sale which was very advantageous to it. Therefore, the Court of Appeal said that damages in lieu of rescission under s 2(2) cannot include loss due to a general decline in market values subsequent to the sale; the proper measure of damages in lieu of rescission is the cost of remedying the defect or the reduced market value attributable to the defect. In *Sindall* the application of this formula would have produced an award based on the figure of £18,000.

An award of damages under s 2(2) is, therefore, calculated by reference to the factors the court is required, by the section itself, to take into account. It is an award of damages which cannot be summarised by reference to any analogous measure within the common law. In this respect, it may be contrasted with the right to damages for misrepresentation created by s 2(1) which, by its reference to the tort of deceit, has been held to incorporate the measure of damages and rules of remoteness appropriate to that tort.[158] However, it has been suggested that s 2(3) has a bearing on the matter. This subsection states that any award of damages under s 2(1) must take account of any award made under s 2(2) thereby suggesting that the award of damages under s 2(1) may be greater than the award under s 2(2).[159] One way in which the s 2(2) award may be less than that under s 2(1) is if the latter

---

[155] [1994] 3 All ER 932.
[156] National Conditions of Sale (20th edn) Condition 14.
[157] That is, at the time of discovery of the sewer.
[158] *Infra.*
[159] *Witter* v *TBP Industries* [1996] 2 All ER 573 at 591 c–d *per* Jacob J.

includes recovery for consequential losses where the former is limited to the loss in value of what is bought under the contract.[160] However, another way in which the award under s 2(2) may be less than that under s 2(1) is if the test of remoteness applicable under s 2(2) is the test of reasonable foreseeability or perhaps even the contractual test[161] when that appropriate to s 2(1) is the more generous (viewed from the perspective of a claimant) one applied in the tort of deceit which permits recovery for all direct losses.

By its terms s 2(2) permits the award of damages 'in lieu of rescission'. Does this mean that damages under the subsection are only available where a *continuing* claim to rescission can be demonstrated? If damages were in this way parasitic upon a claim to rescission, then in any circumstances where the claim to rescission is lost, e.g. one of the bars to rescission has arisen, the claim for damages in lieu would also be lost. The contrary view is that the reference to rescission only imports a requirement that the claimant was at one point in time entitled to rescind and the fact that he is no longer able to do so should not affect his ability to claim damages under s 2(2). Indeed, the intervention of innocent third-party rights so as to bar rescission might be thought to be the most compelling circumstances for an award of damages. In a recent case at first instance,[162] the seller of a business made several misrepresentations to the buyer which induced the latter to purchase the business. The purchaser sought, *inter alia*, to rescind the contract of purchase. In the High Court Jacob J held that rescission was barred on the basis that due to changes in key personnel the representee would be unable to make restitution of the business and the business had been mortgaged so that rescission would affect innocent third-party rights (the mortgagees). However, Jacob J preferred the second view referred to above and held that the power to award damages under s 2(2) did not depend on the right to rescind still being extant but on the claimant having had such a right in the past. Interestingly, Jacob J exercised the recently recognised[163] power to resolve an ambiguity in the interpretation of a statute by reference to what was said in Parliament. In Parliament, the Solicitor General had expressed the view that damages could be awarded under s 2(2) even when restitution was impossible.

---

[160] Atiyah and Treitel, [1967] MLR 369 at 376.

[161] That the appropriate test of *remoteness* is the contract one may be implicit in the view that the appropriate *measure* of damages is the contractual one, as to which see *William Sindall plc* v *Cambs CC* [1994] 3 All ER 932 at 954 H *per* Hoffman LJ and at 961 J *per* Evans LJ, Russell LJ agreeing *contra* the view in the text that the measure of damages cannot be summarised by reference to any pre-existing measure. There is also some evidence derived from the legislative history of the Misrepresentation Act that the contractual measure was not intended because an amendment to introduce the contractual measure of damages was withdrawn without discussion. Standing Committee G, 23 February 1966 referred to by Treitel, p. 337, n. 81.

[162] *Thomas Witter* v *TBP Industries* [1996] 2 All ER 573. Not followed in *Floods of Queensferry Ltd* v *Shand Construction Ltd* [2000] BLR 81.

[163] *Pepper (Inspector of Taxes)* v *Hart* [1993] AC 593.

Indemnity

As we have seen, if the requirements of s 2(2) are satisfied, damages may be given in lieu of rescission. It follows that it is not possible to claim both rescission *and* damages under s 2(2). Rescission may be combined with a claim for damages under s 2(1) if the latter's more stringent requirements are satisfied and the two remedies would not involve compensating the claimant twice for the same loss.[164] Rescission may not be combined with a claim for contractual damages, i.e. damages for breach of contract as that would involve asserting two inconsistent things: that there has been a breach of a subsisting contract[165] and that the contract should be set aside retrospectively, i.e. rescinded because of a defect in the process leading to its formation.

It is possible to claim both rescission and a financial award called an indemnity. It is, therefore, important to distinguish this claim for an indemnity from a claim for damages. The difference may be illustrated simply by reference to the facts of *Whittington* v *Seale-Hayne*.[166] The defendant leased premises to the claimant for the purpose of poultry rearing, which premises the defendant had represented were in a sanitary state. In fact, the premises and water supply were not and as a consequence the claimant's manager became ill and many of the birds died. The claimant sued for his loss of profits, loss of stock, medical expenses, rent and rates paid and repairs effected to the premises. Rescission was granted and the claimant received an indemnity in respect of the rent, rates and repair expenses; the other claims for damages were not recovered.[167] An indemnity may only be claimed for expenses incurred in discharging obligations *created by the contract*; the tenant's obligations to pay rent and rates and to effect repairs to the premises were all created by the lease.

The reason for this limited recovery is that the indemnity seeks to recompense the representee for sums expended which were in effect part of the price paid; it seeks to perfect the mutual re-exchange of property required by the remedy of rescission to restore the parties to the position they were in before they entered the contract. An example will help illustrate this.[168]

A landlord lets two identical flats which he represents to be in a 'sanitary state'. Flat 1 he lets at a rent of £100 per week and the lease makes the landlord responsible for all repairs. Flat 2 he lets at a rent of £80 per week and the lease makes the tenant responsible for all repairs. After ten weeks the tenants seek to rescind the leases when the flats prove to be insanitary.

---

[164] *Infra.*
[165] That is, subsisting at the time of breach, so even if the contract is *terminated* i.e. there has been a breach of a condition or a fundamental breach of an innominate term, the contract is only set aside prospectively; at the time of breach it was a fully valid contract sufficient to support an action for breach. See below.
[166] (1900) 82 LT 49.
[167] But could now be recovered under s 2(1).
[168] *Newbigging* v *Adam* (1886) 34 Ch D 582.

Rescission would involve the mutual re-exchange of property and monies. The tenants would give up possession of the flats and the landlord would return £1,000 to the tenant of flat 1 and £800 to the tenant of flat 2. However, the objective of rescission, subject to any 'bars' arising, is to return the tenant to the position he was in before he entered the lease and if matters rested there this objective might not be fulfilled. The obligation assumed by the tenant to repair the premises is as much a part of the price paid for the right to occupy the premises as is the rent paid directly to the landlord. In our example, the landlord has obviously valued the cost of the repairing obligation at £20 per week which was reflected in the reduced reserve in respect of flat 2. If his estimate had proved correct, the tenant would have expended £200 on repairs during the ten weeks. Hence, rescission is supplemented in the case of flat 2 by the award of an indemnity to the tenant in respect of the monies spent on repairs as required by the lease to properly restore him to the position he was in before the lease was entered.

A case that is sometimes thought to permit recovery of an indemnity beyond the principles described above is *Newbigging v Adam*[169] where the claimant was induced to join a partnership by fraudulent misrepresentation. The claimant was granted rescission of the contract which made him a partner and so the monies he paid into the partnership had to be returned. However, the troublesome aspect of the case is that the Court of Appeal held that he was entitled to an indemnity in respect of any liabilities he had in- curred whilst a partner. It is thought that statements in the Court of Appeal justifying this result may expand the previous operation of an indemnity. Fry LJ said that an indemnity was available both in respect of obligations created by the contract which is rescinded but also those which are entered under the contract and are within the reasonable contemplation of the parties.[170] However, it is suggested that the Lord Justice may have confused the origin of the primary liability of the partnership with a partner's secondary liability to contribute towards it. The former may be created by contracts between the partners and third parties while the latter is created by the contract of partnership and as such an order to relieve the consequences of it falls within the accepted domain of an indemnity.

It can be seen that an indemnity perfects the remedy of rescission to make the restoration of the parties to the position they were in before the contract was entered more accurate. The role of an indemnity is, therefore, supplemental to the remedy of rescission. Hence, it will not be available where a bar has arisen so as to preclude rescission. This is in contrast to the availability of damages under s 2(2) which we have seen only require the proof of a historic claim to rescission.[171]

---

[169] *Ibid.* The indemnity was not considered in the House of Lords: *Adam v Newbigging* (1888) 13 App Cas 308.
[170] At p. 596.
[171] *Supra.*

The recovery of damages

The tort of deceit

Deceit is a tort, that is, an independent legal wrong which is redressable by an action for damages. It is also known as the tort of fraudulent misrepresentation or sometimes simply as fraud. However, the latter word is often used to denote criminal conduct which fraudulent misrepresentation frequently amounts to. The link between the tort of deceit and the criminal law is an important one because many judgments and sub-rules in this area seem to be more concerned with the punishment of the fraudulent representor than the compensation of the representee.[172] Yet, the general aim of damages in the law of tort is to compensate the victim of the tort; exemplary and punitive damages are wholly exceptional.

The major distinguishing feature of an action for deceit is the mental state of the representor which a claimant must prove. In *Pasley* v *Freeman*, Buller J stated that:[173] 'knowledge of the falsehood of the thing asserted is fraud and deceit'. A distinction is sometimes drawn between the knowledge and the motive of the representor; the former is key, the latter is irrelevant. Therefore, a representor may be liable for a fraudulent misrepresentation if he had the required state of mind even though he did not intend to benefit himself or cause loss to the representee.[174]

A scenario which varies a little Robin Hood's *modus operandi* will illustrate this distinction. Suppose that legendary figure proceeded by way of deceiving the rich into parting with their property rather than by taking it. That Robin Hood intended to distribute the property to the poor would be as irrelevant to the nature of the misrepresentation as a belief that his rich victims would be benefited by his activities by securing reward in another life; if the statement which induced the victims to part with their property was made with the requisite intent, that alone is proof of deceit.

The early cases on the tort of deceit were examined by the House of Lords at the end of the last century in *Derry* v *Peek*.[175] A company was authorised by an Act of Parliament to run horse-drawn trams and, if the Board of Trade consented, steam-driven trams. A prospectus was issued by the directors of the company which claimed that the company had the right to run steam powered trams. However, the required permission was never granted. The claimants purchased shares in reliance upon the representation in the prospectus. The claimants were undoubtedly entitled to claim rescission of the contract allotting them shares in the company and therefore were entitled to the return of the monies paid for them. However, the parties to that contract were the claimants and the company, which had been

---

[172] For example, *Pearson* v *Lord Mayor of Dublin* [1907] AC 851, above.
[173] (1789) 3 TR 51 at 57.
[174] *Foster* v *Charles* (1830) 7 Bing 105 at 107 *per* Tindal CJ; *Derry* v *Peek* (1889) 15 App Cas 337 at 374 *per* Lord Herschell.
[175] (1889) 14 App Cas 337.

subsequently wound up, and so the remedy was worthless. This is the reason why the claimants brought an action in deceit for damages against the directors personally.[176]

This is still one of the attractions to claimants of the action in deceit: it may permit a representee (the investors) to recover from a representor (the directors) when the former incurs a loss by entering a contract[177] with a third party (the company) in reliance upon the misrepresentation. This feature of permitting recovery in 'three party' situations is shared with the tort of negligent misrepresentation and explains the continued popularity of these actions in circumstances when as we have seen rescission is not possible because a statement made by A to B cannot be a ground for re-scinding a contract with C, and as we will see, an action for damages under s 2(1) is unavailable because that subsection requires the misrepresentation to be made by someone with whom the representee subsequently contracts.

In *Derry* v *Peek* Lord Herschell expanded upon previous statements describing the mental state of the representor which the claimant must prove:[178]

> ... fraud is proved when it is shown that a false representation has been made (1) knowingly, or (2) without belief in its truth, or (3) recklessly, careless whether it be true or false.

The first and possibly the second mental state describe what might be called 'telling a deliberate lie'. The third mental state might be thought to describe simple negligence. That this is not so is stated explicitly by Lord Herschell:[179]

> I cannot assent to the doctrine that a false statement made through carelessness, and which ought to be known to be untrue, of itself renders the person who makes it liable to an action for deceit.

He also makes the same point when he describes what mental state of the representor will *preclude* a finding of fraud:[180]

> To prevent a false statement being fraudulent there must, I think, always be an honest belief in its truth ...

Therefore, the proof of negligence alone will never suffice to ground an action in deceit. I may represent that a desk I sell to you is a Chippendale, my only ground for saying so being the assurance given to me by the owner of the junk shop I bought it from for £1. If I genuinely believe that it is a Chippendale, I am not fraudulent, though I am surely negligent because no reasonable person would entertain that belief on the scant evidence I have.

So in *Derry* v *Peek* itself the honest belief of the directors that the consent of the Board of Trade was a mere formality was sufficient to protect them

---

[176] The problem was subsequently dealt with by statute see Director's Liability Act 1890 and now the Financial Services Act 1986, ss 150 and 166.

[177] Or in any other way, e.g. making a gift to the third party.

[178] (1889) 14 App Cas 337 at 374.

[179] *Ibid.* at p. 373.

[180] *Ibid.*

from liability for damages in deceit.[181] Similarly, in *Witter* v *TBP Industries*[182] the vendors of a carpet manufacturing business exaggerated the amount set aside in the previous year's accounts in respect of a complaint by a major customer and also falsely represented that expenditure in compiling pattern books had already been written off. These misrepresentations induced the purchaser to offer too high a price for the business on the basis of an overly optimistic view of the company's profit in the next year of trading. Although both misrepresentations were negligent, neither was made fraudulently. In respect of both misrepresentations, the relevant company officers believed the statements to be true and so were not fraudulent.[183]

Claimants who choose to bring an action in deceit are faced with an uphill struggle. They must prove that the defendant foresaw the risk that the statement was untrue: the action cannot succeed when the defendant had a genuine belief in the truth of the statement. However, the difficulties of claimants must not be exaggerated. For although the proof of carelessness on the part of the representor does not itself amount to the required mental state, carelessness, particularly gross carelessness, may be *evidence* from which the required mental state may be inferred. In the Chippendale example above, my conduct might be evidence from which the required degree of foresight can be implied. An analogy can be drawn with the crime of rape where the prosecution must prove that non-consensual intercourse took place and that the perpetrator knew that the victim did not consent or was reckless[184] (in the sense that he foresaw the risk that the victim did not consent). Proof that a reasonable man in the position of the defendant would have realised that there was no true consent is not alone sufficient to support a conviction unless that is regarded as *evidence* from which the jury infer that this defendant foresaw the risk that the victim did not consent.[185]

When an award of damages is considered, two different measures of damage are sometimes contrasted. These are the contract measure and the tort measure. It is important to understand the difference between them before we proceed to a more detailed discussion of the rules applicable in deceit. The contractual measure of damages seeks to put the claimant in the position he would have been in if the contract had been performed;[186] the tortious measure seeks to put the claimant in the position he was in before the wrong occurred.[187] The former is prospective, looking forward to the fulfilment of the promisee's expectations,[188] while the latter is retrospective,

---

[181] Now there might be liability under Misrepresentation Act 1967, s 2(2) or in the tort of negligent misstatement. See below.

[182] [1996] 2 All ER 573.

[183] *Ibid.*, p. 587 J *et seq.*

[184] Sexual Offences Act 1956, s 1(1).

[185] Sexual Offences Act 1956, s 1(2).

[186] The classic definition is that of Parke B in *Robinson* v *Harman* (1848) 1 Exch 850 at 855: 'The rule of the common law is that where a party sustains a loss by reason of a breach of contract he is so far as money can do it, to be placed in the same situation with respect to damages as if the contract had been performed.'

[187] *Ibid.* Tort, by contrast, seeks to put the victim in the position he was in before the tort.

[188] And so is said to protect his expectation interest.

looking to restore the innocent party to the position he was in before the wrong occurred (his status quo ante).[189] Therefore, if a contractual measure of damages was available in respect of a misrepresentation, the claimant would be placed in the position he would have been in if the representation had been true and, if a tortious measure was applied, the claimant would be placed in the position he was in before he relied upon the misrepresentation.[190] A simple example will illustrate their application.

> A pays B £1,000 for a stone B represents to be a one carat diamond. If the stone were as described, it would be worth £1,500 but in fact it is a fake worth only £50. If the contractual measure of damages were awarded, A would receive £1,450: if the representation were true, he would have received a stone worth £1,500, whereas what he has received is only worth £50, so to restore him to the position he would have been in if the representation had been true he must receive the difference between those two figures. If the tortious measure were awarded, A would receive £950: before entering the transaction he had £1,000, whereas he now has a stone worth £50, therefore, he needs £950 which together with the stone gives a combined total of £1,000 – his status quo ante.[191]

Deceit is a tort and so the measure of damages awarded is the tortious one.[192] In a simple case the ascertainment of the basic award should be straightforward. This can be illustrated by reference to a colourful recent case. In *The Siben* the claimant agreed to exchange his luxury yacht, a De Lorean sports car and a sum of money for a villa and discotheque in Portugal as well as an 'escort' business run from the villa. The vendor of the Portuguese property made two fraudulent misrepresentations in the course of negotiations: that he was the owner of the discotheque (in fact it stood on land owned by a third party); and that it was making a profit of £1,500 per weekend. The claimant received damages in respect of these misrepresentations prima facie assessed by reference to the value of the yacht, car and money transferred by the claimant to the defendant with credit being given for the villa transferred by the defendant to the claimant. The discotheque was left out of account because the claimant never got the benefit of its business and the 'escort' business was ignored because this was an immoral business supplying women for money.[193]

It is trite to observe that a person may one day be answerable before a

---

[189] And so is said to protect the *status quo ante*, or when applied to promises, the reliance (interest) of the promisee.

[190] A third measure of damages the restitution measure is not relevant to the present discussion.

[191] For further discussion of the different interests protected by the different measures of damage, see Fuller and Perdue, 'The Reliance Interest in Contract Damages' (1936) 46 Yale LJ 52 and 373; Atiyah (1986) *Essays on Contract*, ch. 2; Burrows, 'Contract, Tort and Restitution – a satisfactory division or not?' (1983) 99 LQR 217.

[192] *Doyle* v *Olby* [1969] 2 QB 158; *East* v *Maurer* [1991] 1 WLR 461; *The Siben* [1996] 1 Lloyd's Rep 35.

[193] The claimant was able to recover damages despite the illegal nature of the 'escort' business because the claimant did not have to rely on or plead the illegality. See below, ch. 6.

'higher' tribunal in respect of the infinite consequences of his actions. However, the earthly courts are somewhat more generous towards miscreants. In the tort of negligence the tortfeasor's legal liability is limited to such consequences of his tort as are reasonably foreseeable, even if only foreseeable as a remote consequence.[194] The excuse that the particular consequence which occasioned the defendant's loss was not one which a reasonable man would foresee does not evoke sympathy when spoken by someone who has told a deliberate lie; justice seems to demand a higher degree of accountability. In line with this sentiment, the test of remoteness of loss adopted by the courts in the tort of deceit is a more generous one (for claimants that is): the claimant is able to recover in respect of 'all the actual damages directly flowing from the fraudulent inducement'.[195]

In *The Siben* the application of this test permitted the recovery of various incidental expenses, e.g. the cost of delivering the yacht. These expenses were almost certainly reasonably foreseeable and so would have been recoverable even if the action had been one for negligent, as opposed to fraudulent, misrepresentation. However, more controversial was the recovery in *East v Maurer*[196] where the vendor of a hairdressing salon represented to the purchaser that he would not be working on a regular basis at another local salon which he retained. Damages were recovered when this representation proved to be untrue and was shown to have been made fraudulently. These damages included all the losses the claimants had suffered but also something in respect of loss of profits. It is this latter item that must be scrutinised carefully. For a claim in respect of loss of profits would seem to be more appropriate if the action was one for breach of contract when of course the contractual measure of damages would be given. Such an award would seek to put the claimant in the position he would have been in if the representation had been true and so would look forward to the fulfilment of the claimant's expectations. However, the award of lost profits in *East v Maurer* is consistent with the tortious measure of damages because, as Mustill LJ stressed,[197] the lost profits were not given in respect of the profits which the claimants would have earned from the business they bought if the vendor had honoured his non-competition pledge; to do so would be to elevate the mere representation to the status of a contractual term. Rather the profits related to the money the claimants would have made from whatever business they would have bought if they had not invested in this one. According to Beldam LJ,[198] with whose judgment Mustill and Butler-Sloss LJJ agreed:

---

[194] *The Wagon Mound (No. 1)* [1961] AC 388.
[195] *Doyle v Olby (Ironmongers) Ltd* [1969] 2 QB 158 at 166–7 *per* Lord Denning MR quoted by the Court of Appeal in *East v Maurer* [1991] 1 WLR 461 at 464–5 and *Downs v Chappell* [1996] 3 All ER 344 at 356–7.
[196] [1991] 1 WLR 461.
[197] *Ibid.*, p. 468 H. See also *Clef Aquitaine SARL v Laporte Materials Ltd* [2000] 3 WLR 1760 (such damages are available where the contract entered is in fact profitable, but less so than the opportunity foregone).
[198] *Ibid.*, p. 464 E.

Damages for deceit are not awarded on the basis that the Claimant is to be put in as good a position as if the statement had been true; they are to be assessed on a basis which would compensate the Claimant for all the loss that he has suffered, so far as money can do it.

The policy which justifies the adoption of a different principle of remoteness in the tort of deceit may have less to do with protecting this claimant's legitimate interests than with punishing the defendant and thereby protecting future victims of deceit. This was the view that was expressed recently, *obiter dicta*, by the House of Lords in *South Australia Asset Management Corporation v York Montague Ltd.*[199] A similar sentiment was expressed in the Court of Appeal in *Downs v Chappell*[200] where Hobhouse LJ, delivering the judgment of the court, stressed the need to check the quantum of recovery to ensure that damages did not exceed compensation for losses in fact suffered. He suggests that to check the assessed loss was in fact consequential on the fault of the defendant a comparison be made between the loss consequent upon entering the transaction with what would have been the position had the represented state of affairs actually existed. In *Downs* v *Chappell* where the representations again related to the profitability of a business, if the representations had been true, the claimants would have been able to cover the interest on the money they borrowed to purchase the business. So the sum awarded as damages which was the difference between the price they paid for the business and the price it would have realised if sold quickly was reasonable.[201] It is important to remember that this reference to what is in effect the contractual measure of damages is merely to ascertain that the tortious measure which is actually awarded does not overcompensate the claimant[202] by permitting recovery of losses beyond those caused by the fault of the defendant, e.g. losses attributable to a decline in the general trading environment.

Even after the prima facie measure of recovery has been ascertained and checked, it may be cut down by a further limiting factor. If the claimant fails to act reasonably to mitigate his own loss, or acts unreasonably to increase his loss, the amount awarded will be reduced accordingly.[203] In *Downs* v *Chappell* the claimants unreasonably turned down two offers to sell the business for a price considerably higher than that eventually obtained. As we have seen, the damages in the case were assessed by reference to the offer which should have been accepted rather than the lower offer which was eventually accepted. The claimants had failed to act reasonably to mitigate their loss when they refused the higher offer and the subsequent fall in the value of the business was attributable to their own indecision rather than the fault of the defendant.

---

[199] [1997] AC 191.
[200] [1996] 3 All ER 344.
[201] For a further discussion of the consequences of the claimants' failure to mitigate their loss, see below.
[202] See p. 362 B.
[203] *Smith New Court Securities Ltd* v *Scrimgeour Vickers Ltd* [1992] BCLC 1104.

We have so far considered two factors which can operate to reduce recovery: remoteness and mitigation. There is a third factor which can operate to reduce recovery of damages but which is inapplicable to the recovery of damages in the tort of deceit: the contributory negligence of the claimant. In *Alliance & Leicester v Edgestop*[204] a fraud was perpetrated upon several lenders by a number of parties. Mummery J refused an application by the employers of a fraudulent surveyor to plead the contributory negligence of the lenders for failing to follow their own internal guidelines on lending and failing to properly scrutinise the loans being made. The judge considered the Law Reform (Contributory Negligence) Act 1945, s 1(1) which states that when someone suffers damage partly as a result of his/her own fault and partly as a result of the fault of another, damages may be recovered subject to a reduction to take account of the fault of the victim. The definition of fault is crucial to the operation of s 1(1). Fault is defined in s 4:

> 'fault' means negligence, breach of statutory duty or other act or omission which gives rise to a liability in tort or would, apart from this Act, give rise to the defence of contributory negligence.

In this case the claimant's conduct does not fall within the first limb as there is no suggestion that the lenders are themselves in any way liable in tort. Therefore, the claimant's conduct only amounts to fault within the 1945 Act if it falls within the second limb whereby it amounts to conduct which, apart from the Act, would amount to the defence of contributory negligence at common law. The judge then considered the position at common law and particularly the statement of Sir George Jessel MR in *Redgrave v Hurd*:[205]

> Nothing can be plainer ... than that the effect of false representation is not got rid of on the ground that the person to whom it was made has been guilty of negligence.

In the judge's opinion, the principle laid down by the Master of the Rolls in *Redgrave v Hurd* has not been altered by any subsequent decision and so the defence of contributory negligence is unavailable in respect of actions for deceit.

The intervention of an agent presents the courts with a further difficulty which they have resolved in the following way. When the agent is aware that the representation is false, the fraud of the agent is imputed to the principal.[206] However, the principal will not be held liable even if he is aware of the untruth of the statement if the agent is not,[207] unless the principal was aware that the representation was being made and 'stood by'.[208]

---

[204] [1993] 1 WLR 1463. See also *Standard Chartered Bank v Pakistan National Shipping Corp (No. 1)* [2000] 3 WLR 1692 (CA).
[205] [1881] 20 Ch D 1 at 13–14.
[206] *S Pearson & Son Ltd v Lord Mayor of Dublin* [1907] AC 351.
[207] *Cornfoot v Fowke* (1840) 6 M & W 358.
[208] *The Siboen and the Sibotre* [1976] 1 Lloyd's Rep 293 *per* Mocatta J at 321.

Misrepresentation Act, s 2(1)

Prior to 1965, a claimant who suffered loss as a result of his reliance upon a misrepresentation could only recover damages if that representation had been made fraudulently or had been incorporated into a contract as a term. However, two parallel developments gave rights of action to the victims of negligent misrepresentations. The first was the right of action introduced by the Misrepresentation Act 1967, s 2(1) considered here, and the second was an action in the tort of negligent misrepresentation (or misstatement), sometimes called a *Hedley Byrne* action, after the House of Lords' case which gave rise to it[209] (see below).

An untrue statement which the representor believes to be true but which no reasonable man would believe to be true will amount to a negligent misrepresentation. Confusingly such a statement is sometimes referred to as an innocent representation. This terminology has its roots in the old law when if damages for misrepresentation were claimed statements could be categorised as either fraudulent and so actionable or non-fraudulent and so non-actionable[210] and in that sense 'innocent'. However, it has not been appropriate since 1964. Therefore, whilst its use in the older cases is unavoidable, it should now be avoided. The phrase innocent misrepresentation will be used in this work to refer to a non-fraudulent *and* non-negligent misrepresentation, i.e. one which the representor believes to be true and which a reasonable man in the position of the representor would have believed to be true. An innocent misrepresentation in this sense is the kind of statement in respect of which an action may be brought for damages under s 2(2) of the Misrepresentation Act 1967.

Section 2(1) provides:

> Where a person has entered into a contract after a misrepresentation has been made to him by another party thereto and as a result thereof he has suffered loss, then, if the person making the misrepresentation would be liable to damages in respect thereof had the misrepresentation been made fraudulently, that person shall be liable notwithstanding that the misrepresentation was not made fraudulently, unless he proves that he had reasonable grounds to believe and did believe up to the time the contract was made that the facts represented were true.

The somewhat convoluted wording of this section must be examined closely as it has important repercussions. Perhaps the most striking feature of the section and the one responsible for its length is the reference to fraud, which is sometimes referred to as 'the fiction of fraud'. Why does the section in effect say that if someone would have been liable to another in the tort of deceit then he/she shall be so liable even if there is no deceit if the statement was made negligently? The reason for this reference to fraud was probably to incorporate into the statutory action the general principles of liability which we have already discussed: that the statement be one of fact, not intention, opinion or law, etc. As we will see, the introduction of the fiction of fraud has

---

[209] *Hedley Byrne & Co Ltd* v *Heller & Partners Ltd* [1964] AC 465.
[210] Unless incorporated as a term of a contract.

had the consequence that the measure of damages and the appropriate test of remoteness to be applied in respect of consequential losses under s 2(1) has been held to be the same as that in the tort of deceit.[211] However, it would surely be inappropriate[212] if the fiction of fraud were used to justify the incorporation into the statutory action of many of the other sub-rules applicable in deceit, which can only really be justified by reference to the pursuit of policies of deterrence and punishment that are only relevant, if at all,[213] to intentional rather than negligent acts.

A key feature of an action under s 2(1) is that the burden of proof is reversed on the issue of negligence. It is not for the claimant to prove that the defendant was negligent rather s 2(1) provides that it is for the representor to prove that he was *not* negligent, i.e. that he had a reasonable belief in the truth of the statement. That this makes an action under the section very attractive to claimants is shown by *Howard Marine & Dredging Co Ltd* v *Ogden & Sons (Excavations) Ltd* [214] where the defendants hired barges from the claimants which the claimants' manager had falsely represented to have a particular capacity. After half a year's use, the defendant refused to pay any further hire and so the claimant brought an action. The claimant sued the defendant for breach of contract. The defendant counterclaimed for damages for misrepresentation under s 2(1). The claimants' manager based his statement as to the barges' carrying capacity upon the figures in the Lloyd's Register of Shipping. Unfortunately for him, the figures in the Lloyd's Register were incorrect. The majority of the Court of Appeal held that the claimants had not discharged the burden cast upon them by the section of showing that they had reasonable grounds to believe in the truth of the statement because the true capacity was recorded in the barges' registration documents. That the burden cast upon a representor by s 2(1) is a heavy one is clear: it was not discharged by consulting the Lloyd's Register which Lord Denning described as the 'bible of the shipping trade', and seemed to require the consultation of documents (the registration papers) which were not available at the representor's office.

In *Howard Marine & Dredging Co Ltd* v *Ogden & Sons (Excavations) Ltd* the misrepresentation was in fact made by the claimants' agent. Although the representor may be liable under s 2(1) in respect of statements made on his behalf,[215] the agent does not incur personal liability under the section.[216]

A further onerous feature of the burden cast upon the representor by the

---

[211] *Royscot Trust Ltd* v *Rogerson* [1991] 2 QB 297.

[212] Lord Reid said in the parliamentary debates on the Act that it would be 'rather unreasonable' if the extended limitation period applied to fraud were also applied to the statutory action 274 HL 936 quoted by Treitel, p. 325. For the limitation period applicable to deceit, see Limitation Act 1980, s 32(1). It seems that Lord Reid's view may have prevailed in *Garden Neptune Shipping* v *Occidental Worldwide Investment Corp* [1990] 1 Lloyd's Rep 330 at 335.

[213] It can be argued that punishment and deterrence are the domain of the criminal rather than the civil law.

[214] [1978] QB 574.

[215] See also *Gosling* v *Anderson* (1972) 223 EG 1743.

[216] *Per* Mustill J in *The Skopas* [1983] 2 All ER 1.

section is that the reasonable belief in the truth of the statement must persist up to the time that the contract was made. This is similar to the principle stated in *With* v *O'Flanagan*,[217] which probably extends to requiring the representor to correct a statement which was reasonably believed to be true when made but where that belief ceases to be a reasonable one at some time before the contract is entered.

In the case of *Jarvis* v *Swans Tours Ltd* [1973] QB 233 Lord Denning suggested that the damages would be the same whether awarded under s 2(1) or for breach of a contractual warranty.[218] As the latter measure of damages is the contractual measure, Lord Denning was plainly of the view that the damages to be awarded under s 2(1) would also be the contractual measure.[219] This would seem to produce a perverse result when compared with the recovery that would be made in respect of the other types of misrepresentation. It might be expected that there would be a 'tariff' of damage measures which reduced according to whether the representor contractually guaranteed the truth of what he said (i.e. it was a term of their contract), whether the statement was made fraudulently, whether it was made negligently and whether it was made with a reasonable belief in its truth. As we know that the first type of statement attracts the contractual measure and the second the tortious one (with responsibility for all direct consequential losses), it would seem odd if negligent misrepresentation were to attract a contractual measure of damages as Lord Denning suggested. In effect, the tariff system would be reversed with the less culpable misrepresentation (a negligent one) resulting in a higher award of damages than a more serious misrepresentation (a fraudulent one). Surely the law should be more sympathetic to the incompetent than to the dishonest. However, put in this way the 'tariff' argument may be thought to place too much emphasis upon the punishment of the misrepresentor which may be thought to be more properly the province of the criminal law; the civil law should only concern itself with compensation. In any event, the controversy over the appropriate measure of damages to be awarded under s 2(1) has now been settled by the Court of Appeal in the next case to be considered and the approach promoted by Lord Denning has been abandoned.

The law is frequently an education in sharp practice (some would perhaps say commercial reality!) for those who study and practise it. *Royscot Trust Ltd* v *Rogerson*[220] was certainly such a case. The claimant was a finance company whose policy was only to finance transactions where the buyer was able to put down a deposit of at least 20 per cent of the purchase price. The

---

[217] [1936] Ch 575, above. Strictly, *With* was a case where the statement *was* true when it was made rather than merely reasonably believed to be true but changes of mental state should fall within the principle as well according to Lord Blackburn in *Brownlie* v *Campbell* (1880) 5 App Cas 925 at 950.

[218] A warranty is a term of a contract the breach of which gives rise to a right to damages but not to a right to terminate the contract.

[219] To similar effect, see Lord Denning's comments in *Gosling* v *Anderson* [1972] EGD 709 and those of Graham J in *Watts* v *Spence* [1976] Ch 165.

[220] [1991] 3 WLR 57.

defendant car dealers were aware of this policy which presumably meant that the claimant company was able to offer a lower rate of interest than would otherwise have been the case as the provision of a large deposit goes some way to demonstrate the means of the buyer and if the buyer did ever default on the repayments the deposit should ensure that the car would be worth more than the outstanding debt. Mr Rogerson wanted to purchase a car for £7,600 with the aid of the claimant's finance but was only able to afford a deposit of £1,600, some 16 per cent of the purchase price. Therefore, to secure the finance, the defendant car dealers 'inflated' the purchase price, falsely representing that the price of the car was £8,000 and that Mr Rogerson had, therefore, paid a 20 per cent deposit. The hire-purchase contract was then entered but, in breach of that agreement, Mr Rogerson sold the car and stopped making payments. The finance company brought an action against the defendants claiming damages under s 2(1). Somewhat surprisingly, no allegation of fraud was made against the defendants.

The main judgment was delivered by Balcombe LJ who closely examined the wording of the section and concluded that, despite what he referred to as 'the initial aberrations'[221] of Lord Denning, the appropriate measure of damages under s 2(1) was the tortious one.[222] According to the Lord Justice, this conclusion followed inexorably from the wording of the section which stated not that the person making the representation shall be liable but rather that he shall be 'so liable' referring to liability in fraud. It followed that not only does the prima facie measure of damages under s 2(1) mirror that in the tort of deceit, but the test of remoteness is also the same.[223] As Mr Rogerson's action in selling the car was regarded as directly attributable to the defendant car dealers' misrepresentation, they were able to recover the difference between the sum of money they had advanced to Mr Rogerson and the instalments which they received from him prior to his default.

Where damages are awarded for breach of contract, there is a prima facie rule that damages are assessed at the date of breach unless justice demands a later date be used.[224] This rule is justified by the principle of mitigation of loss. To take the simple example of a purchaser of a defective good the contractual measure of damages would be an award of the difference between the value of the good as promised and the value of the good supplied, both values being ascertained at the date of breach (i.e. delivery). If there is a rising market in the good, the so-called 'breach date rule' assumes that the disappointed purchaser will go out into the market and buy a substitute at the date of breach so that any further losses through delay may be said to be consequent upon the purchaser's failure to mitigate his loss. However, where the action is one for damages under s 2(1), the 'wrong' for which the

[221] *Ibid.*, p. 63 B.
[222] At p. 63 A–B. This follows an earlier poorly reported case in the Court of Appeal: *Chesneau* v *Interhome Ltd* [1983] 134 NLJ 341.
[223] *Ibid.*, p. 63 B–C and *per* Ralph Gibson LJ at p. 66 G–H. See also *Cemp Properties (UK) Ltd* v *Dentsply Research and Development Corporation* [1991] EG 62.
[224] *Johnson* v *Agnew* [1980] AC 367.

claimant seeks redress may be said to have occurred when the claimant was induced to enter a contract with the representor. However, it would be unfair to assess damages at that time because the untruth of the statement will only be apparent later and it will only be when that untruth is discovered that it is reasonable to expect the representee to mitigate his loss.[225] Therefore, the date at which a reasonable person in the position of the representee would have become aware of the untruth of the statement is the usual date at which damages for misrepresentation will be assessed. In *Naughton v O'Callaghan*[226] the claimants were induced to purchase a horse to race in reliance upon a misrepresentation as to its pedigree. Considerable training expenses were incurred before the true pedigree emerged and the value of the horse had declined considerably as it had proved itself a failure on the racecourse. The damages were assessed as the difference between its purchase price and its value at the time the misrepresentation was discovered as well as expenses incurred up to that time.

We have seen that damages recovered in the tort of deceit may not be reduced to take account of the contributory negligence of the representee. In *Gran Gelato Ltd v Richcliff (Group) Ltd*[227] the same question was raised in relation to a claim under Misrepresentation Act, s 2(1). The claimants agreed to take a lease of property from the defendant in reliance upon the defendant's representation, communicated through the defendant's solicitors, that there were no terms in the head lease which would affect the claimants' enjoyment of the underlease. In fact, the head lease contained a 'redevelopment clause' which permitted the lessor to terminate the head lease for redevelopment upon giving 12 months' notice. The lessor exercised this option when the underlease still had four-and-a-half years to run, so the claimants brought an action against the defendant and its solicitors claiming damages for negligent misrepresentation at common law[228] and against the defendant, the under-lessor, under Misrepresentation Act, s 2(1).

The case further illustrates the principles governing the liability of agents under s 2(1). As we have already seen, no action would lie against the solicitors personally,[229] though an action could be brought against the defendant in respect of the misrepresentation communicated to the claimants by the solicitors on behalf of the defendant.[230]

However, the most controversial aspect of the case was the assertion by the defendant that if the claimants were successful in any claim, then any damages recovered should be reduced to take account of their contributory negligence. The court accepted without argument that contributory negligence is available as a defence to a claim for negligent misrepresentation at

[225] See the discussion of Hobhouse LJ in *Downs v Chappell* [1996] 3 All ER 344 at 359 F.
[226] [1990] 3 All ER 191.
[227] [1992] 1 All ER 865.
[228] As to which, see below.
[229] *Per* Mustill J in *The Skopas* [1983] 2 All ER 1.
[230] *Howard Marine & Dredging Co Ltd v Ogden & Sons (Excavations) Ltd* [1978] QB 574; *Gosling v Anderson* [1972] 223 EG 1743.

common law[231] but went on to consider the same defence in relation to s 2(1) and concluded that if the defence was available in respect of negligent misrepresentation at common law, it should be available in respect of the statutory action for negligent misrepresentations. This reasoning, based upon parity between the two actions for negligent misrepresentation, was further said to be supported by reference to the position adopted with regard to actions for breach of contract where the defence is available if there is concurrent liability in negligence.[232] However, this conclusion is open to a number of criticisms.

First, arguments of parity always beg the question of parity with what? There is certainly an intuitive appeal to the idea that actions for negligent misrepresentation should share similar characteristics, irrespective of whether they are the product of statute or the common law. However, in other regards, parity has not prevailed e.g. a statement of opinion is actionable at common law but not under s 2(1)[233] and the applicable principles of remoteness differ.[234] Indeed, a consideration of remoteness may suggest a different parity to be more appropriate. The adoption of the test of remoteness used in the tort of deceit was justified by the Court of Appeal by reference to the 'fiction of fraud' used in the statute.[235] By the same argument, the fiction of fraud may be thought to suggest that the approach to contributory negligence under s 2(1) should mirror that in the tort of deceit where it has recently been held to have no role[236] rather than that in the tort of negligent misstatement and an action for breach of contract.

Second, one of the premises upon which the judge proceeded may be open to question. He suggested that contributory negligence may act to reduce recovery in the tort of negligent misstatement. However, it is arguable that where the claimant relies upon advice given by the defendant in circumstances where a reasonable man would not have so relied, then it is not the case that the damages of the representor are reduced, rather the representor fails to recover anything. This appears to be the import of the House of Lord's decision in *Smith* v *Eric S Bush*[237] where it was held that a duty of care was owed by a valuer acting for a mortgagee to the mortgagor in respect of a valuation of the house to be purchased with the assistance of a mortgage. It was suggested that where the mortgage was used to finance the purchase of a modest dwelling house it was reasonable for the purchaser to rely upon the valuation but it would not be reasonable to do so if a less modest house was bought or commercial premises were bought. In those

---

[231] A conclusion that is not itself without difficulty. See below pp. 71–3.

[232] *Forsikringsaktieselskapet Vesta* v *Butcher* [1986] 2 All ER 488 (affirmed without discussion of this issue [1989] AC 852).

[233] Unless it conceals a statement of fact, *supra*.

[234] At common law the *Wagon Mound* test of reasonable foreseeability is applied, while under s 2(1) the test applicable is the tort of deceit, which permits the recovery of all direct losses; see above.

[235] *Royscot Trust Ltd* v *Rogerson* [1991] 3 WLR 57.

[236] *Alliance and Leicester Building Society* v *Edgestop Ltd* [1993] 1 WLR 1463.

[237] [1990] 1 AC 831.

circumstances the reasonably prudent purchaser would have had his own survey and valuation made. If the argument based on *Smith* v *Eric S Bush* is accepted, and in relation to an action for negligent misrepresentation at common law, the principle of contributory negligence operates as a complete defence,[238] it should be understood why this argues against its role as partial defence, i.e. as a means of reducing rather than denying recovery. In *Forsikringsaktieselskapet Vesta* v *Butcher* the court was impressed by the absurdity of the situation where if on a given set of facts the defendant owed the claimant a duty of care in tort but the claimant's damages would be reduced on account of the contributory negligence of the claimant, the claimant could avoid that reduction by simply framing his action as one for breach of contract instead. This possibility of avoiding the reduction in damages by crossing out tort in the statement of claim and substituting breach of contract would arise whenever there was a concurrent duty to take care in contract and tort. Therefore, contributory negligence as a defence to an action for breach of contract was only to apply when such concurrent liability existed; it was co-terminous with the absurdity it was meant to avoid. However, the argument loses all force if, as *Smith* v *Bush* suggests, contributory negligence acts as a complete defence; there is then no concurrent liability and so no absurdity to avoid. It may be useful to recap the steps in this difficult argument: if contributory negligence acts as a complete defence to an action for negligent misrepresentation at common law there cannot be any concurrent liability and so there should not be any reduction of damages in such an action on account of the contributory negligence. If this is the position in the tort of negligent misrepresentation, ‚should not the same rule apply when the action is brought under s 2(1)? Parity between the tort of negligent misrepresentation and s 2(1) would seem to require the opposite conclusion to the one the judge in *Gran Gelato* thought it justified.

However, even if the law laid down by the Vice-Chancellor in *Gran Gelato* is upheld, its practical impact may not be great, for courts may be expected to show a considerable reluctance to find conduct on the part of a victim of a breach of contract which is sufficiently 'unreasonable' to amount to contributory negligence. That this may be so is supported by the application of the principle of contributory negligence to the facts of the case itself. For it was held that, although it would be possible in law to do so on the facts of the case, nothing in the conduct of the claimant justified a reduction in the damages he could claim. Further, it was said that the claimant's failure to make further enquiries (about the head lease) 'provides no answer to a claim when the claimant has done that which the representor intended he should do'.[239] Therefore, it seems that the common law principle associated with the case of *Redgrave* v *Hurd* [240] that the failure to avail oneself of an

---

[238] Or perhaps more accurately, but with the same practical effect, to negate the existence of a duty of care.

[239] At p. 877 b–c.

[240] (1881) 20 Ch D 94.

opportunity to verify the truth of a statement does not affect the availability of rescission is to be applied to an allegation of contributory negligence in relation to an action under s 2(1). On this basis, it is difficult to imagine what circumstances may amount to contributory negligence.

The tort of negligent misrepresentation

We have seen that the case of *Derry* v *Peek*[241] defined the mental state which must be proved in order to bring an action in the tort of deceit. For many years after the case was decided it was thought to support a wider proposition that no action could be brought in respect of a negligent statement. However, in 1914 in *Nocton* v *Lord Asburton*,[242] the House of Lords said that this was not the case. As well as liability in contract and under statute,[243] there could be liability in equity in respect of negligent misstatements. According to the House of Lords, this liability may arise when there is a fiduciary relationship between the parties, such as exists between a solicitor and his client. In 1964 in *Hedley Byrne & Co Ltd* v *Heller & Partners Ltd*[244] the House of Lords pointed to its decision of half a century earlier to justify the view that their Lordships were not prevented by precedent from holding that a tortious duty of care may exist when making statements, the breach of which may enable the representee to recover damages in respect of his economic loss.

On the facts of the case, which concerned a misleading credit reference given by the defendant bank to the claimant advertising agency in respect of one of the former's clients, it was held that damages would have been awarded but for an express disclaimer of responsibility which accompanied the reference.[245]

Unfortunately, it has proved difficult to discern in *Hedley Byrne* a simple principle sufficient to justify the imposition of a duty of care in tort in respect of negligent misstatements. Broadly, two different approaches to the imposition of liability may be discerned in subsequent cases.

Several cases[246] emphasise the need for a special relationship to exist between the parties. Statements of the requirements of such a relationship emphasise the representor's knowledge as to whom the statement will be communicated and for what purpose. In *Caparo* v *Dickman*[247] Lord Bridge said that the adviser must know the statement will be communicated to the claimant as an individual or as a member of an ascertainable class in respect of a particular transaction. Similarly, Lord Oliver stated that the requirement is that the adviser knows his advice is required for a purpose and will be communicated to the claimant or a member of an identifiable class and is likely to be relied upon. This emphasis that the statement be intentionally

---

[241] *Supra.*
[242] [1914] AC 932.
[243] Director's Liability Act 1890 and now the Companies Act 1985. Of course, the modern statute with widest effect is the Misrepresentation Act 1967.
[244] [1964] AC 465.
[245] Such a disclaimer might now be unenforceable under the Unfair Contracts Terms Act 1977.
[246] *Smith* v *Eric S Bush* [1990] 1 AC 831 and *Caparo* v *Dickman* [1990] 2 AC 617.
[247] *Ibid.*

made to a particular person or persons for a particular purpose (all the Ps) may be illustrated by contrasting the facts of two cases.

In *Caparo* itself the defendants were auditors who had certified the accounts of a client company as being true and accurate. These accounts, which proved to be misleading, were relied upon by Caparo when attempting to take over the target company with the consequence that Caparo suffered loss. It was held that no duty of care was owed by the auditors to Caparo. The purpose of the statutory requirement to audit company accounts was to safeguard the interests of existing shareholders as such and not to provide information to facilitate takeovers. In contrast, in *Morgan Crucible Co plc* v *Hill Samuel & Co Ltd* [248] it was held that a 'defence' document produced by auditors at the request of the company directors, advising rejection of a takeover bid should be treated differently. This document was produced in relation to a particular transaction in the knowledge that it would be relied on by the predator company. Therefore, there was no ground to strike out [249] the action of the company which, in reliance upon misleading statements in the defence document, increased its take-over bid and thereby suffered loss.

Many of the professionals who, under the *Hedley Byrne* principle, have been held to owe a duty of care to clients, may, to a greater or lesser extent, be said to be in the business of providing information, e.g., accountants, [250] banks, [251] barristers, [252] insurance managing agents, [253] solicitors [254] and valuers of businesses [255] and residential property. [256] However, there is no requirement to this effect. [257] None the less, it is questionable whether liability will arise when a social acquaintance holds himself out as having a particular skill. Although such a duty of care was held to be owed between friends when one undertook to advise the other on the purchase of a second-hand car, [258] this was based upon a concession made by the defendant's counsel which was itself criticised by one member of the Court of Appeal.

---

[248] [1991] Ch 259; see also *Galoo* v *Bright Graheme Murray* [1995] 1 All ER 16.

[249] The defendants asked the court to strike out the claimant's claim as disclosing no cause of action.

[250] The decision to the contrary in *Candler* v *Crane, Christmas & Co* [1959] 2 QB 164 was overruled in *Hedley Byrne & Co* v *Heller & Partners Ltd* [1964] AC 465.

[251] *Hedley Byrne & Co* v *Heller & Partners Ltd* [1964] AC 465.

[252] Barristers no longer have immunity in the tort of negligence in respect of court work and preparations connected therewith. *Rondel* v *Worsley* [1969] 1 AC 191 has been overturned by *Arthur J. S. Hall & Co* v *Simons* [2000] 3 All ER 673.

[253] *Henderson* v *Merrett Syndicates Ltd* [1995] 2 AC 145.

[254] *Ross* v *Caunters* [1980] Ch 297 and *White* v *Jones* [1995] 2 AC 207.

[255] *Esso Petroleum* v *Mardon* [1976] QB 801.

[256] *Smith* v *Eric S Bush* [1990] AC 831.

[257] See *Esso* v *Mardon* [1976] QB 801 at 827 *per* Ormrod LJ and *Howard Marine & Dredging Co Ltd* v *A Ogden & Sons (Excavations) Ltd* [1978] QB 574 at 591 and 600 *per* Lord Denning MR dissenting and Shaw LJ respectively endorsing the dissenting opinions of Lords Reid and Morris in *Mutual Life & Citizens Assurance Co* v *Evatt* [1971] AC 793 to the effect that it was sufficient that considered advice was sought from a businessman in the course of business. The minority view in *Evatt* was also effectively confirmed by the House of Lords in *Spring* v *Guardian Assurance* [1995] 2 AC 296 (employer owes duty of care when writing a reference about a former employee).

[258] *Chaudhry* v *Prabhakar* [1988] 3 All ER 718.

More recent cases have taken a different approach and have not based liability under *Hedley Byrne* upon the discovery of a special relationship as discussed above. Rather they have emphasised that liability for negligent mis-statement in tort is dependent upon an assumption of responsibility by the representor. However, there is force in Lord Griffith's[259] objection that 'assumption of responsibility' states a conclusion of law justified on other grounds (because of X, the representor may be said to have assumed re-sponsibility) rather than providing itself a workable test to identify situations where a duty of care arises in respect of things said. In any event, it may only be relevant where negligent conduct is involved[260] or where a statement is made concerning, rather than directly to, the complainant.[261]

This discussion of the requirements of the tortious action established in *Hedley Byrne* has ranged far beyond the context of pre-contractual nego-tiations. However, it is clear that when those requirements (whatever they are) are satisfied parties negotiating a contract may be held to owe a duty in tort to each other to refrain from making misleading statements. *Esso Petroleum Co Ltd v Mardon*[262] was such a case where a prospective tenant of a petrol station was induced to enter a lease after an assurance had been given by an expert valuer as to the expected petrol sales at the particular site. It was held that the expert valuer owed a duty of care to the tenant at common law.[263]

From the perspective of a claimant, the difficulty of establishing, in law and in fact, the existence of a duty of care make the action an unattractive one. Indeed, when compared to the statutory action for negligent misrepre-sentation, there are two further disadvantages. First, under *Hedley Byrne* the burden of proof is borne by the claimant who must prove all the elements of his cause of action. Under the Misrepresentation Act, s 2(1) the claimant has the benefit of a reversed burden of proof.[264] The claimant need only prove that a misrepresentation has been made to him, it is then up to the defendant to show that he had reasonable grounds to believe in the truth of the statement and also that those grounds continued until the contract was entered. Second, as *Hedley Byrne* liability is tortious, the measure of damages recoverable in such an action is the tortious one; the claimant is, so far as money can do so, restored to the position he was in before the wrong occurred. Although this measure is the same as that applicable to the statutory action, a different rule of remoteness applies. In a *Hedley Byrne* action the claimant may only recover for such items of loss as may be said to

---

259 *Smith* v *Bush* [1990] AC 831.
260 *Henderson* v *Merrett Syndicates Ltd* [1995] 2 AC 145 (negligence of managing agents in managing the risks to which Lloyd's 'Names' were exposed).
261 *Spring* v *Guardian Assurance* [1995] 2 AC 296.
262 [1967] 2 All ER 850.
263 *Cf.* 'Certainly *Hedley Byrne* liability provides a broad base from which particularised duties could develop in pre-contractual bargaining but it is suggested that the vagaries of the tortious duty of care are inappropriate as instruments with which to dissect the intricacies of commercial negotiations.' Ian Brown, 'The Contract to Negotiate: A Thing Writ in Water', Bus Law Rev 353 at 355.
264 See above *Howard Marine Dredging Co Ltd* v *A Ogden & Sons (Excavations) Ltd* [1978] QB 574.

be reasonably foreseeable even if only as a remote possibility. Whereas under s 2(1) of the Misrepresentation Act 1967, as in an action to deceit, the claimant may recover for all the direct consequences of breach, even if they were not reasonably foreseeable.[265]

The computation of the tortious measure of damages has given rise to difficulty where there has been a breach, on the part of a valuer[266] and solicitor,[267] of a duty to take reasonable care to ensure that information they provided was accurate. In such cases[268] the adviser is not liable to the full extent of the defendant's losses which would not have occurred[269] if accurate information had been given because this might require the defendant to indemnify the claimant in respect of losses caused by a fall in the value of the property purchased. The valuer or solicitor provides information to enable the recipient to make a decision; they do not usually undertake to advise as to what decision to make. On this basis, a valuer has been held to be liable only to the extent of the information provided proving wrong; he is only responsible for the 'initial security shortfall', i.e. the difference between the negligent valuation and the real value of the property at the time when the claimant's cause of action accrues.[270] In torts such as negligence, where damage is an essential part of the claimant's cause of action, that action will not accrue until he suffers actual[271] and relevant[272] loss. Where a claimant purchases property in reliance upon a negligent overvaluation or his solicitor's assurance that the property is unencumbered, this will be the date of completing the purchase.[273] The situation where a lender, rather than a purchaser, relies upon a negligent over-valuation presents greater difficulty. Here it seems that damage occurs when the lender can show that he is worse off than he would have been if the security had been worth the sum advised by the valuer probably the time at which the borrower defaults on the loan.[274]

A question can arise as to the effect upon the damages otherwise recoverable by the claimant of any contributory negligence on his part. Statements of the *Hedley Byrne* principle which refer to the *reasonable* reliance[275] of the representee would appear to suggest that where reliance is not reasonable

[265] See above *Royscot Trust Ltd* v *Rogerson* [1991] 2 QB 297.

[266] *South Australia Asset Management Corpn* v *York Montague Ltd* [1997] AC 191.

[267] *Bristol & West BS* v *Mathew* [1997] 2 WLR 436.

[268] The adviser would be so liable if he had warranted, i.e. contractually guaranteed, the accuracy of the information provided.

[269] *Banque Keyser Ullman SA* v *Skandia (UK) Insurance Co Ltd* [1991] 2 AC 249 and *Swingcastle Ltd* v *Alistair Gibson (a firm)* [1991] 2 AC 233, as explained in *South Australia Asset Management Corpn* v *York Montague Ltd* [1997] AC 191.

[270] *South Australia Asset Management Corpn* v *York Montague Ltd* [1997] AC 191.

[271] *Forster* v *Outred & Co* [1982] 1 WLR 86 at 94–6 *per* Stephenson LJ.

[272] Namely, loss which is within the scope of the duty of care owed by the defendant to the claimant. *Nykredit plc* v *Edward Erdman Ltd* [1997] 1 WLR 1627 at 1630–1 *per* Lord Nicholls. Such loss must be measurable even if only with difficulty. *Ibid.*, p. 1632.

[273] *Ibid.*, p. 1630.

[274] *UBAF Ltd* v *European American Banking Corporation* [1984] QB 713; *First National Commercial Bank Plc* v *Humberts* [1995] 2 All ER 673 and *Nykredit plc* v *Edward Erdman Ltd* [1997] 1 WLR 1627 especially at 1638–9 *per* Lord Hoffman.

[275] *Hedley Byrne* v *Heller & Partners* [1964] AC 465 *per* Lord Reid at 486.

Table 2.1 Actions for misrepresentation

	Rescission	s 2(2), MA 1967	s 2(1), MA 1967	*HB v H*	Deceit	Breach
Mental state of representor	Any	Non-fraudulent	Negligent (NB: burden of proof on representor)	Negligent (NB: burden of proof on representee)	Knowingly, without belief in its truth, or recklessly	Any
Must statement be one of fact?	Yes	Yes	Yes	No	Yes	No
Must misrep. be material, i.e. must reliance be reasonable?	Probably not: *Museprime v Adhill*	Probably not: *Museprime v Adhill*	Probably not: *Museprime v Adhill*	No	No	No
Relationship of close proximity between rep'tor and rep'tee	No, but see below	No, but see below	No, but see below	Yes	No	No, but see below
Contract between rep'tor and rep'tee	Yes	Yes	Yes	No, loss may be suffered in any way, e.g. by entering a contract with a third party	No, loss may be suffered in any way, e.g. by entering a contract with a third party	Yes
Remedy	Mutual re-exchange and indemnity	Discretionary damages	Tortious measure of damage	Tortious measure of damage	Tortious measure of damage	Contractual measure of damage
Rule of reasonableness	–	–	All direct losses	All reasonably foreseeable losses	All direct losses	All losses within the *Hadley v Baxendale* test
Can contributory negligence operate to reduce recovery?	No, indemnity not affected	Yes, because damages are discretionary	Yes	Yes	No	Yes, exceptionally

the claimant's contributory negligence is a bar to recovery altogether. However, later cases appear to accept that contributory negligence operates in relation to negligent advice, as it does in respect of negligent conduct, to reduce[276] rather than prevent recovery.

Although a claimant who has a choice whether to pursue a common law or statutory action will, generally and sensibly, choose the latter, still the *Hedley Byrne* action remains vital where exceptionally the Misrepresentation Act action is unavailable. This will be the case where the statement is one of opinion only. It has always been accepted that a statement of opinion may give rise to liability under *Hedley Byrne*.[277] More significant is the fact that the common law, but not the statutory, action is available when the claimant has suffered loss in a way other than by entering a contract with the representor, e.g. by entering a contract with a third party. This is the situation which occurred in the auditor cases[278] which have proved a fruitful source of litigation based on the *Hedley Byrne* principle. In these cases the claimant has suffered loss by relying upon statements made by the defendant auditors when entering contracts with third parties (companies or existing shareholders) to purchase an interest in a company.

Misrepresentation in overview

Liability for misrepresentation in English law is a large and complex topic comprising a number of discrete, but overlapping, methods of redress. These actions are characterised and distinguished one from another by subtle distinctions which are explicable historically but, often, otherwise indefensible. However, it is necessary to master these points of similarity and distinction in order to be able to say what avenues of redress are available in any given factual situation. Table 2.1 summarises the principal points of comparison and contrast. The action for breach of contract is also included in the final column.

PROPRIETARY ESTOPPEL

An estoppel is said to arise when a person is prevented (or 'estopped') from denying something.[279] In the past writers have expressed wildly different opinions about the proper classification of estoppels; from Williston[280] who described nine different types to Ewart[281] who denied its existence at all. In

---

[276] *Banque Bruxelles* v *Eagle Star* [1995] 2 All ER 769 at 819–20 *per* Phillips J. This question was not considered by the Court of Appeal and House of Lords.

[277] *Hedley Byrne & Co* v *Heller & Partners Ltd* [1964] AC 465.

[278] For example, *Caparo* v *Dickman* [1990] 2 AC 617; *Morgan Crucible Co plc* v *Hill Samuel & Co* [1991] Ch 259; *Galoo* v *Bright Graheme Murray* [1995] 1 All ER 16.

[279] Spencer, Bower and Turner.

[280] (1936) *Williston on Contracts*. Revised edn, sections 678–9.

[281] Ewart (1917) *Waiver Distributed*, part of whose analysis was adopted by Rose J in *Danforth Heights* v *McDermid Bros* (1922) 52 OLR 412 at 426–7. See also *Stackhouse* v *Barnston* (1805) 10 Ves 453 at 466, *per* Grant MR.

the present no-one seeks to deny its existence but the debate continues as some commentators[282] and judges,[283] particularly in Australia,[284] seek to construct a single unified doctrine of estoppel. At the outset it should be recognised that great dangers attend such a process. The law becomes over-general and uncertain, ill adapted to deal with particular problems arising in distinct contexts.

In the present context, the negotiation stage of the contracting process, two doctrines are encountered: proprietary estoppel and estoppel by convention.[285] In contrast, so-called promissory estoppel[286] is relevant to a later period in the life of a contract when the parties seek to adapt a pre-existing contract to changing circumstances or preferences. The different environments in which promissory and other estoppels have evolved demand that any attempt to follow the lead of the Australian courts and force a mating between promissory and other estoppels should be resisted lest expertise gained in addressing the distinct problems involved in the negotiation of prospective, as opposed to the modification of existing, contracts, be squandered or at least disguised in the pursuit of an uncertain doctrine of general application.[287] Indeed, even though proprietary estoppel and estoppel by convention have recently been developed to 'police' negotiations, their origins and emphasis remain distinct: the former provides a means to enforce informal contracts to create interests in land; the latter is a more general doctrine to prevent parties departing from a shared assumption or convention operating in relation to contracts with any subject matter. In *The Indian Endurance*[288] Lord Steyn recently said:

> The question was debated whether estoppel by convention and estoppel by acquiescence [a type of proprietary estoppel] are but aspects of one overarching principle. I do not underestimate the importance in the continuing development of the law of the search for simplicity. I also accept that at a high level of abstraction such an overarching principle could be formulated. But Mr Rokison QC, for the owners, persuaded me that to restate the law in terms of an overarching principle might tend to blur the necessarily separate requirements, and distinct terrain of application, of the two kinds of estoppel.

---

[282] For example, Thompson [1983] Camb L Rev 257; Duthie (1988) 104 LQR 362; Kirk (1991) Adelaide Law Rev 225; Lunney [1992] Conv 239; and Halliwell (1994) 14 LS 15.

[283] *Crabb v Arun DC* [1976] 1 Ch 179 at 193 B *per* Scarman LJ; *Taylor Fashions Ltd v Liverpool Victoria Trustees Co Ltd* [1981] 1 QB 133 at 151–2 *per* Oliver J; *Habib Bank Ltd v Habib Bank Ltd* [1981] 1 WLR 1264 at 1285 *per* Oliver LJ. See also *Sledmore v Dalby* [1996] 72 P & CR 204.

[284] See *Walton's Stores (Interstate) Ltd v Maher* (1988) 164 CLR 357 and subsequent cases considered in Carter and Horland (1996) *Contract Law in Australia*, 3rd edn, paras 378–88 and in Halsbury's *Laws of Australia*, Vol. 6, Contract, section 110.

[285] See above.

[286] See Chapter 12.

[287] See Halson, 'The Offensive Limits of Promissory Estoppel' [1999] LMCLQ 256.

[288] *The Indian Endurance (No. 2), Republic of India and Others v India Steamship Co Ltd* [1997] 4 All ER 380 at 392e. See also the note of caution in *Re Basham (dec'd)* [1987] 1 All ER 405 at 414 a–b, *per* Edward Nugee QC sitting as deputy judge in the High Court; *Taylor v Dickens* [1997] *The Times*, 24 November.

A proprietary estoppel arises when a person acts to their detriment in reliance upon his belief that he has acquired, or will, in the future, acquire rights in the property of another. Such an estoppel may be of two kinds: estoppel by acquiescence and estoppel by encouragement.[289] In the former, the property owner does not directly induce the belief of the party asserting the estoppel, but rather culpably 'stands by' and so may thereby be said to have acquiesced in it. In contrast, the latter type of estoppel arises when the belief of the mistaken party arises from the words or conduct of the other. In this way, estoppel by encouragement, like the law of misrepresentation, is a part of the arsenal deployed by the courts to 'police' the negotiation of contracts. However, unlike the law of misrepresentation, estoppel by encouragement is a narrow doctrine subject to a number of strict preconditions.

A typical example of the application of the doctrine is provided by *Matharu v Matharu*.[290] Following their marriage, the defendant and the claimant's son moved into property owned by the claimant. The claimant's statements to relatives and friends encouraged the defendant's belief that the house belonged to her and her husband and in reliance upon this belief she borrowed money from her family to spend on various works of improvement. Following the breakdown of the marriage and the death of the husband, the claimant's suit for possession of the property was refused by the Court of Appeal on the basis that a proprietary estoppel had arisen in favour of the defendant.[291]

For a proprietary estoppel to be established, there must be both encouragement by one party and detrimental reliance by the other. The encouragement may be a direct promise as in *Dillwyn v Llewelyn*[292] a father presenting land to his son to enable the latter to build a house upon it or may, as in *Matharu v Matharu*, comprise representations made to third parties. In contrast, the requisite degree of encouragement was not established by the Hong Kong government who were seeking to purchase a large number of flats when throughout protracted negotiations the seller, to the government's knowledge, retained the right to walk away without obligation.[293] In any event, the expectation excited must be sufficiently ascertained to enable the court to fashion a remedy.[294]

---

[289] See generally *Ramsden v Dyson* (1866) LR 1 HL 129, *Wilmott v Barber* (1880) 15 Ch D 96 and Spencer-Bower, and Turner, ch. 12, 'Encouragement and Acquiescence'.

[290] [1994] 2 FLR 697.

[291] Interestingly, the Court of Appeal established the existence of the estoppel by reference to the five conditions laid down by Fry J in *Wilmott v Barber* (1880) 15 Ch D 96 rather than by reliance upon any broader statement of principle. The *Wilmott v Barber* conditions are: (1) a person has made a mistake as to his or her legal rights; (2) that person has expended money or done some act in reliance on this mistaken belief; (3) the possessor of the legal right must be aware of it and also of; (4) the other person's mistake; (5) the possessor of the legal right must have encouraged the other's expenditure or reliance, either directly or by refraining from asserting his legal right.

[292] (1862) 4 De GF & J 517.

[293] *A-G of Hong Kong v Humphreys Estate* [1987] AC 114.

[294] *Orgee v Orgee* [1997] EGCS 152.

The requirement of detrimental reliance may be satisfied as in *Matharu* and *Dillwyn* by expenditure upon the property in question.[295] However, other acts may suffice. In *Crabb* v *Arun District Council*[296] the claimant sold part of his land in reliance upon the council's representation that the land he retained would enjoy a right of access over the council's land. When this was refused, the claimant found himself in possession of a landlocked plot. Fortunately, the purchase of a helicopter was avoided by the Court of Appeal holding that the council was estopped from denying the right of access. It has been convincingly argued that where, as in cases of estoppel by encouragement, the 'understanding' between the parties is clear, the requirement of reliance is more easily satisfied.[297]

Encouragement and detrimental reliance are not alone sufficient to establish proprietary estoppel; there must also be a sufficient causal link between them.[298] This is established in the same way as in misrepresentation.[299] It is not necessary that the conduct complained of be the sole inducement for the reliance; it is enough that it is *an* inducement.[300] Once it is established that there was encouragement and detrimental reliance, the burden of proof is cast on the 'guilty' party to show that there was no reliance upon his encouragement.[301] Thus, a party was unable to rely upon an estoppel when she gave up a lawful tenancy to become a squatter in other premises owned by the landlord who assured her that she would not be evicted before she was offered reasonable alternative accommodation. The assurance given did not induce the lady to give up her tenancy because it was something she was going to do anyway as a result of racial harassment in the area.[302] On the authorities above the landlord would bear the burden of proving this.[303]

---

[295] Detrimental reliance upon an assurance is more difficult to establish when the parties are related or have a relationship because in such cases they will inevitably change their positions in all sorts of ways and for all sorts of reasons. See Lawson, 'The Things we do for Love: Detrimental Reliance in the Family Home' (1996) 218, 230.

[296] [1976] Ch 179.

[297] Howard and Hill, 'The Informal Creation of Interests in Land' (1995) 15 LS 356. See also Davis, 'Informal Acquisition and the Loss of Rights in Land: What Justifies the Doctrines' (2000) 20 LS 198.

[298] *Eves* v *Eves* [1975] 1 WLR 1338 at 1345 C–F *per* Brightman J; *Grant* v *Edwards* [1986] Ch 638 at 648–9, 655–7 and 656 *per* Nourse LJ and Browne Wilkinson VC.

[299] *Edgington* v *Fitzmaurice* (1885) 29 Ch D 459 at 480, 483 and 485 *per* Cotton, Bowen and Fry LJJ respectively; *McCullagh* v *Lane Fox & Partners Ltd* [1994] 1 EGLR 48 at 51.

[300] *Wayling* v *Jones* (1993) 69 P & CR 170 at 173 *per* Balcombe LJ, Legatt and Hoffman LJJ agreeing; *Amalgamated Investment & Property Co (in liq)* v *Texas Commerce International Bank* [1982] QB 84 at 104–5 (estoppel by convention case).

[301] *Greasley* v *Cooke* [1986] 1 WLR 1306 and *Grant* v *Edwards* [1986] Ch 638 at 657. *Cf. Smith* v *Chadwick* 187 at 196 (misrepresentation).

[302] *Southwark London Borough Council* v *Logan* [1995] Times LR 565. The landlord's promise could not be enforced as a contractual obligation because the defendant did not at the request of the claimant do any act, or forbear from any action, sufficient to constitute consideration. For consideration see Chapter 4.

[303] The question of who bears the burden of proving causation was not explored in the brief judgment in this case. For a careful application of the relevant principles to more complicated factual situations, see *Wayling* v *Jones* (1993) 69 P & CR 170.

As the title of the doctrine suggests, 'proprietary' estoppel only operates in relation to promises concerning land. Indeed, despite a scintilla of authority[304] to the effect that it may extend to cover other types of property,[305] e.g. personal property, the overwhelming majority of cases limit its operation to promises where the subject matter comprises only real property, i.e. land.[306] Exceptionally, it has been held to operate in relation to 'mixed' promises to confer an interest in real and personal property but the latter seem incidental to, and parasitic upon, the former.

Once a proprietary estoppel has been established, 'the court has a wide, albeit of course judicial, discretion to what extent relief should be given and what form it should take'.[307] When exercising this discretion, the court must weigh the encouragement to and reliance of one party against the needs and circumstances of the other. In *Sledmore* v *Dalby*[308] the defendant occupied rent-free property owned by the claimant for 13 years after the death of his wife, the claimant's daughter. A proprietary estoppel arose in favour of the defendant when he and his wife were encouraged to improve the house on the basis that it would one day be theirs. However, the equity that arose in favour of the defendant was satisfied by 18 years of rent-free occupation. An order for possession was granted to the claimant who was living on Income Support in accommodation in urgent need of repair while the defendant was in full-time employment and occupied the property on only a few nights each week as he was living elsewhere with his new partner. At the other extreme, it has been held that the equity in favour of the party who has established the estoppel, cannot be satisfied by anything less than a conveyance of the property in question[309] or an entitlement to the full proceeds of sale.[310] Other cases, such as *Matharu* v *Matharu*, adopt an inter-

---

304 *Western Fish Products* v *Penrith DC* [1981] 2 All ER 204 at 218 *per* Megaw LJ. In *The Henryk Sif* [1980] 2 Lloyd's Rep 245 it was suggested that estoppel by acquiescence can operate more broadly, in that case in relation to a promise not to rely on a relevant limitation period. In *Shearson Lehman Hutton Inc* v *MacLaine Watson* [1989] 2 Lloyd's Rep 570 Webster J casts doubt on his earlier decision at pp. 596 and 604.

305 In *Re Basham* [1986] 1 WLR 1498 the estoppel operated in relation to a cottage and its contents.

306 *Wayling* v *Jones* (1993) 69 P & CR 170 at 173 *per* Balcombe LJ. Legatt and Hoffman LJJ agreeing; *Amalgamated Investment & Property Co (in liq)* v *Texas Commerce International Bank* [1982] QB 84 at 104–5 (estoppel by convention case).

307 *Holiday Inns Inc* v *Broadhead* (1974) 232 EG 951 at 1087 *per* Robert Goff J. See also *Price* v *Hartwell* [1996] GCS 98. See generally Gardner, 'The Remedial Discretion in Proprietary Estoppel' (1999) 115 LQR 438.

308 (1996) 72 P & CR 204.

309 For example, *Dillwyn* v *Llewelyn* (1862) 4 De G F & J 517 (conveyance ordered of land upon which owner encouraged his son to build a house); *Pascoe* v *Turner* [1979] 1 WLR 431 (conveyance to claimant ordered of house she improved which she occupied with claimant for whom she did small administrative tasks before he moved in with another woman); *Re Basham (dec'd)* [1987] 1 All ER 405 (claimant who worked unpaid for stepfather for 30 years was encouraged to do so by promises that on his death his estate would be hers – she was entitled to his estate comprising property and cash).

310 *Wayling* v *Jones* (1993) 69 P & CR 170 (claimant who assisted his homosexual partner run a variety of businesses for over 15 years was entitled to proceeds of sale of a hotel following many assurances that on his partner's death the business would be his).

mediate position where the party asserting the estoppel is granted a licence to occupy the property for life.[311] Any conveyance ordered or interest granted in satisfaction of the equity raised by the estoppel may be accompanied by a financial order requiring the recipient to pay monies to the grantor.[312]

The considerable range of orders available to satisfy the equity raised by the estoppel allows the court to do what it perceives to be justice between the parties. However, two notes of caution must be sounded. First, close attention to the language of the courts would seem to suggest that on occasion the remedy granted goes beyond the satisfaction of any expectation excited and seeks to punish the original owner for conduct the Court does not approve of. In *Pascoe* v *Turner* Lord Denning stated that 'The Court must grant a remedy effective to protect her against the future manifestations of his ruthlessness'.[313] Again, the local authority in *Crabb* v *Arun DC* was accused of 'high-handedness'.[314] These statements contrast markedly with the careful separation of moral and legal principle by Dillon LJ dissenting in *Matharu* v *Matharu* who said:[315]

> I find it repugnant that the claimant should be seeking to evict his widowed daughter-in-law and grandchildren and render them homeless ... [but] I do not believe that I am entitled to regard that as *per se* enough to render his conduct so unconscionable in the eyes of equity to grant him possession of [the property].

It is not appropriate to discuss further the difficult question of the relationship between law and morality in the process of judicial decision making. However, it should be noted that to applaud the naked expression of moral indignation when the perpetrator is a dishonourable man or officious authority might be to invite the same in contexts where it is less easy to predict how a traditionally conservative judiciary would act, e.g. gay relationships[316] or cultures where it is acceptable for a man to have more than one 'wife'.[317] However, it must be said that the cases instanced do not give cause for concern.

The second objection to remedial flexibility is more simply stated. It creates uncertainty: neither party can predict accurately in advance what remedy will be granted if the estoppel is proved. This unpredictability has important consequences for parties who are negotiating an out of court

---

[311] For example, *Inwards* v *Baker* [1965] 2 QB 29 (son built house on father's land).

[312] *Lim Teng Huan* v *Ang Swee Chuan* [1992] 1 WLR 113 (defendant who built house on land jointly owned with claimant entitled to conveyance upon payment of value of undeveloped land) and *Price* v *Hartwell* [1996] EGCS 98 (defendant who improved and contributed to the mortgage entitled to licence for life of house shared with parents conditional upon the reimbursement of mortgage payments made by them).

[313] [1979] 1 WLR 431 at 438–9.

[314] [1976] Ch 179 at 199.

[315] [1994] 2 FLR 597 at 603.

[316] *Wayling* v *Jones* (1995) 69 P & CR 170.

[317] *Philip Lowe (Chinese Restaurant) Ltd* v *Sau Man Lee* [1985] *The Times*, 9 July (relationship between a Chinese man and his second or 'little' wife).

settlement.[318] It has the effect of lowering the level of such settlements which are 'discounted' to reflect the uncertainties of continued litigation. As most cases are settled out of court, it is apparent that the justice achieved by remedial flexibility in the few cases which run to trial is purchased at the cost of lesser settlements for the many which do not.

An important feature of proprietary, as opposed to any other,[319] estoppel is that it gives rise to a cause of action. The party asserting the estoppel may not only use it as a defence to an action for possession[320] or trespass[321] he may himself sue upon it and will probably have to when he is not in physical possession of the disputed property or claims an entitlement to the proceeds of sale.

It is doubtful whether it is possible, other than 'at a high level of abstraction'[322] to identify a single principle to explain the various applications of the doctrine. It has been suggested that 'proprietary estoppel bears a close relationship to restitutionary principles where one party has acquiesced or encouraged another in conduct whereby that other ... would have, if no remedy were granted, unjustly enriched the former'.[323] This is certainly a feature of many cases particularly those where works of improvement[324] or construction[325] were carried out on the property or land or where other services[326] were rendered by the party asserting the estoppel. However, the explanation is at least incomplete and probably defective for two reasons. First, in some cases where an estoppel was established there was no undue enrichment present. In *Crabb* v *Arun District Council*[327] in the absence of the doctrine the council would not have been unjustly enriched by its actions. Second, the remedy granted in many cases goes beyond the reversal of unjust enrichment (e.g. paying for the improvements, building or services) and rather seeks to fulfil the expectations excited in the party encouraged by requiring the conveyance of the interest promised.[328]

A different explanation of the doctrine builds upon the subject matter of the promise. It cannot be denied that the traditional doctrine of proprietary estoppel has, in this jurisdiction, operated almost exclusively against those who seek to resile from an assumption which operated in relation to a dealing with real property. Why is it that the doctrine should have been applied in

---

[318] See generally Harris and Veljanouski, 'Remedies Under Contract Law: Designing Rules to Facilitate Out of Court Settlements' (1983) Law and Pol 97.

[319] See above and below the discussion of promissory estoppel and estoppel by convention.

[320] For example, *Pascoe* v *Turner* [1979] 1 WLR 431.

[321] For example, *Lim Tong Huan* v *Ang Swee Chuan* [1992] 1 WLR 113.

[322] See above n. 287.

[323] *Sledmore* v *Dalby* (1996) 72 P & CR 204 at 208 *per* Roche LJ. See also Hayton and Marshall (1991) *Cases and Commentary on the Law of Trusts*. 9th edn, p. 512.

[324] For example, *Matharu* v *Matharu* [1994] 2 FLR 697.

[325] For example, *Dillwyn* v *Llewelyn* (1862) 4 De GF & J 517.

[326] For example, *Re Basham (decd)* [1987] 1 All ER 405.

[327] [1976] Ch 179.

[328] See Getzler, 'Unconscionable Conduct and Unjust Enrichment as Grounds for Judicial Intervention' (1990) 16 Monash Univ Law Rev 283 at 305–14 and Burrows (*Restitution*), p. 122.

relation to dealings with land? What is particularly distinctive about such transactions sufficient to justify limiting the operation of the doctrine in this way? The answer to both these questions may lie in the formality which attends the transfer of an interest in land.[329] For to the extent that the doctrine of proprietary estoppel gives rise to rights in property, it is operating to subvert the formalities which usually attend the creation of such rights. Thus, perhaps it should occasion no surprise that the doctrine has been applied almost exclusively to the creation of interests in or over land: its operation is thereby conterminous with the formal requirements it is meant to circumvent. This has led some commentators to emphasise the role of proprietary estoppel as a vehicle for the law to recognise the informal creation of proprietary interests in land.[330]

Again, such an explanation is incomplete and defective, because while it is a feature of many cases where the doctrine has been held to operate that there was a contract except for the failure to record or evidence in writing, the doctrine may be relied upon when there is written evidence of a contract but what is lacking is some other contractual requisite, such as consideration[331] or certainty.[332]

It may be that it is not possible to articulate a simple principle to explain the operation of proprietary estoppel. If this is so it would seem to follow a fortiori that no useful single principle can account for a unified doctrine of estoppel of which proprietary estoppel forms only a part. The doctrine has and will hopefully continue to offer protection to those who have been encouraged by another to believe they have acquired or will in the future acquire rights in property owned by that party. To the extent that such discussions may be considered pre-contractual negotiating, proprietary estoppel is a limited, but none the less powerful, weapon in the legal armoury which the courts may use when 'policing' pre-contractual negotiations.

RESTITUTION: FAILED CONTRACT CASES

When negotiations prove inconclusive, the negotiators do not become subject to the contractual obligations originally anticipated. The contract has 'failed' because the discussions that took place neither support the existence of such a contract[333] nor give rise to an estoppel by convention[334] whereby

---

[329] The Law of Property Act 1925, s 40(1) required contracts for the disposition of an interest in land to be evidenced in writing. This is now repealed by the Law of Property (Miscellaneous Provisions) Act 1989, s 2(8). See now s 2(1) of the same Act which requires such contracts to simply be in writing.

[330] Lawson and Rudden, (1982) *The Law of Real Property*. 2nd edn, pp. 217–23; Moriaty, 'Licenses and Land Law: Legal Principles and Public Policies' (1984) 100 LQR 376.

[331] For example, *Crabb v Arun District Council* [1976] Ch 179 at p. 50: '... this relief can be granted although the agreement or understanding between the parties was not sufficiently certain to be enforceable as a contract ...'.

[332] See *Holiday Inns Inc v Broadhead* [1974] 232 EG 951 at 1087 *per* Robert Goff J and *Yaxley v Gotts* [1999] 2 FLR 941 *per* Clarke and Beldom LJJ. *Contra: Orgee v Orgee* [1997] EGCS 152 (expectation of an agricultural tenancy too uncertain to be given legal effect).

[333] See below.

[334] See above.

one party is prevented from denying the existence of a contract. None the less, the law of contract may provide a more limited protection to the expectations of one party if he is able to prove the existence of a collateral or subsidiary contract.[335] However, it is not only the law of contract that might operate to protect the expectations of the negotiators. The doctrine of proprietary estoppel may also operate to protect the expectation interest[336] in relation to promises to confer an interest in land. In addition, the law of tort may be of assistance to a disappointed party to inconclusive negotiations if he is able to prove that the other was fraudulent (the tort of deceit)[337] or in breach of a duty of care (*Hedley Byrne* v *Heller*).[338] The damages recoverable in these actions are said to protect the reliance rather than the expectation interest; the award seeks to compensate the claimant for his reliance upon the defendant with a sum of money sufficient to restore him to the position he was in before the wrong occurred. In contrast, the contractual remedies seek to place the innocent party in the position he would have been in if the promise had been fulfilled and thereby protect his expectation interest. However, another possibility arises which is that the law may protect the restitution interest of a participant to failed negotiations. The object of such an award would be to prevent one party from being unjustly enriched at the expense of the other by requiring the former to 'pay' for any benefit conferred by the latter. The consideration of this award requires some broader knowledge of the law of restitution.

The law of restitution is, like the law of contract and tort, a distinct head of civil liability. As it was only recognised as such by the House of Lords in 1991,[339] any discussion on this subject must refer to 'academic writing which in this sphere [has] gone ahead of the decisions of the courts'.[340] The unifying theme of the area of civil law is the reversal of unjust enrichment.[341] From this theme two essential elements of a restitutionary claim are immediately obvious.[342] First, the defendant must be enriched, i.e. have benefited; second, the enrichment must be unjust. A third[343] less obvious requirement that the enrichment is at the claimant's expense explains a major division within the law of restitution between unjust enrichment resulting from an independent legal wrong, e.g. a tort or breach of contract, and where no

---

[335] See above.
[336] The interest terminology derives from an influential article by Fuller and Perdue, 'The Reliance Interest in Contract Damages' (1936) 46 Yale LJ 52 and 373 at 52–7. *Contra*: Friedman, 'The Performative Interest in Contract Damages' (1995) 111 LQR 628.
[337] See above.
[338] See above.
[339] *Lipkin Gorman* v *Karpnale* [1991] 2 AC 548.
[340] *Marston Construction Co Ltd* v *Kigass Ltd* [1989] 15 Con LR 116.
[341] The word restitution merely describes the legal response to unjust enrichment. For this reason 'unjust enrichment' would be a better description of the area of civil law under discussion. However courts have failed to do so possibly because they believe it to be too uncertain. See generally Birks (1989) *An Introduction to the Law of Restitution*, pp. 1–25.
[342] See Birks, *op.cit.* at p. 21 and Burrows (*Restitution*), p. 7.
[343] Strictly, there is a fourth requirement that there should be no applicable defence.

wrong has to be established.[344] In the former case of unjust enrichment by wrongdoing, the defendant's gain is at the claimant's expense in the sense of having been acquired as a consequence of committing a wrong against him. In the latter case of so-called 'autonomous' unjust enrichment, the defendant's gain is by 'subtraction' from the claimant's wealth.[345]

Having outlined the general structure of the law of restitution, we must now apply its initially strange vocabulary and concepts in the context of failed negotiations.[346] We have already seen that the first step to establishing a restitutionary claim is to ask whether the defendant has been enriched, i.e. benefited. The clearest case of benefit would be the payment of money or transfer of property by one negotiator to another. In all cases involving the payment of monies and whenever the property transferred can be sold[347] the recipient may be said to be 'incontrovertibly benefited'. This is important because the moral force of the recipient's obligation to make restitution derives from *his* enrichment, i.e. a subjective concept. In the cases considered, he cannot deny ('subjectively devalue'[348] in restitution jargon) that such money and property is of worth to him. The same does not hold when the claimant has performed a service for the defendant or given him a non-realisable good. Rather the defendant's assertion that what he received was of no value to him must be rebutted in a different way. A 'bargained for'[349] test has been suggested whereby the defendant is not allowed to deny the value to him of a performance he requested in the expectation that it would be paid for. The 'bargained for' test simultaneously demonstrates that the defendant both wants the performance tendered and that he is prepared to pay for it,[350] leaving no room for any argument based on subjective devaluation.

These problems can be illustrated by reference to the simple facts of the leading case in this area which somewhat surprisingly is a 40-year-old decision at first instance on a £250 claim thought fit for inclusion in volume 1

---

[344] See especially Birks *op.cit.* at pp. 12, 23–5, 40–44 and 313–14.

[345] This distinction is important because in the category of unjust enrichment by wrongdoing restitution, in the sense of the defendant having to give up to the claimant the gains made, is only one possible remedial consequence. Other remedies may be available in respect of the underlying wrong, e.g. damages in tort. For other consequences, see Burrows (*Restitution*), pp. 17–21.

[346] See generally Jones [1980] 18 University of Western Ontario Law Review 447.

[347] Birks, pp. 121–4, who states that the sale must have actually taken place.

[348] The phrase is Birks', *op.cit.* p. 109.

[349] Burrows [1988] 104 LQR 576 and (*Restitution*), pp 14–15. Other writers prefer the concept of 'free acceptance' whereby the defendant will not usually be regarded as benefited by the receipt of goods or services unless he has accepted services or retained goods in circumstances where rejection was possible with actual or presumed knowledge that they would be paid for. The subject of 'free acceptance' has produced a subtle and esoteric, but none the less, impassioned debate amongst restitution lawyers. For a taste of their fury, see also Beatson (1991) *The Use and Abuse of Unjust Enrichment* at pp. 21–44; Birks' Essay 5 in Burrows (ed.) (1991) *Essays on the Law of Restitution*; Burrows (*Restitution*), pp. 11–14.

[350] A different test must be adopted where the defendant's conduct demonstrates that he wants the performance but is *not* prepared to pay for it e.g. he obtained it by duress. See Burrows *op.cit.* pp. 15–16. This is more likely to occur when a pre-existing contract is modified.

of the *Weekly Law Reports*.[351] In *William Lacey (Hounslow) Ltd* v *Davis*[352] the claimants, who tendered for building work on premises damaged in the war, were assured by the defendant landowner that the contract was theirs. At the defendant's request, the claimant prepared bills of quantities and detailed estimates to enable the defendant to claim the maximum contribution from the government. The defendant then changed his mind and sold the property in its unrepaired state. Barry J concluded that the defendant had benefited from the claimant's work because it had enabled him to negotiate a higher contribution from the government thereby enhancing the price at which it was ultimately sold.

William Lacey was applied in a later case where the claimants tendered for a design and build contract to provide a replacement factory for one that was burnt down.[353] No contract was in fact placed as the insurance on the property was insufficient to cover the cost of rebuilding to the required standard. However, the claimants successfully claimed for preparatory work beyond the preparation of the tender; the work had been implicitly[354] requested by the defendant and it was contemplated that it would be paid for. As a result of the preliminary work, the defendants obtained working drawings which assisted with obtaining consents necessary for building and so constituted a benefit to them. More dubious, however, was a suggestion made by Denning LJ in another case[355] that a landlord who carried out alterations to his property at the request of a potential tenant thereby conferred a benefit on him even though the contemplated lease was never entered.

The second step to establishing a restitutionary claim is to show that the enrichment was unjust. Actions for restitution are usually categorised by reference to the factor which renders the enrichment unjust,[356] e.g. that it was obtained as a result of duress, mistake, etc. In the case of failed contracts, the unjust factor is not immediately obvious but is generally thought to be 'a failure of consideration'.[357] In Chapter 4 we will meet the contractual doctrine of consideration, which states the requirement that a contract requires a mutual exchange of value; a promise is enforceable under the law of contract when it is given in consideration of a return promise or

---

[351] More important cases are generally collected in volumes 2 and 3 and then 'upgraded' to inclusion in The Law Reports.

[352] [1957] 1 WLR 932. See also *Fanning* v *Wicklow CC* (unreported, 30 April 1984).

[353] *Marston Construction Co Ltd* v *Kigass* [1989] 15 Con LR 116. This decision was questioned in *Regalian Properties plc* v *LDDC* [1995] 1 All ER 1005 at 1022, *per* Ratee J. See below.

[354] *Cf. William Lacey* where the request was express.

[355] *Brewer Street Investments Ltd* v *Barclays Woollen Co Ltd* [1954] 1 QB 428. Somervell and Romer LJJ appeared to find for the claimant on the basis of a contractual rather than a restitutionary obligation.

[356] For example, Burrows (*Restitution*), chs 3–14.

[357] For example, Birks, Essay 5 in Burrows (ed.) (1991) *Essays on the Law of Restitution* pp. 111 and 114; Burrows (*Restitution*), pp. 293–99; Tettenborn (1996) *Law of Restitution in England and Ireland*. 2nd edn, at pp. 135–6, 155–9; *cf.* McKendrick, 'The Battle of the Forms and of Restitution' [1988] 8 OJLS 197 at 207–8 reflecting Birks' earlier analysis at pp. 114–16 and ch. 8.

act. However, in the law of restitution consideration bears a special meaning.[358] Viscount Simons explains:[359]

> In English law, an enforceable contract may be formed by an exchange of a promise for a promise, or by the exchange of a promise for an act[360] ... thus, in the law relating to the formation of a contract, the *promise* to do a thing may often be consideration, but when one is considering the law of failure of consideration and of the [restitutionary] right to recover money on that ground, it is, generally speaking, *not the promise which is referred to as the consideration, but the performance of the promise.* [emphasis added]

Consideration may be said to have failed, in the special restitutionary sense[361] (referring to the fact, rather than the mere promise, of performance), when a party fails to receive the performance to which he was contractually entitled, e.g. a contract to buy a motorbike and pay a deposit. The dealer refuses to deliver the bike. The 'consideration' given in exchange for my promise to pay has totally failed because the dealer is refusing to perform his promise.

However, where negotiations fail, *ex hypothesi* no contract ever comes into existence and so the definition of failure of consideration must extend beyond 'contracted for performance' to encompass 'bargained for performance'.[362] Consideration may be said to have failed when a party fails to receive the performance he bargained for but which the anticipated provider never become obliged to deliver.[363]

Again, the requirements of a restitutionary claim are best illustrated by the facts of a case. In *British Steel Corporation* v *Cleveland Bridge and Engineering Co Ltd*[364] the parties were negotiating for the sale of steel nodes to be manufactured by the claimants for incorporation in a building being built by the defendants. Although the defendants sent a letter stating their intention to order the nodes, the terms they proposed were rejected by the claimants and no formal contract was executed. None the less, the nodes were manu-

---

[358] It seems that the special restitutionary meaning of 'consideration' pre-dates the more commonly used contractual meaning. Simpson (1975), *A History of the Common Law of Contract.* p. 321; Birks, *op. cit.* at p. 223.

[359] *Fibrosa Spolka Akcyjna* v *Fairbairn Lawson Combe Barbour* [1943] AC 32 at 48.

[360] Respectively known as a bilateral and a unilateral contract. See below.

[361] There is a second less publicised peculiarity to the restitutionary concept. In contract consideration is traditionally defined in terms of an act or promise which is *either* beneficial to the recipient *or* detrimental to the performer/promisor, see *Currie* v *Misa* [1875] LR 10 Eq 153 considered in Chapter 4. In the law of restitution only the benefit to the recipient is considered. Thus, in *Rowland* v *Divall* [1923] 2 KB 500 there was said to be a 'total failure of consideration' when the hirer of a car failed to get good title to it from the seller, despite the fact that he used it for two months, which use was detrimental (through decreased value) to the seller.

[362] Burrows (*Restitution*), pp. 250–3. Some commentators prefer the language of payments made and benefits conferred on the basis of an assumption that proves unjustified to cover both contracted and bargained for performance. See Tettenborn, *op. cit.* p. 109.

[363] Burrow's suggestion (*Restitution*) at p. 293 that where a contract would exist but for a lack of certainty or an absence of an intention to create legal relations 'parties ... can often be said to have struck some kind of bargain' is difficult to understand unless meant to refer to a collateral contract of some sort.

[364] [1984] 1 All ER 504.

factured to an agreed specification and delivered to the defendants. Robert Goff J held that there was no contract binding the parties. The claimants had not promised to supply, and the defendants to purchase, the nodes[365] because it was not realistic to regard the claimants as unable to cease the work if agreement could not be reached on outstanding matters such as the production schedule and liability for late delivery. Nor could there be said to be a contract whereby the defendants promised to pay in exchange for the acts of manufacture and delivery;[366] this was negatived by the fact that all work was done, pending a formal contract.

In the absence of a contract, it was the law of restitution which would regulate the rights and liabilities of the parties. Robert Goff J held that the claimants were entitled to recover a *quantum meruit*[367] for the reasonable value of their work. Although the statements of principle are cast in broad terms, the requisite elements can be isolated.[368] The judge clearly considered that the defendants had been enriched by the receipt of the nodes which had been supplied at their request in the expectation that they would be paid for.[369] This enrichment was unjust because the claimants did not receive any of the benefit (i.e. payment) they bargained for. There was a total failure of consideration in the sense discussed above.[370]

This case also illustrates the third requirement of a restitutionary claim: the defendant's gain must have been at the claimant's expense. Here the gain was made at the claimants' expense in the subtractive sense, i.e. the defendants were enriched by subtraction from the claimants' wealth.

Advantages and disadvantages of a restitutionary analysis

It has already been noted that in this country the law of restitution has only recently been recognised as an independent head of civil liability. As may be expected with such a new subject, it may only be understood once some basic tools of analysis are mastered. A further characteristic of a nascent subject is that its very content and limits are ill defined despite the best efforts of many commentators. As a subject, the law of restitution arouses passion both amongst its proponents[371] and its detractors.[372] The author is

---

[365] A so-called bilateral contract involving the exchange of mutual promises (here to pay and to manufacture/deliver).

[366] A so-called unilateral contract whereby a promise (here to pay) is exchanged for an act (here to manufacture/deliver).

[367] A *quantum meruit* (so much as is deserved) is the form of action to recover the value of services or goods (strictly 'quantum valebat' values goods but more modern usage uses quantum meruit to cover both benefits).

[368] Especially at p. 511, a–d.

[369] *Ibid.*

[370] Commentators strenuously argue against the principle established in the case law that only a total failure of consideration is sufficient. For example, see Burrows (*Restitution*) pp. 253–7.

[371] For example, Beatson, Birks and Burrows.

[372] For example, Atiyah (1979) *The Rise and Fall of Freedom of Contract*, p. 768; (1986) *Essays on Contract*, Essay 2, 'Contracts Promises and the Law of Obligations' and pp. 47–52; Hedley (1985) Legal Studies 56.

neither of these. He accepts that there is a law of restitution but suggests that it must learn to live peaceably with its neighbours in the land of obligations (tort contract). Any practising lawyer will confirm that disputes between neighbours, particularly boundary disputes, inevitably generate more heat than light. Therefore, it is hoped that what follows is a dispassionate but not agnostic account of the law of restitution in relation to failed negotiations with particular emphasis on the interplay between restitutionary and contractual principles.

A distinct advantage of a restitutionary approach is that when a court is faced with a claimant which it considers deserving of a remedy, it is freed from having to 'invent a contract'.[373] This was probably what happened in a case[374] where the claimant obtained mining concessions for the defendant seeking to be paid by a proportion of the profits. However, no agreement was reached on the appropriate percentage. None the less, the House of Lords upheld the claimant's claim to a *quantum meruit* based upon an implied (invented?) promise to pay a reasonable remuneration. The somewhat strained finding of an implied contract can be contrasted with the approach of Robert Goff J in *BSC v Cleveland Steel*[375] where without predisposition, he was able to analyse the communications and conduct of the parties to see if any contract had been concluded in the knowledge that a negative finding would leave the law of restitution to do justice between the parties.[376]

A criticism which is sometimes levelled at a restitutionary approach to failed contracts is that it is insufficiently sensitive to the disappointed expectations of the defendant.[377] What if that which the claimant provides proves defective? As there is no contract, he cannot claim damages for breach of contract. Does he, therefore, have to pay for something he received in respect of which he can raise no complaint? In *BSC v Cleveland Steel* the defendant's counter-claim for late delivery failed because there was no contract, hence no breach of which the defendant could complain. However,[378] if there had been an unreasonable delay in delivery, would this be ignored by the law of restitution? It appears not. It has been suggested[379] that the restitutionary claim might be reduced to reflect the loss which the defendant suffers as a

---

[373] Or expressed in language disguising their constructive role but ultimately meaning the same thing 'squeezing the facts into a contractual matrix'.

[374] *Way v Lotilla* [1937] 3 All ER 759.

[375] *Supra*. See also *Mathieson Gee (Ayrshire) Ltd v Quigley* 1952 SLT 239 considered by McKendrick 1988 8 OJLS 197 at 208–9.

[376] *Cf.* Atiyah who thinks it was 'unreal' and 'absurd' to say that there is no contract 'where ... goods are manufactured and delivered and accepted'. He suggests other commentators might exaggerate the frequency of occurrence of circumstances where no contract ensues. When parties are each pressing for a contract on their own terms their disguised but common intention may be to enter a contract on whatever terms a judge should impose. See Atiyah (1995) *Introduction to the Law of Contract*. 5th edn, pp. 67–9 and Staughton J in *Chemico Leasing SpA v Rediffusion plc* (1985) unreported, cited in *Kleinwort Benson Ltd v Malaysia Mining Corp* [1988] 1 All ER 714 at 720.

[377] See Atiyah *ibid.*, p. 69.

[378] In *BSC v Cleveland Bridge* Robert Goff J held that even if the claimants had assumed an obligation to deliver within a reasonable time on the facts of the case, such a period had expired.

[379] *Crown House v Amec* [1989] 48 Build LR 37 at 54 *per* Slade LJ *obiter dicta*.

result of the defective performance. However, even this latest refinement does not completely remove the problem. Although defects in the performance received may reduce the restitutionary award to nil, the defendant will be 'uncompensated' when he suffers further losses, e.g. if the steel nodes caused the collapse of the building exposing the defendant to massive claims from the building owner. For this reason, Atiyah[380] concludes that 'it is dangerous to decide too readily that a contract does not exist in the belief that any gaps can be dealt with by the law of restitution'.

A theme running through the law of restitution is that its principles should respect any allocation of risk contractually agreed between the parties. However, where negotiations fail and no contract is entered, this does not mean that the parties have not agreed that the risk of certain expenses should be borne by a particular party. It is suggested that the law of restitution should not upset such an agreed allocation even if after the event one party regrets it. It seems that English law embraces such a principle. In *Regalian Properties* v *London Docklands Development Corp*[381] property developers sought to recover the expense of preparing and modifying plans for the development of land owned by the defendants when the defendants abandoned the development. Although the alterations were executed at the request of the defendants, it was held that all such preparatory expenses were at the risk of the claimants. This was the clear implication of the deliberate stance of negotiating subject to contract.

Therefore, it seems that English courts will not embrace any more generalised regulation of pre-contractual negotiations[382] which would involve placing the risk on the party whose fault causes the negotiations to founder. A court prefers to ask at whose risk was the expenditure incurred rather than whose act caused it to be lost.

COLLATERAL CONTRACTS

Parties usually engage in negotiations with a purpose in mind, the conclusion of a contract. If they are able to reach agreement, the main contract (or perhaps contracts) will then come into existence. However, the negotiations between the parties may give rise to a subsidiary or collateral contract which binds the parties in some way. A party who enters a contract with another may bring an action asserting the breach of a term contained in a collateral contract. The breach asserted is typically that the contract goods are defective because they do not possess a quality guaranteed by the collateral, but not the main, contract.[383] However, a collateral contract may

---

[380] (1995) *Introduction to the Law of Contract.* 5th edn, p. 69.
[381] [1995] 1 WLR 212.
[382] *Sabemo* v *North Sydney Municipal Council* [1977] 2 NSWLR 880.
[383] For example, *Miljus (T/A A & Z Engineering)* v *Yamazaki Machinery UK Ltd* [1997] Current Law Digest, July, 125 (milling machine failed to cut gears at a rate guaranteed by the vendor in a conversation evidencing a collateral warranty antecedent to the main contract of purchase).

also come into existence where negotiations upon the terms of the main contract are inconclusive. Indeed, it is when one party feels particularly disadvantaged by the failure to conclude the main contemplated bargain that he may seek redress by asserting that there has been a breach of a collateral obligation. Although the proof of such a contract requires the application of principles of contract formation, it should be remembered the collateral contract precedes the contemplated main contract and so may operate to control the conduct of parties involved in negotiating the main contract. In this way the case law on collateral contracts represents another weapon in the legal armoury which may be called in aid by the courts to give expression to a standard of fair dealing in pre-contractual negotiations. This usage is not apparent when the collateral contract is an express one because then the duties imposed by the contract may be properly described as assumed by the parties rather than imposed by the courts. However, where the collateral contract is implied, there is greater scope for the expression by the court of its own view of 'proper' behaviour by those negotiating the formation of a contract.

In *Walford* v *Miles*[384] the House of Lords had to consider whether the vendors of a photographic business were in breach of the terms of any collateral contract when they declined to sell the business to prospective purchasers. At first, the disappointed purchasers alleged that there was a breach of an oral agreement collateral to the anticipated sale whereby the claimants *inter alia* undertook to obtain a so-called 'comfort letter' from their bank indicating that they could obtain sufficient funds to complete the sale in exchange for the defendants' promise not to negotiate with any third parties. An agreement which imposes a *negative* obligation on the seller, i.e. *not* to sell to any third party is referred to as a 'lock-out agreement'. Later, counsel for the claimants amended their pleadings to assert a 'lock-in agreement' whereby the vendors assumed a *positive* obligation to negotiate in good faith with the claimants. The reason for this change was presumably[385] to justify the £1m damages (the difference between the proposed purchase price of £2m and £3m, the true value of the business) claimed by the claimants. If the claimants were only able to prove the existence of a lock-out agreement whereby the only obligation assumed was not to sell the business to third parties, consistently with such an agreement the vendors could have decided not to sell the business to anyone, i.e. to retain it for themselves. If this had happened, the claimants would have suffered the 'loss' they in fact suffered and had no action to recover it from the defendants because the loss was not caused by the breach of the lock-out agreement. In fact, the defendants did sell the business to a third party. However, it seems that the possibility that in different circumstances the claimants could have suffered, but had no right of redress in respect of, the loss for which they now claimed compensation,

---

[384] [1992] 2 WLR 174.
[385] The reason for the amendment is not clear from the report which only records that the claimants' counsel thought that an action based upon breach of a lock-out agreement would be 'futile'. See Lord Ackner at p. 183 A.

persuaded them that they would have difficulty convincing a court that this loss was caused by the defendants' breach of the lock-out agreement.

The amendment to the claimants' statement of claim asserted that it was an implied term[386] of the collateral agreement that the defendants would continue to negotiate in good faith with the claimants. The claimants appealed to the House of Lords against the decision of the Court of Appeal overturning, by a majority, the decision of the trial judge who found for the claimants. The only full judgment was given by Lord Ackner who said that the obligation of the defendants to negotiate in good faith with the claimants, which was said to result from the agreement that the defendants would deal exclusively with the claimants, lacked certainty[387] and so was unenforceable. This uncertainty derives from the need to determine what would constitute 'a proper reason' to break off negotiations. One of the factors which apparently persuaded the defendants to sell their business to a third party resulted from a proposed term of the contract of sale that the business would produce at least £300,000 profits in its first year. The claimants were concerned that there might be a clash of personalities between the existing staff and the new owners so that the warranted profits would not be achieved. Lord Ackner's difficulty with a duty to negotiate in good faith may be illustrated by asking whether the reason proffered by the defendants for breaking off negotiations was a 'proper' one. How can the court work out whether this was a sufficient reason to justify the defendants in breaking off negotiations with the claimants? Any attempt to define a 'proper' reason involved restricting the defendant's freedom to act at a time before he had given up that freedom by assuming obligations under the main contract of sale. Lord Ackner said:[388]

> ... the concept of a duty to carry on negotiations in good faith is inherently repugnant to the adversarial position of the parties when involved in negotiations. Each party to the negotiations is entitled to pursue his (or her) own interest ...

The approach of the House of Lords in *Walford* v *Miles* which has been aptly labelled 'the repugnancy thesis'[389] may be criticised at a technical as well as a theoretical level. At a technical level Lord Ackner distinguished between a duty to negotiate in good faith and a duty to use best endeavours in negotiations. Although he considered the former to be too uncertain to form the subject matter of a contractual obligation, he did not think the same was true of the latter.[390] Recent case law appears to support the view that an agreement to use best endeavours should not be regarded as unenforceable for uncertainty. In *Queensland Electricity Generating Board* v *New Hope Collieries Pty Ltd*[391] the Privy Council held that a 15-year coal-supply

---

[386] To be implied on the basis of business efficacy. See below ch. 10.
[387] For a discussion of the requirement of certainty, see below ch. 5.
[388] At p. 181 F–G.
[389] Adams and Brownsword (1995) *Key Issues in Contract*, p. 199.
[390] At p. 181 E.
[391] [1989] 1 Lloyd's Rep 205.

contract which failed to provide key terms to govern the parties' relationship after an initial five-year period was sufficiently ascertained to be enforceable because '... by the agreement the parties undertook implied primary obligations to make reasonable endeavours to agree on the terms of supply beyond the initial five-year period ...'. More recently in *Lambert v HTV Cymru (Wales) Ltd* [392] the Court of Appeal held that a term of a contract which obliged the assignee of copyright in certain cartoon characters to use all reasonable endeavours to secure certain rights for the assignor if there was a subsequent assignment was sufficiently certain to be enforceable. However, it is difficult to understand why an obligation to negotiate in good faith is too uncertain to be enforceable when an obligation to use best endeavours is not.[393] Whatever difficulties confront a court in trying to ascertain the former surely apply to the latter. In other words, they are indistinguishable.

A possible distinction may be that the obligation cast upon a party by a best endeavours clause is much weaker than that imposed by an obligation to bargain in good faith. This view is supported by *Phillips Petroleum Co UK Ltd v Enron Europe Ltd* [394] which suggests that a party is not required to ignore his own financial position when he is under an obligation to use best endeavours to reach agreement. In *Walford v Miles* the seller could not be said to have failed to use his best endeavours to secure agreement when he terminated negotiations because of his concerns about the profit warranty. In this way, the repugnancy thesis is met. However, the obligation cast upon the party subject to such an obligation appears to be so weak that it offers minimal protection to his contractual partner. It is perhaps because of these difficulties that there is no mention of this distinction in *The Antclizo*,[395] the first appellate decision to consider *Walford v Miles*.

Perhaps a better explanation for the stark contrast between the results of these two lines of authority can be found. It will be noted that both of the 'reasonable endeavour' cases involved parties who were bound to each other by a main contract the existence, as opposed to the extent, of which was not in dispute. Where the parties are indisputably bound by the terms of the main contract, it might be the case that their interests are more harmonious and so they may not be characterised as taking up 'adversarial' positions. This explanation would suggest that courts should be reticent to impose an obligation to negotiate (in good faith or with best endeavours) upon parties who have not yet reached any agreement on the main terms of their bargain but that this reticence should turn to enthusiasm when the parties are so agreed. This approach at least avoids semantic debate about whether there is any real distinction between promising to negotiate in good faith or with best endeavours.

---

[392] [1998] *The Times*, 13 March and [1998] Current Law Digest, April, para 106.

[393] See Lord Steyn writing extra-judicially who says '... the decision is even more curious when one takes into account that the House of Lords regarded a best endeavours undertaking as enforceable ...' in 'Contract Law: Expectations of Honest Men' (1997) 113 LQR 433 at 439.

[394] Unreported, Court of Appeal, 10 October 1996.

[395] [1992] 1 Lloyd's Rep 558.

The theoretical objection to *Walford* v *Miles* is that even this limited reticence may go too far. The adversarial paradigm described by Lord Ackner may to a degree, or at least in certain sectors, misrepresent commercial realities. The few empirical studies which have been undertaken commonly reveal a high degree of co-operation between contractors.[396] In a memorable phrase, they are said not to 'go for the jugular when trouble arises'.[397] The adversarial model of contracting is also at odds with many theoretical writings which emphasise the emerging importance of norms of co-operation.[398]

Whether there is sufficient evidence to justify Lord Ackner's assertions about the diametrically opposed interests of contractors is unclear. It certainly seems inapplicable to the performance of existing contracts and it is suggested that the approach of the courts to such cases supports this view. Whether Lord Ackner's view is justified in relation to all parties negotiating a new contract is also open to question. Here it may be necessary to distinguish between different kinds of transactions. On the facts of *Walford* itself the view would seem to be justified. The claimants were seeking to make the maximum profit possible by purchasing a business for a price that they thought grossly undervalued the assets of the business; the defendants were seeking the best price for a business they wished to sell because of personal illness. However, elsewhere it will be seen that even though parties are apparently negotiating the formation of a new contract, there may be a history of past dealings sufficient to displace the view that their interests are diametrically opposed.[399] What can be said with confidence is that the unqualified comments of Lord Ackner should not be regarded as endorsing a model of contracting which is universally applicable.

Before leaving *Walford* v *Miles*, it should be noted that whatever the merits of the decision on the facts, its strictures will not apply to arrangements between entities which are not regarded as analogous to parties negotiating contracts. On this basis it has been held[400] that Lloyd's was restricted in its freedom of action by a principle resembling the constraints imposed on certain bodies by public law. Lloyd's was acting in the general public interest and so was to be distinguished from private contractors. On this basis, it was arguable that Lloyd's was subject to an obligation to negotiate in good faith.

---

[396] Macaulay, 'Non-Contractual Relations in Business: A Preliminary Study' (1963) 28 Am Soc Rev 45; Beale and Dugdale 'Contracts Between Businessmen: Planning and the Use of Contractual Remedies' (1975) 2 Brit J Law & Soc 18.

[397] MacNeil, 'Economic Analysis of Contractual Relations: Its Shortfalls and the Need for a Rich Classificatory Apparatus' (1981) 75 NW Univ L Rev 1018, 1048.

[398] For example, MacNeil, 'The Many Futures of Contracts' (1974) 47 S Cal L Rev 691; Williamson, 'Contract Analysis: the Transaction Cost Approach' in (1981) Burrows and Veljanovski (eds) *The Economic Approach to Law*; Collins (1997) *The Law of Contract*. 3rd edn, chs 10 and 15.

[399] For example, *Blackpool and Fylde Aero Club Ltd* v *Blackpool Borough Council* [1990] 1 WLR 1195 considered below, where the claimants had operated a concession to operate pleasure flights from the defendant's airport eight years prior to their tender to continue operations, which was the subject of the litigation in that case.

[400] *Re Debtors (Nos 4449 and 4450 of 1998)* [1999] 1 All ER (Comm) 149.

The Master of the Rolls has remarked: 'For very many people their first and closest contact with the law is when they come to buy or sell a house. They frequently find it a profoundly depressing and frustrating experience.' Purchasers have turned to lock-out agreements to remove some of this frustration in order to protect themselves from sellers who may be tempted to solicit higher offers elsewhere after the original purchaser has incurred legal and survey costs. This practice is known as 'gazumping' and becomes more common when house prices are rising quickly.[401] The potential for gazumping arises from the way in which the sale of real property is usually effected and the lengthy time it takes.[402] The vendor and purchaser reach agreement on a price 'subject to contract'. Such an agreement is binding in honour only;[403] no legally binding agreement arises at this point.[404] The purchaser arranges or finalises finance and usually also commissions a survey. The arrangement only becomes binding upon 'exchange of contracts' when the legal searches necessary to validate the vendor's ownership are complete.

For two reasons the protection from gazumping that is offered by entering a lock-out agreement is not unlimited.[405] First the lock-out agreement would appear to suffer from the same problem that caused the claimants in *Walford* to amend their pleadings. If, contrary to the terms of the lock-out agreement there is a sale to a third party, can the claimant prove that his loss[406] was caused by that breach when he might have suffered the same loss if, consistently with the agreement, the defendant had decided not to sell the property to anyone? In practice this does not seem to have caused any problems. In *Pitt* v *PHH Asset Management Ltd* the Court of Appeal heard a

---

[401] When property prices are falling, it is the vendor who is vulnerable to a purchaser who reduces his offer just before he becomes bound (on exchange of contracts). This process is known as 'gazundering'. It is possible for buyers and sellers to protect themselves from, respectively, gazumping and gazundering by entering into a conditional contract at an earlier stage in proceedings. This would bind the buyer and seller to proceed so long as specified conditions were fulfilled, e.g. that the buyer is able to obtain finance and the survey reveals no major defects. Such conditional contracts have not proved popular.

[402] It has been described in these terms 'part of the trouble is that so many things can go wrong with a sale in these days of repossessions, caution and recession economics. The building societies, burnt by the carefree lending policies of the eighties, make copious checks on borrowers, which take time – and the valuers they send to examine the properties they lend on are more wary than valuers have ever been. Then the structural surveyors step in, also covering their backs against possible losses with doom-laden reports cataloguing every flake of peeling paint ... Then the solicitors arrive on the scene, shielded by receptionists and secretaries, moving at the pace of second class post, vanishing to spend mornings in court at pivotal moments.' *Independent on Sunday*, 22 August 1993.

[403] One estate agent has suggested that honour has a price and that is about 5 per cent of the purchase price. Whenever a vendor can 'make' an extra 5 per cent or more by offering the property to a third party, he will do so. See *Independent on Sunday*, 22 August 1993.

[404] See below.

[405] *Cf.* the general press reaction to the *Pitt* case. 'Gazumping is likely to be well and truly a thing of the past', Sue Fieldman predicted in the *Independent*, and James Landale writing in *The Times* said that 'Gazumping could become a thing of the past'.

[406] Presumably the difference between the contract price and the purchase price of similar property at the time of breach and possibly also wasted expenses. See *infra* for a discussion of the extent to which a claimant may combine a claim for different items of loss.

preliminary appeal on the question whether such an agreement was enforceable and unanimously held that it was. Due to the form of the appeal the issue of damages was not addressed. However, various press reports suggest that damages were awarded of between £7,000 and £15,000.[407] Second, it is necessary to limit the duration of any lock-out agreement, otherwise this alone will render it uncertain and so unenforceable.[408] In *Walford* v *Miles* the agreement was not specified to operate for a definite period and this was a further reason why the agreement relied on by the claimants was unenforceable and a sufficient reason why the lock-out agreement which the claimants in that case originally relied on was also unenforceable.[409] In contrast, in *Pitt* the lock-out agreement was only stated to operate for a fixed period of 14 days. From the perspective of the purchaser, the problem with placing a fixed time limit, particularly one as short as that in *Pitt*, is that the vendor who changes his mind within the period may, consistently with the lock-out agreement, simply postpone approaches to third parties until the expiry of the specified period.

Two fairly simple lessons emerge from this long discussion for anyone who seeks to draft a pre-contractual agreement which cannot be impeached for being too uncertain. These are: lock out but do not lock in, and incorporate a fixed time period.[410]

Before leaving the topic of collateral contracts, a final comparison can be made with *Blackpool and Fylde Aero Club Ltd* v *Blackpool Borough Council*[411] where the Court of Appeal held that a local council which invited tenders to operate a pleasure flight concession from an airfield it owned had impliedly promised that all conforming tenders would be considered. The disappointed tenderer in this case succeeded in an action against the local authority which had failed to consider at all the tender submitted in the required form. The imposition of a duty to consider falls short of an obligation to consider fairly (in good faith) any conforming tender and so viewed narrowly the *Blackpool* case is not inconsistent with *Walford* v *Miles*. Indeed, the duty imposed by the *Blackpool* decision does not require those inviting tenders to make difficult subjective judgments (i.e. what is a proper reason for rejecting a tender) of the sort which Lord Ackner thought were antithetical to the opposed interests of parties negotiating a contract. However, if the tender had been read and then rejected for some irrational reason (on the basis of the tenderer's sporting allegiance) the Court of Appeal today would, as a matter of precedent, be bound by *Walford* v *Miles* and so deny that the invitor owed tenderers a duty to consider fairly (or in good faith) all conforming tenders.

---

[407] [1994] *Mail on Sunday*, 26 September (£15,000) and *Daily Mail* 2 March 1994 (£7,000).

[408] In *Walford* v *Miles* Bingham LJ in the Court of Appeal suggested that the obligation should endure for a reasonable period of time. This attempt to save the agreement was rejected by Lord Ackner in the House of Lords at p. 183 A–B.

[409] 'The agreement alleged in … the unamended statement of claim contains the essential characteristics of a basic lockout agreement, save one. It does not specify for how long it is to last.' (*Per* Lord Ackner at p. 183 A.)

[410] See Halson, 'Locking on to Lock-Out Agreements' (1993) Solicitors Journal 594.

[411] [1990] 1 WLR 1195.

It seems strange that the law would grant redress to a tenderer whose tenderswas not considered at all but refuse it to a tenderer whose tender was considered but rejected for some extraneous reason.

A DUTY TO DISCLOSE?

In many of the cases we have already considered it is easy to identify the behaviour of the defendant which the law considers objectionable. Perhaps the clearest cases involve deceit and proprietary estoppel. Nobody is likely to spring to the defence of a vendor who contracts to sell as his own property that which he knows is owned by a third party[412] or a man who seeks to renege upon a promise to the lover he lived with and who provided him with housekeeping and clerical services that 'the house is yours and everything in it' in reliance upon which she spent her savings on redecoration and improvement.[413] Where the defendant seeks to renege upon an express assurance that was made negligently, or even wholly innocently, rather than intentionally, this would also constitute a convincing case for relief. Beyond such express assurances the moral claim of the party seeking relief is perhaps less strong but still convincing. These include cases where parties have premised their dealings upon an unarticulated common assumption (estoppel by convention) or where the defendant's obligation derives from a subsidiary contract which is usually implied rather than express (collateral contract). It has been argued[414] that the claim of a party who is seeking a remedy in the law of restitution asserts a stronger case for judicial intervention than someone who is 'merely' seeking to have his expectations made good[415] or his detrimental reliance compensated.[416] Despite the high authority of its proponents,[417] this claim is vehemently disputed[418] and does not seem wholly convincing in the context of failed negotiations where the remedy granted should respect any allocation of risk accepted by the parties when unsuccessfully negotiating their contract.

However, beyond all these instances of the legal control of contractual negotiations are cases where the alleged fault of a negotiating party lies not in doing something wrong but rather in his failure to do something. It is a general feature of the common law of obligations that legal consequences are

---

[412] *The Siben* [1996] 1 Lloyd's Rep 35.

[413] *Pascoe* v *Turner* [1979] 1 WLR 431.

[414] Fuller and Perdue 'The Reliance Interest in Contract Damages' (1936) 46 Yale LJ 52, 373.

[415] For example, the claimant in *Pascoe* v *Turner* who sought to have 'ownership' of the property conveyed to her.

[416] The measure of damages granted in the torts of deceit and negligent misrepresentation as well as under Misrepresentation Act 1967, s 2(1) compensate the claimant to the extent of his reliance upon the defendant's misrepresentation. The extent of recovery will also depend upon the applicable test of remoteness of loss.

[417] Fuller and Perdue's article (cited above) has been described as the most famous (Linzer (1989) *A Contracts Anthology*) and significant (Birmingham, 'Notes on the Reliance Interest' (1985) 60 Wash L Rev) contract article ever written.

[418] For example, Friedmann 'The Performance Interest in Contract Damages' (1995) 111 LQR 628.

more readily attached to acts than to omissions.[419] In the tort of negligence this finds expression in the principle that one must take care to avoid harm to others but there is no general duty to act for their benefit.[420] It has been said that 'there are sound reasons why omissions require different treatment from positive conduct'.[421] However, it is recognised that the rule is subject to a number of exceptions[422] and qualifications.[423]

The distinction between misfeasance and non-feasance is usually applied in relation to physical harm suffered by the claimant. However, in *Banque Financière de la Cité SA* v *Westgate Insurance Co Ltd*[424] Slade LJ said: '... the same reluctance on the part of the courts to give a remedy in tort for pure omission applies, perhaps even more so, when the omission is a failure to prevent economic harm'. The case concerned an insurance underwriter who was aware that an insurance broker was making fraudulent representations to various banks that insurance policies had been taken out as security for money owing to them. The Court of Appeal held that the underwriter was not liable to the banks in the tort of negligence for the failure to inform them about the fraud. The Court of Appeal rejected the judge's conclusion that because of the ongoing and profitable business relationship between the underwriters and the banks this was not 'a case of pure omission' and concluded that no liability could arise on the facts in the absence of an express undertaking by the underwriter to be responsible to the banks for such frauds.

In *Banque Financière* it was said that a duty to disclose would conflict with the general rule that parties in contractual negotiations do not owe to each other positive duties of disclosure. The rule of non-disclosure is itself often

---

[419] See generally Honoré, 'Are Omissions Less Culpable?' in Cane and Stapleton (eds) (1995) *Essays for Atiyah.*

[420] 'The very parable of the good Samaritan ... illustrates in the conduct of the priest and the Levite who passes by on the other side, an omission which was likely to have as its reasonable and probable consequence damage to the health of the victim of the thieves, but for which the priest and the Levite would have incurred no civil liability in English law.' *Home Office* v *Dorset Yacht Co Ltd* [1970] AC 1004 at 1060 *per* Lord Diplock.

[421] *Stovin* v *Wise* [1996] AC 923 *per* Lord Hoffmann. *Cf. Smith* v *Littlewoods Organisation Ltd* [1987] AC 241 at 271. See also the more neutral comment of Slade LJ in *Banque Financière de la Cité SA* v *Westgate Insurance Co Ltd* [1989] 2 All ER 952 at 1007–12 that 'For better or worse, our law of tort draws a fundamental distinction between the legal effects of acts on the one hand and omissions on the other ...'.

[422] Mainly arising out of particular relationships between the claimant and the defendant, especially where the former is under the care or control of the latter (schools and pupils, the police and prisoners), or between the defendant and the person causing harm to the claimant (e.g. a borstal and its neighbours) or where the defendant derives a more general benefit from his relationship with the claimant (e.g. employer–employee and carrier–passenger) but also arising from the occupation of property.

[423] For example, the omission may form part of a larger chain of events which can be properly characterised as conduct and the defendant is liable to the extent that his action makes the position of the claimant worse. 'Both the priest and the levite ensured performance of any common law duty of care to the stricken traveller when by crossing to the other side of the road they avoided any risk of throwing up dust in his wounds,' *per* Deane J in *Jaensch* v *Coffey* (1984) 54 ALR 417 at 440.

[424] [1989] 2 All ER 952 at 1007–12. The case is also known as *Banque Keyser Ullmann SA* v *Skandia (UK) Insurance Co Ltd.*

described by the Latin maxim 'caveat emptor' (let the buyer beware). This rule is well illustrated by *Keates* v *The Earl of Cadogan*[425] where a landlord was held to be under no duty to disclose to a prospective tenant that the property to be let 'was in such a ruinous and dangerous state and condition as to be dangerous to enter, occupy, or dwell in, and was likely wholly or in part to fall down, and thereby do damage and injury to persons and property therein'.

Although the law as stated *Keates* v *The Earl of Cadogan* and re-affirmed in *Banque Financière* denies the existence of any general duty to disclose information to your negotiating partner, this is subject to a number of exceptions and qualifications.

Disclosure of terms

Legal doctrine appears to draw a clear distinction between the non-disclosure of material facts and the non-disclosure of contract terms;[426] while the former will not generally attract legal sanctions the latter is more aggressively 'policed'. We have already seen this distinction in the cases dealing with the 'snapping up' of mistaken offers. A unilateral mistake by one party[427] will affect the validity of a contract at law when the mistake is one as to the terms of the contract even if the mistake is not a fundamental one. If the mistake is simply one of quality which the party seeking relief does not think is contractually guaranteed, the mistake is not operative at common law. This is the basis of the decision in *Smith* v *Hughes*.[428] The case concerned the sale of a parcel of oats which turned out to be 'new' rather than 'old' oats and so were valueless to the purchaser. The judge left two questions to the jury which may be paraphrased as:

1. Did the vendor describe the oats as old? If so, judgment for the purchaser.
2. If not, did the purchaser believe the oats to be old and was the vendor aware of this? If so, judgment for the purchaser.

The jury found for the purchaser. This was overturned on appeal because the direction to the jury was deficient. If the jury answered the first question affirmatively then the verdict was correct. In these circumstances it would be a term of the contract that the oats were old and if they were not the vendor could not maintain an action against the purchaser. In fact, the vendor would himself be in breach of an express term of the contract. However, if the jury's verdict for the purchaser was reached on the basis of the second question it could only be supported if the purchaser believed the oats to be old *and also believed it was a term of the contract that the oats were old* and the

---

[425] (1851) 10 CB 591.
[426] This distinction is rarely acknowledged. For an exception see Collins (1997) *The Law of Contract*. 3rd edn, pp. 185–95.
[427] Meaning one party is mistaken and the other is aware of the mistake.
[428] (1871) LR 6 QB 597.

vendor was aware of this. As the jury's verdict did not reveal the basis on which it was reached, a new trial was ordered. This principle was applied in *Hartog* v *Colin & Shields*[429] and *Scriven Bros* v *Hindley*[430] respectively to prevent offerees from accepting offers which they knew, or should have known, were mistaken.

The legal requirement to disclose the terms of a contract is enforced by a number of other disparate common law and statutory measures. These include the rules which determine whether an unsigned document or notice may be relied upon as evidence of the terms of a contract between the parties. The common law rules of incorporation require that any such document must be of a type which might reasonably be expected to contain contractual terms and, most importantly that, before or at the time of contracting, reasonable steps are taken by the party relying upon the notice or document to bring it to the attention of the party subject to it.[431] This common law principle is now reinforced by the Unfair Terms in Consumer Contract Regulations 1999[432] which regard as presumptively unfair[433] and so unenforceable[434] any term in a contract between a seller or supplier and a consumer[435] which has not been individually negotiated and which has:[436]

> the object or effect of ... irrevocably binding the consumer to terms with which he had no real opportunity of becoming acquainted before the conclusion of the contract.

Statutes enact a number of other duties to disclose the terms of contracts in order to protect consumers in their dealings with businesses. The most detailed rules concern the granting of credit and are enacted by the Consumer Credit Act 1974.[437] The complex provisions of the Act seek to ensure that a consumer is fully appraised of the contract he is entering by requiring the creditor to provide the debtor with a copy or copies[438] of the agreement which itself must make clear the amount and timing of payments, the rate of interest and the protection and remedies available under the Act.[439] In addition, many agreements may be cancelled within a statutory 'cooling off' period[440] and the creditor must notify the debtor of this right.[441]

A further example of a statute encouraging the disclosure of contractual

---

[429] [1939] 3 All ER 566.
[430] [1913] 3 KB 504.
[431] *Interfoto Picture Library* v *Stiletto Visual Programmes Ltd* [1989] QB 433.
[432] SI 1999 No. 2083.
[433] Regulation 5(5).
[434] Against the consumer, regulation 8(1).
[435] Regulation 4(1). Regulation 3 effectively defines a seller or supplier as a business and a consumer as a person acting for non-business purposes.
[436] Schedule 2, para 1(i).
[437] Broadly the Act applies to most agreements for the provision of credit not exceeding £25,000.
[438] Sections 62–3.
[439] See Consumer Credit (Agreements) Regulations 1983, SI 1983 No. 1553.
[440] Section 67.
[441] Section 63.

terms is the Employment Rights Act 1996. Section 1 imposes a duty on employers to provide employees with a written statement of the contract terms. Both the consumer credit and employment legislation fulfil obligations imposed by EC law.[442]

Contracts *uberrimae fidei*

Where a contract is characterised by the law as one requiring 'the utmost good faith' (*uberrimae fidei*) a duty to disclose material facts is imposed. The main category of contracts subject to the duty are contracts of insurance[443] where the person taking out the insurance is under a duty to disclose all matters which would be taken into account by the underwriter when assessing the risk.[444] Material facts are those facts which would have had an affect on the mind of a prudent insurer in weighing up the risk he was assuming.[445] Further, in order for the insurer to avoid the policy it is necessary for the non-disclosure, like any positive misrepresentation, to have induced the contract.[446] On this basis, a policy of marine insurance may be avoided if the assured does not declare the true value of the cargo[447] and a policy of life insurance if the assured fails to inform the insurer that other companies had declined to insure his life.[448]

The policy of insurance may also be avoided by the assured if the insurer fails to disclose facts material to the risk. This was one of the ways in which the banks that had advanced loans in *Banque Financière* put their case; the insurer had failed to alert them about the fraudulent activities of an insurance broker. It was held in that case that the facts were not material to the risk assumed by the insurer. Even if they were and they could be regarded as having induced the contract of insurance, this would not entitle the banks to damages. This is because in contracts *uberrimae fidei* the duty to disclose is not based upon an implied term of the contract or upon tort but grew out of a jurisdiction originally exercised by courts of equity. As a result, the appropriate remedy is rescission. Neither were damages available under the Misrepresentation Act 1967, s 2(1) because it refers to a misrepresentation having been 'made' and so does not extend to cover 'true'[449] cases of non-disclosure.

It might be thought that insurers are well protected by the duty to disclose in contracts *uberrimae fidei*. However, this is usually reinforced by stipulation

---

[442] EC Directives 87/102 and 91/533 respectively.
[443] Of any kind: *Rozanes* v *Bowen* (1928) 32 Ll L R 98.
[444] *Pan Atlantic Insurance Co Ltd* v *Pine Top Insurance Co Ltd* [1994] 3 All ER 582.
[445] Marine Insurance Act 1906, s 18(2) as interpreted in *Pan Atlantic Insurance Co Ltd* v *Pine Top Insurance Co Ltd* [1994] 3 All ER 582. The House of Lords accepted that the principles applicable to marine insurance are the same as those applicable to other types of insurance. See Lord Mustill for the majority at p. 610.
[446] At pp. 610–18 *per* Lord Mustill.
[447] *Ionides* v *Pender* (1874) LR 9 QB 531.
[448] *London Assurance* v *Mansel* (1879) 11 Ch D 363.
[449] That is, excluding half-truths and the *With* v *O'Flanagan* duty considered further below.

that the answers to questions posed in the application for insurance form the basis of the agreement.[450] This has the effect of making these answers 'conditions'[451] of the contract with the consequence that any trivial but incorrect information supplied will entitle the insurer to avoid the contract. These 'basis of contract' clauses have attracted much criticism[452] not least because they tend to undermine the requirement of materiality, i.e. that the non-disclosure must be such as would have influenced a prudent insurer. As a result, such clauses are interpreted strictly against insurance companies and may now be controlled by the Unfair Terms in Consumer Contracts Regulations 1999.[453] Only contracts between consumers and suppliers are within the regulations.[454] However, the regulations exempt from review so called 'core terms'[455] and it is unclear whether this exemption will cover these 'basis of contract' clauses.[456]

Contracts of insurance form the main category of contracts *uberrimae fidei*. However, there is old authority to the effect that a duty of disclosure arises in family arrangements. In *Gordon* v *Gordon*[457] a settlement of family property which was agreed on the basis that an elder son was probably illegitimate was set aside because his brother failed to disclose that the parents had in fact been through an unpublicised ceremony of marriage. The older authorities are probably less important now because of statutory inroads[458] and changing social circumstances.[459]

Undue influence[460]

Where a party enters a contract acting under the undue influence of his contractual partner, the court may set the contract aside.[461] Relief for undue influence is subject to the same 'bars' as rescission for misrepresentation.[462]

---

[450] For example, *Magee* v *Pennine Insurance Co Ltd* [1969] 2 QB 507 considered further in Chapter 7.

[451] See Chapter 15.

[452] For example, *Joel* v *Law Union & Crown Insurance Co* [1908] 2 KB 863 at 885 *per* Fletcher Moulton LJ: 'I wish I could adequately warn the public against such practices ...'.

[453] SI 1999 No. 2083. See generally Chapter 11. *Cf.* Unfair Contracts Terms Act 1977 which does not apply to any contract of insurance. See Sch 1, para 1(a).

[454] Regulation 3.

[455] Regulation 6(2).

[456] The European Directive that the regulations enforce sought to exclude from review terms in insurance contracts which 'clearly define or circumscribe the insured risk and the insurer's liability'. See 93/13/EEC, Recital 19.

[457] (1821) 3 Swan 400.

[458] Full and frank disclosure of circumstances and assets is required when parties to matrimonial proceedings seek a consent order approving the settlement of their financial and property affairs. See *Jenkins* v *Livsey* [1985] AC 424.

[459] See *Wales* v *Wadham* [1977] 1 WLR 199 at 218 where a man and his estranged wife were regarded as dealing at arm's length, i.e. as independent individuals with no need for protection.

[460] See generally Birks and Chin, 'On the Nature of Undue Influence', ch 3, in Bealson and Friedmann (eds) (1995) *Good Faith and Fault in Contract Law*.

[461] The affect of undue influence upon third parties to the contract and the doctrine of notice are not discussed in this book. For a summary of the applicable principles, see *Royal Bank of Scotland* v *Etridge (No 2)* [1998] 4 All ER 705.

[462] See above.

Undue influence[463] may be actual[464] or presumed. The latter category may be further sub-divided into cases of relationships (e.g. doctor and patient[465]) where there is a presumption that undue influence was exercised and other relationships where as a matter of fact one party routinely reposed trust and confidence in another (e.g. the relationship between an individual and a *particular* bank manager[466] or an employer and a junior employee[467]). In the case of actual undue influence there is no longer a further requirement that the contract be to the 'manifest disadvantage' of the party seeking relief[468]; in the case of presumed undue influence the requirement persists.[469] A manifest disadvantage is one that is clear and obvious, more than minimal but does not have to be large or even 'medium sized'.[470]

The present state of the law appears to strike a sensible balance between protection of the vulnerable and the security of market transactions. If a party is subjected to actual undue influence or relies upon a misrepresentation, that alone is a sufficient ground for setting the transaction aside. Whether the resulting contract was 'fair' or not is irrelevant. In each case relief is granted because of the wrongdoing which induced the transaction and no more should be required to be proved. However, if the case is one of presumed undue influence, no wrongdoing has been demonstrated. The transaction might or might not have been obtained as a result of wrongdoing. What the law does is to try to identify those transactions where it is sufficiently likely that there was wrongdoing to justify further explanation. This suggests the need for further evidence of impropriety which is provided where the transaction is a disadvantageous one. On this basis, a doctor who purchased at undervalue a painting from a patient would be required to rebut the inference of undue influence, whereas if he purchased it at full value he would not.

In order to rebut the presumption of undue influence, it is necessary to prove that the person subject to it exercised a free will. This requirement is not satisfied by mere disclosure. Rather the party seeking to discharge the burden must go further.[471] Usually it will be necessary to show that the other party had independent advice before entering the transaction.[472]

---

[463] The categorisation derives from *BCCI v Aboody* [1992] 4 All ER 955 and was adopted by Lord Browne-Wilkinson in *Barclays Bank v O'Brien* [1993] 4 All ER 417.

[464] *Re Craig* may be such a case [1971] Ch 95 (elderly widower employed a young woman as secretary and companion and made her gifts of £28,000 over six years).

[465] *Hylton v Hylton* (1754) 2 Ves Sen 547.

[466] *Lloyds Bank v Bundy* [1975] QB 326.

[467] *Crédit Lyonnais Bank Nederland v Burch* [1997] 1 All ER 144.

[468] *CIBC Mortgages v Pitt* [1993] 4 All ER 433 overruling *BCCI v Aboody* [1992] 4 All ER 955 on this point.

[469] *National Westminster Bank plc v Morgan* [1983] 3 All ER 85 as interpreted in *Aboody*. *Dunbar Bank plc v Nadeem* (1998) 31 HLR 402 at 409 and 412.

[470] *Barclays Bank plc v Coleman* [2000] 3 WLR 405.

[471] The rules applied to transactions between a solicitor and his client and between a trustee and a beneficiary are particularly rigorous. These require the solicitor or trustee to show that the transaction was a fair one. In comparison in a case of presumed undue influence the burden of showing a manifest disadvantage is borne by the 'victim'.

[472] *Allcard v Skinner* (1887) 36 Ch D 145 at 190.

Exceptionally, it may be rebutted in a different way, such as by showing that the motivation of the donor was independent and spontaneous.[473] For this reason, undue influence may be said to present a stronger case for relief than the other exceptions to the non-disclosure rule.

Fiduciary relationships

Certain relationships do not give rise to a presumption of undue influence but may none the less be classified as 'fiduciary' relationships by the law. Examples include principal and agent[474] and business partners.[475] As these relationships are thought to present a less strong case for relief than those involving presumed undue influence, they only give rise to a duty to disclose. Nothing further need be done by the party seeking to enforce the transaction.

Inequality of bargaining power[476]

It has been suggested by academics that some of the doctrines already considered should be recast as a more general principle. This would hold that a contract should be set aside whenever there is a general inequality of bargaining power.[477] Such a general provision of the Uniform Commercial Code has been adopted in all but one American state. Section 2-302 states:

> Unconscionable contract or clause
> (1) If the court as a matter of law finds the contract or any clause of the contract to have been unconscionable at the time it was made the court may refuse to enforce the contract, or it may enforce the remainder of the contract without the unconscionable clause, or it may so limit the application of any unconscionable clause as to avoid any unconscionable result.

Although this provision only applies to 'transactions in goods', an analogous approach has been taken to other types of contract. The American Restatement 2d, s 208 has a more general provision which reflects the dual role played by the doctrine in the United States: it aims to control unfair clauses such as exemption clauses as well as incorporating the older categories of exploitation.

Attempts in this country to create a similar overarching doctrine have been less successful. In *Lloyds Bank Ltd* v *Bundy*[478] Lord Denning articulated

---

[473] *Re Brocklehurst* [1978] Ch 14.
[474] *Armstrong* v *Jackson* [1917] 2 KB 822.
[475] Pollock, *Law of Partnership* (1952). 15th edn, p. 8.
[476] Thal, 'The Inequality of Bargaining Power Doctrine: The Problem of defining Contractual Unfairness' (1988) 8 OJLS 17.
[477] See Waddams, 'Unconscionability in Contracts' (1976) 39 MLR 369 and Capper, 'Undue Influence and Unconscionability: A Rationalisation' (1998) 114 LQR 479. *Contra*: Birks and Chin, 'On the Nature of Undue Influence', ch. 3 in Beatson and Friedmann (eds) (1995) *Good Faith and Fault in Contract Law*.
[478] [1974] 3 All ER 757.

such a doctrine to set aside a guarantee and charge over his home granted by an elderly farmer who was unversed in business affairs in favour of a bank to which his son's ailing business was heavily indebted. Lord Denning aggregated a number of existing categories where relief has been granted from disadvantageous contracts.[479] He said:

> Gathering all together, I would suggest that through all these instances there runs a single thread. They rest on 'inequality of bargaining power'. By virtue of it, the English law gives relief to one who, without independent advice, enters into a contract upon terms which are very unfair or transfers property for a consideration which is grossly inadequate, when his bargaining power is grossly impaired by reason of his own needs or desires, or by his own ignorance or infirmity, coupled with undue influences or pressures brought to bear on him by or for the benefit of the other.

Such a doctrine results from what Lord Goff has described as 'the temptation of elegance'.[480] However, elegant solutions are often not practical ones. Over-general statements conceal rather than resolve difficulties of application and so create uncertainty. The doctrine crafted by Lord Denning seeks to amalgamate different concerns arising in very different contexts. Is a case dealing with the consideration supporting a salvage agreement of relevance when considering a case of undue influence? A distinction which is sometimes drawn between substantive and procedural unconscionability may be of help.[481] The former is an argument which justifies the setting aside of a contract by reference to its result (e.g. the salvage agreement where the test is effectively whether there was equivalence of exchange), the latter by reference to a defect in the process of agreement (e.g. undue influence). This distinction raises two related questions. The enforcement of standards of substantive fairness effectively means that the private law of contract is being used as a mechanism to redistribute societal wealth. Is this appropriate? Charles Fried has argued that it is inappropriate to pursue a policy of redistribution through the accidents of litigation. He says:[482]

> Why should just this one representative [i.e. the person who has his contract set aside] of the more fortunate classes be made to bear the burden of our re-distributive zeal? ... Redistribution is not a burden to be borne in a random, ad hoc way by those who happen to cross paths with persons poorer than themselves. Such a conception, heartwarmingly spontaneous though it may be, would in the end undermine our ability to plan and to live our lives as we choose ... The provision of a just social minimum should be society's general responsibility ...

---

479 The categories are: duress of goods, as to which see below; the old cases on unconscionable transactions, such as those with 'expectant heirs'; and undue influence, as to which see above, pp. 99–100, undue pressure covering isolated old cases such as *Williams* v *Bayley* (1866) LR 1 HL 200 (father of son who forged a promissory note was pressured by the bank to give security) and the 'salvage exception' to the rule that courts will not enquire into the adequacy of consideration, as to which see below, p. 163.

480 *Henderson* v *Merrett Syndicates Ltd* [1994] 3 WLR at 781 when considering the issue of concurrent liability in contract and tort.

481 The value of this distinction is doubted by Atiyah in 'Contract and Fair Exchange', ch. 11 in Atiyah (1986) *Essays on Contract*.

482 Fried (1981) *Contract as Promise*, pp. 105–6.

A related question is, if it is appropriate to use the private law of contract in this way, should it be left to unelected judges to fashion standards of substantive fairness? Judges always seem more comfortable when setting aside a contract on the ground of procedural, as opposed to substantive unfairness presumably because it less obviously involves them in overriding the intentions of the parties.

A counter-argument[483] to these concerns is that a doctrine of inequality of bargaining power would only make explicit what judges already do and transparency of reasoning is a good thing. Judges applying the principles of the law of contract do not slavishly give effect to the intentions of the parties. Sometimes it is true to say that, though unelected, they none the less have a creative role in 'making the law'. The application of many doctrines of the law of contract involves the imposition of standards of substantive fairness upon the parties. A doctrine of inequality of bargaining power would simply enable them to do so consistently and transparently.

Although the argument and counter-argument seem equally powerful, in this country, the forces of conservatism have prevailed. Despite its adoption elsewhere,[484] Lord Denning's approach in *Lloyds Bank* v *Bundy*[485] has been disapproved by Lord Scarman in the House of Lords[486] who preferred the orthodox route (undue influence) followed by the other two members of the Court of Appeal. However, this still leaves open the possibility that the old equitable basis of intervention,[487] e.g. in the case of expectant heirs,[488] could be developed to meet more modern demands. Such a development is suggested by *Creswell* v *Potter*[489] which concerned a wife who in the course of divorce proceedings agreed to transfer her share in the matrimonial home to her husband at undervalue, and *Crédit Lyonnais Bank Nederland NV* v *Burch*[490] where an employee of moderate means guaranteed her employer's overdraft up to £270,000. Whether this development can proceed on clear principle grounds which respect the needs of commercial certainty remains to be seen.[491]

---

[483] For an argument that sometimes private law should be used to implement distributional objectives, see Kronman, 'Contract Law and Distributive Justice' [1980] 89 Yale LJ 472. See also Smith, 'In Defence of Substantive Fairness' (1996) 112 LQR 138.

[484] See Enman, 'Doctrines of Unconscionability in England, Canada and the Commonwealth' (1987) 16 Anglo-Am LR 191. An expanded doctrine of unconscionability has survived in Ireland. See Clark, 'The Unconscionability Doctrine Viewed from an Irish Perspective' (1980) 31 NILQ 114.

[485] Which he repeated in *Mathew* v *Bobbins* [1980] EG 421 at 425.

[486] *National Westminster Bank* v *Morgan* [1985] AC 686. See also the comments of Lord Scarman in *Pao On* v *Lau Yiu Long* [1980] AC 614.

[487] See generally the excellent survey by Dawson, 'Economic Duress, An Essay in Perspective' (1947) 45 Mich L Rev 253 at 267–79.

[488] For example, *Fry* v *Lane* (1888) 40 Ch D 312. See also the analogous category of dealing with poor and improvident persons, e.g. *Evans* v *Llewellin* (1787) 1 Cox CC (poor man sold share in estate worth £1,700 for 200 guineas).

[489] [1978] 1 WLR 255.

[490] [1997] 1 All ER 144 (transaction was 'harsh and unconscientious' at p. 151, though decision was based on undue influence).

[491] The old equitable jurisdiction did appear to get out of hand. Meagher, Gummow and Lehane (1992) *Equity: Doctrines and Remedies*. 3rd edn, describe it in this way: 'So tender

Statutory disclosure requirements

Various statutes require the disclosure of information. Two examples provided by the Financial Services Act 1986 are the duty not to dishonestly or recklessly withhold material facts in order to induce someone to enter an investment agreement[492] and the duties of disclosure imposed on those applying for Stock Exchange listing[493] or those issuing a prospectus inviting subscriptions for unlisted securities.[494] The first provision like many others[495] encourages disclosure by the imposition of criminal sanctions. However, the second two provisions may give rise to statutory liabilities to pay compensation.[496]

Further examples are the Package Travel, Package Holidays and Package Tour Regulations 1992 which require the organisers and retailers of such services to provide the consumer with a wide range of information relating to health and visa requirements,[497] intermediate stop-overs and connections[498] and details of the destination itself.[499]

Quasi exceptions: conduct, half-truths and *With* v *O'Flanagan*[500]

We have seen that in general the law of misrepresentation attaches legal consequences to false statements (usually of fact); it does not act on a mere failure to disclose material facts. However, three aspects of the law of misrepresentation may amount to a duty to disclose.

First, we must remember that conduct as well as words might be construed as a positive representation. Compare *Keates* v *The Earl of Cadogan*[501] with the American case of *Obde* v *Schlemeyer*[502] where the seller of a house which he knew was infested with termites was held liable to the purchaser. In both cases there was no express assurance capable of amounting to a term of the contract or a misrepresentation. Yet, in the American case, the vendor was liable for the buyer's losses, whereas in the English case the lessor was held to owe no obligation to the tenant. The distinction lies in the fact that in *Obde* the vendor had covered up and

---

was the concern of equity that by the mid-nineteenth century ... inadequacy of price alone was sufficient ground for setting aside such transactions ...'. This excessive indulgence threatened to upset bona fide commercial transactions and statutory reform became necessary. See Law of Property Act 1925, s 174.

[492] Section 47(1).
[493] Section 146.
[494] Section 163.
[495] For example, the Hallmarking Act 1973 and the General Product Safety Regulations 1994, SI 1994 No 2328.
[496] See respectively Financial Services Act 1986, ss 150 and 166.
[497] Regulation 7.
[498] Regulation 8.
[499] Regulation 9 and Sch 2.
[500] [1936] Ch 575.
[501] (1851) 10 CB 591. See above, p. 96.
[502] (1960) 353 P 2d 672. Another example is *Gordon* v *Selico* (1986) 11 HLR 219, (1987) Conv 121 (vendor of property liable to purchaser when independent contractor employed to eradicate dry rot in property merely concealed it).

repaired all visible signs of infestation. This concealment, like that of the party selling the gun in *Horsfall* v *Thomas*,[503] amounted to a misrepresentation by conduct which is actionable in the same way as an express misrepresentation.

Second, liability might arise where a representor fails to correct a half-truth. A half-truth is a statement which is literally true but which conveys a misleading impression, e.g. a solicitor's statement to the purchaser of property that he was not aware of any restrictive covenants affecting his client, the vendor's, land when the solicitor had never checked to see if there were any.[504] Whether this is regarded as a true exception to the general principle of non-disclosure depends upon whether the half-truth itself is interpreted literally when liability must be imposed for the failure to correct or whether it is interpreted as a reasonable person would in which case liability is imposed on the basis of an untrue implied statement (e.g. that the solicitor had checked).

Third, there is the rule derived from *With* v *O'Flanagan*.[505] This case admits of two possible explanations. Only the alternative ground put by Lord Wright (i.e. the duty to correct when a change of circumstances between utterance and contracting which renders the statement untrue) would amount to a true exception. The 'continuing representation approach favoured by Romer LJ would found liability upon an untrue statement which (by a fiction) is to be regarded as being continuously remade up to the time of contracting.

Other encouragements to disclosure: Sale of Goods Act 1979

The Sale of Goods Act, s 14 implies two terms into contracts for the sale of goods where the vendor is selling goods in the course of a business.[506] Both provisions provide powerful incentives for parties to disclose information. Section 14(2) implies a term that the goods are of satisfactory quality except in relation to defects already drawn to the buyer's attention and, where the buyer examines the goods, in relation to any defects that examination should reveal. Both exceptions encourage sellers to make known any potential defects either by express notice or by ensuring that they are apparent upon inspection. Where the buyer makes known to the seller any particular purpose for which the goods were bought, s 14(3) implies a term that the goods are reasonably fit for that purpose. This measure provides an incentive for the buyer to make known any unusual use to which he intends to put the contract goods. The practical importance of these two provisions should be emphasised. Unlike some of the 'true' exceptions to the non-disclosure rule, the encouragement offered by these provisions applies to a huge area of every-

---

[503] (1862) 1 H & C 90 (a metal plug concealed a defect in the barrel of a gun – although this amounted to a misrepresentation by conduct it did not affect the buyer because he failed to inspect the gun). See further text accompanying note 102 above.

[504] *Nottinghamshire Patent Brick and Tile Company* v *Butler* (1866) 16 QBD 778.

[505] [1934] 1 Ch 575. See above, pp. 31–2.

[506] See Chapter 10.

day commercial activity, i.e. all contracts for the sale of goods in the course of a business. In addition, in relation to sales to consumers, the liabilities arising under these sections cannot be excluded by other contract terms.[507]

A WIDER DUTY TO DISCLOSE

The approach of the law of contract to non-disclosure is undoubtedly untidy. A general principle is stated that there is no duty to disclose and then numerous exceptions and qualifications are elaborated. This type of approach is typical of the common law and in a different context was memorably characterised by Arthur Corbin[508] as one where a court 'states hard-bitten traditional rules and doctrines and then attains an instinctively felt justice by an avoidance of them that is only half-conscious, accompanied by an extended exegesis worthy of a medieval theologian'. Yet, the law is correct to resist what Lord Goff has described, again in a different context, as 'the temptation of elegance'[509] because a lot is at stake here. Those who argue for a more extensive duty of disclosure, perhaps as part of an even broader duty to negotiate in good faith[510] or with proper care,[511] start from and so elaborate particular philosophical premises about what the law of contract should do. We will now briefly examine some of these competing views.

Kronman[512] argues that many features of the present law may be justified by reference to the creation by the law of incentives for parties to 'invest' in the acquisition of information. Information gathering should be encouraged because this is necessary for the pursuit of economic efficiency,[513] defined as the movement of resources to their most highly valued uses. An example might help.

> A is a stamp dealer. B spots a rare 'plate number'[514] among a selection of cheap stamps in A's shop. He purchases the rarity at a low price.
>
> Kronman would argue that if the stamp collector's expertise in the value of rare plate numbers was the result of deliberately acquired information, then the contract should be enforceable. In this way the law creates an incentive for people like B to invest in efficient information generation.

---

[507] Unfair Contract Terms Act 1977, s 6. For a definition of dealing as a consumer for these purposes, see s 12. See further Chapter 11.

[508] (1950) *Corbin on Contracts*, Vol. 3, para 561 discusses the pre-existing duty doctrine of consideration, as to which see Chapter 12. Corbin's multi-volume treatise on the law of contract is a superb and entertaining work. Little can be said about the subject today which he did not say or anticipate and, as will be seen, his criticisms were always as to the point as they were amusing.

[509] *Henderson* v *Merrett Syndicates Ltd* [1994] 3 WLR 761 at 781 discussing concurrent liabilities in contract and tort.

[510] See generally under the next heading: A duty to negotiate in good faith.

[511] See Collins (1997) *The Law of Contract*. 3rd edn, ch. 10.

[512] Mistake, Disclosure and Information (1978) 7 J Leg Stud 1.

[513] A later more general article, 'Contract Law and Distributive Justice' (1980) 89 Yale LJ 472 seems to place greater emphasis upon distributional questions, i.e. *who* is made better off as a result of particular rules.

[514] A number concealed in the margins of the stamp.

A contrary argument derives from the transaction costs associated with contracting. It suggests that a duty of disclosure is desirable where this has the effect of requiring one party, say, the vendor of property, to investigate a particular matter rather than requiring all potential purchasers to do so. Such a desire to avoid increasing the cost of transactions lay behind the provisional proposal of the Law Commission's Conveyancing Standing Committee that a vendor of land should be subject to a positive duty to disclose all material facts relating to the property which he was, or should have been, aware of.[515] This was not endorsed in the full report, *Let the Buyer Be Well Informed*, and has not been acted upon by the courts or the legislature.

A different approach is taken by Charles Fried, the author of *Contract as Promise: A Theory of Contractual Obligation* (1981).[516] Fried emphatically denies that 'economic efficiency'[517] is or should be the basis of the law of contract. Rather, he asserts that the law of contract should be regarded as the elaboration of a moral principle, which he calls the 'promise principle', whereby individuals may impose obligations on themselves. The reason why an individual is morally obliged to perform his contract is because by promising to do so he has appealed to a societal convention that promises should be observed which gives the promisee ground to expect the promise to be performed. To decline to perform the promise is to abuse the trust and autonomy of the promisee.

> An individual is morally bound to keep his promises because he has intentionally invoked a convention whose function it is to give grounds – moral grounds – for another to expect the promised performance. To renege is to abuse a confidence he was free to invite or not, and which he intentionally did invite. To abuse that confidence now is like (but only *like*) lying: the abuse of a shared social institution that is intended to invoke the bonds of trust.[518]

Such a theory of contract appears to run out of explanatory power when confronted with non-disclosure cases. This is because the dispute is about matters which lie beyond the promises exchanged by the parties. Therefore 'it is ... not promise but the competing equities [which] must be used to resolve the inevitable dilemma caused by a contractual accident'.[519] How then does one work out what these respective equities are? The answer according to Fried is by reference to societal conventions. Therefore, Fried suggests that the principle to be applied is:[520]

> ... where the better-informed party cannot compensate for the other's defects without depriving himself of an advantage on which he is conventionally entitled to count, his failure to disclose will not cause the equities to tilt against him.

On this basis, Fried[521] suggests that where costly aerial investigations by an oil company specialising in high-risk operations suggest that certain land

---

[515] *Caveat Emptor in Sale of Land*, para 4.1.
[516] The spine of the book reads: '*Fried Contract as Promise*' and was found in the cookery section of a bookshop in Oxford.
[517] *Ibid.*, pp. 5 and 15.
[518] *Ibid.*, p. 16.   [519] *Ibid.*, p. 81.   [520] *Ibid.*, p. 83.   [521] *Ibid.*, pp. 79–82.

may contain oil and the oil company offers to purchase the land from a large company it is not under a duty to reveal its suspicions to that company. However, if the oil company, through an agent, offers to purchase the land from a small farmer, the equities may point the other way. A response[522] to this approach is to say that social conventions must be specified with great precision if they are to distinguish between such marginal cases.[523]

A third and different approach is taken by Gordley.[524] This historical analysis recognises that in the past most legal systems have supported an Aristotelian principle of corrective justice whereby parties should gain equally from an exchange in order to preserve the pre-existing distribution of wealth. He suggests that the common law only departed from this approach in the last century as a result of the incursion of individualist approaches and in practice not even then to the extent which many statements of principle would lead you to believe. His thesis is that any imbalances in the values of the performances exchanged should invalidate the contract, i.e. the oil company contracts discussed by Fried should be set aside.

Overall, it would seem that Kronman's approach is the one that most clearly explains the law we have. Fried's approach argues for greater disclosure than English law presently provides. Gordley's thesis is in this sense the most radical and argues for the most extensive duty to disclose. However, each of these authors seeks to offer something more than a description of the law we have; each purports to offer a theory about the law we should have.[525] It is suggested that one cannot choose between the various views[526] until one resolves the prior questions about the larger role of the law of contract. Is it there to promote economic efficiency or does it give

---

[522] A further objection is that to the extent such conventions are a product of particular societies (capitalist, socialist, etc.) at a particular point in time this appears to conflict with Fried's claim to have produced a moral theory of contract where '[t]he validity of a moral, like that of a mathematical truth, does not depend on fashion or favour': *ibid.*, p. 2.

[523] See Trebilcock (1993), *The Limits of Freedom of Contract*, p. 107 for an elaboration of this criticism.

[524] 'Equality in Exchange' (1981) 69 Calif Law Rev 1583 and (1992) *The Philosophical Origins of Contract Doctrine*.

[525] It is sometimes difficult to ascertain whether Fried's theory of contract purports only to account for the law we have or whether is also prescriptive. The first sentence of the preface (*op. cit.*) tends to the former: 'This book ... has a theoretical purpose, to show how a complex legal institution, contract, can be traced to and is determined by a small number of basic moral principles ...' In contrast, at p. 37 he writes: 'I conclude that the life of contract is indeed promise, but this is not exactly a statement of positive law.'

A possible reconciliation is that the latter statement merely records that the promise principle does not explain all the law of contract. Rather some of its features can only be explained by reference to 'residuary' principles ('... the tort principle to compensate for harm done, ... the restitution principle for benefits conferred [and] ... a distinct third principle for apportioning loss and gain ... the principle of sharing ...', see pp. 69–70) or, as with the doctrine of consideration to which this comment was particularly directed, cannot and need not be explained because of basic contradictions in its definition; see ch. 3 especially pp. 28–30. It is this incoherence which justifies Fried's view that the consideration in its present form is unsupportable.

[526] Other variants and intermediary positions can also be identified, e.g. Scheppele (1988) *Legal Secrets: Equality and Efficiency in the Common Law* and Trebilcock (1993) *The Limits of Freedom of Contract*, pp. 111–15.

expression to some basic moral principle and if so which? If it is considered that the law of contract should simultaneously reflect all these considerations, how is a conflict between them to be resolved? Even if they are capable of final resolution, these evaluative questions cannot be taken further here. My purpose has been simply to show that when at the margins of settled principle the law has to confront difficult questions, it must have resort to deeper philosophical questions which in turn may reflect or suggest very different attitudes to self reliance.

In conclusion, it is probably wise to return to the law that we have in this country. The general principle that denies any duty between parties negotiating a contract to disclose information is premised upon the idea of individualism where a party considering entering a contract is expected to take all reasonable steps for his own protection. This is immediately apparent from the leading case of *Keates v The Earl of Cadogan*[527] where dismissing the purchaser's claim for relief in a judgment consisting of a single paragraph[528] Chief Justice Jervis notes that he failed to 'do what any man in his senses would do, viz. make proper investigation, and satisfy himself as to the condition of the house before he entered upon the occupation of it'.

A DUTY TO NEGOTIATE IN GOOD FAITH[529]

Discussions of the duty to disclose in contract negotiations often go further to consider a broader obligation to negotiate in good faith. This then prompts three questions which may be summarised as: What is it?; Do we have it?; and Do we need it?.

What is it?

The answer to the first question varies according to context and author. Sometimes the requirement of good faith is discussed in relation to contract negotiation[530] and sometimes in relation to the performance[531] or modification[532] of pre-existing contracts[533] and occasionally in relation to all

---

[527] (1851) 10 CB 591 at 601. See above for the facts.

[528] Maule J at p. 601 managed only a sentence: 'The declaration struck me, at first sight, as a perfectly bad one; and it does not improve upon acquaintance.'

[529] There is a voluminous literature. For a number of different approaches contained in a single volume see Beatson and Friedmann (eds) (1995) *Good Faith and Fault in Contract Law* and Forte (ed.) (1999) *Good Faith in Contract and Property Law*. For a simple but authoritative overview, see Mason, 'Contract, Good Faith and Equitable Standards in Fair Dealing' (2000) 116 LQR 66.

[530] Cohen, 'Pre-contractual Duties: Two Freedoms and the Contract to Negotiate' and Fabre-Magnan, 'Duties of Disclosure and French Contract Law', respectively chs 2 and 4 in Beatson and Friedmann, *op. cit.*

[531] Farnsworth, 'Good Faith in Contract Performance', ch. 6 in Beatson and Friedmann, *op. cit.*

[532] Rakoff, 'Implied Terms: Of "Default Rules" and "Situation Sense"' ch. 8 in Beatson and Friedmann, *op. cit.*

[533] Eisenberg, 'Relational Contracts'; McKendrick 'The Regulation of Long Term Contracts in English Law'; Lorenz, 'Contract Modification as a Result of Change of Circumstances', respectively chs 11, 12 and 14 in Beatson and Friedmann, *op. cit.*

episodes in the life of a contract.[534] Often the standard of behaviour which is imposed by the definition of good faith used in relation to one stage in a transaction is not appropriate to a different stage in the contracting process.

Unfortunately, definitions are rare in discussions of good faith.[535] The following definitions have been proposed though it should be noted that the second, third and fourth were proposed in relation to the obligation to *perform* a contract in good faith.[536] They are ranked in terms of increasing judicial intervention. The minimum content that can be given to the concept of good faith is an obligation to be honest in which sense the concept has been used in this country[537] and also apparently in the United States. If honesty simply requires someone to refrain from telling lies, it adds nothing to the protection already afforded by the tort of deceit. The next least ambitious definition proposed is that good faith simply aggregates a number of existing and familiar common law doctrines[538] such as the implication of terms.[539] Other commentators side-step the difficulty of describing what good faith is by focusing on what it is not i.e. by describing instances of bad faith.[540] To the extent that these instances do not extend beyond the existing case law, this approach is the mirror image of the previous one. However, to the extent that it leaves room for the creation of new categories, it reaches beyond the previous definition. Such an approach is described in the American Restatement[541] which recognises that:[542] 'A complete catalogue of

---

[534] Ebke and Steinhauer, 'The Doctrine of Good Faith in German Contract Law', ch. 7 in Beatson and Friedmann, *op. cit.*

[535] See Goode's comment: 'good faith ... we do not quite know what [it] means ...' in 'The Concept of "Good Faith" in English Law' 2 Saggi Conferenze e Seminari 3, 3. In the 18-page introduction to the collection of essays on good faith, Beatson and Friedmann (*op. cit.*) do not attempt to define the concept.

[536] For a recent discussion of good faith in relation to the performance of contracts, see *Balfour Beatty* v *Docklands Light Railway* (1996) 78 BLR 42 at 57–8.

[537] This is the definition given to the phrase in relation to the Leasehold Reform Act 1967, Sch 3, para 4(1) which provides that where a tenant in good faith makes a claim to acquire the freehold of the property the landlord is prevented from enforcing any right of forfeiture or re-entry. See *Central Estates (Belgravia) Ltd* v *Woolgar* [1971] 3 All ER 647 (tenant who had used leased premises as a brothel lacked the necessary good faith).

[538] Farnsworth, 'Good Faith Performance and Commercial Reasonableness Under the Uniform Commercial Code' (1963) 30 U Chi LR 666. See also Clarke, 'The Common Law of Contract in 1993: Is there a General Doctrine of Good Faith?' (1993) 23 HKLJ 318.

[539] On the implication of terms, see Burrows, 'Contractual Co-operation and the Implied Term' (1968) 31 MLR 390 and Collins (1992) 55 MLR 556. See *Blackpool and Fylde Aero Club* v *Blackpool Borough Council* [1990] 1 WLR 1195 considered further in Chapter 3. Australian courts have gone further. In *Hughes Aircraft Systems International* v *Airservices Australia* (1997) 146 ALR 1 at 37–4 Finn J held that a duty of good faith is implied in law into all contracts (public body inviting tenders). See also *Livingstone* v *Roskilly* [1992] 3 NZLR 230 at 237 *per* Thomas J for a similar approach in New Zealand.

[540] Summers, 'Good Faith in General Contract Law and the Sales Provisions of the Uniform Commercial Code' (1968) 54 Virg Law Rev 195.

[541] The Restatement is an attempt by the American Law Institute, a private group of judges, lawyers and academics to state the rules of the common law. The first Restatement of Contracts was published in 1932 and the second in 1979.

[542] 2d Contracts, Art 205, Comment D.

types of bad faith is impossible ...'.[543] However, the most far-reaching definitions derive from continental law[544] and have been described as a complete reversal of the common law approach:[545]

> The principle of good faith which was adopted by Continental law postulates an *a priori* limitation of freedom of action in the bargaining process, subject to excuses or justifications exempting from liability. On the other hand, the position of English law is just the opposite: it is an *a priori* assumption of freedom in the bargaining process, subject to special rules imposing liability.

In France it has been said that: 'one of the most striking recent evolutions of French contract law has been the multiplication of pre-contractual duties of disclosure'.[546] Many duties are imposed by legislation[547] with a movement towards a general duty to disclose.[548] This statutory regulation is reinforced by case law interpreting provisions of the Civil Code relating to lack of consent (*vices du consentement*). A failure to disclose may be actionable on the basis of mistake (*erreur*) or fraud (*dol*) which extends to cover a failure to correct a known misunderstanding.[549]

Under German law[550] the parties to a contract are said to be under a primary obligation to perform. Additionally, they are subject to secondary obligations including an obligation to bargain in good faith and to deal fairly with each other (*Aukfklarungspflicht*).[551]

---

543 Other commentators have criticised the conservatism of this negative analysis. Burton, 'Breach of Contract and the Common Law Duty to Perform in Good Faith' (1980) 94 Harv L Rev 369 argues that the obligation to perform in good faith operates to limit contractual discretions whereby it is bad faith to seek to regain any opportunities forgone on contracting. Such a definition is only applicable to (and was only intended to be applicable to) the duty to perform in good faith.

544 The classic account is Kessler and Fine, 'Culpa in Contrahendo [Fault in Negotiations], Bargaining in Good Faith and Freedom of Contract: A Comparative Study' (1964) 77 Harv L Rev 401.

545 Cohen, 'Pre-contractual Duties: Two Freedoms and the Contract to Negotiate', ch. 2, pp. 31, 31 in Beatson and Friedman, *op. cit.*

546 Fabre-Magnan, 'Duties of Disclosure and French Contract Law', ch. 4 in Beatson and Friedmann, *op. cit.* See generally Ghestin, 'The Pre-Contractual Obligation to Disclose Information – French Report' in Harris and Tallon (eds) (1989) *Contract Law Today – Anglo-French Comparisons.*

547 Many of these duties relate to the disclosure of terms and have obvious English parallels, e.g. the requirement to inform debtors about the rate of interest applicable to their agreement (Law no. 66-1010, dated 28 December 1966 on Usury, Moneylending and Certain Acts Relating to Canvassing and Advertising, Art 4 on the disclosure of interest rates (*cf.* Consumer Credit (Agreements) Regulations 1983, SI 1983, No 1553), but others extend further to cover the disclosure of material facts, e.g. the disclosure requirements imposed upon issuers of publicly traded securities under the regulations of the Commission des Opérations de Bourse (*cf.* Financial Services Act 1986, s 146) and the duties of disclosure imposed upon parties to contracts of insurance by the Insurance Code (*cf.* the common law doctrine of *uberrimae fidei*).

548 *Ibid.*, p. 101.

549 By a decision of the Cour de Cassation dated 1 April 1954, Bull Civ, Section Sociale, no. 223 p. 171. The Cour de Cassation exercises a supervisory jurisdiction over all civil, commercial, social and criminal courts in France. Though technically only persuasive (there is no doctrine of binding precedent in France), its decisions are regarded as authoritative.

550 See generally Ebke and Steinhauer, 'The Doctrine of Good Faith in German Contract Law' in Beatson and Friedmann, *op. cit*, ch. 7.

551 See judgment of 12 November 1969, BGH, NJW 1970, 653, 655.

Do we have it?

The answer to this question follows *a fortiori* from our examination of the duty to disclose; if the English common law does not recognise a general duty of disclosure between parties negotiating a contract it must follow that it disclaims any wider concept of a duty owed between them. However, it should be noted that the present day position did not always pertain. In *Hodgson* v *Richardson*[552] Yates J laid down the general proposition that 'the concealment of material circumstances vitiates all contracts, upon the principles of natural law'. Better known perhaps is the reference by Lord Mansfield to good faith as the 'governing principle ... applicable to all contracts and dealings'.[553] However, this general conception did not survive long and is now confined to insurance contracts where it has meta-morphosed into the principle of *uberrimae fidei*.[554]

Rather what the common law now has are a number of disparate principles which do the work which a general doctrine of good faith in negotiations might be expected to do. These include, in addition to the situations considered above where, exceptionally, the common law imposes a duty to disclose on parties negotiating a contract, estoppel by convention, the law of misrepresentation, proprietary estoppel, the law of restitution in relation to 'failed' negotiations and collateral contracts. Other exceptional doctrines may also be said to represent the endorsement of a duty to negotiate in good faith. A good example is provided by the exception to the general rule that the courts will not enquire into the adequacy of consideration which is said to apply to salvage contracts.[555] Only a 'reasonable' consideration will be permitted in such contracts because otherwise the salvor might extract an extortionate price from a stricken vessel to tow it away from danger.[556] The result of this is that the practical difference between the civil law and common law is not as great as it may first appear. Thus, it would seem that the observation of Bingham LJ in *Interfoto Library* v *Stiletto*, with which we began our discussion of the negotiation stage of contracting, is amply justified.[557]

Express references to good faith are becoming a more common feature of

---

[552] 1 W Blac 463.

[553] *Carter* v *Boehm* (1766) 3 Burr 1905 at 1910.

[554] For a detailed description of this transformation, see Lord Mustill's judgment in *Pan Atlantic Insurance Co Ltd* v *Pine Top Insurance Co Ltd* [1994] 3 All ER 582.

[555] *The Kingalock* (1854) 1 Sp Ecc & Ad 263 and *The Port Caledonia* [1903] P 184.

[556] Further examples might be the restriction placed upon a party's election to tender his contractual performance and claim the contract price following a repudiatory breach by the other party; see *White and Carter (Councils) Ltd* v *McGregor* [1962] AC 413 and below pp. 456–66, or the protection offered to a party who in good faith purports to exercise a non-existent contractual power to terminate a contract; see *Woodar Investment Development Ltd* v *Wimpey Construction (UK) Ltd* [1980] 1 All ER 571 and below pp. 432–3. Of course, both doctrines deal with good faith performance rather than good faith negotiation.

[557] It is further supported by a fascinating study comparing the way different jurisdictions would deal with a number of hypothetical problems which concluded that 'there is a very considerable degree of harmony of result': Whittaker and Zimmermann, paper delivered at the SPTL annual conference in 1997.

English law.[558] Regulation 5(1) of the Unfair Terms in Consumer Contract Regulations 1999[559] defines an unfair term as 'any term which contrary to the requirement of good faith causes a significant imbalance in the parties' rights and obligations to the detriment of the consumer'. In general,[560] the regulations are not designed to police contractual negotiations but they do represent an explicit incorporation of good faith into the mainstream of English contract law.

It is sometimes said that 'one volunteer is worth ten conscripts'. Similar logic might suggest that the willing enthusiasm displayed by the Court of Appeal towards the concept of good faith in a number of recent cases[561] might be a more significant portend of how our law will develop than the explicit adoption of good faith in the regulations which were only enacted to fulfil our obligations under a European Community Directive.[562] Although the decisions broadly concerned the performance rather than the negotiation of contracts, the enthusiasm for embracing the concept of good faith might be significant.

Do we need it?

The answer to this question depends crucially upon which definition of good faith is being proposed and to which stage in the life of a contract it is meant to apply. In order to consider the full range of definitions of good faith, we examined those proposed in relation to the performance of contracts. Now we will consider whether English law should adopt any of these general principles in order to 'police' the negotiation stage of contracting. The minimal definition of good faith requires parties to be honest in their dealings. This requirement is unobjectionable and enforced by the tort of deceit. More contentious[563] is the proposal that English law should embrace a further requirement requiring parties to observe reasonable standards of

---

558 And also international commercial law. See the United Nations Convention on Contracts for the International Sale of Goods, Art 1.7 which requires regard to be had to the observance of good faith in international trade when interpreting its provisions. The 'Vienna Convention' as it is known seeks to bring a degree of uniformity to international trade by operating as a set of 'default rules' (i.e. they are to apply unless excluded) to regulate international trade contracts. It has been ratified by many major trading nations including China, France, Germany and the USA, but not yet by the United Kingdom.

559 SI 1999 No 2083.

560 With the exception of Sch 3 para 1(i) which deals with the disclosure of terms and is considered above.

561 *Timeload Ltd v British Telecommunications Ltd* [1995] EMLR 459; *Philips Electronique Grand Publique SA v British Sky Broadcasting Ltd* [1995] EMLR 472; *Balfour Beatty Civil Engineering v Docklands Light Railway* [1996] 78 BLR 42; *Zockoll Group Ltd v Mercury Communications Ltd* [1998] FSR 354.

562 Directive on Unfair Terms in Consumer Contracts (93/13/EEC).

563 Though, as we have seen, there is considerable debate as to whether, and if so to what extent, this is simply a novel packing for old established doctrines. A proponent of this view is Scalia J in the USA who described good faith as 'simply a rechristening of fundamental principles of contract law' in *Tymshare Inc v Covell* 727 F 2d 1145 at 1152 referring to the view of Farnsworth considered above.

fair dealing of the sort contemplated by the Uniform Commercial Code[564] which provides with respect to the sale of goods by a merchant that[565] good faith imports a requirement of honesty in fact as well as 'the observance of reasonable standards of fair dealing in the trade'.[566] There is undoubted enthusiasm for such change from academics[567] and an open mind towards the issue on the part of the government agencies charged with law reform[568] and latterly perhaps also the judiciary.[569] Yet, there are equally numerous and vociferous opponents.[570]

The outcome of this debate is not clear. It may be argued that such a broad principle is alien to the common law method whereby development is pragmatic and incremental, expanding a jurisdiction only by small departures from existing precedents. In other words, the way of the common law is to develop from the bottom upwards and not from the top down. As a historic statement this is certainly true, but, in the same way, it is also true to say that there must come a point when individual principles with a common purpose are welded together to yield a simpler, broader principle. The modern tort of negligence emerged in *Donoghue* v *Stevenson*[571] in this way. The proponents of good faith argue that the law relating to contractual negotiations now stands, as the law of tort of negligence did in 1932, in need of such unification.

---

[564] The Uniform Commercial Code is a statutory code that aims to unify the common law across the United States. All the states except Louisiana, which has a civil law tradition, have adopted it.

[565] Article 2-103(1)(b). See also Art 3-103(a)(4) where in relation to negotiable instruments good faith is defined as 'honesty in fact and the observance of reasonable commercial standards of fair dealing'.

[566] See also the Restatement (2d) of Contracts which provides: 'Every contract imposes upon each party a duty of good faith and fair dealing in its performance and its enforcement.'

[567] See Powell writing as long ago as 1956: 'Good Faith in Contracts' [1956] CLP 16. However, most of the enthusiasm is more recent, e.g. Adams and Brownsword (1995) *Key Issues in Contract* ch. 8 who distinguish between good faith as an exception to the usual freedom to indulge in self-interested behaviour and their preferred formulation of good faith as a rule where good faith in the sense of co-operative behaviour displaces self-interest as the predominant contract ideology. See also Brownsword, '"Good Faith in Contracts" Revisited' [1997] CLP 111. For a less theoretical appeal, see Harrison (1997) *Good Faith in Sales* who appears to suggest that we already have such a doctrine. This author appears to draw the conclusion that we have such a doctrine from the existence of principles that are compatible with it rather than from legislation or case law supporting such a general duty. It is suggested that if there exist principles consistent with such a duty there must still be an explicit recognition of such a duty before it can be said to exist.

[568] See Office of Fair Trading (1986), *A General Duty to Trade Fairly. A Discussion Paper*, especially paras 5.2 and 5.14.

[569] In addition to the four Court of Appeal cases cited above, see Lord Steyn writing extra-judicially in 'Contract Law: Fulfilling the Reasonable Expectations of Honest Men' (1997) 113 LQR 433, who at p. 439 discusses the case of *Walford* v *Miles* [1992] AC 128 and says, 'If the issue were to arise again, with the benefit of fuller argument, I would hope that the concept of good faith would not be rejected out of hand.'

[570] Bridge, 'Does Anglo Canadian Contract Law Need a Doctrine of Good Faith?' (1984) 9 Can Bus LJ 385, which question the author answers negatively at p. 413: 'because it has evolved sufficiently towards the protection of justified expectations'. See also Shell, 'Opportunism and Trust in the Negotiation of Commercial Contracts: Toward a New Cause of Action' (1991) 44 Vanderbilt L Rev 221.

[571] [1932] AC 562.

Another argument against the doctrine of good faith is that contempt which is born of unfamiliarity. The doctrine is seen as a continental intrusion which common lawyers will struggle to define and apply. Some of this reaction is simple xenophobia. Our legal system is insular in a literal sense only. We are a part of the European Union and thereby committed to the pursuit of a single market unencumbered by barriers and promoted by common practice. Already this has produced express reference to good faith in domestic legislation in the Unfair Terms in Consumer Contract Regulations 1994 and 1999. There also exist other pressures to unify our legal systems and in this regard the United Kingdom may not be able to 'hold out' against the uniform adoption of good faith by continental legal systems. Two different unifying projects already demonstrate this. First, for some years the Commission on European Contract Law (a non-governmental body comprised of lawyers from different European states) has been working on a Statement of the Principles of European Contract Law.[572] Article 1.102 provides that 'parties are free to enter into a contract and to determine its contents, subject to the requirements of good faith and fair dealing'. Further, Art 1.201 requires parties 'to co-operate in order to give full effect to the contract' and in Art 1.202 the obligation to act in good faith is made non-excludable. The precise ambit of these principles is not yet apparent and their impact upon pre-contractual negotiations will have to be worked out when they are invoked. Although the principles only necessarily apply when they are expressly adopted, courts may nonetheless refer to them when considering domestic disputes.[573] There are similar provisions contained in a code published by the International Institute for the Unification of Private Law (known as Unidroit).[574] This code is similar to the European code in a number of ways: it preserves the parties' freedom to enter a contract[575] but imposes on the parties an obligation to act in accordance 'with good faith and fair dealing' which duty is unexcludable.[576] Again, the effect of these principles upon pre-contractual negotiations will have to be worked out. Like the European code they will only necessarily apply when expressly adopted but may also be referred to by courts in other cases.[577] However, an important distinction is that the Unidroit code is designed to regulate international commercial contracts.

A more convincing argument against the introduction of a doctrine of good faith emphasises the uncertainty which such a doctrine would introduce into our law. Although it has become fashionable in recent years amongst academics to decry arguments of certainty as the last-ditch attempts of legal conservatives to maintain the status quo, none the less the objection is a powerful one. The common law does not like uncertainty for

---

[572] This is helpfully reproduced in Rose (ed.) (1998–9) *Blackstone's Statutes on Contract, Tort and Restitution*. 9th edn, pp. 424–45.
[573] Article 1.101.
[574] Unidroit Principles for International Commercial Contracts. Again, this code is helpfully reproduced in Rose *op. cit.* See pp. 445–61.
[575] Article 1.1.   [576] Article 1.7.   [577] Preamble.

good reason. To the extent that rules are uncertain, the costs of transactions increase. Greater sums are spent on drafting agreements to try to make good the deficiencies of the law but testing the efficacy of these measures in the courts is a most costly affair for everyone concerned. We are sometimes told that the average supermodel (is there such a thing?) will not get out of bed for less than £10,000, but such an offer might not even induce a top commercial lawyer to turn over to ask for more! Litigation is expensive. Further, most cases settle out of court. The effect of uncertainty in legal entitlements is to depress the level of out of court settlements. A litigant who is sure to win his day in court would not be prepared to accept less than the net value to him of the court award. However, a litigant who is not sure to win must discount that award by a factor reflecting the likelihood of losing, or more if like most litigants he is risk averse (not a risk taker).

The Israeli experience is instructive here. The Contracts (General Part) Law 1973, s 12(a) provides: 'in negotiating a contract, a person shall act in customary manner and in good faith'. One commentator[578] has observed that:

> the scope of this duty and its application under Israeli law are not altogether clear, either to litigants or to the judiciary and legal scholars … Hence, almost any negotiation is susceptible to future litigation, the results of which are unpredictable.

CONCLUSION

Drawing a conclusion from this prolonged examination of the negotiation process is difficult. The common law undoubtedly has a considerable armoury which it can deploy against those who seek to abuse the negotiation process. This armoury is indeed more extensive than many contract textbooks would suggest. This lack of publicity arises from the fact that the common purpose of some of these doctrines is often disguised because they feature in different parts of a traditional textbook or are only considered in textbooks on another branch of the law of obligations. That common purpose would be recognised and fostered if the existing doctrines were brought together under the umbrella of good faith. Such an aggregation might have resulted in a more sympathetic reception to parties who want their dealings to be conducted with reciprocal obligations of good faith.[579] It might also demystify the concept of good faith sufficiently to make common lawyers more comfortable with continental jurisprudence in general, which will only benefit us as a member of the European single market. Yet, there remains the powerful counter-argument of uncertainty which is not easily overcome. Perhaps the time has come to recognise such a duty but the problem of uncertainty would need to be met by only applying the new duty in circumstances which fell within or were closely analogous to the pre-existing doctrines.

---

[578] Cohen, ch. 2, pp. 53–4 in Beatson and Friedmann (eds) (1995) *Good Faith and Fault in Contract Law.*

[579] *Cf.* the discussion of *Walford* v *Miles* above.

PART II

THE BIRTH OF THE CONTRACT

3

AGREEMENT: OFFER AND ACCEPTANCE

INTRODUCTION

At this point it is necessary to observe a technical distinction, namely that between a 'simple' contract and a deed. The former is a contract constituted by the elements of agreement, an intention to create legal relations and supporting consideration. The first and second prerequisites of a simple contract are self-explanatory. Agreement states the law's insistence upon corresponding offer and acceptance; the requirement of contractual intention means that purely social and domestic arrangements are not usually enforceable in the courts. Perhaps the third prerequisite, that of consideration, needs further explanation. At its most basic, consideration is the price paid for a promise, i.e. that which is given in 'consideration' of it. This consideration may itself be another promise, in which case the contract is called a 'bilateral' one, or it may consist in the performance of an act, in which case the contract is described as 'unilateral'. Unilateral and bilateral contracts may, subject to some exceptions,[1] be written or oral. This book is concerned solely with simple contracts which, for the sake of brevity, we will henceforth simply describe as contracts. The phenomenon of agreement will be the subject of this chapter; the requirements of consideration and contractual intention will be examined in succeeding chapters.

By contrast, a deed must be written and needs no consideration. It provides a mechanism by which gratuitous promises (i.e. these not made in return for anything) can be made binding. Therefore, deeds have more in common with the law of gift than the law of contract, the latter being based upon mutual exchange, i.e. upon 'bargain'. Deeds tend also to be used in connection with more formal dealings, the purchase of land, building and engineering contracts. Although a deed is not a requirement of such

---

[1] For example, a contract for the sale or other disposition of an interest in land must be made in writing: Law of Property (Miscellaneous Provisions) Act 1989, s 2. See below for an examination of the other formal requirements.

contracts,[2] and the contracts described will always be enforceable as 'simple' contracts, none the less, the use of a deed offers an important advantage. This is that the time within which an action for breach of any obligation assumed must be brought is longer when that obligation is contained in a deed. In the case of deeds, the 'limitation' period is 12 years;[3] for simple contracts it is generally six years;[4] and only three years if damages are claimed in respect of personal injury suffered as a result of negligence, nuisance or breach of duty.[5] This longer limitation is especially attractive in such contracts when a breach of contract may not manifest itself for a number of years.

A number of important points emerge from this general discussion which bear repetition. First, the law of contract is concerned with the enforcement of bargains and not with gifts. Another is that there is a divergence between the lawyers' vocabulary and common usage of the word contract. To the lawyer a contract is a bundle of legal obligations created by agreement, contractual intention and consideration. However, many people use the word contract to refer to a written document. In other words, the common usage seems to rest upon confusion between the form and substance of legal obligation. This may explain why people are not immediately aware how often in their daily lives they enter contracts; it is not only when they start a new job or rent a house but also each time they buy a newspaper or catch a bus.

As you consider the cases which follow, try to think about two related questions which we will take up during the course of the chapter. First, how well does the law of offer and acceptance deal with the great diversity of factual situations, which fall within its ambit? These range from complex, high-value transactions between nationals of different countries, e.g. international sale contracts to low-value consumer contracts, such as buying a train ticket or putting money into a ticket machine in a car park. Second, how do the courts arrive at a resolution of the dispute they are called upon to adjudicate? Is it by the application of clear rules or do they reach an instinctive justice, aided by little more than an intuitive but unarticulated sense of fairness concealed by a smokescreen of rule, sub-rule and exception so malleable that it could be moulded to support any conclusion? As it is sometimes put, do the courts reason *to* a conclusion or *from* one?

OFFERS AND INVITATIONS TO TREAT

An offer is a definite promise to be bound, provided that certain terms are met. A vague invitation to begin negotiating does not amount in law to an

---

[2] As they are, for example, in respect of the creation of a lease for more than three years; see Law of Property Act 1925, ss 52, 54(2).
[3] Limitation Act 1980, s 8(1).
[4] Limitation Act 1980, s 5.
[5] Whether the injury arises out of a breach of contract or not: Limitation Act 1980, s 11. However, this period may be extended under s 33.

offer and is referred to as an invitation to treat. This can be illustrated by reference to the famous case of *Carlill* v *Carbolic Smoke Ball Co.*[6]

The defendant company manufactured a product called the 'Carbolic Smoke Ball'. In an advertisement it offered to pay £100 to anyone who caught influenza after having used the Smokeball in a specified way, and stated that it had deposited £1,000 with its bankers to demonstrate the company's 'sincerity' in this matter. The claimant, who had used the Smokeball in the prescribed way and caught influenza, claimed the £100.

The defendant advanced a number of arguments in order to avoid liability, including the suggestion that the advertisement was a mere sales 'puff' and not intended to have legal effect. From this argument and the way it was rejected by the Court of Appeal it can be seen that there is a close relationship between the distinction we are presently considering and the requirement of an intention to create legal relations. In *Carlill* the Court of Appeal pointed to the deposit of money the defendant claimed to have made with its bankers in order to reject the argument that the promise was not a serious one. Two consequences followed from this: the advertisement was an offer and there was an intention to create legal relations.

Unfortunately, the distinction between offers and invitations to treat is as easy to state as it is, in some situations, difficult to apply. Ultimately, the proper classification of a statement as either an offer or an invitation to treat is said to depend upon the intention of the parties. However, the question then simply becomes how do the courts ascertain whether a statement was intended to be an offer or an invitation to treat? The answer to this question depends upon whether there is any direct evidence of that intention. In *Gibson* v *Manchester City Council*[7] the courts examined closely the language of the communications between the parties in order to discover their intention. The council treasurer replied in the following terms to an expression of interest by the claimant tenant in purchasing his house, which was owned by the council:

> The Corporation may be prepared to sell the house to you at the purchase price of £2,725 less 20% = £2,180 (freehold) ... If you would like to make a formal application to buy your council house, please complete the enclosed application form ...

Following a change of political control of the council, the new majority party wished to halt the sale of all council houses which it was not already contractually obliged to complete. The House of Lords considered that the use of the non-committal phrase '*may* be prepared to sell' (emphasis added) was, in Lord Diplock's words, 'fatal' to the claimant's assertion that the council's letter was a contractual offer which was accepted by the claimant's submission of a formal application. This despite the fact that the most important contractual term, the price, was precisely specified. The House of

---

[6] [1892] 2 QB 484. See the fascinating discussion of the background to the case by Simpson at (1985) 14 LS 345.
[7] [1979] 1 WLR 294.

Lords drew a distinction between an agreement about the price at which the vendor would be prepared to sell and his preparedness to sell in the first place; the first was established but the second was not.[8] This conclusion was supported by the reference to a further formal application. The consequence of this interpretation was that the council had not entered a binding contract to sell the council house. This result may be contrasted with the outcome of *Storer* v *Manchester City Council*,[9] another case arising out of the change of policy on the part of Manchester City Council. In this case the Court of Appeal held that there was a binding contract for the sale of a council house when the tenant completed and returned the formal agreement for sale. The unequivocal language of the formal agreement was sufficient to demonstrate the intention that it be a contractual communication and the council's letter disclosed an intention to bring forward the date of contracting. In contracts for the sale of land the usual rule that parties become bound upon the 'exchange of contracts' (meaning the exchange of completed, signed formal contracts) was displaced by the treasurer's letter which advised the tenant to *immediately* insure the property.

Two caveats

Even where there is direct evidence of the parties' intention, two caveats must be entered. First, the language used by the parties is never determinative. That a communication is expressed to be an 'offer' does not conclude the question; the courts look to the substance rather than the form of the communication. So when the defendant wrote to the claimant stating that he was 'prepared to offer' him property at a particular price, this letter may none the less be held not to constitute an offer.[10] A further example is provided by the situation where a company 'offers' shares for public sale. Such 'offers' are in fact treated as invitations to members of the public to themselves offer to buy the shares.[11]

The second caveat is simply a reminder that, as we have seen, the

---

[8] See also *Bigg* v *Boyd Gibbons Ltd* [1971] 2 All ER 183 where the Court of Appeal expressly drew this distinction. In *Harvey* v *Facey* [1893] AC 552 the House of Lords relied upon the distinction in dubious circumstances. The appellants telegraphed the respondents 'Will you sell us Bumper Hall Pen? [a property in Jamaica] Telegraph lowest cash price', to which the respondent replied: 'Lowest cash price for Bumper Hall Pen, £900'. The appellants then replied: 'We agree to buy Bumper Hall Pen for £900 asked by you ...'. The House of Lords held that the first telegram asked two questions but that only the second was answered. However, on the facts of the case it could be said that a positive answer to the first question was implicit in the reply to the second question.

[9] [1974] 3 All ER 824.

[10] *Clifton* v *Palumbo* [1944] 2 All ER 497 and *Spencer* v *Harding* (1870) LR 5 CP 561 where a circular containing an 'offer ... for sale by tender ...' was held to be an invitation to treat only. See also *Bigg* v *Boyd Gibbons Ltd* [1971] 2 All ER 183, although the statement was made *obiter dicta* as the relevant communication was in fact held to be an offer.

[11] *Hebb's Case* (1867) LR 4 Eq 9; *National Westminster Bank plc* v *IRC* [1994] 3 All ER 1 at 7. *Cf.* a letter to a shareholder announcing a rights issue (where a company 'offers' new shares to shareholders in proportion to their existing shareholding) which was held to constitute a contractual offer in *Jackson* v *Turquand* (1869) LR 4 HL 305.

intentions of the parties are ascertained *objectively*. The secret uncommunicated subjective intentions of the parties are not usually relevant. Rather parties are considered to intend what a reasonable interpretation of their words and deeds would suggest.[12]

Where there is no direct evidence of the parties' intention, the proper classification of a communication as either an invitation to treat or an offer is an even more difficult task. This difficulty arises in part because the distinction is not one of kind but rather one of degree; the more vague and 'woolly' the communication is, the more likely it is to be intended to be an invitation to treat. As with all judgements of degree, clear cases are easy to characterise but in between there lies a grey area which is more difficult. It is only possible to get an insight into where the courts are likely to draw the line by examining their approach to particular factual situations in the past.

Advertisements

In an American case *Lefkowitz* v *Great Minneapolis Surplus Store*[13] the defendants placed an advertisement in a newspaper which said:

Saturday 9 am sharp; 3 brand new fur coats, worth to $100, First come first served, $1 each.

In response to this and another similar advertisement, the claimant was the first customer to present himself at the appointed times but the defendant refused to sell a coat to him. The claimant was successful in his action for breach of contract, the Supreme Court of Minnesota held that the advertisement amounted to an offer. More precisely, the offer was a unilateral one, i.e. a 'reward' was promised in exchange for an act by the promisee (use of the smoke ball and catching influenza, being first in the queue at the sale) who did not herself or himself assume an obligation. In each case the only obligation assumed by the promisee derived from separate contracts to purchase the goods in question. The difference between the cases lies in the fact that in *Carlill* the contract to purchase the smoke ball was part of the condition stipulated by the promisor, whereas in *Lefkowitz* entering the contract for the purchase of the coat was the reward offered if a different condition was satisfied.

In *Partridge* v *Crittenden*[14] the court had to consider the status of an advertisement which the defendant placed in the classified advertisements section of a specialist periodical which read 'Bramblefinch cocks and hens, 25s each'. The question of whether the advertisement was an offer or an invitation to treat arose in the context of criminal proceedings as under Protection of Birds Act 1954 it was an offence to offer these birds for sale. If the advertisement was an offer, the defendant was guilty; if it was an

---

[12] *Smith* v *Hughes* (1871) LR 6 QB 597 and *Centrovincial Estates* v *Merchant Investors* [1983] Com LR 158.

[13] (1957) 86 NW 2d 689.

[14] [1968] 2 All ER 421.

invitation to treat, he was not. The Divisional Court quashed his conviction.

The differing conclusions of the courts in *Carlill* and *Lefkowitz* where the advertisements were held to be offers, and *Partridge* v *Crittenden* where it was not, means that there can be no sweeping generalisation about the status of advertisements. However, the following factors seem to be important. First, in *Carlill* there was other evidence to support the implication of an offer, the deposit of £1,000. Second, the status of the statement seems to be linked with the status of the defendant. Where the defendant is a manufacturer of goods, it is easier to conclude that the advertisement was intended to be an offer capable of acceptance by anyone to whom it was addressed because as a manufacturer he may be supposed to be in a position to satisfy the anticipated demand. However, where the good advertised is not manufactured but produced with the assistance of some natural process, as in *Partridge* v *Crittenden*, it is not so easy to assume that the supplier intends to be bound to supply the good to everyone who replies to the advertisement lest he become subject to a demand he cannot satisfy. Another way to reconcile and generalise the decisions of *Carlill*, *Lefkowitz* and *Partridge* v *Crittenden* is by reference to the type of contract that the advertisement immediately contemplated. In *Carlill* and *Lefkowitz* it included a *unilateral* one involving the exchange of a promise for an act (see above); in *Partridge* v *Crittenden* only a *bilateral* contract was envisaged involving the mutual exchange of promises (a promise to buy and a promise to sell). In *Carlill* Bowen LJ said:

> [This] is not like cases in which you offer to negotiate or you issue advertisements that you have got a stock ... to sell ... in which case there is no offer to be bound by any contract. Such advertisements are offers to negotiate – offers to receive offers – offers to chaffer ...

This factor may be further illustrated by a New Zealand case[15] where a local authority placed newspaper advertisements stating that it intended to sell plots of land at advertised prices and that if there were too many bids for any plot a ballot would be held. The advertisement was held to amount to a unilateral offer to hold a ballot and enter a contract for sale with the winner which offer was accepted by parties who replied stating their preparedness to pay the price demanded.

A different approach would be to emphasise what the defendant in each case received. In *Carlill* and *Lefkowitz* the advertisements were supposed to stimulate consumer interest *which the very facts of the case* reveal that they did. Why should the defendants receive the benefit of their marketing strategies and at the same time deny any liability to pay for them? By contrast, the court in *Partridge* v *Crittenden* was not confronted with a defendant who was simultaneously claiming the benefit of and disclaiming the burden of a marketing strategy.[16] If this consideration influenced the courts, the cases provide an example of courts reasoning *from* a conclusion.

---

15 *Markholm Construction Ltd* v *Wellington City Council* [1985] 2 NZLR 520.
16 Although in other respects he was not particularly deserving of sympathy.

The courts' approach to circulars and price lists provides a good example of the application of the above factors. In *Grainger & Son* v *Gough*[17] a price list issued by a wine merchant was considered to be an invitation to treat on the basis that a merchant could not be taken to have intended his list to constitute an offer which could be accepted by a large number of customers when he only had finite supplies of each vintage. Perhaps the position would have been different if he was the château owner in control of the means of production. The court might also have been influenced by the fact that the list contemplated the formation of a bilateral contract only.

It should be stressed that the checklist of factors considered above will often be influential but that sometimes decisions in this area seem a little quixotic. For instance, it is difficult to explain the classification of a notice advertising deck chairs for hire as an offer.[18] Perhaps the fact that the claimant suffered personal injury when the deckchair collapsed evoked particular sympathy in the court and, therefore, caused it to favour recovery, though this seems unlikely. Hence, the case must stand as a warning about the danger of relying upon generalisations in this area.[19]

Advertisements are subject to legal control beyond that exercised by the civil law considered above. As we saw in *Partridge* v *Crittenden*, the law may attach criminal consequences to certain types of advertisement. However, other criminal provisions are of more general application than the Protection of Birds Act 1954 which was discussed in that case. For example the Consumer Protection Act 1987, s 20 makes it 'an offence … in the course of any business … [to give] to any customers an indication which is misleading as to the price at which any goods, services, accommodation or facilities are available …'. A store's claim that it will 'beat any TV HiFi and video price by £20 on the spot' was held to have contravened this enactment.[20]

Displays of goods

Similar considerations have certainly influenced courts when they have considered whether the display of goods in shop windows amounts to an offer for sale. In *Fisher* v *Bell*[21] this question arose, again in the context of a criminal prosecution, when the defendant displayed in his shop a 'flick-knife' the sale of which is a criminal offence. It was held that the display did not amount to an offer for sale. The court was heavily influenced by the fact that a shopkeeper could not normally be taken to intend to commit himself to supply the displayed good to everyone who walks into the shop and 'accepts' the offer constituted by the display.

---

[17] [1896] AC 325. The question arose out of legislation which sought to subject to tax those exercising a trade in the United Kingdom.

[18] *Chapelton* v *Barry UDC* [1940] 1 KB 532.

[19] See, for example, *Denton* v *GN Ry* (1856) 5 E & B 860, considered below, where a railway timetable was held to constitute an offer to run trains at the times contained therein.

[20] *R* v *Warwickshire County Council, ex parte Johnson* [1993] AC 583.

[21] [1961] 1 QB 394.

In *Pharmaceutical Society of Great Britain* v *Boots*[22] the Court of Appeal had to identify the precise time when a contract was concluded in a self-service store. The court considered that this required them to decide whether the display of goods on open shelves in a self-service shop amounted to an offer of goods for sale. The question arose because a statute required certain substances to be sold only under the supervision of a registered pharmacist. In the store the pharmacist was near the cash desk and could intervene if necessary to prevent a customer from taking any medicine. The claimants, who were responsible for enforcing the statutory provisions, argued that placing goods on open display constituted a contractual offer which was accepted by the customers when they placed them in their basket and that, as the sale was concluded before the pharmacist had the opportunity to intervene, Boots had failed to comply with the statute. The Court of Appeal held that the display of goods was an invitation to treat and that the customer at the cash desk made the offer[23] and so the pharmacist was afforded an adequate opportunity to intervene and, if necessary, prevent the sale.

This analysis was justified by reference to the perceived absurdity that would result if the display of the goods on open shelves was considered to be an offer. The court thought that 'one of the most formidable difficulties' of such a view would be that the placing of the goods in the customer's basket would amount to an acceptance and thereby, in theory at least, preclude him from changing his mind and replacing the goods on the shelves. This is open to two objections. First, it simply does not follow from the hypothetical premise that the display is an offer and that the customer placing the goods in his basket is the acceptance. The acceptance might still take place at the cash desk thereby permitting the customer to change his mind. Indeed, a conclusion as to the exact time of acceptance was no part of the decision in *Boots* and so does not form part of the *ratio decidendi* of the case.[24] Second, the concern for the customer seems overstated and unsupported by any empirical evidence. It is apparently premised upon 'greedy' behaviour on the part of shopkeepers which is inconsistent with the increasingly generous replacement policies operated by larger retailers.

Interestingly, in a number of cases decided in the United States the courts have held that the contract was concluded before the customer reached the cash desk. In *Sancho-Lopez* v *Fedor Food Corp,*[25] the claimant was injured when a carbonated drink exploded when he was removing it from his basket and approaching the cashier's desk. The court held that the contract had already been concluded at the time of the injury and so the claimant successfully sued for breach of an implied warranty in the contract of sale.

---

[22] [1952] 2 QB 795.
[23] *Cf.* the criminal case of *R* v *Morris* [1984] AC 320 where for the purposes of the offence of theft it was held that the switching of labels on goods and removing them from the shelf amounted to an 'appropriation' of the goods.
[24] See Jackson [1979] 129 NLJ 775.
[25] (1961) 211 NYS (2d) 953.

Other cases in the United States support the view that a contract is concluded before the goods are accepted for payment.[26] The apparent inconsistency between the decisions in *Boots* and *Sancho Lopez* may be resolved if they are both regarded as expressions of a desire to protect consumers. In *Boots* the English Court of Appeal thought, wrongly,[27] that the protection of a dithering consumer's freedom of action required that the contract be concluded at the cash desk, but the decision in *Sancho-Lopez* recognises that the moment of contractual formation must be brought forward to offer the consumer effective redress[28] in the event of personal injury.[29] Again, the courts appear to be reasoning from, rather than to, just solutions.

Auctions

At common law an auctioneer's call for bids is an invitation to treat and the bidders make the contractual offers which the auctioneer accepts by the fall of the hammer, at which point a bilateral contract comes into existence.[30] It follows from this that until the fall of the hammer, a bidder is free to withdraw his offer. The Sale of Goods Act 1979, s 57(2) confirms that this is the case:

> A sale by auction is complete when the auctioneer announces its completion by the fall of the hammer, or in other customary manner; and until the announcement is made any bidder may retract his bid.

Auctions may be subject to a reserve (minimum price).[31] Where this is so, no contract is formed between the buyer and seller if the auctioneer purports to accept a bid below the reserve price.[32] However, where the auction is not subject to any reserve, it is unlawful for the seller, or anyone acting on his behalf, to bid for the property.[33] In such circumstances contractual relations

---

[26] *Gillespie v Great Atlantic & Pacific Stores* (1972) 187 SE 2d 441 and *Sheeskin v Giant Food Inc* (1974) 318 A 2d 874, but *cf. Lasky v Economy Grocery Stores* (1946) 65 NE (2d) 305 where in similar circumstances a claimant failed in her action for personal injury suffered as she was placing the bottle in her basket the court preferring the view that no contract was concluded before the customer reached the cashier's desk.

[27] In both *Gillespie v Great Atlantic & Pacific Stores* (1972) 187 SE 2d 441 and *Sheeskin v Giant Food Inc* (1974) 318 A 2d 874 the acceptance was said to be subject to a power to cancel at any time before reaching the cash desk.

[28] Liability in contract would be established without proof of fault on the part of the shopkeeper (i.e. so-called 'strict liability'), whereas at common law the liability of the manufacturer would be dependent upon the proof of fault on his behalf. See *Grant v Australian Knitting Mills* [1936] AC 85 (itchy underwear). Since 1987 the manufacturer may be liable under the provisions of the Consumer Protection Act of that year. Although liability is not fault-based, it is limited by certain defences and restrictions inherent in the definition of a 'defective' good. See generally Howath (1995) *Textbook on Tort*, pp. 410–30.

[29] *Cf.* above the discussion of *Chapelton v Barry UDC* [1940] 1 KB 532.

[30] *Payne v Cave* (1789) 3 Term Rep 148.

[31] If land is to sold by auction, it is a requirement that the auction be expressed to be with or without reserve. See Sale of Land by Auction Act 1875, s 5.

[32] *McManus v Fortescue* [1907] 2 KB 1.

[33] Sale of Goods Act 1979, s 57(4).

might exist between the auctioneer and a bidder. It has been held[34] *obiter dicta*[35] that where an auction is held 'without reserve', if the auctioneer fails to accept the highest bid, he will be in breach of contract towards the disappointed bidder.[36]

Where an auction is advertised, it has been held, consistently with the other advertisement cases considered above, that the advertisement does not constitute an offer. Therefore, someone who travels to an auction to bid for an advertised lot which was subsequently withdrawn cannot recover damages for breach of contract.[37] This result is consistent with the other advertisement cases to the extent that a bilateral rather than a unilateral contract was contemplated by the advertisement but inconsistent in so far as the facts of the case reveal that the claimant suffered loss by responding to the advertisement in the manner contemplated; why should defendants receive the benefit of their marketing strategies and at the same time deny any liability to pay damages caused by reliance upon it?[38]

Tenders

A statement that goods are to be sold by tender and an invitation to tender for the supply of goods do not usually constitute contractual offers. Rather the offer is considered to be made by the party who submits a tender, which may be accepted by the original invitor. In *Spencer* v *Harding*[39] the defendants published a circular 'to offer ... for sale by tender' the stock in trade of a business. The claimants' contention that the circular amounted to a contractual offer to sell to the highest bidder was rejected by the court of Common Pleas on the ground that 'there is a total absence of any words to intimate that the highest bidder is to be the purchaser' rather '[i]t is a mere attempt to ascertain whether an offer can be obtained ...'.[40] If the invitation contains any express language reserving the right of the invitor to refuse any tender, it follows *a fortiori* that the invitation cannot amount to a contractual offer. This was the situation in an Australian case where a prospectus issued

---

[34] *Warlow* v *Harrison* (1859) 1 E & E 309, applied by the Court of Appeal in *Barry* v *Davies* [2000] 1 WLR 1962 (auction without reserve – auctioneer refused two bids of £200 as too low; bidder entitled to over £27,500 damages based on market value of goods less amount bid and expenses). This principle was implicitly approved by the House of Lords in *Harvela Investments Ltd* v *Royal Trust Co of Canada Ltd* [1986] AC 207, a case involving a sale by tender rather than by auction considered below.

[35] Because the claimant's pleadings were defective.

[36] *Per* Martin B on the basis that the seller has warranted that the sale will be without reserve, *per* Bramwell and Willes JJ on the narrower ground that the auctioneer was in breach of a warranty that he had authority to sell without reserve.

[37] *Harris* v *Nickerson* (1873) LR 8 QB 286.

[38] Would the application of this criterion support the advertisement being an offer in a case like *Harris* v *Nickerson* where the auction took place but not where the auction was cancelled altogether?

[39] (1870) LR 5 CP 561.

[40] See also *Rookes* v *Dawson* [1895] 1 Ch 480 where the claimant, who secured the highest mark in a scholarship examination but was none the less refused the scholarship, failed in his action for breach of contract. Quaere whether he would have succeeded if the scholarship was awarded to a candidate with lower marks.

by a local authority inviting financial institutions to advance it loans of money contained language which reserved a right to the authority to decline to accept any particular tender[41] and in a New Zealand case where a notice from a local authority advertising a sale of property by tender contained the phrase 'highest or any tender not necessarily accepted'.[42]

In contrast, where the invitation to tender expressly states that the invitor will accept the highest (in the case of a sale[43]) or lowest (in the case of an invitation to supply goods or do work[44]) tender, the invitation will be held to constitute a contractual offer. In *Harvela Investments Ltd v Royal Trust Co of Canada*[45] the House of Lords had to consider whether an invitation to tender for the purchase of shares which stated that the vendor would accept the highest 'offer' was itself an offer to sell. Given the expressed intention of the vendor that he would sell to the highest bidder, the House of Lords concluded that the invitation to tender was a contractual offer.[46] More precisely, it was a unilateral offer,[47] a promise (to accept the highest bid) given in exchange for an act (the submission of a bid). The main contract for the sale of the shares which the vendor[48] was obliged to enter with the party who submitted the highest bid submitted in conformity with the invitation[49] would itself be a bilateral contract whereby the tenderer promised to pay the sum bid in exchange for vendor's promise to transfer the shares.

Exceptionally, an invitation to tender may be held to constitute a contractual offer even though the invitation does not expressly oblige the invitor to accept any tender. In *Blackpool and Fylde Aero Club v Blackpool Borough Council*[50] the defendants invited tenders for a pleasure flight

---

41 *Meudell v Mayor etc. of Bendigo* (1900) 26 VLR 158.
42 *Gregory v Rangitikei District Council* [1995] 2 NZLR 208.
43 For example, *Harvela Investments Ltd v Royal Trust Co of Canada* [1986] AC 207 considered below.
44 *Pratt Contractors Ltd v Palmerston North City Council* [1995] 1 NZLR 469 (invitation to submit tenders for the construction of a flyover).
45 [1986] AC 207.
46 A similar result would be reached if the invitor stated that he would *purchase* goods or services at the *lowest* tendered price. *William Lacey (Hounslow) Ltd v Davis* [1957] 1 WLR 932 at 939.
47 Somewhat puzzlingly, Lord Diplock refers to the telex containing the invitation to tender as a contract rather than an offer. *Cf. MJB Enterprises v Defence Corporation Ltd* [1999] 1 SCR 619 which doubts whether the invitation to submit tenders should be considered to be a unilateral contract on the ground that such a contract would leave the tenderer free of obligation.
48 The highest tenderer did not come under any obligation until his tender was accepted, although, of course, the vendor was obliged to accept the tender. Again, somewhat puzzlingly, Lord Diplock seems to suggest that a bilateral contract comes into existence independently of the vendor's acceptance of the tender.
49 The invitation was held to impliedly exclude referential bids (any bid which can only be quantified by reference to rival bids). This aspect of the case is considered below at p. 131. An invitation may also be held to exclude the correction after submission of contradictions or ambiguities discovered in the bids according to *Vachon Construction v Cariboo (Regional District)* (1996) 136 DLR (4th) 307 at 316 *per* Finch JA, or bids containing hand-written additions to the required form of tender according to *MJB Enterprises v Defence Corporation* [1999] 1 SCR 619.
50 [1990] 1 WLR 1195. Adams and Brownsword, 'More in Expectation than Hope; The Blackpool Airport Case' (1991) 54 MLR 281.

concession but failed to consider a tender submitted by the claimants in conformity with the procedure laid down. The Court of Appeal held that on the facts of the case the invitation to tender constituted a contractual offer to consider all tenders submitted in accordance with the procedure prescribed by the defendants. In the view of the court, this was justified by a number of exceptional features,[51] the contractual significance of which is open to question. What distinguishes the case from the contention of the claimant in *Spencer* v *Harding* and justifies its earlier treatment is the nature of the contractual offer. In *Spencer* v *Harding* the claimant argued that the invitation to tender constituted a contractual offer to sell to the highest tenderer, in the *Blackpool* case the claimants alleged that the invitation to tender constituted a contractual offer to consider all conforming tenders. The obligation contended for by the claimants in the *Blackpool* case fell short of an obligation to enter the main contract with them.[52] In this sense they were claiming that there had been an abuse of the negotiating process (by the breach of a contractual obligation which was collateral to the main contemplated contract), which is why we examined the case earlier[53] where we saw that the English courts were prepared to accept the idea of a duty to consider but have authoritatively rejected as unworkable the concept of a duty to negotiate in good faith (i.e. to consider fairly).[54] The *Blackpool* decision may be criticised on a number of grounds. The exceptional features said to justify the imposition of a duty to consider are unconvincing; such a duty would not preclude the council from examining the tender[55] and then

---

[51] Tenders were solicited from selected parties known to the invitor, where the invitation prescribes a clear procedure (common form of tender, anonymity secured by the provision of special envelopes) and an absolute deadline. See also the New Zealand case of *Pratt Contractors Ltd* v *Palmerston North City Council* [1995] 1 NZLR 469 at 478 where a similar duty arose because the tendering process 'was not ... a mere calling for tenders ... contractors [were required] to register their interest and pay a ... non-refundable deposit [and] the tender documents were extensive, detailed and substantial'.

[52] The duty imposed by foreign courts would appear to be more extensive: In Canada, see *MJB Enterprises* v *Defence Corporation Ltd* [1999] 1 SCR 619 '*At a minimum*, the respondent offered ... to consider bids ...' (emphasis added); in New Zealand, see *Pratt Contractors* v *Palmerston North City Council* [1995] 1 NZLR 469 at 483 where it was conceded that '... the council was obliged to proceed in a manner which met the general requirements of that rather indefinable term "fairness" ...;' and in Australia, see *Hughes Aircraft Systems International* v *Airservices Australia* (1997) 146 ALR 1 where it said that a term could easily be implied to the effect that the invitor should conduct the tender process fairly (though this referred to fairness in the sense of equal treatment for all tenderers rather than a duty to consider fairly each individual tender).

[53] See above, p. 93.

[54] *Walford* v *Miles* [1992] 2 AC 128. *Cf.* the Canadian courts which have no problem with the concept and will impose such a duty even where a so called 'privilege clause' expressly reserves to the invitor the right not to accept the lowest, or indeed any, tender. See *Best Cleaners and Contractors Ltd* v *Canada* [1985] 2 FC 293 at 306–7 *per* Mahoney JA; *Chinook Aggregates Ltd* v *Abbotsford (Mun. Dist)* [1989] 40 BCLR (2d) 345 at 350 *per* Legg JA; and *Vachon Construction* v *Cariboo (Regional District)* (1996) 136 DLR (4th) 307 at 316 *per* Finch JA.

[55] Regulations have been introduced to give effect to EC Directives which aim to ensure that there is no discrimination between nationals of member countries when considering tenders for major public works: SI 1991 No. 2679.

rejecting it for some irrational ground[56] and, in the event of a successful action, damages would be difficult to assess.[57]

In *Harvela* a second issue dominated the House of Lord's discussion of the contractual implications of the tendering process. This was the status of a 'referential bid' that is one which cannot be quantified other than by reference to another bid. In the case two bids were submitted: the first $2.175m and the second referential bid of $2.1m or $0.101m in excess of any other offer, whichever is higher. The vendor accepted the second bid of $2.276 ($2.175m + $0.101m). The House of Lords held that the vendor should have accepted the first bid as the object of the process was to secure the highest bid and this would be undermined if referential bids were admitted.[58] For instance, what would have been the outcome if both parties bid $1 or $1 more than any other party? If such bids were valid, has each party bid $infinity? Enforcing such a judgment would be a taxing job for the bailiffs!

It is interesting to compare the approaches of Lords Diplock and Templeman in the House of Lords. Lord Diplock sought to apply the traditional analysis of offer and acceptance to reason to a conclusion as to the existence and content of any contractual obligations assumed. In contrast, Lord Templeman begins with an examination of the policy basis of the tendering process and then stipulates a contractual analysis that is consistent with those underlying policies. In other words, he appears to be reasoning from a conclusion about what the tendering process is meant to achieve.

A different factual setting for the use of tenders is in building and civil engineering where for large projects a general contractor will employ a number of sub-contractors who submitted tenders for part of the work. To the question 'At what point does the sub-contractor become bound by the terms of the tender he submits?' the traditional answer is 'Assuming the tender to be a contractual offer, when it is accepted'. This may produce a problem for the general contractor who has already relied on the sub-contractor's bid in order to compute his own bid for the job. Different jurisdictions have devised different techniques to deal with this apparent problem. In Canada it has been held that the sub-contractor is contractually

---

[56] It could, of course, reject the tender after consideration e.g. on the basis of a conflict of interest between a tenderer and a council executive *Fairclough Building* v *Port Talbot BC* [1990] 62 BLR 82.

[57] The difficulty in assessing damages is a result of the nature of the obligation breached. Where the offer is to contract with the party who submits the highest (sale) or lowest (supply) tender, damages may be awarded on a full expectation basis, e.g. in *Pratt Contractors Ltd* v *Palmerston North City Council* [1995] 1 NZLR 469 the disappointed tenderer was awarded damages based upon the benefit to him of the contract to build the flyover. However, as in the *Blackpool* case where the offer is to consider all conforming tenders, the invitor's breach of contract has deprived the invitee of the opportunity of having his bid considered, a much less valuable thing.

[58] See also the New Zealand case of *Pratt Contractors Ltd* v *Palmerston North City Council* [1995] 1 NZLR 469 where a tender to build a flyover for $250,000 less than any other conforming tender was considered invalid.

bound not to withdraw his tender[59] and in the United States the doctrine of promissory estoppel has been used to justify a similar conclusion.[60] In this country the Law Commission has provisionally recommended that a party who, in the course of a business, makes an offer which he states will not be revoked for a particular length of time should be liable to pay damages to the offeree for the breach of such promise.[61] However, an empirical study by Lewis[62] revealed interesting evidence about the behaviour of general and sub-contractors. The study reveals that it is common practice for general contractors to show the lowest bid to other tenderers in order to persuade other tenderers to reduce their bids (so-called 'bid shopping'). Indeed, unsuccessful sub-contractors may themselves seek details of the lowest bid in order to re-tender at a more competitive price (so-called 'bid pedalling'). Therefore, it would seem that neither general contractors nor sub-contractors would welcome the introduction of an obligation upon a 'sub' not to withdraw his bid or any further obligation on a 'general' to accept the lowest bid on the basis that both parties prefer to preserve their freedom of action. This limited study emphasises a very important lesson for those proposing law reform (including the writers of textbooks!). Empirical need must be *demonstrated* and not simply *asserted* to justify law reform.

The United Kingdom's membership of the European Union has had a considerable impact upon the award of major procurement contracts. Regulations have been introduced over recent years to give effect to European Directives, which aim to secure equality of opportunity for the nationals of all member countries in relation to the award of major contracts of public work. These regulations include the Public Works Contracts Regulations 1991,[63] Public Services Contracts Regulations 1993,[64] Public Supply Contracts Regulations 1995[65] and the Utilities Contracts Regulations 1995.[66] The commercial significance of these regulations should not be underestimated.[67] Within their areas of application they massively curtail the freedom of action previously enjoyed by bodies awarding such contracts by providing remedies in damages for those who are subject to discrimination as a result of a failure to comply with the regulations. In a book on the

---

[59] The Queen in Right of *Ontario* v *Ron Engineering & Construction Eastern Ltd* (1981) 119 DLR (3d) 267 (sub-contractor was not entitled to the return of a deposit when he realised that he had made an error in the computation of his tender).

[60] *Drennan* v *Star Paving Co* (1958) 333 P 2d 757 (sub-contractor estopped from withdrawing his mistaken bid to do paving work in school which had been relied on by general contractor). In this country no action could be maintained by the general contractor on the basis of promissory estoppel as the doctrine does not, of itself, create a cause of action. *Combe* v *Combe* [1951] 2 KB 215 considered below in ch. 12.

[61] (1975) Working Paper No. 60, 'Firm Offers'.

[62] (1982) 12 JL & Soc 153.

[63] SI 1991 No. 2680.

[64] SI 1993 No. 3228.

[65] SI 1995 No. 201.

[66] SI 1993 No. 3228.

[67] It has been estimated that within the European Union the public procurement of goods and services amounts to approximately 15 per cent of Gross Domestic Product. See Quigley, *European Community Contract Law* (1998) Vol. 1, p. 326.

general principles of contract it is easy to give the impression that regulations such as these which are applicable only to certain types of contract represent only a minor gloss upon the general principles of the common law. However, a moment's anecdotal reflection upon the value of the contracts described above will make it clear that although the regulations are contract specific they are of huge economic significance.

Standing offers

The cases above all consisted of invitations to supply or purchase specified goods or services at a particular time. However, a different situation arises where there is an invitation to supply unspecified quantities of goods or services which may be required within a certain time period. In such cases it has been held that the invitation is not a contractual offer. Rather the invitee who responds positively is considered to be making a 'standing offer' to supply or purchase the goods or services. This offer is then accepted upon each occasion that the original invitor orders goods or services. Although generally[68] the party who made the standing offer is able, like any other offeror,[69] to revoke his offer for the future,[70] once an order is placed, he is obliged to deliver on that order.[71]

Tickets and machines

An examination of the cases in which the courts have been called upon to identify who makes a contractual offer in relation to travel on a bus or train reveals a number of different analyses. In *Wilkie* v *London Transport Board*[72] Lord Greene MR suggested that a bus company made an offer to passengers by running a bus service. In a case involving a railway it has been held that an offer was made in the timetables announcing the times of services.[73] A different approach again is to regard the issuing of the ticket as the contractual offer.[74] Associated with these different suggestions as to when an offer is made is a variety of times at which acceptance is said to be made. It could be the act of embarkation,[75] the request for,[76] or the retention of,[77] a ticket.

---

[68] This will not be the case if the standing offer was not simply to supply the goods or services but also to hold the offer open throughout the specified period: *Percival* v *London County Council Asylum, etc. Committee* (1918) 87 LJKB 677. However, there must be consideration sufficient to support the promise to hold the offer open. See *Dickinson* v *Dodds* (1876) 2 Ch D 463 considered below.

[69] *Byrne* v *Van Tienhoven* (1880) 5 CPD 344.

[70] *Offord* v *Davies* (1862) 12 CB (NS) 748.

[71] *Great Northern Ry* v *Witham* (1873) LR 9 CP 16.

[72] [1947] 1 All ER 258.

[73] *Denton* v *GN Ry* (1856) 5 E & B 860.

[74] *Cockerton* v *Naviera Axnar SA* [1960] 2 Lloyd's Rep 450.

[75] *Pitcaithly & Co* v *Thacker* (1903) 23 NZLR 783 and *Wilkie* v *London Transport Board* [1947] 1 All ER 258.

[76] *Moral* v *Northern Steamship Co* [1922] NZLR 966 (case involved the request that goods be transported).

[77] *Thornton* v *Shoe Lane Parking Ltd* [1971] 2 QB 163 at 169.

This diversity of approaches has led Treitel[78] to conclude that 'the authorities yield no single rule: one can only say that the exact time of contracting depends in each case on the wording of the relevant document and the circumstances in which it was issued'. However, the apparent lack of consistency on the part of the courts may be explained better when attention is focused upon the reason why the exact moment of contract formation is important. Many of these cases raise the question whether a defendant is protected by an exemption clause contained in an unsigned document or notice which in turn depends *inter alia* upon whether, before the contract was entered into, the defendant took reasonable steps to bring the clause to the attention of the party subject to it. Given the hostility which the courts have historically displayed towards such clauses, it seems reasonably clear that the cases cannot simply be approached as if the courts have applied an objective set of criteria in a dispassionate way to ascertain the moment of contractual responsibility. Rather the suspicion is that the courts are on occasion tempted to specify the exact time of contract formation in a way that renders an exclusion clause effective or ineffective according to the perceived merits of the case. Further, the cases seem to display a particular generosity towards those who have suffered personal injuries.[79] This is well illustrated by the approach of Lord Denning in *Thornton* v *Shoe Lane Parking*[80] where the claimant suffered personal injuries attributable in part to the defendants' negligence when he returned to the defendants' car park to collect his vehicle. Lord Denning held that the defendants were unable to rely upon an exclusion clause printed on the back of a ticket obtained from an automated vending machine:

> the offer is made when the proprietor of the machine holds it out as being ready to receive the money. The acceptance takes place when the customer puts his money into the slot ... He is not bound by the terms printed on the ticket ... because the ticket comes too late.

Again, the courts seem to be reasoning from rather than to a conclusion. It is in this sense that Treitel's observation that the time of contracting depends upon the circumstances of each case should perhaps be understood.

THE TERMINATION OF AN OFFER

Prior to acceptance a contractual offer may be terminated in a number of ways.

Revocation – bilateral contracts

First an offer may be withdrawn by the offeror. Revocation is only effective

---

[78] Treitel, p. 14.
[79] For example, the claimants in *Wilkie* v *London Transport Board* [1947] 1 All ER 258; *Thornton* v *Shoe Lane Parking* [1971] 2 QB 163; *contra* the unsuccessful claimant in *Thompson* v *London Midland & Scottish Ry Co* [1930] 1 KB 41.
[80] [1971] 2 QB 163 at p. 169 D–F. Megaw LJ and Sir Gordon Wilmer reserved their view as to the exact point of time at which a contract came into existence.

when it is communicated to the offeree. In *Byrne* v *Van Tienhoven*[81] a letter was posted by the defendant on 1 October offering goods for sale and followed on 8 October by a letter seeking to revoke the original offer. However, on 11 October the claimants received the defendant's first letter and telegraphed their acceptance, which they subsequently confirmed by letter on 15 October. The defendant's second letter (of revocation) did not reach the claimants until 20 October. The court held that a contract having been concluded on 11 October the purported revocation was ineffective.

Although it is settled law that communication of withdrawal is necessary, there is room for debate as to what amounts to communication. What would the position have been if in *Byrne* the claimants received the letter of revocation on 10 October but correctly anticipating its contents declined to open it until they had telegraphed their acceptance the following day. In such circumstances the withdrawal is effective from such time as the offeror could reasonably expect the offeree to read the message. This principle is supported by a case dealing with the communication of a notice by the owners of a ship withdrawing it from a charter party.[82] Therefore, if the withdrawal is received on a Sunday and it is not reasonable to expect the office to be operating at the weekend, it will not be regarded as communicated until Monday morning.

After acceptance, assuming the other contractual requisites to be satisfied (intention to create legal relations and consideration), the offeror may not himself extinguish the contract between the parties. From the moment that acceptance is effective, the contractual obligations created may only be discharged with the consent of the offeree, i.e. by agreement. Such an agreement whereby each party agrees to give up against the other any enforceable rights created by the contract is called a compromise agreement.

A questionable extension of the requirement that withdrawal be communicated is the principle that it need not be communicated *by the offeror*. So in *Dickinson* v *Dodds*[83] the defendant offered to sell his house to the claimant for £800 promising to hold the offer open for two days.[84] The following day the defendant sold the property to a third party and a fourth party communicated this fact to the claimant on the same evening. It was held that the defendant was not obliged to sell the property to the claimant[85]

---

[81] (1880) 5 CPD 344.

[82] *The Brimnes* [1975] QB 929.

[83] [1876] 2 Ch D 463.

[84] The offeror promised that the offer would be 'left over' until Friday. This phrase is interpreted as meaning that the offer is irrevocable until Friday. However, it could plausibly be construed as meaning that the offeree had until Friday at the latest to accept but that in the interim the offeror was free to withdraw the offer. See Gilmore (1974) *The Death of Contract*, pp. 28–9.

[85] Nor was he in breach of any subsidiary obligation not to offer the property to any third party, even if the words used can support such a promise, as the claimant did not provide consideration in order to generate an enforceable option to purchase. *Cf. Mountford* v *Scott* [1975] 2 WLR 114 where for £1 an option was granted to purchase a house for £10,000 within six months. The option could not be withdrawn before the end of the period as it had been purchased for good consideration (£1). As long ago as 1937 the Law Revision

as the defendant's offer to sell was revoked when the sale to the third party was communicated to the claimant. The suggestion in the head note to the case that 'the sale of the property to a third person would itself amount to a withdrawal of the offer ...' must be wrong. Rather it follows from the undoubted requirement of communication that withdrawal will only be effective when the offeree learns[86] of the sale to the third party. However, this principle may be criticised on the basis that a heavy burden is cast upon the offeree who must ascertain whether the facts reported to him about the offeror's sale of the property to another are in fact true.[87]

Revocation – unilateral contracts

We have already encountered an essential difference between unilateral and bilateral contracts; the former involves the exchange of a promise for an act and the latter the exchange of two promises. It is of the essence of such an exchange that the offeree does not assume any obligation himself; he is free to perform the act stipulated or not. Unilateral contracts *typically but not necessarily* have a number of other features. As in *Carlill*, it is frequently the case that the offeror promises to pay a sum of money if a particular act is performed though the offeror might agree to sell property.[88] Again, as in *Carlill*, the offer *typically but not necessarily*[89] is published to a large number of people, as this is usually necessary to achieve its overall purpose.[90] However, in a typical 'reward' case it would be most imprudent of an offeror to phrase his offer in a way that could be accepted by a large number of people (£100 to whomever can tell me the whereabouts of my stolen motorcycle); rather the offer should be phrased in a way that can only result in liability to one person (£100 to the first person to tell me the whereabouts of my stolen motorcycle).

We have already seen that the general rule in bilateral contracts is that revocation must be communicated to the offeree. Such a requirement would not be appropriate in the case of most unilateral contracts where the offer is publicised to a very large number of people. An offeror could never be sure that he had communicated the revocation to everyone who was aware of the original offer. Although an English court has never considered the question, it is suggested that the American rule should be followed. In *Shuey* v *United*

Committee's Sixth Interim Report recommended the abolition of the requirement of consideration in relation to agreements to keep an offer open for a specified period of time or until the happening of a particular event.

[86] Or should learn, see above.

[87] See Treitel, p. 40.

[88] For example, as in *Levkovitz* or *Harvela* considered above. See also *Daulia Ltd* v *Four Millbank Nominees Ltd* [1978] Ch 231.

[89] For example, *Errington* v *Errington* [1952] 1 KB 290 and *Daulia Ltd* v *Four Millbank Nominees Ltd* [1978] Ch 231 considered below.

[90] In *Carlill* presumably to stimulate sales of the smokeball in the typical reward cases, e.g. *R* v *Clarke* [1927] 40 CLR 227 to secure a criminal conviction.

States[91] the Supreme Court held that an offer of a reward for information leading to the arrest of certain criminals was revoked by a presidential decree. There was no requirement or indeed any realistic possibility that the revocation would be communicated to every person who read the original offer. Rather it was enough that the 'same notoriety [be] given to the revocation that was given to the offer'.

A further difference between unilateral and bilateral contracts is in the rules that have been developed to control the withdrawal of unilateral offers once the offeree has embarked upon the performance of the act stipulated in the offer. The need for such rules may be illustrated by the facts of a Canadian case *Dale et al.* v *Government of Manitoba*[92] where:

> A programme was implemented to encourage members of disadvantaged groups to study at university. Students who began to study under this initiative were subsequently informed that the level of support was to be reduced.

The students affected were successful in their action against the university. Relying upon *Carlill* it was held that the university made a unilateral offer to the students to maintain a certain level of support which was accepted by the students when they took up their places. Argument in the Manitoba Court of Appeal centred on whether under the law of agency the university staff administering the programme had the authority of the government to bind them to the continuance of the scheme, and this question was resolved in favour of the students. However, the facts of the case, where the student claimants were in the third year of their studies, provide an excellent illustration of the injustice that may be caused to someone who begins performance of an act which is stipulated to be acceptance of a unilateral offer if the offeror is able to withdraw the offer after the performance has begun.

A possible solution to this problem, suggested in an early work on the law of contract,[93] is to say that the unilateral offer is accepted, and so irrevocable, as soon as the offeree has begun to perform the act stipulated, but that it is not enforceable by the offeree until he has provided consideration for it by completing the stipulated act. The Law Revision Committee endorsed this solution in 1937 as did the Restatement 2d Contracts.[94]

However, this solution has been criticised for a number of reasons. First, it proceeds by way of assertion rather than deduction.[95] Second, the concern for the interest of the offeree may have been overstated. Is it always unjust to offerees, who themselves assume no obligation to complete the performance

---

[91] (1875) 92 US 73.

[92] (1997) 147 DLR (4th) 605.

[93] *Pollock on Contract*, p. 19.

[94] Restatement of the Law, Second, Contracts: this is a codification of the common law prepared by the American Law Institute and published as a multi-volume work. Revision is ongoing and work is advanced upon the third edition.

[95] See McGoverney in *Selected Readings on the Law of Contracts*, p. 300.

upon which they have embarked, invariably to hold that revocation is impossible once performance has begun. Also, in many of the perceived cases of injustice where the offeror has sought to revoke his offer once performance has begun (e.g. A promises to pay B £10 if he washes his windows; A purports to revoke when A has washed the front but not the rear windows), the offeree will be able to maintain a restitutionary[96] action against the offeror for the benefit he has conferred. These criticisms would seem to commend a solution which derives from pre-existing contract doctrine which is flexible enough to offer protection to the offeree when justice so demands.

The approach of the English courts appears to meet these criteria. In *Errington* v *Errington*[97] a father bought a house with the help of a mortgage. He told his son and daughter in law that if they paid the mortgage repayments the house would become theirs. They moved into the house and made the payments. After the father died his personal representatives tried to revoke the arrangement. Denning LJ said that:

> The father's promise was a unilateral contract – a promise of the house in return for their act of paying the instalments. It could not be revoked by him once the couple entered on performance of the act because it is clear that the father expressly promised the couple that the property should belong to them as soon as the mortgage was paid, and by implication promised that, so long as they paid the instalments to the building society, they should be allowed to remain in possession.

This approach was endorsed in *Daulia* v *Four Millbank Nominees*[98] where the Court of Appeal held that a unilateral contract (or 'if' contract according to Goff LJ) was entered into between the mortgagee of a portfolio of properties with the power to sell and the prospective purchaser to the effect that if the purchaser attended the mortgagee's office at particular time with his signed contract and a banker's draft for the deposit, the properties would be sold to him. The Court of Appeal held that the prospective purchaser performed the act stipulated and so was entitled to demand conveyance of the properties. However, Goff LJ said *obiter dicta* that if the purchaser had not fully performed that act requested by the mortgagee 'it was too late for the offeror to revoke his offer' because 'there must be an implied obligation on the part of the offeror not to prevent the condition becoming satisfied, which obligation it seems to me must arise as soon as the offeree starts to perform'.

This solution which depends upon the implication of a second subsidiary promise by the offeror to the effect that he will not revoke the unilateral offer or do anything inconsistent with the completion of the requested act by the offeree is a flexible one, as such a term can only be implied where it is necessary to give business efficacy to the contract. This means that no such

---

[96] The law of restitution, like the law of contract, is a distinct branch of the law of obligations. It is based upon the principle of reversing unjust enrichment. In the example described, B would be able to maintain a *quantum meruit* (so much as he deserves) action against A.

[97] [1952] 1 KB 290.

[98] [1978] 2 All ER 557.

term need be implied where it is not necessary to avoid injustice to the offeree. *Luxor (Eastbourne) Ltd* v *Cooper*[99] was such a case where the owner of two cinemas offered an agent £10,000 if he should introduce a purchaser with whom the seller concludes a sale. The agent introduced a party who was prepared to purchase the properties but the owner declined to sell thereby preventing the agent from completing the act stipulated. The House of Lords held that the agent could not maintain an action for breach of a subsidiary promise not to prevent the condition from becoming satisfied. Such a condition would only be implied when necessary to give commercial efficacy to the arrangement. Such an implication was not necessary where the agent had been offered a very large sum of money (more than the annual salary of the Lord Chancellor it was noted!) for comparatively little work. It was worthwhile for the agent to effect an introduction in the hope that the owner would sell; it was worthwhile despite the fact that the owner might change his mind.

Irrevocable banker's credits may operate as a special exception to the rules discussed above. These instruments are designed to facilitate trade between nationals of different countries who do not necessarily trust each other or have sufficient capital to pay for goods before their onward sale has been effected. Therefore, an entity whose creditworthiness is beyond dispute, a bank[100] is instructed by a purchaser of goods to open a credit in favour of the seller. The bank notifies the seller that the credit is set up and the seller can then obtain payment for the goods against the tender of certain specified documents (usually including the bill of lading which operates as a title document for the goods). It is accepted that the bank is not able to revoke the credit once it has been notified to the seller, otherwise confidence in the system would be irrevocably damaged. Usually the seller may be said to have commenced performance of some act, which may be said to have been stipulated as a condition of the credit, e.g. arranging shipment of the goods. In this way the irrevocability of the credit may be said to be an application of the principles discussed above with the bank as the offeror of a unilateral contract. However, the credit is thought to be irrevocable from the moment of notification, i.e. even if the seller has done nothing in reliance. Such a result cannot be explained by reference to unilateral contracts and is simply a naked application of commercial policy.

Rejection

At its simplest, a rejection may be a simple statement by the offeree that he has no interest in the offer made to him. Or it may implied from a counter-offer, made by the offeree. A counter-offer, therefore, has two distinct effects: it acts as a rejection of the original offer and stands as a new offer capable of acceptance by the offeror. The facts of *Hyde* v *Wrench*[101] illustrate this. The

---

[99] [1941] AC 108.
[100] Though this oft repeated statement rings a little hollow in the age of Johnson Mathey, BCCI and Barings.
[101] [1840] 3 Beav 334.

defendant offered to sell land to the claimant for £1,000. The claimant offered to purchase the land for £950. This was a counter-offer, which rejected the offer to sell for £1,000, and stood as an offer to purchase the land for £950. The defendant then refused to sell the land for £950. This was a simple rejection unaccompanied by any counter proposal. The claimant then purported to accept the original offer of sale at £1,000. However, this offer was no longer in existence following its rejection by the claimant's counter-offer. The most that the purported acceptance of the original offer of sale could be is an offer to purchase the land for £1,000. As the defendant did not accept this, no contract of sale came into existence. The characterisation of the final communication as an offer when it was phrased as an acceptance is an application of a broad principle that the law looks to the substance rather than the form of contractual communications. In other words, the 'label' used by the parties themselves to describe a communication is not conclusive as to its legal effect.[102]

It will be apparent from the above discussion that it is important to characterise each communication chronologically because the character of subsequent communications is dependent upon that of prior ones. The final communication in *Hyde* v *Wrench* could not amount to an acceptance because there was no offer left to accept. For this reason it is useful to summarise the parties' communications in some way and to incorporate the effect of each one as it is noted. The following is offered as my own way of doing this.

D – P	offers to sell land for £1,000 X	O
P – D	offers to purchase for £950 X	CO
D – P	refuses to sell for £950	RE
P – D	accepts offer to sell at £1,000	O
Where:	O = offer	
	CO = counter-offer	
	RE = rejection	
	X = no longer available for acceptance, and is added when the subsequent communication directly or indirectly (i.e. by counter-offer) rejects an earlier offer.	

We have seen that a communication, which is at variance with an offer, cannot amount to an acceptance and will constitute a counter-offer. When we examine acceptance we will see that an acceptance is defined as an unequivocal assent to the terms proposed by the offeror. However, an intermediate category of communication exists which is not sufficiently inconsistent with the offer to constitute a counter-offer but which also does not amount to a sufficiently unequivocal assent so as to constitute an acceptance. Such an intermediate response is termed a mere inquiry and its effect was considered in *Stevenson* v *McLean*[103] where two parties were

---

[102] Compare use of the words 'condition' (Chapter 15) and 'deposit' (Chapter 17).
[103] (1880) 5 QBD 346.

negotiating about the sale of a quantity of iron. McLean wrote to Stevenson '… I would now sell for 40s net cash'. Stevenson replied by telegraph 'Please wire whether you would accept forty for delivery over two months, or if not, longest limit you would give'. McLean argued that Stevenson's reply was a counter-offer leaving him free to sell the goods elsewhere. Lush J disagreed and said:[104]

> … the form of the telegram is one of inquiry. It is not 'I offer forty for delivery over two months', which would have likened the case to *Hyde* v *Wrench* … Here there is no counterproposal … here is nothing specific by way of offer or rejection, but a mere inquiry, which should have been answered and not treated as a rejection …

Two important conclusions can be drawn from the case respectively about the classification and effect of an offeree's response to a contractual offer. First, it seems that the courts are more likely to conclude that a response was intended to be a mere enquiry when it relates to a matter like delivery, which may be considered less important than, say, price.[105] It is interesting to note that in this context the courts appear to attach considerable importance to the form of the response, i.e. whether the offeree himself described it as an enquiry.[106] Second, an enquiry does not affect an offer which remains available for acceptance by the offeree.

The cases that defined the concepts of counter-offer and inquiry were decided in the last century. However, the modern practice of dealing on standard forms provides a contemporary challenge to the continued usefulness of these categories. The problem is well illustrated by the facts of the leading case *Butler* v *Ex-Cell-O Corporation*.[107] The claimants offered to sell a machine to the defendants on the claimants' standard terms of sale, which included a clause that reserved to them the right to increase the price to reflect increased manufacturing costs (the price escalation clause). The defendants responded and ordered the machine on their own standard terms, which did not include a price escalation clause. The claimants detached, signed and returned a tear-off slip at the bottom of the defendant's order, which said: 'We accept your order on the terms and conditions stated thereon.' The machine was manufactured and delivered by the sellers who claimed that under the price escalation clause they were entitled to a further payment.

The majority of the Court of Appeal applied the traditional rules of offer and acceptance which require acceptance to be an unequivocal assent to the offer (the so called 'mirror image' theory of agreement) and held that this

---

[104] At p. 350.
[105] See also *G Percy Trentham* v *Archital Luxfer Ltd* [1993] 1 Lloyd's Rep 25 where a response to an offer (itself a counter-offer) which requested information concerning dispute resolution procedures was held to amount to a mere enquiry.
[106] See *Northland Airliners Ltd* v *Dennis Ferranti Meters* (1970) 114 SJ 845 (defendant responded to an offer to sell an aircraft which required delivery within a reasonable time. The response stated that delivery should take place within 30 days. This was intended to be a mere enquiry but the telegram failed to state this and was treated as a counter-offer).
[107] [1979] 1 WLR 401.

was found in the claimants' act of returning the tear-off slip. The contract was, therefore, concluded on the defendants' terms and so the claimants were not entitled to compensation for the increased cost of manufacture. What makes this analysis unconvincing is the letter of the claimants referring to their original offer, which accompanied the tear-off slip. The majority thought that the letter's reference back to the claimants' original offer was inserted merely to enable defendants to locate in their files the original correspondence; in their view it was not inserted to reinstate those terms. With respect, this is not convincing. One cannot help but think that this case is one of the clearest instances where courts reason from, rather than to, a conclusion reached on other grounds. It would not be difficult to conclude that considered together the return of the tear-off slip and the accompanying letter constituted a counter-offer to deal on the claimants' original terms.

The Court of Appeal may have been reluctant to adopt this alternative analysis because it thought that this would require it to conclude that no contract at all bound the parties. In the course of argument by counsel, Lawton LJ pointed out that:

> ... if the letter ... which accompanied the form acknowledging the terms which the buyers had specified amounted to a counter-offer, then in my judgment the parties were never *ad idem*. [i.e. agreed]

This conclusion is probably correct. It is sometimes possible to infer acceptance of contractual terms from conduct such as taking delivery of goods. On this basis a contract came into existence between a coal merchant and a customer who regularised their previous informal practices by drawing up, approving and acting upon a contract which was never executed (i.e. signed by each party).[108] In *Butler* the machine was completed and delivered but, as Lawton LJ goes on to explain, the latter act could not be relied upon as unequivocal acceptance of the supplier's terms because:

> It cannot be said that the buyers accepted the counter-offer by reason of the fact that ultimately they took physical delivery of the machine. By ... [that] time they had made it clear by correspondence that they were not accepting that there was any price escalation clause in any contract that they had made with the [claimants].

However, in a case like *Butler* it is not necessary for the courts to strain to find a contract where one cannot easily be made out.[109] Rather the courts could look to the law of restitution to provide the unpaid supplier of goods with a cause of action. In Chapter 2 we saw that another branch of the law of obligations, the law of restitution, may require a defendant to compensate a claimant for any unjust enrichment the defendant has gained at the expense of the claimant. The law of restitution comprises many different types of action generally classified according to the factor that makes the defendant's

---

[108] *Brogden v Metropolitan Railway Co* (1877) 2 App Cas 66. See also *G Percy Trentham v Archital Luxfer Ltd* [1993] 1 Lloyd's Rep 25 (completion of work by sub-contractor was acceptance of main contractor's standard sub-contract).

[109] See McKendrick, 'The Battle of the Forms and the Law of Restitution' [1988] 8 OJLS 197.

enrichment unjust. In this context it is of interest to note that such an action might be available where negotiations fail to result in a contract but goods have none the less been delivered. There are both advantages and limitations to the using the law of restitution here. In *Butler* the Court of Appeal went to considerable lengths to find (invent?) a contract. This approach of forcing the facts to fit the template of a contractual action would not be necessary if a restitution based approach is followed.[110] It is interesting to contrast the approach of the Court of Appeal in *Butler* with that of Goff J in *BSC* v *Cleveland Steel*,[111] the leading modern case on restitutionary actions in respect of failed negotiations. Goff J appeared to analyse the facts dispassionately, without any 'panic' that the failure to find the existence of a contract would leave the supplier without a claim to payment. However, a limitation of a restitutionary approach is that its concentration on the enrichment of the defendant might leave the claimant unprotected if the goods supplied are defective.[112] Further, even the claimant might be better protected if a contractual action were available. This is because only a contractual action seeks to protect the claimant's expectations, i.e. to put him in the position he would have been in if the contract had been performed.[113] In a restitutionary claim an unpaid supplier would be entitled to claim the reasonable cost of manufacture. In a contractual claim the damages recovered could be greater and extend to the recovery of the profit the claimant would have made if the contract had been performed.[114]

Lord Denning in *Butler* took a different approach to the problem of the 'battle of the forms'. He disliked the all or nothing approach of the old 'mirror image' test applied by the majority which meant that any contract was concluded on either the buyer's or the seller's terms. He said that:[115]

> The better way is to look at the communications passing between the parties and glean from them, or from the conduct of the parties whether they have reached agreement on all material points, even though there may be differences between the forms and conditions printed on the back of them ... If [the] differences are irreconcilable, so that they are mutually contradictory, then the conflicting terms may have to be scrapped and replaced by a reasonable implication.

An empirical study[116] of transactions involving engineering businesses

---

[110] The Court of Appeal in *Butler* should not be blamed for their oversight because that case predated by some 12 years the authoritative recognition of restitution as a distinct head of civil liability in *Lipkin Gorman v Karpnale* [1991] 2 AC 548.

[111] [1984] 1 All ER 504.

[112] See Chapter 2 for elaboration and a partial answer.

[113] 'A theme that runs through our law of contract is that the reasonable expectations of honest men must be protected ... It is the objective which has been and still is the principal moulding force of our law of contract', *per* Steyn LJ in *First Energy* v *HIB* [1993] 2 Lloyd's Rep 194 at 196. See also Lord Steyn writing extra-judicially in 'Contract law: Fulfilling the Reasonable Expectations of Honest Men' (1997) 113 LQR 433.

[114] See *BSC* v *Cleveland Steel* [1984] 1 All ER 504 at 511. This would not be the case if, from the perspective of the claimant, the contract was not a profitable one.

[115] At pp. 404–5.

[116] Beale and Dugdale, 'Contracts between Businessmen' (1975) 2 Brit J Law & Soc 45 at 48–51.

supports Lord Denning's approach. The study found that the businesses were more concerned that there was a common understanding on major points than exact agreement on all details.

The disadvantage of the approach proposed by Lord Denning is that it is uncertain. It is important in this context and others[117] not to underestimate the importance of certainty. In commercial dealings certainty often appears to be a more prized value than fairness.[118] The effect of uncertainty must be considered *ex ante* (i.e. prospectively) as well as *ex post* (i.e. retrospectively). *Ex ante* uncertainty as to potential transactors' legal rights is wasteful in two ways. First, where parties are not sure of their rights, they may 'waste' money on advice to clarify their position. Such expenses will eventually be passed on to the consumer in the form of an increased price. In addition, the prospect of such costs may dissuade some contractors from trading at all. *Ex post* costly litigation may occur to ascertain the parties' legal rights. However, it must be remembered that most legal disputes are actually settled out of court and any uncertainty is exploited by the party resisting liability to force a lower settlement. Therefore, the often unnoticed effect of legal uncertainty is to depress the level of compensation received by most parties.[119]

Different bodies have framed statutory solutions to the conundrum posed by the battle of the forms. The Vienna Convention on Contracts for the International Sale of Goods[120] provides that a reply to an offer which adds to, limits or varies it is a counter-offer unless the differences do not 'materially alter' the terms of the offer. In the latter case the reply takes effect as an acceptance unless the offeror promptly objects to the changes.[121] Similar proposals have been made as part of the Unidroit Principles for International Commercial Contracts,[122] the Statement of Principles of European Contract Law[123] and the Uniform Commercial Code.[124]

Lapse of time

An offer may expressly be made valid for a stated length of time, until a

---

[117] See also the discussions of exclusion clauses benefiting third parties (ch. 11) and the classification of contractual terms by reference to their remedial effect (ch. 15).

[118] A typical general statement is that of Lord Brandon in *Leigh & Sullivan* v *Aliakmon Shipping* [1986] 2 All ER 145 at 155: 'Yet certainty of the law is of the utmost importance, especially but by no means only, in commercial matters.'

[119] See Harris and Veljanovski (1987) 5 Law and Policy Q 97.

[120] Also called The United Nations Convention on Contracts. This has not yet been ratified by the UK.

[121] See Art 19 but note that under Art 19.3 differences relating to price and payment terms, time and place of delivery and some other matters are always 'material'.

[122] See Art 2.11. The principles are usefully reproduced in *Blackstone's Statutes on Contract, Tort and Restitution 1998–9*. 9th edn.

[123] See Art 2.209 reproduced as above. The principles are intended to be incorporated into domestic as well as cross-border contracts.

[124] Section 2-207. The UCC is a model statute, designed to 'simplify, clarify and modernise ... commercial transactions in the United States'. It has been adopted in full by all states except Louisiana (which has a civil-law-based system) and the District of Columbia.

given date or until a specified event occurs.[125] Such an offer may be accepted within the stipulated period. If the offeror revokes the offer before the period has expired, this will not, without more, amount to a breach of contract unless the offeror agreed, for good consideration, to keep the offer open. Such an arrangement is often called a contractual option. In *Dickinson v Dodds*[126] the defendant offered to sell a number of houses to the claimant: 'This offer to be left over until Friday, 9 o'clock am, June 12 ...'. We have already seen that the claimant's action on the main contract to sell failed because the offer was revoked before it was accepted. Neither could he bring an action for breach of the collateral promise not to revoke the offer to sell before the stated time because he had not provided any consideration in exchange for that promise.

An offer may by implication state a time within which it must be accepted. Such an implication may arise from the medium used to transmit the offer. It has been held that when an offer was made by telegram this required a quick response.[127]

Where an offer does not state either expressly or impliedly a time within which it must be accepted, it must be accepted within a reasonable time. Various factors will be relevant to the determination of what is a reasonable time including the nature of the goods being sold or the service supplied as well as the prevailing market climate. An offer to sell a quantity of chicken giblets will 'expire' before that to sell a quantity of stone. Similarly, an offer to sell a commodity against a volatile market will 'expire' before one to sell the goods where a stable market is operating.

Death of offeror and offeree

Statements to the effect that the death of either the offeror[128] or the offeree[129] automatically terminates an offer are too sweeping. Perhaps the better view is that the death of the offeree, like that of the offeror,[130] will only terminate an offer when the personal qualities of the deceased were important to the offer.

ACCEPTANCE

The traditional view is that acceptance is an unequivocal assent by the offeree to the terms proposed by the offeror. Several of the detailed rules we have examined in this chapter (the orthodox approach to counter-offers, the inability to accept non-conforming tenders illustrated by the *Harvela* case)

---

[125] An example of the latter is provided by *Financings Ltd* v *Stimson* [1963] 1 WLR 1184 (it was an implied condition of an offer to sell a car on hire-purchase terms that the offer would terminate if the car's condition should change substantially before the offer was accepted).
[126] (1876) 2 Ch D 463.
[127] *Quenerduaine* v *Cole* (1883) 32 WR 185.
[128] *Dickinson* v *Dodds* (1876) 2 Ch D 463 at 475 *per* Mellish LJ.
[129] *Reynolds* v *Atherton* (1922) 127 LT 189.
[130] *Bradbury* v *Morgan* (1862) 1 H & C 249 especially at 255 *per* Bramwell B.

and elsewhere (the principles governing cases of mistaken identity) can be regarded as elaborations of this basic definition of acceptance. We will now examine other principles of acceptance as applied in the different contexts of bilateral and unilateral contracts.

ACCEPTANCE IN BILATERAL CONTRACTS

The general rule is that acceptance must be communicated.[131] It should be emphasised that this is the general proposition from which certain exceptions, particularly the postal rule, depart and not the other way round. As Lord Wilberforce observed in a leading case, 'the general rule' has important implications for 'when and where' the contract was made.[132] In cross-border contracts, it will be necessary to ascertain where the contract was made in order to establish what law governs the contract and whether English courts have jurisdiction to hear the case.[133]

The general rule is applicable to all forms of instantaneous communication including face-to-face discussions, telephone conversations and the use of telexes.[134] Therefore, if the offeree does not hear the acceptance, perhaps in the first case because of an aircraft passing overhead or in the second and third cases because of the line going dead no contract comes into existence. In each case the offeree must repeat his acceptance to create a contract. The rationale behind this rule was explained by Lord Denning in this way:[135] in each case the offeree either is, or should be, aware that the communication of the acceptance has failed and so he is required to repeat it. Additionally, Lord Denning said that the offeror is 'clearly bound' where the communication failed but the offeree thinks it was successful and the failure to receive it was the fault of the offeror, e.g. because the offeror is daydreaming and so fails to hear the spoken or telephoned acceptance or because the offeror's teleprinter runs out of ink. This exception is justified by the relative culpability of the parties. The offeree has done all that can reasonably be expected of him but the offeror has not. The exception will not apply when the offeror is not at fault. There will be no contract if the communication fails through no fault of either party, e.g. the telex line fails but the offeree's teleprinter records that the message was sent successfully and the offeror's teleprinter does not record that there has been a failed communication.

It is suggested that acceptance by fax and e-mail should also be subject to the principles stated by Lord Denning.[136] However, a further question may

---

[131] *Entores v Miles Far East Corp* [1955] 2 QB 327 and *Brinkibon Ltd v Stahag Stahl* [1983] 2 AC 34.

[132] *Brinkibon v Stahag Stahl* [1983] 2 AC 34.

[133] *Entores v Miles Far East Corp* [1955] 2 QB 327.

[134] Telex communication involves a message being sent by a teleprinter, a device like a typewriter, and almost simultaneously being typed by the receiving teleprinter.

[135] *Entores v Miles Far East Corp* [1955] 2 QB 327 at 332–3.

[136] For the argument as to why these modes of communication should be regarded as falling outside the postal rule, see below.

arise as to what amounts to communication to the offeror when the message is received by an unstaffed receptor. It may be difficult to lay down a universal rule here. Lord Wilberforce has warned that:[137]

> No universal rule can cover all such cases; they must be resolved by reference to the intentions of the parties, by sound business practice and in some cases by a judgment where the risks should lie.

On this basis it is suggested that an acceptance sent by fax or e-mail should be regarded as communicated when it is received by the offeror's machine only where it is reasonable to expect the offeror to immediately become aware of the receipt. In other cases, e.g. communication to an office outside normal trading hours, the message should be regarded as communicated when a reasonable person in the position of the offeror would have become aware of it.[138]

We have seen that in a number of cases it has been held that the law recognises so-called 'acceptance by conduct'.[139] It is not absolutely clear whether the general rule requiring the communication of acceptance is applicable or if they form an exception to it.[140] This is because the conduct relied upon is typically taking delivery of goods proffered by the offeror which act is both an external manifestation of assent by the offeree and a communication of that fact to the offeror. A further reason is that in these cases the courts appear predisposed to find that a contract of some kind exists and so would be unsympathetic to any 'technical' argument to the contrary. None the less, the expression of acceptance by conduct and the requirement of communication are separate requirements. The facts of the leading case on acceptance by conduct may support the view that they are separate requirements. In *Brogden*[141] the act of marking a contract 'approved', signing it and placing it in a drawer was held not to amount to acceptance, but making deliveries and generally conducting business upon the terms contained in the contract did amount to acceptance by conduct. If the former act is regarded as a sufficient manifestation of assent, it may be that it did not constitute acceptance only because it was uncommunicated. However, this interpretation is difficult to support for a number of reasons. First, the deposit in the drawer of a signed contract may not be sufficiently unequivocal to amount to a manifestation of assent.[142] Second, the case contains a number of contrary statements.[143] Third, despite being a decision

---

[137] *Brinkibon* v *Stahag Stahl* [1983] 2 AC 34 at 42.

[138] *Cf. The Brimnes* [1975] QB 929 (notice of withdrawal of ship) considered above in relation to the revocation of an offer.

[139] See above, p. 142.

[140] Perhaps being further examples of acceptance by silence, as to which see below.

[141] *Brogden* v *Metropolitan Railway Co* (1877) 2 App Cas 666.

[142] This view is stated most forcefully by Lord Gordon at p. 697: 'In this case we have no evidence whatever of consent by putting the document into a drawer, an operation of the meaning of which we really know nothing whatever.' See also Lord Cairns at pp. 674–5 who notes that the word 'approved' might have been added to signify concurrence with the form and expression rather than the substance of the contents.

[143] For example, Lord Blackburn at p. 688 rejects the view that mere mental assent can amount to acceptance but may be understood to suggest that a contract can be concluded by further action by the offeree which is not communicated to the offeror.

of the House of Lords, the case was treated as raising a question of fact rather than law.[144] Whatever the proper interpretation of *Brogden*, further support for the view that communication is an additional requirement in cases of acceptance by conduct may derive from *Felthouse v Bindley*.[145] In *Felthouse* there was an external manifestation of assent by the nephew (telling the auctioneer to 'hold back' the horse) but this was not communicated to the uncle. The finding of the court that there was no contract in that case supports the view that communication is an additional requirement.

The postal rule of acceptance

The postal rule is an exception to the general rule that acceptance must be communicated to the offeror. The postal rule of acceptance holds that when it is reasonable to use the post as a means of communicating acceptance of a contractual offer the acceptance is complete when a properly addressed[146] letter of acceptance is deposited in the post box.[147] The rule, therefore, brings forward the time of contracting by dispensing with the need for actual communication to the offeree. The facts of *Henthorn v Fraser*[148] provide a simple illustration of the operation of the rule. The claimant posted a letter[149] accepting the defendant's offer to sell property to him. It was held that a contract was concluded when the letter of acceptance was posted despite the fact that the defendant had already posted a revocation of the offer. Under the postal rule the contract was concluded before the revocation was effective.[150]

Rationale of the postal rule

It is difficult to find a convincing argument to support it but many have been proffered. It has been suggested that the post office should be regarded as the common agent of both parties with the consequence that communication to the agent concludes the contract.[151] However, such an agency is surely a convenient fiction. The Post Office receives a sealed envelope and so must at most be considered an agent for the transmission of letters but not for their

---

[144] See Lord Selborne at p. 687, Lord Blackburn at p. 690 and Lord Gordon at p. 697.
[145] *Felthouse v Bindley* (1862) 11 CB (NS) 869. See below pp. 152–4.
[146] There is no direct authority requiring the letter of acceptance to be properly addressed. See below for a discussion of principle.
[147] *Adams v Lindsell* (1818) 1 B & Ald 681 (although it may be questioned to what extent this often quoted case in fact supports the postal rule); *Ex Parte Harris* (1872) LR 7 Ch App 567; *Henthorn v Fraser* [1892] 2 Ch 27; *Bruner v Moore* [1904] 1 Ch 305.
[148] [1892] 2 Ch 27.
[149] It was held to be reasonable for the claimant to use the post as a method of acceptance even though the offer to sell was not made by post. For this aspect of the case see below.
[150] Revocation of an offer is only effective upon communication to the offeree. See above.
[151] *Household Fire Assurance Co Ltd v Grant* (1879) 4 Ex D 216 at 220; *Byrne & Co v Van Tienhoven & Co* (1880) 5 CPD 344 at p. 348.

receipt.[152] In *Adams* v *Lindsell* it was said that if communication was required:[153]

> ... no contract could ever be completed by post. For if the defendants were not bound by their offer when accepted by the [claimants] till the answer was received, then the [claimants] ought not to be bound till after they had received the notification that the defendants had received their answer and assented to it. And so it might go on *ad infinitum*.[154]

What this passage shows is that in the case of postal communications there is a need to identify a point of time at which a contract is concluded which relieves the parties of any need for further confirmation. What the passage does not demonstrate is why that time should be the posting of a properly addressed letter of acceptance. However, it might be argued that in the absence of any compelling argument in favour of a later date, the law should (as it does) bring forward the moment of contract formation. This would reduce the chances of a communication going astray and reduce the risks to parties who are negotiating against a volatile market. Another practical argument in favour of the present rule is that it reduces difficulties of proof because an offeree can easily adduce evidence of posting. Such a view seems to be premised upon a clerk taking a letter to a post office and obtaining a stamped receipt of posting. It is questionable whether it is sensible to premise a rule on such an antiquated view of commerce. In modern times commercial concerns with large post rooms would have to rely upon their own records for evidence of posting and these lack the objectivity of the post office receipt.

In the end, it may be the case that the postal rule of acceptance can only be explained historically but not defended rationally. It has been argued[155] that the rule can only be explained by reference to historical context. In the mid-nineteenth century the introduction of an inexpensive prepaid post combined with the widespread use of domestic letter boxes created a public perception that a letter once posted would reliably and speedily reach its destination. In the age of computerised communication it might seem strange to regard the post as 'near instantaneous' communication. However, it was so perceived at the time and so this might explain why the courts effectively brought forward the moment of contractual responsibility.

It is interesting to conclude this section by noting that the postal rule is not found elsewhere in the European Union except in Scotland and Ireland

---

[152] See Farwell J's interjection into the argument of counsel for the defendant in *Bruner* v *Moore* [1904] 1 Ch 305 at 308.

[153] (1818) 1 B & Ald 681 at 683. See also Ferson 'The Formation of Simple Contracts' (1924) 9 Cornell Law Quarterly 402.

[154] *Cf.* the European's Commission's proposed Directive on Electronic Commerce, which apparently succumbs to this absurdity. Article 11 provides that, '... the contract is concluded when the recipient of the service has received from the service provider, electronically, an acknowledgement of receipt of the recipient's acceptance'. Indeed, the original proposal required an acknowledgement of receipt of the acknowledgement!

[155] 'Trashing with Trollope: A Deconstruction of the Postal Rules in Contract' (1992) 12 OJLS 170.

and the former's Law Commission has recommended its abolition.[156] As a consequence, it is not retained in either the Unidroit Principles or the Principles of European Contract Law, which both unequivocally enact acceptance principles requiring communication to reach the offeree.[157]

When does the postal rule apply?

Where an offer was made by post it will usually be possible to accept it by post. The postal rule may apply even where the offer was not made by post. The guiding principle seems to be that it will apply whenever it is reasonable to use the post as a method of acceptance.[158] In *Henthorn* v *Fraser*[159] it was held that an oral offer could be accepted by post because the parties lived some distance apart. It will not be reasonable to accept by post when the postal service is in a state of disruption.[160]

Acceptance by post will not be reasonable where as in *Holwell Securities* v *Hughes*[161] the offeror has made it clear that acceptance must be notified to him. An offer to sell a house which was 'to be exercisable by notice in writing to the ... Vendor' could only be accepted when the acceptance was communicated. Acceptance by post will not be reasonable where the offeror expressly[162] or by implication requests a speedy response. Indeed, the means of communicating the offer may itself be sufficient to make clear that the offeror needs a quick response. On this basis an offer made by telegram could not be accepted by post.[163] It would seem likely now that the same could be said of an offer made by fax or e-mail. Even where a particular means of communication is prescribed by the offeror, the offeree will generally be able to use a different means if it is 'just as good' from the offeror's point of view.[164]

We have already seen that the postal rule of acceptance is not applicable to the revocation of offers[165] or to acceptances communicated by instantaneous means.

The postal rule is only applicable when the letter of acceptance is received

---

[156] Scottish Law Commission Report, No 144, 1993.

[157] See Unidroit Principle 2.6(2); Principles of European Contract Law, Art. 2:205.

[158] According to Lord Herschell in *Henthorn* v *Fraser* [1892] 2 Ch 27 at p. 33, the postal rule may be relied on whenever '... the circumstances are such that it must have been within the contemplation of the parties that ... the post might be used as a means of communicating ...'. See also *Holwell Securities* v *Hughes* [1974] 1 WLR 155 *per* Russell LJ. *Cf.* the more restrictive approach in *Household Fire etc. Insurance* v *Grant* (1879) 4 Ex D 216 at 233 *per* Thesiger and Baggaley LJJ (postal rule requires the actual or implied authority of the offeror).

[159] [1892] 2 Ch 27.

[160] *Bal* v *Van Staden* [1902] TS 128.

[161] [1974] 1 WLR 155.

[162] A good example is provided by a famous American case. In *Eliason* v *Henshaw* (1819) Wheat 225 the defendant gave the driver of the claimant's wagon a written offer to buy flour requesting a response '... by return of wagon ...'. It was held that the claimant's reply by mail was outside the terms of the offer.

[163] *Quenerduaine* v *Cole* (1883) 32 WR 185.

[164] *Tinn* v *Hoffmann & Co* (1873) 29 LT 271 (acceptance requested by return of post any equally speedy method acceptable).

[165] *Supra*.

by the Post Office. Placing the letter in an official post box will be sufficient, but giving it to an employee of the Post Office who is authorised to distribute but not to collect letters will not be.[166] Further, it has recently been said that the postal rule will not apply where it would produce 'manifest inconvenience or uncertainty'.[167]

It has been held that the postal rule is applicable to telegrams[168] of acceptance.[169] More relevant to modern commerce is the use of e-mail. This system of communication may superficially be regarded as a modern version of the letter post. Common features include: an intermediary (the telephone company) who transmits the message and a recipient, who will not always be aware that his message has failed to get through. However, these features are also possessed by some methods of instantaneous communication. Further, the postal rule is clearly anomalous and the trend in recent times has been to limit[170] or ignore[171] it. Therefore, it is suggested that e-mails should not come within the postal rule. If this suggestion is accepted, it establishes that no contract is made when an e-mail acceptance is sent; it does not establish when a contract is formed. This depends upon the principles discussed earlier particularly those relating to the use of 'unmanned receptors'.

The consequences of the postal rule

The postal rule produces the possibility that a contract will come into existence when the letter of acceptance is lost in the post. While the loss of a properly addressed letter is surely a less frequent occurrence than many debtors would want you to believe ('I posted the cheque last week, honest') it must occur. When it does, the offeror is bound to a contract even though he is not, and without more, never will be, aware of that fact. English courts appear to be happy to apply the full rigour of the postal rule in this circumstance.[172] Perhaps this application of the rule is not too unfair to the offeror because he could have avoided it by expressly or impliedly requiring notification of acceptance.[173] However, it is suggested that even though the offeror takes the risk of a properly addressed letter of acceptance being lost, he should not be treated as having assumed the risk of an improperly

---

[166] *Re London & Northern Bank* [1900] 1 Ch 220.

[167] *Holwell Securities Ltd* v *Hughes* [1974] 1 All ER 161 at 166 *per* Lawton LJ, following a suggestion made in Cheshire and Fifoot (1972) *Law of Contract*. 8th edn.

[168] Telegrams were typed communications delivered by the Post Office and are no longer used. They were replaced by telemessages which were also delivered (somewhat more slowly – this was progress?) by the Post Office. The postal rule probably applied to telemessages as well, but the question is academic as they are also now obsolete.

[169] *Stevenson, Jacques & Co* v *McLean* (1880) 5 QBD 346 and *Bruner* v *Moore* [1904] 1 Ch 305.

[170] *See Holwell Securities Ltd* v *Hughes* [1974] 1 All ER 161 discussed below.

[171] See Principles of European Contract Law, Art. 2:205.

[172] *Household Fire Assurance* v *Grant* (1879) 4 Ex D 416 (party who applied for shares in a company had contracted to purchase them even though the letter of allotment (i.e. acceptance) never reached him). *Cf. Kelly* v *Cruise Catering Ltd* [1994] 2 ILRM 394 (Irish Supreme Court said *obiter* that the postal rule should not apply where the letter of acceptance is lost in the post).

[173] As in *Holwell Securities Ltd* v *Hughes* [1974] 1 All ER 161.

addressed letter failing to reach him.[174] Permitting the post to be used to communicate acceptance may just indicate willingness on the offeror's part to assume the risk of negligence or accident on his/her own part. It is surely going too far to argue that the selection of the post as a means of communication is a sufficient demonstration of a desire to assume the burden of your prospective contractual partner's incompetence.

Another circumstance where the strict application of the postal rule has been questioned is where the offeree seeks to revoke his posted acceptance. When the offeree uses a speedier means to communicate the 'revocation', the offeror may receive the revocation before the acceptance. In such circumstances it can be argued that the offeree would not be in any way prejudiced if, contrary to the strict application of the postal rule, the court held that no contract came into existence. In the absence of clear domestic authority,[175] it is suggested that the argument of principle we have just described should prevail that an 'overtaking revocation' should be regarded as effective. The objection that such a rule unduly favours the interests of the offeree who is thereby allowed a brief period to gamble on market movements[176] may be met by pointing out that the offeror enjoys the same privilege with regard to his offer[177] and that the offeror can always stipulate that acceptance must be communicated within a particular time or by an expeditious means.

Silence as acceptance

To the extent that an offer may be accepted by the silence of the person to whom it is directed it constitutes a further exception to the general rule requiring the communication of acceptance. However, it is difficult to state with certainty the extent to which silence can be relied upon as evidence of acceptance. This difficulty arises for two reasons: first, the leading cases often only address the issue indirectly; second, they often fail to state or take account of the policy objective which lays behind the law of contract's hostile approach to the recognition of silence as evidence of acceptance. This

---

[174] There is no direct authority on the point. See the analogy of *Getreide-Import Gesellschaft* v *Contimar etc.* [1953] 207 at 793.

[175] *Morrisson* v *Thoelke* (1963) 155 So 2d 889 and *A to Z Bazaars (Pty) Ltd* v *Minister of Agriculture* (1974) (4) SA 392(c) support the strict application of the postal rule and *Dick* v *US* (1949) 82 F Supp 326 opposes it. The difficult Scottish case of *Dunmore* v *Alexander* (1830) 9 Shaw 190 is often discussed in this context. A letter of revocation arrived at the same time as another letter. If the second letter was an acceptance it would follow *a fortiori* from the court's decision that the revocation was effective that a letter of revocation which arrived before an acceptance would be effective. However, the majority appear to have regarded the second letter as an offer in which case the decision is not relevant to the question of whether a revocation can overtake an acceptance. See generally, Treitel, p. 27.

[176] That is, if while his posted acceptance is in the hands of the Post Office the terms he has 'accepted' become unattractive he can revoke the acceptance by a speedier means of communication.

[177] Which can be revoked by a speedier means than that by which it is communicated if subsequently the terms offered prove disadvantageous to the offeror.

difficulty is illustrated by the case of *Felthouse* v *Bindley*[178] where a man was discussing the purchase of a horse belonging to his nephew. The nephew wrote to his uncle saying that there was a misunderstanding between them about the price of the horse; the uncle thought he had bought the horse for £30 when the nephew believed he had sold it for 30 guineas.[179] The uncle wrote back offering to split the difference adding: 'If I hear no more about him, I consider the horse is mine at £30 15s.' There were no more communications between the parties. Six weeks later the nephew employed an auctioneer to sell some farming stock and instructed him to leave out the horse which had already been sold. Unfortunately, the horse was included in the auction and sold to a third party. The question whether a contract existed between the uncle and nephew was raised indirectly when the uncle brought an action against the auctioneer in the tort of conversion.[180] The uncle's action failed. The uncle's letter was only 'an open offer' which was never accepted.

Although *Felthouse* v *Bindley* is often regarded as the leading authority on acceptance by silence in the law of contract, the proper principle to be derived from the case is open to question. First, the issue of acceptance by silence was only raised indirectly in the context of a tortious action. Second, the decision would appear to be wrong on its facts. In the Court of Common Pleas[181] Willes J correctly expressed the policy behind the court's approach to the question whether silence can be relied upon as evidence of acceptance but then failed to apply it. He said: '... the uncle had no right to impose upon the nephew a sale of his horse ...'. The policy is that no person should be able to 'force' a contract upon an unwilling party.[182] If I were to say to my contract class (and I do, annually), 'I offer to sell you a copy of a certain contract textbook signed by the author for £100. If you do not object in the next three seconds I will assume that you want to accept my offer. One, two, three,' it would as morally wrong as it would be personally impoverishing if I could not rely upon my students' three seconds of silence as acceptance of my generous offer. I should not be permitted to force a contract upon my class in this way.[183] However, in *Felthouse* v *Bindley* there was adequate evidence (the instruction to the auctioneer) that the nephew wanted to contract with his uncle. Indeed, Willes J notes 'that the nephew in his own mind intended his uncle to have the horse at the price which he (the uncle)

---

[178] [1862] 11 CB (NS) 869.

[179] A guinea was one pound one shilling equivalent to £1.05 in post-decimal currency. The guinea is still widely used in connection with the sale of horses.

[180] Conversion is the assertion of rights over another's property.

[181] The decision of the Court of Common Pleas was confirmed by the Court of Exchequer Chamber on the basis that the agreement alleged did not comply with the formal requirements then imposed by the Statute of Frauds 1677. See below.

[182] The Unsolicited Goods and Services Act 1971 enforces a similar policy. Effectively it provides that unsolicited goods become the property of the recipient six months after receipt or 30 days after he informs the sender that he is in possession of the goods if the sender does not collect them.

[183] Recommending the book as essential reading is, of course, another matter altogether.

had named, £30 15s ...' On this basis it is difficult to see why no contract existed between the uncle and the nephew.

It is suggested that the true rule is that silence cannot be regarded as evidence of acceptance when this would involve forcing a contract upon an unwilling party. This statement is consistent with the policy that the rule seeks to enforce and accommodates the exceptional situations where silence has been held to amount to acceptance. The case of *Rust* v *Abbey Life*[184] supports this statement of the rule. The simplified facts of the case were that Mrs Rust applied for property bonds, which Abbey Life issued and sent to her. After seven months, during which the investment proved unprofitable, Mrs Rust claimed her money back on the basis that she had never contracted to buy the bonds. The Court of Appeal rejected her argument on the basis that her application was an offer and the sending of the bonds an acceptance or alternatively,[185] if the sending of the bonds was a counter-offer,[186] Mrs Rust's prolonged silence was an acceptance of it. Mrs Rust's application for the bonds showed that treating her silence as acceptance would not involve forcing a contract on an unwilling party. It is true that she later regretted her decision to buy the bonds but only in the same sense that a purchaser of a lottery ticket would be pleased to receive a refund after the draw fails to reward him with a prize. Mrs Rust was a willing party to the contract to purchase the bonds before she realised they were providing a poor return on her money, just as the hypothetical purchaser of a lottery ticket is a willing party prior to the draw.

Further examples when exceptionally silence has been held to constitute acceptance[187] are where the custom of the trade or business being transacted recognises it as such.[188] In such cases a willingness to contract may be inferred from the offeree's knowledge of the business he is involved in. In the exceptions so far considered we have made inferences about the offeree's willingness to enter a contract from his previous communications with the offeror and his knowledge of the custom of his trade. A stronger case for inferring that the offeree wants his silence to be regarded as acceptance is where he says so. In *Re Selectmove Ltd*[189] it was said *obiter dicta*:[190]

> Where the offeree himself indicates that an offer is to be taken as accepted if he does not indicate to the contrary by an ascertainable time, he is undertaking to

---

[184] [1979] 2 Lloyd's Rep 334.
[185] And so *obiter dicta*.
[186] It seems that the terms on which the bonds were issued may have been sufficiently different to those proposed in her application to constitute a counter-offer.
[187] It is sometimes suggested that a line of cases which hold that an offer to abandon arbitration proceedings may be accepted by the silence of the other party to them provide another example of acceptance by silence. See particularly, *The Hannah Blumenthal* [1983] AC 854. A better view is that these cases turn upon policy considerations peculiar to their own facts, i.e. a desire to avoid protracted arbitration proceedings. In any event, the matter is now dealt with by the Arbitration Act 1996, s 41(3).
[188] *Minories Finance Ltd* v *Afribank Nigeria Ltd* [1995] 1 Lloyd's Rep 134.
[189] [1995] 1 WLR 474.
[190] *Per* Peter Gibson LJ at p. 478, Stuart Smith and Balcombe LJJ agreeing. See also *Gebr. Van Weelde Scheepvaartkantor BV* v *Compania Naviera Sea Orient SA* [1985] 2 Lloyd's Rep 496 at 509 *per* Evans J.

speak if he does not want an agreement to be concluded. I see no reason in principle why that should not be an exceptional circumstance such that the offer can be accepted by silence.

In this case it was apparently assumed that an offer by a taxpayer to pay by instalments his arrears of taxes could be accepted by the silence of the tax inspector if the latter had agreed to revert to the taxpayer if the proposal was unacceptable.[191]

It has been observed that '... in the practical world ... an omission to act may be as pregnant with meaning as a positive declaration ...'.[192] However, it will not always be so. The exceptional situations identified above are those where the courts have held that silence can provide evidence of acceptance. Whether it does is, of course, a question of fact. Put another way, falling within one of the recognised exceptions is a necessary but not sufficient ground for holding that there was acceptance of a contractual offer. In addition, it must be shown that the silence was of such duration and in such circumstances as to amount to an unequivocal acceptance.

ACCEPTANCE IN UNILATERAL CONTRACTS

Someone who was unaware of the offer at the time he performed the stipulated act cannot accept a unilateral offer, such as that of a reward. In *R v Clarke*,[193] a reward was offered for information leading to the conviction of the person or persons who murdered two policemen. The claimant who supplied the information had seen the offer of a reward but frankly admitted that at the time of supplying the information she had forgotten about it. Her honesty did not serve her well because the High Court of Australia held that the claim must fail because the offer was not in the claimant's mind when she did the stipulated act.[194]

A number of cases that appear to contradict this principle may in fact be explained on a different basis.[195] In *Williams* v *Carwardine*[196] a woman gave information in circumstances similar to those in *R* v *Clarke* and successfully

---

[191] For the purposes of the Appeal, it was assumed that such an agreement could be made out. Even so, it would be unenforceable if the agreement was with someone who did not have sufficient authority to grant such concessions and, even if he did, it was not supported by good consideration.

[192] *Vitol SA* v *Norelf Ltd* [1996] 3 WLR 105 at 114 *per* Lord Steyn with whom the other members of the House of Lords agreed (dealing with the analogous question of whether the victim of a breach of contract had to elect expressly to terminate the contract or whether such election could be inferred from his silence or inactivity).

[193] (1927) 40 CLR 227; see also *Fitch* v *Snedaker* (1868) 38 NY 248 and *Bloom* v *American Swiss Watch Co* [1915] App D 100 (Supreme Court of South Africa).

[194] The decision seems to endorse the view of Lord Parker CJ that when accepting a unilateral offer the offeree would be well advised to 'go to the length of saying that he knew of [it and acted] in reliance on it': *Taylor* v *Allon* [1965] 1 All ER 557 at 559 (court rejected the defendant's argument that he had accepted an offer of temporary insurance cover by simply driving his car).

[195] Though perhaps not *Neville* v *Kelly* (1862) 32 LJ CP 118.

[196] (1833) 5 C & P 566.

claimed the reward. She provided the information with knowledge of the reward but her motive was to salve her conscience because she thought she was going to die. The case may be distinguished[197] on the basis that it merely demonstrates the irrelevance of motive.[198] *Gibbons* v *Proctor*[199] may also be reconciled with *R* v *Clarke*. Again, a reward was involved. In this case a policeman gave the information to a colleague at a time when the policeman was not aware of the reward. However, he did become aware of the reward before the information was communicated to his superior officers. There is no contradiction between the successful claim of the policeman in *Gibbons* and the principle laid down in *R* v *Clarke* if the acceptance in *Gibbons* was the communication to the superior officer.[200]

It is suggested that a better approach to the reward cases would have regard to the policy objective that the law should pursue. This implies that doing the act stipulated as the precondition for the receipt of a reward should always be regarded as acceptance when the information would not have been proffered but for the offer of a reward. Such a principle would support the result in *R* v *Clarke* but not that in the other two cases. In *Williams* and *Gibbons* the information would have been proffered even if no reward had been offered. A rule of non-recovery would not create a disincentive to come forward with valuable information.[201]

The principle that an offer may not be accepted unless the offeror is aware of it is usually discussed in relation to unilateral contracts. However, *Upton RDC* v *Powell*[202] suggests that the offer of a contract may be accepted even though the offeree was not aware of the offer. The defendant, whose house was ablaze, telephoned the local police and asked them to send 'the fire brigade'. The police sent the Upton fire brigade, who later claimed payment because the house was outside their usual service area. The court upheld the claim on the basis that the telephone call was an offer of a bilateral contract (to pay) which was accepted by the conduct of the offeree (attending) even though the offeree was ignorant of it.

However, the rule that the offeree must be aware of the offer at the time of his purported acceptance may explain the court's refusal to recognise a contract constituted by so-called 'cross-offers'.[203] This refers to the situation

---

[197] See especially the judgments of Littledale and Patterson JJ. However, it could be argued that the cases are indistinguishable. *Clarke* may also be characterised as a case involving the issue of motive. The claimant was himself suspected of the offence and his motive was to clear his own name. In *Williams* it was found that the claimant had forgotten about the reward when she gave her statement.

[198] However, it seems that if the performance of the stipulated act is entirely motivated by factors other than the unilateral offer it is not accepted by that performance. See *Lark* v *Outhwaite* [1991] 2 Lloyd's Rep 132 at 140. This is consistent with *Carlill* v *Carbolic Smoke Ball Company* [1893] 1 QB 256 where Mrs Carlill's prime motivation in using the smoke ball was presumably to avoid catching influenza but where she was nevertheless influenced by the maker's offer of a reward.

[199] (1891) 64 LT 594.

[200] See Treitel, p. 34 and the report in (1891) 55 JP 616.

[201] *Contra* the view expressed in Furmston (ed.) (1999) *The Law of Contract* at para 2.219.

[202] [1942] 1 All ER 220.

[203] *Tinn* v *Hoffmann & Co* (1873) 29 LT 271 at 278–9 *per* Blackburn, Brett and Grove JJ.

where the parties simultaneously exchange corresponding offers, e.g. A writes to B offering to sell his car for £10,000 and before it is received B writes to A offering to buy his car for the same price.

CONCLUSION

The principles of offer and acceptance are largely the product of the last century. We have seen that in many situations (e.g. contracts with machines, the battle of the forms, etc.) they sometimes struggle to deal with the realities of modern life. None the less, they remain important to the general law of contract. It is sometimes asked whether we still have a general law of contract when so many areas that were once thought to fall within the general law of contract have now developed their own jurisprudence.[204] Employment law is one example and landlord and tenant law another. However, the distinct doctrines which justify the separate consideration of some of these topics often deal with the content of the contractual obligation and the remedies available for its breach. It is still the principles of agreement honed in the last century, which govern the formation of such agreements.

This is not to say that there will not be continual tensions as the old principles are adapted to new challenges. However, such adaptation is a sign of a responsive law rather than an outdated one. An example from the emerging world of electronic commerce will be used to illustrate this. In 1999 due to 'a software error' a major high street retailer advertised Sony TVs on its Website at £3 each when the correct price should have been £299.99. Unsurprisingly this 'offer' was 'accepted' by a large number of people, including one person who ordered 1,700 sets and, according to press reports, by many lawyers employed by City of London firms of solicitors. The press statement issued by one of the City law firms acting for its employees said that a contract was concluded on the basis that the 'advert' was an offer which the employee accepted by the order. It would seem to be absurd if the retailer were obliged to honour all these 'contracts'. However, the old rules do not dictate this. It has long been established that a party cannot 'snap up' an offer which he knows to be mistaken.[205] The prediction of Brownsword and Howells might well prove correct when they say:[206]

> At all events, complex and messy formation questions, albeit in a revolutionary electronic environment, look like more grist to a familiar mill than the stuff out of which radically new principles will need to be forged.

It is suggested that a responsive law of contract formation should be able to meet the new challenges of an electronic era. What is really at issue is simply

---

[204] See McKendrick, 'English Contract Law. A Rich Past, An Uncertain Future' (1997) 50 CLP 25 at 62.

[205] See *Hartog* v *Colin & Shields* [1939] 3 All ER 566 discussed in Chapter 2.

[206] 'When Surfers Start to Shop: Internet Commerce and Contract Law' (1999) 19 Leg Stud 287 at 298–9.

how responsive it must be. Early indicators may well have overstated the degree of adaptation required. In 1998 the European Commission published a draft directive on certain aspects of electronic commerce[207] which provides that contracts concluded at a distance which involve the customer signifying agreement on his computer shall not be binding until the customer has received an acknowledgement of his order and has in turn confirmed the order.[208] On first reading this appears to be a radical rewriting of the process of contract formation but from another perspective it is no more revolutionary than the 'cooling off period' required by statute in relation to contracts for the provision of credit.[209] What is clear, however, is that the means to deal so effortlessly with those in different jurisdictions may require an approach to such contracts which itself is no respecter of national boundaries. It is this pursuit of a unified law of contract or at least a number of harmonious separate systems which in this context and others might require the abandonment of some of the eccentricities of our own law of contract[210] and force us to question whether some of the new challenges require more flexible responses.[211]

---

[207] COM (1998) 586; OJ 1999/C 30/04.
[208] Article 11.
[209] See Consumer Credit Act 1974, ss 67–73.
[210] See the omission from the Principles of European Contract Law of the postal rule of acceptance.
[211] See above, p. 144, the solutions to the problem of the battle of the forms proposed by the Vienna Convention, Unidroit, the Principles of European Contract Law and the American Uniform Commercial Code.

4

CONSIDERATION AND ITS SUBSTITUTES

Few things seem to provoke such divergent opinions amongst contract lawyers as the doctrine of consideration. They disagree about what the doctrine tells us about the general law of contract, even more fundamentally about what it is and indeed about whether any of this matters at all! We will briefly examine these oppositions before considering which views find support in the case law.

In his classic *History of English Law* Holdsworth wrote: 'The theory of the English Law of Contract is contained in the doctrine of consideration'.[1] A contemporary writer has expressed a similar sentiment, certainly less reverentially and perhaps less seriously: 'Consideration is to contract law as Elvis is to rock-and-roll: the King'.[2] Perhaps its detractors would continue the analogy and say both are dead and buried. In his account of the moral basis of contract Charles Fried considers whether the doctrine of consideration provides a rival explanation for the enforcement of contracts and concludes that 'the standard doctrine of consideration ... does not pose a challenge to my conception of contract law as rooted in promise, for the simple reason that that doctrine is too internally inconsistent to offer an alternative at all'.[3]

The traditional definition in *Currie* v *Misa* describes consideration as:[4]

> ... either ... some right profit or benefit accruing to one party, or some forbearance, detriment, loss or responsibility given, suffered or undertaken by the other.

This definition is said to emphasise the idea of reciprocity. The business of the law of contract is the enforcement of bargains not gifts. When the case

---

[1] Vol. 3, p. 413.
[2] Gordon, 'A Dialogue about the Doctrine of Consideration' (1990) 75 Cornell Law Rev 987 at n. 2 (an eminently readable article which to give a further flavour of its style describes in n. 4 a conversational article by two leading 'critical legal scholars' as 'like a pair of old acid-heads chewing over a passage in Sartre'). See also the more circumspect historical comments of Gilmore: 'The balance-wheel of the great machine *was* the theory of consideration ...', (1974) *The Death of Contract*, p. 18 (again, eminently readable) and Ibbetson: 'Consideration, in the sense of reciprocity, *had* been for centuries the linchpin of the English law of contract', (1999) *A Historical Introduction to the Law of Obligations*, p. 236. When lawyers begin to express the worth of something by simile and metaphor, one should examine closely their motives and evidence.
[3] Fried (1981) *Contract as Promise*, p. 35.
[4] (1875) LR 10 Ex 153 at 162.

law is examined we will see that this broad definition is not applied to every situation that might fall within it. As Grant Gilmore said in his punchy account of the origins of contract, 'it is clear that there are benefits and benefits, detriments and detriments'.[5] Sometimes a benefit or detriment in fact is not recognised as one in law;[6] sometimes the court recognises as a benefit or detriment in law something which was not so regarded by the parties.[7] Because the traditional definition is not always determinative, some commentators have suggested that it should be abandoned. They regard the doctrine of consideration is an amalgam of policy reasons sufficient to justify the enforcement of a promise.[8] On this view, consideration is no more than a reason, any reason, for enforcing a promise. Treitel disputes this approach which he regards as 'a negation of any applicable rules of law'.[9]

Does any of this theoretical and definitional debate matter? From an early time it was clear that the doctrine would always be applied in a way that seeks to give effect to the parties' intentions, whatever the rigid definitions would seem to dictate. In what may be the first serious English work on the law of contract,[10] Sir Jeffrey Gilbert recognised that the courts would 'strain to find a consideration, since men were presumed not to have been acting in vain in purporting to enter a contract'.[11] The same sentiment was well expressed in an early Canadian case:[12]

> In this situation as in many others, the rule of reason will at last prevail, that if the parties do in truth agree ... effect will be given to the bargain which they have voluntarily made rather than to any fanciful rule of law, laid down at a time when the fashion of the courts was to thwart all contracts ...

This approach is even more prevalent in the modern cases. The technical doctrine appears to be the last resort of the scoundrel according to Donaldson J who said: 'A defence of lack of consideration rarely has merit.'[13] We will now see how the courts have applied, disapplied and redefined the doctrine of consideration to avoid giving aid to unmeritorious claimants and in order to give effect to various policy prescriptions.

---

[5] *Op. cit.*, p. 20. Gilmore maintains that the modern doctrine of consideration originates in the deliberate misrepresentation of past precedent by the United States' most eminent contemporary judge, Oliver Wendell Holmes.

[6] See the discussion of *Wade* v *Simeon* (1846) 2 CB 548 below.

[7] See the discussion of *The Atlantic Baron* in Chapter 12.

[8] Atiyah, 'Consideration: A Restatement', ch. 8 in Atiyah (1988) *Essays on Contract*. This is an amended version of an inaugural lecture published in 1971.

[9] See 'Consideration: A critical Analysis of Professor Atiyah's Fundamental Restatement' (1976) 50 Australian LJ 439. See also Reiter, 'Courts, Consideration and Common Sense' (1977) 27 U Toronto LJ 439. Significantly Treitel supplements the traditional definition in terms of benefit and detriment with the concept of 'invented' consideration. This is used to explain cases where the courts have regarded an act as consideration when the parties apparently did not, e.g. *Shadwell* v *Shadwell* (1860) 9 CB (NS) 159 at 174 *per* Erle CJ who says that the promisor 'may have made a most material change in his position'.

[10] See British Library MS 265 and Ibbetson (n.2 above) p. 216.

[11] *Ibid.*, p. 238, n. 122.

[12] *Gardner et al.* v *Ford et al.* (1863) 13 UCCP 446 at 449 quoted by Reiter (n. 9 above) p. 439.

[13] *Thoresen Car Ferries Ltd* v *Weymouth Portland Borough Council* [1977] 2 Lloyd's Rep 614.

THE TRADITIONAL DEFINITION

The traditional definition of consideration refers to benefit to the promisee or detriment to the promisor as alternatives. Either alone would be sufficient. Suppose that I agree to sell my motorcycle for £10,000 but that I ask the purchaser to pay the money to an impoverished friend. The purchaser's promise would be as much a detriment to him as if it had been made to me. However, it is less clear that the promise to pay a third party is a benefit to me.

None the less, in many circumstances, such as the simple exchange of mutual promises, both benefit and detriment will be present on both sides. Each promise will be simultaneously a detriment to the promisor and a benefit to the promisee. This was illustrated when the Court of Appeal[14] applied the traditional definition to an auction which was said to be without reserve. It was held that there was a collateral contract between the auctioneer and the bidder under which the auctioneer promised to sell the goods to the highest bidder. This undertaking was detrimental to the auctioneer and beneficial to the bidder. The consideration moving from the bidder was his bids which, to his detriment, could be accepted unless withdrawn, and which benefited the auctioneer by raising the bidding.

CONSIDERATION AND GIFT

The law draws a clear distinction between a contract and a gift. Agreement, consideration and an intention to create legal relations constitute a contract. A gift is constituted by a clear intention of the donor to transfer his interest in property together with physical or symbolic delivery.[15] The crucial distinction between a contract and a gift is therefore reciprocal consideration.[16] This has very important practical consequences because if a promise is classified as a gift it will not be enforceable in the absence of delivery or, perhaps, the finding of a trust. English law may be thought to be committed to a rather narrow law of gift and a comparatively wide law of contract. Like many legal distinctions, that between contract and gift is easier to state than to apply to marginal cases. The difficulty is distinguishing between a contract and a conditional gift. An example from a newspaper not known for its law reports will suffice: 'A bingo fan who won £30,000 was ordered to pay two pals £10,000 each yesterday after she welshed on a deal to share prize money.'[17]

---

[14] *Barry* v *Davies* [2000] 1 WLR 1962.
[15] See Bridge (1996) *Personal Property Law.* 2nd edn, pp. 80–88.
[16] One consequence of dismissing the doctrine of consideration from his theory of contract is that Fried brings within his theory many promises, which would presently fall within the law of gift. See Fried (1981) *Contract as Promise*, ch. 3.
[17] Less amusing but of rather greater precedential value is *Wyatt* v *Kreglinger and Fernau* [1933] 1 KB 793 (pension subject to not working in wool trade – restriction void for being in unreasonable restraint of trade. *Obiter dicta* Slesser and Greer LJJ stated that the offer was contractual; Scrutton LJ stated that it was a conditional gift.

The question for the court[18] was whether the winner's promise to share her winnings was a conditional gift to her pals (i.e. conditional upon them doing the same) which was not perfected by symbolic delivery (perhaps sharing the cards used to play the game) or whether it was a contractual promise accepted by a reciprocal undertaking. The court obviously took the second view. Where a party makes an offer which is contingent upon some happening which is not within the control of the offeree, this will be presumed to be a conditional gift (e.g. if you catch flu I will pay you £100). If the contingency involves some action or inaction of the offeree, then it will more readily constitute a contract (e.g. if you use my smokeball and catch flu I will pay you £100). At base the issue is one of finding the promisor's true intention. Did he intend to ask for something in return for his promise or did he merely offer a gift, which was qualified in some way?[19]

CONSIDERATION NEED NOT BE ADEQUATE

This requirement expresses the general policy of the law of contract to enforce a contract even if there is no equivalence of exchange. That the sale was at a gross undervalue or overvalue[20] does not of itself render it unenforceable. Such an agreement might suggest that there has been an abuse of the bargaining process, that the purchaser and vendor respectively misrepresented the value of the thing being sold. If this is so, then the law of misrepresentation might provide a ground for setting aside a contract that was otherwise enforceable.

On this basis an agreement to rent property for £1 per annum would be enforceable as being made for sufficient, if not adequate, consideration.[21] In contrast, a husband's bare promise to pay his wife on separation £100 p.a.

---

18 The scenario is not a new one. Gamblers have long had difficulty keeping promises to share their winnings. See *Scot* v *Haughton and Fuller* (1706) 2 Vern 560 (master gave servant lottery ticket on understanding that master's daughter would get half the prize if it was greater than £1 – won £1,000).

19 The question is sometimes asked whether the act of the promisee was requested by the promisor. In *Southwark London Borough Council* v *Logan* [1995] TLR 565 at 565 Neill LJ delivering the judgment of the court said: 'It was true that ... forbearance to act could constitute ... consideration ... But the forbearance must be at the express or implied request of the other party ...'. This is probably linguistic subterfuge because a request can be express or implied and an implied request is as difficult to identify as it is to distinguish a conditional gift from a contract.

20 A contrary suggestion may have been made unintentionally by Lord Templeman in *Lipkin Gorman* v *Karpnale* [1991] 2 AC 548. The case involves a solicitor who stole money from his practice and lost it gambling at a casino. In order to defeat the victim of the theft's claim for the return of the money, the casino owners argued that they had given good consideration for it. The House of Lords rejected this argument. Lord Templeman said that even if, as he was entitled to, the gambler had bought drinks with some of the £150,000 worth of chips, this would not constitute good consideration. This may be interpreted to suggest that it was the difference in value between the drinks and the chips, which would prevent it being good consideration. It is difficult to generalise from this apparently incautious statement and it might mean no more than the gambling and refreshment contracts fall to be considered separately. See Treitel, pp. 81–2.

21 *Thomas* v *Thomas* (1842) 2 QB 851.

would not be enforceable unless she gave something, even of minimal value, in return.[22] This rule is the origin of the phrase 'peppercorn' rent, which refers to a minimal rent in the past often literally a peppercorn. Indeed, it has been said that the peppercorn 'does not cease to be good consideration if it is established that the promisee does not like pepper and will throw away the corn'.[23] This comment was made in a case where it was held that three chocolate wrappers were part of the consideration tendered in a transaction.[24] The principle may also be illustrated by bailment[25] cases such as *Bainbridge* v *Furmston*[26] where the claimant allowed the defendant to weigh two boilers. Whatever the motive[27] of the defendant, the removal of the boilers was perhaps a benefit to the defendant and certainly a detriment to the claimant sufficient to support a promise that they are returned in good order.[28]

This principle is apparently contradicted by the decision in *Lipkin Gorman* v *Karpnale*[29] where it was held that gambling chips provided by a casino did not constitute good consideration for the money paid to obtain them.[30] Perhaps the best explanation of the case[31] is to limit its application to the context in which it arose; an action to recover stolen money. The interests of the victim of the theft are best served by adopting a narrow definition of consideration. The same approach is not appropriate when the transaction does not affect third parties in any way.

Salvage agreements provide an exception to the adequacy principle. When such agreements are entered in necessitous circumstances there is considerable opportunity for extortion. Consider a disabled yacht about to drift on to rocks whose crew is offered a tow to safety by a passing fishing boat for a very high fee. Such agreements are only enforced to the extent that the consideration agreed was reasonable taking into account such factors as the value of the property salvaged, the danger to which the salvor was exposed, the resources of the salvor consumed, etc.[32] The problem is one of monopoly. In the circumstances in which the yacht finds itself the fishing

---

[22] *Combe* v *Combe* [1951] 2 KB 215.

[23] *Chappell & Co Ltd* v *Nestlé Co Ltd* [1960] AC 87 at 87 *per* Lord Somervell.

[24] The issue arose indirectly under Copyright Act 1956, s 8, which provided for royalty payments to be levied on the 'ordinary retail selling price'. As part of a promotion to encourage chocolate sales, the defendants offered records in exchange for a small sum and three wrappers. The House of Lords held that the wrappers must be taken into account when calculating the royalty payable.

[25] Bailment is the relationship established between one party (the bailor) who delivers his property to another (the bailee) with the intention that the bailee should return the property or deal with it in a certain way.

[26] (1838) 8 Ad & El 743.

[27] Motive should be distinguished from consideration. See *Thomas* v *Thomas* (1842) 2 QB 851 at 859 *per* Patteson J.

[28] *Per* Patteson J.

[29] [1991] 2 AC 548.

[30] See above n. 19 for the relevance of this finding.

[31] Treitel points out that the explanation of the case could not be that the chips were themselves worthless (so were the wrappers in the *Chappell* case) or that they remained the property of the club (the boilers in *Bainbridge* remained the property of the bailor). See pp. 81–2c.

[32] *The Kingalock* (1854) 1 Sp Ecc & Ad 263 and *The Caledonia* [1903] P 104.

boat enjoys a monopoly of towing services and like many monopolists will be tempted to extract a monopoly rent. In New Zealand an analogous common law principle has been applied to other monopolists such as suppliers of electricity[33] and air traffic control services.[34]

PAST CONSIDERATION

Past consideration is consideration which predates the promise it is now said to support. In *Eastwood* v *Kenyon*[35] the guardian of a young girl borrowed money to pay for her education. After she was married her husband undertook to pay back the loan. The guardian was unable to enforce this promise because the consideration he had supplied for it, maintaining and educating the girl, was past. Past consideration should be distinguished from executed consideration. Executed consideration refers to a promise, which was made at the same time as the counter-promise, which it is said to support but which, after that time, has been performed. Suppose a neighbour sees my garden and spontaneously comes and mows the lawn and I later promise to pay her for doing so. The only consideration for my promise is past and so it is unenforceable. Suppose instead my neighbour and I agree that she will mow the lawn for £20 and she later mows the lawn. Then the consideration, which supports my promise to pay, is executed but not past.

The doctrine of past consideration supports the view that consideration helps define enforceable contracts as bargains. A promise to pay for something in the past is closer to a gift than a bargain. In so far as the doctrine admits of exceptions, it might be said to undermine the bargain theory of consideration. A colourful application of this exception occurred in *Lampleigh* v *Brathwait*[36] where the defendant who was to be hanged asked a friend to ride to Royston to seek the pardon of King James I. The friend did this and the pardon was granted. The recipient then promised to pay his friend £100 which he later refused to do. It was held that the friend could recover the promised payment because the act, though performed in the past, was requested by the defaulting party. This exception was developed in *Re Casey's Patents*[37] where someone was granted a share of certain patents for having managed them in the past. The promise of a share in the patents was said to be enforceable because the manager's work despite being past was performed at the request of the other party and also in the expectation that it would be paid for. This second precondition grafted upon the exception was confirmed by the Privy Council in *Pao On* v *Lau Yiu Long*[38]

---

[33] *Auckland Electric Power Board* v *Electricity Corporation of New Zealand Ltd* [1994] 1 NZLR 551.

[34] *Airways Corp of New Zealand* v *Geyserland Airways Ltd* [1996] 1 NZLR 116.

[35] (1840) 11 A & E 438. See also *Roscorla* v *Thomas* (1842) 3 QB 234 (sale of horse agreed – seller later gave written warranty of soundness) and *Re McArdle* [1951] Ch 669 (promise made in consideration of carrying out work – work specified already completed).

[36] [1615] Hob 105.

[37] [1892] 1 Ch 104.

[38] [1980] AC 614.

which added a third, that the subsequent promise must have been legally enforceable if it had been made in advance.

MORAL AND ECONOMIC CONSIDERATION

In the late eighteenth century Lord Mansfield[39] considered the prevalent doctrine of consideration too rigid. At first he regarded consideration as playing an evidentiary role.[40] It provided evidence of the parties' intention to be bound but was not alone determinative. If that serious intention could be proved by other means that was sufficient.[41] However, this frontal attack upon the citadel of consideration was soon repulsed.[42] A flank attack was then launched. According to Lord Mansfield, whenever someone is under a moral obligation to do something, the pre-existing moral obligation provides consideration sufficient to justify the enforcement of the promise to do that thing. However, a promise is an acknowledgement of that pre-existing moral obligation. The 'Catch 22' of its time, a promise could no more escape enforceability than a 'crazy' airman could avoid combat missions in Joseph Heller's classic.[43] A promise would always generate its own consideration. The concept of moral consideration endured for a while but was then, sometime after its champion, finally laid to rest.[44]

Some promises are simply too vague and nebulous to constitute consideration. A promise made in consideration of 'natural affection' will not be enforceable.[45] This principle is sometimes expressed as a requirement that the consideration has some economic value[46] though, as we have seen, the law is uninterested in its adequacy. This has been proposed as a possible explanation of *White* v *Bluett*[47] where it was held that a son who promised not to bore his father with complaints had not provided sufficient consideration to support the father's promise not to enforce a promissory note against his son. Most parents would value the promise of their offspring not to complain and so to them the decision proves that the traditional test of benefit and detriment is not applied to all the situations, which it ostensibly covers. That the decision is actually based upon some undisclosed policy perhaps best expressed by the Victorian ideal that children should be seen but not heard is amply supported by the language of Pollock CB. He said: 'The son had no right to complain.' In what sense? The son committed no legal wrong by doing so. Perhaps in Pollock CB's view he committed a moral wrong but we have seen that this no longer constitutes good consideration.

[39] Chief Justice from 1756.
[40] *Cf.* Fuller, 'Consideration and Form' (1941) 41 Columbia LR 799.
[41] *Pillans* v *Van Mierop* (1782) 1 Cowp 289 at 290.
[42] *Rann* v *Hughes* (1778) 7 Term Rep 350.
[43] 'Crazy' pilots must be grounded. All they had to do was ask, except that *Catch 22* states that a concern for one's own safety was the act of a sane mind. Corgi ed. at p. 54.
[44] *Eastwood* v *Kenyon* (1840) 11 A & E 438.
[45] *Bret* v *JS* (1600) Cro Eliz 756 and *Mansukhani* v *Sharkey* [1992] 2 EGLR 105.
[46] See Treitel, pp. 78–9. *Cf.* Smith, 'The Law of Contract – Alive or Dead' (1979) 13 The Law Teacher 73 at 77.
[47] (1853) 23 LJ Ex 36.

In a number of other cases promises with no obvious economic value have been enforced. These include, in an American case, an undertaking to stop smoking.[48] Another recent case appears to be inconsistent with *White* v *Bluett*. In *Pitt* v *PHH Asset Management Ltd*[49] the Court of Appeal had to consider a 'lock-out' agreement in which the seller of a house undertook not to negotiate with any third parties. It was held that the prospective purchaser provided good consideration for the seller's promise. Three items of consideration were identified: the purchaser withdrew his (empty) threat to obtain an injunction to restrain any sale to a rival bidder, the purchaser said that he would otherwise withdraw and tell the rival bidder he was so doing with the consequence that she could reduce her own bid and the purchaser promised to exchange contracts within 14 days of receiving draft contracts. The first two items identified were of undoubted economic value to the seller and so on that basis the decision may be said to be consistent with one explanation of *White* v *Bluett*. However, both items emphasised the practical benefit to the seller of the purchaser's forbearance from doing something. We have already criticised *White* v *Bluett* for its failure to recognise the practical value of the son's promised forbearance. Further, the second item of consideration emphasised the detriment to the purchaser of not doing what he was otherwise entitled to do. Properly analysed, the son in *White* was also promising not to do what he was otherwise entitled to do and yet he was said not to have provided sufficient consideration.

However, the greatest contrast with the result in *White* v *Bluett* is provided by *Ward* v *Byham*[50] where it was said that a mother's promise to look after a child and keep it happy was sufficient consideration to support the illegitimate father's promise to pay the mother a weekly allowance. It is difficult to see why the son's promise not to complain and thereby make his father happy was not good consideration when the promise of a mother to ensure that her child was happy did constitute good consideration. Perhaps Lord Mansfield's ghost holds the key to reconciling the two cases because few would deny that the father of an illegitimate child had a moral duty[51] to support the child.

COMPROMISE AGREEMENTS

When legal disputes are compromised the agreement to end the dispute is enforceable as a contract. Typically, in exchange for the payment of a sum of money, one party agrees to give up its untested legal claim against the other. Powerful arguments of policy support the enforcement of such compromises.[52]

---

[48] *Hamer* v *Sidaway* (1891) 27 NE 256.
[49] [1994] 1 WLR 327.
[50] [1956] 1 WLR 496.
[51] The mother of an illegitimate child has a statutory duty to maintain that child (National Assistance Act 1948, s 42) and so the mere act of supporting the child could not constitute good consideration. See below, pp. 172–3.
[52] In his recent overhaul of the civil justice system, Lord Woolf considered the encouragement of out-of-court settlements of disputes to be a cardinal principle.

The conflict is brought to an end and further litigation is avoided. The overworked courts are spared another case and the public purse is thereby saved expense.[53] This is illustrated by *Cook* v *Wright*[54] where the claimant agreed not to take proceedings against the defendant for a statutory contribution towards street improvements if the defendant agreed to pay a reduced amount by instalments. The complicating factor was that as the owner's agent the defendant was not actually personally liable to make the payment. The claimant erroneously thought that the defendant was liable to make a contribution. The court held that the compromise agreement was enforceable. To promise to give up a cause of action against another which, the claimant wrongly but honestly believes to be well grounded, is good consideration for a reciprocal promise. This conclusion can be justified by the traditional definition of consideration according to which consideration may consist of either a benefit to the promisee or a detriment to the promisor. Promising to give up a non-existent cause of action against another is a benefit to the promisee who is freed from the time and trouble of having to defend the claim. It does not matter that giving up such an action was not a detriment to the promisor[55] because, in the traditional definition, benefit and detriment are alternatives. The position is not changed when normal costs are considered. Although a successful defendant will usually be awarded costs against the claimant, court costs do not usually operate on an indemnity basis. Rather the costs awarded against an unsuccessful claimant are assessed by reference to a notional scale and the defendant's actual costs will invariably exceed the amount he recovers.

In contrast, in *Wade* v *Simeon*[56] the party who promised to give up a non-existent cause of action was actually aware that his action was ill founded. The court held that the compromise agreement was not supported by good consideration. The language of the court made it clear that they could not lend any support to someone who abuses the process of the courts and asserts a cause of action they know to be non-existent. Tindal CJ said it was '*contra bonos mores* [against good morals] and certainly contrary to all the principles of natural justice' to do so. Put in policy terms, it seems that the policy of encouraging the out of court settlement of disputes yields to a higher policy of curbing fraud.[57] This result simply cannot be explained by reference to the traditional benefit/detriment definition. It is as beneficial to a party not to have to defend an ill-founded claim which the claimant thinks

---

[53] The costs of running the court system and the costs of funding legal aid.

[54] (1861) 1 B & S 559.

[55] In fact, it is a benefit to the *promisor* not to bring an ill-founded action.

[56] (1846) 2 CB 548.

[57] The most important statute in the law of contract is surely The Dastardly Deeds Act which has a single provision stating that the courts should do nothing to assist and everything to frustrate and even punish those who seek to perpetrate fraud. A fictitious Act but a serious point. Whatever technical doctrines would seem to dictate, fraudsters will not receive assistance from the courts. We have already seen several manifestations of this policy in the sub-rules and exceptions applicable in the tort of deceit (more generous rules of remoteness, etc., no requirement of materiality, etc.) and the same policy is implemented here.

is well founded as it is not to defend an ill-founded claim which the claimant knows to be so. In short, if there was consideration in *Cook* v *Wright* there was equally consideration in *Wade* v *Simeon*. Of course, the result reached in the latter case is sensible. The point is simply that it cannot be justified by reference to the orthodox definition of consideration.[58] The area of compromises therefore provides powerful evidence to support the approach of Atiyah that the doctrine of consideration is no more than a loose amalgam of policy reasons for enforcing or denying legal effect to promises.

PRE-EXISTING DUTIES

A particular problem is posed for the doctrine of consideration when someone performs an act or promises something that they were already under a pre-existing legal obligation to do. The approach of the law differs according to the source of the pre-existing duty. The pre-existing duty may arise from a contract with a third party,[59] from a contract with the subsequent promisor[60] or from the law generally.[61] The first and third of these situations are dealt with here and the second in a later chapter. This is because cases within the first and third situations raise issues of contract formation while those in the second situation necessarily raise issues of contractual modification. In a traditional doctrinally arranged textbook all three situations would be discussed together in a chapter on contract formation. The policy factors which are relevant to contract formation are not the same as those which are raised by modifications of existing contracts.

In a classic article Lon Fuller described three functions performed by the doctrine of consideration.[62] These were an evidentiary function, to provide evidence of the existence of the contract; a cautionary function, to prevent incautious commitments; and a channelling function, to provide the parties with a means of signalling to the court that the agreement was to be enforceable. Fuller described this latter function as 'the facilitation of judicial diagnosis'. It is suggested that these three functions are more appropriate to the consideration as a requirement for the formation of contracts than to consideration as a requirement for a contractually binding modification. In cases where the existence as opposed to the effect of a modification is in issue other evidence is available independent of the consideration required.

---

[58] In *Pitt* v *PHH Asset Management Ltd* [1994] 1 WLR 327 the purchaser's empty threat to obtain an injunction was treated as good consideration without any enquiry whether the purchaser was, or was not, aware that the action was bound to fail. If he was aware, *Wade* v *Simeon* suggests that promise not to seek an injunction, cannot constitute good consideration whereas, if he honestly thought he was entitled to an injunction, *Cook* v *Wright* suggests that the promise would be valid consideration. Neither case nor principle was cited by the court or counsel.

[59] For example, A contracts with B to do something which A is already bound to do under a contract with C.

[60] For example, A contracts with B to do something; later B promises to pay a further sum to A to complete the same service.

[61] For example, A contracts with B to do something which A is under a statutory duty to do.

[62] 'Consideration and Form' (1941) 41 Colum L Rev 799.

Writings or testimony of the parties are surely more trustworthy forms of evidence. If for any reason a party is falsely trying to prove the existence of a modification, little protection is afforded to the other party by an insistence that consideration be required when the court refuses to investigate the adequacy of that consideration. The cautionary protection of consideration is less necessary in the modification setting; this function is served by the requirement of consideration when the contract was initially formed. The giving of consideration in the original contract adequately guarded against the entering of incautious commitments; there is little need for the parties to be further cautioned about the seriousness of their agreement at the modification stage.[63] There seem to be great dangers which may attend the use of consideration as a 'signal' to the courts. It has been observed that:[64]

> the consideration signal produced by a party of superior bargaining power can be a smokescreen for overreaching, often accepted by the courts as conclusive proof that the agreement should be enforced.

The law relating to contractual modifications comprises several legal doctrines of which the pre-existing duty doctrine of consideration is only one. The proper policies to be pursued by the law of contractual modifications are developed in Chapter 12. This discussion is intended only to emphasise the point that the doctrine of consideration functions very differently in different contexts.

We will now examine two of the sources of pre-existing obligations. The third source of pre-existing duty is a contract with the subsequent promisor which raises issues of contractual modification rather than formation and so is examined in Chapter 12. When considering pre-existing duties it is useful to bear in mind a distinction between factual and legal definitions of consideration. A factual definition of consideration emphasises the fact of benefit or detriment that may result from the mere performance of the pre-existing duty. A legal definition of consideration requires something in excess of the pre-existing legal duty.

The pre-existing duty arises from a contract with a third party

Three cases decided in the 1860s are said to support the proposition that the act of performing a contractual duty owed to a third party can constitute good consideration.[65] The cases are not wholly satisfactory[66] and a flavour of

---

[63] See Restatement Contracts 2d 1981, s 89(a), comment A.
[64] Crocker, 'Contracts. Modification Agreements; Need for New Consideration. Economic Duress: Note' (1975) 50 Wash L Rev 960 at 964–5.
[65] *Shadwell* v *Shadwell* (1860) 9 CB (NS) 159; *Scotson* v *Pegg* (1861) 30 LJ Ex 225; *Chichester* v *Cobb* (1866) 14 LT 433.
[66] In the first two the promisor might have in fact done acts in excess of the duty owed to the third party. In *Pfizer Corp* v *Paton* [1965] AC 512 at 536 Lord Reid may be taken to suggest the contrary when he says that the supply of NHS drugs to a patient does not create a contract between the recipient and the chemist because the latter is already under a contractual obligation to supply them. However, it is likely that at the time Lord Reid was not thinking about consideration but rather about contractual intention.

this can be obtained by looking at one: *Shadwell* v *Shadwell*. This involved an uncle's promise to his nephew to 'make up' his earnings to a given level in view of his intended marriage. At the time a promise to marry was legally enforceable[67] and so the consideration provided by the nephew was the performance of an act he was already obliged to do under the terms of a contract with a third party (his fiancée). Erle CJ and Keating J held that the nephew provided good consideration but did so without reference to the pre-existing duty. Byles J who did refer to the pre-existing obligation held that the promise was not binding.[68] However, the matter can now be said to be clarified by the Privy Council in *The Eurymedon*[69] where it was held that the stevedores' act of unloading goods was a sufficient consideration to support an exemption of liability from damage even though the unloading was something that the stevedores were already contractually obliged to do by their contract with the carrier.[70]

In *The Eurymedon* Lord Wilberforce did not distinguish between the performance of a pre-existing contractual duty owed to a third party and the promise to perform one. However, the collateral contract under which the goods owners extended to the stevedores an exemption from liability for damage to the goods was described as a unilateral one. A unilateral contract involves the exchange of a promise (here the exemption) for an act (here the unloading). Therefore, the *ratio decidendi* of the case only strictly extends to the proposition that the performance, as opposed to the promise of performance, of a contractual duty owed to a third party can constitute consideration. However, the *ratio decidendi* of a further Privy Council decision addressed this circumstance.

The exchange contemplated in *Pao On* v *Lau Yiu Long*[71] was a very simple one. An individual, LY, wanted to obtain a property. Unfortunately, the way the transaction was effected, by an exchange of shares, makes it seem complicated. A property was owned by a private company (SO) all of whose shares were in turn owned by an individual (PO). A contract (the main agreement) was entered between PO, SO and a public company (FC) the majority of whose shares were owned by LY, who was not personally a party to this contract. The main agreement provided that all the shares in SO (and so the property) would be transferred to FC in exchange for a number of FC

---

[67] And surprisingly remained so until Law Reform (Miscellaneous Provisions) Act 1970 s 1(1). As a contract of 'personal service', it could not be specifically performed. See generally Chapter 16.

[68] On the basis that there was no contractual intention. This was approved in *Jones* v *Padavatton* [1969] 1 WLR 328 at 333 *per* Salmon LJ.

[69] [1975] AC 154.

[70] *The Eurymedon* has been approved in *The New York Star* [1981] 1 WLR 138 and *The Mahkutai* [1996] AC 650.

[71] [1980] AC 614. This case does not fit easily in the category of pre-existing contractual duties owed to third parties. Three parties were involved only because of the separate legal personalities of LY and the public company of which he was a majority shareholder. If the corporate veil is lifted, the case becomes analogous to the cases considered later involving a modification of an existing contract. See generally the discussion of economic duress in this case and in Chapter 12.

shares. PO further promised to retain a certain number of these shares for a stipulated period. PO sought to protect himself against a fall in the value of FC shares during the retention period by entering a separate agreement with LY under which LY agreed to buy back the shares at the end of the retention period for the original transfer price. This arrangement would have been effective to protect PO against any fall in the value of FC shares but would also have forced him to give up any increase. When he realised this, PO refused to proceed with the main agreement unless the 'buy-back' arrangement with LY was replaced with a true indemnity (i.e. which protected PO against a decline in FC shares but left him with any gains). To protect public confidence in FC, LY agreed to the indemnity. The main agreement was performed. FC shares fell in value during the retention period and PO sought to enforce the indemnity.

LY took three objections to the enforcement of the indemnity: the consideration for it was past,[72] the only consideration was the promise to perform a pre-existing contractual duty owed to a third party (FC) and the agreement was obtained by economic duress.[73] The Privy Council held that the second objection failed because the promise to perform a pre-existing contractual duty owed to a third party does constitute good consideration.[74]

The position now seems to be that it is good consideration either to perform (*Eurymedon*) or to promise to perform (*Pao On*) a contractual duty owed to a third party. Both propositions emerge from cases where practical good sense demands that the doctrine of consideration should not operate to frustrate an arm's length commercial agreement. Both decisions categorically reject the application of a legal definition of consideration described earlier.[75] Because both are broad-based policy decisions which admit no counter-argument,[76] the principles laid down do not even seem to require the presence of a factual benefit or detriment. In both cases lip service is paid to the need for consideration but its 'discovery' does appear to be little more than assertion.

The pre-existing duty arises from the law generally

This is a residual category for pre-existing duties that do not arise from either a contract with a third party or a contract with the subsequent promisor. The general approach of the cases is to apply a legal definition of consideration. On this approach the promise or performance of a contractual duty owed to a third party will not itself amount to good consideration.

---

[72] That is, entering the main agreement which had already occurred. This argument failed because the facts fell within the exception to past consideration. See above, p. 164.

[73] This argument failed because the pressure was not sufficiently compelling to amount to compulsion. See further Chapter 12.

[74] Departing from the earlier contrary decision in *Jones* v *Waite* (1839) 5 Bing NC 341 at 351.

[75] That is, one which requires something in excess of the pre-existing duty.

[76] See, in particular, the hostility of the courts to 'technical' arguments, which might subvert the broad principle of third-party immunity, established in *The Eurymedon*.

Therefore, a witness who was required under a subpoena[77] to attend to give evidence at a hearing could not enforce a promise to pay a fee.[78] However, it is true to say that this old case is out of line with modern practice where expert witnesses are paid an agreed fee and even other witnesses required to attend are paid compensation.

A further illustration is provided by *Glasbrook Bros Ltd v Glamorgan CC*[79] where during a strike of mineworkers the mine owners agreed to pay a sum of money to have a force of police officers stationed at the mine. This promise was held to be enforceable. Although the police are under a general duty to protect people and property, the House of Lords thought that this duty could have been adequately discharged by having a modest mobile force ready to go to the mine at short notice if trouble was anticipated. The provision of a larger force billeted at the mine was in excess of the police authority's pre-existing duty and so amounted to legal consideration sufficient to support the mine owner's promise of payment. The provision of police services is now regulated by statute in a way that reflects the common law rule: police authorities are allowed to charge for 'special police services'.[80] In deciding whether police services are special, the court can take account of the following: whether attendance is required at a private or public place, whether violence has already occurred or will imminently occur, the nature of the event and whether adequate protection can be assured without diverting officers from other duties. Applying these factors a football club has been required to pay for police attendance at its matches.[81]

Lord Denning has consistently opposed a legal definition of consideration in cases where the pre-existing duty derives from the law generally. In *Ward v Byham*[82] he approached the case '... on the footing that, in looking after the child, the mother is only doing what she is legally bound to do. Even so, I think there was a sufficient consideration.' However, Morris and Parker LJ reached their conclusion on the basis of a legal definition. Both thought that the mother was doing something in excess of her strict statutory duty to maintain the child when she promised to prove that the child was well looked after and happy[83] and to allow the child to choose for herself whether she wished to live with the mother. A year later in *Williams v Williams*[84] Lord Denning reiterated his view that legal consideration was not necessary. The case concerned a wife's claim for sums due under a maintenance agreement in which she undertook to support herself. Lord Denning said that '... in

---

[77] Now called a witness summons.

[78] *Collins v Godefroy* (1831) 1 B & Ad 950.

[79] [1925] 2 AC 270.

[80] Police Act 1996, s 25(1).

[81] *Harris v Sheffield United FC* [1988] QB 77 applying Police Act 1964, s 15(1).

[82] [1956] 1 WLR 496. See above for the facts of this case.

[83] To say that the act of making the child happy constituted consideration is inconsistent with *White v Bluett* (1853) 23 LJ EX 36 considered above. Under the National Assistance Act 1948 a duty was cast upon a mother to care for an illegitimate child; the duty did not require her to prove that it was well cared for. The mother's offer to *prove* the child's wellbeing is a more convincing ground for finding legal consideration.

[84] [1957] 1 WLR 148.

promising to maintain herself while in desertion, the wife was only promising to do that which she was already bound to do. Nevertheless, a promise to perform an existing duty is, I think, sufficient consideration to support a promise ...'. Again, the other two members of the Court of Appeal supported the result on the grounds of a legal definition of consideration. They thought that by 'deserting' her husband she had suspended but not extinguished her right to support from him; her promise not to revive her claim to support constituted legal consideration sufficient to support his promise to pay maintenance.

The requirement of legal consideration in this situation would also appear to be inconsistent with the old reward cases. These held that offers of reward were enforceable even though the criminal law made it an offence not to report a felon[85] to the police.[86] This exception may be justified by the considerable public interest in encouraging those with knowledge of criminal activity to make it known to the proper authorities. At a more general level it shows again how the application of the doctrine of consideration has been influenced by policy factors. The reason put forward for a more generous definition of consideration in the reward cases does not of itself support the more general reform proposed by Lord Denning.

THE SUBSTITUTES

A promise contained in a deed need not be supported by consideration. A deed is a written instrument which is intended to operate as a deed and which is validly executed. Deeds were originally sealed with molten wax. The requirement of a seal has been abolished for individuals.[87] However, the deed must be signed, witnessed and delivered.[88] Similarly, the old requirements have been relaxed for many companies[89] and charities.[90]

To 'avoid' the doctrine of consideration it is not necessary to embody a contract in a deed. Some nominal consideration, the adequacy of which the courts cannot investigate, could be introduced to render an otherwise gratuitous promise enforceable. However, a major advantage of using a deed is the greater limitation period which is available to bring an action. An action for breach of contract must presently[91] be brought within six years of the breach.[92] An action on a deed must only be brought within twelve years from the date of breach of contract.[93] Deeds are widely used in the

---

[85] A felon was someone who had committed a serious crime.

[86] That is, misprision of felony, which was abolished by Criminal Law Act 1967, s 5(1).

[87] Law of Property (Miscellaneous Provisions) Act 1989, s 1(2).

[88] Respectively ss 1(4), 1(3)(a) and 1(3)(b).

[89] Companies Act 1985, s 36A(4).

[90] Charities Act 1993, ss 50 and 60.

[91] The Law Commission have proposed a new three-year period to run from when the claimant knows or should know that he has a cause of action subject to a 'long stop' of ten years or 30 years for personal injury claims from breach.

[92] Limitation Act 1980, s 5. Where damages are claimed for personal injury, it is three years from the later of the date of breach or the date of knowledge as defined in s 14(1).

[93] Limitation Act 1980, s 8(1).

construction industry and elsewhere where a breach of contract may cause damage that only manifests itself many years later. This presents the problem that a claimant could lose his action for breach of contract (other than one for personal injury) before he was even aware that he had one.[94] This occurred in *Lynn v Bamber*[95] where plum trees were purchased in 1921 but it was not until 1928 that the buyer discovered they were not the warranted variety. An example of the value of the longer limitation period applicable to deeds is provided by the litigation following the heavy liabilities incurred by Lloyd's 'Names', the individuals whose assets underwrite the risks assumed by insurers at Lloyd's of London. The Names were exposed to these liabilities because of the negligent advice they were given by advising agents many of whom owed the Names a contractual duty of care. In many cases the contractual limitation period had expired by the time that the Names were aware of the losses to which they were exposed. Some Names managed to sue their advisers in tort[96]; others who had embodied their contracts in deeds were able to take advantage of the full twelve-year limitation period.[97]

If deeds are the oldest substitute for consideration, estoppel is the latest. A person is said to be estopped when he is prevented from denying something. There are many varieties of estoppel. We have already discussed estoppel by convention, which may prevent a party from departing from an assumption made by the other when negotiating a contract and proprietary estoppel which may require a promisor to give effect to representations which he made in negotiations.[98] Both types of estoppel are part of the legal control of the negotiating process. Estoppel by representation operates to prevent a person from denying the truth of a representation of fact, which he/she has made.[99] This limitation means that it cannot operate to give effect to statements as to the future and cannot operate as an alternative to a contract supported by consideration as a means of giving legal effect to promises. The doctrine of promissory estoppel does give effect to promises but the modern doctrine originates and has been developed in cases dealing with promises to modify existing contracts. For this reason it is examined in Chapter 12 with other legal doctrines which collectively constitute the law on contractual modifications. In any event, where the doctrine applies the modifying promise is given a limited legal effect which falls short of a contract modification supported by consideration. In other jurisdictions promissory estoppel has been developed, sometimes in amalgamation with one or more

---

[94] Section 14A contains a provision similar to that applicable to personal injury (s 14(1)) which starts time running from the date of knowledge. However, s 14A has been interpreted to apply only to latent damage arising from the breach of a tortious as opposed to a contractual duty of care. *Iron and Trade Mutual Insurance Co Ltd v JF Buckenham* [1990] 1 All ER 808 and *Société Commerciale de Réassurance v ERAS (International) Ltd* [1992] 1 Lloyd's Rep 570.

[95] [1930] 2 KB 72.

[96] *Henderson v Merrett Syndicates Ltd* [1995] 2 AC 145.

[97] *Aiken v Stewart Wrightson Members' Agency Ltd* [1995] 1 WLR 1281.

[98] See Chapter 2.

[99] *Jorden v Money* (1854) 5 HL Cas 185.

of the other types of estoppel to provide a means of enforcing promises without any restriction to modifying ones.[100] Such a unified doctrine of estoppel provides a substitute for the doctrine of consideration as a means of giving legal effect to promises. In this country there are mounting pressures to move in the same direction. Indeed some tentative steps have been taken. Later I argue that such a development should be resisted because it will produce an over-general doctrine that is insufficiently responsive to the different contexts to which it is required to apply.[101] At this point we will simply illustrate the development by reference to the Australian case that marked the creation in that jurisdiction of such a unified doctrine.

The facts of *Walton's Stores (Interstate) Ltd* v *Maher*[102] are fairly straight-forward. The owner of premises was negotiating with a major retail chain to build a shop on his land for lease to them. Both parties thought that a deal had been finalised but the relevant documents were never executed. The owner demolished the existing building and began to construct the new shop before the retail chain said it did not intend to proceed. In the High Court the majority[103] held that the owner had acted upon an assumption that a contract would come into existence[104] and that the doctrine of promissory estoppel prevented the retail chain from going back on the assumption made. Although no contract was entered, the owner was in this case protected by the expanded doctrine of promissory estoppel as if there had been such a contract.

What then is the relationship between such an expanded doctrine of estoppel and consideration? The High Court addressed this question and concluded that the two are not inconsistent. Estoppel justifies the enforcement of the promise to the extent necessary to prevent detriment being suffered by the promisee. In contrast, a promise supported by consideration is enforced to the extent necessary to make good the expectations excited in the promisee. However, experience in Australia, and in the United States, which also has a more extensive doctrine of estoppel, would suggest that this theoretical distinction is not observed in practice.[105] If this is so, the relationship between the traditional conception of a contract supported by consideration and any expanded doctrine of estoppel will prove problematic.

---

[100] See Halson, 'The Offensive Limits of Promissory Estoppel' [1999] *LMCLQ* 256, especially pp. 261–8.

[101] See Chapter 12.

[102] (1988) 164 CLR 387.

[103] Mason CJ and Wilson J in a joint judgment and Brennan J.

[104] A minority of Deane and Gaudron JJ held that the owner had relied upon a statement of existing fact that the contracts had been exchanged and so could rely upon a traditional estoppel.

[105] See the article by Halson, cited in n. 100 above.

5

FORM, INTENTION AND CERTAINTY

FORM

Non-lawyers sometimes think that there is a requirement for all contracts to be in writing. This misimpression is reinforced by the way we talk about contracts. Questions such as: 'Have you seen the contract? Have you signed the contract?', etc. assume a written document. In reality, a contract is a juristic creation, a bundle of rights and obligations. Indeed, a moment's reflection upon the number of contracts concluded in the average day (buying a paper, a bus ticket, etc.) would reveal the practical inconvenience of requiring all contracts to be written.

In the past many more transactions than now were required to be in writing. The Statute of Frauds 1677 provided that a wide variety of contracts were to be unenforceable if not in writing or evidenced in writing including contracts for the sale of land,[1] contracts of guarantee[2] and contracts for the sale of goods of £10 or more.[3] In the preamble the purpose of the statute was stated to be the avoidance of 'many fraudulent practices, which are commonly endeavoured to be upheld by perjury and subornation of perjury'. It was thought that the forensic processes of the courts were not sufficiently developed to be able satisfactorily to find the truth between competing testimonies[4] and that such difficulties would be reduced if a requirement of writing were imposed. The formal requirements imposed by the statute may be said to perform an evidentiary function.[5] This may be the reason why requirements of form are associated with legal systems in an early stage of their development.[6] However, we will see that modern legal systems also impose requirements of form but do so in relation to narrower categories of contract with the purpose of furthering particular policy objectives.

As the forensic abilities of the courts improved and certain restrictive rules of evidence were abolished e.g., that a person was not allowed to testify in

---

[1] Section 4.

[2] Section 4. This section also covers promises by personal representatives to personally pay damages, contracts made in consideration of marriage and contracts to be performed more than a year in the future.

[3] Section 17.

[4] Ibbetson (1999) *A Historical Introduction to the Law of Obligations*, p. 203.

[5] See Chapter 4 for a discussion of the evidentiary, cautionary and channelling functions of formalities and consideration.

[6] For example, Atiyah (1995) *Introduction to Contract*. 5th edn, p. 162.

any proceedings in which he was interested, the original 'evidentiary' rationale for the Statute of Frauds was no longer applicable. Indeed, the statute itself became a trap for the unwary denying enforceability to unobjectionable bargains.[7] The courts fought against this and developed ingenious doctrines and distinctions to avert its harsher effects. A doctrine of part performance was developed which operated as an alternative to writing in relation to contracts for the sale of land.[8] In relation to contracts for the sale of goods, the statute was evaded by distinguishing between a variation and a rescission of a contract. Although the former, like the contract it amended, was required to be in writing, the latter was not. This distinction was used by the courts to give effect to otherwise unobjectionable modifications.[9] Collins has described this evasion of the 1677 statute[10] in this way:

> ... the rules invariably become diluted and attenuated, for convincing non-documentary evidence of serious though informal undertakings based on trust will inevitably occur and induce a court to abandon its requirement of formality for the sake of protecting the genuine expectations of the parties ...

In view of the widespread dissatisfaction[11] with the statute, which Lord Wright described as an 'excrescence on the common law',[12] it is surprising how long it endured. Its longevity was probably in part attributable to the success of the courts in evading it. It was not until 1954[13] that s 4 of the Statute of Frauds was repealed (except in relation to guarantees) and the general requirement of writing for contracts for the sale of goods worth more than £10 was abolished.[14] The Law of Property Act 1925, s 40 substantially re-enacted the 1677 requirement that any contract for the sale of land or any interest in it must be in writing or evidenced in writing. In 1989, s 40 was repealed and the Law of Property (Miscellaneous Provisions) Act 1989, s 2 now requires all such contracts to be in writing rather than merely evidenced in writing.

We will now examine the formal requirements currently in force. These have been arranged to reflect their primary purpose.

---

[7] '... had [the Act] ... always been carried into execution according to the letter, it would have done ten times more mischief than it has done good, by protecting rather than preventing, frauds': *per* Wilmot J in *Simon* v *Metivier (or Motivis)* (1766) 1 Wm Bl 599 at 601.

[8] *Steadman* v *Steadman* [1976] AC 536. The doctrine of part performance was recognised by the Law of Property Act 1925, s 40(2). This section was repealed by the Law of Property (Miscellaneous Provisions) Act 1989, s 2(8), and part performance though a judicial creation cannot have survived this repeal.

[9] See the discussion in Chapter 12.

[10] (1999) *Regulating Contracts*, p. 206.

[11] The catalogue of criticism is recorded in Cheshire, Fifoot and Furmston, pp. 208–10.

[12] (1939) *Legal Essays and Addresses*, p. 226.

[13] Law Reform (Enforcement of Contracts) Act 1954, following a report by the Law Reform Committee.

[14] It survives in some Australian states. In Tasmania and Western Australia it is still in force and the limit is $20 while in the Northern Territory it has been raised to $50.

Cautionary formal requirements

The requirement that all contracts for the sale of an interest[15] in land be in writing[16] was enacted on the recommendation of the Law Commission.[17] The Law Commission declined to leave it to the parties to decide whether such contracts should be reduced to writing. The requirement of writing performs a cautionary function. It effectively requires resort to legal advice, which hopefully causes the parties to reflect upon the nature of the obligations which they are assuming. However, the protection thereby afforded to many is purchased at the cost of a few. Parties who enter agreements, which are not in writing, will not be able to enforce their agreements. In the past if they had done acts in reliance upon the contract, they could rely upon the doctrine of part performance but this doctrine has not survived the 1989 Act. Where a party is prevented from proving a term of the contract, which was omitted from the written document the original contract may be rectified,[18] or the omitted term might take effect as a collateral contract.[19] Where the whole of the contract is informal, it may be given effect by the doctrine of proprietary estoppel[20] which represents a major qualification to the new requirement of writing.[21] It is suggested that the development of proprietary estoppel and its unique quality as, of itself, constituting a cause of action is best viewed as a means of avoiding the restrictive formal requirements imposed on contracts for the sale of interests in land.[22] For this reason attempts to force a mating between proprietary and other estoppels should be resisted.[23]

Contracts of guarantee are still governed by the Statute of Frauds, s 4, which requires such contracts to be evidenced in writing. The agreement itself need not be in writing; it is sufficient if there is a written 'note or memorandum' of it. The Law Reform Committee whose report[24] led to the repeal of the other formal requirements imposed originally by the Statute of Frauds[25] considered that contracts of guarantee were deserving of special treatment in order to protect '[i]nexperienced people from undertaking obligations which they did not fully understand'. Although the section covers

---

[15] That is, including a lease or a charge.

[16] A lease for more than three years must be made by deed to create a legal estate Law of Property Act 1925, ss 52 and 54(2). An informal lease operates in equity as an agreement to enter a lease which may be specifically enforced if the requirements of the Law of Property (Miscellaneous Provisions) Act 1989 are satisfied.

[17] Law Com., No. 164 (1987).

[18] *Commission for New Towns* v *Cooper (GB) Ltd* [1995] Ch 259.

[19] For example, *Record* v *Bell* [1991] 1 WLR 853.

[20] See above ch. 2.

[21] Law Com., No. 164 (1987), paras 5.2–5.5.

[22] 'Estoppel ... has additional potential when the estoppel claimant is seeking an interest in land. There is no simple explanation for that extra potential, but it appears to have developed in response to certain limitations in the law, in particular the need for formalities to convey an estate in land ...': Cooke (2000) *The Modern Law of Estoppel*, p. 170. See also Halson, 'The Offensive Limits of Promissory Estoppel' [1999] LMCLQ 256.

[23] See generally Halson above.

[24] Law Reform Committee First Report, Cmd 8809.

[25] Other than that embodied in Law of Property Act 1925, s 40.

contracts of guarantee, whereby one person undertakes a subsidiary liability to make good the default of another, it does not extend to so-called contracts of indemnity where a party undertakes a personal liability as principal debtor.[26] The distinction has been explained in this way. Suppose two people going into a shop, the first of whom intends to buy goods and the second, to help his friend get credit, offers to pay the shopkeeper if the first defaults. This is a guarantee. However, if the second effectively says to the shopkeeper 'give my friend the goods I will pay' he has entered a contract of indemnity.[27]

Informational formal requirements

The primary purpose of many modern formal requirements is to encourage the disclosure of information. Several statutory disclosure requirements have already been encountered when we asked to what extent the law imposes a duty of disclosure upon parties negotiating a contract.[28] Regulated agreements under the Consumer Credit Act 1974[29] must comply with detailed formal requirements. The objective is to make sure that the debtor is fully aware of his rights and obligations. Agreements must make clear the amount and timing of payments, the APR (annual percentage rate)[30] and the protection and remedies under the Act. In particular, the creditor is usually[31] required to provide one or two copies[32] of a notice informing the debtor of his cancellation rights. If the creditor fails to comply with the formal requirements, the agreement cannot be enforced without a court order.[33] However, if the creditor fails to provide the required notice of cancellation rights, the agreement is in all circumstances unenforceable against the debtor.[34] This drastic 'penalty' is highly effective in ensuring that creditors comply with the statutory requirements.

[26] *Moschi* v *Lep Air Services* [1973] AC 331 at 348 *per* Lord Diplock.

[27] *Birkmyr* v *Darnell* (1805) 1 Salk 27.

[28] See Chapter 2.

[29] Regulated agreements are agreements to provide less than £25,000 credit but excluding most first mortgages and some short term credit arrangements, e.g. usual trade credit and 'credit' cards requiring a single payment, such as Diner's Club cards. See ss 8 and 16. See also *Zoan* v *Rouamba* [2000] 1 WLR 1509 (agreement to hire car, while hirer's own car was repaired, which allowed hire to be deferred for 12 months, was a regulated agreement).

[30] The annual percentage rate is a standardised way of calculating the interest payable and allows customers to compare the interest charged by different lenders.

[31] That is, when oral negotiations take place away from the creditor's or associated party's premises: s 67. This provision was aimed at 'door-step' sales but is cast in sufficiently wide language to cover many other situations, e.g. negotiations at a car showroom.

[32] In the usual situation the agreement is not executed when the debtor signs it because the creditor does not commit himself until he has made enquiries about the creditworthiness of the debtor. See s 62. In the usual situation the creditor must give two copies to the debtor. Exceptionally, the agreement is executed when the debtor signs and here only one copy must be given by the creditor to the debtor. See s 63.

[33] Section 65. The court will generally exercise the discretion in favour of the creditor unless the position of the debtor was thereby prejudiced. For example, *National Guardian Mortgage Co* v *Wilkes* [1993] CCLR 1 (failure to supply copy caused prejudice to buyer – interest rate reduced by 40%). *Cf. Nissan Finance UK* v *Lockhart* [1993] CCLR 39 (copy sent few days late – agreement enforced).

[34] Section 127(4)(b).

Another example is provided by the Package Travel, Package Holidays and Package Tours Regulations 1992[35] which require contracts for the provision of package holidays[36] to contain[37] specified information[38] and for a written copy to be given to the consumer.[39]

Contracts of employment need not be in writing but an employer is obliged to provide his employee with a 'Section 1' statement.[40] This is a written record of the terms and conditions of the contract of employment. The statement is only evidence of the contract and does not contain contractual terms. Similarly, a landlord is required to supply a tenant with a rent book containing certain information.[41] This requirement of disclosure is additional to any formal requirement imposed by any other enactment.[42]

Transferable formal requirements

In relation to some transactions a written document is essential to aid the transferability of obligations. Negotiable instruments are legal instruments intended to represent money, such as bills of exchange, promissory notes and including cheques. It is of the essence[43] of such documents that they like the money they represent can be transferred. This is their utility and it is furthered by a requirement of writing.[44] Bills of lading issued by a ship's master to the shipper of cargo perform three functions. They act as a receipt for the goods to be carried, as evidence of the terms upon which they are to be carried and as a document of title. The recognition of the bill of lading as a document of title was crucial to the development of international trade because it permitted the goods to be bought and sold and ownership passed while still on the high seas. This was achieved by endorsing the bill of lading to the new owner who could then present it to obtain possession of the goods at the destination port. Clearly a written document is essential to fulfil this function.

INTENTION

An agreement supported by consideration, which conforms to any applicable formal requirements, is still not binding if it does not disclose an

---

[35] SI 1992 No. 3288.
[36] Package holidays are defined in reg 2 as holidays that involve two or more of the following elements: transport, accommodation or other tourist services.
[37] Regulation 9(1)(a).
[38] Listed in Sch 2: destination, transport, standard of accommodation, meals included, minimum numbers, itinerary, included visits and services, name and address of organiser/retailer and insurer, price and payment method, special items requested by customer and any time limits applicable to complaints.
[39] Regulation 9(1)(c).
[40] Employment Rights Act 1996, s 1.
[41] Landlord and Tenant Act 1985, s 4.
[42] For instance, Law of Property Act 1925, ss 52 and 54(2) and Law of Property (Miscellaneous Provisions) Act 1989, s 2.
[43] '... formality is constitutive rather than merely evidentiary ...': Collins (1999) *Regulating Contracts*, p. 207.
[44] Bills of Exchange Act 1882, s 3(1).

intention to create legal relations. The judgment of Atkin LJ in *Balfour* v *Balfour*[45] is generally considered to be the authoritative statement of an intention to create legal relations as a separate requirement for the formation of a contract. The case concerned an agreement between spouses whereby a man who worked abroad agreed to pay his wife £30 per month when she decided not to follow his work and stay in England. When 18 months later he wrote to suggest that they make their separation permanent she sued to enforce the agreement. Warrington and Duke LJJ were apparently happy to dismiss the wife's action possibly on the basis of a lack of consideration recognised by the law.[46] However, Atkin LJ said: '... even though there may be what as between other parties would constitute consideration ... [agreements between spouses] are not contracts ... because the parties did not intend that they should be attended by legal consequences'. The need for a separate requirement of an intention to create legal relations may be doubted. It could be argued that it merely restates a part of the law of agreement because the only offer and acceptance recognised by the principles of agreement are those intended to create legal relations.[47] However, the requirement has been restated and acted upon many times in a number of different contexts.[48] Before examining these decisions and contexts we will briefly discuss the nature of the requirement that the agreement must disclose an intention to create legal relations.

The main question here is whether the requirement of an intention to create legal relations states a rule of policy or describes a genuine search for the intention of the parties.[49] If it states a rule of policy that certain types of agreement should not be enforced, then it functions like the rules of illegality and should apply irrespective of the parties' intentions. If the law disapproves of a particular transaction, the rule of illegality – often expressed by the Latin maxim of *ex turpi causa oritur non actio* (no action shall arise from a base cause) – will deprive it of legal force. If the law considers it inappropriate for certain types of agreement to be the subject of litigation and expresses this by saying that they are not supported by an intention to create legal relations, the absence of such an intention states a conclusion of law. Its expression as the parties' intention is really just a smokescreen for judicial interference with the parties' supposed freedom of contract. When illegality is involved, the courts are not similarly embarrassed to interfere with the parties' agreement because they are often protecting their own processes from being used by those whose contract offends an independent

---

[45] [1919] 2 KB 571.
[46] See Hepple [1970] Camb LJ 122 at 125–6.
[47] *Williston on Contracts.* 3rd edn, s 21 and Hamson, 'The Reform of Consideration' (1938) 54 LQR 234.
[48] For instance, *Jones* v *Padavatton* [1969] 1 WLR 328 and *Ford Motor Co* v *AUEW* [1969] 2 QAB 303.
[49] Which one commentator terms the 'pure' theory. See Hedley, 'Keeping Contract in its Place – *Balfour* v *Balfour* and the enforceability of Informal Agreements' [1985] 5 OJLS 391, especially at 393–9.

rule of law. The case for non-assistance is less strong when the parties' contract does not breach any other rule of law. None the less, some statements of the requirement of an intention to create legal relations are put in a way which would not give way readily to the parties' actual intention that their agreement should be enforceable. In *Balfour* v *Balfour*, for instance, Atkin LJ said: 'In respect of these promises each house is a domain into which the King's writ does not seek to run, and to which his officers do not seek to be admitted.'[50]

The question posed at the beginning of the preceding paragraph is not expressed explicitly or even answered implicitly by the courts. Rather a compromise is reached whereby the requirement of an intention to create legal relations is said to operate as a presumption. To the extent that a presumption may be rebutted by the contrary intent of the parties it would seem that the courts are favouring the view that the requirement is simply part of the court's quest to discover the true intentions of the parties. However, the courts sometimes appear to make it very difficult to rebut the prima facie presumption and so appear to be covertly stating and imposing a rule of policy.

Domestic and social arrangements

Agreements between spouses such as that in *Balfour* v *Balfour* are presumed not to be contractually binding. The presumption established by that case may be rebutted and appears to be weaker than it was. It has been held not to apply when the spouses are no longer 'in amity'.[51] The same principle is applicable to unmarried partners. In *Ward* v *Byham*,[52] which was considered earlier in relation to the requirement of consideration, the court enforced an agreement between the estranged father of an illegitimate child and its mother in which the father promised to pay regular sums of money to the mother. The harsh effects of this presumption are mitigated by a number of overlapping doctrines. Where the promisee has acted upon the assurance the court may find that it gives rise to a proprietary estoppel or constructive trust.[53] In general, it can be said that the requirement of an intention to create legal relations rarely seems to be applied in a way that denies legal force to executed as opposed to executory agreements.[54]

Even in this qualified form the continued application of the requirement of an intention to create legal relations to the fact situation in which it was first judicially considered is questionable. A social revolution has occurred since the consecration of the Victorian marriage at the centre of the litigation in

[50] At p. 579.
[51] See also *Merritt* v *Merritt* [1970] 1 WLR 1211 and *Re Windle* [1975] 1 WLR 1628.
[52] [1956] 2 All ER 218.
[53] For example, *Eves* v *Eves* [1975] 3 All ER 768 and *Hardwick* v *Johnson* [1978] 1 WLR 683 *per* Lord Denning MR. For a general discussion of proprietary estoppel, see Chapter 2.
[54] *Tanner* v *Tanner* [1975] 1 WLR 1346.

Balfour v *Balfour*,[55] nor has the law stood still. One commentator has highlighted the trend in family law towards the private ordering and 'contractualisation' of intimate relationships.[56] *Balfour* v *Balfour*, which marks the intersection of family and contract law, does not seem to reflect modern day values and so may be ripe for review. Indeed, there are signs of judicial dissatisfaction with the case. In the House of Lords *Balfour* v *Balfour* has been described as 'extreme' and stretching the doctrine of intention to create legal relations 'to its limits'.[57]

Other family agreements have also been held not to disclose an intention to create legal relations. In *Jones* v *Padavatton*[58] a mother who worked in America promised her daughter an allowance and rent-free accommodation if her daughter, who was working as a secretary, would go to England to study for the Bar. Danckwerts and Fenton-Atkinson LJJ[59] applied *Balfour* v *Balfour* and concluded that the agreement was not intended to be binding. Salmon LJ thought that the arrangement must originally have been intended to be legally binding because the parties could not have meant it to be possible for the mother with impunity to withdraw the allowance immediately after the daughter moved to England. In this conclusion he was supported by an earlier case[60] where a couple sold their house to move in with older relatives. This arrangement was held to be contractual because the younger couple would not have sold their home in reliance upon a non-binding arrangement. However, in *Jones* Salmon LJ concluded that the contractual arrangement was only intended to endure for a reasonable time which had in fact elapsed by the time of the litigation.

The courts have considered the question of whether a social arrangement constitutes a binding contract as a subsidiary question raised by other litigation. As a consequence, it is probably wrong to generalise too widely from such cases. Several cases deal with arrangements between work colleagues to offer one another lifts. Most concern claims against the Motor Insurers Bureau,[61] which pays compensation to those injured in car accidents caused by uninsured drivers. The decisions in these cases generally favour the claimant who is seeking compensation from the Bureau.[62] In

---

[55] As an illustration *Balfour* v *Balfour* was decided 14 years before women were accorded full contractual capacity in the Law Reform (Married Women and Tortfeasors) Act 1935.

[56] See Freeman, 'Contracting in the Haven: *Balfour* v *Balfour* Revisited', ch. 4 in Halson (ed.) (1996) *Exploring the Boundaries of Contract*.

[57] *Pettit* v *Pettit* [1970] AC 806.

[58] [1969] 1 WLR 328.

[59] Salmon LJ held that the agreement was intended to be binding but that it was not to endure beyond a reasonable period which had in any case expired (surely the mother was not free to withdraw the allowance immediately after the daughter moved, which would be the consequence of the majority decision).

[60] *Parker* v *Clark* [1960] 1 All ER 93.

[61] *Buckpitt* v *Oates* [1968] 1 All ER 1145 did not (two teenagers had a habit of riding in each other's cars. No contractual agreement despite the claimant who was injured by the defendant's negligent driving having contributed 'petrol money').

[62] *Connell* v *MIB* [1972] AC 301; *Coward* v *MIB* [1963] 1 QB 259; *Albert* v *MIB* [1972] AC 301.

another case[63] an arrangement under which the victim of a road accident undertook to make payments for nursing care provided by his brother and mother was held to be an enforceable one. However, this finding may be explained by the fact that it enabled the victim to recover the costs of those services from the driver who caused the accident.

Where family members have business dealings the usual presumption will be held to be rebutted and their agreement enforceable. This was the case when brothers who were directors in a family firm agreed that if any of them resigned monies owed to them by the firm would be forfeit.[64] This principle may also explain the enforceability of promises made in consideration of marriage.[65]

From the cases there emerges a trend that the looser the ties between parties entering an agreement and the more certain the terms of that agreement the more likely it is to constitute a contract. If the relationship between the parties can be represented as a continuum, the relationship of spouses (*Balfour*) or parent and child (*Jones*) represent the closest ties of kinship. At the other extreme are arm's-length dealings between strangers, which will be examined in the next section. Many intermediate points might be identified, such as an arrangement between unrelated persons living in a family-type situation[66] where logically no presumption or a weaker presumption will apply. As a result, it is more difficult to predict in advance and rationalise in retrospect the outcome of the cases.[67]

Business agreements between strangers

Business agreements between strangers are generally presumed to be intended to create legal relations. However, this presumption may be rebutted expressly or impliedly. In this context when considering whether the presumption has been rebutted, the courts take great care to ascertain and give effect to the parties' actual intentions.

An example of express rebuttal is provided by *Rose and Frank Co v Crompton Bros*[68] where the defendants authorised the claimants to distribute their goods in the United States. The agreement contained the following:

Honourable Pledge Clause
This arrangement is not entered into, nor is this memorandum written, as a formal

---

[63] *Haggar v de Placido* [1969] 1 WLR 328.
[64] *Snelling v John G Snelling Ltd* [1972] 2 WLR 588.
[65] For example, *Shadwell v Shadwell* (1860) 9 CB (NS) 159 (uncle's promise to nephew to support him following marriage).
[66] *Simpkins v Pays* [1955] 1 WLR 975 (persons sharing a house formed a 'syndicate' to enter a competition and agreed to share winnings held enforceable).
[67] Compare the previous case with *Lens v Devonshire Club* [1914] The Times, 4 December, noted by Scrutton LJ in *Rose and Frank Co v Crompton Bros* [1923] 2 KB 261. In *Lens* a golf-club member unsuccessfully tried to enforce the alleged terms of a golf competition. See the criticism of this case by Hedley, 'Keeping Contract in its Place – *Balfour v Balfour* and the Enforceability of Informal Agreements' [1985] 5 OJLS 391 at 391, n. 9.
[68] [1923] 2 KB 261.

or legal agreement, and shall not be subject to legal jurisdiction in the law courts of the United States or England, but it is only a definite expression and record of the purpose and intention of the three parties concerned to which each honourably pledge themselves with the fullest confidence, based on past business with each other, that it will be carried through by each of the three parties with mutual loyalty and friendly co-operation.

The Court of Appeal held that this amounted to an express and unequivocal negation of an intention to create legal relations and so the defendants were not in breach of contact when they terminated it without notice.[69]

To the same effect are two cases[70] involving football pools coupons, which contained the following clause:

It is a basic condition of the sending in and acceptance of this coupon that it is intended and agreed that the conduct of the pools and everything done in connection therewith and all arrangements relating thereto (whether mentioned in these rules or implied) and this coupon and any agreement or transaction entered into or payment made by or under it shall not be attended by or give rise to any legal relationship, rights, duties or consequences whatsoever or be legally enforceable or the subject of litigation, but all such arrangements, agreements and transactions are binding in honour only.

The clause was sufficient to expressly negative any intention to create legal relations between a customer and the pools company.

In both of the above cases the parties' intention not to enter a legally enforceable agreement was clear if not laboured. Where ambiguous or equivocal language is used the courts are not so willing to interpret the clause as negating a contractual intention. In one case it was held that describing a payment as *ex gratia* was not sufficiently clear to negative an obligation to make the payment.[71]

Agreements for the sale of land are often expressed to be 'subject to contract'. This time honoured phrase has 'acquired a definite legal meaning'[72] to the extent that it should be considered to amount to an express negation of any intention to create legal relations at that point in time. As a result, such agreements are not binding upon either the purchaser or seller.[73] This rule has recently been described as 'deeply embedded in statute and authority'.[74] The phrase 'subject to details' seems to have the same effect when used in relation to charter parties.[75]

---

[69] However, the defendants were obliged to satisfy orders for goods which they had already accepted.

[70] *Jones* v *Vernon's Pools Ltd* [1938] 2 All ER 626; *Appleson* v *H Littlewood Ltd* [1939] 1 All ER 464.

[71] *Edwards* v *Skyways Ltd* [1964] 1 All ER 494.

[72] *Chillingworth* v *Esche* [1924] 1 Ch 97 at 114 *per* Sargant LJ.

[73] *Winn* v *Bull* (1877) 7 Ch D 29.

[74] *Pitt* v *PHH Asset Management Ltd* [1994] 1 WLR 327 at 334 *per* Bingham MR and like other deeply embedded objects can inflict considerable pain. See Bingham MR at p. 333: 'For very many people their first and closest contact with the law is when they come to buy or sell a house. They frequently find it a profoundly depressing and frustrating experience.'

[75] *The Junior K* [1988] 2 Lloyd's Rep 583.

The presumption that business agreements between strangers are intended to create legal relations might also be impliedly rebutted. This may be illustrated by a careful analysis of *Kleinwort Benson Ltd* v *Malaysia Mining*[76] where the Court of Appeal had to consider the legal effect of a so-called 'comfort letter'[77] from a parent company to a bank which agreed to make a loan to a subsidiary of the former. The letter stated:

> It is our policy to ensure that the business of [our subsidiary] ... is at all times in a position to meet its liabilities to you ...

The Court of Appeal held that this statement did not have contractual force. Reference to the language used and the course of negotiations justified this conclusion. The language of the letter was not promissory.[78] It did not give any guarantee of the parent company's future intention; it merely stated their policy at the time of writing.[79] That this was recognised by the bank is apparent from the course of negotiations. At first the bank proposed joint and several liability on the part of the parent and subsidiary for the sums advanced. This was then modified to propose a guarantee by the parent in respect of all monies advanced to the subsidiary. In both cases the bank was to be paid an 'accepting commission/margin' of $3/8$ per cent per annum. The defendant rejected the bank's proposals and offered the letter of comfort instead. The bank's representative said that a letter of comfort 'would not be a problem' but that a higher rate would be levied. In the event the accepting commission/margin was increased by $1/8$ per cent to $1/2$ per cent per annum. This increase must be taken to reflect the greater risk assumed by the bank when the only assurance it was to receive from the parent was a letter of comfort. This was, therefore, an indirect acknowledgement by the bank that it was not receiving a contractually binding guarantee.

Two important points emerge from this discussion of the *Kleinwort* case. First, each case will depend upon its own facts. There is no rule of law that all letters of comfort lack contractual force. Indeed, it should be emphasised that letter of comfort is not itself a legal term. Rather it describes a common business practice the effect of which will vary depending upon the evidence from which the presence or absence of a contractual intention can be inferred. In an Australian case[80] it was held that a letter of comfort proffered

---

[76] [1989] 1 All ER 785.

[77] In business, so-called 'letters of comfort' are not notes of condolence sent to grieving relatives but generally refer to assurances given by parent companies to parties trading with their subsidiaries.

[78] See also *Bank of New Zealand* v *Ginivan* [1991] 1 NZLR 178 ('Our policy is that this Company will conduct its affairs in a responsible manner ... and will use our "best endeavours" to see that the Company continues to do so' – element of futurity in assurance sufficient to distinguish *Kleinwort*). *Contra: Bowerman* v *Association of British Travel Agents Ltd* [1996] CLC 451 (ABTA 'guarantee' held to give rise to contractual relations with customers who booked holidays despite the use of the present, rather than the future, tense 'ABTA arranges').

[79] In this it differed from the preceding provision in which the parent company undertook not to reduce its holding in the subsidiary until the loans were repaid.

[80] *Banque Brussels Lambert SA* v *Australian National Industries* (1989) 21 NSWLR 502.

in circumstances analogous to those in *Kleinwort* gave rise to a contractually binding obligation.[81] Indeed, an intermediary position can be identified. In *Re Atlantic Computers plc*[82] a letter of comfort was held to give rise to a limited *contractual* warranty that the declared present intention of the writer was sincere but offered no assurance that it would remain so. Second, even though the letter of comfort does not give rise to a contractual obligation, it may still have some legal effect. It will amount to a representation which if untrue at the time of utterance, or perhaps if it subsequently becomes untrue,[83] will give rise to liability for misrepresentation.[84]

Although neither is a legally defined term, letters of comfort should be distinguished from letters of intent. Letter of intent refers to a broader category of assurance usually where a party negotiating a contract states his intention to eventually enter a contract with the recipient. Whether a letter of intent or any other preliminary agreement[85] gives rise to contractual obligations will depend upon the proper construction of the parties' intention.[86] In *British Steel Corp* v *Cleveland Bridge and Engineering Co Ltd*[87] Goff J held that a letter stating the customer's intention to place an order on its standard terms of business for 'steel nodes' at a quoted price could not have been intended to constitute the offer of a bilateral[88] or unilateral contract,[89] and so it had no contractual effect at all.

CERTAINTY

An agreement supported by consideration and disclosing an intention to create legal relations which complies with any applicable formal requirements will not be enforceable as a contract if it lacks certainty. A lack of certainty may be caused by the vagueness of what is said or the failure to specify important matters. Although it is convenient to consider cases as depending upon vagueness or incompleteness, there is considerable overlap between these concepts. We will illustrate this with a case that haunted the author during the writing of this book.

In *Malcolm* v *Chancellor, Masters and Scholars of the University of Oxford*[90] an author[91] whose philosophical work was initially rejected by a publisher received a firm commitment to publish his manuscript if it was substantially revised. The author did the revisions but the publisher refused to publish it.

---

[81] To give notice of any reduction of the parent company's shareholding in the subsidiary.
[82] [1995] BCC 696.
[83] See Chapter 2.
[84] *Per* Ralph-Gibson LJ at p.790.
[85] Other common descriptions are 'memorandum of understanding' or 'heads of agreement'.
[86] See Chapter 3.
[87] [1984] 1 All ER 504 considered in Chapter 2.
[88] Because the manufacturer could not have intended to become bound to supply goods of unspecified quality. *Ibid.*, p. 510.
[89] Because the work was done pending a contemplated contract rather than under an extant one. *Ibid.*
[90] [1990] *The Times*, 19 December.
[91] Who represented himself.

Gavin Lightman J held that the agreement was too incomplete to be enforceable. Many important terms were left to be agreed: How many copies were to be printed? Hardback or paperback? What royalty was the author to receive? The first two questions could also be described as arising from the vagueness of the publisher's only undertaking, i.e. to publish the work. The case, therefore, illustrates the considerable area of overlap between the two causes of contractual uncertainty. The case also illustrates a decision against the merits. The judge reached his conclusion with 'considerable regret' agreeing that the claimant had been 'harshly and unfairly treated' in a way that put the defendants 'under a strong moral obligation to make amends'.

Vagueness

In *G Scammell & Nephew Ltd v Ouston*[92] the House of Lords held that an agreement to purchase goods 'on hire-purchase' was too vague. There were too many different types of hire-purchase agreement to be able to say which type the parties intended. None the less the courts will often go to considerable lengths to try to 'save' an agreement which would otherwise fail upon the agreement.[93] Vagueness may be removed by reference to trade custom.[94] Vagueness may also be resolved by the imposition of a standard of reasonableness. In *Hillas & Co Ltd v Arcos Ltd*[95] agreement was reached for the sale of timber 'of fair specification'. A standard of reasonableness was applied to make the requirement sufficiently certain to be enforceable. Perhaps the most dramatic technique available to the courts is that of severance. Where a term is so vague as to be meaningless it is sometimes jettisoned altogether. In *Nicolene Ltd v Simmonds*[96] a quantity of steel bars was bought on 'the usual conditions of acceptance'. As there were no usual conditions of acceptance and the rest of the contract was sufficiently certain to be enforceable, the clause was simply ignored.

Incompleteness

A contract must be sufficiently complete so as to be workable. On the other hand, it need not specify every last detail of the parties' dealing. Therefore, a contract will not be enforceable if it fails to specify some important matter. In *May and Butcher Ltd v R*[97] an agreement was reached for the sale of tent

[92] [1941] AC 251.
[93] *Tito v Waddell (No. 2)* [1977] Ch 106 at 314 (the longest case in The Law Reports, almost a full volume of the Chancery Reports) and *Sudbrook Trading Estate v Eggleton and Others* [1982] 3 All ER 1.
[94] *Ashburn Anstalt v Arnold* [1989] Ch 1 at 27 (vagueness of promise to grant shop lease 'in prime position' could be resolved by expert trade evidence) overruled on another ground in *Prudential Assurance Co Ltd v London Residuary Body* [1992] AC 386.
[95] (1932) 147 LT 503.
[96] [1953] 1 QB 543.
[97] [1934] 2 KB 17.

material the timing and amount of payment to 'be agreed upon from time to time'. The House of Lords held that no enforceable contract could come into existence while those important matters were still outstanding. However, where the parties have acted upon an incomplete agreement, the courts will not easily conclude that it is unenforceable. In *Foley* v *Classique Coaches*[98] the claimant agreed to sell land to the defendant to build a bus depot in exchange for the defendant's promise to buy all his petrol from the claimant 'at a price to be agreed by the parties in writing and from time to time'. The land was sold and the agreement acted on for three years after which the defendant sought to 'escape' the petrol agreement. It was held that the petrol agreement was binding. This result is intuitively sound. The defendant was effectively seeking to avoid paying part of the 'price' charged for the land upon which it built its coach station. Also, when the agreement has been operated successfully for a considerable period the suggestion that it is so uncertain as to be unenforceable simply does not ring true.[99] However, the result, though distinguishable[100] from that in *May*, does not sit easily with it.

Again, there are several ways in which the courts are able to avoid the conclusion that an apparently uncertain agreement is unenforceable. The Sale of Goods Act 1979, s 8(2) provides that where the price of goods is not 'determined' by the contract the buyer must pay a reasonable price. Similarly, where the contract is one for the supply of a service and the contract does not specify the price of the service the Supply of Goods and Services Act 1982, s 15(1) provides that the supplier shall pay a reasonable charge.

The agreement itself might provide criteria by reference to which the 'missing' term can be formulated.[101] In *Hillas & Co Ltd* v *Arcos Ltd*[102] an option to purchase timber was enforceable despite the failure to specify a price because it provided for the price to be calculated by reference to a designated price list. Similarly an agreement may provide a mechanism for the provision of matters which the contract fails to specify. In *Sudbrook Trading Estate Ltd* v *Eggleton*[103] a lease gave the lessee an option to purchase

---

[98] [1934] 2 KB 1.
[99] See also *British Bank for Foreign Trade* v *Novinex* [1949] 1 KB 623.
[100] In addition to the above two factors, the Court of Appeal in *Foley* distinguished *May* on the wholly unconvincing ground that the petrol agreement was contained in a deed and that the agreement contained an arbitration clause of an unusual kind which was interpreted to apply to any failure to agree as to price.
[101] This could include a provision that the price was to be fixed by the seller or buyer. It would certainly be an unwise contract to enter where the consideration you are obliged to pay was in the discretion of the other party but it would not necessarily be an invalid one. Clauses in loan contracts whereby the creditor is able unilaterally to change the rate of interest charged are valid. See *Lombard Tricity Ltd* v *Paton* [1989] 1 All ER 918. This is not affected by the Unfair Terms in Consumer Contract Regulations 1999, No 2083, reg 5(5) and Sch. 2, para 2(b).
[102] [1932] 147 LT 503.
[103] [1983] 1 AC 448.

the reversion at a price to be agreed by two valuers one to be nominated by each party or if they cannot reach agreement by an umpire. The House of Lords interpreted this provision as an agreement to sell at a reasonable price which the court could itself fix when the lessor refused to appoint a valuer.

6

ILLEGALITY IN FORMATION

INTRODUCTION

It is perhaps self-evident that when someone employs another to kill a lover or business partner, the courts should not entertain an action by the hired killer to recover the price of the 'hit' if the proposer subsequently refuses to pay.[1] In case it is thought too preposterous that such a claimant would ever present himself to the court, the famous 'Highwayman's Case'[2] should be remembered, where one robber brought an action against another for a fair share of the profits of their joint activities. Indeed, the maxim used to express the court's refusal to countenance such an action is no less compelling for being expressed, as it usually is, in Latin: *ex turpi causa oritur non actio* (no action shall arise from a base cause). At the other end of the spectrum it is perhaps also self-evident that a party who contracts for the carriage of his goods should not be able to resist payment because the carrier exceeded the speed limit (and so committed a criminal offence) in the course of delivering the goods. Our intuition about the unenforceability of the first contract and the enforceability of the second reflects the fact that a major criminal offence was central to the first contract, whereas the lesser offence involved in the second was only incidental to its performance.

Between these polar cases is to be found the full spectrum of reprehensible conduct which might affect the enforceability of any contract. The task of cataloguing the range of circumstances and conduct sufficient to render a contract 'illegal' is the first problem encountered when examining this subject. That this is a difficult and controversial job is evidenced by the fact

---

[1] The example in the text follows *a fortiori* (reasoning from the weaker to the stronger case) from cases involving agreements to commit lesser crimes: *Allen* v *Rescous* (1676) 2 Lev 174 (assault); *Ashton* v *Turner* [1981] QB 137 (burglary); *Pits* v *Hung* [1991] 1 QB 24. However, in *Tappenden* v *Randall* (1801) 2 BOS 2 Pul 467 Heath J said *obiter* at p. 471: 'Undoubtedly there may be cases where the contract is of a nature too grossly immoral for the court to enter into any discussion of it; as where one man has paid money by way of hire to another to murder a third person.'

[2] *Everet* v *Williams* (1725) reported at (1893) 9 LQR 197.

that no two textbooks address the question in the same way.[3] In a recent consultation paper, the Law Commission observed that:[4]

> in some areas the uncertainty and complexity is such that we have found it very time consuming and difficult to ascertain and set out what the present law is ... [and that the] result is a body of case law which is uncertain, at times inconsistent, and which is by no means readily comprehensible.

These difficulties result from the range of conduct and circumstances which are said to fall within the doctrine. Both of the examples considered above involved the commission of a crime. However, the doctrine of illegality extends much further to include such diverse contracts as one to purchase a lottery ticket,[5] the hire of a carriage by a prostitute with which to advertise her services,[6] a 'solus' agreement under which a garage undertook for a considerable time to purchase all its petrol from a single source[7] and contracts for the sale of goods entered by sellers who are in breach of statutory licensing requirements.[8]

However, a few simple distinctions emerge from the two examples which may be used to categorise the case law. The first is that between common law and statutory illegality. Murder is a crime at common law whereas speeding is a statutory offence. It may be useful for the purposes of exposition to distinguish between situations where the category of illegal conduct is prescribed by the common law and where it is prescribed by statute.[9] This distinction may have relevance beyond exposition because there may be techniques appropriate to the examination of one source of illegality which are inappropriate to the other (e.g. rules of statutory interpretation). Further, it may be the case that for constitutional reasons the courts who are subordinate to the legislature feel more inhibited when developing the category of statutory illegality than when considering common law illegality.[10]

A second useful distinction which emerges from the two examples is that between contracts which are illegal as formed and those which are illegal as

---

[3] *Anson's Law of Contract* (1998, 27th edn) follows a three-fold division between statutory illegality, gaming and wagering contracts and illegality at common law; Cheshire, Fifoot and Furmston (13th edn) distinguish between contracts illegal by statute or the common law and contracts merely rendered void by statute or on the grounds of public policy by the common law; Treitel's account (10th edn) divides illegal contracts into those involving the commission of a legal wrong and those contrary to public policy and deals separately with contracts which are declared by statute to be void or unenforceable.

[4] (1999) *Illegal Transactions: The Effect of Illegality on Contracts and Trusts*, No. 154, paras 1.13 and 1.12.

[5] *Re Senator Hanseatische Verwaltungsgesellschaft GmbH* [1997] 1 WLR 515.

[6] *Pearce* v *Brooks* (1866) LR 1 Ex 213.

[7] *Esso Petroleum Co Ltd* v *Harpers Garage (Stourport) Ltd* [1968] AC 269.

[8] *Re Mahmoud and Ispahani* [1921] 2 KB 716.

[9] However, it seems as if contracts to commit a crime are usually categorised as illustrations of common law illegality irrespective of the source of the criminality.

[10] *Cf.* Greig and Davis (1987) *The Law of Contract*, p. 1116: '[the distinction] no longer serves any useful purpose and ought to be abandoned'.

performed.[11] In the 'hit man' example, the law takes exception to the object of the contract (the commission of murder); it is illegal as formed. In the second example, no objection could be taken to the object of the contract (the carriage of goods). Rather, it is the manner of its performance which is illegal, but as we have seen, also irrelevant. It might be expected that the courts would be more lenient towards cases where it is merely the manner of performance which is illegal and this appears to be the case. This reinforces the point that different considerations and policies are relevant to different episodes in the life of a contract. For this reason, illegality in performance is considered later in the book.[12]

If cataloging the varieties of illegality which may affect a contract is the first difficult task in examining this area, the second is stating the effects of such contracts. Again, the courts refer to a Latin maxim: *in pari delicto, potior est conditio defendentis* (where the parties are equally guilty, the defendant is in a stronger position). On this basis, the courts will not generally help a claimant recover property transferred pursuant to an illegal contract. Such an unqualified principle 'would create manifest injustice'[13] by always placing the losses on the shoulders of the transferor. Therefore, the courts demonstrate a 'willingness to manipulate [the rule] and to create exceptions to [its] application in such a way as to reach the preferred outcome'.[14] The chief difficulty in describing the effect of illegality upon contracts is ascertaining when the exceptions to the general rule apply.

Before proceeding with a full catalogue of the various types of illegality and a description of their effects and consequences, we must consider what policies the legal regime should seek to effect. For it is the tension between competing and opposed policy objectives that causes the account of the law to appear so rich in exceptions and sub categories.

POLICY OBJECTIVES

Deterrence is the first policy encountered. By refusing to aid the claimant, the courts warn others that if they indulge in similar behaviour they will not be able to seek the assistance of the court in respect of claims arising from the illegal transaction. Others may thereby be deterred from entering such transactions. The principle of deterrence was recently stated by Millet LJ in a claim brought by a builder for work done under a building contract where

---

[11] See e.g. *Re Mahmoud and Ispahani* [1921] 2 KB 716, 725 *per* Bankes LJ and 729 *per* Scrutton LJ. *Cf.* Furmston (1999) *The Law of Contract*, para 5.30: 'the distinction is apt to generate ... confusion'.

[12] A contract is illegal as performed where its performance contravenes a legal rule which was in existence when the contract was entered. Such illegality in performance is considered in Chapter 13 and should be distinguished from supervening illegality where a contract is entered the performance of which would be legal at the time of contracting but which becomes illegal as a result of subsequent events. Such supervening illegality is dealt with under the doctrine of frustration considered in Chapter 14.

[13] Law Com., No. 154 of 1999, para 1.12.

[14] *Ibid.*

the builder had agreed to provide a false estimate to assist the owner in defrauding his insurance company. He said:[15]

> [I]t is time that a clear message was sent to the commercial community. Let it be clearly understood if a builder or a garage or other supplier agrees to provide a false estimate for work in order to enable its customer to obtain payment from his insurers to which he is not entitled, then it will be unable to recover payment from its customer and the customer will be unable to claim on his insurers even if he has paid for the work.

Deterrence also explains one of the exceptional situations when the court will permit a party to an illegal transaction to maintain an action. This exception applies when the party seeking the court's help can demonstrate that he has repented of its illegal purpose; the claimant has a *locus poenitentiae*, i.e. a time for repentance. The *locus poenitentiae* is said to encourage second thoughts and to create an incentive for the parties not to implement or persist in their illegal purpose.[16]

Although it is true that deterrence is a policy more usually associated with the criminal law rather than the civil law and its general efficacy[17] may be open to doubt, on occasion it might be very significant. For example, under the Consumer Credit Act 1974, if an agreement can be cancelled[18] and the creditor fails to make the debtor aware of his cancellation rights, the agreement is unenforceable by the creditor.[19] In this case the agreement is unenforceable because the statute says so rather than because of the *ex turpi* rule. Nevertheless, it demonstrates clearly how a strict rule of non-enforceability brings discipline to the market. Any creditor flouting these provisions would find he had no way of recovering monies advanced to a creditor.

The second policy, punishment, is also more frequently enforced by the criminal rather than the civil law. However, it is exceptionally regarded as a valid aim of the civil law, as for example when exemplary damages are awarded. The Law Commission has recently recommended that such awards remain exceptional but that nevertheless their availability should be expanded and that they should be renamed 'punitive damages'.[20] However, it recommends that such damages should not be available in respect of a breach of contract *inter alia* because[21] a contract is a private arrangement in

---

[15] *Taylor* v *Bhail* [1996] CLC 377 at 383–4. *Cf.* the same judge in *Tribe* v *Tribe* [1996] Ch 107 at 133–4.
[16] See the argument of counsel for the claimant in *Tinsley* v *Milligan* [1994] AC 340 at 345.
[17] *Ibid.*
[18] A cancellable agreement is defined to include agreements concluded in circumstances where the debtor might feel pressurised, e.g. face-to-face in the debtor's home. See ss 56 and 67.
[19] Section 127(3).
[20] Law Commission Report, No. 247 of 1997, *Aggravated, Exemplary and Restitutionary Damages* at paras 5.40–5.43. It recommends that such damages be available for any tort or equitable wrong which is committed with conduct which evinces a deliberate and outrageous disregard of the claimant's rights.
[21] See para 5.72. The other reasons given are the historic refusal to award such damages, the fact that contractual losses are usually pecuniary (and so presumably merit lesser protection), the greater need for certainty in contract and the desire to allow parties to sell

which parties negotiate rights and duties, whereas the duties which obtain under the law of tort are imposed by law; it can accordingly be argued that the notion of state punishment is more readily applicable to the latter than the former.

Such an objection to the award of exemplary damages for breach of contract would also seem to argue against the implementation of a policy of punishment by means of the principles governing the enforceability of illegal contracts.[22] This may be one of the reasons why punishment is rarely mentioned in the case law. However, a more significant reason may be the indiscriminate nature of the punishment meted out by the doctrine of illegality. When the law refuses to enforce an illegal contract, it is little more than a matter of chance which of the two equally guilty parties will be punished by being saddled with a loss. Consider again the highwayman's case. Only the claimant highwayman was punished by the court's refusal to allow an action against his equally culpable partner in crime. This was recognised by Lord Mansfield as long ago as 1775. His authoritative account of the principles bears reading in full.[23]

Lord Goff reiterated the point more succinctly when he observed recently that the law relating to contractual illegality 'is indiscriminate and so can lead to unfair consequences as between the parties to litigation'.[24] For it to be a legitimate policy for the law to pursue, the punishment must be just. Justice in this context means not only deserved but fair in the sense that all infractors should be treated equally. As this is not the case with regard to illegal contracts, it is suggested that punishment alone cannot be considered a sufficient policy to justify the court's general refusal to enforce illegal contracts.[25]

The third policy which is said to be pursued by the contractual principles of illegality is the desire to ensure that the claimant should not profit from his own wrong. Such a policy objective has an obvious appeal which helps explain our instinctive reaction to the paid assassin's claim. However, in other situations the law's refusal to entertain an action based on an illegal contract will act to ensure, rather than to prevent, a party profiting from his own wrong. In *Upfill* v *Wright* [26] a landlord let a flat to a woman whom he knew was the lover of a married man who would pay for the rent. The landlord's action to recover the rent failed because the contract was said to be tainted by illegality (it was 1911!). In other words, the woman and her

---

their contractual performance to third parties who are prepared to pay more than the original promisee, out of the proceeds of which that promisee may be fully compensated (so-called 'efficient breach').

[22] In other words, it is suggested that the Law Commission's approaches to exemplary damages and illegality are inconsistent.

[23] *Holman* v *Johnson* (1775) 1 Cowp 341 at 343.

[24] *Tinsley* v *Milligan* [1994] 1 AC 340 at 355.

[25] *Cf.* the more sympathetic approach of the Law Commission in Report No. 154 of 1999, *Illegal Transactions: The Effect of Illegality on Contracts and Trusts*, para 6.11.

[26] [1911] 1 KB 506.

lover were able to enjoy the premises rent-free.[27] Despite the fact that this policy is sometimes frustrated rather than furthered by the court's refusal to enforce an illegal contract when it is resorted to, it is often in strong terms.[28]

The final policy said to support the illegality rules is the need to uphold the dignity of the courts. It is thought to be demeaning for the courts to be involved in enforcing or valuing such contracts. In one case[29] a contract was entered whereby the defendant agreed to exchange a discotheque, villa and 'escort' business in Portugal for a sports car and yacht owned by the claimant as well as some cash. The claimant succeeded in his action for fraudulent misrepresentation because this could be made out and a remedy granted without reference to the illegal escort business which involved the supply of women for sex. If the escort business could not have been left out, the court would have had to place a value upon it which would have been improper. However, it must be remembered that many so-called cases of illegality do not involve the kind of exploitation present in *The Siben*. Rather they may involve the breach of a technical statutory regulation.[30] In such circumstances, the court could not really be said to be demeaned if it enforced the contract.

The complete picture appears to be that no single policy can provide a complete justification for the rules governing illegal contracts. In different circumstances, each of the policies examined may provide a partial explanation of the court's stance. The complex set of rules and exceptions which collectively comprise the topic of contractual illegality have been fashioned by a number of distinct and sometimes conflicting policy objectives. Some principles are not explicable on the basis of any policy and can only be explained historically.

A final general point must be made for the benefit of readers who are still indignant at the court's characterisation as immoral the extramarital affair in *Upfill* v *Wright*. This is that the principles of illegality to some degree reflect general social morality and so will vary through time. The Victorian moral indignation displayed in that case would be unlikely to be repeated today. More recently, the Court of Appeal quickly dismissed the claim of a landlord that a flat occupied by an unmarried couple was being used for immoral purposes.[31]

---

[27] The law of restitution, together with the law of contract and tort, form the law of obligations. The law of restitution seeks to reverse unjust enrichment. The landlord in *Upfill* would prima facie be entitled to restitution on the basis that he has conferred a benefit on the tenant which has not been paid for at all (in technical language there is said to be a total failure of consideration). However, illegality is regarded as a general defence to a restitution action unless certain exceptions can be made out and none is applicable here.

[28] It is an 'absolute rule ... that the Courts will not recognise a benefit accruing to a criminal from his crime': *Boresford* v *Royal Insurance Company Ltd* [1938] AC 386 at 599 *per* Lord Atkin.

[29] *The Siben* [1996] 1 Lloyd's Rep 35.

[30] See under the next heading: Statutory illegality.

[31] *Heglibiston Establishment* v *Heyman & Others* [1977] 36 P & CR 351.

STATUTORY ILLEGALITY

In *St John Shipping Corp* v *Joseph Rank Ltd*, Devlin J said:[32]

[T]he court will not enforce a contract which is expressly or impliedly prohibited by statute. If the contract is of this class it does not matter what the intent of the parties is, if the statute prohibits the contract, it is unenforceable whether the parties meant to break the law or not.

The making of a contract (we are dealing with illegality in formation) may, therefore, be either expressly or impliedly prohibited by a statute. A good example of express prohibition can be found in (now repealed) legislation which sought to restrict the availability of credit by requiring the payment of substantial (25 per cent) deposits. Agreements which failed to stipulate for the required deposit were expressly illegal as formed.[33]

A statute may declare that certain conduct is to be a criminal offence (speeding in a car, etc.). Where the prohibited conduct is the making of a contract, any such contract may be considered to be expressly prohibited by statute. Statutes currently in force prohibit the sale of a flick-knife[34] and the trade for profit in human organs.[35]

Ascertaining whether a statute impliedly prohibits the making of a contract is a more difficult task. Various approaches may be found in the case law. Before examining these, a note of caution should be entered. The distinction between illegality in formation and illegality in performance which is supported in the case law[36] and followed in this book is sometimes difficult to apply in relation to statutory illegality. Devlin J makes this point in the *St John Shipping* case when he observes the difficulty of distinguishing between contracts which are illegal because 'in the course of performing a legal contract an illegality was committed' and contracts where 'the way in which the contract was performed turned it into the sort of contract that was prohibited by the statute'.[37]

Courts tend to treat the question of implied statutory prohibition as a question of construction. They must simply ascertain whether Parliament intended the statute to prohibit the making of such a contract. This approach, like that of discovering the intention of the contractors when interpreting a term of the contract, may be a genuine enquiry. Or it may be a smokescreen designed to disguise the law-making activity of the unelected judiciary. The theme of a judiciary who are constitutionally embarrassed to admit the extent of their creative or policy making role is a recurring one in the law of contract. Here we can perhaps lament the passing of Lord Denning[38] who felt no such embarrassment.

---

[32] [1957] 1 QB 267 at 283.
[33] For example, *Stoneleigh Finance Ltd* v *Phillips* [1965] 2 QB 537.
[34] Restriction of Offensive Weapons Act 1959 s 1(1)(a).
[35] Human Organs Transplants Act 1989, s 1.
[36] See n. 12 above.
[37] [1957] 1 QB 267 at 284. See also *Fitzgerald* v *FJ Leonhardt Pty Ltd* (1997) 71 ALJR 653 at 655 *per* Dawson and Toohey JJ.
[38] Lord Denning died in 1999.

An example of this process is provided by *Re Mahmoud and Ispahani*[39] where the Court of Appeal had to consider the effect of the Seeds, Oils and Fats Order 1919 which provided that anyone who buys or sells linseed oil must be licensed to do so. A buyer of oil misrepresented to a licensed seller that he was also properly licensed. The buyer refused to accept delivery of the oil he ordered and so the seller brought an action for non-acceptance. This action failed because the Court of Appeal considered it clear that the order prohibited the sale of licensed oil where the buyer, seller or both do not have the necessary licence.

Mahmoud was applied by the Privy Council in *Chai Sau Yin* v *Liew Kwee Sam*[40] where the seller of rubber brought an action to recover the balance of the purchase price for rubber sold. The buyer argued that the contract was illegal and so unenforceable against him because he did not possess a licence as required by the Rubber Supervision Enactment. This argument was accepted and the action failed.

Two features of these cases should be emphasised. First, they represent 'easy' cases where the language of the statutory provisions readily convinced the courts that their enactors' intention was to prohibit such contracts being entered.[41] This, despite the fact that *Mahmoud* involved secondary legislation when it might be thought that evidence was more scarce from which the court could make inferences about legislative intent.

The second feature is the observation that the doctrine will often work to the advantage of unmeritorious parties such as the purchaser in *Mahmoud* who was free of obligation.[42] It is the capricious nature of an unqualified application of the doctrine which has prompted the courts to create the exceptions to the rule of non-enforceability which we later examine.

From these strong cases it must not be concluded that a statutory prohibition will be too readily inferred.[43] In modern times when legislative control of commerce is more prevalent than in the past, there is a danger that if the courts too readily infer that contracts are prohibited by statute, the capricious effects of the doctrine will also be magnified.

A subsidiary test which is sometimes referred to here is to ask whether the object of the statute was to increase national revenue. Licensing requirements which only serve this limited fiscal purpose may be interpreted as not

---

[39] [1921] 2 KB 716.

[40] [1962] AC 304.

[41] For this reason, *Mahmoud* is sometimes classified as a case of express statutory illegality. Atkin LJ's language at p. 724 would appear to support this view. However, it is suggested that because the order did not in terms state that unlicensed dealings were prohibited the case should be considered as a clear case of implied statutory illegality.

[42] Bankes LJ's characterisation of the purchaser's conduct as shabby (p. 724) was probably an understatement. It would also appear to be fraudulent with the result that the seller could bring an action in the tort of deceit according to Williams, 'The Legal Effect of Illegal Contracts' (1942–4) 8 CLJ 51 at 59.

[43] '... a court ought to be very slow to hold that a statute intends to interfere with the rights and remedies given by the ordinary law of contract ...': *per* Devlin J in *St John Shipping Corp* v *Joseph Rank Ltd* [1957] 1 QB 267 at 288. See also *Shaw* v *Groom* [1970] 2 QB 501 at 523 *per* Sachs LJ.

involving any implied statutory prohibition of entering contracts of a particular kind. On this basis, an unlicensed tobacconist was not precluded from enforcing a contract against a purchaser.[44] The opposite conclusion would be reached where the legislation had as its purpose the protection of the public. Therefore, an unlicensed broker was unable to enforce a brokerage contract because 'the legislature had in view ... the benefit and security of the public in ... important transactions which are negotiated by brokers'.[45] However, the High Court of Australia has recently said that the 'revenue test' cannot be pushed too far. It suggests that even where a statute is enacted to protect the public, that purpose may be sufficiently served by the imposition of a penalty short of rendering all contracts unenforceable.[46]

A second subsidiary test involves asking whether the provision in question seeks to penalise a certain commercial activity or each individual manifestation of it. If the former is the case, this may be evidence that no implied prohibition was intended.[47] In an Australian case[48] this was applied in relation to unauthorised banking business where a daily fine was imposed which did not take account of the number of unauthorised transactions. This was sufficient to justify the conclusion that the statute aimed to control unauthorised business in general and not to prohibit individual contracts.

Finally, it has been argued that a simpler all encompassing test should be adopted. This would ask simply whether the statute necessarily contemplates the prohibited acts as being done in the performance of a contract.[49] Applying this test we can see that in *Mahmoud*, the prohibited acts (unlicensed buying and selling of oil) would necessarily involve contractual dealings. In contrast, in relation to our earlier example of the speeding carrier, we can say that the prohibited act does not necessarily involve the performance of a contract. However, it is suggested that this test is itself only a partial one as it would fail to explain the enforceability of the contract in *Smith* v *Mawhood*. Surely in that case the prohibited act (unlicensed dealings in tobacco) necessarily contemplated contractual arrangements.

ILLEGALITY AT COMMON LAW

A number of types of contract are treated by the common law as illegal. A quick review of these categories (e.g. contracts contrary to good morals, contracts injurious to family life) will reveal that illegality at common law has a wide application. These various manifestations are all based upon the idea that the courts should not enforce contracts which are contrary to public policy. The question then arises who must determine the needs of public

---

[44] *Smith* v *Mawhood* (1845) 14 MAW 452.
[45] *Cope* v *Rowlands* (1836) 2 MAW 149 at 158–9 *per* Partie B.
[46] *Fitzgerald* v *F J Leonhardt* [1997] 189 CLR 215.
[47] *Victorian Daylesford Syndicate Ltd* v *Dott* [1905] 2 Ch 624 especially at 630 *per* Buckley J.
[48] *Yango Pastoral Company Pty Ltd* v *First Chicago Australia Ltd* [1978] 139 CLR 410, especially at 415 *per* Gibbs ACJ and 435 *per* Murphy J.
[49] Buckley, 'Implied Statutory Prohibition of Contracts' (1975) 38 MLR 535.

policy and translate them into aggregations of prohibited contracts. On this occasion, there is only one answer, the courts. Unlike statutory illegality, they cannot legitimise their decisions by reference to the search for the intention of the legislature. This introduces a valuable flexibility into the doctrine which we have already seen will vary through time to reflect changing social conditions and community values.[50] This necessary flexibility itself threatens commercial enterprise and social relations. In business, when transactors are considering large sums of money, certainty is regarded as a key value.[51] Commercial incentive is stifled whenever contractors are uncertain about the legal effect of the contractual arrangements they put in place. In the social sphere, the dangers arise from permitting so unrepresentative a group as the judiciary to be arbiters of morality. These dangers are well recognised and most famously summarised by Burroughs J when he described public policy as 'a very unruly horse, and when once you get astride it you never know where it will carry you. It may lead you from sound law.'[52] Characteristically, Lord Denning thought this to be only a problem when the jockey (judge) is unskilled.[53]

One result of this tension between the need for flexibility and the desire for certainty has been a cautious approach by the courts. However, it would be misleading merely to refer to statements such as Lord Halsbury's denial that any court could 'invent a new head of public policy'.[54] This is not merely because it prompts the obvious question: 'Where did the existing heads come from?', but also because it conceals much judicial invention.

First, judges do not feel inhibited from developing existing heads of public policy to meet changing social and economic needs. This is seen clearly in relation to the court's treatment of cohabitees and employees. Second, some novel applications come close to admitting new heads of public policy. An example is a decision that a moneylending contract is illegal if it reduces the borrower to a 'servile' position.[55] Third, there have been several suggestions that public policy might require contracts promoting discrimination of some sort to be unenforceable. The suggestion is clearly sensible but in most spheres statutory protections have made any development of the common law otiose. For example, in *Nagle* v *Feilden*[56] the Court of Appeal thought that a contract which discriminated against women would be against public policy and in unreasonable restraint of trade. This case predated the Sex Discrimination Act 1986 which now offers statutory protection against sex

---

[50] What the law recognises as contrary to public policy turns out to vary greatly over time.
[51] See also the discussion of conditions in Chapter 15.
[52] *Richardson* v *Mellish* (1824) 2 Bing 229 at 252.
[53] 'With a good man in the saddle, the unruly horse can be kept in control. It can jump over obstacles': *Enderby Town FC Ltd* v *The Football Association* [1971] Ch 591 at 606.
[54] *Jonson* v *Driefontein Consolidated Mines Ltd* [1902] AC 484 at 491. See also *St John Shipping Corp* v *Joseph Rank Ltd* [1957] 1 QB 267 at 274–5 *per* Devlin J: '… public policy is not a doctrine which ought to be extended in the service of making new heads …'.
[55] *Neville* v *Dominion of Canada News Co Ltd* [1915] 3 KB 556. *Cf.* Human Rights Act 1998, which incorporates into domestic law rights under the European Convention on Human Rights, Article 4 of which prohibits slavery and forced labour.
[56] [1966] 2 QB 633.

discrimination. In addition, the Race Relations Act 1976 offers protection against discrimination on the basis of colour, race, nationality or ethnic or national origins. Discrimination on the basis of religious or political grounds was not protected by domestic law outside Northern Ireland[57] until the Human Rights Act 1998 gave effect to Article 9 of the European Convention on Human Rights' protection for freedom of thought, conscience and religion.

Contracts to commit a crime or a tort

A contract to commit a crime or a tort is self evidently an illegal contract. This principle has been applied widely to agreements to assault a third party[58] and to obtain goods by false pretences.[59] In this context it should be noted that every agreement to commit a crime is itself a crime – that of conspiracy.

A related principle is that no person shall be assisted to recover the product of his crime. This is a naked expression of one of the policy factors which are thought to justify more generally the rules of illegality. The principle applies equally to the personal representatives of the criminal. On this basis, the personal representatives of a man who fatally shot himself were unable to recover under an insurance policy which was construed to cover self-inflicted death.[60]

At the time of the case, suicide was, but no longer is, a crime.[61] If the facts of the case were to recur, the result might be different but the reasoning is still valid. The continuing public interest in depriving the criminal of access to the proceeds of his criminal activities was recently reaffirmed by the House of Lords in *A-G v Blake*.[62] Blake had been a spy working for British Intelligence who defected and became an agent for the Soviet Union. He was convicted of unlawfully communicating information contrary to Official Secrets Act 1911, s 1(1)(c) and sentenced to 42 years' imprisonment. After 15 years he escaped to Moscow. A majority of the House of Lords held that, where justice so demands, a court can take the exceptional step of requiring a party to a contract to account for any benefits he derived from its breach. In this case such a remedy was appropriate *inter alia* because the Crown had a legitimate interest in preventing the defendant from profiting from his serious and damaging breach of contract. A similar policy has been recognised by the legislature in enacting a number of measures designed to deprive drug traffickers of the proceeds of their crimes.[63]

Most crimes are also torts but the reverse is not true. However, a contract

---

[57] See Fair Employment (Northern Ireland) Act 1989, s 49, which amends the Fair Employment (Northern Ireland) Act 1976, s 16.
[58] *Allen v Rescous* (1676) 2 Lev 174.
[59] *Berg v Sadler & Moore* [1937] 2 KB 158. See now Theft Act 1968, ss 15 and 16 (obtaining property by deception and obtaining a pecuniary advantage by deception).
[60] *Boresford v Royal Exchange Assurance* [1938] AC 586.
[61] Suicide Act 1961, s 1.
[62] [2000] 3 WLR 625.
[63] Criminal Justice Act 1988, Part VI as amended by the Proceeds of Crime Act 1995.

to commit a tort is itself illegal[64] unless neither party is aware that performance of the contract would constitute a tort.[65]

Contracts promoting sexual indecency

If this section were written a 150 years ago, it would have been more extensive. For the then prevailing morality would condemn a wider range of contracts than that which pertains now. Contracts involving prostitution were regarded as illegal even though they could only be regarded as indirectly promoting immorality. On this basis, the contract to hire an ornamental carriage by a prostitute was held illegal.[66] However, there comes a point when the connection between the contract and the prostitution is too loose to justify non-enforcement. The courts have enforced contracts to let a room to a prostitute who does her business elsewhere[67] and to do laundry despite the fact that the linen contained a number of gentlemen's nightcaps![68]

The decisions which seem most at variance with modern values are those concerning cohabitees where, for example, a landlord failed in his action to recover rent from a female tenant who was having an affair with a married man who provided money for the rent.[69]

The approach of the courts has undoubtedly changed and the modern decisions generally reflect a less strict moral code. However, the enforceability of contracts involving prostitution has only been indirectly considered by the courts and it appears that traces of the old approach still remain.[70] Elesewhere, judges have sought to reflect contemporary standards. In a case concerning undue influence,[71] Lord Browne-Wilkinson said, 'Now that unmarried cohabitation, whether heterosexual or homosexual, is widespread in our society, the law should recognise this.' Indeed, the court's approach may almost be described as dismissive when it detects echoes of the outdated strict approach. In a case concerning cohabitation by an unmarried couple, Roskill LJ said:[72]

---

[64] Compare *Allen v Rescous* (1676) 2 Lev 174 (assault – also a crime) and *Clay v Yates* (1856) 1 H&N 73 (libel – not a crime).

[65] To contract to sell goods owned by a third party would amount to a tort (called conversion) against the third party. However, the Sale of Goods Act, s 12 (which implies a term that the goods offered are owned by the seller) appears to presume that such a contract is not illegal.

[66] *Pearce v Brooks* (1866) LR 1 Exch 213. See also *The Dowager Marchioness of Annondale v Ann Harris* (1727) 2 PWms, affd 1 Bro PC 250.

[67] '[B]ecause persons of that description must have a place to lay their heads': *Appleton v Campbell* (1826) 2 C & P 347. See also *Crisp v Churchill* cited in *Lloyd v Johnson* (1798) 1 Bos & P 340. Whether the case is considered a liberal decision is perhaps a question of perspective. A different view is that the court sought to protect the interests of the property-owning classes by enabling a landlord to recover rent from a prostitute tenant.

[68] *Lloyd v Johnson* (1798) 1 Bos & P 340.

[69] *Upfill v Wright* [1911] 1 KB 506.

[70] *Coral Leisure Group Ltd v Barnett* [1981] 1 CR 503.

[71] *Barclays Bank plc v O'Brien* [1994] 1 AC 180 at 198.

[72] *Heglibiston Establishment v Heyman* (1978) 36 P & CR 351 at 361.

if that user is to be interpreted as using premises for an immoral purpose there must be a great many breaches of covenant being committed in London and elsewhere today.

Perhaps the most amusing account of the modern approach comes from an Australian case where Stable J asked:[73]

> are the actions of people today to be judged in the light of the standards of the last century? ... cases discussing what was then by community standards sexual immorality appear to have been decided in the days when for the sake of decency the legs of tables wore drapes ... I do not accept that immoral today means precisely what it did in the days of *Pearce* v *Brooks*; I am ... entitled to look at the world under modern social standards ... What was apparently regarded with pious horror when the cases were decided would ... today hardly draw a raised eyebrow ... [T]he social judgements of today upon matters of 'immorality' are as different from those of the last century as is the bikini from a bustle.

However, it should be noted that morality may vary between countries as much as it does through time. While of no direct authority in English law, the recent comments of the Malaysian Court of Appeal at least serve to emphasise the degree to which courts seek to reflect domestic moral standards. Gopal Sri Ram JCA said:[74]

> The views expressed in *O'Brien's* case merely reflect the law's attempt to keep in tandem with the moral standards of the society in which an English court functions. Our society ... has an entirely different set of moral standards. It would therefore be quite wrong to blindly follow all foreign decisions if the result would facilitate moral decadence within our social structure.

Contracts prejudicial to the administration of justice

This head of illegality, like the preceding one, covers a wide range of conduct. One obvious example is where parties agree to 'stifle' a prosecution, i.e. to prevent it from proceeding, such as where two men bribed a prosecution witness to withdraw a charge of rape.[75] This case illustrates another feature of illegality – that conduct will frequently offend more than one head of illegality. Such an agreement would itself amount to the crime of conspiracy to pervert the course of justice, which would provide a further ground for holding the agreement to be illegal.

There are limits upon this head of illegality where a party seeks to use the threat of criminal prosecution as an 'encouragement' to settle an associated civil claim. Where the agreement itself does not amount to a conspiracy to pervert the course of justice or other[76] crime, courts are likely to regard the

---

[73] *Andrews* v *Parker* [1973] Qd R 93 at 102–4.
[74] *Tengku Abdullah Sultan Abu Bakan* v *Mohd Latiff bin Shah* [1996] 2 MLJ 265 at 309–10.
[75] *R* v *Panayiotoy* [1973] 3 All ER 112.
[76] Criminal Law Act 1967, ss 1 and 5(1) make it a crime to conceal an arrestable offence. There is a saving where the disclosure results from an attempt to make good loss or injury caused by the offence.

agreement as fully enforceable when it only affects the private interests of the parties concerned.[77]

This general head of illegality strikes at the very *raison d'être* of the courts and so is 'policed' with special vigour. A typically robust statement of the court's approach is that of Tindal CJ when considering the enforceability of an agreement to compromise a claim which the claimant knew he had no right to assert:

> It is almost *contra bonos mores* and certainly contrary to all the principles of natural justice, that a man should institute proceedings against another, when he is conscious that he has no good cause of action ... The [compromise] therefore, altogether fails.[78]

A different policy often referred to by the courts is the desire to protect themselves from 'floods' of litigation. Variants of this policy are used to justify the refusal of novel claims in the law of tort[79] and to explain features of the doctrine of consideration said to encourage out of court settlements.[80] This policy of self-protection may conflict with that expressed by Tindal CJ and give some encouragement to parties to assert doubtful claims. This conflict is resolved by the courts enforcing agreements which compromise doubtful claims but refusing to enforce agreements compromising claims known to be invalid. It also justifies the exception to this head of illegality in respect of 'private arrangements'.

Any agreement which seeks to oust the jurisdiction of the courts will be invalid. An example would be a clause in a separation agreement ... between spouses which stated that '[t]he wife shall not [bring] ... matrimonial proceedings' so long as payments are made under the agreement.[81] This rule is necessary to prevent parties from evading the judicial control of such contracts. The jurisdiction is distinct from, but based upon the same policy as, the principles developed to control so called exemption and limitation clauses.[82] These are clauses in a contract which do not seek to usurp the court's jurisdiction; rather they implicitly accept the court's jurisdiction. Exemption and limitation clauses are designed to exclude or limit any

---

[77] For example, *Fisher & Co v Apollinaris* (1875) LR 10 Ch App 297 (agreement to end private prosecution under Trade Marks Act in exchange for apology and transfer of trade mark valid) and *McGregor v McGregor* (1888) 21 QBD 424 (agreement by spouses to compromise mutual allegations of assault valid).

[78] *Wade v Simeon* (1846) 2 CB 548. See ch. 4 for a criticism of the alternative ground for the decision (absence of consideration) offered by the court.

[79] For instance, *Spartan Steel & Alloys Ltd v Martin & Co (Contractors) Ltd* [1973] QB 27, 38–9 *per* Lord Denning MR denying liability for 'pure' economic loss in the tort of negligence and *McLoughlin v O'Brien* [1983] 1 AC 410 limiting liability for nervous shock in the tort of negligence.

[80] See generally *Cook v Wright* (1861) 1 B & S 559 considered below in ch. 4.

[81] *Williams v Williams* [1957] 1 WLR 148. See also *Wales v Wadham* [1977] 1 WLR 199. The rule as applied to agreements between spouses now has a statutory basis. See Matrimonial Causes Act 1973, s 34. Even though such agreements are unenforceable against the party subject to the restriction, it is provided by the statute that that party can sue to recover sums promised but unpaid. Similar rules now apply to some maintenance agreements concerning children. See Child Support Act 1991, s 9.

[82] See Chapter 11.

remedy which would otherwise be available from the courts, or even to prevent a liability that would give rise to such a remedy, from arising.

The court's obvious distaste for agreements which seek to oust its jurisdiction may be a self-protective reflex. It would also appear to be inconsistent with the cardinal principle of classical contract law, often expressed simply as 'freedom to contract', that competent parties to a valid contract are free to regulate their relations.[83]

This tension between competing policy considerations explains why the courts will exceptionally regard as valid clauses which clearly oust their jurisdiction. The major exception concerns arbitration clauses, i.e. contracted undertakings that disputes should be submitted to arbitration rather than subject to court proceedings. It would perhaps be immodest of the courts too readily to interfere with the parties' express wish to have their dispute resolved in a rival forum. However, such immodesty pertained for many years in the common law's hostile attitude towards arbitration clauses. Such interference by the courts meant that some of the advantages of arbitration, speed and cost were lost. Parliament then intervened and the Arbitration Act 1979[84] permits the parties, once arbitration proceedings have commenced, to enter agreements excluding the court's powers to review arbitration proceedings. In the absence of such an exclusion agreement, the court's role is limited to hearing appeals on a point of law[85] and the House of Lords has held that leave to appeal should only be granted sparingly, i.e. where an important or pervasive question of law is involved.[86] The law relating to arbitration was consolidated in the Arbitration Act 1996.[87]

Another type of agreement which is regarded as prejudicial to the administration of justice is any agreement which amounts to 'wanton or officious intermeddling with the disputes of others'.[88] This category of contracts arose from the old common law crimes of 'maintenance' and 'champerty'. Maintenance referred to the stirring up of litigation by assisting a party to bring or defend a claim. Champerty was a more specific crime where someone agreed to provide such help in exchange for a share of the proceeds of litigation.[89] Lord Mustill recently described maintenance and champerty as necessary protections for an immature legal system which:

> in medieval times ... lacked the internal strength to resist the oppression of private individuals fomented and sustained by unscrupulous men of power.[90]

In modern times, courts are more powerful and so better equipped to detect

---

[83] That is, those with full contractual capacity (e.g. sane adults) who enter contracts which are not affected by any negativing factors (e.g. undue influence, etc.).

[84] See generally Kerr (1980) 43 MLR 45.

[85] Section 1(2).

[86] *The Noma* [1982] AC 724. An example would be the proper construction of standard form contract in wide usage. *The Rio Sun* [1981] 2 Lloyd's Rep 489 and [1982] 1 Lloyd's Rep 404.

[87] See generally Saville [1997] LMCLQ 502.

[88] *Giles v Thompson* [1994] 1 AC 142 at 164.

[89] See *Camdex International v Bank of Zambia* [1996] 3 WLR 759 at 765 *per* Hobhouse LJ.

[90] *Giles v Thompson* [1994] 1 AC 142, p. 153.

abuses of process with the result that the criminal and tortious actions have been abolished.[91] What remains is the principle that a champertous agreement is regarded as illegal for the purposes of the law of contract.[92]

According to Lord Mustill, another remnant of the old actions is the rule, largely enforced as a standard of professional conduct, that prevents a solicitor from accepting payment for professional services calculated as a proportion of the sum recovered from a defendant.[93] This prohibition has been held to apply to an agreement between a solicitor and an interpreter under which the former was to pay the latter a share of legal aid fees earned from clients introduced,[94] but not to an agreement between a claimant and a company providing services to help with personal injury litigation even though the company was run by and employed solicitors.[95]

In addition to the case law developments relaxing former constraints on solicitors, there have been statutory measures. The Courts and Legal Services Act 1990, s 58[96] permitted solicitors to enter conditional fee agreements under which, if the litigation was successful, the solicitor would typically become entitled to his fees plus an agreed 'uplift'. This provision has now been extended to cover a wider range of litigation.[97] The enhanced fees payable by a winning party may now be recovered from the losing party as costs[98] as may any insurance premium paid by the winner for a policy to indemnify him against his liability in the event he lost.[99] However, the Court of Appeal has held that an agreement by a solicitor to charge her normal fee if she won but a lower fee otherwise was not within the statutory saving and so was unenforceable.[100] Although the statutes only extend protection to solicitors entering agreements in relation to litigation in the courts, it has been held that an analogous approach should be taken in respect to agreements contemplating reference to arbitration.[101]

Contracts injurious to the institution of marriage or prejudicial to family life

When asked what he thought about the institution of marriage, Groucho Marx replied that it was fine for people who like living in institutions. Such

[91] Criminal Law Act 1967, ss 13(1) and 14(1).

[92] Criminal Law Act 1967, s 14(2).

[93] [1994] 1 AC at 153. Lord Mustill suggested that champerty explains another legal rule: the 'refusal to recognise the assignment of a bare right of action'. Recently this rule has been interpreted so as not to render unenforceable assignment for good commercial reasons. See *Trendtex Trading Corp* v *Crédit Suisse* [1982] AC 679.

[94] *Mohamed* v *Alaya & Co* [2000] 1 WLR 1815.

[95] *Quantum Claims Compensation Specialists Ltd* v *Powell* [1998] SC 316.

[96] See now the Access to Justice Act 1999.

[97] The Courts and Legal Services Act 1990, s 58A permitted conditional fees in relation to property and financial matters.

[98] Courts and Legal Services Act 1990, s 58A(6).

[99] Section 28.

[100] *Anuad* v *Geraghty & Co* [2000] 3 WLR 1041, not following *Thai Trading Co (a firm)* v *Taylor* [1998] 3 All ER 65. See also *Hughes* v *Kingston-upon-Hull City Council* [1999] 2 All ER 49.

[101] *Bevan Ashford* v *Geoff Leandle (Contractors) Ltd (in liquidation)* [1998] 3 WLR 173 confirmed by later amendment to the Courts and Legal Services Act 1990. See now s 58A(4).

irreverence expresses a fact of modern life which has been noted judicially: that in contemporary Britain people live openly in a wider variety of relationships than they did in the past. For this reason, many of the older cases cannot now safely be relied upon.

That many of the older cases are out of step with modern life is well illustrated by *Hermann v Charlesworth*.[102] The defendant was the publisher of *The Matrimonial Post and Fashionable Marriage Advertiser*. The claimant entered an agreement under which she paid a fee in exchange for being introduced to suitable marriage partners, with a further sum payable on marriage. No marriage resulted from these introductions and the claimant sought the return of the initial fee. It was held that the agreement was a marriage brokerage contract which was injurious to the institution of marriage and so unenforceable. The case appears to be premised upon a view of the sanctity of marriage which would not pertain today. Indeed, it is inconceivable that the contracts entered between individuals and 'computer-dating' agencies would now be considered unenforceable.

Three further observations can be added. First, the case may have been open to question when decided. It followed a number of older cases which presented far stronger cases for unenforceability being characterised by one commentator as contracts 'to "kidnap" an heiress'.[103] Second, the claimant did recover the initial fee on the basis of a broad equitable power (which has not been much exercised outside this context)[104] to order the return of money. Third, the point could again be made that different cultures view similar contracts in different ways. In Malaysia marriage bureaux are regarded as performing a valuable social function and in Singapore they receive government support.[105] This would suggest that in a multicultural, pluralistic society such as ours the law should not too readily impeach such contracts.

In this country agreements to marry were, but are no longer,[106] regarded as legally enforceable. The old cases[107] which held that a promise by a married person to marry was illegal are no longer of direct relevance. However, the statute which abolished the contractual action for breach of promise to marry also provided that for some disputes concerning property, a formerly engaged couple are to be treated as if they were married.[108] Thus an agreement which, prior to 1970 was unenforceable for illegality in respect

---

[102] [1905] 2 KB 123. The case was characterised at p. 130 as involving 'the introduction of the consideration of a money payment into that which should be free from any such taint'.

[103] Furmston, 'The Analysis of Illegal Contracts' (1966) U of Tor LJ 267 at 299.

[104] In the past the equitable jurisdiction was applied more generally, e.g. *Morris v McCulloch* (1763) Amb 432 (money paid to secure a military commission to be repaid).

[105] See Phang (1998) *Cheshire, Fifoot and Furmston's Law of Contract – Second Singapore and Malaysian Edition*, pp. 691–2.

[106] Law Reform (Miscellaneous Provisions) Act 1970, s 1. See Cretney (1970) 33 MLR 534. They are still enforceable in Malaysia, Singapore and Brunei, *ibid.* at pp. 889–90.

[107] For example, *Spiers v Hunt* [1908] 1 KB 720.

[108] Section 2.

of which no contractual action could be brought, after that date may for certain limited purposes be treated as if it had been performed.[109]

Agreements between spouses which, in some way, provide for their future separation have been held to be invalid. This rule is based upon the view that such arrangements may discourage parties from marrying or continuing in wedlock. Thus, it is said to apply both to agreements made before[110] and during[111] marriage but not to arrangements concluded after[112] or even immediately prior to, separation.[113] In the latter cases, the courts take the pragmatic view that there is nothing left to protect.

A variation of such agreements has received a lot of recent publicity. So-called 'pre-nuptial contracts' are agreements entered into in anticipation of marriage and which are only effective upon marriage. These contracts have received much popular attention because the parties are often celebrities who are seeking to protect their pre-existing wealth. The status of such agreements is unclear. An unquestioning application of the older cases would hold such arrangements to be illegal and so unenforceable. However, there have been powerful calls for the recognition of such contracts even from within the 'establishment'.[114] Arguments for the enforceability of such contracts include:[115] parties are free to personalise their arrangements to match their own needs; recourse to the courts is reduced, tensions within the marriage avoided and public money saved; such agreements serve a cautionary function causing the parties to think seriously about the commitments of marriage; equality between the parties may be promoted *if* the agreement serves to protect the assets of the weaker party; and pre-nuptial agreements reflect the view of many couples that they, rather than the state or church, should regulate their own private lives.

An agreement which is inconsistent with the proper discharge of parental responsibility is illegal. On this basis the courts[116] and later the legislature[117] have provided that a parent cannot by contract transfer to a third party his or her rights and duties regarding a child. Statute also provides that a surrogacy agreement (i.e. one whereby a woman agrees to conceive a child with a view to another party assuming parental responsibility) is unenforceable.[118]

---

[109] See *Shaw* v *Fitzgerald* [1992] 1 FLB 357.
[110] *Brodie* v *Brodie* [1917] P 271.
[111] *H* v *W* [1857] 3 K & J 282.
[112] *Hart* v *Hart* [1881] 18 Ch D 670.
[113] *Wilson* v *Wilson* [1848] 1 HLC 538.
[114] For instance, Law Society Family Law Committee, Sands (1991) Law Soc Gazette 2.
[115] See Trebilcock (1993) *The Limits of Freedom of Contract*, pp. 43–4 and Conway, 'Pre-Nuptial Contracts' [1995] 145 NLJ 1290.
[116] *Humphreys* v *Polak* [1901] 2 KB 385.
[117] Children Act 1989, s 2.
[118] Human Fertilisation and Embryology Act 1990, s. 36. See also *Re P* (*Minors*) (*Wardship Surrogacy*) [1987] 2 FLR 42.

Contracts liable to affect adversely the state's relations with other states

The first group of cases concerns trading with the enemy in times of war.[119] Such contracts are illegal on the ground that their performance will tend to assist the hostile state's economy. Very different considerations are said to justify the non-enforcement of contracts which involve the performance in a friendly country of an act which is illegal under its domestic law. The maintenance of friendly relations with non-hostile states is the relevant policy here. On this basis, contracts to finance an attack upon a friendly country[120] and to smuggle whiskey into the USA during the prohibition era have been held to be illegal.[121]

Contracts inconsistent with good government

The law of contract recognises the public interest in good government which in turn requires its officials to discharge their duties without seeking personal gain. On this basis, the courts have refused to enforce agreements under which a Member of Parliament received a salary in exchange for voting in accordance with the payer's wishes[122] and a contract to 'purchase' a knighthood.[123]

Contracts in restraint of trade[124]

There is a sense in which all contracts restrain the future freedom of action of its parties. If I contract to sell you my house, I am not at liberty to sell it elsewhere. If I do so, you may recover damages for my breach of contract or obtain a court order requiring me to specifically perform my obligation to you. However, the law of contract takes objection to only some types of restraint. There are two main areas where the doctrine operates: in relation to promises by employees not to compete with their employer, and undertakings by the sellers of businesses not to carry on in competition with the purchaser. Beyond these settled applications, it is difficult to state when the doctrine may apply. In one case the doctrine of restraint of trade was applied to a solus agreement under which a garage agreed to buy all its petrol for a long period from one supplier.[125] In this case Lord Wilberforce declined to state the exact limits of the doctrine but preferred to describe it

---

[119] *Potts* v *Bell* (1800) 8 Term Rep 548. *Kuenigl* v *Donnersmarck* [1955] 1 QB 515. See also Trading with the Enemy Act 1939.

[120] *De Wutz* v *Hendricks* (1824) 2 Bing 314.

[121] *Foster* v *Driscoll* [1929] 1 KB 470.

[122] *Osborne* v *Amalgamated Society of Railway Servants* [1910] AC 87.

[123] *Parkinson* v *College of Ambulance* [1925] 2 KB 1.

[124] Restraint of Trade is covered in more detail in a number of specialist works. Heydon (1971) *The Restraint of Trade Doctrine*; Trebilcock (1986) *The Common Law of Restraint of Trade*; Jefferson (1996) *Restraint of Trade*.

[125] *Esso Petroleum Co Ltd* v *Harpers Garage (Stourport) Ltd* [1968] AC 269.

as 'one to be applied to factual situations with a broad and flexible rub of reason'.[126]

If an agreement is subject to the doctrine of restraint of trade, the party seeking to rely upon the disputed clause must prove that it is reasonable. This test has two aspects: it must be reasonable as between the parties and reasonable as being in the public interest.[127]

Employment contracts

Any restraint upon an employee will only be enforceable if it is reasonably necessary to protect a proprietary right of the employer such as trade secrets, other confidential information or to avoid solicitation of his customers. An example of a trade secret is the knowledge possessed by a plastics research technologist employed by a manufacturer of specialised PVC tape.[128] Other confidential information would extend to cover the knowledge of a senior employee responsible for compiling the biannual catalogue upon which a mail order business depended.[129] Customer lists are clearly very valuable commercial information and so the House of Lords have held that a restraint was enforceable against a solicitor's managing clerk who had acquired influence over his employer's clientele.[130]

What an employer is not entitled to restrain is the exercise by an employee of his own skill even where that skill was learned from his employer.[131] However, there remains the possibility that the courts might expand the traditional categories of protected 'proprietary' interests to include wider 'commercial'[132] interests. Wilberforce J[133] appeared to consider this possibility in a case examining the 'retain and transfer system' operating to prevent football clubs from employing players retained by rival clubs. Although he held that there was no sufficient justification for the arrangement, he did canvass possibilities outside the usual categories, e.g. that otherwise richer clubs would have a monopoly of the best players. It has been suggested[134] that a promise by an actor not to appear on the stage for three months which is made to promote a new film may represent the protection of a valid commercial interest rather than a proprietary interest.

A second requirement of a restrictive clause in a contract of employment is that the restraint must be reasonable in terms of subject matter, locality and duration. In general, a restraint must not extend beyond the activity which the employee was employed to do.[135] Similarly, the clause must not seek to

---

126 *Ibid.*, p. 331.
127 *Nordenfelt v Maxim Nordenfelt Guns and Ammunition Co Ltd* [1894] AC 535.
128 *Commercial Plastics Ltd v Vincent* [1965] 1 QB 623 (restraint was ultimately unenforceable for being too wide).
129 *Littlewoods Organisation v Harris* [1978] 1 All ER 1026.
130 *Fitch v Dewes* [1921] 2 AC 158.
131 *Herbert Morris Ltd v Saxelby* [1916] 1 AC 688.
132 The phrase is that of Treitel, p. 41.
133 *Eastham v Newcastle United Football Club Ltd* [1964] Ch 413.
134 Treitel, p. 417.
135 *Attwood v Lamont* [1920] 3 KB 571 (tailor cannot be restrained from working as a 'hatter').

operate over a larger geographical area than is necessary for the protection of the employer's proper interests.[136] However, it seems that it is easier to justify a restraint of long duration than one of wide coverage. Indeed, a lifelong restraint may be permissible where the nature of the business justifies it,[137] i.e. where clients have infrequent dealings. Where the covenant does not extend beyond a promise not to disclose confidential information, this may not – indeed, sometimes, to be efficacious, must not – be limited as to time.[138]

The final requirement is that the clause must be reasonable in the interests of the public appears to be virtually irrelevant in relation to restrictions upon employees.[139] In one exceptional case[140] it was given as one reason for the invalidity of the clause. The case involved a wool broker who was offered a retirement pension on condition that he did not engage in the wool trade. The Court of Appeal held that this restraint was both unreasonable between the parties and unreasonable for being contrary to the public interest because it unnecessarily deprived the nation of a worker with valuable expertise.

Contracts for the sale of a business

When someone purchases a business it is understandable that he or she will want to protect it from competition on the part of the vendor. The law meets this need by enforcing covenants in contracts for the sale of a business which restrict the future activities of the seller. Clauses must pass the same tests as those inserted in employment contracts (i.e. they must protect a proprietary interest and be reasonable both between the parties and in the public interest). However, it is generally the case that the courts approach such clauses in contracts for the sale of a business in a less hostile way than they do in employment contracts.

The purchaser of a business is not able to restrain the vendor from competition *per se*. Rather the law enables the purchaser to do so to the extent necessary to protect his or her proprietary interest in the goodwill of the business he or she has bought. For this reason, a clause is unenforceable if it goes beyond what is necessary for protection of the business actually sold. The question of what business has been sold appears to be one of substance rather than form. Therefore, a clause which restrained the assignor of a licence to brew beer from brewing beer for 15 years was unenforceable

---

136 *Mason v Provident Clothing and Supply Co Ltd* [1913] AC 724 (salesman employed to sell in Islington cannot be prevented from doing the same within 25 miles of London).

137 *Fitch v Dewes* [1921] 2 AC 158 (solicitors' managing clerk).

138 *A-G v Barker* [1990] 3 All ER 257. Members of the intelligence services owe a lifelong duty of confidentiality to the Crown: *A-G v Guardian Newspapers (No. 2)* [1988] 3 All ER 545 and *A-G v Blake* [1998] 1 All ER 833, both concerning members of the SIS (Special Intelligence Service).

139 *A-G of Commonwealth of Australia v Adelaide Steamship Co* [1913] AC 781 at 795.

140 *Wyatt v Kreglinger and Fernau* [1933] 1 KB 793.

when the only business actually carried out was the production of Japanese rice spirit, *sake*.[141]

The reasonableness between the parties of any restriction in a contract for the sale of a business is, like a restriction imposed on an employee, judged by reference to subject matter, locality and duration. This is well illustrated by the leading case of *Nordenfelt* v *Maxim Nordenfelt Guns and Ammunition Co Ltd*.[142] In this case the appellant, an ammunition inventor and manufacturer, sold his business and covenanted not to manufacture guns or ammunition (other than torpedoes) and explosives (other than gunpowder). The restraint was upheld despite being worldwide and stated to last for 25 years. The breadth of this constraint was said to be justified by the small number of companies engaged in the business.

The courts' approach to contracts for the sale of a business is less hostile than the way they deal with employment contracts. This difference of approach is justified by reference to two factors.[143] First, it might be frequently the case that parties negotiating the sale of a business have equal bargaining power, whereas the employer–employee relationship is usually characterised by an inequality of bargaining power. While this has been referred to in a number of cases (especially those involving young songwriters/performers),[144] it will not always apply, e.g. where the employee is represented by a powerful professional association or trade union.[145] The second factor is that the failure to enforce a restriction in a business sale as opposed to an employment contract would, in a more immediate sense, deprive the purchaser of the very thing he was paying for. The employee's breach of covenant does not deprive the employer of that which he primarily bargained for (labour) rather it deprives him of a collateral and perhaps contingent benefit (freedom from competition).[146]

Other anti-competitive practices

The doctrine of restraint of trade extends beyond the two established categories of cases already considered. Unfortunately, it is difficult to articulate clearly the limits of the jurisdiction.

Modern cases have held that a number of 'exclusive dealing' arrangements are unenforceable for being in unreasonable restraint of trade. Examples include so-called solus agreements whereby garages agree to purchase all

---

[141] *Vancouver Malt and Sake Brewing Co Ltd* v *Vancouver Breweries Ltd* [1936] AC 181.

[142] [1894] AC 535.

[143] See generally Treitel, pp. 414–15.

[144] *A Schroeder Manis Publishing Co Ltd* v *Macauly* [1974] 1 WLR 1308; *Clifford Davies Management* v *WEA Records* [1975] 1 WLR 61.

[145] A point made by Treitel at p. 415 who also refers to a managing director who may technically be an employee. 'A managing director can look after himself': *M & S Drapers* v *Reynolds* [1957] 1 WLR 9 at 19.

[146] *Cf.* Treitel p. 415 who appears to suggest that *all* an employer bargains for is the labour of his employee.

their petrol supplies from a particular oil company.[147] In *Esso Petroleum Co Ltd v Harpers Garage*,[148] the House of Lords had to consider the validity of two such agreements respectively expressed to last for five and 21 years. It held that while the former was enforceable, the latter was not.[149]

The *Esso* case did not clearly indicate what exceptional features of the agreements in question qualified them for review under the doctrine of restraint of trade. Subsequent cases have made it clear that courts attach considerable importance to the relative bargaining powers of the parties. This is well illustrated by a case concerning an agreement entered between a then unknown song writer and a publisher under which the former pledged his exclusive services for five years (with an extension option) but the latter assumed no obligation to publish the writer's songs.[150] The agreement also provided for termination upon one month's notice by the publisher but no right of termination was allowed the writer. The agreement was held invalid. Similarly, an agreement between a record company and pop group which allowed for six further extensions by the record company and which was entered before the group became famous was held invalid.[151]

A further relevant factor is whether the party for whose benefit the restriction operates becomes subject to a conflict of interest. In one case, a party contracted to act as both the manager and promoter for a boxer.[152] The agreement was to run for three years and was renewable for the same period. It was held that the two capacities assumed by the defendant were incompatible: as the boxer's manager, he was obliged to obtain the highest fee possible; as promoter he was liable to pay that fee! As a result, the agreement was unenforceable.

The doctrine of restraint of trade does not generally operate to protect a purchaser or lessee who takes land subject to a restrictive covenant. The purchaser or lessee is not thereby deprived of any right he previously enjoyed. However, the doctrine does apply where, as in the *Esso* case, someone who already does business at a particular location accepts some restriction on his freedom to continue to do so. To similar effect is the *Alec Lobb* case[153] where the 'owner' of a garage entered a refinancing arrangement with Total Oil whereby he leased the premises to Total for 51 years at a nominal rent in exchange for a sub-lease and a capital payment. The court was prepared to look into the realities of the situation and ignore the fact

---

147 Usually accompanied by subsidiary promises providing for minimum opening hours and requiring the garage proprietor to extract similar promises from anyone he sells the business to. Prospective garage owners are usually induced to accept these restrictions by the offer of development finance from the oil company.
148 [1968] AC 269.
149 The problem presented by these cases is unlikely to recur. Following a Monopolies Commission Report undertakings concerning solus agreements were given to the government by the major oil companies. See Treitel, p. 428.
150 *Schroeder Music Publishing Co Ltd v Macaulay* [1974] 3 All ER 616.
151 *Silverstone Records v Mountfield* [1993] EMLR 152.
152 *Watson v Prager* [1991] 1 WLR 726.
153 *Alec Lobb (Garages) Ltd v Total Oil GB Ltd* [1985] 1 WLR 173.

that, technically, the garage owner had no pre-existing legal interest in the site (it was in fact owned by a company he controlled).

The *Alec Lobb* case illustrates an important point about the restraint of trade doctrine which, put simply, is that it is difficult to evade. The courts take a pragmatic approach and investigate thoroughly formal arrangements which aim to place a contract outside the doctrine.[154] Another illustration of this purposive approach concerns agreements between employers which effectively restrict the freedom of workers. In one case,[155] the court declared void resolutions passed by the governing body and employers' association to disqualify from international and county matches any player accepting a contract from a private promoter. In contrast, trade unions still enjoy a considerable degree of statutory protection from the restraint of trade doctrine.[156] The Trade Union and Labour Relations (Consolidation) Act 1992, s 11 provides that the restraint of trade doctrine does not itself justify finding that because of the purposes of a trade union, its rules, or agreements entered by it, are void and unenforceable.

STATUTORY CONTROL OF ANTI-COMPETITIVE PRACTICES

The courts' willingness to control anti-competitive practices is, however, limited. There are three closely related reasons for this reluctance. First, the constitutional argument: judges are not elected, so in a democracy it is not appropriate for them to determine economic policy. Second, the competence argument: courts are not well-suited or properly staffed to conduct broad ranging economic investigations into particular sectors of the economy. Third, the contractarian argument: courts are too influenced by the *laisser faire* (literally 'leave to do', i.e. non-interventionist) basis of classical contract law. This results in reluctance to challenge anti-competitive practices.

The legislature has intervened, enacting a number of measures and empowering several bodies and individuals to control cartels and monopolies. Only a brief outline of these measures can be given here. At the outset, it should be noted that this area of law (usually called competition law) is a late developer on this side of the Atlantic. The courts of the United States have been far more vigorous in the pursuit of free trade and have built up a strong control of anti-competitive practices which is known as anti-trust law.[157]

In 1956 legislation was introduced outlawing restrictive agreements

---

[154] In a different context, see *Kores Manufacturing Co Ltd* v *Kolak Manufacturing Co Ltd* [1959] Ch 108 (arrangement between two *employers* not to 'poach' each other's staff was reviewable because it effectively restricted the employees) and *Bull* v *Pitney Bowes Ltd* [1967] 1 WLR 273 (doctrine not evaded by placing restriction in the company's pension scheme). *Cf. Wyatt* v *Kreglinger & Fernau* [1933] 1 KB 793.

[155] *Greig* v *Insole* [1978] 1 WLR 302.

[156] This 'protection' has survived the erosion elsewhere of the privileges formerly enjoyed by trade unions, e.g. in relation to the economic torts.

[157] A good example is the availability of so-called 'triple indemnity suits' where damages are recoverable at the rate of three times the actual loss.

controlling the supply, acquisition or manufacture of goods unless the agreement is demonstrated to be in the public interest.[158] However, the United Kingdom's membership of the European Union has brought more wide-ranging restrictions. European competition law was directly applicable in English law but is now re-enacted in the new Competition Act 1998. Responsibility for enforcing the Act lies initially with the Director-General of Fair Trading[159] who can impose penalties of up to 10 per cent of an organisation's turnover.[160]

The main provisions of European law which define its competition policy are Arts 81 and 82 (formerly 85 and 86) of the European Community Treaty. The former prohibits 'all agreements … and concerted practices … which have as their object or effect the prevention, restriction or distortion of competition'. In particular, several types of agreement are expressly controlled.[161] Any agreement which contravenes Art 81 is void and unenforceable[162] in the UK and may result in the imposition of fines.[163] However, some prima facie infringements may be permitted if the agreement falls within an individual or block exemption.[164] An example of the application of Art 85 was provided by a case[165] where a manufacturer was forbidden from imposing on national distributors an obligation not to trade outside the country's boundaries.

Further control is provided by Art 82 which prevents the 'abuse of a dominant position'. In particular, this seeks to prevent mergers and practices which will effectively reduce competition.[166]

The body formerly known as the Monopolies and Mergers Commission was renamed in the Competition Act and is now called the Competition Commission.[167] It is an independent investigative body which has cases referred to it by the Government or the Director-General of Fair Trading.[168] It has no power to give effect to its own recommendation and so depends upon governmental implementation.

It is convenient to consider at this point one other body of law outside the common law restraint of contract cases but which similarly controls

---

[158] Restrictive Trade Practices Act 1956.
[159] Section 25.
[160] Section 26.
[161] That is, agreements which fix prices, control or limit production, markets, technical development or investment, divide markets or supply sources, treat equivalent contracts dissimilarly and impose irrelevant supplementary obligations. See Competition Act 1998, s 2.
[162] Article 85(2).
[163] That is, by the Commission of the European Communities.
[164] The agreement or practice must: (a) improve production/distribution, or promote technical/economic progress, (b) give the consumer a fair share of such benefits, (c) consist of only indispensable restrictions and (d) not create the possibility of eliminating competition in respect of a substantial part of the products in question.
[165] *Consten and Grundig* v *Commission of the European Communities* (cases 56/64, 58/64) [1966] ECR 299.
[166] See Competition Act 1998, s 18.
[167] Section 44.
[168] An officer appointed by the government.

anti-competitive practices. Unlike the measures considered above, these principles are not domestic or European legislation. Rather they form part of what is known as public law, which is the collective term for the rules and processes which regulate the relationship between government bodies and, more significantly, between government bodies and individuals.[169] Where a person is adversely affected by the decision of a body which discharges a quasi-judicial function, public law may provide grounds upon which to challenge this decision. Thus public law supplements the law of contract which might also regulate relationships between persons subject to the control of the body and between those persons and the body itself. On this basis, the Court of Appeal have refused to strike out a claim that a rule of the jockey club which prevented a female from being a horse trainer was invalid[170] and a rule of the pharmaceutical regulatory body which imposed limits upon the goods which their members could sell was held to be invalid.[171] Indeed, it has been argued that these cases represent a breaking down of the boundary between private law and public law. Once it is recognised that a contract is only partly the creation of the parties, that much of the law of contract is concerned with the imposition upon the parties of certain standards of fairness and this is coupled with a public law which imposes its own standards of fairness upon individuals' contractual relationships with regulatory bodies, the borderline between the private law of contract and public law becomes blurred and meaningless.[172] The suggestion has been made that there are more procedural than substantive points of difference between private and public law.[173]

GAMBLING CONTRACTS

The legal 'control' of gambling contracts derives from statute. However, unlike the statutes we encountered earlier, the Gaming Act 1845 does not, expressly or impliedly, prohibit the formation of such contracts.[174] It simply provides that henceforth they will be 'null and void'.[175] This hybrid character

---

[169] See generally Le Sueur and Sunkin (1997) *Public Law*, pp. 3–6.

[170] *Nagle* v *Feilder* [1966] 2 QB 633.

[171] *Pharmaceutical Society of GB* v *Dickson* [1970] AC 403.

[172] See generally Oliver (1999) *Common Values and the Public–Private Divide*. For a less ambitious suggestion that contract law already does and to a greater extent should adopt public law principles, see Beatson, 'Public Law Influences in Contract Law', ch. 10 in Beatson and Friedmann (eds) (1995) *Good Faith and Fault in Contract Law*. Cf. *R* v *Disciplinary Committee of the Jockey Club ex parte Aga Khan* [1993] 1 WLR 909 at 933 *per* Hoffmann LJ.

[173] *Shearson Lehman Hutton* v *MacLaine Watson & Co Ltd* [1989] 2 Lloyd's Rep 570 at 625 *per* Webster J.

[174] '… ordinary betting [is] treated as a thing of neutral character, not to be encouraged, but on the other hand, not to be absolutely forbidden … an ordinary bet [is] a mere debt of honour, depriv[ed] … of all legal obligation, but not … illegal', *per* Lush J in *Haigh* v *The Town Council of Sheffield* (1874) LR 10 QB 102 at 109.

[175] Section 18.

of gambling contracts is thought to justify their inclusion in a chapter on illegality[176] but to require separate treatment within that chapter.

Gambling contracts are not described as such by the common law or statute which tend to use the more antiquated language of 'wagering' and 'gaming' contracts. The proper definition of these two categories is not as easy as it might first seem.

A wagering contract is:[177]

> one by which two persons, professing to hold opposite views[178] ... agree that ... one shall win from the other ... a sum of money or stake; neither ... having any other interest in that contract than the sum or stake he will so win or lose.

One very important feature of this definition is that a contract is not a wager if one party cannot win or one party cannot lose. The latter part of the exclusion prevents many contracts which would commonly be described as betting or gambling from technically being so. These include the submission of a football pool,[179] the purchase of a lottery ticket,[180] the placing of a 'tote' bet on a horse[181] and playing bingo,[182] all of which do not amount to wagers with the person running the 'game' or 'book' because they simply re-distribute a portion of the stakes to the winners.[183] The law acts upon the truism that the 'bookie never loses'.

It is not only the requirement of loss which excludes from the definition of wagering many common forms of gambling. It is also a requirement of wagering that there are only two parties to any wager. However, games with many participants such as roulette may be viewed as a series of wagers between the players and the casino. The same might not be true of a game of cards played between more than two friends where there is no 'house'.

Another aspect of the definition of a wagering contract needs amplification. This is the requirement that the parties have no other interest in the outcome than that created by the bet. This factor is used to distinguish between contracts of insurance and gambling. A genuine insurance contract is one where the party seeking protection against uncertainty has an 'insurable interest'.[184] If I take out 'comprehensive' insurance on my motorcycle, my

---

[176] *Cf.* the approach of the Law Commission, Consultation Paper, No. 54 of 1999, which felt that this justified omitting the subject from its proposals.

[177] Per Hawkins J in *Carlill* v *Carbolic Smoke Ball Co* [1892] 2 QB 484 at 490, affirmed [1893] 1 QB 256.

[178] In the original *dictum* the opposing views had to concern 'a future uncertain event'. However, it is clear that this is too restrictive and that there can be a wager in relation to a past or present fact upon which the parties hold different views (e.g. the number of pages in this book). See Cheshire, Fifoot and Furmston, p. 335.

[179] A subject which is surprisingly free of authority.

[180] See *Re Senator Hanseatische Verwaltungsgesellschaft GmbH* [1997] 1 WLR 515.

[181] The Horseracing Totalisation Board divides the net proceeds of bets between winners.

[182] *Peck* v *Lateu* [1973] SJ 185.

[183] An agreement to divide the proceeds of any 'win' will itself not be a wager for the same reason. See *Slot* v *Haughton & F Fuller* (1706) 2 Vern 560 (master gave servant a lottery ticket on condition that the latter gave the former's daughter half of any prize over £1. £1,000 was won).

[184] Life Assurance Act 1774, s 1 (non-marine insurance) and Marine Insurance Act 1906, s 4.

ownership of it is the insurable interest. Contracts of insurance are obviously of huge commercial importance and so it is obvious that their enforceability should be beyond doubt. What to the layman may be less obvious is how they could be confused with gambling. Surely the difference between a bet with a friend and the insurance of a house is clear. As with all distinctions, such polar cases present a clearer picture than the grey area is in between. What about a contract to pay out in the event of crop failure. Is the farmer gambling on next season's weather or insuring against it? The requirement of an insurable interest would be satisfied by the farmer's ownership of the trees which would produce the crop.[185]

Another type of dealing which on close inspection may resemble a gambling contract is the purchase and sale of stocks and shares. Again, there is a need to clearly identify commercially valuable activity and to ensure that its enforceability is beyond question. This is certainly the case when stocks and shares are bought and sold. However, a more difficult case is presented by a 'contract to pay differences', i.e. where the parties do not actually contemplate the delivery of and payment for the shares but where one shall receive from the other the difference between the contract price of the share specified and its market price on the settlement day. Such a contract for differences is regarded as a wagering contract[186] but there are restrictions upon who can plead such a defence.[187]

Similar problems are encountered in relation to the sale of commodity futures. Where there is a sale of goods to be delivered in the future at the then prevailing market price, the uncertainty thereby introduced does not transform the contract into a wager. However, if both parties are merely speculating on future price movements, the result will be different. The test is, therefore, one of intention[188] and this does introduce uncertainty into commercial dealings which has been avoided elsewhere by the requirement of an insurable interest.

A modern phenomenon which the courts have had to consider in the light of these principles is interest-rate swap transactions.[189] Interest-rate swaps may be, but are not necessarily, wagering contracts. Again, the determining factor is the intention of the parties. Where the purpose of the parties is not speculative, the agreement will not be treated as a wager.[190]

---

[185] *Thacker* v *Hardy* [1878] 4 QBD 685 at 695.
[186] *Thacker* v *Hardy* [1878] 4 QBD 685.
[187] The Gaming Act may not be pleaded by a licensed dealer in securities according to Licensed Dealers (Conduct of Business) Rules 1983: SI 1983 No. 585, r 18(2).
[188] *Ironmonger & Co* v *Dyre* [1928] 44 TLR 497 at 499 *per* Scrutton LJ.
[189] An interest-rate swap is a financial instrument whereby two parties pay each other interest (one fixed, the other variable) upon a notional sum usually accompanied by an additional payment at the commencement of the agreement. Such 'swaps' were in effect disguised loans designed to evade the restrictions imposed by central government upon borrowing by local government.
[190] *Morgan Grenfell* v *Welwyn Hatfield District Council* [1995] 1 All ER 1. Even if the 'swap' in this case was a wager, it was 'saved' by the Financial Services Act 1986, s 63. As to which, see following note and accompanying text.

Agreements which would otherwise be classified as wagers may be saved by other legislation. For example, the Financial Services Act 1986 'saves' contracts involving the buying and selling of investments where such purchase and sale is the business of one party.[191] In one case,[192] a company which provided gambling facilities in relation to financial indices such as the FT30 was protected by the 1986 Act.

'Gaming' adds little to the definition of a wager. It implies the playing of a game[193] for money or money's worth.[194]

The effects of a gambling contract

We have not yet considered the consequences for the parties of entering an illegal contract beyond the general description that it is unenforceable. In this regard, gambling contracts are distinct because the Gaming Act 1845 definitively states the effect of a gambling contract. For this reason we will examine the consequences of gambling contracts before we generalise about the effects of other types of illegal contract.

The Gaming Act 1845, s 18 states:

All contracts or agreements ... by way of gaming or wagering, shall be null and void, and no suit shall be brought or maintained in any Court of Law or Equity for recovering any sum of money or valuable thing alleged to be won upon any wager or which shall have been deposited in the hands of any person to abide the event on which any wager shall have been made.

The section has three aspects. First, the consequence of all gaming and wagering contracts being void is that neither party can sue upon it. A party who places a winning bet is prevented from enforcing it just as a party placing a losing bet who has not yet paid the stake is free from suit.[195]

Second, the section prevents the enforcement of any supplementary promises.[196] The House of Lords has held that the prohibition which begins 'no suit' was not redundant; it did not merely restate in different words the effect of the contract being null and void. Rather, it applied to any supplemental promises as where a defaulting debtor agreed to pay his past debts to avoid being excluded from racecourses.

---

[191] Section 63 and Sch 1, para 12.
[192] *City Index Ltd v Lesle* [1991] 3 All ER 180. A typical bet would be one against the company's forecast for a particular index. If the client thought it was too optimistic, he would place a sell bet giving him a payment equivalent to the extent to which the company's forecast exceeded what actually transpired. If the client's judgement was wrong, he would have to pay the amount by which the index lagged behind events. If the client thought the company's prediction too pessimistic, he would place a buy bet which would have the opposite effect.
[193] Including horse racing: *Applegarth v Colley* (1842) 10 M & W 723.
[194] *Ellesmere v Wallace* [1929] 2 Ch 1 at 55. *Cf.* Gaming Act 1968, s 52(1) which adds that it must be a game of chance. The 1968 definition is only applicable to that enactment.
[195] *Abery v Chandler* [1948] 64 TLR 394.
[196] *Hill v William Hill* [1949] AC 530.

Money paid under a void contract can usually be recovered.[197] However, it has been held that the normal rule is reversed in this context and so a losing gambler is unable to recover any stake paid.[198] It is difficult to justify this by reference to the express words of the section which are limited to actions by the winner. It has been explained on the basis that the act of payment is itself a waiver by the payor of his right to the money.[199]

Third, the section expressly deals with the situation where money or something of value is deposited with a third party 'stakeholder'. However, this has been interpreted as not preventing a party from demanding the return of money or something of value from the stakeholder at any time before he has handed it over to the winner.[200]

THE CONSEQUENCES OF ILLEGALITY

The catalogue of reprehensible conduct we have compiled is large and varied. We now examine the consequences for the parties of inclusion in one of the categories of illegal contracts. We will see that with some caution we can generalise about the effects upon the parties of illegality.

Enforcement of the contract

The Latin maxim we encountered at the beginning of this chapter, *ex turpi causa oritur non actio* (no action can arise from a base cause) implies that neither party can bring an action to enforce the illegal contract. In the highwayman case[201] mentioned earlier, one highwayman was not permitted to enforce an agreement with another to split the proceeds of their robberies. A more recent illustration involved an agreement between a solicitor and another under which the latter was to receive a share of the former's fees for preparing applications for asylum by individuals he introduced to the solicitor.[202] The contract was illegal because it involved a breach of the Solicitors Practice Rules which forbid solicitors from sharing fees and so the action to recover the agreed share of fees failed.[203]

In Chapter 9 we will see that the courts have resorted to the device of the collateral contract in order to enable a meritorious party to evade a harsh legal rule.[204] The same device is used in relation to illegal contracts. In *Strongman (1945) v Sincock*[205] an architect employed a company to modernise

---

[197] It was assumed in *Bell* v *Lever Bros* [1932] AC 161 that *if* the contracts of compromise had been void, the sums paid pursuant to them could be recovered from the employees.
[198] *Lipkin Gorman* v *Karpnale* [1991] 2 AC 548 at 561.
[199] *Bridger* v *Savage* (1884) 15 QBD 363 at 367.
[200] *Diggle* v *Higgs* (1877) 2 Ex D 422.
[201] *Everet* v *Williams* (1725) reported at (1893) 9 LQR 197.
[202] *Mohamed* v *Alaya & Co* [1998] 2 All ER 720.
[203] A restitutionary action also failed.
[204] For example, the doctrine of privity of contract. See *Shanklin Pier Ltd* v *Detel Products Ltd* [1951] 2 KB 854.
[205] [1955] 2 QB 528.

some houses. This work required a licence from the Ministry of Works which the architect undertook to obtain. In fact he only obtained a licence for £2,150 worth of work when £6,000 was the value of what was done. The builders only received £2,000 from the architect and sued for the balance. The Court of Appeal held that the main agreement was illegal and so unenforceable. However, the claimant succeeded on the basis that there was a breach of a collateral promise by the defendant – that he would obtain the necessary licences. It should be emphasised that this principle may only be used by an innocent party.

In the case just considered, the builders would have been entitled to recover as damages for breach of the collateral contract the sum necessary to put them in the position they would have been in if that contract had been performed. This is called the contractual measure of damages[206] and would be £6,000 (value of work done) less £2,900 (amount already received). This measure of damages is the maximum a claimant can recover in respect of a breach of contract.[207] If the breach of contract involves the commission of a tort, the claimant may recover damages which are typically less than those for breach of contract.[208] However, where the tort is fraud, the courts, unsurprisingly, dislike 'liars' and although the 'lesser' tortious measure is awarded, it is assessed in a generous way (i.e. generous to claimants).[209] Tortious damages in deceit for fraudulent misrepresentation may be the second best recovery available to the victim of a breach of an illegal contract. On this basis, the purchaser of a flat recovered damages against a vendor who had fraudulently misrepresented that the flat included a roof terrace.[210]

The recovery of money and property

Although a party to an illegal transaction will not generally be able to enforce it, he may none the less be able to recover benefits he has conferred upon the other party to the illegal contract. Such a remedy will be less valuable to the claimant because it operates only to restore him to the position he was in before the transfer was made rather than fulfil the expectations excited by the contract.[211] In the case concerning the hire of an

---

[206] See generally Chapter 17.

[207] Exemplary damages are not available for breach of contract. So-called restitutionary damages might, in exceptional circumstances, exceed contractual damages. See Chapter 17.

[208] Confusingly, so-called 'tortious' damages may exceptionally be awarded in respect of a breach of contract.

[209] *East* v *Maurer* [1991] 1 WLR 461.

[210] *Saunders* v *Edwards* [1987] 1 WLR 1116 (the contract was illegal because the purchase price was incorrectly apportioned to evade liability to pay stamp duty). See also *Shelley* v *Paddock* [1980] QB 348 where the defendant swindled the claimant out of the price of Spanish property which the defendant had innocently paid for in breach of currency regulations.

[211] Like the award of the tortious measure of damages, the recovery of money and property will restore the recipient to his precontractual position. The former achieves this solely by the award of a sum of money; the latter operates literally (with regard to property) and requires the return of the very property in question.

ornamental carriage by a prostitute,[212] the owners of the carriage having failed
to recover unpaid hire would certainly appreciate the return of their property.

The general rule is that the courts will not order the return of money paid
or property transferred under an illegal contract.[213] In effect the law simply
lets losses fall where they lie. The principle, like so much of this subject, is
usually expressed in Latin: *in pari delicto potior est conditio defendentis* (where
the parties are equally guilty the defendant is in the best position).[214] It was
expressed in antiquated but colourful language thus:[215]

> [No] polluted hand shall touch the pure fountains of justice. Whoever is a party to
> an unlawful contract, if he hath once paid the money stipulated to be paid ... he
> shall not have the help of a court to fetch it back again.

If this rule were strictly applied it might undermine the policy of deterrence
pursued by the law in this area. If the owner of the ornamental carriage were
unable to recover it from the prostitute, prostitutes might be encouraged to
hire conveyances safe in the knowledge that they could neither be required
to pay for their hire nor ordered to return them. Therefore, the general rule
admits three exceptions which are: where a party withdraws from the illegal
enterprise, where the parties are not equally guilty and where the claimant
does not need to rely on the illegal contract.

Before examining the scope of the three exceptions, a problem of
classification arises. A party's claim that he should have property returned to
him is a claim in the law of restitution rather than the law of contract.
Restitution is concerned with the reversal of unjust enrichment. Here the
party seeks the return of property to avoid the unjust enrichment of the
party in *de facto* possession. As the claim for the return of property arises
because of an illegal contract, our treatment of illegality would be
incomplete if it were not examined here.

Unfortunately, restitution lawyers disagree how these exceptions fit within
the broader framework of their subject. The simplest approach is to regard a
restitutionary action as unavailable for the same policy reasons as justify the
refusal of a contractual one. The exceptions are then justified by reference to
circumstances which rebut the policies justifying non-enforcement and non-
recovery.[216] This approach may be criticised because it fails to distinguish
between illegality operating as a defence to an otherwise valid claim to
restitution (e.g. failure of consideration or mistake) and the situation where
the unequal participation in the illegal purpose itself provides a sufficient
justification for ordering the return of money or property.[217] The criticism is

---

[212] *Pearce v Brooks* (1866) LR 1 Ex 213.

[213] *Scott v Brown* [1892] 2 QB 724.

[214] See Grodecki (1955) 71 LQR 254.

[215] *Collins v Blanton* [1767] 2 Wilson 341 at 350 *per* Wilmot CJ, quoted in (1998) *Anson's Law of Contract.* 27th edn, at p. 388.

[216] Goff and Jones (1998) *The Law of Restitution.* 5th edn, ch. 24.

[217] The criticism is that of Birks (1989) *An Introduction to the Law of Restitution.* Rev. edn, pp. 299–303 and 424–32. See also Burrows (*Restitution*), pp. 333–4 and Burrows and McKendrick (1997) *Cases and Materials on the Law of Restitution*, p. 511.

probably well founded but the debate is a sterile one so far as we are concerned. The two different approaches do not disagree upon how the law would apply to particular factual circumstances rather the controversy surrounds how these factual circumstances are accommodated within a coherent account of the law of restitution. As the latter is beyond our brief we will simply note the squabble and move directly to an account of the law.

Withdrawal from the illegal enterprise

A party to an illegal contract will be able to recover any benefit he has conferred if he withdraws in time. The law grants the transferor a 'time for repentance' or *locus poenitentiae*. If no such opportunity was available, the law would be favouring the interests of the more culpable party who has continued with the illegal contract. This exception is meant to discourage illegality by giving parties an incentive to repudiate the illegal contract. In the language of restitution (introduced above), it is the exception rather than the rule from which it departs which is necessary to prevent the unjust enrichment of the transferee. The *locus poenitentiae* operates as a restitutionary cause of action.

It is not easy to state the limits of this exception. There appear to be three requirements. First, it is necessary that the illegal purpose has not yet been effected. In *Tribe* v *Tribe*[218] the claimant owned a company and was personally liable on repairing covenants contained in two leases for shops used by the company. The claimant transferred shares in the company to his son. This transfer was a sham: the stated consideration was never paid nor intended to be paid. It was entered to make the claimant look as if he had no valuable assets and thereby strengthen his bargaining position with regard to his personal liabilities on the leases. The Court of Appeal held that the claimant was entitled to reclaim his shares because in the event no creditors were deceived. The claimant bought the reversion[219] on one shop and surrendered the lease on the other and during negotiations neither the vendor nor lessor were made aware of the share transfer. It seems that the *locus poenitentiae* is lost once the illegal purpose has been fully or *partly* effected.[220]

The second requirement, which has been emphasised in some cases, is the need for 'repentance'.[221] In *Tribe* v *Tribe* the Court of Appeal unanimously

---

[218] [1996] Ch 107. The case dealt with the *locus poententrae* in relation to the law of trusts but it is suggested that the law of contract and trusts should be the same in this regard.

[219] That is, the landlord's interest.

[220] 'If [the transferee] ... is seeking to carry out the illegal purpose, or has already carried it out in whole or in part, then he fails': *per* Issacs, Gavan Duffy and Rich JJ in *Perpetual Executors and Trustees Association of Australia Ltd* v *Wright* [1917] 23 CLR 185; and 'where the illegal purpose has been wholly or partially effected, the law allows no *locus poenitentiae*': *per* Romer LJ in *Alexander* v *Ragson* [1936] 1 KB 169 at 190.

[221] *Parkinson* v *The College of Ambulance Ltd and Harrison* [1925] 2 KB 1; *Alexander* v *Ragson* [1936] 1 KB 169; *Berg* v *Sadler and Moore* [1937] 2 KB 158; *Harry Parker Ltd* v *Mason* [1940] 2 KB 590.

rejected[222] this requirement. Millett LJ explained this rejection on the basis that the court is concerned with the achievement of justice and this should not be limited to the 'penitent'.[223]

The third requirement is that the withdrawal must be voluntary. If the only reason for the claimant's withdrawal is that it is no longer possible to carry out the illegal purpose, then recovery may not be permitted. This is illustrated by *Bigos* v *Boustead*[224] which involved an agreement to supply foreign monies, by way of a loan, in breach of currency regulations, the loan secured by a share certificate deposited with the supplier. The foreign currency was never supplied and so the disappointed borrower unsuccessfully sought the return of his certificate. He had only sought to withdraw from the transaction when its illegal purpose was 'frustrated' by the other party's refusal to perform. This principle reflects the underlying policy justification for the *locus poententiae* exception. It is meant to provide an incentive for parties to abandon their illegal enterprise. To the extent that it has been frustrated by other factors there is simply no need for legal intervention.[225] However, it may be objected that if withdrawal is unavailable in the 'frustration' cases, the only way in which someone like the claimant in *Bigos* can avoid a loss is to persuade the other party to carry through the original illegal purpose. Thus the law creates an incentive for the transferor to try to cajole an initially hesitant transferee to continue with the illegal agreement.[226]

Where the parties are not equally guilty (*in pari delicto*)

Where parties' involvement in the illegal contract is unequal, the 'innocent' party may be able to bring an action for the return of money or property. The basis of this action will be one of the recognised heads of restitution. Illegality operates as a defence to this action unless the claimant is less culpable.

The general defence is illustrated by *Parkinson* v *The College of Ambulance Ltd and Harrison*[227] where the claimant was encouraged to make a large charitable donation in exchange for a knighthood. When the honour was not forthcoming, the claimant sought to recover his donation. If the agreement had not been one which was inconsistent with good government (e.g. it

---

[222] 'All that matters is that no deception was practised ...': *per* Nourse LJ at p. 122; 'I would hold that genuine repentance is not required': *per* Millett LJ at p. 135. It should be noted that Nourse LJ limited his comments to the effect of illegality upon the law of trusts, whereas Millett LJ intended his comments to apply generally. A difficulty is presented by Otton LJ who simply says, 'I agree' and so gives no indication as to the scope of the principles he agrees with.

[223] This follows the argument of several academics. See Grodecki (1955) LQR 254 at 263. Beatson (1975) 91 LQR 313 and Merkin (1981) LQR 420. *Contra*: Birks (1989) *An Introduction to the Law of Restitution*, p. 301.

[224] [1951] 1 All ER 92.

[225] See especially Burrows (*Restitution*), p. 339.

[226] *Cf.* Burrows, *ibid.*, pp. 339–40.

[227] [1925] 2 KB 1.

concerned the sale of a suit of knight's armour rather than a knight's honour), the payor would have been able to recover the money in an action for restitution. The factor which would justify the reversal of the defendant's enrichment (the 'unjust factor' in 'restitution speak') is said to be a failure of consideration. In short, he did not receive what he had bargained for.

This may be contrasted with the case of *Kiriri Cotton Co Ltd* v *Dewani*[228] where a landlord, in breach of statutory rent restrictions, demanded and received a 'premium' from a sub-tenant. The sub-tenant's action to recover the premium was successful. The ground upon which the sub-tenant claimed restitution of the premium was that it was paid under an operative mistake. Mistake, like failure of consideration, is a recognised head of restitution. However, the sub-tenant was successful because he was not regarded as equally guilty as the landlord. The obligation not to charge a premium was imposed upon the landlord for the protection of tenants. As a victim, the sub-tenant was not regarded as culpable to the same extent as the landlord. To similar effect is a case[229] where an insurer entered contracts of insurance in breach of the provisions of the Insurance Companies Act 1974. This statute imposed obligations upon insurers for the benefit of the insured and the latter had no reason to have knowledge of its provisions so they could reclaim the premiums paid.

The *in pari delicto* maxim cannot be taken literally. It seems that the courts' concern is simply with the innocent state of mind of the claimant *per se* rather than requiring a comparison of the states of mind of both parties. In one case[230] the claimants insured a cargo of goods being shipped from Russia to England. Unknown to both parties, war had broken out between the countries.[231] The claimants recovered the premium paid because 'no fault [was] imputable to them'. However, the defendant's state of mind was probably just as innocent so the parties were in fact *in pari delicto*.

Where a person is coerced into making a payment or handing over property, the oppressed party may reclaim it in a restitutionary action. Where duress is the ground justifying restitution, the victim is not *in pari delicto* and so illegality will not operate as a defence. On this basis, friends who paid money to 'replace' that taken by an employee were able to recover the sums paid.[232] It was held that the payments were made under duress to avoid the employee's prosecution by his employer and that they were recoverable notwithstanding that they were paid under an illegal contract whose purpose was to suppress a crime. The principle may extend beyond duress to cases involving undue influence,[233] or, more controversially, to cover vulnerability

---

[228] [1960] AC 192 (PC).
[229] *Re Cavalier Insurance Co Ltd* [1989] 2 Lloyd's Rep 430.
[230] *Oom* v *Bruce* (1880) 12 East 225.
[231] The outbreak of war 'frustrated' the contract between the parties. Frustration like failure of consideration is another unjust factor justifying restitution.
[232] *Davies* v *London and Provincial Marine Insurance Co* (1878) 8 Ch D 469.
[233] *Andrews* v *Parker* [1973] Qd R. 93.

where the illegality consists of a breach of a statutory measure whose purpose is to protect members of a class to which the claimant belongs.[234]

Earlier we considered cases where one party was induced to enter an illegal transaction in reliance upon the other party's fraudulent mis-representation. Where the representation was to the effect that the putative transaction was legal (e.g. that the vendor had obtained the necessary permits when he had not) the situation might be described as one where the parties are not *in pari delicto*. However, it is suggested that such cases were more appropriately considered earlier because they involve an independent cause of action in the tort of deceit, which may come close to the effective enforcement of the contract. Under the next heading we consider cases where a party is able to reclaim money or property transferred pursuant to an illegal contract because his action is said not to involve reliance upon the illegal contract. The exception may be said to be a part of the law of property which determines what interest individuals have in real property (e.g. land) or personal property (e.g. goods). Although it is principles of property law which determine the relative titles of parties arguing about the ownership of property, it is the law of tort which enforces them. The party with a superior title will bring an action in tort (trespass if land, conversion if goods) to assert that title and recover his property or damages in lieu.

Recovery without reliance upon the illegal contract

It is hard to categorise the variety of circumstances where a party to an illegal transaction is able to recover money or property because he is able to make out a right to it 'without' reliance upon the illegal contract. However, the following categories find support in the cases.

Transferor can recover because the transferee did not thereby obtain any interest

This is illustrated by an appeal to the Privy Council from the Court of Appeal for Eastern Africa[235] concerning local legislation forbidding the lease of land to non-Africans. A lessor was able to evict a non-African lessee because the legislation was interpreted as rendering all contravening agreements ineffective to transfer any interest to the lessee.

---

[234] *Gray v Southouse* [1949] 2 All ER 1019 (payment by tenant of prohibited premium – returnable notwithstanding tenant's knowledge of illegality). *Cf. Kiriri Cotton* considered earlier where the claimant had no such knowledge.

[235] *Amar Singh v Kulubya* [1964] AC 142. 'All the claimant has got to say is: "These were my goods. I was possessed of these goods in 1868. I have never parted with them to anybody. They are my goods still. I never sold them and I have never given them to anybody in such a way as to deprive myself of the right to possession of them"', *per* James LJ in *Taylor v Bowers* (1876) 1 QBD 291 at 298.

Transferor can recover because the transferee's interest in the property was subsequently terminated

In the difficult case of *Bowmaker Ltd v Barnet Instruments Ltd* [236] a finance company 'sold' three machine tools to the claimant on hire purchase terms. [237] These agreements were illegal because they were prohibited under wartime pricing and licensing regulations. The hirers defaulted upon the payments due under the contracts, sold two of the tools and refused to return another. The finance company successfully claimed damages in the tort of conversion in respect of *all* three machines. This result is readily explained in relation to the two machines sold. The hirer's act of 'selling' the goods before he himself owned them amounted to a repudiatory[238] breach of contract. This automatically terminated the right to retain possession (called a special property) enjoyed by the hirer or pledgee of goods. The finance company was able to establish its title to the goods sold by reference to the transfer of the goods to it and so was not forced to rely on the illegal contract. However, it is unclear how the same can be said of the goods retained by the hirer where the only wrong was the continuing non-payment of hire. Such non-payment was of course a breach of contract but the contract could not be enforced by the finance company and non-payment alone would not operate to terminate the hirer's special property. Therefore, it is difficult to see on what basis the finance company could assert an unqualified right to possession. [239] Even though the application of the law to some of the facts in *Bowmakers* may be doubted, the general principle stated has been accepted and acted on. [240]

Transferee may recover because the illegal contract was effective to transfer property to him

An illegal contract is effective to transfer property despite the fact that the court would not enforce it by way of an action for breach of contract. Therefore, if for some reason the transferee under an illegal contract finds himself dispossessed of the contract property he may still recover it. In *Singh v Ali* [241] the Privy Council held that property in a lorry had passed to the purchaser despite the fact that it was registered in the vendor's name in order to secure a haulage licence which the purchaser would have been unable to secure. The purchaser was able to successfully sue the vendor who retained the lorry and refused to deliver it. In *Singh*, the purchaser had obtained possession of the

---

[236] [1945] KB 65. For criticism, see Hamson (1949) 10 CLJ 249; *contra*: Coote (1972) 35 MLR 38.

[237] Hire purchase is a way of financing a credit sale. It typically involves a finance company buying goods and then hiring them to the 'purchaser' who only technically becomes owner when the final payment of hire and a nominal fee to exercise the options to buy is made.

[238] A repudiatory breach is one which justifies the other party in terminating the contract; see further Chapter 15.

[239] Treitel at p. 453 suggests that there might have been an express clause which terminated the special property upon the hirer's default in payment.

[240] Most recently in *Tinsley v Milligan* [1994] 1 AC 340.

[241] [1960] AC 167.

property and operated the lorry for a period. However, the principle may apply even though the purchaser does not take possession, e.g. where the goods are delivered to a third party.[242] It seems that in both cases property will pass when the illegal agreement is performed.[243]

THE NON-RELIANCE PRINCIPLE AND THE LAW OF TRUSTS

The general non-reliance principle (i.e. upon the illegal agreement) of which the three situations just discussed are sub-categories was recently examined by the House of Lords in relation to the law of trusts. In *Tinsley* v *Milligan*,[244] Ms T and Ms M were lovers who with joint funds bought a house. The intention was that they had equal interests in it. In fact, the legal title was registered in T's name to enable M to make fraudulent claims for social security benefits. M later informed the Department of Social Security about the fraud. The relationship ended and T moved out. T claimed possession of the property.

The majority[245] of the House of Lords held that M was able to assert an equitable title to the property because she could do so without reliance upon the illegal (fraudulent) arrangement. In this case, it was a presumption of the law of trusts which permitted M to assert her title without direct reliance upon the illegality. Where purchase money for property is provided by two persons but the legal title is recorded in a single name, the latter is presumed to hold the property on trust for all contributors in shares proportionate to those contributions (the presumption of resulting trust). M was able to rely upon this presumption to establish her title but T could not rebut it without reference to the illegal arrangement.

The case sought to bring some order to this area of law. It applied the non-reliance principle in the context of trusts and so refused to apply different rules to legal and equitable claims. However, the result of reliance upon the presumptions of trust law was purely fortuitous for M. If M and T had been husband and wife, M's action would have failed. In these circumstances, it is assumed that money advanced by a man to his wife is given as a gift (the presumption of advancement) which M could not have rebutted without reference to the illegal agreement.

Critique of the non-reliance exception

There is a general difficulty with the non-reliance principle which is that it is easy to state but difficult to apply. In what sense can we say that the

---

[242] [1971] 1 QB 210.

[243] The cases use the term 'execution'. However, it is unclear whether this will cover the situation where it is executed on one side only, e.g. goods are delivered but not yet paid for.

[244] [1994] 1 AC 340.

[245] Lords Jauncy, Lowry and Browne-Wilkinson. Lords Keith and Goff dissenting would have refused M relief on the basis of the equitable maxim that 'equity will not assist a claimant who does not come to equity with clean hands' at p. 362 (i.e. with a clear conscience).

successful parties in the cases we have analysed did not rely on the illegal contract? The finance company in *Bowmakers* certainly had to refer to the illegal hire purchase contracts as part of their case. Does this amount to reliance? One commentator has urged that the courts should 'come clean' and admit that they permit some reliance upon the illegal transaction.[246]

It seems difficult to resolve many cases involving illegality and the transfer of money or property in a way that commands universal respect. The division of opinion in *Tinsley* v *Milligan* is evidence of this. The common law approach is an all or nothing one. Either M succeeds and receives her share in the property notwithstanding her earlier participation in the illegal scheme (as the majority held) or T succeeds and effectively gets a windfall gain from her unqualified title despite the contribution M made to the purchase price (the solution favoured by the minority).

It has been suggested that a more flexible approach is needed which can do better justice between the parties. This is illustrated by a case[247] in which the High Court of Australia refused to follow *Tinsley* v *Milligan*. The claimant provided money to purchase a house which was registered in the names of her son and daughter. This was in order to 'protect' her future entitlement to a 'subsidy' which was conditional upon her having no other interests in property. With the assistance of the subsidy the claimant purchased another house in her own name. The parties fell out and the first house was sold by the son and daughter. The claimant argued that they held the sale price on trust for her. The court held that the presumption of advancement applied but that this could be rebutted by the mother despite being a party to the illegal scheme. The proceeds of sale were held on resulting trust for the claimant subject to a condition that she repay the subsidy she had fraudulently obtained.

Both the end and the means merit close examination. Justice was done between the parties by effectively requiring each to give up any gain made as a result of the fraudulent scheme. This was achieved by adapting the presumptions of the law of trusts to reflect contemporary reality and introducing remedial flexibility. In the past, the presumption of advancement had only been applied to gifts from a father, rather than a mother, to a child. Partial justice could have been achieved by simply applying the outdated presumption; the claimant would not be entitled to the sale proceeds and so would be deprived of the benefits of her fraud. However, this would be to endorse an outdated presumption and would produce an ill-deserved gain for the children. Therefore, the presumption was applied to gifts from a female as well as a male parent, but the claimant was permitted to rebut it by reference to the illegal scheme. Complete justice was then achieved by depriving the claimant of the fruits of her deception when she was required to reimburse the subsidy she had fraudulently obtained.

Two objections may be taken to the Australian approach. First, it might be

---

[246] Enonchong, 'Title Claims and Illegal Transactions' (1995) 111 LQR 138.
[247] *Nelson* v *Nelson* [1995] 70 ALJR 47; Enonchong [1996] RLR 78; Rose (1996) 112 LQR 386.

said to encourage, or at least fail to deter, illegal contracts because the fraudulent party knows that the worst that could happen is that she will be deprived of her gain. Secondly, such remedial flexibility introduces considerable uncertainty into the law.[248] The first criticism may be answered by saying that in this context, deterrence is best left to the criminal law.[249] The second by the observations that this may be a price worth paying for justice.[250]

SEVERANCE

Sometimes an otherwise unenforceable contract can be saved if the court is able to 'sever' the illegal part. Severance may operate in two ways. First, the courts may simply strike out an objectionable contract term. In one case,[251] a husband promised to pay money to his estranged wife in exchange for her (1) maintaining herself and indemnifying him if she pledged his credit[252] and (2) not bringing any matrimonial proceedings. The wife's second undertaking was illegal but could be severed, allowing the court to consider the enforceability of the first. Severance may operate in a second way where parts of a single clause are pencilled out (hence the blue-pencil test). Where the seller of imitation jewellery undertook for two years not to sell real or imitation jewellery in London or at named places abroad, the covenant as written was held to operate over too wide an area and too broad a subject.[253] The business sold only fake jewellery and operated only in London. The court severed the offending party of the clause and enforced what was left.

A few observations must be made about this doctrine. First, severance will not be permitted where the illegality is particularly serious, such as a contract to defraud the revenue.[254] In practice, it is most frequently encountered in relation to covenants in restraint of trade. Second, severance may operate as a trap for the layman. Where contracts are drafted professionally, it is usual to present the obligations assumed as a series of single undertakings. This means that if one operates in restraint of trade, it

---

[248] See Phang (1998) 11 JCL 53.

[249] See Shand, 'Unblinkering the Unruly Horse: Public Policy in the Law of Contract' [1972A] CLJ 144 at 155. *Cf.* the comments of Nicholls LJ in the Court of Appeal in *Tinsley v Milligan* observing that no action was taken by the Department of Social Security against M after she had confessed her fraud. 'Apparently the DSS did not regard the situation with any alarm. The judge observed that no doubt this was because it had become inured by daily experience of much worse forms of fraud being practised upon it than any which could be laid at the door of these two women', [1992] Ch 310 at 315–17.

[250] The objection becomes more convincing when it is realised that the price of the just resolution of the litigants' dispute is the uncertainty faced by others who find themselves in a similar position in the future. *Cf.* 'It is important to observe that ... [illegality] is not a principle of justice; it is a principle of policy whose application is indiscriminable and so can lead to unfair consequences as between the parties to litigation', *per* Lord Goff in *Tinsley v Milligan* [1994] AC 340 at 355.

[251] *Williams v Williams* [1957] 1 WLR 148.

[252] A wife was able to 'pledge' her husband's credit.

[253] *Goldsoll v Goldman* [1915] 1 Ch 292.

[254] *Miller v Korinsk* [1945] 62 TLR 85.

may be severed from the rest. Severance is not possible where what is left after the 'blue pencilling' is incomprehensible.[255] Third, the court will not redraft the contract[256] by adding to it or rearranging what is left after severance other than when removing discriminating provisions.

REFORM OF THE LAW

The body of law which defines those contracts considered to be illegal in formation and which describes their effect is undoubtedly 'technical and complex'.[257] This might be acceptable if the law of illegality resolved cases in a way which was just, consistent and comprehensive. However, we have seen that this is clearly not so. Therefore, there is a need to reform the law in this area.

The courts themselves sought to introduce more flexibility and justice by adopting a 'public-conscience' test under which the court had to balance the consequences of granting or refusing relief.[258] Under this approach the rules and exceptions we have examined above are relegated to non-binding indicators as to how the courts' discretion might be exercised.[259]

However, the public-conscience test was emphatically rejected by both the majority and the minority in the House of Lords. Lord Goff thought that it was far from obvious that such a test would be preferable to the existing strict rules.[260] Lord Browne Wilkinson considered that the consequences of illegality should not depend 'on such an imponderable factor'.[261]

It would seem that any further general reform of the law in this area must be undertaken by the legislature. This has occurred in New Zealand where, following a brief Law Reform Committee Report, a short Act was introduced.[262] The economy of the report and Act was partly made possible because neither sought to define what amounts to an illegal contract. Rather the common law categorisation of illegality was left in place; the reform replaced all the common law rules as to the effects of illegality with a broad discretion to effect substantial justice between the parties.

---

[255] Though the test is sometimes applied with some latitude. See *T Lucas & Co Ltd* v *Mitchell* [1974] Ch 129 as discussed in Treitel at p. 468 where it was held that the geographical coverage of a constraint was invalid and could be severed despite the fact that another clause could not be properly understood other than by reference to the severed provisions.

[256] *Cf.* the New Zealand Illegal Contracts Act 1970, s 8(1) which provides 'where any provision [is] an unreasonable restraint of trade, the court may ... (b) so modify the provision that at the time the contract was entered into, the provisions as modified would have been reasonable ...'.

[257] Law Commission (1998) *Illegal Transactions: The Effect of Illegality on Contracts and Trusts Consultation Paper*, No. 154, para 1.18.

[258] The test was first used by Hutchison J in *Thackwell* v *Barclays Bank plc* [1986] 1 All ER 676. It was endorsed by the majority of the Court of Appeal in *Tinsley* v *Milligan* [1992] Ch 310.

[259] See *Tinsley* v *Milligan* [1992] Ch 310 at 319–20 *per* Nicholls LJ.

[260] [1994] 1 AC 340 at 363.

[261] *Ibid.*, p. 369.

[262] The Illegal Contracts Act 1970 has only 11 sections. *The Report on Illegal Contracts* by the Contracts and Commercial Law Reform Committee which preceded it runs to 11 small pages and cites only 16 cases.

To an English lawyer, the conferral of such a broad discretion seems dangerous. It makes explicit that which a conservative judiciary prefer not to draw attention to, that they have a creative, i.e. law-making, role. Further, it creates considerable uncertainty, particularly in its early years of implementation. It seems that these fears were well founded.[263] A long-standing member of the Committee whose report resulted in the Act considers that the discretion conferred by the Act has been exercised more enthusiastically by the courts than its inventors intended. He has written that:[264]

> If powers are being given and constraints on them are intended, the New Zealand experience suggests that those constraints should not be left to be inferred, but should be spelled out in the legislation as clearly as possible.

In *Tinsley* v *Milligan*, Lord Goff,[265] no doubt mindful of the New Zealand experience, effectively issued an invitation to our own Law Commission to conduct 'a *full* enquiry into the matter' (emphasis added). A consultation paper was published in 1999[266] containing a thorough[267] examination of the existing law. The Law Commission's provisional recommendation is that the present rules regulating the effect of illegality in contracts and trusts should be replaced by a discretion under which the court could decide whether or not to enforce an illegal transaction, to recognise that property rights have been transferred or created by it, or to allow benefits conferred under it to be recovered.[268] However, to avoid the dangers described by the New Zealand writer, the Law Commission recommends that this discretion be 'structured'[269] to provide guidance for the courts exercising it and so to reduce uncertainty. In particular, the courts are directed to consider: the seriousness of the illegality, the knowledge and intention of the party seeking to enforce the illegal contract or recover benefits conferred under it or asking for the recognition of legal or equitable rights, whether refusing relief which would otherwise be awarded will act as a deterrent, whether refusing relief will promote the policy of the rule which renders the transaction illegal and whether refusing relief is proportionate to the illegality involved.

---

[263] Furmston, 'The Illegal Contracts Act 1970 – An English View' (1972) 5 NZULR 150.
[264] Cooke, 'Validation Under The Illegal Contracts Act' (1992) 15 NZULR 80 at 105.
[265] At p. 364.
[266] (1999) *Illegal Transactions: The Effect of Illegality on Contracts and Trusts*, No. 154.
[267] It runs to 181 pages! *Cf.* the report which resulted in the New Zealand Act. Of course, it is quality, not quantity, that counts. However, as has become usual, the Law Commission's consultation paper contains a *thorough* excellent detailed examination of the present law before considering the case for reform. The only omissions are the restraint of trade and gambling contracts.
[268] Paragraph 1.18: i.e. 'illegality should contrive to be used only as a defence to what would otherwise be a standard claim for a contractual or restitutionary remedy or for the recognition of legal or equitable property rightly ... [with] one possible exception (withdrawal during the *locus poenitentiae*), where illegality may act as a cause of action'.
[269] See paras 1.19 and 7.27–7.43. See generally Buckley, 'Illegal Transactions': Chaos or Discretion?' (2000) 20 LS 155 supporting the approach of the Law Commission.

7

NON-AGREEMENT MISTAKES

When parties enter a contract one or both may be labouring under a mistake. Three different situations must be distinguished. First, where the parties are at cross-purposes, one party means one thing, the other another. As an example, A offers to sell her 'computer' to B. A intends to sell her desktop computer; B intends to buy A's laptop computer. Second, one party may have made a mistake and the other may be aware of this mistake.[1] A offers to sell her only computer for 'two hundred pounds'. English is not A's first language and she often confuses the numbers two and seven. In fact, she meant to say 'seven hundred pounds'. B is aware that A has made this mistake. Third, both parties may share a common misapprehension. For example, unknown to A and B, A's only computer was destroyed by a fire at her home before she contracted to sell it to B. Both A and B think that the computer is still in existence at the moment of contracting. Before proceeding further a note of caution should be entered. Writers and courts use different labels to describe the three different factual situations just described. It is wrong to assume that different writers and judges use the same label to describe the same thing. The terminology followed in this book describes the first situation as *mutual mistake*, the second as *unilateral mistake* and the third as *common mistake*.[2] Unfortunately, many writers and judges use the descriptions of 'mutual' and 'common' interchangeably to refer to the third situation.[3]

There is an important difference between, on the one hand, the first two classes of mistake and, on the other, the third class of mistake. In the first two types the court is concerned to discover whether the parties have reached an agreement. Where no agreement can be discerned, the mistake is said to have *negatived* consent. For this reason the first two types of mistake were considered in Chapter 2 of this book which deals with contractual negotiations. In contrast, when the third type of mistake is made, the parties have a clear agreement, but the question is what effect their common misapprehension has upon that undoubted agreement. This question is

---

[1] Typically, because the other induced the mistake of the first party. For such cases see the discussion of misrepresentation in Chapter 2. However, the category is wider as the hypothetical case shows.

[2] The terminology used in this chapter was developed by Cheshire, Fifoot and Furmston, pp. 235–6.

[3] Grammatically the words are distinct. Common means 'shared'. Mutual was once used as a synonym for common but now means possessed by each of two persons/things towards the other.

sometimes put in the form: 'Does the mistake operate to *nullify* consent?' For this reason the third category of mistake will be described as a 'non-agreement' mistake and is considered in this chapter. Three different sub-categories of common mistake will be considered.

COMMON MISTAKE AS TO THE EXISTENCE OF THE SUBJECT MATTER OF THE CONTRACT[4]

The case of *Couturier* v *Hastie*[5] concerned the sale of a cargo of corn en route for England which, unknown to both parties at the time of sale, had fermented and been sold at an intermediary port by the master of the carrying vessel. The action was effectively that of the seller seeking payment for the price of the goods.[6] The courts which considered the case[7] differed about the proper interpretation of the bargain that was concluded between the parties. A majority of the Court of Exchequer Chamber held that the contract was one for the sale of the cargo *if it existed* at the date of the contract. Such a contract is described as the sale of an 'adventure'. Why would anyone purchase the mere chance that the goods exist? In this instance the answer is simple because if the goods were damaged or lost, the purchaser would be entitled to the benefit of the insurance on the goods. In the absence of insurance, the sale of goods if they exist may still be a valuable contract. If goods guaranteed to exist cost £100, a 1 in 2 chance that the same goods may exist would be valued at £50. A risk-neutral trader would regard the purchase of such a chance for any sum less than £50 as a profitable contract. It is worth 'taking a chance' if 'the price is right'.

In contrast, the Court of Exchequer and the House of Lords held that the contract in question was one for the sale of goods supposed to exist. In such circumstances the seller was unable to maintain an action for the price of the goods when, in fact, at the time of contracting, they did not exist. As Lord Cranworth put it, 'the whole question turns upon the construction of the contract that was entered into between the parties ...'. There are three different constructions which might be put upon the parties' contract. First, it might allocate to the buyer the risk of the goods' non-existence. This was the approach of the majority of the Court of Exchequer Chamber. On this approach the seller's action for the price would succeed. The buyer bought a chance and got a chance. His gamble was not successful but that is the risk of gambling. The buyer of such a chance is no more entitled to resist an action for the price than a disappointed 'punter' is entitled to demand the return of his stake when the horse he bets on fails to win. However, the

---

[4] Sometimes known as cases of *res extincta*.
[5] (1856) 5 HLC 673.
[6] The defendant was not the buyer but a *del credere* agent of the seller. A *del credere* agent is someone who guarantees the performance of anyone he introduces to his principal. Therefore, the case may be treated as if the action was one against the buyer directly.
[7] The court of first instance was the Court of Exchequer which found for the claimant. The defendant successfully appealed to the Court of Exchequer Chamber. The claimant then unsuccessfully appealed to the House of Lords.

dismissal of the seller's action for the price is consistent with one of two other possible interpretations of the parties' contract. The contract might have allocated the risk of the non-existence of the subject matter of the contract to the seller. In other words, the seller guaranteed the existence of the goods. Alternatively, the contract might have failed, expressly or impliedly, to allocate that risk. In both cases the seller would not be able to sue for the price. However, in the former but not the latter situation the buyer would be able to sue for non-delivery. The buyer can legitimately complain when the seller fails to honour his guarantee; the buyer has no cause for complaint against the seller when the essential, but unguaranteed, basis of their bargain fails. It is often assumed that *Couturier* is an example of the second alternative and that the buyer would not have been able to sue for non-delivery.

A clear example of a contract of sale, which allocated to the buyer the risk of non-existence of the contractual subject matter, is provided by an Australian case. In *McRae v The Commonwealth Disposals Commission*,[8] the defendants sold to the claimants a wrecked tanker, which they stated to be lying at a particular location. The claimants mounted a salvage operation. In fact, there was no tanker lying at or near the stated location. The claimants successfully sued for damages for breach of contract[9] and recovered both the cost of the abortive salvage operation and the price paid for the salvage rights.[10] The High Court of Australia carefully considered the reason for the failure of the claimants' action in *Couturier* and emphasised that this followed from the House of Lord's interpretation of the contract. The High Court recognised that *Couturier* cannot properly be said to support any wider proposition that contracts for the sale of a non-existent subject matter are always void. If such a view were accepted, the buyer would not be able to bring an action for damages for non-delivery. When we say a contract is void, we mean that no contract ever came into existence. If there was no contract, clearly there could be no breach.

It may seem as if the proper interpretation of the *Couturier* case has been somewhat laboured. The reason is that the case became associated with the proposition that a common mistake as to the existence of the contractual subject matter rendered the contract void. Unfortunately, this misinterpretation was given statutory force in the Sale of Goods Act 1893, s 6. The current provision is contained in the Sale of Goods Act 1979, s 6:

> Where there is a contract for the sale of specific goods, and the goods without the knowledge of the seller have perished at the time when the contract is made, the contract is void.

In *McRae* the court had to consider the effect of an equivalent statutory provision.[11] It concluded that the reference to goods perishing meant that

---

[8] [1951] 84 CLR 377.
[9] The claimants' action to recover damages for deceit failed because the defendants were considered to have acted in a grossly negligent, but not fraudulent, way.
[10] For this aspect of the case, see Chapter 17.
[11] Victoria Goods Act 1928, s 11.

the provision could only apply to contracts for the sale of goods which once existed; it had no application to contracts for the sale of goods, like the one in *McRae*, which *never* existed. Indeed, it could be argued that the section may be excluded by the contrary intent of the parties, which is adequately evidenced by the contractual allocation of the risk of non-existence of the subject matter to either the seller (goods guaranteed to exist) or the buyer (sale of a chance).[12] The argument derives indirect support from the Sale of Goods Act 1979, s 55, which states the general principle[13] that provisions in the Sale of Goods Act which would otherwise give rise to a 'right, duty or liability' may be 'negatived' by express agreement between the parties. The support is indirect because s 6 does not give rise to a 'right, duty or liability', rather it prevents a right, duty or liability that would otherwise arise from arising. The argument is that if the Act expressly permits the exclusion of sections giving rise to duties, it would be contrary to the policy of the Act not to allow the exclusion of sections which prevent duties from arising. The answer to this subtle attempt to outflank the statute and reinstate the true *ratio decidendi* of *Couturier* is very simple. Many sections of the Act expressly provide that they are subject to the contrary intent of the parties but s 6 does not. Where a section is silent on this point, the more reasonable inference is that the section was intended to apply even if the parties purport to provide otherwise.

The above discussion may usefully be summarised. Where there is a common mistake as to the subject matter of the contract, the rights and liabilities of the parties depend upon whether the Sale of Goods Act 1979, s 6 applies. The precise ambit of s 6 is unclear. If s 6 does not apply, it is necessary to see whether the parties' contract has allocated the risk that the goods do not exist. If it allocates that risk to the seller, the seller cannot sue for the price but the buyer can recover damages for non-delivery. If it allocates the risk to the buyer, the seller can sue for the price but the buyer cannot sue for non-delivery. If the contract is silent, then neither party can sue the other.[14] However, if s 6 does apply, then neither party can bring an action against the other in any circumstances. The following tables show the different possibilities.

---

[12] See Atiyah, '*Couturier* v *Hastie* and the Sale of Non-existent Goods' (1957) 73 LQR 340.

[13] This ability has been much qualified by subsequent legislation such as the Unfair Contract Terms Act 1977, ss 6–7, which severely restricts the freedom of contractors to exclude liabilities arising under the terms implied into contracts by the Sale of Goods Act, ss 11–15.

[14] This is the extent to which the common law recognises a doctrine of common mistake as to the existence of the subject matter of the contract. See Steyn J's careful judgment in *Associated Japanese Bank (International) Ltd* v *Crédit du Nord SA* [1989] 3 All ER 902 at 912. Further illustrations include *Strickland* v *Turner* (1852) 7 Ex 208 (contract to buy annuity void when the subject matter, i.e. the annuity, no longer existed after the death of the annuitant) and *Galloway* v *Galloway* [1914] 30 TLR 531 (separation deed between two parties who were not in fact married was void because subject matter of the deed, i.e. the marriage, was non-existent).

Table 7.1 Where Sale of Goods Act 1979, s 6, does not apply

Was the risk of non-existence of the goods allocated by the parties to:

	The seller?	*The buyer?*	*Neither seller nor buyer?*
Seller sues for price	No action *Couturier* (HL) ?	Action possible *Couturier (Excheq)*	No action *Couturier* (HL) ?
Buyer sues for non-delivery	Action possible *McRae*	No action	No action

Table 7.2 Where Sale of Goods Act 1979, s 6, does apply

Was the risk of non-existence of the goods allocated by the parties to:

	The seller?	*The buyer?*	*Neither seller nor buyer?*
Seller sues for price	No action	No action	No action
Buyer sues for non-delivery	No action	No action	No action

COMMON MISTAKE AS TO QUALITY

This describes the situation where two parties contract for the sale of something which both believe has a certain quality. If the contract goods lack the quality they were supposed to have, the avenues of redress available to the buyer depend upon whether the assumption of the buyer arises as a result of the seller's misrepresentation and if so the status of that representation. If the seller's representation was incorporated into the contract as a term, the buyer can sue for breach of contract. If the representation did not amount to a term, the buyer may bring an action for misrepresentation. However, if a remedy for misrepresentation was never available (e.g. no representation was made), has subsequently become unavailable (e.g. the misrepresentation was wholly innocent and a bar to rescission has arisen and no damages are available under the Misrepresentation Act 1967 s 2(2)) or is simply worthless (e.g. the misrepresentor cannot be traced), a party to an ostensible contract might rely on the doctrine of mistake. However, at the outset it should be emphasised that the doctrine of common mistake is a very narrow and ungenerous one.

In *Bell* v *Lever Bros* Lord Atkin stated that a common mistake as to quality will render a contract void if it 'is as to the existence of some quality which makes the thing without the quality essentially different from the thing as it was believed to be'.[15] In *Bell* the claimant employed the two defendants as

---

[15] This statement of the law is supported by the judgments of Lords Thankerton and Blanesburgh.

chairman and vice-chairman. The claimant wanted to terminate the defendants' contracts of employment and agreed to pay them compensation of £30k and £20k. The claimant was unaware that the defendants, by speculating in the company's business, had breached their contracts of employment in a way that entitled the claimant to terminate the defendants' contracts without payment. The jury found that the defendants themselves were unaware of the breaches of contract they had committed. It is perhaps not obvious why the case involved a mistake as to quality at all. The reason is that the subject matter of the compensation agreements was the underlying contracts of employment. Both parties believed the employment contracts to have a quality, unimpeachability, which they did not in fact have. However, the majority[16] held that the mistake as to quality was not a sufficiently fundamental one to render the compensation agreements void.

A common criticism of *Bell* is that if the mistake made by the parties in that case is not sufficiently fundamental to render the contract void, it is difficult to know what is. This view is supported by many cases where the doctrine has been said not to apply. These include contracts for the sale of shares in a company understood to have secured a valuable contract[17] and a 1939 motor car believed to be a 1948 model.[18] However, in *Bell* the sums advanced by the claimants were massive ones and they were apparently paid as the only way to procure the termination of the two contracts of employment. Professor J.C. Smith has written that '... it is impossible to envisage a mistake as to quality which is more fundamental than that in *Bell* v *Lever Bros* ...'.[19] This led Cheshire, Fifoot and Furmston to suggest that there is no common law doctrine of mistake as to quality.[20] However, this line of argument was rejected by Steyn J in *Associated Japanese Bank (International) Ltd* v *Crédit du Nord*.[21] The case concerned a fraud perpetrated by someone who falsely raised money against the security of non-existent industrial tooling. Money was raised against the non-existent machines by a 'lease and sale back'. This involved the fraudster selling them to the claimant bank for over £1m and immediately leasing them back. The fraudster persuaded the defendant bank to guarantee the payments due under the lease. Neither bank asked to inspect the machines. Predictably, the fraudster disappeared with the £1m and defaulted on the lease payments. The claimant bank then sought to enforce the guarantee. Superficially, the case looks like one involving a common mistake as to the existence, rather than the quality, of the contractual subject matter. Both parties to the

---

[16] Lords Atkin and Thankerton. Lord Blanesburgh said that when the claimants' action for fraud failed this debarred them from asserting the existence of a common mistake because this involved the opposite assertion, i.e. of good faith on the part of the defendants. However, if he was wrong on this technical question of pleading, he agreed with Lords Atkin and Thankerton. Lord Warrington, with whom Lord Hailsham agreed, held that the mistake was sufficiently fundamental to do so.

[17] *Kennedy* v *Panama, etc. Royal Mail Co* (1867) LR 2 QB 580.

[18] *Oscar Chess Ltd* v *Williams* [1957] 1 WLR 370.

[19] Smith (1998) *The Law of Contract*. 3rd edn, p. 178.

[20] See now p. 246.

[21] [1988] 3 All ER 902.

guarantee clearly thought that the machines existed when they did not. However, the subject matter of the guarantee was not the machines but the fraudster's obligations under the lease. Both banks thought that these obligations had a quality, i.e. they related to machines owned by the claimant bank, which in fact they lacked. In a most careful judgment Steyn J held that the claimant bank's action failed. The main ground for this conclusion was the proper interpretation of the guarantee, which he said was subject to an express or implied condition that the machines in fact existed. If this was not so, he held that the guarantee was void for common mistake as to quality.[22] Further, Steyn J pointed out that criticism of the result in *Bell* may not be wholly justified. It was clearly a borderline decision but there was certainly some evidence that in order to secure the future co-operation of the employees, Lever Bros might have agreed to pay the 'golden handshakes' even if they had been aware of their breaches of contract.[23]

Cases where a sufficiently fundamental mistake as to quality has been made so as to render the contract void are undoubtedly rare. Other examples include the sale of napkins which were believed to be the property of Charles I when they were in fact only Georgian,[24] a policy of insurance upon the life of someone who both seller and buyer assumed to be living but who had in fact died[25] and a short letting of a room from which to view King Edward VII's coronation procession which had in fact been cancelled before the letting was agreed.[26]

What the cases so far considered have established is that there is undoubtedly a doctrine of common mistake at law but that it operates within very narrow limits. This strict position is to a certain extent modified by the intervention of equity, although there is some tension between the common law and equitable principles. When a contract is void at common law, equity cannot 'revive' the contract. However, when a contract is valid at common law, e.g. because there was a common mistake as to quality which was not sufficiently fundamental to render the contract void at common law, the contract may none the less be set aside in equity. In equity contracts are voidable, rather than void, for mistake. This distinction has important remedial consequences. When a contract is void, it simply never comes into existence. When a contract is voidable it is liable to be set aside. Until it is set aside, the contract is valid. This means that when the court sets aside a contract for mistake, it may attach such conditions to its order as it deems

---

22 See also *William Sindall plc v Cambs CC* [1994] 3 All ER 932 at 952 *per* Hoffmann LJ and at 957 *per* Evans LJ, Russell LJ agreeing (contract for sale of development land allocated to buyer risk of incumbrances not known to seller which might affect land – doctrine of common mistake, therefore, not applicable).

23 See Lord Blanesburgh at p. 181 and Lord Thankerton at p. 223.

24 *Nicholson & Venn v Smith-Marritt* (1947) LT 189. The buyer actually recovered damages because the mistake was induced by the seller's carelessness and in these circumstances the seller is not allowed to rely on his mistake to escape liability. See Treitel, p. 267.

25 *Scott v Coulson* [1903] 2 Ch 249. If the insured was living, the policy's value was its 'surrender' value; when the insured died, the policy 'matured' and so was worth more.

26 *Griffith v Brymer* [1903] 19 TLR 434.

necessary to do justice between the parties. In *Solle v Butcher*[27] property was let and a rent agreed based on the belief that it fell outside of Rent Act control. In fact, the landlord who had considerably improved the property could have increased the rent before the new lease was granted but was precluded from doing so afterwards. The court set aside the lease on condition that the tenant was offered the option of staying on at the higher rent. Similarly, in *Grist v Bailey*[28] a contract for the sale of a house was set aside. The price agreed of £850 was based upon the house being occupied by a protected tenant. In fact, the tenant had died before the sale was agreed and the house with vacant possession was worth £2,250. The sale was set aside subject to the condition that the vendor offer the property at full market value to the disappointed purchaser.[29]

The precise ambit of the equitable jurisdiction is unclear. As nothing can revive a contract which is void at common law, the test applicable in equity must be one more generous to relief. A mistake must be fundamental before a contract is void at common law. In equity it need only be sufficiently basic to justify setting aside the contract on terms. Unfortunately, the courts have proposed no simple test sufficient to identify such cases. To describe the relevant category of mistake as 'material' is perhaps over-inclusive[30] and to substitute the word 'basic' is perhaps under-inclusive. What is clear is that the claim to have a contract set aside in equity may be lost in circumstances analogous to those which 'bar' a claim to rescind a contract for misrepresentation.

MISTAKE AS TO OWNERSHIP OF PROPERTY

An unusual, almost unbelievable, type of mistake is where a party agrees to purchase property which he already owns. Such a mistake occurred in *Cooper v Phibbs*[31] when a tenant agreed to take the lease of a fishery to which, unknown to either party, he was already entitled as a tenant for life. The House of Lords set aside the lease in equity on condition that the 'lessor' was to have a lien over the property for improvements he had effected. Although the case appeared to be the exercise of an equitable jurisdiction, it has subsequently been treated as a decision that the contract was void rather

---

[27] [1950] 1 KB 671.
[28] [1967] Ch 532. See also *Laurence v Lexcourt Holdings* [1978] 2 All ER 810 (building let for office use when planning permission for that purpose did not extend to whole premises – was a misrepresentation and in alternative a common mistake).
[29] In *Magee v Pennine Insurance Co Ltd* [1969] 2 QB 507 an insurance claim was compromised in circumstances when, because of innocent misrepresentations in the original proposal, the insurer could have avoided any liability. The equitable jurisdiction was invoked to set aside the compromise but surprisingly no conditions (e.g. that all premiums be returned) were imposed.
[30] See *Clarion Ltd v National Provident Institution* [2000] 1 WLR 1888, at 1906, suggesting that the equitable jurisdiction should not be framed so broadly as to allow parties to escape from 'bad' bargains.
[31] (1867) LR 2 HL 149. Matthews (1989) 105 LQR 599.

than voidable.[32] Indeed, it was used as one of the two illustrations proffered in *Bell* by Lord Atkin as examples of mistakes which are fundamental enough to render a contract void.[33] The basis of this principle, often referred to as *res sua*, is said to be based upon the legal impossibility of the vendor fulfilling his ostensible obligation.[34]

CONCLUSION

By now it will be apparent that the subject of mistake is not an easy one. The case law is difficult to interpret and the law is complicated by the uneasy co-existence of statutory, common law and equitable principles. However, two more caveats should be noted. First, the categories of mistake considered above may not be mutually exclusive. The case of *Bell* v *Lever Bros*, which was analysed as one involving a common mistake as to quality, could be represented as one of *res extincta* (Lever Bros were buying the employees' indefeasible right to continue their employment which right did not exist) or as raising a *res sua* (Lever Bros were buying something they already owned, the right to terminate their employees' contracts). Second, the relationship between common mistake and frustration should be noted but not pressed too far. A fashionable line of argument emphasises the link between the doctrines by describing the former as initial impossibility and the latter as subsequent impossibility. The argument proceeds that whether an event occurs moments before contracting and so is addressed by the doctrine of common mistake or moments after and so addressed under the rubric of frustration should not affect the outcome. Such a unified approach is not reflected in the present law where relief is less readily granted under the doctrine of mistake than under that of frustration. Further, the remedial consequences of the two doctrines differ significantly. Moreover, there may be grounds to justify these differences because, as any racing pundit will tell you, it is much easier to investigate and ascertain existing facts than it is to predict the future.[35]

---

[32] *Bell* v *Lever Bros Ltd* [1932] AC 161 at 218 *per* Lord Atkin and in the Court of Appeal [1931] 1 KB 557 at 585 *per* Scrutton LJ and at 591 *per* Lawrence LJ. On this approach the court would not be entitled to impose conditions.

[33] The other example is based upon the then current view of *Couturier* v *Hastie* that all common mistakes as to the existence of the contractual subject matter rendered the contract void.

[34] *Debenham* v *Sawbridge* [1901] 2 Ch 98 at 109 *per* Byrne J.

[35] See Treitel, pp. 362–3.

8

CAPACITY

A sober adult of sound mind enjoys full contractual capacity. In contrast, minors, the mentally incapacitated and companies have limits upon their ability to enter contracts. The limits placed upon minors and those suffering from mental incapacity seek to strike a balance between the need to protect vulnerable individuals and a respect for open market transactions. The rules relating to corporate capacity also seek to strike a balance, in this case between the need to protect shareholders and those who do business with the company.

MINORS

A minor is someone under 18 years of age. The general rule is that any contract made between an adult and a minor is binding upon the former but not the latter. Although the contract is not binding on the minor, it is not void. A minor who pays money or transfers property pursuant to a contract with an adult cannot reclaim the money or property merely because he is a minor. In other words, minority itself is not a ground for restitution. On this basis a foolish[1] minor who exchanged his motorcycle for a car could not get his bike back when the car needed repair.[2] However, these general rules are subject to a number of exceptions and qualifications.

Contracts for necessaries

A minor is obliged to pay a reasonable sum for so called necessaries.[3] Necessaries are defined as 'goods suitable to the condition of life' of the minor.[4] The minor's 'condition of life' depends upon two things: his social status and his immediate needs. What might be a necessary for a prince will not be so for pauper. In a number of cases which have recently been

---

[1] On this point the author admits to considerable prejudice.
[2] *Pearce v Brain* [1929] 2 KB 310.
[3] Sale of Goods Act 1979, s 3.
[4] *Ibid.*

described as 'quaint examples of a bygone age'[5] many seemingly extravagant items have been held to be necessaries including 'rings, pins and a watch chain',[6] a servant's uniform,[7] a horse used for transport[8] and 'champagne and wild ducks'.[9] However, no item can be a necessary if the minor does not at the time of purchase have a need for them. In *Nash* v *Inman*[10] a tailor failed to recover the price of clothes, including 11 fancy waistcoats, supplied to a minor because[11] there was no evidence that he was not already adequately supplied with suitable clothing.[12] Services, particularly the provision of education, as well as goods may constitute necessaries.[13] The burden of proving both that the goods or services are suited to the minor's status and also immediately needed is cast upon the supplier.[14] It is an open question whether executory, i.e. unperformed, contracts for the provision of necessaries are binding on the minor.[15]

Beneficial employment contracts

A minor is bound by service contracts which taken as a whole are to his benefit. A contract under which a minor was employed as a railway porter required him to give up any potential claim for personal injury under the Employer's Liability Act 1880. However, it substituted an insurance entitlement the premiums for which were partly met by the employer. In some respects the statutory scheme was more generous, in others the insurance provision. Overall it was considered that the contract operated for the benefit of the minor and so the contract was binding.[16] Similarly,[17] a boxer who turned professional while still an infant was bound by a contract which required him to forfeit his 'purse' if disqualified. When the boxer was disqualified for low punches, the provision operated against him. None the less, the contract was enforceable because by upholding the dignity of the sport it generally benefited him.

---

[5] *Allen* v *Bloomsbury Health Authority* [1993] 1 All ER 651 at 661.

[6] *Peters* v *Fleming* (1860) 6 M & W 42.

[7] *Hands* v *Slaney* (1800) 8 TR 578.

[8] *Barber* v *Vincent* (1860) Freem. KB 497.

[9] According to (1874) Hansard, Vol. 219, Ser. 3, col 1225, quoted by Treitel at p. 499.

[10] [1908] 2 KB 1.

[11] And because there was no evidence that the clothes were appropriate to the minor's status.

[12] Shopkeepers in the environs of Eton College would do well to take heed of these requirements because press pictures showed the then 17-year-old Prince William sporting garish Union Jack waistcoats.

[13] *Roberts* v *Gray* [1913] 1 KB 520.

[14] *Nash* v *Inman* [1908] 2 KB 1.

[15] *Ibid.* at p. 8 *per* Fletcher Moulton LJ (not binding); *Roberts* v *Gray* [1913] 1 KB 520 at 530 *per* Hamilton LJ (binding).

[16] *Clements* v *London & North Western Railway* [1894] 2 QB 482.

[17] *Doyle* v *White City Stadium Ltd* [1935] 1 KB 110.

Ratification

A person is bound by any contract which he entered as a minor and which he expressly or impliedly ratifies after attaining full contractual capacity.[18]

Voidable contracts

When a minor receives property with obligations attached to it, e.g. a leasehold where he must pay rent or shares when he is liable to 'calls', the minor is bound by the obligations for as long as he retains the property.[19] However, during his minority and for a reasonable time thereafter[20] the minor can repudiate the contract and thereby avoid any future liability under it.[21] A minor cannot claim back money already paid over at the time of repudiation unless there has been a total failure of consideration, i.e. he has received nothing in return for it.[22] In this respect the minor is in the same position as an adult who can claim restitution of money paid where the consideration has failed.[23] The minor does not receive special treatment[24] beyond the fact that he can claim restitution for total failure of consideration, even though the adult is ready, willing and able to perform.[25] As a result, it has been said that this aspect of the law relating to minors is unjustifiably harsh[26] though in other ways the approach of the law is more indulgent.[27]

Restitution by a minor

Parties who contract with minors are placed in an unenviable position. As a general rule they can neither sue for the price of goods or services supplied

---

[18] *Williams* v *Moor* (1843) 11 M & W 256.

[19] *London & North Western Railway* v *M'Michael* (1850) 5 Ex 114.

[20] *Edwards* v *Carter* [1893] AC 360 (five years too long even though for most of period party was unaware of right to repudiate).

[21] *Keteley's Case* (1613) 1 Brownl 120 (also reported as *Ketsey's Case* (1613) Cro Jac 320 and *Kirton* v *Eliot* (1613) Roll Abr 731), *Blake* v *Concannon* (1870) IR 4 CL 323 (an Irish case). However, there are *dicta* to suggest that repudiation has retrospective effect and so frees the minor from obligations which have already accrued. See *North Western Ry* v *McMichael* (1850) 5 Ex 114 at 125 *per* Parke B and *Steinberg* v *Scala (Leeds) Ltd* [1923] 2 Ch 452 at 461 *per* Younger LJ.

[22] *Steinberg* v *Scala (Leeds) Ltd* [1923] 2 Ch 452 (minor who applied for and was allotted shares repudiated contract – able to avoid liability for future calls but not entitled to purchase price back because no total failure of consideration – she got the shares).

[23] For a discussion of restitution claims arising from a failure of consideration, see Chapter 2 (under heading of Restitution: failed contract cases) and Chapter 14.

[24] Compare the position of those suffering from mental incapacity who are entitled to restitution of benefits conferred even if there has been no total failure of consideration, namely the lack of contractual capacity alone justifies restitution.

[25] This would usually operate to prevent restitution, see *Thomas* v *Brown* (1876) 1 QBD 714.

[26] See Burrows (*Restitution*), pp. 324–5.

[27] For example, contracts are only set aside on the basis of mental incapacity when that incapacity was apparent to the other party: *Hart* v *O'Connor* [1985] AC 1000; contracts with minors are not subject to such a requirement.

nor get their property back. Therefore, the Minors' Contracts Act 1987, s 3(1) provides that:

> ... the court may, if it is just and reasonable to do so, require the defendant to transfer to the [claimant] any property acquired by the defendant under the contract or any property representing it.

This provision is clearly meant to cater for cases like *Nash v Inman* where the minor could be required to return the waistcoats to the tailor. If the minor had swapped the waistcoats with a friend for 11 striped jackets, the court could order that the jackets be given to the tailor as property representing the waistcoats. Beyond such obvious examples, the effect of the subsection is unclear. Particular problems are posed where the original goods are sold for cash and others purchased. Are those replacement goods prevented from being 'property representing' the original goods because the replacement was effected by two cash transactions rather than one barter? If the answer is 'no', then it can be argued that where the original goods are sold and no replacement purchased the money received should also be regarded as 'property representing' the original goods.[28]

MENTAL INCAPACITY

Mental incapacity might result from various causes. Case law dealing with self-inflicted mental incapacity, perhaps as a result of excessive consumption of alcohol or drugs, is rare. A contract would not be unenforceable merely because it was signed 'after a good lunch' when both parties had consumed sufficient wine to cloud their business judgment.[29] To be relevant the self-inflicted impairment must prevent the defendant from understanding the transaction.[30] Despite the fact that the drunkard or addict is in a sense the author of his own misfortune, the protection afforded such persons is apparently the same as that extended to those whose mental incapacity results from causes beyond their control.

A contract will not be binding upon someone suffering from impaired mental capacity if the other party is aware of this impairment.[31] This requirement of knowledge contrasts starkly with the approach to minors' contracts, which invalidates contracts even if the adult is unaware of the minority. It is for the party alleging incapacity to prove it.[32] The contract becomes binding if it is ratified at a time when the incapacity has ended.[33]

---

[28] The 1987 Act does not affect old equitable rules, which required a fraudulent minor to return identifiable property. As to which, see *Stocks v Wilson* [1913] 2 KB 235 (minor liable to account for proceeds of goods obtained by fraud). However, such rules may well be redundant after the 1987 Act, particularly if a generous construction is put upon s 3(2).

[29] Though this may be a sufficient ground to refuse an equitable remedy such as specific performance. See *Malins v Freeman* (1837) 2 Keen 25 at 34.

[30] *Re Bevan* [1912] 1 Ch 196.

[31] *Imperial Loan Co v Stone* [1892] 1 QB 599 and *Re Beavan* [1912] 1 Ch 196 (drunkenness).

[32] *Re K* [1988] Ch 310.

[33] *Manches v Trimborn* (1946) 115 LJKB 305 and *Matthews v Baxter* (1873) LR 8 Ex 132 (ratification when sober).

Where a person suffering from mental incapacity would not otherwise be bound to pay for necessaries, the Sale of Goods Act 1979, s 3(2) requires him to pay a reasonable sum for them. As with minors' contracts, necessaries comprehend services as well as goods and so might include private medical services as well as privately prescribed drugs.

Where a person is suffering from mental incapacity his property may be subject to the protection of the court under the Mental Health Act 1983, Part VII. In such cases any purported disposition of property is not binding on the person suffering the incapacity but is binding on the other.[34]

COMPANIES

It was the case that a company incorporated under the Companies Acts could only make such contracts as were authorised by its memorandum of association. Any activity not so authorised was *ultra vires*.[35] The original rationale for the doctrine of *ultra vires* was that it operated to protect shareholders and those who advance money to the company who by consulting the memorandum of association could tell how their investment would be applied. However, it operated to the detriment of innocent third parties who unknowingly entered *ultra vires* contracts with the company. The original strict rule was departed from in order to benefit such persons who now enjoy statutory protection under Companies Act 1985, s 35.

CONCLUSION

In the introduction to this chapter it was suggested that the policy issues underlying the subject of contractual capacity were different when individuals and corporate bodies were concerned. However, it is surprising that the approach to individuals who lack contractual capacity is not more uniform. Whether capacity is lacked because it has not yet been acquired (minors) or once gained is later lost as a result of external or internal factors (respectively mental disorder and drunkenness) should make little difference to the approach of the law. This is surely a corner of the law of contract in need of reform or at least 'tidying up'.

---

[34] *Re Walker* [1905] 1 Ch 60.
[35] *Ashbury Railway Carriage and Iron Co* v *Riche* (1875) LR 7 HL 653.

9

THIRD PARTIES

INTRODUCTION

The doctrine of *privity of contract* states that only those who are parties to a contract can enforce the contract for their benefit or be subject to burdens under it. We can immediately see that the doctrine has two aspects: the first concerns the extent to which contracts are enforceable *by* strangers and the second the extent to which they are enforceable *against* strangers. If we think about the two parts of the rule, the justification for the second part is more self-evident than that for the first. It is intuitively obvious that a contract concluded between A and B should not, without his consent, be capable of creating any obligation for C. However, it is less obvious why A who receives good consideration from B in exchange for his (B's) promise to confer a benefit on C should not be liable to C if he (B) refuses to do so. This intuition is reflected in the attitude of the courts, academics and law reform agencies.

Judicial dissatisfaction with the rule that third parties cannot enforce a contract for their benefit is not new. Lord Diplock referred to it as an 'anachronistic shortcoming ... a reproach to English private law'.[1] However, criticism has become more strident in recent years. A typical recent statement is that of Steyn LJ in *Darlington Borough Council* v *Wiltshier Northern Ltd*:[2]

> The case for recognising a contract for the benefit of a third party is simple and straightforward ... The law of contract should give effect to the reasonable expectations of contracting parties ... there is no doctrinal, logical or policy reason why the law should deny effectiveness to a contract for the benefit of a third party where that is the expressed intention of the parties. I will not struggle with the point further since nobody seriously asserts the contrary.

There have been many similar statements in this country[3] and abroad. In the

---

[1] *Swain* v *Law Society* [1983] 1 AC 598 at 611. See also *Beswick* v *Beswick* [1968] AC 58 at 72 *per* Lord Reid calling for the implementation of the Law Revision Committee's 1937 proposals (see below); *Woodar Investment Development Ltd* v *Wimpey Construction UK Ltd* [1980] 1 WLR 277 *per* Lord Scarman at 300 ('... this unjust rule ...') and Lord Salmon dissenting at 291 demanding reform; *Forster* v *Silvermere Golf and Equestrian Centre Ltd* (1981) 125 SJ 397.
[2] [1995] 1 WLR 68 at 76.
[3] See also Lord Goff's comments in *The Pioneer Container* [1994] 2 AC 207 at 335 and *White* v *Jones* [1995] 2 AC 207 at 262–3.

High Court of Australia Toohey J in *Trident General Insurance* v *McNeice Bros* said that the rule 'lacks a sound foundation in jurisprudence and logic'[4] and the Canadian courts have also sought to avoid its rigid application.[5] In the common law world it was the United States' courts which early on moved decisively against the doctrine. In *Lawrence* v *Fox*[6] it was decided that a third party was able to enforce a contractual obligation meant to benefit him.

Academic criticism of the rule is also widespread[7] and longstanding[8] with some commentators suggesting that the law of tort has had to make good deficiencies in the law of contract.[9] A further pressure for reform comes from Europe. The legal systems of most of the member states of the European Union openly recognise the rights of third parties to enforce contracts.[10] The pursuit of a single market in Europe may require member states' domestic contract law to become more uniform and easily intelligible to other member states. This impetus would seem to require the abandonment of some of the more eccentric features of our law of contract such as, perhaps, the doctrine of privity. For instance, the latest edition of the Principles of European Contract Law provides that a third party can require performance of a contractual obligation when the right to do so was expressly agreed between the original contracting parties.[11]

Responding to this groundswell of opinion, the Law Commission issued a consultation paper outlining the case for reform of the third-party rule.[12] The case was persuasively made out and met with general acceptance. Some objection was raised by the construction industry which had become (too?) accustomed to dealing with privity problems by a complicated scheme of cross indemnities. It was feared that the new third-party right proposed by the Law Commission might be uncertain in its operation compared to the

---

[4] (1988) 165 CLR 107. See also *Olsson* v *Dyson* (1969) 120 CLR 365 at 392 *per* Windeyer J.

[5] *London Drugs Ltd* v *Kuehne & Nagel International Ltd* (1992) 97 DLR (4th) 261 (employee effectively obtained the benefit of exemption clause in a contract to which he was not a party by limiting the (tortious) duty of care owed by him to the property owner). See below.

[6] (1859) 20 NY 268 (New York Court of Appeals). See now Restatement (Second), s 302, which permits all 'intended' as opposed to 'incidental' beneficiaries to enforce contractual obligations contained in contracts to which they are not a party.

[7] Andrews, 'Does a Third Party Beneficiary have a Right in English Law?' (1988) 6 Legal Studies 14; Reynolds, 'Privity of Contract, the Boundaries of Categories and the Limits of the Judicial Function' (1989) 105 LQR 1; Adams and Brownsword, 'Privity and the Concept of a Network Contract' (1990) 10 Legal Studies 12; Beyleveld and Brownsword, 'Privity, Transitivity and Third Parties' (1991) 54 MLR 48.

[8] Corbin, 'Contracts for the Benefit of Third Parties' (1930) 46 LQR 12; Dowrick, 'A *Jus Quaesitum Tertio* by Way of Contract in English Law' (1956) 19 MLR 374; Furmston, 'Return to *Dunlop* v *Selfridge*?' (1960) 23 MLR 373.

[9] Markesinis, 'An Expanding Tort Law – The Price of a Rigid Contract Law' (1987) 103 LQR 354 and Whittaker, 'Privity of Contract and the Tort of Negligence: Future Directions' (1996) 16 Ox JLS 191.

[10] For example, see French Code Civil, Art 1121 and German Burgerliches Gesetzbuch, Art 328.

[11] Principles of European Contract Law, Art 6.110.

[12] No. 121, *Privity of Contract: Contracts for the Benefit of Third Parties* (1991).

devices presently used to circumnavigate the doctrine. In its full report[13] the Law Commission said that it thought that the concern about a lack of certainty could be met by modifying their proposal for an exception to the privity doctrine. The Law Commission was convinced that a general exception remained necessary for parties who do not have access to or whose contracts do not justify the expense of the legal advice needed to 'get round' the doctrine.[14] The statutory exception proposed by the Law Commission[15] became law as s 1 of the Contracts (Rights of Third Parties) Act 1999.

The importance of the Law Commission's Report and consequent Act should be emphasised at the outset. It is not the first time a law-reform body in this country has proposed reform of the third-party benefit rule.[16] It is not the first statutory provision to confer a right to enforce a contract upon a third party.[17] It was not intended to give a direct right of action to everyone who can presently bring himself within one of the existing exceptions to the rule.[18] It does not in terms abolish the doctrine of privity of contract.[19] However, it is the first *general* statutory exception to the third-party benefit rule; it is not restricted to particular types of contract or particular classes of claimant. The breadth of the exception fully justifies its treatment at the beginning of the next section.[20] However, it is first necessary to describe in more detail the rule from which that exception departs.

THE FIRST RULE: STRANGERS CANNOT ENFORCE CONTRACTS

The rule that third parties to a contract cannot in their own name enforce for their benefit provisions in it is associated with two cases: *Tweddle* v *Atkinson*[21] and *Dunlop Pneumatic Tyre Co Ltd* v *Selfridge & Co Ltd*.[22] In the

---

[13] (1996) *Privity of Contract: Contracts for the Benefit of Third Parties*, No. 242. This report continues the trend of recent Law Commission reports of containing an excellent and exhaustive account of the law in this country and an abbreviated description of the approach taken in other jurisdictions by courts and law reform agencies.

[14] Paras 1.7–1.10.

[15] With minor amendment.

[16] (1937) *Law Revision Committee Sixth Interim Report*, Cmd 5449, paras 41–9.

[17] For example, Married Women's Property Act 1882, s 11 (life insurance taken out for the benefit of a spouse or children and expressed to be for their benefit creates a trust in their favour which can be enforced by them). See below.

[18] For instance, the claimants in *White* v *Jones* [1995] 2 AC 207 (beneficiaries under will who were deprived of their gift when a solicitor negligently failed to execute a new will in their favour before the testator died). See below.

[19] Section 7(1) expressly preserves all existing exceptions to the third-party benefit rule. Section 4 expressly preserves any right of the promisee which if exercised might effectively secure a benefit for a third party. See below.

[20] When I proposed this book to the publishers this chapter was to be called 'Privity of Contract'. The change of title to 'Third Parties' reflects the author's view that the exception is now more important than the rule and, indirectly, the length of time it has taken to complete the book!

[21] (1861) 1 B & S 393.

[22] [1915] AC 847.

first case the father of a son who was engaged to be married promised the intended bride's father that he would pay a sum of money to his son upon marriage in return for the bride's father doing the same. The bride's father failed to do so and was sued by the son.[23] The action failed. However, the reason appears to be that the son had provided no consideration for his father-in-law's promise not because the son was not a party (not *privy*) to the contract between the fathers. Therefore, the case is not strictly about the doctrine of privity of contract at all.[24] As Steyn LJ recently put it: 'The genesis of the privity rule is suspect ... It ... originated in the misunderstanding of *Tweddle* v *Atkinson*'.[25]

The second case would also appear to be wrongly associated with the doctrine of privity of contract. The claimant wanted to maintain a minimum price level for its products. Therefore, it extracted a promise from all its wholesalers that they would not sell the claimant's products below a certain price and required them to extract a similar promise from the parties they sold to. Dew was a wholesaler who complied with these obligations when he sold tyres to Selfridge. However, Selfridge did sell the tyres on at below the specified price in breach of the promise it had made to Dew. The claimant's action to enforce that promise failed. Viscount Haldane and Lords Dunedin, Atkinson, Parker and Sumner held that the claimant was unable to enforce the promise because it had not provided good consideration for it. Only Viscount Haldane mentioned the doctrine of privity and even then only as an alternative ground for his decision; the claimant could not enforce the promise made by Selfridge because it was not a party to the contract in which it was embodied.[26]

However, what was actually decided in these two leading cases may only be of historic interest because the privity principle with which they are often associated has been stated and acted upon (though with admitted reluctance) by the House of Lords in *Scruttons Ltd* v *Midland Silicones Ltd*[27]

---

[23] Strictly by his executor, but nothing turns on this.

[24] See Atiyah (1979) *Rise and Fall of Freedom of Contract*, p. 414.

[25] *Darlington Borough Council* v *Wiltshier Northern Ltd* [1995] 3 All ER 895 at 904.

[26] Closely related to the descriptive question: were these cases resolved by the application of the doctrine of consideration or the doctrine of privity? is an analytical question: are the doctrines of consideration and privity distinct? In other words, is the doctrine of privity subsumed by the doctrine of consideration which requires that consideration must move from the promisee? While we retain a doctrine of consideration, the question is of no practical significance. An unsuccessful claimant will be as indifferent to learn whether he has failed for one reason or two as the successful claimant will be to know whether he has cleared one hurdle or two. Indeed, in the one case when it might be expected to be discussed its impact has been reduced by the concept of joint promisees. If A makes a promise to B and C in exchange for consideration provided by C, can B enforce the contract against A? It would seem that B was a party to the contract but provided no consideration. The doctrines must be distinct because one is satisfied (privity) when the other is not (consideration). However, if B and C are regarded as joint promisees (suggested *obiter* in *Coulls* v *Bagot's Executor and Trustee Co Ltd* [1967] ALR 385 and supported by *McEvoy* v *Belfast Banking Co Ltd* [1935] AC 24) it could be argued that the consideration supplied by C moves from B as well. In this way the two rules are again brought into alignment.

[27] [1962] AC 446.

and *Beswick v Beswick*.[28] In *Beswick* v *Beswick* a coal merchant sold his business to his nephew in exchange for *inter alia* retaining him as a consultant and, after the uncle's death, paying a pension to his widow. The uncle died and when the pension was not paid the widow brought an action against the nephew. In the Court of Appeal Lord Denning grandiosely dismissed the doctrine of privity as 'only a rule of procedure' and said that the widow could enforce the promise in her own right.[29] The House of Lords held that the widow was entitled to enforce the contract but only because she was her husband's personal representative.[30] Ghoulish though it might sound, as her husband's personal representative, the widow stood in her dead husband's shoes. She was able to enforce the contract as her dead husband. The doctrine of privity was no longer relevant because it was then an action by a contracting party.

Whether the House of Lords was right not to follow the lead of Lord Denning and seek to judicially abolish the doctrine of privity is open to debate. Steyn LJ has said that he thought judicial reform might be possible if the House of Lords were to take the lead.[31] However, the experience overseas would suggest the contrary. In *Trident Insurance Co Ltd v McNeice Bros Pty Ltd*[32] the High Court of Australia considered the doctrine in the context of a claim under a policy of liability insurance by someone who was not a party to the contract of insurance. The majority who upheld the claim did so on different bases: Deane J on the basis of the 'trust' exception to the doctrine (as to which see below), Gaudron J on the basis of the need to reverse the unjust enrichment of the insurer, Mason CJ, Wilson and Toohey JJ on the basis of the inapplicability of the doctrine of privity though this might be limited to the insurance context. What is clear is that judicial reform of the doctrine of privity carries with it the danger that it might produce great uncertainty. Well-drafted legislation would seem to offer the best hope of modifying the doctrine in a way that remedies the injustice of the third-party benefit rule at the same time avoiding commercial uncertainty. We will now examine how successful the English Law Commission has been in fulfilling these hopes.

---

[28] [1968] AC 58.

[29] [1966] Ch 538 at 557. For other cases where Lord Denning fought against the doctrine of privity, see *Smith and Snipes Hall Farm Ltd* v *River Douglas Catchment Board* [1949] 2 KB 500 and *Drive Yourself Hire Co (London) Ltd* v *Strutt* [1954] 1 QB 250.

[30] Upon death most existing causes of action against and for the deceased survive respectively against and for the benefit of his estate. The estate is represented by executors (female executrix) appointed under a will or an administrator (female administratrix) appointed by the court if the deceased died intestate. Collectively administrators, administratrixes, executors and executrixes are known as personal representatives.

[31] *Darlington Borough Council* v *Wiltshier Northern Ltd* [1995] 1 WLR 68 at 76.

[32] (1988) 165 CLR 107.

EXCEPTIONS TO NON-ENFORCEABILITY
Contracts (Rights of Third Parties) Act 1999

The Law Commission concluded that the case for reform of the third-party benefit rule was overwhelming. Two main arguments were said to support this conclusion:[33]

> If the theoretical justification for the enforcement of contracts is seen as the realisation of the promises or the will or the bargain of the contracting parties, the failure of the law to afford a remedy to the third party where the contracting parties intended that it should have one frustrates their intentions, and undermines the general justifying theory of contract.

The difficulty with this argument is that it is conditional. To the extent that the theoretical justification put forward does not explain the enforcement of contracts, this argument for third-party rights fails. Unfortunately, the Law Commission does not explore at all the proper justification for the enforcement of contracts. However, it does put forward a second non-conditional argument for the enforcement of third-party benefits which:[34]

> ... focuses on the injustice to the third party where a valid contract, albeit between two other parties, has engendered in the third party reasonable expectations of having the legal right to enforce the contract particularly where the third party has relied on that contract to regulate his or her affairs.

Although both arguments have a different focus, the first upon the original contractors and the second upon the third party, to the extent that they overlap they will not dictate different results.[35] However, it is to be regretted that such a radical change to the common law should be seen to rest, even partially, upon an unsubstantiated assertion. Indeed, it can be argued that this theoretical vacuum in the Law Commission's report has been the cause of the Commission's major dilemma which is: in what circumstances should the original contracting parties be precluded from modifying their contract in a way which removes or reduces the benefit they first agreed to confer on the third party?[36]

More particularly, the Law Commission highlighted three defects of the present law. First, in many situations the right to sue for breach of contract and the loss which it causes become separated.[37] Second, even if the promisee can obtain a satisfactory remedy for the third party, the promisee

---

[33] At para 3.1.

[34] Paragraph 3.2.

[35] The second argument applies to the third party the explanation for the enforcement of two party contracts associated with Patrick Atiyah. The practical difference between the two arguments for the enforcement of third-party benefits, like that between the view of Patrick Atiyah and Charles Fried, though fundamental would only dicate a different result in a small number of cases.

[36] See Halson, 'Variation, Privity and Law Reform' in (1996) *Exploring the Boundaries of Contract*, p. 83.

[37] Paragraph 3.3.

cannot be compelled to do so.[38] The facts of *Beswick* v *Beswick* illustrate both of these concerns. The right to sue upon the contract was possessed by the deceased; the third party, his widow, suffered the loss. The promisee could not personally obtain a remedy for obvious reasons. Fortunately, on the unusual facts of that case, the House of Lords was able to achieve justice for the third party. The third-party, Mrs Beswick in her personal capacity, was also the contracting party (Mrs Beswick as her husband's administratrix). When the contracting party and third-party beneficiary are housed in the same physical body, one is sufficiently motivated to act for the benefit of the other! The third defect of the present law is that it is complex and the various exceptions and subterfuges used to avoid injustice are both artificial and uncertain.[39] Given that the Act expressly preserves all existing exceptions and enforcement by a contracting party for the benefit of the third party, it might be thought that the new Act, by creating a new exception and not abrogating any existing ones, renders the law more complex and uncertain. However, over time it is hoped that the breadth of the new exception will cause some of the old avoidance techniques to be forgotten and it will no longer be necessary for the courts to create new ones.

Section 1 provides:

[A] person who is not a party to a contract (a 'third party') may in his own right enforce a term of the contract if –
(a) the contract expressly provides that he may, or
(b) ... the term purports to confer a benefit on him.

The section creates two categories of third party that can enforce a contract to which they are not privy. An illustration of the first category would be where A promises B that in exchange for B's car A will pay C £10k 'who shall have the right to enforce this promise'.[40]

Importantly, this provision is intended to cover an exclusion clause, which names the parties who are to be free from liability.[41] However, it does not extend to cover cases such as *Beswick* where it could not be said that the contract between the uncle and his nephew expressly provided that after his death his widow could enforce it for her benefit. That it did expressly provide that she should after his death receive a benefit would not be enough to come within s 1(1)(a).

An illustration of the second category of third party would be where A promises B that in exchange for B's car A will pay C £10k. The effect of the test is to establish a rebuttable presumption in favour of there being a third

---

[38] Paragraph 3.4. Some of the cases give a false impression of selfless conduct here. In a number of cases the legally distinct promisee and third party are in fact associated in some way, e.g. in *The Eurymedon* [1975] AC 154 and *Linden Gardens Trust Ltd* v *Lenesta Sludge Disposals Ltd* [1994] 1 AC 85 (associated companies). Faced with heavy legal costs, altruistic behaviour towards strangers is not common.

[39] Paragraph 3.6.

[40] Or the right to sue on it, see para. 7.10.

[41] *Ibid.* and so avoiding some of the technical difficulties associated with *The Eurymedon*, explored below.

party right where a contractual provision seeks to confer a benefit upon an expressly designated third party.[42] The Act expressly states that no enforceable third-party right will be created if 'on a proper construction' of the contract it is clear that the original parties did not intend the term to be enforceable by the third party.[43] The onus of proof will effectively be on the promisor, i.e. doubts will be resolved in favour of the third party. It will always be open to the contractors to state in the contract that the third party shall not thereby receive an enforceable right. However, even in the absence of any such express provision, the Law Commission thought that someone who contracted with a main contractor would be unable to use this provision to sue a sub-contractor employed by him. It was thought that the well-known practice within the construction industry of establishing a chain of contracts where each party only had available to him remedies against the next party in the chain would be sufficient to exclude the presumption.[44] For similar reasons the Commission thought that this category would not extend to permit a purchaser of goods from a retailer to sue the manufacturer directly.

The third party need not be expressly identified by name but could be identified as a member of a class or by description. In the *Trident* case a third party claimed to be entitled to benefits under a contract of liability insurance to which he was not a party. Although the insurance contract identified the third party by description ('all contractors and sub-contractors') rather than by name, this would still come within the new Act.[45] Indeed, it is not even necessary for the third party to be in existence when the contract is entered.[46]

It is interesting to apply this second category to some of the existing cases establishing exceptions to the third-party benefit rule. Mrs Beswick would come within it. She was expressly named and it is unlikely that the nephew would be able to show that he and his uncle intended that Mrs Beswick should not be able to enforce the contract. In *Woodar Investment Development Ltd v Wimpey Construction UK Ltd*[47] Woodar agreed to sell land to Wimpey for a consideration, part of which was to be paid to a third party. There are *obiter dicta*[48] in the judgments of the House of Lords to the effect that Woodar would not have been able to claim substantial damages for Wimpey's failure to pay the third party. Following the new Act, the third party, who was expressly named and upon whom Wimpey and Woodar intended to confer a benefit, would be able to bring an action to recover the

[42] Paragraph 7.17, following the single category of third-party claimant in New Zealand. See New Zealand Contracts (Privity) Act 1982.
[43] Section 1(2).
[44] Paragraph 7.18(3).
[45] Paragraph 7.50.
[46] Section 1(3).
[47] [1980] 1 WLR 277.
[48] By a majority the House of Lords held that Wimpey's incorrect but bona fide belief that the contract entitled it to withdraw meant that Wimpey was not liable to Woodar for breach of contract.
[49] Paragraph 7.49.

money owed to him.[49]

However, it seems that under the new provisions a party who employs a main contractor to do building work who in turn contracts with a sub-contractor to do all or part of the work will not be able to sue the sub-contractor directly even where the sub-contractor was 'nominated' by the employer.[50] Where, as in the building trade, it is generally accepted that under the chain of contracts typically established the employer's contractual rights should be exercised against the main contractor, it would be possible for the sub-contractor to rebut the presumption that the third-party (employer) should obtain an enforceable right against the sub-contractor. Another case that will fall outside the new Act concerns the negligent drafting of a will by a solicitor which results in a beneficiary not receiving a gift which the testator intended him to have. The tort of negligence now gives a remedy to the disappointed beneficiaries.[51]

From the beginning an issue which has been 'central'[52] to the new right of action is the extent to which the original contracting parties can vary or cancel their contract in a way which adversely affects the third party. The Act seeks to strike a compromise between the right of the original parties to vary their contract as they wish and the right of a third party to confidently rely upon rights conferred upon him. The former is preserved by s 2(3), which effectively provides that the contracting parties can expressly reserve the right to cancel or vary the contract without the consent of the third party.[53] When the contract is silent on this question, the Act provides a number of 'default' rules designed to protect the rights of the third party. Section 2(1) provides that where under s 1(a) the third party has obtained an enforceable right, in three circumstances the original parties may not without his consent[54] 'cancel ... or vary the contract' so as 'to extinguish, or alter' his rights. These are where:

(a) the third party has communicated his assent to the term to the promisor; or
(b) the promisor is aware that the third party has relied on the term; or
(c) the promisor can be reasonably expected to have foreseen that the third

---

[50] These were the facts of *Junior Books Ltd v Veitchi & Co Ltd* [1983] 1 AC 520 when exceptionally the employer was given a right of action against the sub-contractor in the tort of negligence. Subsequent to this case there has been a marked reluctance on the part of the courts to permit the recovery of 'pure economic loss' in the tort of negligence. It, therefore, seems that the *Junior Books* case, though never formally overruled, will never be expanded and probably never even applied. See *Simaan General Contracting Co v Pilkington Glass (No. 2)* [1988] QB 758.

[51] *Ross v Caunters* [1980] Ch 297 (solicitor negligently failed to warn testator that will would be invalid if witnessed by spouse of one of beneficiaries) and now *White v Jones* [1995] 2 AC 207 (solicitor negligently failed to draft a new will reinstating gifts to his two daughters with whom he had fallen out but subsequently made up).

[52] Consultation paper No. 121, 1991, para 5.28.

[53] Or they require the third party's consent only in certain specified circumstances. See s 2(3)(b).

[54] The court has a discretion to dispense with the consent of the third party if his whereabouts are not reasonably ascertainable or he is not mentally capable of giving consent or if it is satisfied that it cannot reasonably be ascertained whether or not the third party has in fact relied on the term. See respectively s 2(4)(a), (b) and (5).

party would rely on the term and the third party has in fact relied on it. The requirement of communication in (a) means actual communication by words or conduct.[55] The third party cannot rely upon a posted but not received letter as a sufficient communication of his assent. In other words the postal rule of acceptance has no application. To hold otherwise would be to unfairly favour the interests of the third party over those of the promisor.[56]

The reference to 'reliance' in (b) is not qualified in any way. It follows that any kind of reliance by the third party will be sufficient to 'crystallise' his rights. For two reasons the Law Commission expressly rejected a requirement of detrimental reliance, i.e. where the third party makes his position worse in reliance.[57] First, such a requirement would not explain why the third party with an enforceable right is entitled to an expectation based remedy, namely one which seeks to place him in the position he would have been in if the original promise had been fulfilled rather than a reliance-based one, in other words, one which seeks to place him in the position he would have been in if no promise to benefit him had ever been made. Second, they referred to the analogy of promissory estoppel which rejects a test of detrimental reliance. This reasoning is not convincing. The 'problem' the Law Commission identifies in its first reason is one that afflicts the law of contract generally. If the purpose of the law of contract is to give effect to the parties' intentions,[58] it is difficult to see why this does not justify the more general availability of specific performance, i.e. a court order that the promisor do the very thing he has promised to do rather than an award of damages. When the general law of contract proceeds upon the basis of a discontinuity between right and remedy, it should not embarrass a third party to do the same particularly where the third party's remedy is expressed to be 'any remedy ... that would have been available to him if he had been a party to the contract'.

Further, the reference to promissory estoppel is incomplete. It is true that the reliance of the promisee necessary to give rise to a promissory estoppel need not be detrimental but it must be reliance sufficient to render it inequitable to allow the promisor to go back on his word.[59] On this test a promisee who has beneficially relied may not be able to claim the benefit of an estoppel. Consider a tenant who is told by a landlord that he may pay half rent next month. The tenant uses the money saved to buy lottery tickets one of which wins a large sum of money. The tenant has certainly relied upon his landlord's promise but it is arguable that the tenant has relied in circumstances where it would not be inequitable to allow the landlord to go back on his word. If a third-party beneficiary anticipates his promised

---

[55] Section 2(2)(a).

[56] Section 2(2)(b) and para 9.20.

[57] Paragraph 9.19.

[58] This is the point where the Law Commission's failure to clarify the theoretical justification for the enforcement of contracts causes difficulty. See above.

[59] *The Post Chaser* [1981] 2 Lloyd's Rep 695 at 701.

investment and buys lottery tickets with the same consequence, is his case for enforcement any more compelling than that of the tenant? However, under the new Act the third party would apparently be able to enforce the contract for his benefit.

The Act makes provision for the third party to obtain an enforceable right even though the promisor is not aware that he has done so. Although this might seem unfair to the promisor, it is a requirement that the act of reliance which in fact took place was one which the promisor could have reasonably expected to occur. In this way the promisor is protected from an opportunistic promisee who might seek to crystallise his right by an unexpected act of reliance. However, he will not be protected from, though he will at least be aware of, an opportunistic promisee who seeks to crystallise his right under (a) or (b) by a swift acceptance or communication of unexpected reliance. Perhaps the new law acts upon the commonplace – 'better the devil you know ...'.

Further limits upon the new third-party right

For the purposes of exercising his right to enforce a term of a contract, the third party is treated as if he was a party to the contract and 'the rules relating to damages, injunctions, specific performance and other relief shall apply accordingly'.[60] The damages recoverable by a third party will, therefore, be subject to the usual limiting factors as applied to the third party. Was the loss of the third party too remote to be recoverable? Did the third party act reasonably to mitigate his loss?[61]

However, for other purposes the third party will not be treated as if he was a party to the contract. This may have important implications when legislative measures controlling exemption clauses and other unfair contract terms are considered. Where an exclusion clause properly construed operates to exclude or restrict the third-party right, the exclusion would not appear to be caught and so controlled by the Unfair Contract Terms Act 1977, s 3. As a matter of interpretation this is understandable, but as a matter of policy it is difficult to defend. It is understandable that the new third-party right is not 'caught' by the wording of an Act that precedes that right by over two decades; it is indefensible because the third party is inexplicably given a lesser level of protection from the destructive effect of exemption clauses than is the original promisee. The Law Commission recognises the problem but thinks that 'practical politics' demand that it should not be resolved at the outset. Despite the number of arguments put forward by the Law

---

[60] Section 1(5)

[61] For the principles of remoteness and mitigation, see below.

[62] Paragraph 13.10. In all, 11 reasons are proffered for declining to reform the Unfair Contract Terms Act 1977 to secure uniform protection for contractors and third parties. These overlapping and sometimes inconsistent reasons include: consumer protection measures are inconsistent with the policy of the new Act; the Act does not set out to secure equality between the contracting and third parties; common law controls on exemption clauses, such as the rules of incorporation, will protect third parties; third parties are better off under the Act than they were before; the 1977 Act will control attempts to exclude liability to a

Commission to support its approach[62] it is suggested that the contrary arguments are more persuasive. We are left with an uneven law, which fails to give equal protection to parties in comparable positions. Indeed, the new Act actually worsens the position of third-party beneficiaries by amending another section of the 1977 Act to take away from third parties a protection from the exclusion of liability for loss or damage to property which they would otherwise enjoy.[63] This change has little to commend it except consistency for consistency's sake. After all, two wrongs do not make a right. The basic criticism is simply that it seems odd to carefully construct a third-party right and then make it so much easier for the contracting parties to exclude it than it is for them to exclude the liabilities they owe each other.

The third party's right is subject to any defence or right of set off arising in connection with the contract which would have been available to him in an action by the promisee[64] so that a contract which is void perhaps for mistake or illegality is no more enforceable by the third party than it would be by the promisee. Further, the third party's right is subject to any defence, set off or counter-claim not arising from this contract that would have been available against the third party if the third party had been a party to the contract,[65] such as a defence arising from the fact that, perhaps unknown to the promisee, the third party fraudulently induced the promisor to enter the contract. Additionally, the third party's right is subject to any defence or set off not covered by the previous provisions when the contract provides for it to be available and it would have been available against the promisee.[66] Where the third party seeks to obtain the benefit of an exemption or limitation clause, similar provisions to those contained in s 3(2)–(5) apply.[67]

As we have already seen, the Act preserves any existing right of the promisee to enforce the contract for the benefit of the third party.[68] The promisor is protected from having to pay out twice, both to the promisee under an existing and preserved right of enforcement for the benefit of the third party and again in a direct action by the third party under the Act. In the second action the court should reduce the damages payable to reflect the recovery in the first one.[69]

There are a number of express exceptions to the third-party rights created

contracting party seeking to enforce the contract for the benefit of the third party; reform of the 1977 Act would be difficult; reform should be gradual; the law should be allowed a period of recuperation after having a major operation; and the Unfair Terms in Consumer Contract Regulations do not extend to third parties.

[63] Section 7(2) amending Unfair Contract Terms Act 1977, s 2(2).

[64] Section 3(2) subject to any express clause in the contract which narrows or widens the defences or set-offs available under this section. See s 3(5).

[65] Section 3(4) subject to any express clause in the contract which narrows the defences, set-offs or counter-claims available under this section. See s 3(5).

[66] Section 3(3), e.g. A contracts to buy B's car for a consideration to be paid to C. B owes A money under an unrelated contract. A and B expressly agree that A can raise against B any matter which would have given A a defence or set-off to a claim by B.

[67] Section 3(6). This extra sub-section is necessary because it is technically incorrect to speak of defences available to the promisor when the promisor will be the party asserting a liability of the third party.

[68] Section 4.

[69] Section 5.

by the Act. The most important are that a third party such as the customer or client of an employer cannot obtain any rights under the Act against an employee.[70] On this basis an overseas student who directly paid full university fees (and so had a contractual relationship with the university) could not obtain any right of action against a lecturer who gave poor lectures! Third parties cannot bring actions to obtain the benefit of clauses in contracts for the carriage of goods by sea[71] except to claim the benefit of exemption clauses contained therein.[72]

Other statutory exceptions

There are other statutory exceptions to the doctrine of privity of contract. The practical and commercial significance of these exceptions is greater than their brief statement would suggest. However, unlike s 1 of the Contracts (Rights of Third Parties) Act 1999, they are of narrow application.

Several of the existing statutory exceptions deal with contracts of insurance. These permit third-party spouses and children to claim the proceeds of life insurance,[73] third-parties specified in motor insurance policies to claim to be indemnified for liabilities covered by the policy,[74] interested parties to demand that the proceeds of property insurance be applied to rebuild property destroyed by fire,[75] third parties to claim under liability insurance when the insured has become insolvent,[76] parties with a limited interest in property to claim the benefit of insurance on that property[77] and shareholders to sue one another and the company as if they were all parties to the registered memorandum and articles of association.[78]

The Package Travel, Package Holidays and Package Tours Regulations 1992[79] impose obligations to provide certain information and to different extents control the advertising, booking, pricing and cancellation of such holidays. In addition, the regulations give the beneficiaries of package holidays a direct right of action against the organiser and/or retailer even if

---

[70] Section 6(3).

[71] Section 6(5)(a) defined in s 6(6) as contracts contained in or evidenced by a bill of lading or other analogous contracts. It was presumably thought that the position of third parties is adequately protected by the Carriage of Goods by Sea Act 1992, s 2, of which effects a statutory assignment of the right to sue the carrier to the subsequent holder of the bill of lading. Section 6(5)(b) also exempts contracts for the carriage of goods by rail, road and air in a similar way.

[72] Section 6(5)(b).

[73] Married Women's Property Act 1882, s 11.

[74] Road Traffic Act 1988, s 148(7).

[75] Fire Prevention (Metropolis) Act 1774, s 11.

[76] Third Parties (Rights Against Insurers) Act 1930, s 1.

[77] Marine Insurance Act 1906, s 14(2) (mortgagee, consignee, etc.) and Law of Property Act 1925, s 47 (seller of property holds proceeds of insurance received between exchange of contracts and conveyance for the buyer).

[78] Companies Act 1985, s 14. The articles and memorandum of association are the fundamental documents necessary to establish a company.

[79] SI 1992 No. 3288, implementing EEC Council Directive 90/314.

[80] See reg 2(1) (defining a consumer to whom the obligations imposed by the regulations are owed broadly to extend beyond the contracting party) and reg 15.

there is no direct contractual relationship between them.[80]

In order to understand the operation of the next statutory exception, a brief account of international trade is necessary. International trade in goods is typically conducted upon certain standard contract terms. The variants most frequently encountered[81] are known as FOB and CIF terms. In FOB contracts the seller's obligation ends when he places the goods free (i.e. of outstanding charges and duties) on board the ship, i.e. the buyer is responsible for arranging the contract of carriage. In CIF contracts the buyer pays the seller a sum of money for the cost of the goods, insurance and freight i.e. carriage, so it is the seller's responsibility to arrange the contract of carriage.

Parties contract for the carriage of goods by sea in two ways. Where the cargo is large a ship may be chartered and the contract of charter called a charter party will be the contract of carriage. Where the cargo is more modest and a whole ship is not required,[82] the cargo might be shipped under a bill of lading contract. A bill of lading is a very important document issued by the ship's captain that may serve three functions. It can be a receipt for the goods shipped, evidence of the terms of the contract of carriage and it functions as a document of title. The last function is important to international trade because it allows parties to buy and sell commodities while they are on the high seas. Property is transferred pursuant to such contracts by making over or endorsing the bill of lading to the purchaser.

When the seller arranged the contract of carriage a difficulty arose at common law because the buyer of goods to whom property in the goods had passed by endorsement of the bill of lading was unable to sue the carrier if the goods were damaged in transit. The cause of action (i.e. right to sue) and the loss had become separated. The seller possessed the right to sue because he was a party to the contract of carriage but the buyer who now owned the goods ultimately suffered the loss. In 1855 this was resolved in favour of the buyer by the Bills of Lading Act.[83] The Act provided that when property in goods passed by the endorsement of the bill of lading the buyer obtained a right of action under the contract of carriage evidenced in the bill of lading.

---

[81] Many hybrids exist all known by equally cryptic abbreviations, e.g. in order of increasing responsibility of the seller ex works, FAS (free alongside), C and F (cost and freight) and delivered.

[82] Or for other reasons the cargo owner does not wish to take upon himself the extra responsibilities involved when chartering a ship. Charter parties may be entered either for a voyage or for a period of time. Voyage charters impose risks and obligations upon the charterer, e.g. he will be liable to pay liquidated (i.e. fixed in advance) damages called demurrage if loading is delayed and the ship stands idle. Time charters expose the charterer to even greater risks and obligations, e.g. 'hire' is payable for the full duration of the charter even if the desired voyage is completed early.

[83] In *Dunlop* v *Lambert* (1839) 6 Cl & F 600 the common law had earlier resolved this problem in favour of the seller by letting the seller sue for the buyer's losses. The common law principle became redundant and so forgotten after the 1855 Act until it was given new life by the House of Lords in *Linden Gardens Trust Co Ltd* v *Lenesta Sludge Disposals Ltd* [1994] 1 AC 85 which is examined below. This interpretation of *Dunlop* v *Lambert* is disputed by Lord Clyde in *Alfred McAlpine Construction Ltd* v *Panatown Ltd* [2000] 3 WLR 946.

[84] See Davenport writing in 1989, 'Like many old people, the Act still copes well with familiar and routine transactions. Dating as it does from early in the age of the steamship, it is hardly surprising that the statute should be showing some signs of geriatric weakness when applied

Unfortunately, the solution proposed by the 1855 Act was not watertight.[84] For instance, the buyer sometimes obtained the property in the goods other than by the endorsement of the bill of lading.[85] In such circumstances the buyer did not obtain any right of action against the carrier and so was left without a remedy when the carrier carelessly damaged the goods.[86] Therefore, the 1855 Act was replaced by the Carriage of Goods by Sea Act 1992, which effects a statutory assignment to inter alia the holder of a bill of lading of the right to sue the carrier. This operates independently of the passing of property and so avoids the difficulties of the old Act.

The trusts exception[87]

The law of property provides a number of exceptions to the doctrine of privity of contract, the most important of which is perhaps the trust. Indeed, though a great oversimplification, it is often said to be 'the distinguishing feature' between the law of property and the law of contract that property obligations are said to be good against all the world, whereas contractual obligations only bind the parties.[88] At one time it seemed as if, because of its breadth, this exception had in practical application displaced the very rule from which it formally departed. Indeed, one famous commentator writing in 1930 suggested that the doctrine of privity only survived in the minds of law teachers who 'rehearse it so frequently that they believe it to have divine authority ... [even though] the living law of decision and application has taken another channel'.[89] However, as we will see, the courts subsequently closed the door firmly in the face of these developments though, in the light of the very latest judicial pronouncements, the portal might more accurately be described as ajar.

A trust is typically established where a donor gives property to a trustee to hold for the benefit of a beneficiary. Although a stranger to the establishment of the trust, under the law of trusts, the beneficiary has always been able to enforce the trust.[90] There is certainly no difficulty in the concept of a trust of

---

to the very different conditions of the late twentieth century': 'Problems in the Bills of Lading Act' (1989) 105 LQR 174 at 174.

[85] The endorsement of the bill of lading to pledgee does not come within the 1855 Act but might give rise to an implied contract between the pledgee and the carrier allowing the former to bring a direct contractual claim against the latter. See *Brandt* v *Liverpool Steam Navigation Co* (1924) 1 KB 575.

[86] *Leigh and Sillivan Ltd* v *The Aliakmon Shipping Co Ltd (The Aliakmon)* [1986] AC 785 (C and F buyer was unable to pay for the goods and so received the bill of lading only to enable him to collect the goods as agent for the seller. When later in funds the buyer obtained property in the goods which had been damaged in transit. No right of action under the 1855 Act because property did not pass by endorsement of the bill of lading but rather under a separate later contract.

[87] See Jaconelli, 'Privity: The Trust Exception Examined' (1998) 62 Conv 88.

[88] See Atiyah (1995) *Introduction to the Law of Contract*. 5th edn, p. 355.

[89] Corbin, 'Contracts for the Benefit of Third Persons' [1930] 46 LQR 12 at 13–14.

[90] An action for the enforcement of the donor's promise or damages for its breach would usually be brought by the trustee. The damages awarded would reflect the loss of the beneficiary and be held for him. If the trustee refuses to bring proceedings, the beneficiary can sue in his own name. See Deane J in *Trident General Insurance Co Ltd* v *McNeice Bros Pty Ltd* (1988) 62 AJLR 508 at 525–6.

intangible property such as shares or a bank account. The argument then proceeds that if a contractual promise can also be regarded as intangible property capable of being the subject matter of a trust, then the restrictions of the doctrine of privity have been avoided. This is best illustrated by the facts of a case where the analogy of the trust was successfully relied on.

In *Walford*'s case[91] Walford, a broker, negotiated a charter between a ship owner and a charterer. In the contract of charter to which Walford was not a party the shipowner undertook to pay him a commission. The House of Lords held that the charterer was a trustee of the shipowner's promise, which could be enforced by the beneficiary, Walford.

However, this development was stopped in *Vandepitte* v *Preferred Accident Insurance Corporation of New York*[92] and this decision was followed in *Re Schebsman*[93] the facts of which were a little more complicated.

> Two companies employed S. When his employment was terminated one of the companies agreed to pay S a sum of money in instalments and if he died to make the payments to his wife and daughter. S became bankrupt and died. S's trustee in bankruptcy[94] sought a declaration that S was the trustee of the company's promise in favour of his wife and daughter.

The trustee in bankruptcy wanted the declaration to enable him to apply to have the trust set aside as an attempt to evade the proper payment of his creditors. The sums payable would then form part of his estate and be available for distribution to his creditors. The Court of Appeal held that there was no trust of the promise. It was said that the courts are not free to find a trust of a promise whenever it suited them in order to evade the doctrine of privity. For a trust to be found, there must be evidence of a clear intention to create one. Lord Greene MR said: '… it is not legitimate to import into the contract the idea of a trust when the parties have given no indication that this was their intention'. It is interesting to note that in this case if there had been a trust of the company's promise, because of the intentions of S's trustee in bankruptcy, the interests of the third party would have been harmed rather than advanced. This point was no doubt emphasised by Denning KC (as he then was) who appeared for the widow and daughter.

A possible objection to the greater use of the trust to evade the doctrine of privity has been the perceived irrevocability of a trust. When parties enter a contract it is always open to them by agreement to bring that contract to an end. In contrast a trust cannot usually be abrogated by the donor and trustee. However, Atiyah points out that this objection proceeds on the basis of an oversimplification of the law of trusts which does in fact recognise the concept of a revocable trust.[95] In this instance he thinks that the courts have

---

[91] *Les Affréteurs Réunis Société Anonyme* v *Leopold Walford (London) Ltd* [1919] AC 801.
[92] [1933] AC 70.
[93] [1944] Ch 83.
[94] A very different type of trustee. The trustee in bankruptcy is the person charged with gathering all the assets of the bankrupt for distribution among his creditors.
[95] Atiyah, *op. cit.* (n. 88 above), pp. 371–2.
[96] Indeed, there are echoes of this lack of imagination in the Law Commission's somewhat cursory dismissal of the trust exception. See paras 2.8–2.9.

simply taken the 'easy (one is tempted to say "lazy") way out'.[96]

To a limited extent Atiyah's criticism has been met in two recent cases where the trust exception has been adopted by a majority of the English Court of Appeal and by a lone member of the High Court of Australia[97] who thought that it was 'difficult to understand the reluctance which courts have sometimes shown to infer a trust'. In *Darlington Borough Council v Wiltshier Northern Ltd*:[98] A local authority wanted to build a recreation centre on land it owned. To avoid government restrictions on local authority borrowing, a bank contracted with a builder for the work. A separate agreement was entered between the bank and the local authority under which the bank agreed to pay the builder sums due under the building contract, which the local authority would repay to the bank. This agreement also provided that the bank was not liable for the building works but would upon request assign to the local authority all rights against the builder. The local authority alleged that the building work was defective.

The Court of Appeal had to consider whether the local authority could recover substantial damages which in turn depended upon whether the bank, which had assigned to the local authority its rights under the building contract, was entitled to such damages. Dillon and Waite LJJ held that the bank was a trustee for the local authority of the rights it had against the builder. As such, the bank could have recovered from the builder substantial damages representing the local authority's loss. Following the assignment, the local authority could recover these same damages directly. It is true that this was only an alternative ground for the decision in the case,[99] which was discussed in under half a page, and that Steyn LJ did not feel it necessary to consider the point. However, the case may signal a new willingness to develop the trusts exception. Whether the courts take this step may depend upon the success of the new statutory exception. Although the Contracts (Rights of Third Parties) Act 1999 expressly preserves all existing exceptions to the privity rule,[100] the courts will be unlikely to develop them further if the Act is regarded as remedying the major injustices caused by the rule. In any event, it seems likely that any development of the exception will be

---

[97] See Deane J in *Trident General Insurance Co Ltd v McNeice Bros Pty Ltd* (1988) 62 AJLR 508 at 525 agreeing with Fullagar J in *Wilson v Darling Island Stevedoring and Lighterage Co Ltd* (1956) 95 CLR 43 at 67.

[98] [1995] 3 All ER 895.

[99] The other ground was an expansion of the *Dunlop v Lambert* principle as developed in *Linden Gardens Trust Ltd v Lenesta Sludge* [1994] 1 AC 85. For this aspect of the case see later in this chapter under headings of Action by the promisee and Damages.

[100] Section 7(1).

[101] '[T]he conception of a trust attaching to a benefit under an exclusion clause extends far beyond conventional limits': *Southern Water Authority v Carey* [1985] 2 All ER 1077 at 1083. *Contra: Swain v Law Society* [1982] 1 AC 598 (Solicitor's Act 1974, s 37 was interpreted as empowering the Law Society to create a contract for the benefit of third parties (its members)) where a promise to provide an indemnity was apparently considered to be a possible subject matter for a trust though the case was decided by application of public law principles. To similar effect, see Deane J in *Trident General Insurance Co Ltd v McNeice Bros Pty Ltd* (1988) 62 AJLR 508 at 526: 'It is difficult to envisage a class of contract in which

limited to promises to pay money or to transfer property[101] and is unlikely to extend to third parties who want to claim the benefit of an exemption clause.[102]

Agency

Agency is the relationship which arises when one party, the principal, authorises another party, the agent, to act on his behalf and the agent agrees to do so.[103] The principal is able to enforce a contract made by his agent even though the principal is not personally a party to it and so avoid the doctrine of privity. This is unobjectionable (except, perhaps, where the agent's acts are ratified retrospectively) when the agent is acting within the prior authority of the principal whose existence is made known to the other contracting party. However, the principles of agency extend much further. First, the agent's authorisation may post-date rather than precede his actions on behalf of his principal; his actions are then said to be 'ratified'. Second, the agent's acts might bind his principal even when he is not actually empowered to do so if he acts within the usual authority which such an agent may be expected to possess ('usual' authority), or if he acts within the authority he appears to have or is held out as having (apparent or ostensible authority), even if his actions are actually prohibited by the principal.[104] However, the most controversial extension of agency is the so-called doctrine of the undisclosed principal. Where this applies, the principal may be able to enforce a contract even though the agent was not openly acting on behalf of the principal. The person with whom the agent contracts[105] may find himself bound to a party with whom he never intended to contract.[106]

In *Midland Silicones Ltd* v *Scruttons Ltd*[107] negligent stevedores employed by the carrier damaged goods. In an action for negligence by the goods owner, the stevedores claimed to be entitled to the benefit of a limitation

---

the creation of a trust would be more readily discernible than the type of contract which is involved in the present case, namely, a policy of liability insurance indemnifying both a party to the contract and others ...'.

[102] For an example of an attempt to harness the trust exception to secure the benefit of an exemption clause, see *The Eurymedon* [1975] AC 154: '... for the purpose of ... this [exemption] clause the carrier is or shall be deemed to be acting as agent or *trustee* on behalf of all ... independent contractors ...'. The stevedores were able to bring themselves within other exceptions to the privity rule.

[103] See generally Treitel, ch. 17, from which the definition is derived.

[104] Though the principal will have an action against the agent for exceeding his authority.

[105] Whom agency lawyers call the third party. This is confusing to contract lawyers considering agency as an exception to the doctrine of privity who would regard the principal as the third party. Be careful.

[106] The doctrine of the undisclosed principal is subject to several limitations. I could not contract to write a book on contract law and then tell the publisher that I had in fact contracted on behalf of my three-year-old son, nor would it be possible for a hypothetical author who had so tried the patience of his publisher with promises of a manuscript that it refused ever to deal with him again to persuade a colleague to contract to write the book with the original author contracting as an undisclosed principal.

[107] [1962] AC 446.

clause in the contract (the bill of lading) between the goods owner and the carrier. Lord Reid considered the possibility that the relationship of agency existed between the stevedore as principal and the carrier as agent so that the former could enforce the contract with the goods owner for his benefit. He said that for agency to be established four criteria must be met: the bill of lading must be clear that its benefits extend to the stevedores; the carrier must have contracted in two capacities, in his personal capacity and as agent for the stevedores; the carrier must be authorised in advance so to act or his actions must later be ratified by the stevedore; and there must be good consideration moving from the stevedore to support the limitation of liability. The stevedores were unable to satisfy the first two criteria because they were not named or described in the class of people to whom the limitation of liability was to extend, nor could they satisfy the second condition because there was no evidence that the carrier was acting on their behalf.

Collateral contracts

A court may find that in addition to the main contract between the promisor and promisee there was a collateral (subsidiary) contract between the promisor and the third party in which the undertaking to the third party is repeated. The third party would then be able to enforce the collateral contract to which he is a party and thereby secure the benefit of a clause in the main contract to which he is not a party. In two types of case there is an obvious temptation for the court to find (really invent) such a contract. The two overlapping categories are based upon respectively the requirements of justice and commerce.

Shanklin Pier Ltd v *Detel Products Ltd* is a good example of the first type. The claimants employed contractors to paint their pier. The defendants assured the claimants that the paint they manufactured would last seven years. The claimants instructed the contractors to use the defendants' paint. The paint did not last. The claimants' action against the defendants was successful. The claimants were not trying to secure the benefit of a term in a contract to which they were not a party (a warranty as to quality in the contract to purchase the paint entered between the contractors and the defendants). Rather they were seeking to enforce a term of a collateral contract to which they were a party. The collateral contract was one whereby the defendants guaranteed the longevity of their paint in exchange for the claimant instructing their contractors to use it. If the claimants had bought the paint from the manufacturers, they would have had an action against them for breach of an express or implied term[108] of the contract of sale and for misrepresentation. It would be unjust if the fact that the manufacturers' assurances induced the claimants to require their contractors to use the

---

[108] That is, breach of the term implied by Sale of Goods Act 1979, s 13, that the goods shall conform to any description given.

paint left them without a remedy.

The Eurymedon provides an example of the second category of collateral contract. The facts of the case were broadly similar to those in *Midland Silicones* but the result was very different. In *The Eurymedon* the stevedores were able to claim the protection of an exemption clause in the bill of lading. There are two possible doctrinal explanations for the success of the stevedores' claim. First, the stevedores were able to enforce the exemption clause in the bill of lading for their benefit because they successfully argued that the carrier had made that contract as their agent. The difficulties that prevented the stevedores from succeeding with this argument in *Midland Silicones* did not afflict the stevedores in *The Eurymedon*. Following the decision in the earlier case, the practice had arisen of drafting exemption clauses in the widest possible way[109] naming or describing all parties who might be involved in the transport of the goods. These became known as 'Himalaya clauses' after the ship involved in one of the early cases[110] and satisfied the first of the conditions laid down by Lord Reid in *Midland Silicones*. The second and third of Lord Reid's conditions were also easily satisfied because the stevedores and the carrier were associated companies. This fact would make it easy to infer that the carrier was contracting both for himself and on behalf of the stevedores, and that the carrier was authorised to do so.

Lord Reid's fourth requirement that consideration must move from the stevedore presented greater difficulties. Lord Wilberforce delivering the opinion of the majority of the Privy Council said:

> There is possibly more than one way of analysing this business transaction into the necessary components; that which their lordships would accept is to say that the Bill of Lading brought into existence a bargain initially unilateral but capable of becoming mutual, between the shippers and the stevedore, made through the carrier as agent. This became a full contract when the stevedore performed services by discharging the goods. The performance of these services for the benefit of the shipper was the consideration for the agreement by the shipper that the stevedore should have the benefit of the exemptions and limitations in the Bill of Lading.

The final sentence of this quotation shows that the performance by the stevedores of the contractual duty they owed to the carrier was good consideration to support the exemption from liability offered to them by the shipper (i.e. goods owner).[111] However, the 'unilateral' bargain described

---

[109] The exemption was expressed to extend to any 'servant or agent of the carrier (including every independent contractor from time to time employed by the Carrier) ...'.

[110] *Adler* v *Dickson* [1955] 1 QB 158.

[111] Exercise caution with terminology when considering this case from the different perspectives of the doctrines of consideration and privity. The consideration issue raised was whether the performance of a pre-existing contractual duty owed to a third party could constitute good consideration. The privity issue raised was whether a third party could claim the benefit of a contract to which he was not a party. In each case the third party is different. The first refers to the carrier who is a third party to the contract between the stevedore and the shipper. The second refers to the stevedore who is a third party to the contract between the shipper and the carrier.

by Lord Wilberforce in the preceding sentence suggests a different and independent justification for the stevedores receiving the benefit of the exemption clause. It seems that there was a collateral and unilateral contract between the stevedores and the shipper under which the former was to be exempted from liability for all damage to the latter's goods in exchange for assisting in the transport of those goods. It was collateral because it ran beside the main carriage and stevedoring contracts; it was unilateral[112] because it involved the exchange of a promise (effectively I will not hold you liable for damage to my goods) for an act (unloading the goods). Under this analysis the exemption from liability which the stevedores sought to enforce against the shipper was then a term of a contract to which the stevedore was a party. In short, Lord Wilberforce's explanation of how the fourth requirement of agency was established provides a different and self-supporting exception to the privity rule.

It is apparent from Lord Wilberforce's judgment that he was keen to extend the benefit of the exclusion clause to everybody named in it whatever the technical requirements of privity might seem to demand. Indeed, he might fairly be accused of over-enthusiasm as he provided two different justifications for this result. It may not be intuitively obvious why a negligent stevedore should not be answerable for his actions even where the shipper has promised that he will be free from liability.[113] As with many commercial disputes, the true effects of legal liability must take account of the existence of undisclosed but ever present insurance. Also, as with many commercial disputes, the aim of the court is commercial convenience rather than justice.[114] Consider the situation if there is doubt about the effectiveness of a Himalaya clause. It would then be necessary for the goods owner to insure the goods against damage (in case the clause is effective). It would also be necessary for the stevedore to insure the goods (in case the clause is not effective). However, the cost of the stevedore's insurance would be passed on to the carrier as part of the charge for his stevedoring services. This would then be passed on to the goods owner as an undifferentiated part of the charge for the carriage services.[115] The goods owner then pays twice for the insurance of his goods, once directly and again indirectly. We can, therefore, justify the counter-intuitive proposition that exclusion clauses should simply be given their stated effect. To refuse to enforce them is against the long-term interests of the very people such a rule might at first be thought to protect.

---

112 Though the agreement might now be regarded as 'bilateral' with the consequence that the stevedore would be liable to the shipper if the stevedore refused to unload the goods. See *The Mahkutai* [1996] AC 650 at 664.

113 Fullagar J was perhaps acting on this intuition when he condemned 'a curious, and seemingly irresistible, anxiety to save grossly negligent people from the normal consequences of their negligence': *Wilson v Darling Island Stevedoring and Lighterage Co Ltd* [1956] 1 Lloyd's Rep 346 at 357, whose remarks were approved by Viscount Simonds in *Scruttons v Midland Silicones* [1962] AC 446 at 472.

114 An amusing attempt to disguise one as the other occurred when a barrister described his client to Lord Denning as 'a God-fearing limited liability company'.

115 In *The Eurymedon* Lord Wilberforce suggests that the effectiveness of such clauses is 'assumed' in the rates of freight set by carriers.

Subsequent cases have endorsed the pragmatic nature of the decision in *The Eurymedon*. Despite that case's reliance upon basic principles of contract and agency, the courts have discouraged:[116]

> ... a search for fine distinctions which would diminish the general applicability, in the light of established commercial practice, of the principle.

Unfortunately for law lecturers, this approach renders redundant a discussion of unusual hypothetical scenarios where the application of the traditional principles of offer and acceptance might defeat the intention of the parties to the bill of lading. One favourite is where goods belonging to shipper A are handled negligently and so fall and damage goods belonging to shipper B. A strict application of the unilateral contract analysis proffered in *The Eurymedon* would not extend to the stevedore the benefit of an exemption clause contained in the contract of carriage between shipper B and the carrier. This is because a unilateral offer is not accepted until the act stipulated as acceptance is complete.[117] In the hypothetical, if the stipulated act is the unloading of shipper B's goods, this has not even begun when B's goods are damaged. Indeed, in *The Mahkutai*[118] Lord Goff suggested that the principle of *The Eurymedon* may soon be regarded as so detached from its roots in the general principles of contract formation and agency that it will soon be regarded as 'a fully fledged exception to the doctrine of privity of contract' thereby 'escaping all the technicalities with which Courts are now faced in English law'.[119]

Assignment

The benefit of a contract may be transferred to a third party. Such a transfer is called an assignment and the transferor and recipient are respectively known as the assignor and assignee. Assignment may be effected without the consent of the promisor.[120] However, there are several limits upon the availability and effect of assignment. It is not possible to assign contracts of a personal nature, so a boxing promoter cannot assign the benefit of promotion and management contracts,[121] nor is it possible to assign a contract which is expressed to be non-assignable. In *Linden Gardens Trust Ltd*

---

[116] *The New York Star* [1981] 1 WLR 138 at 144.

[117] See generally Chapter 3. That the offer is not usually revocable once performance of the stipulated act has begun is irrelevant.

[118] [1996] 2 Lloyd's Rep 1 at 8.

[119] *The Suleyman Stalskiy* [1976] 2 Lloyd's Rep 609 (stevedore not protected because there was an insufficient connection between carrier and stevedore to regard the latter as the former's agent) was an early case which did not escape.

[120] Neither is it strictly necessary to give notice of the assignment to the promisee. However, for a number of reasons (e.g. prior to the notice the debtor could be discharged from the debt by the assignor) it is prudent to give notice.

[121] *Don King Productions Inc v Warren* [1998] 2 Lloyd's Rep 176 at 194 *per* Lightman J, affirmed [1999] 2 All ER 218. However, the parties to such a contract could create a trust for the benefit of third parties and this would not be precluded by a contractual provision preventing assignment.

[122] [1993] 3 All ER 417.

v *Lenesta Sludge Disposals Ltd*[122] actions were brought by the assignees of the benefit of standard form building contracts. The House of Lords held that these assignments were ineffective because there was a contractual prohibition on assignment in the standard form and that the prohibition was not itself void for being against public policy.[123] The right to sue for damages to be assessed by the court for breach of contract cannot be assigned unless the assignee has a genuine or substantial interest in the outcome.[124] An assignee is said to 'take subject to equities' meaning any defences available to the promisor and any defects in the rights assigned. In common parlance the assignor can 'only give what he has'.

The Law Commission was obviously influenced by the analogy of assignment when considering the reform of the privity doctrine. At a level of policy the Commission found it to be a persuasive argument for reform that if an immediate assignment is valid, what objection can there be to allowing a third party right of enforcement without an assignment. At the level of detail, the provisions which limit the third-party right by reference to the defences, set-offs and counter-claims available to the promisor mirror the 'taking subject to equities' principle of assignment.[125]

The law of tort

The law of tort may indirectly permit a third party to a contract to effectively obtain the benefit of a contract to which he is not a party. Where that benefit is a positive obligation this is achieved by permitting the third party to bring an action in the tort of negligence for the recovery of an economic loss. In *White* v *Jones*[126] a negligent solicitor failed to give prompt effect to his client's instruction to reinstate two gifts under his will in favour of his daughters with whom he had 'fallen out' and subsequently 'made up'. When the solicitor's client died before an amended will was executed the daughters failed to receive legacies as the testator intended. The disappointed beneficiaries were not parties to the contract under which the solicitor undertook to draft a will giving prompt effect to the testator's instructions. However, the daughters were able to effectively enforce that obligation against the solicitor when they successfully sued him in the tort of negligence. That the tort action was effectively enforcing a contract for the benefit of a third party is emphasised by two features of the case which are

---

[123] An assignment of wages which would deprive the employee of his only means of support is against public policy and so void *King* v *Michael Faraday & Partners Ltd* [1939] 2 KB 753 as is the proceeds of matrimonial proceedings *Watkins* v *Watkins* [1896] P 222.

[124] *Martell* v *Consett Iron Co Ltd* [1955] Ch 363. If the benefit of a contract is assigned before it is breached (e.g. to perform a service) the assignee can later recover damages if the service is sub-standard. Similarly, liquidated (fixed) claims (e.g. for unpaid rent) can be assigned even if the debtor disputes liability *Camdex International Ltd* v *Bank of Zambia* [1996] 3 All ER 431. There is a thriving industry based upon the assignability of such debts which are 'purchased' at a discount to their full value by concerns who with varying degrees of legality 'enforce' them against the debtor.

[125] See para 2.17.

[126] [1995] 2 WLR 187.

unusual for an action in the tort of negligence but which would not be so if the action was one for breach of contract. First, the loss suffered by the claimants was pure economic loss. Such losses are often contrasted with physical damage to property or the person. Economic loss is what is typically but not exclusively claimed in an action for breach of contract.[127] Physical damage is, typically but not exclusively, claimed in an action in the tort of negligence.[128] Second, the damages paid to the two daughters represented the value of the lost gifts. Damages in the tort of negligence usually, but not always, seek to restore the claimant to the position he was in before the tort occurred. Damages for breach of contract, usually but not always, seek to put the claimant – as did the award in *White* v *Jones* – in the position he would have been in if the promise broken had been kept.

In *White* v *Jones* Lord Goff emphasised the exceptional nature of the case before him:[129]

> In the forefront stands the extraordinary fact that, if such a duty is not recognised, the only persons who might have a valid claim (i.e. the testator and his estate) have suffered no loss, and the only person who has suffered a loss (i.e. the disappointed beneficiary) has no claim.

Lord Goff thought that the best way to do 'practical justice'[130] would be to grant the disappointed beneficiaries a remedy in the tort of negligence on the basis that 'the assumption of responsibility by the solicitor towards his client should be held in law to extend to the intended beneficiary'.[131] Lord Browne-Wilkinson said that when the solicitor undertook to give effect to the testator's intentions he thereby assumed responsibility for a 'task' which if performed negligently would adversely affect identified third parties.[132] The approach[133] of Lord Browne-Wilkinson may be regarded as a broader one but is none the less restricted by the requirement of an assumption of responsibility for the task and so is much more limited than that taken in previous cases[134] to impose liability upon negligent drafters of wills.[135]

Although this 'exception' to the doctrine of privity is narrow in application, it will continue to be of importance. It is narrow because it is only in exceptional circumstances that damages for pure economic loss can be

---

[127] Personal injury may but does not typically result from a breach of contract, e.g. one to service the brakes on a car.

[128] *D & F Estates Ltd* v *Church Commissioners* [1989] AC 177 and *Murphy* v *Brentwood DC* [1991] 1 AC 398.

[129] [1995] 2 WLR 187 at 199.

[130] At p. 198.

[131] At pp. 206–7.

[132] At p. 212.

[133] Lord Nolan, the third member of the majority, agreed with both Lords Goff and Browne-Wilkinson.

[134] *Ross* v *Caunters* [1980] Ch 297 where liability was imposed upon the ordinary principles of negligence applicable to the recovery of damages, e.g. for personal injury in road accidents.

[135] *White* v *Jones* has been applied beyond the drafting of wills. In *Carr-Glynn* v *Frearsons* [1998] 4 All ER 225 a solicitor was found liable under the principle when she failed to advise her client to sever a joint tenancy to avoid the client's share in the property passing on her death to the surviving tenant.

recovered in an action in the tort of negligence. However, it will continue to be of importance because the new statutory right of action will not extend to cover disappointed beneficiaries such as the claimants in *White* v *Jones*.

The tort of negligence may also provide a way for third parties to indirectly claim the benefit of an exemption clause. In *Norwich City Council* v *Harvey and Others*[136] where the claimant employed contractors to extend a swimming pool. The contract allocated the risk of fire damage to the employer and required him to maintain adequate insurance. Work on the roof was sub-contracted under a contract which said that the provisions of the main contract regarding fire damage should apply. An employee of the sub-contractor started a fire. The employer's action[137] in the tort of negligence against the sub-contractor and his employee failed. The duty of care owed to the employer by the sub-contractor and his employee was qualified by the exemption from liability in the main contract which was 'the clear basis upon which all the parties contracted'.[138] This technique of limiting the duty of care owed by the third party to the claimant in a way which reflects any clear assumption of risk by the claimant provides an effective mechanism for avoiding the doctrine of privity and giving the intended effect to exemption clauses expressed to extend to third parties. It would also avoid the technical problems associated with the solutions proposed in *The Eurymedon*.

ACTION BY THE PROMISEE

If the promisee is prepared to bring an action the third party may be able to effectively secure the benefit of a clause in the contract to which he is not a party. There are three different remedies which the promisee might seek.

Specific performance

Specific performance is an order of the court that the promisor shall do the very thing he undertook to do.[139] If such an order is made and complied with, the third party will receive the benefit of a contract to which he was not a party. If such an order is made but not complied with, the rules of civil procedure permit the third party to enforce it. The decision of the House of

---

[136] [1989] 1 WLR 828.
[137] If, as the contract required, the employer had taken out a policy of insurance under which the employer claimed, the action would in fact be that of the insurance company. Where an insurer has paid a claim under a policy of insurance he may exercise any right of action of the assured against whoever caused the injury or loss for which the insurer paid out under the policy. The insurer is said to be 'subrogated' to the rights of the insured. As the subrogation claim is brought in the name of the insured it is not apparent who is really bringing the action.
[138] At p. 837. A similar conclusion was reached *obiter dicta* in *Pacific Associates Inc* v *Baxter* [1990] 1 QB 993.
[139] Where the promisor has undertaken to pay a sum of money, the equivalent remedy is an action in debt. See generally Chapter 16.
[140] [1968] AC 58.

Lords in *Beswick* v *Beswick*[140] is an example of the use of specific performance to avoid the injustice that a strict application of the privity rule would otherwise cause. The House of Lords granted specific performance to the promisee (Mr Beswick deceased, represented by his administratrix, Mrs Beswick) against his nephew who had *inter alia* promised that after Mr Beswick's death he would pay a pension to his widow.

The facts of this case also illustrate the limitations of the remedy as a 'way round' the doctrine of privity. First, specific performance is regarded as an exceptional remedy, damages being the 'usual' remedy for a breach of contract. The availability of specific performance is restricted by a number of rules the most important of which is that it is not available where damages would be an adequate remedy. On the facts of *Beswick* the majority of the House of Lords[141] held that the promisee would only be entitled to nominal damages because he had suffered no loss as a result of the promisor's breach of contract. In addition, specific performance will not be granted where the service promised is of a personal nature and where the court's order would require constant supervision by the court. Indeed, after a period during which the grip of these restrictive rules was gradually relaxed by the courts, the latest House of Lord's decision[142] has reasserted the vitality of the latter restriction, which may be taken to signal a return to a strict application of the other restrictions.

Second, the third party may experience difficulty persuading the promisee to seek the remedy on his behalf. On the exceptional facts of *Beswick*, this was not a problem because the promisee (Mrs Beswick as administratrix) and the third party (Mrs Beswick in her personal capacity) were housed in the same physical body! Other cases can be envisaged where the promisee might be willing to seek the remedy for the benefit of the third party perhaps because they are associated companies but such altruism in the face of possibly substantial legal costs[143] is not the norm in commercial or social dealings.

Stay of action

A third party may effectively obtain the benefit of a negative promise (such as an undertaking not to sue the third party) in a contract to which he is not a party if the promisee is able to obtain a stay of action. A stay of action is a court order stopping proceedings brought by the promisor which he has promised not to bring. The stay of action can be given permanent effect if the court is further prepared to dismiss the action once and for all.[144] The stay of action is therefore similar to an order of specific performance. Both

---

[141] Lord Pearce thought otherwise though he acknowledged at p. 88 that damages would be a 'less appropriate' remedy; damages would be an award of a lump sum to compensate for the loss of a periodic payment.

[142] *Co-operative Insurance Society Ltd* v *Argyll Stores (Holdings) Ltd* [1998] AC 1.

[143] Perhaps the promisee would ask the third party to indemnify him.

[144] As in *Snelling* v *John G Snelling Ltd* [1973] QB 87.

are orders of the court directing promisors to do the very thing they have undertaken to do. Specific performance enforces positive undertakings and the stay of action gives effect to certain negative undertakings.[145]

In *Gore* v *Van der Lann*[146] Mrs Gore was injured while travelling on a bus operated by Liverpool Corporation. The accident was caused by the negligence of the bus conductor. Mrs Gore travelled with a free bus pass issued by Liverpool Corporation which exempted the corporation and its employees from liability for injury. Mrs Gore brought an action in the tort of negligence against Van der Lann, the conductor, personally.[147] The Corporation applied for a stay of this action. The application failed because of a statutory provision invalidating the exclusion of liability for injury to passengers carried in public service vehicles.[148] The Court of Appeal distinguished an earlier decision[149] which held that such a pass constituted a licence rather than a contract and so was not subject to a predecessor of the statutory provision applied in *Gore*. The Court of Appeal went on to consider, *obiter*, what the position would have been if the exemption had not been rendered void by statute. For A to be entitled to a stay of action in respect of B's promise to A not to sue C, it was said to be necessary to satisfy two preconditions: B has expressly promised A not to sue C, and A has a sufficient legal interest in the enforcement of that promise.

The first requirement was given an excessively narrow interpretation in *Gore* where Willmer and Salmon LJJ said that an exemption from liability was not sufficient. It is suggested that there is no substantive difference between a promise by A to B not to sue C and a promise by A to B to exempt C from liability. To hold otherwise is to have excessive regard to the form rather than the substance of the promise. This more liberal approach has been supported in subsequent cases such as *Snelling* v *John G Snelling Ltd*.[150] Three brothers, owed money by the company of which they were directors, agreed that if any of them resigned the money owing would be forfeit. One brother resigned and sued the company for the debt. The company was a third party to the brothers' agreement. Ormrod J was prepared to grant the two other brothers a stay of action which he made

---

145 Negative undertakings other than promises not to sue third parties are enforced by the grant of an injunction.

146 [1967] 2 QB 31. See Davies, 'Mrs Gore's Legacy to Commerce' (1981) 1 LS 287.

147 She was presumably inhibited from suing the corporation (which is vicariously responsible for torts committed by its employees in the course of their employment) by the exemption clause contained in her application for a free pass. In view of the decision of the Court of Appeal on the applicability of Road Traffic Act 1960, her reticence was not justified.

148 Road Traffic Act 1960, s 151. See now Public Passenger Vehicles Act 1981, s 29.

149 *Wilkie* v *London Passenger Transport Board* (1946) 62 TLR 327 on the unconvincing ground that Wilkie was an employee and the pass was issued as a privilege of employment. The fact that Wilkie had an undisputed contract with the defendant (his contract of employment) should make it more, not less, likely that a benefit given to him by the defendant was conferred as a matter of contractual right.

150 [1973] QB 87.

permanent by dismissing the action. The agreement to forfeit the debt was not in the form of a promise not to sue the company but it amounted to the same.[151]

The requirement of a sufficient legal interest is less obvious. The idea appears to be that the promisee will have a sufficient legal interest if the promisor's breach of promise would expose the promisee to a legal liability to reimburse the third party for any sums recovered from him by the promisor. This would be satisfied if in *Gore* it was a term of Van der Lann's contract of employment that his employer would indemnify him against any damages he became liable to pay while acting as a conductor. This example will also make clear the underlying rationale of the stay of action. Consider the consequences if there was no doctrine of a stay of action and Mrs Gore's undertaking did not violate any statutory prohibition. Mrs Gore would recover substantial damages from Van der Lann. He would then enforce his indemnity against Liverpool Corporation. Liverpool Corporation would then sue Mrs Gore for the breach of her promise not to sue Van der Lann and would quantify its loss as the amount it had to pay him under the indemnity. To permit such litigation is futile and wasteful. Ignoring the legal and emotional cost of the litigation nobody would benefit; each party's bank balance would end up exactly where it began. When legal costs are considered, the only parties to benefit from such circular litigation are the lawyers. Therefore, the courts take the very sensible step of permitting the promisee to have the first action by the promisor against the third party stayed if the promisee can show that the promisor expressly or impliedly promised not to sue the third party and that he (the promisee) had a sufficient legal interest in the enforcement of that promise. It can be seen that the two requirements effectively describe the two actions which would result in the circular litigation which the grant of a stay of action avoids.

This explanation given of the policy which justifies the grant of a stay of action would suggest that the requirement of a sufficient legal interest should be satisfied by an obligation to indemnify the third party which is practically, if not legally, compelling. Consider the example above based on the *Gore* case where the agreement to indemnify Van der Lann is contained in a collective agreement with his trade union rather than his employment contract. Even though the collective agreement was expressed to be 'binding in honour only', it may be more effective in 'persuading' the corporation to indemnify its employee than a contractually binding term in his contract of employment. In other words the corporation may be more moved by the ultimate threat of collective industrial action than it would be by an

---

[151] See also *European Asian Bank v Punjab and Sind Bank* [1982] 2 Lloyd's Rep 356 at 369 *per* Ackner LJ (express or *implied* promise not to sue sufficient) and *Deepak v ICI* [1998] 2 Lloyd's Rep 139 at 165 *per* Rix J: '... a promise to hold harmless ... is wholly incompatible with a right to sue'.

individual threat of legal action. However, in *Gore* all three members of the Court of Appeal were of the view that a legal obligation must be proved.[152] Again, it seems that the strict approach in *Gore* may have been relaxed in subsequent cases. For example, in *Snelling v John G Snelling*[153] what was the sufficient interest which the remaining directors had in the enforcement of the promise made by the resigning director? Breach of that promise would not expose them to any legal obligation to make good to the company the debt it paid to the parting director. However, as a small family business, its members may feel a morally binding but not legally enforceable obligation to do so. The test formulated by Ackner J in *The Elbe Maru*[154] that the applicant for a stay of action must show a real possibility of prejudice if the action is not stayed would seem to be a preferable one.

Damages

It is often thought to be a first principle of contract law that the promisee is only entitled to damages in respect of his own loss and not that of a third party. Like most first principles this is more frequently acted upon than stated and is subject to a number of exceptions. It also begs the question as to how a promisee's loss is defined.[155] These exceptions and the proper definition of loss are explored in the rest of this section.[156]

In *Jackson v Horizon Holidays*[157] the claimant contracted with the defendants to provide a family holiday. The holiday proved to be sub-standard and the claimant recovered damages greater than he would have received if the holiday had only been booked for himself. Was the first principle stated above violated? Lord Denning's judgment was characteristically bold. He simply saw no reason why in certain contracts the contracting party should not recover damages in respect of a third party's loss. The examples he used, a host taking his friends to dinner and the vicar booking a coach outing for the church choir, like the facts of *Jackson* itself, suggest informal situations where it is usual for one party to contract on behalf of others. The case of *Jackson*, in particular the approach of Lord Denning, was scrutinised by the House of Lords in *Woodar Investment*

---

152 'It has not been shown that there was any contract between the corporation and the defendant rendering the corporation liable in law to indemnify the defendant ...', *per* Willmer LJ. 'There is no ... contract between the corporation and the defendant making the corporation liable for the torts of the latter ...', *per* Harman LJ; and '... the corporation would have had to establish that ... [it] would in law be obliged to indemnify its servant ...', *per* Salmon LJ.

153 [1972] 2 WLR 588.

154 [1978] 1 Lloyd's Rep 206 at 210. *Contra: The Chevalier Rose* [1983] 2 Lloyd's Rep 438 at 443 where Parker J questions whether this test is stringent enough. See also *Deepak v ICI* [1998] 2 Lloyd's Rep 139 at 166 *per* Rix J supporting a more liberal approach.

155 See generally McKendrick, 'Breach of Contract and the Meaning of Loss' [1999] 52 CLP 37.

156 See also below.

157 [1975] 1 WLR 1468.

158 [1980] 1 WLR 277.

Development Ltd v *Wimpey Construction UK Ltd*.[158] The House of Lords held[159] that if the purchaser of land's failure to complete the transaction had been a breach of contract, the vendor would not be entitled to damages in respect of part of the unpaid purchase price which, under the terms of the contract, was payable to a third party. Their Lordships disapproved of the broad principle stated by Lord Denning but added that the result in *Jackson* was supportable on one of two grounds: either the claimant recovered for his own losses throughout (he recovered more than he would have recovered if he had contracted for a holiday for himself only because his own disappointment was increased at witnessing the disappointment of his family); or, more tentatively, it was suggested there might be certain types of contract such as ordering meals in restaurants, family holidays or ordering taxis for a group which call for special treatment. On this approach, Lord Denning's illustrations of what he may have perceived as a wider principle become restricted categories in which that principle may operate. However, the House of Lord's decision does at least give these applications of the principle a greater legitimacy.[160]

An exception to the rule that a promisee may not bring an action to recover damages for a third party was established in *Dunlop* v *Lambert*.[161] It has been authoritatively summarised in this way:[162]

> the consignor may recover substantial damages against the shipowner if there is privity of contract between him and the carrier ... although, if the goods are not his property or at his risk, he will be accountable to the true owner for the proceeds of his judgment.

The case seeks to solve the problem of the separation of the right of action (possessed by the consignor) and the property interest (possessed by the consignee) in favour of the former. The rule fell into desuetude after the Bills of Lading Act 1855 solved the problem in favour of the consignee who by s 1 had transferred to him 'all rights of suit' contained in the contract of carriage when property in the goods passed to him by endorsement of the bill of lading.[163]

The *Dunlop* exception was given new life by a novel application or

---

[159] By a majority their Lordships held that the purchaser was not in fact in breach of contract because he honestly but erroneously thought that he was exercising an express right to cancel the contract.

[160] Lord Denning had relied upon a *dictum* in *Lloyd's* v *Harper* (1880) 16 Ch D 290 at 291: '... where a contract is made with A for the benefit of B, A can sue on the contract for the benefit of B and recover all that B could have recovered ...'. However, Lush LJ was almost certainly considering one of the recognised exceptions such as the trust where it has always been accepted that the trustee can bring an action to recover substantial damages on behalf of the trustee. See above.

[161] (1839) 6 Cl & F 600.

[162] *The Albazero* [1977] AC 774 at 844 *per* Lord Diplock.

[163] See now Carriage of Goods By Sea Act 1992 which repealed the Bills of Lading Act 1855, s 1, and was introduced to remove technical anomalies in the operation of the 1855 Act and specifically to deal with problems posed by cargoes shipped in bulk. See generally Wilson (1993) *The Carriage of Goods by Sea*. 2nd edn, pp. 148–58.

[164] [1994] 1 AC 185. See the discussion in Law Commission Report, No. 242 (1996) at pp. 26–9.

extension in *Linden Gardens Trust Co Ltd* v *Lenesta Sludge Disposals Ltd*.[164] In this case a company was in breach of a contract it entered with the owner of a building for the removal of asbestos. The complicating factor was that the building had already been sold by the time the company breached its contract. The House of Lords held that the original owner of the building was entitled to substantial damages even though he was no longer the owner of the property and the cost of remedial work had been borne by the subsequent owner.[165] The majority[166] adopted the explanation of the *Dunlop* exception given by Lord Diplock in *The Albazero* that:[167]

> ... in a commercial contract concerning goods where it is in the contemplation of the parties that the proprietary interests in the goods may be transferred from one owner to another after the contract has been entered into and before the breach which causes loss or damage to the goods, an original party to the contract, if such be the intention of them both, is to be treated in law as having entered into the contract for the benefit of all persons who have or may acquire an interest in the goods before they are lost or damaged, and is entitled to recover by way of damages for breach of contract the actual loss sustained by those for whose benefit the contract is entered into.

Lord Browne-Wilkinson concluded that the company and the original building owner entered the contract in the knowledge that the building would be occupied and possibly purchased by third parties.[168] In addition, the prohibition on assignment (which prevented the subsequent owner from obtaining rights of action against the company) convinced him that it must have been the parties' intention that the original building owner should 'be entitled to enforce contractual rights for the benefit of those who suffered from defective performance'.[169] The only extension of the *Dunlop* exception that was required to apply it to the facts of *Linden Gardens* was to cover the transfer of rights in real property but it was suggested that it would not apply '[i]f the ultimate purchaser is given a direct cause of action against the contractor ...'.[170] This was confirmed by the majority of the House of Lords in *Alfred McAlpine Construction Ltd* v *Panatown Ltd*. A company employed a contractor to build an office block on land owned (for tax reasons) by an associate company. The employing company was not entitled to substantial damages in respect of the deficient building works because the damage was suffered by the associate company, which had a direct right of action against the contractor under a duty of care deed.

---

[165] To whom the original owner had made an invalid assignment of the contract with the company.

[166] Lord Browne-Wilkinson, with Lords Ackner, Bridge and Keith agreeing.

[167] At p. 847e–f. *Cf. Alfred McAlpine Construction Ltd* v *Panatown Ltd* [2000] 3 WLR 946 *per* Lord Clyde.

[168] Interestingly at p. 437e–f Lord Browne-Wilkinson suggests that the possibility that a large development might need to be sold before completion was something which was more likely, and so more foreseeable, at times of recession in the property market than in a more buoyant economic climate.

[169] At p. 437b–c.

[170] At p. 437g, *per* Lord Browne-Wilkinson.

[171] Lords Ackner and Bridge appeared to have some sympathy with his approach. In *Darlington*

Lord Griffiths'[171] approach was very different. In his opinion, the promisee had 'suffered loss because he did not receive the bargain for which he contracted'[172] and so was entitled to 'the cost of securing the performance of that bargain'.[173] However, he limited his principle in two respects. First, it was stated only to apply to contracts for 'work, labour and the supply of material'.[174] Second, it was dependent on the court being satisfied 'that the repairs have been or are likely to be carried out'.[175]

In *Darlington Borough Council* v *Wiltshier Northern Ltd*[176] a local authority wanted to build a recreation centre on land it owned. In order to circumvent government restrictions on local-authority borrowing, a bank contracted with a builder for the work. A separate agreement was entered between the bank and the local authority under which the bank agreed to pay the builder sums due under the building contract which the local authority would reimburse to the bank. In addition, this agreement provided that the bank was not liable for the building works but would upon request assign to the local authority any rights against the builder. The local authority alleged that the building work was defective and the Court of Appeal had to consider whether the local authority could recover substantial damages, which in turn depended upon whether the bank, which had assigned to the local authority its rights under the building contract, was entitled to such damages.

The facts of the *Darlington* case differed from those of *Linden Gardens* in one significant respect. In *Darlington* the promisee (the bank) *never* had a proprietary interest in the land; in *Linden Gardens* (and *Dunlop*) the promisee (respectively the original owner of the building and the consignor of the goods) had transferred ownership before the breach. The Court of Appeal thought that the principle should be extended to cover all cases where it is:[177]

> contemplated by the parties that a third party *was*, or would become, owner of the property and that owner has no direct right to sue for breach of contract. (emphasis added)

THE SECOND RULE: CONTRACTS CANNOT IMPOSE OBLIGATIONS UPON STRANGERS

The second aspect of the doctrine of privity of contract is that a third party to a contract should not be subject to burdens by it. It is certainly intuitively obvious that A and B should not by the mere act of contracting be able to

Borough Council v *Wiltshier Northern Ltd* [1995] 3 All ER 895 at 908a Steyn LJ said that he was in agreement with the wider principle propounded by Lord Griffiths, subject to a qualification considered below. See also the dissenting judgment of Lords Goff and Millett in *Panatown* above.

[172] At p. 422a.
[173] *Ibid.*
[174] At p. 421h.
[175] At p. 422g. In *Darlington Borough Council* v *Wiltshier Northern Ltd* [1995] 3 All ER 895 Steyn LJ disagreed with this restriction, as did Lords Goff and Millett in their dissenting judgments in *Panatown*.
[176] [1995] 3 All ER 895.
[177] Law Commission Report, 242 (1996) p. 28.

oblige C to do anything. For this reason the Contract (Rights of Third Parties) Act 1999, following the Law Commission's proposals, does not affect this aspect of the doctrine. None the less, the rule that a contract cannot impose obligations on third parties is not an absolute one and the following exceptions are well recognised.

Land law

According to the rule in *Tulk* v *Moxhay*,[178] third parties are bound by restrictive covenants affecting land. This rule now applies where the claimant owns land capable of being affected by the covenant. If I sell half of my garden to a builder, I might insert into the contract of sale an undertaking that the land cannot be used for industrial purposes. According to the rule in *Tulk* v *Moxhay*, the restrictive covenant will bind not only the builder but also anyone to whom he sells the plot of land.

The possibility of applying the *Tulk* v *Moxhay* principle to promises other than restrictive covenants affecting land was raised by the decision of the Privy Council in *Lord Strathcona Steamship Co Ltd* v *Dominion Coal Co Ltd*.[179] In this case it was held that a time charter agreed between a charterer and a shipowner also bound a purchaser of the vessel who bought with notice of the prior charter. In a subsequent case[180] Diplock J refused to follow the *Strathcona* decision on the basis that it was wrongly decided because the analogy of land law was inexact and undesirable. It was inexact because the land law principle would only apply where land was divided and undesirable because it might apply when the purchaser has only constructive as opposed to actual notice of the prior contract. Alternatively, Diplock J was prepared to distinguish the case on the basis that the buyer of the ship in *Port Line*, unlike the buyer in *Strathcona*, knew that the ship was under charter but did not know the details of the charter.

The tort of interference with contractual rights

A third party commits a tort if, without legal justification, he interferes intentionally or recklessly with a contract. This is known as an economic tort and would be committed by a trade union which persuaded its members, in breach of their contracts of employment, to take industrial action. Trade

---

178 (1848) 2 Ph 774 (claimant who owned plots in Leicester Square, London sold the garden in the middle to the appropriately named Elms who covenanted not to build on it. The garden was sold and resold to the defendant who was restrained by injunction when he proposed to build on it).

179 [1926] AC 108. In *De Mattos* v *Gibson* (1858) 4 De G & J 276 it had already been held that the charterer of a ship is entitled to an injunction to restrain anyone to whom the vessel is subsequently mortgaged from interfering in the performance of the charter.

180 *Port Line* v *Ben Line Steamers* [1958] 2 QB 146 (while time charter to claimants was still running shipowners sold ship and took immediate bare boat charter back from defendant purchasers – bare boat charter was to terminate if ship was requisitioned. Ship was requisitioned – claimants claimed to be entitled to compensation for requisition paid to defendants as owners.).

unions previously enjoyed extensive statutory protection from liability for the economic torts but this was dramatically reduced during the recent period of Conservative government.[181]

In *Swiss Bank Corp v Lloyds Bank Ltd*[182] Browne-Wilkinson J[183] sought to explain the result but not the reasoning of the *Strathcona* and *Port Line* cases by reference to this tort. He thought that the *Strathcona* case was rightly decided as an application of the tort of interference with contractual rights or a close analogy to it.[184] In *Strathcona* the purchaser was rightly restrained from interfering with the charter of which he was aware because to do so would amount to a tort against the charterer. However, the tort only prevents deliberate interference and so would not seem to be made out on the facts of *Port Line* where the defendant had only limited knowledge of the charter.

The application of the *Strathcona* principle in a non shipping context was considered by Hoffman J in *Law Debenture Trust Corporation v Ural Caspian Oil Corp*.[185] The case concerned the longstanding claims for compensation of four companies which traded in Russia and had their assets confiscated after the 1917 revolution. In 1986 the shares in the companies were sold to L subject to a condition that any compensation subsequently paid by the Russian government would go to the original shareholders. L sold the shares to H who in turn sold them to C. The Russian government paid compensation to the companies who failed to hand it over to the original shareholders. Hoffmann J held that one of the original shareholders had an arguable case[186] based on the novel claim that there had been an interference with *the remedies* arising out of a broken contract. His reasoning was that on existing authority[187] the claimant would have been entitled to an order against H requiring the re-transfer of the shares to L because H had induced L to breach its covenant to the claimant. The transfer of shares to C effectively deprived the claimant of this remedy and C was accountable for this loss of remedy. Hoffmann J held that the broader principle derived from the *Strathcona* case was inapplicable. It only extended to the grant of an injunction to prevent a purchaser from dealing with the property in a way that was inconsistent with the original contract. It has never been used, as the claimant sought to in this case, to enforce against a purchaser a positive

---

[181] See discussion of *The Evia Luck (No. 2)* [1992] 2 AC 152 in Chapter 12.
[182] [1979] Ch 581.
[183] The Court of Appeal and the House of Lords did not discuss the correctness of these decisions.
[184] See also *Mac-Jordan Construction Ltd v Brookmount Erostin Ltd* [1992] BCLC 350.
[185] [1993] 1 WLR 138.
[186] The issue was whether the claim disclosed a good cause of action. This was resolved in favour of the claimant on the basis that, on the ground discussed in the text, the claimant had an arguable case.
[187] *Esso Petroleum Co Ltd v Kingswood Motors (Addlestone) Ltd* [1974] 1 QB 142.
[188] The distinction between the permissible enforcement of negative covenants and the impermissible enforcement of positive obligations also arises in relation to the enforceability of negative covenants in contracts to provide services. See the discussion below where it is clear that this is a formal distinction that is easier to state than to apply.

duty to perform covenants entered into by a predecessor in title.[188] Indeed, Hoffmann J admitted that it is very difficult to state clearly what are the limits of the principle to be derived from the *Strathcona* and *Swiss Bank* cases.

Bailment

A bailment exists when one party called the bailor delivers goods to another, the bailee with the intention that the bailee should return them to the bailor or deal with them in a certain way, e.g. leaving shoes with a cobbler to be repaired or clothes at a dry cleaners. It is a principle of the law of bailment that in some circumstances the bailor is bound by the terms of any further bailment (called a sub-bailment) entered by the bailee. In *Scruttons Ltd v Midland Silicones Ltd*[189] Lord Denning relied upon this principle to limit the liability of the stevedores. Lord Denning thought that the key question raised in that case was not whether the stevedores were entitled to obtain the benefit of a clause in a contract (the bill of lading) to which they were not a party but rather whether the goods owner was subject to the burden of a clause in a contract to which he was not a party (the contract for the provision of stevedoring services) which repeated the limitation clause contained in the bill of lading. In other words, his suggestion was that the second aspect of the doctrine of privity (contracts cannot impose obligations on third parties) rather than the first (strangers cannot enforce contracts) was involved. The goods owner (bailor) bailed the goods to the carrier (bailee) who then bailed the goods (thereby becoming a sub-bailor) to the stevedore (sub-bailee). In the circumstances of the case, as an exception to the usual rule that contracts cannot impose obligations or burdens on strangers, the sub-bailee was entitled to rely on the terms of the bailment, including the limitation clause, against the bailor. Lord Denning explained that the doctrine of privity was developed at a time when general liability in the tort of negligence was not recognised. He pointed to the irony inherent in the judgments of the majority in the case. The law had swung from one extreme to another. In the past, before the development of a general tort of negligence in *Donoghue v Stevenson*,[190] a stevedore would never be liable to the goods owner because his only liability would be in contract. In the present, in the opinion of the majority, the stevedores were always liable because there was available an action against them in the tort of negligence, to which the doctrine of privity denied them any defence.

> What an irony is here! This 'fundamental principle' which was invoked 100 years ago for the purpose of holding that the agents of the carrier were 'not liable at all' is now invoked for the purpose of holding that they are inescapably liable, without the benefit of any of the conditions of carriage. How has this come about?[191]

---

[188] [1962] AC 446.
[190] [1932] AC 562.
[191] *Per* Lord Denning: *Scruttons Ltd v Midland Silicones Ltd* [1962] AC 466.

Lord Denning later applied this principle *obiter*[192] to hold that the owner of a fur coat (the bailor), who sent the coat to a furrier (the bailee and sub-bailor) to be cleaned, who then sent it to a specialist cleaner (sub-bailee), would be bound by any exemptions contained in the sub-bailment. Lord Denning explained the basis of the principle, as he had in *Scruttons*, as being founded upon the consent of the bailor. Whenever the bailor can be regarded as having expressly or impliedly consented to the terms of the sub-bailment, he is to be regarded as bound by them.

The 'consent'[193] explanation[194] of the principle of bailment on terms has been approved by the Privy Council in *The Pioneer Container*.[195] This case also suggested that this principle or something analogous to it is the true explanation for the elusive concept of 'vicarious immunity' associated with the puzzling[196] old case of *Elder Dempster & Co Ltd* v *Patterson Zochonis & Co Ltd*[197] where the House of Lords held that a shipowner was entitled to rely upon an exclusion clause in the bill of lading, despite the fact that the contract of carriage was between the shipper and a charterer.[198] The facts of *Elder Dempster* do not strictly raise the question of a bailment on terms because the goods were bailed directly to the shipowners. None the less, the Privy Council said that the result in *Elder Dempster* would have been the same if the shippers had delivered the goods to agents of the charterers (bailees and sub-bailors), who had then delivered them to the shipowner, who would then truly be a sub-bailee.

---

[192] Because the actual terms of the exemption only extended to cover goods owned by the furrier and even then would only apply to loss or damage during processing, not, as it happened, to a theft which took place before processing began.

[193] Consent in bailment must, like intention in contract, be ascertained objectively rather than subjectively.

[194] Rejecting the view of Donaldson J in *Johnson Matthey* v *Constantine Terminals Ltd* [1976] 2 Lloyd's Rep 215 at 221 that the bailor is bound by the terms of the sub-bailment even if he has not consented to them.

[195] [1994] 2 All ER 250. See also the Court of Appeal's decision in *The Captain Gregos* [1990] 2 Lloyd's Rep 395.

[196] In *Midland Silicones Ltd* v *Scruttons Ltd* [1962] AC 446 at 479 Lord Reid described trying to extract a *ratio decidendi* from *Elder Dempster* as 'unrewarding'. See also the descriptions of Donaldson J in *Johnson Matthey* v *Constantine Terminals Ltd* [1976] 2 Lloyd's Rep 215 at 219: 'something of a judicial nightmare' and Ackner LJ in *The Forum Craftsman* [1985] 1 Lloyd's Rep 291 at 295: 'heavily comatosed, if not long interred'.

[197] [1924] AC 522.

[198] This explanation of *Elder Dempster* was also apparently accepted by the House of Lords in *The Mahkutai* [1996] 2 Lloyd's Rep 1 at 6 *per* Lord Goff, delivering the opinion of the Privy Council.

PART III

THE LIFE OF THE CONTRACT

10

THE CONTENT OF THE CONTRACT: EXPRESS AND IMPLIED TERMS

A contract is comprised of terms. The terms of a contract may be classified according to their source or their remedial effect. In this chapter we are concerned with the source of contract terms. Later, in Chapter 15, we will examine in detail the classification of terms according to whether a breach of that term gives rise to a right in the innocent party to terminate the contract. At this point, a brief overview of that discussion would be useful. When terms are classified according to their remedial effect, three types of term are considered: *conditions, warranties* and *innominate terms*.

A condition is a term any breach of which gives rise to a right in the innocent party to terminate the contract, i.e. to treat his obligations as at an end. This is in addition to a claim for damages.

A warranty is a term any breach of which gives rise to a right for the innocent party to recover damages only. If the innocent party has suffered no loss, only nominal damages can be recovered.

An innominate or intermediate term is one where it cannot be said in advance what remedy will arise upon its breach. Rather it is necessary to wait and see how serious the breach is. If it is a serious breach, like the breach of a condition, it will give rise to a right in the innocent party to terminate and seek damages. If the breach is not a serious one then, like a warranty, it will only give rise to a claim for damages.

EXPRESS TERMS

The terms of a contract may be either express or implied. Express terms arise from what the parties said or wrote. In contrast, implied terms may arise from statute, custom or the common law. However, not everything said by the parties during negotiations will become a term of the contract. It is of considerable practical importance to be able to identify things said during contractual negotiations, which are incorporated into any eventual contract, and those which are not. Where an untrue statement is made which is not incorporated into the contract, it can only give rise to remedies for misrepresentation. Where such a statement is incorporated into the contract as a term, the innocent party has a choice as to whether to pursue a remedy for misrepresentation or for breach of contract.[1] There may be an advantage in pursuing one set of remedies rather than the other. If the claimant only wants financial compensation, he may prefer to sue for breach of contract

---

[1] Misrepresentation Act 1967, s 1(a).

because the usual measure of damages[2] is more generous than that applicable to a claim for misrepresentation. If the statement, though incorporated as a term, does not give rise to a right of termination (i.e. it is a warranty or an innominate term and the breach has not been a serious one), the claimant may prefer to exercise his right to rescind for misrepresentation in order to 'escape' the contract.

Term or representation?

Whether a statement made during negotiations is a term or a mere representation will depend upon the intention of the parties. However, to say this simply regresses the inquiry one stage. The question then becomes, how do the courts ascertain the intention of the parties? The courts have developed a number of 'pointers', which they use in order to ascertain the parties' presumed intention. The description as 'pointers' of the factors emphasised by the courts is important. These pointers are not rules. A rule is a statement, which, unless an exception applies, is dispositive of all circumstances falling within its stated application. A pointer is different and simply 'inclines' the court to a conclusion. If more than one pointer applies, they may support opposite conclusions about the parties' intention (i.e. one factor might suggest that the parties intended a term, another that they must have intended a representation). In such a case it would be necessary to 'weigh' the contrary indicators to consider which is/are the most compelling. The pointers used by the courts are:

Verification

When the representor tells the representee that he should verify the truth of the statement made, this indicates that the statement was intended to operate as a representation only. In *Ecay* v *Godfrey*[3] someone selling a boat assured the purchaser that the hull was sound but also advised him to get it surveyed. The assurance was held to be a representation only. This principle extends to situations where the representor does not advise verification but where it would be usual for the representee to verify what was asserted. This is why statements made by sellers of houses in response to pre-contract enquiries do not usually amount to terms of the contract.[4] In this context buyers are expected to commission a survey to verify or disprove any claims made by the seller.

Importance

The more important the thing said the more likely it was intended to operate as a term. In *Bannerman* v *White*[5] the court held that a farmer's assurance

---

[2] Such a sum as is necessary to put the claimant in the position he would have been in had the contract not been breached. It is usually called the expectation measure because, as far as award of money can, the court seeks to make good the expectations of the party in breach.
[3] (1947) 80 Lloyd's LR 286.
[4] *Green* v *Symons* (1897) 13 TLR 301.
[5] (1861) 10 CB 844.

that his hops had not been treated with sulphur was a term because the purchaser, a brewer, had made it clear that the hops were useless to him if they had been so treated. The same principle has been applied in a number of cases involving the sale of animals. In *Couchman* v *Hill*[6] a heifer for sale at auction was described in the catalogue as 'unserved'.[7] This was important to the buyer who sought and received confirmation of this from both the seller and the auctioneer. The buyer bought the animal but it soon died giving birth at too young an age. The buyer successfully sued for breach of warranty after the animal died giving birth.[8] Again, in *Schawel* v *Reade*[9] the purchaser of a horse was induced to curtail his examination of a horse by the seller's insistence that the animal was sound. When the horse proved unfit for stud purposes, the buyer successfully sued for breach of contract.

Time

The time at which the statement was made has an affect upon its status. The closer in time the making of the statement and the conclusion of the contract the more likely it is that the court will think that it was intended to be a term. Conversely, the longer the period between the making of the statement and the contract, the more likely it was intended to be a mere representation. In *Routledge* v *McKay*[10] a party who offered a motorbike for sale told a prospective purchaser that it was a 1942 model. A sale was concluded over five weeks later. This time lag was taken to indicate that the parties did not intend the statement to be a term.

The relative skill and knowledge of the parties

A famous American jurist, Karl Llewellyn,[11] once said that 'leading cases hunt in pairs'. For each case that falls within a rule, there is usually another which falls just outside it. The following are two such cases. In *Oscar Chess* v *Williams*[12] a private seller sold his car to a garage. He said it was a 1948 model and this was supported by the car's logbook. In fact it was a much earlier model and, unknown to the seller, the logbook had been forged by a previous owner. At first instance the garage succeeded in its action for breach of contract. This decision was reversed in the Court of Appeal where Lord Denning said that the county court judge had directed his mind to the wrong question. He had concerned himself with the question of whether the statement of the car's year was a condition or a warranty, i.e. what type of

---

[6] [1947] KB 554. See also *Harling* v *Eddy* [1951] 2 KB 739 (at auction sick-looking cow drew no bids until seller intervened to guarantee its condition – held to be a term).

[7] That is, not bearing a calf.

[8] The decision has been criticised because participants at an auction 'without reserve' are entitled to expect to be bidding on equal terms. In *Hopkins* v *Tanqueray* (1854) 15 CB 130 concerning the sale of a horse the court denied that a private conversation before an auction could give rise to a warranty.

[9] [1913] 2 Ir Rep 81.

[10] [1954] 1 All ER 855.

[11] Llewellyn was the driving force behind the American Uniform Commercial Code.

[12] [1957] 1 WLR 370.

term it was, when what he should have asked himself was whether it was a term at all. The garage had greater skill and knowledge in relation to the thing: '[t]hey are the experts' according to Lord Denning, whereas 'the seller had himself no personal knowledge of the year when the car was made ... He must have been relying on the registration book.' He concluded that '[i]t is unlikely that such a person would warrant the year of manufacture'.[13]

In *Dick Bentley Productions Ltd* v *Harold Smith (Motors) Ltd*[14] a dealer sold a 'well-vetted' Bentley car that he said had covered 20,000 miles. The car was in fact more well-petted than well-vetted. It was in good cosmetic condition but had covered many more miles than was claimed. Again, the dealer could be expected to have greater skill and knowledge, but in this case the dealer was the representor not the representee. This justified the conclusion that the statement was intended to be a term of the contract of sale.

This pair of cases neatly illustrate the following two propositions. When the representee has greater skill and knowledge in relation to the thing said, the statement is more likely to be a representation (*Oscar Chess*); when the representor has greater skill and knowledge in relation to the thing said, the statement is more likely to be a term (*Dick Bentley*).

In *Dick Bentley* Lord Denning put forward the principle that if a person made a statement in order to induce another to enter a contract, there was a presumption that the statement was a contractual term unless the representor is able to show that he was not at fault in making it. This proposition is contradicted rather than supported in the cases.[15] In addition, it seems to proceed on a wrong basis. Liability in the law of contract is generally considered strict, i.e. it arises independently of fault on the part of the defendant. It is suggested that Lord Denning's principle should not be followed.

It is instructive to apply these principles to the facts of *Beale* v *Taylor*[16] where a private seller sold to a private buyer a car described as a 'Herald convertible, white, 1961, twin carbs'. This was literally a half-truth. The back of the car was indeed that of a 1961 Triumph Herald but the front was not. The front that had been welded on was from an earlier car. The court held that the statement was a term. Between a buyer and seller with the same status, the seller who has had the car and its documentation in his possession must have greater skill and knowledge in relation to the identity of the car. Applying the principle of *Dick Bentley* (representor's greater skill and

---

[13] See also *Harlingdon & Leinster Enterprises Ltd* v *Christopher Hull Fine Art Ltd* [1990] 3 WLR 13 (dealer in contemporary British paintings attributed a work to a leading German impressionist and sold it to a dealer specialising in that school – attribution was not contractually binding).

[14] [1965] 1 WLR 623.

[15] For example, *Royscot Trust Ltd* v *Rogerson* [1991] 3 WLR 57 (car dealer exaggerated deposit paid by customer to obtain more advantageous credit terms for him). Would this not be a breach of contract on Lord Denning's principle?

[16] [1967] 1 WLR 1193.

knowledge – term), we can support the court's conclusion that the statement was a term.[17]

Before leaving *Oscar Chess* we should emphasise one more feature of the case. The statement was classified as a representation because of the relative skill and knowledge of the parties. This was despite the fact that the importance of the car's age and absence of a time lag between the making of the statement and the contract would suggest that the statement was intended to be a term. This would seem to suggest that the relative skill and knowledge of the parties is given more weight when in competition with the other pointers.

Parol evidence rule

When parties reduce their bargain to a written document, the parol evidence rule states that other, usually oral, evidence cannot be relied on to contradict the written document.[18] The rule is subject to many exceptions[19] when parol evidence can be relied upon such as to prove the existence of an implied term or a collateral contract. One exception appears to be wider than the rule it departs from. The parol evidence rule will not apply when the written document does not record the totality of the parties' bargain.[20] The exception describes the only circumstance when anyone would want to rely upon parol evidence. For this reason the Law Commission described the rule as 'no more than a circular statement'.[21] The Law Commission's Working Paper[22] had originally recommended the abolition of the rule. In its full report it concluded that because of the breadth of the exception just discussed, it was not meaningful to talk about a parol evidence rule at all. How can you abolish a non-existent rule? If you try to do so by legislation, someone will think that there is something to abolish. Therefore, abolition was not recommended in the full report.[23]

Collateral contract[24]

A statement which does not appear to be part of a contract or which offends, if there is such a thing, the parol evidence rule may take effect as a collateral

---

17 *Cf.* Treitel at pp. 328–9 who says the case 'is hard to reconcile' with *Oscar Chess* because both cases involved private sellers but reached opposite results (*Oscar Chess*: representation, *Beale*: term) perhaps because *Oscar Chess* was not cited in *Beale*, which might in turn be due to the fact that the seller was not legally represented. It is suggested that this analysis gives too much weight to the status of the seller. It is the *relative* skill and knowledge of the parties which is important not the *absolute* knowledge of one party.

18 *Jacobs v Batavia & General Plantations Trust Ltd* [1924] 1 Ch 287 at 295.

19 Treitel lists 13.

20 *Allen v Pink* (1838) 4 M & W 140 (oral warranty relied on despite written record of sale containing no warranty).

21 Law Commission (1980) *The Parol Evidence Rule*, No. 154, para 2.7. See also Beldam LJ's description of it in *Youell v Bland Welch & Co Ltd* [1992] 2 Lloyd's Rep 127 at 140 as 'the rule, if rule it be'.

22 No. 76, 1976.

23 *Cf.* Contract (Scotland) Act 1997 which gives statutory form to the rule (s 1(1)) and the exception discussed above (s 1(2)).

24 See generally Wedderburn (1959) Camb LJ 58.

contract. In such cases there is a main contract and a collateral or subsidiary one. In *City and Westminster Properties* v *Mudd*[25] a lessor sought to forfeit a lease because a tenant was in breach of his covenant to use the premises for business purposes only. It was held that there was an agreement collateral to the main one in which the lessor agreed to allow the tenant to live on the premises in exchange for the tenant entering the main agreement. In *Esso* v *Mardon*[26] a statement made by the oil company to the franchisee of a petrol outlet about the estimated throughput of petrol on his site was held to be part of a contract collateral to the main lease.[27]

IMPLIED TERMS

Terms which are implied into contracts derive from three sources: statute, custom and the common law.

Statute

Legislation implies terms into different classes of contract. The most important provisions are those contained in the Sale of Goods Act 1979, ss 12–15 and the Supply of Goods and Services Act 1982, s 13. The Sale of Goods Act 1979 implies terms into contracts for the sale of goods that the owner has title to the goods he is selling (s 12(1)), that the goods conform to any description given (s 13(1)), that the goods are of satisfactory quality (s 14(2)), that the goods are reasonably fit for any purpose disclosed by the buyer (s 14(3)) and that the contract goods conform to any sample supplied (s 15(2)). The Supply of Goods and Services Act 1982, s 13 implies a term into contracts for the provision of a service that the supplier will exercise reasonable care and skill. For a number of reasons, these statutory implied terms are of great practical importance. First, the implied terms as to ownership, satisfactory quality, conformity to sample and quality of service do not require the party seeking to rely on such a term to prove that anything in particular was said by himself[28] or the other party.[29] In the real world this is a very important advantage in relation to oral contracts where the first response of a seller or supplier who gave some assurance as to quality will often be to deny that he did so. It will then be very difficult for the other party to prove what was actually said. Second, breach of the statutory implied terms give rise to valuable rights. The terms implied into contracts for the sale of goods[30] are conditions simply because the statute

---

[25] [1959] Ch 129.
[26] [1976] QB 801.
[27] Collateral contracts have been used to evade the doctrine of privity of contract. For examples see Chapter 9.
[28] *Cf.* the implied term as to fitness for particular purpose.
[29] *Cf.* the implied term as to description.
[30] The implied term that the supplier of any service will exercise reasonable care and skill is an innominate term. Whether the innocent party is entitled to terminate the contract will, therefore, depend upon how serious a breach of contract has occurred. See Chapter 15.

says they are. This frees the innocent party from having to prove that the term was intended by the parties to operate as a condition[31] and entitles him or her to terminate the contract, i.e. to reject the goods.[32] Third, the Unfair Contract Terms Act 1977 makes it more difficult to exclude the terms implied into contracts for the sale of goods than it does express terms.[33]

Implied term as to title

It may be thought to be an obvious requirement that a party who is contracting to sell goods should actually own them. However, the Sale of Goods Act 1979, s 12(1) does not refer to the ownership of the seller. Rather it requires the seller to have a 'right to sell' the goods. A contract of sale from A to B can be performed by A causing a third party, C, to transfer title to B. It seems that the right referred to in s 12(1) is a power to vest property in the goods. However, this statement must be qualified by the case of *Niblett Ltd v Confectioners' Materials Co Ltd*[34] where the sellers contracted to sell a quantity of tinned milk bearing one of three brand names including 'Nissly' which infringed the claimant Nestlé's trade mark. The Court of Appeal held that although the seller had the right to sell the goods there was none the less a breach of s 12(1) because a third party (Nestlé) was entitled to cause the detention of the goods. The true proposition appears to be that the right to sell referred to in s 12(1) will be satisfied by a mere power to vest property except where a third party is able to restrain the sale.

Two further terms are implied by Sale of Goods Act, s 12 into contracts for the sale of goods. These are the implied warranties that the goods are free of undisclosed encumbrances (i.e. charges, mortgages) until property is due to pass[35] and that the buyer shall enjoy quiet possession of the goods.[36] Both are warranties and so their breach gives rise to a right to damages only. It is difficult to understand what case might fall within the first warranty that would not offend s 12(1) and so amount to a breach of condition. However, the ambit of the second warranty has given rise to concern. The seller cannot be taken to be guaranteeing the buyer against any future disturbance of his enjoyment of the goods which is unrelated to their relationship of buyer and seller. The limits of this warranty were considered in *The Playa Larga*[37] which concerned a C & F sale[38] of sugar between a Cuban state company

---

[31] See Chapter 16.

[32] See *Barber* v *NSW Bank* [1996] 1 WLR 641 for an illustration of the 'extra' proof required of a claimant who seeks to rely upon an express as opposed to an implied statutory term as to ownership.

[33] See especially s 6 and Chapter 11 below. The same cannot be said of the implied term that the supplier of any service will exercise reasonable care and skill is an innominate term.

[34] [1921] 3 KB 387.

[35] Section 12(2)(a).

[36] Section 12(2)(b).

[37] *Empresa Exportadora de Azúcar* v *Industria Azucarera Nacional SA* [1983] 2 Lloyd's Rep 171. The case also provides an interesting guide to communist writing etiquette where letters open with 'Dear Comrade' and end with 'Yours Revolutionarily'.

[38] That is, one where the buyer paid an inclusive price to cover the cost of the goods (C) as well as their transport (F – freight).

and a Chilean purchaser. Following the coup which overthrew Dr Allende's left-wing Chilean government and replaced it with General Pinochet's right-wing dictatorship, the Cuban government decided to withdraw the *Playa Larga* which had already partly discharged its cargo at Valparaiso. Ignoring the warnings of a pursuing destroyer and helicopter, the *Playa Larga* left port. It was held that there had been a breach of the implied warranty as to quiet possession even as regards the part of the cargo that was delivered because the buyer was deprived of the opportunity to inspect the whole cargo, which might have justified the rejection of the part delivered. Although the right to quiet enjoyment does not endure indefinitely, the case establishes that it may endure after delivery until the buyer has an opportunity to inspect the goods.

Implied term as to description

The apparently simple implied term that goods sold should conform to any description given has given rise to contradictory case law. In a number of older cases the courts came close to abolishing the distinction between representations and terms by treating any words of description as a condition within s 13. Examples include *Arcos v Ronaasen*[39] where the buyers agreed to purchase a quantity of wooden staves which the sellers were aware they required for making cement barrels. The contractual specification required them to be $1/2$ an inch thick. In fact only 5 per cent conformed to this specification, though the rest were all less than $9/16$ of an inch thick and were reasonably fit for the purpose for which they were purchased. None the less, the House of Lords held that there had been a breach of s 13 on the basis that 'A ton does not mean about a ton, or a yard about a yard. Still less when you descend to minute measurements does $1/2$ inch mean about a $1/2$ inch'.[40] An even more severe example is provided by *Re Moore & Co and Landauer & Co*[41] where the seller's only deviation from the contractual specification was that tinned peaches were delivered in cases containing 24 rather than 30 tins. The buyer successfully rejected the goods on this basis even though it was clear that his real motive was to escape a 'bad' bargain.

More recently a less expansive approach to s 13 has been taken. In *Ashington Piggeries Ltd v Christopher Hill Ltd*[42] the House of Lords held that a statement of quality that did not identify an essential characteristic of the goods sold was not part of the description of the goods within s 13. In *The Dianna Prosperity*[43] the House of Lords was confronted with a similar

---

[39] [1933] AC 470.
[40] At p. 479. Even Lord Atkin would disregard 'microscopic' variations.
[41] [1921] 2 KB 519.
[42] [1972] AC 441 (consignment of mink food was made with herring meal obtained from a third party which contained a substance poisonous to mink). The main issues in the case concerned the quality of the mink food supplied under the contract between the seller and buyer. The issue of description arose in relation to the contract between the seller and the third party who agreed to provide herring meal of 'fair average quality'. Seller unsuccessfully claimed that these were words of description within s 13.
[43] *Reardon Smith Line Ltd v Yngvar Hansen-Tangen* [1976] 1 WLR 989.

problem in relation to time charters of a ship. A number of charters were arranged for a vessel which was still under construction. However, market movements made these contracts unattractive to charterers who sought to escape from them. In the charters the vessel was described by its yard and number as Osaka 354. In fact the ship was too large to be constructed at the Osaka yard and so was built at the Oshima yard where it was ship no. 4. The charterers pressed an analogy with the old strict cases on s 13 and claimed that they were entitled to terminate the charters because of the builders' failure to construct a vessel which corresponded to the contractual description. This opportunistic ploy was rejected by the House of Lords which described some of the old cases as 'excessively technical'.[44] Words of description will only fall within s 13 or outside that section operate as a condition if they constitute 'a substantial ingredient of the "identity" of the thing sold'.[45] However, it was emphasised that the old approach may be appropriate where the contract is one for the sale of 'unascertained future goods (e.g. commodities) as to which each detail of the description must be assumed to be vital ...'.[46]

For a contract to be a sale by description within s 13, it is necessary for the buyer to rely upon the description given. In *Harlington and Leinster Enterprises Ltd* v *Christopher Hull Fine Art Ltd*[47] a painting attributed to a German expressionist painter called Munter, which later turned out to be a forgery, was sold by one dealer to another. The seller was not a specialist in that school of painting but the buyer was. The majority of the Court of Appeal held that the sale was not one *by* description because the buyer had relied upon his own examination of the painting.

Satisfactory quality

There is an important precondition to the implication of the term under Sale of Goods Act, s 14(2) that the goods sold are of satisfactory quality. The same precondition applies to the other term implied by that section (fitness for particular purpose) as well as the term implied by Supply of Goods and Services Act 1982, s 13 that the supplier of a service should exercise reasonable care and skill in its provision. This precondition is that the sale must have been concluded in the course of a business. Two questions are then raised. Do the seller's activities amount to a business at all? Here the Act provides an inclusive definition that extends to 'a profession and the activities of any government department ... or local or public authority'.[48] If the answer to this question is 'yes', the next one is, does the sale arise in the course of that business?. Similar words are used in a number of statutes[49] and a common definition was emerging which required some regularity or

---

[44] At p. 998 *per* Lord Wilberforce.
[45] *Ibid.*
[46] At p. 999 *per* Lord Wilberforce.
[47] [1991] 1 QB 564.
[48] Section 61(1)(b).
[49] For example, the Trade Descriptions Act 1968 and the Unfair Contract Terms Act 1977.

repetitiveness to constitute a business dealing.[50] However, this trend has properly been halted by the decision of the Court of Appeal in *Stevenson* v *Rogers*[51] where it was held that the phrase 'in the course of a business' in s 14 did not impose a requirement of regularity of dealings. On this interpretation, a fisherman who in 1988 sold a boat he had purchased five years earlier was regarded as selling it in the course of his business. This different approach may be justified by reference to a policy of consumer protection which requires the phrase 'in the course of a business' in Sale of Goods Act 1979, s 14 to be given a wider definition to ensure that a larger number of persons may rely upon the terms implied by that section.

Where there is a sale in the course of a business, the obligation to supply goods of satisfactory quality does not extend to defects specifically brought to the buyer's attention before the contract is made[52] or, if the buyer examines the goods before the contract is made, defects which that examination ought to reveal.[53] The first qualification requires the attention of the buyer to be drawn to the specific defect. This would not be satisfied where the seller simply said that the goods are 'sold as seen'. The second qualification is difficult to rationalise. It seems to put the reckless buyer who fails to examine the goods he is buying in a better position than the prudent purchaser who does examine the goods but does so in a negligent manner.[54]

The standard of 'satisfactory' quality was introduced in 1994[55] to replace the old standard of 'merchantable' quality. The old term of merchantability was thought to be outdated and ill-suited to the consumer, as opposed to the commercial, context. In fact the courts had begun to accommodate consumer interests by interpreting merchantability as importing acceptability rather than mere usability. The Law Commission had originally favoured the term 'acceptable' quality but 'satisfactory' was eventually preferred because it was thought to extend greater protection to buyers on the ground that a buyer might be said to be prepared to accept goods which he regarded as unsatisfactory.[56]

According to ss 14(2A) and 14(2B) a number of factors should be considered when determining whether the goods are of satisfactory quality. These include any description of the goods. The description may operate to increase (e.g. 'first class') or decrease ('seconds') the standard that would otherwise need to be achieved. It is also stated that courts should take

---

[50] *Davies* v *Sumner* [1984] 1 WLR 1301 (isolated sale of car by self-employed courier who misrepresented the mileage not an offence within Trade Descriptions Act 1968); *R & B Customs Brokers Ltd* v *United Dominions Trust Ltd* [1988] 1 WLR 321 (private company disposed of car bought for private and business use of one of its directors did not deal in the course of a business for purposes of the Unfair Contract Terms Act 1977, despite fact that it had done so two or three times before).

[51] [1999] 2 WLR 1064.

[52] Section 14(2C)(A).

[53] Section 14(2C)(B).

[54] See Bridge (1997) *The Sale of Goods*, pp. 314–15. It is questionable whether this paradox will, as Bridge suggests, operate to dissuade buyers from conducting examinations when a competent examination would save the buyer from entering a disastrous contract.

[55] Sale and Supply of Goods Act 1994.

[56] Another reason is that 'satisfactory' avoids confusion with acceptance as used to describe circumstances when the buyer might lose the right of rejection.

account of 'the price (if relevant)'. The introduction of 'if ...' might be meant to prevent a seller from arguing that goods offered at a 'sale price' can be of a lower quality than full price goods. Further, goods are required to be fit for all the purposes for which goods of the kind in question are commonly supplied.[57] In addition, courts may have regard to the appearance and finish of the good,[58] freedom from minor defects,[59] safety[60] and durability.

Two issues which are not specifically mentioned in s 14 are second-hand goods and the effect of warnings and instructions. However, if the goods are described as 'second-hand' and/or sold at a lower price than new goods, these factors may be taken into account. Any warnings or instructions which accompany the goods may be taken into account when considering whether the goods are of satisfactory quality.[61]

Fitness for a particular purpose

The term implied by Sale of Goods Act 1979, s 14(3) that goods should be reasonably fit for 'any particular purpose' made known to the seller will, like the term implied by s 14(2), only arise when the goods are sold in the course of a business. If the buyer wishes to fasten the seller with an obligation that the goods are reasonably fit for something other than their normal purpose the buyer must make that purpose known to the seller.[62] It is necessary that the purpose to which the buyer intends to put the goods be communicated to the seller but this need not be with great particularity.[63] If I asked a salesperson whether a dinner service was suitable for putting in a dishwasher, I would not be required to give details of its make and the programme I intended to run. Liability is strict under this section in the sense that a supplier may be liable even though he has taken all reasonable care to ensure that the goods are suitable for the purpose disclosed.[64] Although liability is strict, the standard of that liability is based on reasonableness, i.e. the goods need only be 'reasonably fit' for the purpose disclosed. On this basis the supplier of an engine for a fishing boat was not liable when components suffered extensive and premature wear as a result of some peculiarity in the boat's design which was not appreciated by the buyers and so not communicated to the sellers.[65]

---

[57] This appears to depart from the earlier authority of *Aswan Engineering Establishment Co* v *Lupdine* [1987] 1 WLR 1 where it was held that if goods had multiple purposes they were merchantable if they were fit for one of those purposes.

[58] *Rogers* v *Parish* [1987] QB 933 (sale of new and expensive car – cosmetic appearance relevant to old standard of merchantability).

[59] *Ibid.*, where other defects included the deterioration of oil seals, gearbox noise and misfiring.

[60] *Bernstein* v *Pamson Motors* [1987] 2 All ER 220 (sealant in oil channels caused extensive damage – car unsafe and so not of merchantable quality).

[61] *Wormell* v *RHM Agriculture (East) Ltd* (1987) 1 WLR 1091 (instructions on weedkiller ignored – seller not liable under s 14(3)).

[62] *Slater and Others* v *Finning* [1996] 3 All ER 398.

[63] *Kendall* v *Lillico* [1969] 2 AC 31.

[64] *Frost* v *Aylesbury Dairy Co* [1905] 1 KB 608 (liability imposed for typhoid infected milk even though its presence was undiscoverable at the time).

[65] *Slater and Others* v *Finning* [1996] 3 All ER 398. See also *Griffiths* v *Peter Conway* [1939] 1 All ER 685 (buyer of coat contracted dermatitis – buyer had particularly sensitive skin and coat would not have affected normal person – no liability).

Sale by sample

Two terms are implied into a contract of sale by sample. These are that the bulk conforms to the sample provided[66] and that the goods are 'free from any defect, making their quality unsatisfactory which would not be apparent on reasonable inspection of the sample'.[67]

Other legislation

The Sale of Goods Act 1979 is the most important piece of legislation concerning the supply of goods. However, the Act only applies to *sales* of goods. Similar terms are also implied into contracts of hire purchase, hire and other contracts for the supply of goods, e.g. barter and the materials elements of work and materials contracts by other legislation.[68] Where someone contracts to provide a service,[69] the Sale of Goods and Services Act 1982, s 13 provides that he also impliedly undertakes to 'carry out the service with reasonable care and skill'.[70]

When considering statutory implied terms, it is necessary to ascertain the type of contract under consideration before the relevant statute can be identified. This is not always an easy task and it is one which the courts sometimes get wrong.[71]

Custom

The accepted custom of the trade or commerce concerned or the locality at which it is transacted may be a source of implied terms. In one case it was accepted that an agricultural tenant who was served with notice to quit should be given an allowance for seed he planted and the labour of doing so.[72] Terms cannot be implied by custom which are in conflict with the express terms of the contract. This was the basis upon which the Court of Appeal and House of Lords dismissed the argument of a shipowner that commission for negotiating a charter was not payable to an agent when the ship was requisitioned and so unable to perform the concluded charter.[73]

The common law

The common law is also a source of implied terms. The process of common law implication may be divided into two sub-categories: implication in fact and implication in law.[74] Implication in fact occurs where the courts imply a

---

[66] Section 15(2)(a).
[67] Section 15(2)(c).
[68] Respectively Sale of Goods (Implied Terms) Act 1973, ss 8–11; Supply of Goods and Services Act 1982, ss 7–10 and 2–5.
[69] Including the service elements of work and materials contacts.
[70] *Wilson v Best Travel Ltd* [1993] 1 All ER 353.
[71] *Shine v General Guarantee* [1988] 1 All ER 911 (car bought on hire purchase terms – term implied under Sale of Goods Act 1979, s 14(2) rather than Supply of Goods (Implied Terms) Act 1973, s 10(2)).
[72] *Hutton v Warren* (1836) 1 M & W 466.
[73] *Walford's Case* [1919] AC 801.
[74] *Lutor v Cooper* [1941] AC 108 at 137; *Ashmore and Others v Corporation of Lloyd's* [1992] 2 Lloyd's Rep 620; *Scally v Southern Health and Social Services Board* [1991] 4 All ER 563; *Equitable Life Assurance Society v Hyman* [2000] 3 WLR 529.

term into a contract because of the presumed, but unexpressed, intention of the parties. In other words, the term is something which the parties would have wanted to include in their agreement.[75] Implication in law is the judicial expression that certain contracts should as a matter of policy contain certain terms even if the parties themselves did not mean to include them and perhaps even if the parties intended to exclude them.

Implication in fact

Two different tests are sometimes relied upon by the courts to justify implication in fact. The first, the business efficacy test, asks whether it is necessary to imply the term in order to make the contract meaningful in a commercial sense. On this basis the courts have implied a term into a contract for the use of a tidal wharf that the wharfowner had taken reasonable steps to see that the river bottom was safe for ships to lay on when the tide receded or at least to warn the master if it was not so.[76] In contrast, the test did not justify the implication into a contract (under which the owner of two cinemas agreed to pay a commission to an agent if he introduced someone who bought the cinemas) of a term that the cinema owner would not refuse to complete a sale with any party introduced who was willing to pay the asking price.[77] The size of the consideration offered which the House of Lords noted was more than the Lord Chancellor's annual salary meant that the agreement entered was commercially viable even though the agent's best efforts might eventually be frustrated by a change of mind on the part of the cinema owner. Where the contract under consideration is similar to one that has operated successfully in the past, it will be more difficult to convince the court that it is now necessary to supplement its express provisions with terms implied on the basis of business efficacy.[78] At all times the court must resist:[79]

> ... the temptation to rewrite the agreement between the parties in a more efficient and attractive way, an exercise which was frequently both easy and tempting with the benefit of hindsight.

---

[75] '*Ad hoc* gap fillers' in the language of Lord Steyn. See *Equitable Life* (n. 74) at 539.Where the agreement that was concluded fails to record the agreement which was in fact reached, the court can be asked to 'rectify' the contract. This equitable jurisdiction only extends to correcting failures to record the agreement actually reached. See *Frederick E Rose (London) Ltd v William H Pim Jnr & Co Ltd* [1953] 2 QB 450 (contract for sale of 'horsebeans' could not be rectified to become a contract for sale of 'feveroles' (which are up–market horsebeans) because at the time of contracting both parties thought the two words were synonymous).

[76] *The Moorcock* (1889) 14 PD 64. The test is sometimes known as the *Moorcock* test. See also *Reigate v Union Manufacturing Co (Ramsbottom) Ltd* [1918] 1 KB 592 at 605 *per* Scrutton LJ: 'A term can only be implied if it is necessary in the business sense to give efficacy to the contract ...'.

[77] *Luxor (Eastbourne) Ltd v Cooper* [1941] AC 108.

[78] *Ashmore and Others v Corporation of Lloyd's* [1992] 2 Lloyd's Rep 620 (no term could be implied into contract between Lloyd's and the 'Names' whose assets ultimately secure the insurance liabilities of Lloyd's to alert the Names about matters affecting their underwriting interests or to monitor the activities of managing agents who were 'in trouble').

[79] *Express Newspapers v Silverstone Circuits Ltd* [1989] *Independent*, 16 June, *per* Purchas LJ.

The second test has become known as the officious bystander test. It has been described in this way by MacKinnon LJ:[80]

> Prima facie that which in any contract is left to be implied and need not be expressed is something so obvious that it goes without saying; so that, if, while the parties were making their bargain, an officious bystander were to suggest some express provision for it in their agreement, they would testily suppress him with a common 'Oh, of course'.

It has been said that for terms to be implied based on this test they must be precise but not overly complex. The officious bystander would only be able to comprehend terms that were not too vague and would be unlikely to agree to those that were too elaborate.[81]

The following summary of the grounds for implication in fact was endorsed in *Philips Electronique* v *British Sky Broadcasting*:[82]

> ... for a term to be implied the following conditions (which may overlap) must be satisfied: (1) it must be reasonable and equitable; (2) it must be necessary to give business efficacy to the contract, so that no term will be implied if it is effective without it; (3) it must be so obvious that 'it goes without saying'; (4) it must be capable of clear expression; (5) it must not contradict any express term of the contract.

Implication in law

In a recent case Sir Thomas Bingham expressed the view that the process of implication of contractual terms 'is so potentially intrusive that the law imposes strict constraints on the exercise of this extraordinary power'.[83]

This comment is particularly relevant to the process of implication in law. If this process is operated without constraint, the courts are simply re-writing the parties' contract for them. This is antithetical to the values of classical contract law, which viewed a contract as the product of the parties' wills to which the courts should give slavish effect.[84] Whether such a contract law ever existed is open to debate. It is certainly true that it does not exist today. None the less, the law of contract is different from the law of tort and restitution, and this difference stems from the consensual nature of the contractual relation. The description of the role of classical contract law is as inaccurate a picture of modern contract law as it would be to describe it as only concerned with the external imposition of obligations on the parties. Modern contract law is a contradictory mix of voluntarily assumed obligations overlain with externally imposed standards of fair behaviour. It is exactly because contract law still has a core that is at least in part justifiable

---

[80] *Shirlaw* v *Southern Foundries Ltd* [1939] 2 KB 206 at 227.

[81] *Ashmore and Others* v *Corporation of Lloyd's* [1992] 2 Lloyd's Rep 620.

[82] [1995] EMLR 472 at 481 repeating the statement of Lord Simon in *BP Refinery (Westernport) Pty Ltd* v *The President, Councillors and Ratepayers of Shire of Hastings* (1978) 52 AJLR 20 at 26.

[83] *Philips Electronique* v *BSB* [1995] EMLR 472 at 481.

[84] See above, ch. 1.

in terms of mutual consent that the courts feel embarrassed to openly reserve to themselves a general power to overturn or supplement the unambiguously expressed intentions of the parties.

In this regard, it is instructive to contrast the approach of Lord Denning in the Court of Appeal with that of the House of Lords in *Liverpool County Council* v *Irvin*.[85] The House of Lords held that it was an implied term of a contract for the lease of a maisonette in a council-owned block that the landlord should exercise reasonable care to ensure that the common parts (e.g. halls and lifts) were maintained in a reasonable state of repair.[86] Lord Wilberforce emphasised two factors, which justified the implication in law of this term. These were the particular relationship of the parties, i.e. landlord and tenant, in relation to a particular type of property, namely high-rise blocks in multi-occupation. The House of Lords emphatically rejected the general power favoured by Lord Denning in the Court of Appeal to imply terms into contracts whenever it appears reasonable to do so.[87] In *Scally* v *Southern Health and Social Services Board*[88] Lord Bridge described the process of implication in law as 'the search, based on wider considerations, for a term which the law will imply as a necessary ingredient of a definable category of contractual relationship'.

Another relationship which is thought to justify the implication in law of various terms is that of employer and employee.[89] It is an implied term of a contract of employment that the employer must take reasonable care to protect the health and safety of his employees. This implied duty might operate to restrain a health authority from requiring junior doctors to work so many hours of overtime that it is detrimental to their health.[90] Indeed, it was suggested by one member of the Court of Appeal that the term implied would take precedence over any contrary inconsistent express provision.[91] The implication of terms into contracts of employment may be more easily justified where the contract of employment contains complex terms negotiated by representative bodies, the details of which the employee could not reasonably be aware. On this basis a term was implied into the contracts of employment of doctors that the employer was obliged to take reasonable steps to alert the employee to any action he ought to take to become entitled to valuable rights, such as an entitlement to a pension.[92]

---

[85] [1977] AC 239.
[86] Which obligation the LCC had in fact discharged.
[87] To similar effect see *Re International Scholarship Foundation and National Trust Co* (1992) 87 DLR (4th) 267.
[88] [1991] 4 All ER 563 at 571.
[89] See generally Rideout in Halson (ed.), (1996) *Exploring the Boundaries of Contract*, ch. 7.
[90] *Johnstone* v *Bloomsbury Health Authority* [1991] 2 All ER 293.
[91] *Per* Stuart Smith LJ at p. 299. *Contra: Duke of Westminster* v *Guild* [1985] QB 688.
[92] *Scally* v *Southern Health and Social Services Board* [1991] 4 All ER 563.

11

THE CONTENT OF THE CONTRACT: EXCLUSION CLAUSES

EXEMPTION CLAUSES

Exemption clauses are clauses that exclude or limit the liability of a party for breach of contract or some other obligation.[1] Such clauses are a part of everyday commercial and domestic life. Exemption clauses are closely associated with the use of 'standard-form' contracts which are the regularised printed terms and conditions upon which commercial transactors seek to do business.[2] Similar standard-form contracts are used by businesses that provide goods and services to consumers such as the utility supply companies (water, gas, and electricity) as well as other service providers, such as telephone companies, banks and bus and rail providers. In this way the use of exemption clauses affects the provision of basic goods and services which are central to our day-to-day life. However, many consumers are unaware of the details and sometimes the existence of these exculpatory provisions. Perhaps ignorance in this regard is bliss because if the consumer objected to any such provision, in reality there is no chance of renegotiating it. Most of these contracts are entered into on a 'take it or leave it' basis because of the inequality of bargaining power between the parties. For this reason the courts have treated such clauses with great hostility and have devised various techniques to curb what is perceived as their undesirable effect upon the contractual rights of consumers.

This judicial hostility and resourcefulness has in some cases been matched by the ingenuity of commercial draftspersons who have sought to achieve the same objective by techniques which outflank the policing mechanisms utilised by the courts. One such response needs to be considered here because it will cause us to redefine the definition of our subject with which this chapter commenced. If exemption clauses are only perceived to operate as exclusions or limits upon the remedy that would otherwise be available in respect of a breach of contract, the techniques used to control them will be similarly focused. The reason for this stems from the exceptional nature of the judicial intervention in this field. To the extent that a contract is regarded as the product of the parties, any judicial interference with their 'freedom to contract' must be justified. We have already noted that the courts have

---

[1] Such as liability imposed by the law of tort, the law of bailment or statute.
[2] We have already examined the problems that can arise when each insists on using its own form. See ch. 3.

intuitively felt that intervention was adequately justified in order to protect consumers from the harsh effects of modern business practice. At the same time, for constitutional, theoretical and pragmatic reasons, courts routinely disclaim any general power to write or rewrite parties' contracts for them. This produces a need to define the occasions when intervention is justified. An example will illustrate the effect of adopting too narrow a definition of exemption clauses. Suppose that I am a marine surveyor. My standard contract excludes liability for negligent surveys. What is the effect of this clause? It could be interpreted as making unavailable to the victim of a breach of contract a remedy that would otherwise be available to him or her. However, parties are generally regarded as free to assume whatever contractual responsibilities they wish. Could the clause be regarded as simply preventing any obligation for negligent surveys from arising in the first place? If so, some of the controls devised by the courts (and later by the legislature) mindful not to create a general power to revise the parties' contract might not apply to the clause. This distinction between what can inelegantly be described as 'remedy-qualifying' and 'obligation-defining' clauses[3] has been exploited by commercial draftspersons to the advantage of their clients. However, the response of the courts and legislature has in many cases been a robust one which extends their control to cover such clauses, whatever the consequences for classical contract theory. To reflect this fact we should expand our opening definition: exemption clauses exclude or limit *or appear to exclude or limit* the liability of a party for breach of contract or some other obligation.

At this point we should consider the effect upon the courts of the increasing legislative control of exemption clauses. The general legislative control derives from two important and overlapping sources: the Unfair Contract Terms Act 1977 and the Unfair Terms in Consumer Contracts Regulations 1999.[4] The 1977 Act built upon and expanded earlier domestic legislation. The 1999 regulations replaced similar 1994[5] regulations that implemented obligations imposed on member states of the EC by the Directive on Unfair Terms in Consumer Contracts. These two measures overlap untidily and imperfectly. None the less, the overall legislative control of exclusion clauses has meant that the courts have been relieved of the need to perform mental gymnastics and doctrinal sophistry in order to protect consumers from the destructive effects of exemption clauses. As a result, the importance of some of the judicial controls has declined.

The overall control of exemption clauses takes three forms.[6] First, exclusion clauses may be denied any legal effect because though recorded in

---

[3] See generally Coote (1964) *Exclusion Clauses*.
[4] SI 1999 No. 2083.
[5] Unfair Terms in Consumer Contracts Regulations, SI 1994 No. 3159.
[6] In the past the doctrine of privity of contract was also used to 'control' exemption clauses when a person sought the protection of an exemption clause in a contract to which he was not a party. The 'control' exercised by the doctrine of privity was only ever partial because it was only relevant to third parties who relied on exemption clauses. Now the Contracts (Rights of

a written notice or document that notice or document was not incorporated into the parties' contract. Second, the courts must interpret any clause that does form part of the parties' contract. The courts have devised an approach to the construction of such clauses, which seeks to limit their effect. Third, the Unfair Contract Terms Act 1977 and the Unfair Terms in Consumer Contracts Regulations 1999 might apply to the clause and so deny or limit its effect.

INCORPORATION

When a party signs a contract he is generally regarded as bound by its terms whether or not he has in fact read them. This principle was applied to deny a remedy to the purchaser of a defective 'slot machine' because the seller had excluded all liability for express and implied warranties.[7] The agreement, which was printed on brown paper, contained a number of clauses including the one in question 'in regrettably small print' and was not read by the claimant. In this country the signature principle is qualified in two ways. First, the Court of Appeal has recently held that it is only applicable if the signed document is one that can reasonably be expected to contain contractual terms. On this basis the act of signing weekly time sheets which referred to standard terms did not vary a prior oral contract.[8] Second, a party may be able to avoid a contract he has signed if he can bring himself within the ancient doctrine[9] of *non est factum* (it was not my deed). This narrow doctrine is available to persons[10] who sign documents under a mistaken belief as to their nature or effect but who have themselves exercised all proper care.[11] In contrast to our qualified but nevertheless strict signature rule, the Canadian courts have held that an exemption clause in a signed document will not bind the signatory unless the party relying on the clause brought it to the attention of the other in such a way that he or she must be taken to have agreed to it.[12]

Where the exemption clause is contained in an unsigned document or

---

Third Parties) Act 1999 will, if the statutory requirements are met, permit third parties to obtain the benefit of exclusion clauses in contracts to which they are not a party. See Chapter 9.

[7] *L'Estrange v Graucob* [1934] 2 KB 394. See Spencer, 'Signature, Consent and the Rule in *L'Estrange v Graucob*' [1973] CLJ 104.

[8] *Grogan v Robert Meredith Plant Hire* (1996) 15 Tr LR 371.

[9] It originally applied to illiterate persons who executed deeds after they had been incorrectly read to them: *Thoroughgood's Case* (1584) 2 Co Rep 9a.

[10] Only exceptionally to those of full age and capacity. Those who are blind or illiterate more easily bring themselves within the doctrine.

[11] *Saunders v Anglia Building Society* (also known as *Gallie v Lee*) [1971] AC 1004.

[12] *Crocker v Sundance Northwest Resorts Ltd* (1989) 51 DLR (4th) 321 and *Trigg v MI Movers International Transport Services Ltd* (1991) 84 DLR (4th) 504, applying *Tilden Rent-a-Car Co v Glendenning* (1978) 83 DLR (3d) 400. In the first case the defendant had misrepresented the effect of the clause. This narrower ground would justify the non-enforcement of the clause under English law. See *Curtis v Chemical Cleaning & Dyeing Co Ltd* [1951] 1 KB 805. See also *Hoffman v Sportsman Yachts Inc* (1992) 89 DLR (4th) 600.

notice, it will only be incorporated into the contract where three pre-conditions are satisfied. First, the document or notice must be of a kind which would reasonably be expected to contain contractual terms. Second, the person seeking to rely on the document must take steps prior to the conclusion of the contract to alert the other to the existence of the term. Third, the steps which must be taken are required to be such as are reasonable in the circumstances. The application of these three principles can be conveniently illustrated by reference to the facts of *Interfoto Picture Library Ltd* v *Stiletto Visual Programmes Ltd*[13] where the clause in question was a penalty, rather than an exemption, clause but nothing turned on this. The claimants ran a library that hired out photo transparencies. The defendants ordered 47 photo transparencies. The claimants sent these accompanied by a delivery note which said that £5.00 per day was payable for each transparency retained for longer than 14 days. The defendants failed to return them within that period and the claimants sued under the clause. The Court of Appeal held that the clause was not incorporated into the parties' contract.

The first requirement of incorporation was satisfied because it was 'an inescapable inference that the defendants would have recognised the delivery note as a document of a kind likely to contain contractual terms'. This contrasts with *Chapelton* v *Barry UDC*[14] where it was held that it was reasonable for a person hiring a deckchair to assume that the ticket he received was a receipt for the hire charge rather than a contractual document. In *Interfoto* the contract was concluded after delivery when the defendants telephoned the claimants to say that some of the transparencies would be of use to them. The notice preceded the contract and so the second requirement of incorporation was satisfied. This was not the case in *Olley* v *Marlborough Court Ltd*[15] where a hotel was precluded from relying upon an exemption clause contained in a notice on the back of the hotel bedroom doors. The contract was concluded at the reception desk before the guest had an opportunity to read the notice. However, the third requirement of incorporation was not satisfied. The steps taken by the claimants to bring the clause to the attention of the defendants fell short of what it was reasonable to expect of them in the circumstances of the case. It seems that a relevant circumstance is how destructive or onerous the clause in question would be if it was enforced. In other words, the more destructive an exemption clause would be to the claimant's rights, the greater steps that must be taken by the defendant to discharge the burden cast on him. This principle is well expressed by Lord Denning who noted that for some clauses to be enforceable the clause would need to be 'printed in red ink with a big red hand pointing to it'.[16]

The requirement that the party seeking to rely on an unsigned notice or

---

[13] [1989] QB 433.
[14] [1940] 1 KB 532.
[15] [1949] 1 KB 532.
[16] *J Spurling Ltd* v *Bradshaw* [1956] 1 WLR 461 at 466 and *Thornton* v *Shoe Lane Parking Ltd* [1971] 2 QB 163.

document must take reasonable steps to bring it to the attention of the other party has been applied harshly in the past. In *Thompson* v *London, Midland & Scottish Railway*[17] an exclusion clause in a railway timetable was held to be validly incorporated despite the fact that the claimant was illiterate and the clause was on page 552 of a timetable that cost 20 per cent of the ticket price to buy. Indeed, some judges still believe that the test should be applied in a way that does not introduce uncertainty into the law. For this reason Hobhouse LJ suggested that the principle should not be more exacting where the clause is a particularly onerous or destructive one.[18]

When, in the past, two parties have regularly and consistently dealt on certain terms their previous course of dealing may, when they contract again, bind them to certain terms. It is difficult to generalise about the frequency and uniformity of dealings which is required to satisfy these requirements. It has been held that 100 dealings within three years are sufficiently frequent to be regular[19] but that three or four transactions over five years are not.[20] In one case the claimant had in the past sometimes been asked to sign a 'risk note' and sometimes not; the course of previous dealing was held to be insufficiently consistent to incorporate an exemption clause contained in that note when, on a later occasion, he was not asked to sign one. Where the contracting parties are both commercial entities, the court may apply these requirements in a less stringent way. In one such case a clause was held to form part of a later contract on the basis of its use on two prior occasions and the fact that its use was customary in the trade in question.[21]

CONSTRUCTION

When the courts have ascertained the terms of the parties' contract they must interpret them to discover their legal meaning. Traditionally the courts have sought to place as narrow a construction as possible[22] on exemption clauses. This approach of construing the exemption clause against the party seeking to rely on it is often referred to as *contra proferentem* (literally against the profferer). The common law *contra proferentem* rule is repeated in the Unfair Terms in Consumer Contracts Regulations,[23] which provide in reg 7(2) that 'If there is doubt about the meaning of a written term, the interpretation which is most favourable to the consumer shall prevail ...'. Unfortunately, the *contra proferentem* principle is much easier to state in the abstract than it is to apply in practice.

Statutory provisions, in particular the Unfair Contract Terms Act 1977, severely restrict the extent to which parties can exclude liability for the

---

[17] [1930] 1 KB 41.
[18] *AEG (UK) Ltd* v *Logic Resource Ltd* [1996] CLC 265.
[19] *Hardwick Game Farm* v *Suffolk Agricultural Poultry Producers Association* [1969] 2 AC 31.
[20] *Hollier* v *Rambler Motors (AMC) Ltd* [1972] 2 QB 71.
[21] [1975] QB 303.
[22] And even narrower the cynic might say.
[23] SI 1999 No. 2083.

negligent breach of their contracts. However, before the Act is applied or where the contract is one which falls outside the Act altogether, the court must interpret any clause which purports to exclude such liability. A party who wants to exclude liability for a negligent breach of contract should make clear this intention by stating that liability for negligence is being excluded although some unambiguous synonym for negligence is also acceptable.[24]

Where the exclusion does not refer to negligence, the situation is more complicated. Here it is necessary to distinguish two different situations. The first is where but for the exclusion clause there would be liability if the breach of contract was caused by the negligence of the offending party and also if it was not.[25] The Sale of Goods Act 1979, s 14(2) imposes such a 'strict' liability'. The seller is regarded as having guaranteed that the goods will be of satisfactory quality. If the goods turn out to be unsatisfactory, it is no defence for the seller to say that he took all reasonable care to ensure that they were satisfactory, for instance by buying from a reputable source and storing them properly. Any attempt to exclude liability for the provision of unsatisfactory goods which did not distinguish between the negligent and the non-negligent provision of unsatisfactory goods, e.g. 'the seller shall not be not liable for the provision of unsatisfactory goods in any circumstance whatsoever', would be interpreted as excluding only the liability for the non-negligent provision of unsatisfactory goods.[26] Such a construction would not affect in any way the liability of the seller for the negligent provision of unsatisfactory goods.[27]

The second situation is where the only liability is for negligent breach of contract, i.e. liability is not strict. This is the case with many contracts for the provision of a service. The term implied into such contracts by Supply of Goods and Services Act 1982, s 13 that the service provider shall exercise 'reasonable care and skill' gives rise to negligence based liability only.[28] The difficulty presented by this situation is that negligence based liability is the only liability there is so if the exemption clause is to have any legal effect it would have to be construed as excluding that liability.[29] Later cases have found a way of avoiding this conclusion by interpreting the exemption clause as having a hortatory function; it is merely a warning that there will be no

---

24 *Canada Steamships Company* v *The King* [1952] AC 192, *Shell Chemicals Ltd* v *P & O Roadtanks Ltd* [1995] 1 Lloyd's Rep 297 and *Smith* v *UMB Chrysler (Scotland) Ltd* 1978 SC (HL) 1.

25 There must be a realistic possibility as opposed to a fanciful one that there is liability in the absence of negligence. See *The Raphael* [1982] 2 Lloyd's Rep 42 and *Dorset County Council* v *Southern Felt Roofing Co Ltd* (1989) 48 BLR 96.

26 Such attempts are the subject of strict statutory control. See Unfair Contract Terms Act 1977, especially s 6.

27 *Canada Steamships Company* v *The King* [1952] AC 192 at 208 and *Upper Lakes Shipping Ltd* v *St Lawrence Cement Inc* (1992) 89 DLR (4th) 722.

28 Again, any attempt to exclude this liability is subject to the Unfair Contract Terms Act 1977. Exclusion is controlled by the general ss 2 and 3. There is no provision in the Act specifically dealing with the exclusion of the term implied by s 13 of the 1982 Act, i.e. there is no equivalent to s 6.

29 *Alderslade* v *Hendon Laundry Ltd* [1945] 1 KB 189 at 192.

liability in the absence of negligence. This was the approach taken *in Hollier* v *Rambler Motors*,[30] where the claimant's car was damaged by fire while being repaired by the defendant garage. The defendant sought to rely upon the exclusion clause contained in its invoice, which the claimant had received on at least two of the previous three or four times he had used the garage. The Court of Appeal held that the exemption clause was not incorporated by such infrequent and inconsistent dealings. However, even if the provision that 'the company is not liable for damage caused by fire to customers' cars on the premises' was incorporated into the contract, it could 'be given ample content by construing [it] as a warning'. It will not be possible to take this approach if the undifferentiated clause is a limitation, as opposed to an exemption, clause. A limitation clause cannot sensibly be regarded as a warning that responsibility will be limited in respect of a liability that can never arise.

It was at one time thought that there was a rule of law that a party could not rely upon an exemption clause when he himself was in fundamental breach of contract.[31] This so-called doctrine of fundamental breach was always indiscriminate but it later became unnecessary. It was indiscriminate because as a rule of law it was dispositive of all circumstances that came within its ambit. The valuable protection it afforded to consumers was purchased at the cost of creating uncertainty in relation to commercial contracts between parties of equal bargaining power. If two such parties contract on the basis that one party is not to be responsible to the other, even in respect of a fundamental breach of contract, this allocation of risk should be respected. The doctrine became unnecessary in the light of the protection offered to consumers by the Unfair Contract Terms Act 1977. As a rule of law, the doctrine of fundamental breach was finally[32] laid to rest by the House of Lords in *Photo Production* v *Securicor*.[33] In this case Securicor contracted to provide security services including night patrols at the claimant's premises. To keep himself warm, the patrolman started a small fire that got out of hand and burnt down the premises. The House of Lords held that Securicor was protected by the exemption clause which provided: 'Under no circumstances shall ...[Securicor] be responsible for any injurious act or default by any employee of the company ... nor, in any event, shall the company be held responsible for (a) any loss suffered by the customer through ... fire ...'. At first sight, it might be thought that the upholding of the clause was hard on the claimant. However, both parties were commercial concerns dealing at arm's length. Securicor contracted to provide visits at a very low cost (about 26 pence per visit). This cost probably reflected the

---

[30] [1972] 2 QB 71.

[31] *Karsales (Harrow) Ltd* v *Wallis* [1956] 1 WLR 936.

[32] Earlier attempts at internment such as the *Suisse Atlantique* case [1967] 1 AC 361 were unsuccessful usually because of Lord Denning's repeated attempts to 'dig up the corpse'. See e.g. *Harbutt's Plasticine Ltd* v *Wayne Tank and Pump Co Ltd* [1970] 1 QB 447 and *Wathes (Western) Ltd* v *Austins (Menswear) Ltd* [1976] 1 Lloyd's Rep 14.

[33] [1980] AC 827.

parties' clear understanding that the risk of damage to the premises and so the obligation to insure them lay with the factory owner.[34] As Hobhouse J observed in another case, 'It is always relevant to have in mind when construing a contract between commercial parties that the primary purpose of the relevant provision may simply be one of the division of risk, often insurable risk.'[35]

The doctrine of fundamental breach now exists as a doctrine of construction only. This means that exemption clauses will, where possible, be interpreted not to apply to a fundamental breach of contract. However, if the parties make clear their intention that the exemption clause is to apply even to a fundamental breach of contract, their intention will be respected by the courts. The doctrine of fundamental breach is now best considered as an aspect of the *contra proferentem* principle.

In *Ailsa Craig Fishing Co Ltd* v *Malvern Fishing Co Ltd* it was suggested that the *contra proferentem* rule is not 'applicable in its full rigour' to limitation as opposed to exemption clauses and that 'one must not strive to create ambiguities by strained construction ... The relevant words must be given, if possible, their natural plain meaning'.[36] This suggestion is open to the objection that limitation clauses vary a lot from those which limit liability to a token sum to those which still permit generous, but not full, compensation for loss. Should the same approach be taken to both types of clause? Should not a more natural approach to the construction of exemption clauses also be taken particularly in relation to commercial transactions? Such an approach has been taken in Australia[37] and Canada[38] and has some support in this country. In *George Mitchell (Chesterhall) Ltd* v *Finney Lock Seeds Ltd*[39] Lord Diplock agreed with Lord Denning in the Court of Appeal that the Unfair Contract Terms Act 1977 'removed from the judges the temptation to resort to ... a tortured meaning so as to avoid giving effect to an exclusion or limitation of liability'.

THE UNFAIR CONTRACT TERMS ACT 1977

The Unfair Contract Terms Act 1977 undoubtedly has a misleading title. It does not enact any general control over unfair or unconscionable terms. Its general provisions apply only to clauses which seek to exclude or restrict liability. Obviously, the liability we are concerned with is liability for breach of contract, but it should be noted that some sections, such as s 2, extend to the exclusion of tortious duties of care. There are many categories of 'unfair'

---

[34] The action might have been brought by the factory owner's insurers who would be 'subrogated' to the rights of their policy holder.

[35] *EE Caledonia Ltd* v *Orbit Valve Co Europe* [1993] 4 All ER 165 at 173.

[36] [1983] 1 WLR 964 *per* Lords Fraser and Wilberforce. To similar effect, see also *Westcoast Transmission Co* v *Cullen Detroit Diesel Allison Ltd* (1990) 70 DLR (4th) 503.

[37] *Darlington Futures Ltd* v *Delco Australia Pty Ltd* (1987) 61 ALJR 76.

[38] *Schenker & Co (Aust) Pty Ltd* v *Malpas Equipment and Services Pty Ltd* [1990] VR 834.

[39] [1983] 2 AC 803 at 810.

term which are not touched by the Act, such as 'penalty' clauses.[40] However, exemption clauses are broadly defined in s 13(a)–(c) to include clauses making liability subject to restrictive or onerous conditions (e.g. requiring a defective car to be returned to the factory), clauses excluding or restricting any right or remedy or penalising someone who pursues a particular remedy (e.g. excluding the right to terminate a contract) and clauses excluding or restricting rules of evidence or procedure (e.g. providing that a signature on a delivery note is to be regarded as conclusive proof that goods conform to the contractual specification).

Further provisions in the Act apply only to indemnity clauses, i.e. clauses under which one party promises to reimburse another for any liability incurred in the performance of a contract. Section 4 subjects to a test of reasonableness any term requiring a person who deals as a consumer to indemnify another in respect of that other's liability for negligence or breach of contract.[41] The Act also controls any attempt to exclude or restrict guarantees of consumer goods given by manufacturers and distributors to consumers. If goods are made by A, distributed by B, sold by C and bought by D, s 5 is only relevant to any claims (in tort or under a collateral contract) which D may have against A or B. In terms s 5 extends to all attempts to exclude or restrict liability for loss or damage but will in practice only be used in relation to damage to property or such other economic loss as may be recoverable. This is because any attempt to exclude liability for negligently inflicted death or personal injury will be invalid under s 2(1).

Scope, concepts and definitions

Some contracts are excluded from the Act altogether. The main categories are contracts of insurance, contracts which concern the transfer of an interest in land and international supply contracts.[42] The general sections of the Act which apply to contracts within its jurisdiction build on and use a number of concepts and definitions which we now need to explore.

Certain provisions in the Act only apply to 'business liability'.[43] Business liability is defined as liability for the breach of obligations or duties arising from things done in the course of a business or from the occupation of premises for business purposes.[44]

Some of the general sections of the Act only apply when a party 'deals as a consumer'. According to s 12, a party deals as a consumer in relation to another if three conditions are satisfied.[45] First, the party does not make the contract in the course of a business. Second, the other party does make the contract in the course of a business. Third, if the contract is one for the sale or hire-purchase of goods, the goods must be of a type 'ordinarily supplied

[40] As to which see Chapter 17.
[41] 'Dealing as a consumer' and 'reasonablness' are discussed below.
[42] Section 26 and Sch 1.
[43] Section 1(3).
[44] Section 1(3)(a)–(b).
[45] Contained in s 12(1)(a)–(c).

for private use or consumption'. Business is defined in the Act only in an inclusive way to extend to 'a profession and the activities of any government department or local or public authority'.[46] It has also been held that 'in the course of a business' in s 12 requires a regularity of transactions and so is not apt to cover persons who engage in 'one-off' or occasional transactions.[47] It will be appreciated that the concept of dealing as a consumer within the Act is an artificial one which does not extend to all dealings by private persons. If a private person purchases a good or service from another private person, neither 'deals' as a consumer within the Act. If a private person buys industrial tooling from a business, the buyer does not deal as a consumer because the goods are not of a kind ordinarily supplied for private consumption. In the case of a sale by auction or competitive tender, the buyer is never regarded as dealing as a consumer.[48] It is for the party asserting that the other does not deal as a consumer to prove that this is the case.[49]

The concept of 'reasonableness' is an element in many of the sections. It is defined in s 11(1) as a requirement:

> That the term shall have been a fair and reasonable one to be included having regard to the circumstances which were, or ought reasonably to have been known to or in the contemplation of the parties when the contract was made.

An important point concerns the time for determining reasonableness. The reasonableness of a term falls to be judged at the time of entering the contract. It is not to be judged with the benefit of hindsight.[50] It follows from this that it is the whole clause and not just the part later relied on which must be reasonable.[51] The burden of proving that a clause is reasonable is borne by the party seeking to rely on the clause.[52]

It is difficult to generalise about the requirement of reasonableness because a discussion of it does not feature in the reports of many appellate decisions. This paucity of appellate comment is due to the fact that the question of reasonableness is regarded as one for the trial judge which 'the appellate court should treat ... with the utmost respect and refrain from interference with it unless satisfied that it proceeded on some erroneous principle or was plainly and obviously wrong'.[53] However, the statute itself provides a number of guidelines.

---

[46] Section 14.
[47] *R & B Customs Brokers Ltd* v *United Dominions Trust Ltd* [1988] 1 WLR 321. *Cf.* the approach to the interpretation of the phrase 'in the course of the business' in the Sale of Goods Act 1979 s 14, discussed in *Stevenson* v *Rogers* [1999] 2 WLR 1064, considered at p. 294 above.
[48] Section 12(2).
[49] Section 12(3).
[50] *Edmund Murray Ltd* v *SP International Foundations Ltd* (1992) 33 Con LR 1 and *Chester Grosvenor Hotel Co Ltd* v *Alfred McAlpine Ltd* (1991) 56 BLR 115.
[51] *Stewart Gill Ltd* v *Horatio Myer & Co Ltd* [1992] 2 WLR 721 and *Overseas Medical Supplies Ltd* v *Orient Transport Services* [1999] 2 Lloyd's Rep 273.
[52] Section 11(5).
[53] *George Mitchell Ltd* v *Finney Lock Seeds Ltd* [1983] 2 All ER 737 at 743 *per* Lord Bridge. The case concerned an earlier repealed statutory measure. See also Adams and Brownsword, 'The Unfair Contract Terms Act: A Decade of Discretion' (1988) 104 LQR 94.

Section 11(4) states that when considering reasonableness in relation to a *limitation* clause the court should have regard to the resources available to the person who would have to meet the liability as well as the extent to which this liability could have been covered by insurance. However, the availability[54] and cost[55] of insurance has also been emphasised in a number of cases where the reasonableness of an exemption clause had to be determined.

Section 11(2) refers to a number of guidelines contained in Sch 2, which are said to be relevant to the determination of reasonableness in relation to ss 6–7 of the Act. However, the trend is to consider the factors in relation to the question of reasonableness in relation to *any* section of the Act.[56] The factors are the relative bargaining positions of the parties,[57] whether the customer received an inducement to agree to the term or had an opportunity to contract with others on a different basis, whether the customer knew or ought reasonably to have known about the term, where the term imposes a precondition the reasonableness of it and whether the goods were made to special order. In *Smith v Eric S Bush*[58] Lord Griffiths described factors similar to the first two in the Schedule but also emphasised the difficulty of the task undertaken for which liability is being excluded and the practical consequences of the finding in relation to reasonableness including the availability of insurance.

Liability for negligence

Section 2 provides as follows:

(1) A person cannot by reference to any contract term or to a notice ... exclude or restrict his liability for death and personal injury arising from his negligence.

(2) In the case of loss or other damage, a person cannot so exclude or restrict his liability except in so far as the term satisfies the requirement of reasonableness.

This section applies to attempts to exclude liability for negligence arising in contract or tort. If the section catches the purported exclusion of liability for negligence, it follows *a fortiori* that it will extend to attempts to exclude liability for deliberate acts, and this is spelt out in s 1(4). However s 2 will not apply to the exclusion of strict liabilities, i.e. liability arising in the absence of negligence. Such exclusions will be subject to s 3.

Section 1(3) provides that s 2 only applies to business liabilities as defined above. The effect of the section differs according to the liability which is purportedly excluded. Where a person tries to exclude liability for negligently caused death or personal injury, he is not allowed to do so. If a person tries to exclude liability for the negligently caused loss or damage to

---

[54] *Smith v Eric S Bush* [1989] 2 WLR 790 at 810 *per* Lord Griffiths.
[55] *Singer Co (UK) Ltd v Tees and Hartlepool Port Authority* [1988] 2 Lloyd's Rep 164 at 169.
[56] *Ibid., Phillips Products v Hyland* [1987] 2 All ER 620 at 628, and *Overseas Medical Supplies Ltd v Orient Transport Services* [1999] 2 Lloyd's Rep 273.
[57] Where the parties are of equal bargaining power, a clause may be considered reasonable if it is common in the trade in question: *Schenkers Ltd v Overland Shoes Ltd* [1998] 1 Lloyd's Rep 498.
[58] [1989] 2 WLR 790 at 809–10.

property, he may do so only if he can satisfy the criterion of reasonableness discussed above.

In a number of cases it was argued that the section was not drafted in a way that would 'catch' contracts which were expressed so as to prevent any liability for negligence from arising at all. In other words, s 2 was only able to catch 'remedy qualifying' rather than 'obligation defining' terms. Such an argument was accepted by the Court of Appeal in *Smith* v *Eric Bush* but roundly rejected in the House of Lords on the basis that it would emasculate the Act and would not be consistent with the Law Commission's report[59] which preceded it.[60]

Contractual liability

Section 3 applies where one party deals as a consumer or on the other's written standard terms of business. We have already examined the first category but the second needs discussion here. There appear to be two requirements: that the relevant party has written standard terms of business and that, on this occasion, he contracted on the basis of them. A party does not fail to deal on the other's written standard terms of business when there are negotiations preceding the conclusion of the contract but the 'general conditions remained effectively untouched'.[61] However, dealing on the basis of a Trade Association's model terms may not fall within the section unless the contractor adopts the terms as his own standard terms.[62]

Section 3(2) goes on to provide that against the party dealing as a consumer or on the other's written standard terms of business the other:

... cannot by reference to any contract term –
(a) when himself in breach of contract, exclude or restrict any liability in respect of the breach; or
(b) claim to be entitled –
    (i) to render a contractual performance substantially different from that which was reasonably expected of him, or
    (ii) in respect of the whole or any part of his contractual obligation, to render no performance at all,
except in so far as ... the contract satisfies the requirement of reasonableness.

It has been said that s 3(2)(a) 'is directed to an exemption clause of the classic type exonerating a contractual party in default from the ordinary consequences of the default'.[63] In other words, it applies to 'remedy

---

[59] (1975) *Second Report on Exemption Clauses*, No. 69, para 127: 'Our recommendations ... are intended to apply to exclusions of liability for negligence ... even in cases where the person seeking to rely on the exemption clause was under no legal obligation ... to carry out the activity.'

[60] [1989] 2 WLR 790 at 809 endorsing the same approach of Slade LJ in *Phillips Products* v *Hyland* [1987] 2 All ER 620.

[61] *St Albans DC* v *International Computers Ltd* [1996] 4 All ER 481 at 491 *per* Nourse LJ, Hirst LJ and Sir Ian Glidewell agreeing.

[62] *British Fermentation Products Ltd* v *Compair Reavell Ltd* [1999] BLR 352.

[63] *Timeload* v *British Telecommunications* [1995] EMLR 459 at 468 *per* Sir Thomas Bingham MR.

qualifying' exclusion clauses. However, s 3(2)(b) has given rise to much greater difficulties. It is obviously intended to apply to situations where the party seeking to rely on the clause is not in breach of contract or it would add nothing to s 3(2)(a). That is to say, it applies to obligation-defining clauses. The major difficulty is to know how the court can ascertain the reasonable expectations of the other party. The question has arisen recently in two decisions of the Court of Appeal concerned with the apparently high-handed actions of dominant suppliers of telecommunication services. In the latest decision, *Zockoll Group Ltd* v *Mercury Communications Ltd*,[64] the claimants believed they had spotted a valuable commercial opportunity by anticipating the introduction of alphanumeric telephone numbers in the UK. They obtained from the defendants a number of selected telephone numbers where the numbers spelt out words on alphanumeric phone pads. The case concerned the withdrawal after 14 days' notice of one number, 0500 35448 (FLIGHT(s)), which the claimants had hoped to franchise to travel agents. The defendants were contractually entitled to withdraw any number they wished. The Court of Appeal held that it was at least arguable that the contractual power of withdrawal relied upon by the defendants was caught by s 3(2)(b), despite the fact that it did require the defendant to give reasonable notice of withdrawal and that this was only one of 53 numbers licensed to the claimants.

The earlier case of *Timeload* v *British Telecommunications*[65] concerned the termination of a contract to use a single telephone number. The Court of Appeal held that it was arguable that the clause permitting termination 'at any time' fell within s 3(2)(b). The defendant's argument that because of the power of termination the claimant could not reasonably expect the number to be available for an indefinite period was rejected. If a customer reasonably expects the power of termination only to be exercised when there exists substantial and objective justification for it, and it is exercised without such justification, this may amount to the tender of a partial or different performance to that which the customer reasonably anticipated. Sir Thomas Bingham also went on to say that even if the 'letter of the statute does not apply' the court could 'treat the clear intention of the legislature expressed in the statute as a platform for invalidating or restricting the operation of an oppressive clause'.[66]

Statutory implied terms

Section 6 controls the extent to which parties to a contract for the sale of goods[67] can exclude liability for breach of the statutory implied terms.[68] Although s 6 can apply to non-business liability, it should be remembered that

[64] [1998] FSR 354.
[65] [1995] EMLR 459.
[66] At p. 469
[67] Or hire purchase.
[68] Section 7 applies in a similar way in relation to the terms implied by statute into contracts of hire and other contracts for the supply of goods.

Table 11.1 A simplified summary of the main provisions of the UCTA 1977

UCTA	Type of liability excluded	Does the section only apply to business liability within s 1(3)?	Must the victim deal as a consumer within s 12?	Effect of the section
s 2(1)	Negligently caused death or personal injury	Yes	No	Ban
s 2(2)	Negligently caused loss or damage to property	Yes	No	Subject to the reasonableness test
s 3	Contractual liability	Yes	Yes or on standard business terms	Subject to the reasonableness test
s 6	Liability for breach of SGA 1979, s 12	No	No	Ban
	Liability for breach of SGA, ss 13, 14 & 15	No[1]	Yes	Ban
		No [1]	No	Subject to the reasonableness test
Misrepresentation Act 1967, s 3	Liability for misrepresentation	No	No	Subject to the reasonableness test

Important Definitions
Business liability: s 1(3) & s 11
Reasonableness: s 11 = Sch 2
Dealing as a consumer: s 12
Exemption clauses: s 13

Notes
1. However, the SGA s 14 itself only applies to businesses.
2. No distinction is here made between the different tests of reasonableness.
3. This summary does not take account of some contracts scope of the Act.

the obligation to supply goods of a satisfactory quality or fit for a particular purpose will only arise if the sale is in the course of a business.[69] Any attempt to exclude liability for breach of the implied term as to title is void.[70] However, the effect of any attempt to exclude liability for breach of the implied

---

[69] Sale of Goods Act 1979, s 14(2) and (3).
[70] Section 6(1).

terms as to description, satisfactory quality, fitness for particular purpose or conformity to sample will depend upon whether the buyer deals as a consumer. If the buyer deals as a consumer, the exclusion is void;[71] if he does not deal as a consumer, the exclusion is subject to the reasonableness test.[72]

THE MISREPRESENTATION ACT 1967, s 3

Section 3 was amended by the Unfair Contract Terms Act to provide that a contract term which excludes or restricts liability in respect of misrepresentations made before the contract was entered or any remedy available in respect of such a misrepresentation is only enforceable if it satisfies the test of reasonableness in s 11(1) of the Unfair Contract Terms Act. As we have seen, this test is applied at the time of contracting and so modifies the previously applicable test which asked whether reliance on the term was fair and reasonable in the circumstances of the case.

THE UNFAIR TERMS IN CONSUMER CONTRACTS REGULATIONS 1999[73]

These regulations implement a European Directive[74] which has as its stated aim the promotion of a single European market. The Directive seeks to do this by requiring member states to enact a minimum level of consumer protection. In the UK it was implemented by the Unfair Terms in Consumer Contracts Regulations 1994.[75] In 1999 these were replaced with new regulations bearing the same name.[76] The major changes in the new regulations concern certain enforcement procedures. They extend to other bodies listed in the statute (Trading Standards Authorities, The Consumer Association, etc.) the power enjoyed by the Director General of Fair Trading to apply for an injunction to prevent continued use of a term. In addition, the Director General and the qualifying bodies are empowered to demand copies of standard agreements.

The manner of implementation is not a tidy one. The technique used was simply to copy out the provisions of the Directive.[77] This means that some of the language of the regulations, e.g. the good faith requirement is unfamiliar to a common lawyer. It also means that no attempt has been made to integrate the regulations with the Unfair Contract Terms Act 1977. The two measures overlap in many ways. The regulations apply to unfair terms in

---

[71] Section 6(2)(a).
[72] Section 6(3).
[73] See generally Beale, 'Unfair Contracts in Britain and Europe' [1989] CLP 229, Beale in Beatson and Friedmann (eds) (1995) *Good Faith and Fault in Contract Law*, and Bright, 'Winning the Battle Against Unfair Contract Terms' (2000) 20 LS 331.
[74] Council Directive 93/13/EEC.
[75] SI 1994 No. 3159. These came into force on 31 December 1994. The date specified in the Directive by which it should be enacted was 1 July 1995.
[76] SI 1999 No. 2083.
[77] Bright and Bright, 'Unfair Terms in Land Contracts: Copy Out or Cop Out' (1995) 111 LQR 655 criticise this approach.

contracts concluded between a seller or supplier and a consumer.[78] A consumer is defined as any natural person who is acting for purposes outside his trade, business or profession. A seller or supplier is a natural or legal person (e.g. a company) who is acting for the purposes of his trade, business or profession, whether publicly owned or not.[79] An unfair term in a contract concluded between a seller or supplier and a consumer is not binding on the consumer.[80] A contractual term is regarded as unfair if it has not been individually negotiated and 'contrary to the requirement of good faith, it causes a significant imbalance in the parties' rights and obligations ... to the detriment of the consumer'.[81] There are four elements here: the term must not be individually negotiated, and there must be an absence of good faith, a significant imbalance and a detriment to the consumer.[82]

A contractual term is always regarded as not having been individually negotiated where it has been drafted in advance and the consumer has not been able to influence the substance of the term.[83] Even if some terms are negotiated, the regulations will apply to the rest of the contract if 'an overall assessment of it indicates that it is a pre-formulated standard contract'.[84] If a seller or supplier claims that a contract was individually negotiated, he bears the burden of proving that it was.

The requirement of good faith has been said to have two aspects: procedural and substantive. A term may be unfair if its existence came as a surprise to the party subject to it. On the other hand, there will be some terms which cause such an imbalance in the parties' rights that they will always be regarded as unfair whatever steps were taken to publicise them. The element of a significant imbalance has been said 'to overlap substantially with that of the absence of good faith'.[85] It has been suggested that a term which gives the seller or supplier a significant advantage without a countervailing benefit to the consumer such as a reduced price might fail this test.[86] Finally, no term will be regarded as unfair unless it causes a detriment to the consumer.

The overlapping nature of these last three elements is revealed by the way they were applied by the Court of Appeal in *Director-General of Fair Trading* v *First National Bank plc*. The case concerned a standard form loan agreement which provided that on default of an instalment the creditor was entitled to demand repayment of the outstanding balance as well as all accrued interest. Further, interest would be payable at the contract rate until payment before and after judgment. The Court of Appeal thought that there was an absence of good faith on the part of the bank because the possibility of having to pay

---

[78] Regulation 4(1).
[79] Regulation 3(1).
[80] Regulation 8.
[81] Regulation 5(1).
[82] Beale in Beatson and Friedmann, *op. cit.*, ch. 5 at p. 245, quoted by the Court of Appeal in *Director-General of Fair Trading* v *First National Bank plc* [2000] 2 WLR 1353.
[83] Regulation 5(2).
[84] Regulation 5(3).
[85] *Director-General of Fair Trading* v *First National Bank plc* [2000] 2 WLR 1353 at 1366.
[86] *Ibid.*

interest even when complying with a court order to pay the debt in instalments was not specifically pointed out by the creditor and would create 'unfair surprise'. Moreover, it creates a significant imbalance in the rights and obligations of the parties by allowing the bank to obtain post-judgment interest in a way it would not usually be entitled to with no countervailing benefit to the debtor. Finally, there is clear detriment to the debtor who has to pay the interest.

Where a term is expressed in 'plain intelligible language', the assessment of fairness cannot relate to the definition of the main subject matter of the contract or the adequacy of the price or remuneration (the core terms).[87] If these provisions were interpreted broadly, they could protect from review many aspects of a contract. However, the Court of Appeal appeared to interpret these provisions restrictively in *Director-General of Fair Trading* v *First National Bank plc*[88] when it rejected the creditor's argument that the clause empowering the creditor to charge interest after judgment was a core term within the regulations. The creditor claimed that the terms of a loan contract which define the rate and duration of interest payments define the main subject matter of the contract and/or the price or remuneration for the loan. This argument was rejected by the Court of Appeal, which accepted that the clause in question dealt with secondary matters. It was a default provision to apply in the exceptional circumstance where there was a breach of contract. It did not define the price or remuneration. The contractual rate of interest was set elsewhere in the agreement; the clause in question merely defined the circumstances in which interest at the contractual rate was payable. The Court of Appeal apparently accepted the debtor's argument that to hold that this provision fell within the 'core term' exception would render most of the contract immune from challenge under the regulations.

The regulations also contain a so-called 'grey list' of terms which are to be considered presumptively unfair.[89] Many of these clauses would also be controlled by Unfair Contract Terms Act 1977. These include terms excluding or limiting the liability of a seller or supplier for the death of, or personal injury to, a consumer,[90] 'inappropriately' excluding or limiting the consumer's rights in the event of the seller's or supplier's non-performance, partial performance or inadequate performance[91] and binding the consumer to terms with which he had no real opportunity of becoming acquainted before he entered the contract.[92]

OVERVIEW

The law relating to the control of exemption clauses is undoubtedly complex

---

[87] Regulation 6(2)(a) and (b).
[88] *Cf. Kindlace* v *Murphy (NI)* (unreported), discussed by Bright, *op. cit.* p. 345, which takes an expansive view of what constitutes 'core terms'.
[89] Regulation 5(5) and Sch 2. The list describes 17 terms. *Cf. Zealander* v *Laing* (unreported), discussed by Bright, *op. cit.* p. 349, which suggests that this might overstate the effect of the list.
[90] Schedule 1, paras 1(a) and 90 respectively.
[91] Schedule 1, para 1(b).
[92] Sch 1, para 1(i).

and untidy. The coexistence of common law and statutory control produces areas of overlap. For instance, the steps taken by a party seeking to rely upon an exemption clause contained in an unsigned document or notice are relevant to the common law doctrine of incorporation as well as the definition of reasonableness in the Unfair Contract Terms Act 1977[93] and that of an unfair term within the Unfair Terms in Consumer Contracts Regulations 1999.[94] It is the relationship between the 1977 Act (the Act) and the 1999 Regulations (the regulations) that is most untidy. While it is clearly true that the two regimes are not mutually exclusive, they are not co-terminous. The overlap between them is imperfect: in some respects the Act is broader than the regulations; in other respects it is not.

When the following questions are asked, the Act is broader. *What parties are subject to the regime?* Some of the Act's provisions will apply to contracts between commercial contractors;[95] none of the regulations do.[96] *Are negotiated clauses controlled?* The Act can apply to such provisions; the regulations do not.[97] *Is the regime confined to the exclusion of contractual liability?* The Act controls the exclusion of some tortious liabilities;[98] the regulations do not.

When the following questions are asked, the regulations are broader. *Are contracts for the sale of interests in land covered?* The former are undoubtedly excluded from the Act,[99] but are probably within the regulations.[100] *Are clauses other than exemption clauses controlled?* Despite its title, the Act only controls exemption clauses.[101] The regulations extend to many other 'unfair' terms, e.g. penalty clauses,[102] and clauses permitting retention of a deposit.[103]

A further important point to remember is that there is considerable overlap between the different provisions *within* each regime. This is most easily illustrated by reference to the Act where an attempt by a business to restrict its liability to a private purchaser of goods for the negligent provision of an unsatisfactory good might be subject to ss 2(2), 3 and 6. This is especially important when applying the different regimes to a hypothetical problem. Consider the effect of each applicable regime and within each consider all relevant provisions. It will usually be the case that some provisions offer advantages over others. In the example above, s 6 will ban reliance on the clause, whereas s 2(2) will simply subject it to a reasonableness test.

[93] See Sch 2, para (c).
[94] See Sch 2, para 1(I).
[95] For instance, ss 2(1), 2(2), 3 (when dealing on written standard terms) and 8 (amending Misrepresentation Act 1967, s 3).
[96] Regulations 3 and 4.
[97] Regulation 5(1).
[98] Sections 2(1), 2(2) and 5.
[99] Schedule 1, para 1(b). See *Unchained Growth III plc* v *Granby Village Management Co Ltd* [2000] 1 WLR 739.
[100] See Bright and Bright, *op. cit.* and Attew, 'Teleological Interpretation and Land Law' (1995) 58 MLR 696.
[101] Section 13.
[102] Schedule 2, para 1(e).
[103] Schedule 2, para 1(d).

12

THE MODIFICATION OF CONTRACTS

INTRODUCTION

Contracts are entered into and contracts are terminated. This is a somewhat simplified account of the life of a contract but one that is reinforced by legal doctrine,[1] for much of the law of contract apparently concerns itself with only two episodes in a contract's life: birth and death. We have already seen that this view fails to recognise the negotiation stage of the contracting process as raising sufficiently distinct problems as to merit separate consideration. Such a view also neglects a whole dimension of contractual activity, the modification of contracts, the practical importance of which is emphasised in the small number of empirical studies which have been conducted.[2] This is the period after a contract comes into existence but before its end when it may be modified by the parties in response to changing circumstances external to it or to reflect the changing preferences of the contractors. The negotiation and modification of contracts are episodes in the life of a transaction as different from its formation and termination as conception and middle age are distinct from birth and death in the life of a human being.

It is as true in law as it is elsewhere that first impressions can be very misleading. It is no more the case that the law fails to respond to the problems raised by contractual modifications than it is that it does not regulate pre-contractual negotiations. However, the law relating to the modification of contracts is, like that relating to pre-contractual negotiations, dispersed. A complete account requires the examination of a number of different rules and doctrines which, in a traditional doctrinally arranged textbook, would be found in an early chapter dealing with the basic requirements of a contract (consideration and promissory estoppel), as part of a list of so-called vitiating factors (economic duress) located in the middle of the book, in a later chapter dealing with the discharge of contracts

---

[1] And by most legal textbooks which do not address modification as a discrete issue: see (1998) *Anson's Law of Contract*. 27th edn; Atiyah (1995) *An Introduction to the Law of Contract*. 5th edn; Cheshire, Fifoot and Furmston (13th edn); McKendrick (2000) *Contract Law*. 4th edn; Treitel (10th edn).

[2] Beale and Dugdale, 'Contracts between Businessmen: Planning and the Use of Contractual Remedies' (1975) 2 Brit J Law and Soc 18 and Macaulay, 'Non-Contractual Relations in Business: A Preliminary Study' (1963) 28 Am Soc Rev 45 and 'Elegant Models, Empirical Pictures and the Complexities of Contract' (1976) 11 J Law & Society Rev 507 and 'Business Practices and the Flexibility of Long Term Contracts' (1950) 36 Virg LR 627.

Fig. 12.1 The current legal response to a contractual modification

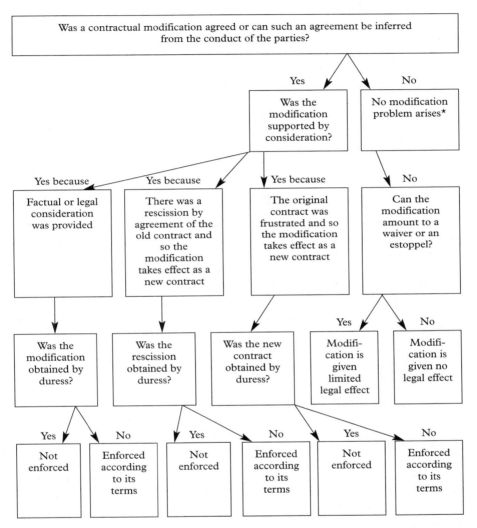

However, under the doctrine of mitigation the refusal of an offer of amended performance may reduce the innocent party's claim to damages for breach.

(frustration) and in a closing chapter devoted to remedies (mitigation). This multi-layered legal response to a contractual modification can best be summarised diagrammatically by Fig. 12.1.

It is a major theme of this book that the dispersal and consequent failure to recognise the common purpose of different doctrines or sub-doctrines is, for a number of related reasons, undesirable. First the policy objectives which the law should pursue are obscured. This produces a risk that doctrines will be applied in inappropriate contexts or in inappropriate ways. It also means that the law may fail to provoke valuable comment from judges and to stimulate relevant debate amongst commentators. Second, it can result in repetition when different doctrines do the same work. Third, confusion may be caused when doctrines appear to suggest different results perhaps as a result of their mechanistic application. Fourth, it is difficult to state and apply the law to resolve real life disputes.

The lack of orchestration of the law relating to contractual modifications will be more easily understood if we briefly examine[3] the policy objectives that should be pursued by the law in this area. Two different objectives can be identified: the promotion of contractual flexibility and the restraint of opportunism.

CONTRACTUAL FLEXIBILITY

Contracting parties are not omniscient. When they contract in an uncertain and complex world it becomes very costly, if not impossible, for them to provide in their contract for all future eventualities. The burden of initial contractual specification can be reduced if the law facilitates and encourages adaptive behaviour by contracting parties.[4] Consideration of this limited capacity of contractors to provide in advance for all possible outcomes would seem to commend enforcement of the modification in the following type of case.[5]

Example 1

A builder, A, contracts to build a house for B on land which B owns. When A is excavating the site, prior to laying the foundations, he discovers unanticipated mine workings beneath the site. Building would be dangerous unless they were filled in. Since construction would now cost A twice as much as the contract price, B agrees to pay him this. The mine workings were not reasonably discoverable before the excavation was started.

Enforcement of the modification in this case would seem to be warranted. It is an adaptation to a circumstance that was unanticipated and therefore not provided for in the original contract. Enforcement will encourage negotiating parties not to waste time providing for every possible contingency in their contracts, since they know that the agreement can subsequently be modified. Moreover, enforcement may allow both parties to realise potential benefits. The benefit to B from the modification is not immediately apparent, and may not amount to consideration, but he could be gaining an enhanced reputation for fair dealing; he may also derive a benefit from acting altruistically or he may wish to avoid the extra expense

---

[3] For a more detailed discussion, see Halson, 'Opportunism, Economic Duress and Contractual Modifications' (1991) 107 LQR 649 (hereafter Contractual Modifications) at 649–56.
[4] Williamson (1975) *Markets and Hierarchies*, p. 25.
[5] *Cf. Linz* v *Schuck* (1907) 67 A 286 and *Watkins & Son* v *Carrig* (1941) 21 A 2d 591.

which would fall upon him if performance on the original terms drove A into bankruptcy and prevented A from completing the work.[6]

OPPORTUNISM

Opportunism refers to the attempt by a party to a contract to exploit a vulnerability of his contractual partner which is created by the contract itself; the attempt is designed to secure a modification of the contract favouring the opportunist. An example will illustrate this.[7]

Example 2

A Co contracts with B Co, a company of shipbuilders, to construct a ship to be delivered on 1 January 2000. Many other shipbuilding companies tendered for the contract. A Co then enters a very lucrative charter with C Co to commence on 7 January 2000. On 1 December 1999 B Co demands an increase of 10 per cent in the contract price. It is aware of the charter and knows that it would cost A Co twice the contract price to get another ship built to fulfil the charter at such short notice. A Co agrees to pay the extra 10 per cent.

B Co has clearly taken advantage of a vulnerability of A Co created by its reliance upon the original contract. The objection to such opportunistic behaviour is its wastefulness. The opportunistic act is wasteful in itself because it consumes resources (the negotiating time of A and B) for no productive purpose, just to transfer further income from A to B.

Opportunistic behaviour may also be wasteful in two further ways. First, it creates a risk that the project will not actually be executed by the resource (B Co) that can do it most efficiently. For strategic reasons, A Co may have the ship built at another yard in order to demonstrate to shipbuilders that it is not prepared to accede to future opportunist demands. Secondly, it creates a risk that A Co will arrange its business inefficiently in an attempt to avoid a situation where opportunism could be exercised. For example, it may arrange a later commencement date for the charter. The law should aim to reduce this waste by refusing to give effect to opportunist modifications. Resources will then be freed for other constructive uses.

From the two examples considered above, it can be seen that there is a tension between the aim of encouraging contractual flexibility and the need to restrain opportunism. This tension may be resolved by the enforcement of non-opportunistic modifications and the non-enforcement of opportunistic ones.

It is apparent from the first example that one criterion which may help the courts to identify non-opportunistic modifications is the occurrence of

---

[6] See Posner, 'Gratuitous Promises in Economics and Law' (1977) 6 J Leg Stud 411 at 421; Muris, 'Opportunistic Behaviour and the Law of Contracts' (1981) 65 Minn L Rev 521. This was the situation in *Citra Constructions Ltd* v *Allied Asphalt Co Pty Ltd*, Supreme Court of New South Wales, unreported but discussed in Spence (1999) *Protecting Reliance*, pp. 128–35 (company which contracted to provide materials from overseas faced liquidation following devaluation of the Australian dollar unless modification was agreed).

[7] *Cf. The Atlantic Baron* [1979] 1 QB 705, discussed below.

circumstances which were not anticipated in the contract. Indeed, the courts already may, to a limited degree, take account of such circumstances through the application of the doctrine of frustration,[8] for if the doctrine applies, the original contract is discharged and the 'modification' is then enforceable as a new contract. It is submitted that when parties agree to a modification in response to unanticipated circumstances, and that modification reasonably reflects the impact of those circumstances, it should be enforced even if the unanticipated circumstances are insufficiently calamitous to cause the doctrine of frustration to apply. If the extent of the modification is reasonably related to the impact of the unanticipated circumstances, there is no suspicion of opportunism.

The second example provides a clue to identifying opportunistic modifications, which is to examine the attractiveness of the alternatives open to the party whose position is ostensibly less attractive as a result of the modification. If all his alternative courses of action are actually less attractive than submission to the modification, this should raise a strong suspicion of opportunism. Conversely, if he consents to a modification when an adequate alternative (a legal remedy or a substitute performance) is available, this may rebut the inference of opportunism.

The analysis of opportunism presented here is not yet complete. In some circumstances it will be seen that the strict non-enforcement of opportunistic modifications may not be the best approach.

Where a rule of non-enforcement works

Consider again Example 2. The acts of B Co were clearly opportunistic since it was seeking a contractual modification by exploiting a vulnerability in A Co created by the contract itself. Here a firm rule of non-enforceability would, in effect, give B Co the choice of performing or breaching. It obviously anticipated making a profit at the original contract price; its later demand was merely a strategic attempt to increase that profit. When given the choice of retaining the original profit by performing or having to pay damages to A Co for a breach, it will obviously prefer the former course. Therefore, the rule of non-enforcement works and will help to discourage parties in the position of B Co from indulging in similar exploitative behaviour in the future.

Where a rule of non-enforcement fails[9]

Example 3

A contracts to build a new workshop for B, a clothes manufacturer, for £100,000. Many other acceptable tenders were rejected. B needs the workshop

---

[8] See below.

[9] *Cf.* Mather, 'Contract Modification under Duress' (1982) 33 S Carol L Rev 615; Robison, 'Enforcing Extorted Contract Modification' (1983) 68 Iowa L Rev 699.

because of a lucrative contract he has obtained from the government. Since B does not tell A of the government contract at the time of contracting, it is 'too remote' for damages for loss of profit under it to be recoverable if A breaches the contract. The construction contract specifically allocates the risk of increases in the cost of construction materials to A. The cost of bricks doubles and A demands £150,000 to build the workshop. No substitute builder can complete the job in time for B to fulfil the government contract.

This example differs from the earlier housebuilding example since here it is not the materialisation of an unanticipated circumstance which has occurred, but the materialisation of a risk that was specifically assigned to one party. Hence, the arguments outlined earlier to support the enforcement of non-opportunistic modifications, where the parties are agreeing upon the allocation of a risk which their original bargain failed to address, do not apply. A is taking advantage of B's reliance upon his punctual performance. He is trying to reallocate a risk which the original bargain assigned to him. Since this is an example of opportunism, a rule of non-enforcement would seem to commend itself. However, this is not so if some further facts are added:

A originally envisaged a profit of £20,000 (i.e. £100,000 – £80,000, the costs of materials and labour). Due to an increase in the costs of bricks, if A performed the contract at £100,000, he would lose £30,000. Hence, to maintain the same profit, he asked for £150,000. There is an effective clause in the contract limiting A's liability in the event of his breach to £10,000.

Here a rule of non-enforcement simply will not work to the advantage of B. Such a rule will not persuade A to perform rather than breach; he will prefer to breach and lose £10,000 rather than perform at the original contract price and lose £30,000. So the rule of non-enforcement will result in B losing the profits on his valuable government contract.

So, where, if a modification is not enforced, a party seeking to take advantage of opportunism will still prefer to breach his contract rather than to perform it, perhaps the modification should be enforced. To adopt a contrary rule would be to injure all future parties in B's position, the very persons whom the anti-opportunism rule is supposed to protect. The non-enforcement rule would prevent these 'victims' of opportunism from offering a credible inducement to secure the performance they prefer to a breach. In other words, they cannot 'buy' the actual performance they want, and are left to a remedy in damages which they do not want.[10] The essential distinguishing characteristic of this type of case, where the opportunistic modification should be enforced, as opposed to the earlier example where it should not, is that here if it is not enforced the opportunist will prefer breach to performance.[11]

This suggestion, that certain opportunistic modifications should be

---

[10] The 'new' definition of consideration endorsed in *Williams* v *Roffey Bros* [1991] 1 QB 1 can be supported on this basis.
[11] For further variations on this example, see Halson, 'Contractual Modifications' (n. 3 herein above) at pp. 654–5.

enforced,[12] is only justified in order to induce performance rather than breach. If this is the sole reason for enforcing such modifications then perhaps they should be enforced only to the extent necessary to induce performance. In the example above, A will prefer to perform rather than breach if paid anything in excess of £130,000. Since the only justification for this rule would be to minimise B's losses, it may be considered wrong legally to sanction any greater wealth transfer from B to A than is necessary to induce the performance which avoids B's losses on the government contract.

However, this would involve the courts in rewriting the parties' contract, a task they frequently refuse to perform.[13] Nevertheless, if they do not, they are forced to choose between a rule of non-enforcement of opportunistic modifications and enforcement of such modifications to their full extent. The former rule will serve only to increase the losses of the party whom it seeks to protect, when faced with an opportunist who prefers breach to performance. The latter sanctions a greater wealth transfer than is necessary to avert the injurious consequences of breach. The middle path of limited enforcement may, therefore, seem to commend itself.

The middle path is itself not without risk. Its success would crucially depend upon an accurate assessment by the court of the extent to which it is necessary to enforce the modification in order to induce the opportunist to perform. If this is underestimated, the opportunist will prefer to breach rather than perform the contract as modified by the court, with the attendant hardship for the original promise. Thereafter, potential future promisees will justifiably have little confidence in the court's ability to ensure that they will receive the promisor's contractual performance following a modification. This may result in future contractors arranging their affairs inefficiently in order to protect themselves from the possibility of opportunistic extortion to a greater extent than if the legal machinery ensured that they were at least able to offer a credible inducement to an opportunistic contractual partner. Since the courts have no experience of this sort of enquiry, and consequently the risk of error is high, it may be preferable in such situations to enforce the modification to its full extent. The court could be confident that the amount stipulated would be sufficient to induce the opportunist to perform, otherwise he would probably not have agreed to the modification.

This discussion of policy objectives may also be summarised diagrammatically (Fig. 12.2). A comparison of Fig. 12.2 with Fig. 12.1 raises questions about whether the legal regime which regulates contractual modifications is overly elaborate and poorly co-ordinated.

---

[12] *Cf.* Smith, 'Contracting Under Pressure: A Theory of Duress' [1997] CLJ 343 at 348–9 who says: 'From an economic perspective, this approach may be acceptable but from a moral perspective it seems wrong as it rewards wrongdoing.' However, what is the value of a protection that actually injures its victims?

[13] For example, 'Nothing is more dangerous than to allow oneself liberty to construct for the parties contracts which they have not in terms made ...', *per* Lord Atkin in *Bell* v *Lever Bros Ltd* [1932] AC 161 at 226; see the discussion below of the extraordinary American case of *Alcoa* v *Essex Group Inc* (1980) 499 F Supp 53, where the court simply redrafted the parties' contract for them.

Fig. 12.2 The opportunism analysis

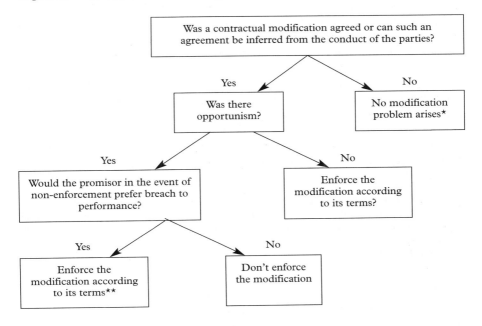

* *Unless it is desired to encourage modifications by limiting recovery for breach of contract when a modification has been refused.*

** *Note the possibility of limited enforcement.*

THE PRE-EXISTING DUTY DOCTRINE

If the legal response to a mutually agreed contractual modification may be expressed as a chronology, the first legal doctrine applied is that of consideration. Until recently a contractual adjustment was said to be unsupported by consideration if the only promise given in return for it was to perform a pre-existing legal duty created by the original contract.[14] This rule was traditionally derived from the case of *Stilk* v *Myrick*,[15] where a sailor sought to recover an extra sum of money promised to him if he would continue to serve on a ship until it returned to England. The sailor was already contractually bound to complete the return voyage and his action to recover the extra sum failed.[16] A distinction is sometimes drawn[17] between two different definitions of consideration: factual and legal. A factual

---

[14] Reynolds and Treitel, 'Consideration for the Modification of Contracts' (1965) 7 Malaya L Rev 1.

[15] (1809) 2 Camp 317; 6 Esp. 129. The name of the defendant is spelt differently in each report. I am following the spelling of Campbell. For an interesting account of the background to the case and its reporting, see Luther, 'Campbell, Espinasse and the Sailors: Text and Context in the Common Law' (1999) 19 LS 526.

[16] That the captain was the defendant is only stated in Espinasse at p. 129.

[17] For example, Treitel, p. 65.

definition emphasises the *fact* of benefit or detriment; a legal definition, recognises as consideration only those acts which the promisor was not already under a *legal* obligation to perform. *Stilk v Myrick* is often cited to support a legal definition of consideration because the only consideration moving from the seaman to support the promise of extra money was his promise to 'work the ship home': something which he was already obliged to do under his original contract of employment.[18] However, only in Campbell's report is the failure ascribed to the absence of consideration, and this rationalisation of the case was expressly disapproved in *Harris v Carter*.[19] The alternative report of Espinasse explains the decision on the basis of the 'just and proper policy',[20] recognised in the almost identical earlier case of *Harris v Watson*.[21] In *Harris v Watson* Lord Kenyon explained the policy of law in this way:[22]

> If this action was to be supported it would materially affect the navigation of the Kingdom ... This rule was founded on a principle of policy, for if sailors were in all events to have their wages and in times of danger entitled to insist on an extra charge on such a promise as this they would in many cases suffer a ship to sink unless the captain would pay any extravagant demand they might think proper to make.

Another early case exposes the policy objective being pursued by the law in this area. This is the case of *Hartley v Ponsonby*[23] which similarly involved a claim by a seaman for extra wages. The claim was successful this time, but only after the jury had found that the captain's offer of extra money was made, 'voluntarily ... not by coercion'.[24] The precise juristic basis of the case

---

[18] See also *Atlas Express Ltd v Kafco Ltd* [1989] QB 833 (road carrier demanded greater payment than originally agreed to distribute small company's product to large national chain – held agreement to pay the extra not supported by consideration) and the New Zealand case of *Cook Island Shipping Co Ltd v Colson Builders Ltd* [1975] 1 NZLR 422 (carrier of goods by sea demanded extra payment in addition to the agreed freight – held agreement to pay extra not supported by consideration). *Contra: The Atlantic Baron* [1979] QB 705 (considered below) and *The Alev* [1989] 1 Lloyd's Rep 138 (purchasers of goods agreed with the owners of the carrying vessel to pay various expenses – ship owners appointment of purchasers as their agent was sufficient legal consideration to support the promise to pay expenses) where a legal test for consideration was applied and satisfied. However, the agreements in *Atlas* and *The Alev* were ultimately unenforceable for being obtained by economic duress. For this aspect, see later in this chapter.

[19] (1854) 3 E & B 559 at 562.

[20] At p. 130. Espinasse's Reports are usually treated with considerable caution. See Blackburn J's comments in *Redhead v Midland Railway Co* [1866–67] LR 2 QB 412 at 437. Of Espinasse and two other reporters he said: 'neither reporter has such a character for intelligence and accuracy as to make it at all certain that the facts are correctly stated, or that the opinion of the judge was rightly understood'. Most damning and amusing is the comment attributed to Maule J that did not care 'for Espinasse or any other ass'. Indeed, it appears that 6 Espinasse may even be the least reliable volume of his reports as it was composed from contemporaneous notes two years after the cases were heard when Espinasse was suffering from a nervous disease (6 Esp. v–vi). However, perhaps on this occasion the report can be trusted as Espinasse did appear as counsel.

[21] (1791) Peake 102.

[22] *Ibid.*, p. 103.

[23] (1857) 7 E & B 872.

[24] *Ibid.*, p. 875.

is unclear, but it seems that a large number of desertions[25] somehow discharged the obligations of the remaining crew under their original contracts, leaving the claimant in the position of a 'free man'[26] to contract afresh. Whether this discharge occurred as a result of a principle analogous to frustration[27] or turns upon a special rule of policy that a seaman should not be held to a promise to work on an unsafe ship[28] is not certain. However, again, the policy of enforcing freely negotiated modifications was respected.

These cases stand therefore as a rare early articulation of the policy consideration underpinning the law in the area of contractual modifications; the non-enforcement of extorted modifications and the enforcement of freely agreed alterations. Judges elsewhere have recently made explicit reference to the policy goals of the law relating to contractual modifications, at the same time recognising the limited role that the doctrine of consideration can play in furthering these policies. In the United States Posner J has said:[29]

> The requirement of consideration has, however, a distinct function in the modification setting – although one it does not perform well – that is to prevent coercive modifications.

Similarly, in Australia Santow J recently noted that:[30]

> If it be assumed that the underlying concern is to prevent coercive modifications, the traditional notion of consideration does not perform that role very well.

These recent restatements of the policy basis of earlier cases[31] are valuable because this underlying policy appeared to be forgotten when the rule was stated in terms of a requirement of legal consideration, since the simple assertion that a promise to do what one is already bound by a contract with the promisor to do cannot be consideration seemed to have both an intuitive appeal and an internal consistency.[32] However, so stated, the pre-existing duty rule has been said to involve either an error of fact or logic.[33] It involves an error of fact if it is taken to mean that actual performance of the pre-existing duty is not a benefit in fact. In comparison with a promise to perform, it is 'a bird in the hand is worth more than a bird in the bush'. If it is conceded that there is a benefit (or detriment) in fact, but asserted that there is not one in law, the error is one of logic. The use of the phrase 'in law'

---

[25] Nineteen crew members out of 36 deserted; *cf. Stilk* v *Myrick* where two crew members deserted, though it is not clear how many sailors constituted a full crew.

[26] *Loc. cit.*, p. 877.

[27] Of course, the case predated the classic articulation of the doctrine of frustration in *Taylor* v *Caldwell* (1863) 3 B & S 826.

[28] Hinted at by Lord Campbell, *loc. cit.*, p. 877.

[29] *United States* v *Stamp Home Specialities Manufacturing Inc* (1990) 905 F 2d 1117 at 1121–2.

[30] *Musumieci* v *Winadell* [1994] 34 NSWLR 723 at 742.

[31] See also *Cook Island Shipping Co Ltd* v *Colson Builders Ltd* [1975] 1 NZLR 422 referring to an older American case *Lingenfelder* v *Wainwright Brewery Co* (1891) 15 SW 844.

[32] This is what Sharp meant when he said that the pre-existing duty rule: 'was very commonly framed in analytical language implying a kind of cogency in the mere assertion that doing what one is bound to do can amount to nothing', 'Pacta Sunt Servanda' (1941) 41 Col L Rev 783 at 786.

[33] (1963) *Corbin on Contracts*, s 172. *Contra*: Spence (1999) *Protecting Reliance*, p. 130.

simply begs the question. It amounts to saying that performance of a duty is not a legally recognised consideration because it is not a consideration that is legally recognised. Thus, Corbin makes explicit the fact that adherence to the pre-existing duty rule is not a logical corollary of the definition of consideration as any benefit or detriment,[34] and so is not necessary to maintain its logical consistency. The enforcement of the rule threatens to frustrate the reasonable expectations of businessmen who have agreed on a modification. It is also inconsistent with all empirical studies of contractual modifications,[35] which reveal a greater willingness to adapt and respond to unanticipated changes than the pre-existing duty rule would apparently 'permit'. Parties rarely insist on their strict legal entitlement. They do not 'go for the jugular when trouble arises'.[36]

However, even the judicial application of the legal definition of consideration reveals a reluctance to apply it mechanistically to all the situations it ostensibly governed. As Santow J observed in the Supreme Court of New South Wales: 'In truth, there has been a continuing trend to side-step the artificial results of a strict doctrine of consideration.'[37] It could be evaded in the English courts by the use of two techniques: the finding of a rescission followed immediately by the conclusion of a new contract or the discovery of some, perhaps nominal, fresh consideration. An investigation into these evasion techniques is instructive.

Rescission and new contract

Where duties on both sides are still outstanding before any breach has occurred, it is possible for the parties to agree to rescind their original agreement. Thus in *Langden v Stokes*,[38] the maxim was approved, *eodem modo quo oritur eodem modo quo dissolvitur*[39] (in the same way the agreement has arisen it may be dissolved). The lines of authority represented by *Langden v Stokes* and *Stilk v Myrick* are, therefore, in potential conflict. The courts can clearly find that the rescission of the old contract was followed immediately by the creation of a new one with identical terms to the original, except for an altered price clause. Thus the pre-existing duty rule is evaded.

This conflict has been partially obscured by the technical confusion of the law in this area.[40] The complicating factor is the formal requirement

---

[34] *Cf.* Cheshire, Fifoot and Furmston, who may fall into the error identified by Sharp, when at p. 93 they write of: 'The somewhat obvious rule that there is no consideration if all that the claimant does is to perform, or to promise the performance of, an obligation already imposed on him.'

[35] See n. 2 above.

[36] A telling phrase used by MacNeil, 'Economic Analysis of Contractual Relations: Its Shortfalls and the Need for a Rich Classificatory Apparatus' (1981) 75 NW Univ L Rev 1018 at 1048.

[37] *Musumeci v Winadell Pty Ltd* [1994] 34 NSWLR 723 at 740.

[38] (1634) Cro Car 383.

[39] *Ibid.*, p. 384.

[40] See generally Stoljar's excellent article, 'The Modification of Contracts' (1957) 35 Can Bar Rev 485 at 509, to which I am indebted. The most important of the formal requirements was

imposed on certain types of contract. Where a contract is required to be in writing to be enforceable, an oral modification may be effective as a rescission of the original contract,[41] but will be ineffective as a variation of it.[42] Yet, the outcome of the cases seems to suggest that the courts, if they possibly can, will enforce what they consider to be a reasonable and non-extorted accommodation, whatever result technical doctrines ostensibly dictate. Thus in *Morris* v *Baron*[43] the House of Lords enforced a modification notwithstanding that no action could be brought on the original contract because it was rescinded and the variation was unenforceable because it did not comply with the relevant formalities. That the courts are prepared to evade technical doctrines and enforce modifications appears to have been admitted by Lord Sumner in *British Benningtons* v *NW Cachar Tea*,[44] an admission which was repeated by Lord Devlin, delivering the judgment of the Privy Council in *United Dominions Corporation (Jamaica) Ltd* v *Shoucair* when he said:[45]

> The choice before the Board lies between solving the problem by means of ... formal logic or solving it by giving effect as far as possible to the intention of the parties as was done in *Morris* v *Baron*. The argument for the respondents assumed rightly that their Lordships would accept the guidance offered in *Morris* v *Baron* ...

The rescission and new contract device has also been used in *Raggou* v *Scougall*[46] to enforce a contractual modification which reduced the contract price. This poorly reported decision of the King's Bench again reveals the manipulations of this technique. Darling J expressed himself to be delighted to be able to prevent the claimant from recovering the difference between his lower amended salary and his original salary, because he was trying to do 'a very dishonest thing'.

In *Schwartzreich* v *Bauman-Basch*[47] the Court of Appeals of New York enforced an agreement to pay the claimant extra wages on the basis of a rescission followed 'shortly afterwards' by a new agreement. However, the court said that the result would be the same whether the rescission occurred shortly before, or at the time of, the new agreement. While this evasion of the pre-existing duty rule may allow courts to enforce reasonable modifications, the legal logic behind it reduces to more tautology. Courts are forced to argue in a circle, making the validity of the new agreement depend on the rescission, when the validity of the rescission depended on the new

---

probably the Sale of Goods Act 1893, s 4, until its repeal in 1954 by the Law Reform (Enforcement of Contracts) Act, s 2. Then it was Law of Property Act 1925, s 40, but see now Law of Property (Miscellaneous Provisions) Act 1989, s 2.

[41] *Halsbury's Laws of England*, 4th edn, Vol. 9, para 565.

[42] *Ibid.*, para. 570.

[43] [1918] AC 1.

[44] [1923] AC 48.

[45] [1969] 1 AC 340, 349A. *Contra: McCausland* v *Duncan Lawrie Ltd* [1996] 4 All ER 995 (oral variation of contract for sale of land not enforced).

[46] (1915) 31 TLR 564. See also *Williams* v *Moss Empires* [1915] 3 KB 242.

[47] (1921) 131 NE 887. See also Dekoven, 'Modification of a Contract in New York: Criteria for Enforcement' (1967) 35 Univ Ch L Rev 173.

agreement.[48] Moreover, courts must take great care when applying this approach. The modification in *Schwartzreich*, for example, may have been extorted, the designer knowing that his employer had to get his samples on the road immediately.

A finding of new consideration

There are two ways in which the court may find new consideration and so avoid the conclusion that a contractual modification is unenforceable for want of consideration. The first way is to find 'legal' consideration. Strictly such a finding takes the case out of the ambit of the pre-existing duty rule.[49] However, in so far as the consideration 'found' is purely nominal, it represents another means by which the courts can enforce meritorious modifications.[50] This is perhaps illustrated by *The Atlantic Baron*[51] where a shipyard demanded that all outstanding instalments due under a shipbuilding contract be increased to 'compensate' them for a currency devaluation. The purchaser, who had concluded a lucrative charter for the ship and who could not reasonably obtain a replacement elsewhere, reluctantly agreed. The purchaser also asked the yard to increase the letter of credit[52] to cover the larger instalment payments. The court held that the increase in the letter of credit was good consideration to support the purchaser's promise to increase the outstanding instalments.[53]

The recognition of nominal consideration as conferring presumptive validity on a modification is dangerous. There is a considerable risk that it will be introduced into the modification by a well-advised opportunist to disguise his extortion as a bargain. Santow J recently expressed this concern in the Supreme Court of New South Wales when he said, 'Consideration expressed in formalistic terms of one dollar can indeed actually cloak duress rather than expose it.'[54] In *The Alev* Hobhouse J bluntly said: [55]

---

[48] Corbin, 'Hard Cases Make Good Law' (1923) 33 Yale LJ 78 at 80.

[49] *Target Holdings v Priestley* (High Court, unreported): mortgagor who accepted immediate personal liability to repay some arrears instead of the conditional liability assumed under the original mortgage thereby provided good consideration for the mortgagee's promise to give up its claim to recover other arrears.

[50] Lord Hailsham in *Woodhouse Ltd v Nigerian Produce Ltd* [1972] AC 741, 757 appears to hint at the courts' ability to 'invent' consideration.

[51] *North Ocean Shipping v Hyundai Construction Co* [1979] QB 705. See also the New Zealand case of *Moyes and Groves Ltd v Radiation (NZ) Ltd* [1982] 1 NZLR 368 (buyer ordered goods which had to be imported from India and were delivered three years later – seller provided good consideration to support buyer's promise of a higher purchase by giving up its claim that the original contract had been abandoned).

[52] The letter of credit was a guarantee by the yard's bank that in the event of the yard's insolvency, the instalment payments would be reimbursed.

[53] *Ibid.*, p. 713E. See to similar effect *Kilbuck Coal v Turner and Robinson* (1915) 7 OWN 673; *contra*: *Gilbert Steel v University Construction Ltd* (1973) 36 DLR (3d) 496 Aff'd (1976) 67 DLR (3d) 606.

[54] *Musumeci v Winadell Pty Ltd* [1994] 34 NSWLR 723 at 742.

[55] [1989] 1 Lloyd's Rep 138 at 147.

The present case illustrates this point. The claimants alleged various items of consideration. None of them had any commercial substance and merely illustrated the poverty of their case. Although I consider that in one respect there was technically consideration, neither that head nor any other went any way towards undermining the conclusion that the agreement was entered into under compulsion.

This risk is recognised in both the Restatement of Contracts 2d and the Uniform Commercial Code in the United States. In the Restatement, the pre-existing duty doctrine is retained. However, to avoid the risks associated with sham consideration, s 73 also requires that there be 'more than a pretence of bargain'. Similarly, the Uniform Commercial Code abolishes the requirement of consideration for a modification under UCC, s 2.209(i) and replaces it with a requirement of good faith, but the presence of technical consideration cannot validate a bad faith modification according to s 2.209, comment 2.

The use of technical consideration in this way is subject to a further criticism; namely that its use to avoid the pre-existing duty doctrine considerably distorts the real nature of the 'bargain' under discussion. In *The Atlantic Baron* the extra money was paid by the purchaser to ensure delivery of their ship on time, not because they wanted an increase in a letter of credit.

It seems that the force of this argument was recognised by the Court of Appeal in an important case which opens up a second way in which the court may find new consideration and so avoid the conclusion that a contractual modification is unenforceable for want of consideration. In *Williams* v *Roffey Bros & Nicholls (Contractors) Ltd*[56] the defendants, the main contractors, were engaged to carry out the refurbishment of a block of flats. They sub-contracted the carpentry to the claimant. He was to be paid £20,000 in stages related to the amount of work done. While carrying out his contractual obligation, the claimant suffered financial difficulties which the judge found were caused by two factors: the claimant's failure to supervise his workmen adequately and the fact that the original price of £20,000 was too low. The defendants, who were themselves subject to a time penalty clause in the main contract, therefore proposed to pay the claimant an additional sum in instalments of £575 at the time of completion of each remaining flat. Shortly thereafter the claimant ceased work, having 'substantially', but not totally, completed the carpentry in eight further flats.

In the Court of Appeal the defendants' principal submission was that their promise to pay additional sums was not supported by consideration.[57] All

---

[56] [1990] 1 All ER 512; Adams and Brownsword, 'Contract, Consideration and the Critical Path' (1990) 53 MLR 536. Chen Wishart 'Consideration: Practical Benefit and the Emperor's New Clothes' in Beatson and Friedman (eds) (1995) *Good Faith in Contract Law*; ch. 5; Halson, 'Sailors, Sub-Contractors and Consideration' (1990) 106 LQR 183; Phang, 'Consideration at the Crossroads' (1991) 107 LQR 21.

[57] A subsidiary submission that the additional payments were only due as each flat was completed, substantial completion not being enough, was quickly dismissed by the court relying upon *Hoenig* v *Isaacs* [1952] 2 All ER 176.

three judges agreed that the promise of additional payments was supported by consideration but did not agree as to where the consideration was to be found.

Glidewell LJ expressly followed the judgment of the majority of the Court of Appeal in *Ward* v *Byham* and of the whole Court of Appeal in *Williams* v *Williams*.[58] These decisions were based upon a legal definition of consideration; the disputed promises were each tendered in exchange for a promise more extensive than the pre-existing duty and so were enforced. The consideration identified by Glidewell LJ comprised: the assurance that the claimant would continue working and not halt work in breach of contract, the avoidance of the penalty clause operating, and the avoidance of the expense of engaging different carpenters to complete the work. It is respectfully submitted that these benefits to the defendants could only have amounted to factual consideration and only then if they represented losses which would not be recoverable as damages in the event of breach (perhaps any penalty payment would have been too remote?). The judgments of Russell and Purchas LJJ also appear to be based upon a factual definition of consideration. Russell LJ referred to the advantages of replacing what had hitherto been a haphazard method of payment by a more formalised scheme. Similarly, Purchas LJ pointed to the reorganisation of working practices which resulted from the promise to pay additional sums, whereby each flat was completed by the claimant in turn, thus allowing the defendants' other tradesmen access to do their work.

Innovations in the law are often introduced in a way that downplays their significance. This protective reflex on the part of the originator is often necessary to avert the premature death of their progeny. An acknowledgement of this in the context of contractual modifications was a typically honest comment of Lord Denning upon his 'invention' of the doctrine of promissory estoppel that '[m]uch as I am inclined to favour the principle stated in the *High Trees* case it should not be stretched too far lest it be endangered'.[59] In *Williams* v *Roffey* a similar reflex can be detected. Glidewell LJ formulated the principle of factual consideration introduced by the case in a defensive way which limited it to the context of contractual modifications. He summarised the law in this way:

> ... the present state of the law on this subject can be expressed in the following proposition:
>
> (i) if A has entered into a contract with B to do work for, or to supply goods or services to, B in return for payment by B; and
>
> (ii) at some stage before A has completely performed his obligations under the contract B has no reason to doubt whether A will, or be able to, complete his side of the bargain; and
>
> (iii) B thereupon promises A an additional payment in return for A's promise to perform his contractual obligations on time; and

---

[58] *Ward*: [1956] 1 WLR 496; *Williams*: [1957] 1 WLR 148.
[59] *Combe* v *Combe* [1951] 2 KB 215 at 219.

(iv) as a result of giving his promise, B obtains in practice a benefit, or obviates a disbenefit; and

(v) B's promise is not given as a result of economic duress or fraud on the part of A; then,

(vi) the benefit to B is capable of being consideration for B's promise, so that the promise will be legally binding.[60]

This formulation may be criticised in a number of respects for being underinclusive and ambiguous. Propositions (iii), (iv)(b), (v) and (vi) are underinclusive. There is no logical reason to limit the third proposition to promises by B to make a payment to A; it should also extend to a promise by B to forgive or reduce a debt owed to him by A. The fourth and sixth propositions also need expansion. Consideration is traditionally defined in terms of either a benefit to the promisee *or* a detriment to the promisor,[61] whereas Glidewell LJ's propositions only allow for the former. The fifth proposition also needs expanding to include other forms of unacceptable conduct besides economic duress (e.g. undue influence).

However, a more serious criticism of Glidewell LJ's account of the law is an inherent ambiguity. Proposition (iv) fails to make clear whether the factual consideration recognised in the case is the practical value to the promisee of a repeated promise of the promisor's original undertaking or the practical value of actual performance. The answer is surely the latter. It is difficult to see what benefit could be said to accrue to the main contractor or detriment be suffered by the sub-contractor simply as a result of the latter's repetition of his earlier promise. The benefit or detriment results from the actual performance of that obligation. Further, the same proposition does not make clear how factual consideration is to be applied in the case of contractual modifications. Here it must be remembered that the subsequent promisor would have available to him the usual remedies for breach of contract against the other party. The ascertainment of factual consideration requires a comparison of the position of the subsequent promisor if he gets the performance he has contracted to receive with his position if all he has is an action for breach of contract against the defaulter. In many cases the former will be more valuable and so amount to factual consideration. In *Williams* v *Roffey* the sub-contractor's performance permitted the main contractor to avoid liability under a clause in the contract he entered with the property owner whereby the main contractor would become liable to make a payment if the work was not completed on time. Such a payment would probably not be recoverable by the main contractor in an action against the sub-contractor because it was probably too remote[62] a consequence of his breach of contract.

---

[60] At p. 15.

[61] *Currie* v *Misa* (1875) LR 10 Ex 153, discussed above.

[62] The law does not hold a person accountable for all the consequences of his wrongful act. Rather as a matter of policy it limits the damages which the wrongdoer must pay. This is called the principle of remoteness of loss. Damages which are irrecoverable are said to be too remote. Remoteness is considered in detail in Chapter 17.

Similarly, if the facts of *The Atlantic Baron*[63] were to recur today, it is possible that Mocatta J would have found that there was factual consideration in the purchaser's promise to increase the instalments because the yard's performance of its obligation (i.e. to build the ship and deliver it on time) permitted the customer to meet its commitments under a lucrative charter it had concluded. Again, it is likely that if the subsequent promisor pursues an action for breach of contract against his contractual partner the principle of remoteness would mean he failed to recover his full losses, i.e. the loss of profit under the charter. *Musumeci* v *Winadell Pty Ltd*[64] involved a rent reduction offered by the landlord of commercial premises when he let an adjacent property to a competitor of the first tenant. Santow J held that there was a practical benefit to the landlord sufficient to constitute good consideration because he thereby retained the original tenant as a viable business. The implication is that without the concession the tenant would have closed down or become insolvent which would have respectively deprived the landlord of future rent and left him unable to recover accrued rent.

In *Musumeci* Santow J helpfully reformulated the principles stated by Glidewell LJ in *Williams* v *Roffey* to meet the criticism of underinclusiveness and ambiguity.[65] It is suggested that this reformulation should be preferred to the original for a coherent statement of the principle of factual consideration introduced in *Williams* v *Roffey*. Santow J said:

> The present state of the law on this subject can be expressed in the following proposition:
> (i)   If A has entered into a contract with B to do work for, or to supply goods or services to, B in return for the payment by B, and
> (ii)   At some stage before A has completely performed his obligations under the contract B has reason to doubt whether A will, or be able to, complete his side of the bargain, and
> (iii)   B thereupon promises A an additional payment or other concession (such as reducing A's original obligation) in return for A's promise to perform this contractual obligation at the time, and
> (iv)   (a)   As a result of giving his promise B obtains in practice a benefit, or obviates a disbenefit provided that A's performance, having regard to what has been so obtained, is capable of being viewed by B as worth more to B than any likely remedy against A (allowing for any defences or cross-claims), taking into account the cost to B of any such payment or concession to obtain greater assurance of A's performance, or
>   (b)   as a result of giving his promise, A suffers a detriment (or obviates a benefit) provided that A is thereby foregoing the opportunity of not performing the original contract, in circumstances where such non-performance, taking into account B's likely remedy against A (and allowing for any defences or cross-claims) is capable of being viewed by A as worth more to A than performing that contract, in the absence of B's promised payment or concession to A.

---

[63] [1979] QB 705; see below for the facts of this case.
[64] (1994) 34 NSWLR 723.
[65] *Ibid.*, p. 747.

(v) B's promise is not given as a result of economic duress or fraud or undue influence or unconscionable conduct on the part of A nor is it induced as a result of unfair pressure on the part of A, having regard to the circumstances, then,

(vi) The benefit to B or the detriment to A is capable of being consideration for B's promise, so that the promise will be legally binding.

The test of factual benefit introduced in *Williams* v *Roffey* has been applied in a small number of cases. In one case[66] the promise of a party to take delivery of a ship in accordance with his obligations under a pre-existing contract was held to confer a sufficient practical benefit or, strictly, avoidance of a disbenefit to the shipbuilder. This meant that a number of concessions granted by the shipbuilder were contractually binding on him. Hirst J found that the purpose of the concessions was to dissuade other key customers from breaching their contracts. If the shipbuilder's actions for breach of these contracts would not fully compensate him for his losses, it is possible that there was good consideration. However, the case appears to be a weaker case than *Williams* v *Roffey* for inferring practical benefit. In *Williams* v *Roffey*, the sub-contractor's timely performance was highly likely to avoid the main contractor's liability under the 'penalty' clause; in *Anangel* the benefit to the shipbuilder was far more speculative. Would one customer taking delivery necessarily persuade others to do so? Where an employer agrees severance terms with redundant employees this may disclose factual consideration. There may be a practical benefit to the employer from the continued performance of the employee's contract and there might also be an avoidance of detriment in the form of harmonious industrial relations at a difficult time.[67] In New Zealand the Court of Appeal referred to *Williams* v *Roffey* as a 'marginal case' but none the less followed it[68] and, as we have seen, it has been followed in Australia in *Musumeci*.

One possible application of the rule in this country has, so far, been firmly rejected by the courts. This is in relation to an agreement to accept part payment in discharge of a larger debt. There is ancient and established[69] authority[70] to

---

[66] *Anangel Atlas Compania Naviera SA* v *Ishikawajima-Harima Heavy Industries Co Ltd (No 2)* [1990] 2 Lloyd's Rep 526. See also *Simon Container Machinery Ltd* v *Emba Machinery MB* [1998] 2 Lloyd's Rep 429.

[67] *Lee v GEC Plessey Telecommunications* [1993] IRLR 383 at 389 *per* Connel J; *Ajax Cooke Pty Ltd t/a Ajax Spurway Fasteners v Nugent* (Supreme Court of Victoria, unreported), referred to in *Musumeci v Winadell* (1994) 34 NSWLR 723 at 746.

[68] *United Food and Chemical Workers Union of New Zealand v Talley* [1993] 2 ERNZ 360 at 376 *per* Hardie Boys J; *Newmans v Ranier* [1992] 2 NZLR 68. Both cases are not totally convincing on the identification of practical benefit as discussed above.

[69] *Pinnel's Case* (1602) 5 Co Rep 117a. The common form of loan was a bond which acknowledged a debt (the 'penalty') to be paid on a certain day unless a lesser sum (the 'true' loan) was paid before that time. In *Pinnel* the defendant, at the claimant's request, paid him a lesser sum than the true loan at an *earlier* (see n. 71 below) time than the true loan became payable. The creditor's action to recover would have failed had it not been for a technical error in the way in which the debtor pleaded his case. Pleadings, the formal recitals of an action, assumed great importance in the older cases. In *Pinnel* the defendant failed to plead that he had *tendered* the lesser sum in complete satisfaction of the debt.

[70] *Foakes v Beer* (1884) 9 App Cas 605. The respondent obtained judgment against the appellant which they subsequently agreed the latter could pay in instalments. When all the instalments

support the proposition that such agreements are not, without more,[71] enforceable. In the days when *Stilk* v *Myrick* and the 'legal' definition of consideration held sway, the ancient rule as to part payment of debts seemed to follow *a fortiori*. If an agreement to perform all your pre-existing duty could not constitute good consideration, it seemed to follow inexorably that a promise to pay only part of your pre-existing duty could not be good consideration.[72] However, when following *Williams* v *Roffey* the mere performance of the pre-existing duty can constitute consideration this opened the question whether the part performance of that duty could also constitute good consideration. Indeed, what may be thought to be the impetus behind *Williams* v *Roffey* that it brings the formal law more closely into line with business practice would also seem to apply to the part payment of debts. In *Foakes* v *Beer* Lord Blackburn said:[73]

> ... all men of business ... do every day recognise and act on the ground that prompt payment of a part of their demand may be more beneficial to them than it would be to insist on their rights and enforce payment of the whole.

However, in *Re Selectmove*[74] the Court of Appeal emphatically rejected the suggestion that the concept of factual consideration introduced in *Williams* v *Roffey Bros* affected the old rule as to the part payment of debts. The Court of Appeal conceded that '[i]n the absence of authority there would be much to be said for the enforceability of such a contract' but thought that any such extension must be made by the House of Lords or 'more appropriately, by Parliament after consideration by the Law Commission'. On this basis it

---

had been paid, the respondent claimed the interest which was owing on the original debt. Since unpaid judgment debts attract interest, the agreement to pay the judgment by instalments was only an agreement to accept part payment in discharge of a larger debt.

71 The following have been held to be enforceable, i.e. fall outside the rule as to part payment of debts: an agreement to pay a lesser sum at an earlier time (*Pinnel's Case* (1602) 5 Co Rep 117a), at a different place chosen for the convenience of the credit (*Vanbergen* v *St Edmund Properties* [1933] 2 KB 223), where the payment is to be made by a third party (*Hirachand Punamchand* v *Temple* [1911] 2 KB 330) or in a different form, e.g. goods to the value of a lesser sum – just as the law will not enquire into the adequacy of a good worth £100 which is sold for £200, it will regard the promise of a good worth £100 as good consideration to support a promise to forgo a debt of £200 – though a cheque is regarded as the same form of payment as cash (*D & C Builders* v *Rees* [1966] 2 QB 617), where there is a bona fide dispute about the debt (*Cook* v *Wright* (1861) 1 B & S 559) and where there is an agreement (called a composition) between creditors to each accept a stated percentage of the debt owing to them (*Cook* v *Lister* (1863) 13 CB (NS) 543). The last exception is hard to accommodate within the traditional definition of consideration as benefit or detriment and is probably best viewed as a triumph of pragmatism over outdated principle. It would clearly be commercially undesirable if creditors could assent to such an agreement and then 'go behind' it to claim the balance owing. Indeed, one explanation of the rule states that such conduct would amount to a fraud upon the other creditors which must be restrained: *Wood* v *Roberts* (1818) 1 Stark 417.

72 The rule in *Pinnel's Case* predates the doctrine of consideration but was explained in *Foakes* v *Beer* in terms of the absence of consideration.

73 [1884] 9 App Cas 605 at 622. Lord Blackburn's judgment was *dubitante*, meaning that he was not prepared to formally dissent from the majority but none the less had considerable doubts.

74 [1995] 1 WLR 474 at 481 *per* Peter Gibson LJ with whom Balcombe and Stewart-Smith LJJ agreed. See also *Amos* v *Citibank Ltd* [1996] QCA 129.

held that even if a taxpayer could rely upon the silence of the Inland Revenue as acceptance[75] of his offer to pay off his tax arrears in instalments,[76] there was no consideration to support the Revenue's promise.[77] In contrast, Santow J in the Supreme Court of New South Wales did not feel inhibited from applying *Williams* v *Roffey Bros* to a promise to accept part payment of rent. He noted the continuing trend to 'sidestep' the formal requirements of the doctrine of consideration and the 'logic' of taking the same approach to the full and partial performance of pre-existing duties.[78]

One very significant effect of the decision in *Williams* v *Roffey* is the impact that it will have upon the relative importance of doctrines which collectively comprise the law relating to contractual modifications.[79] To the extent that a factual rather than a legal definition of consideration is more easily satisfied, it is the presence or absence of pressure amounting to economic duress which ultimately will determine the enforceability of a modification. Thus the developing principles of economic duress assume a more significant role. It is these principles we will now examine.

DURESS

Introduction

In the past duress operated within narrow limits.[80] The first form of duress recognised by the common law involved actual or threatened violence to the person.[81] This limited notion was closely associated with the legal control of criminal and tortious conduct.[82] Its operation was further restricted by the requirement that the pressure be such as would overcome a 'constant' man.[83] This had the effect of preserving the emphasis on the wrongfulness of the threatened conduct rather than on the consequences to the party coerced. Traces of the standard survive in French law[84] but it was abandoned in England[85] and the United States.[86]

---

[75] For a discussion of silence as acceptance, see above.

[76] Paying the full amount of the arrears would, like the payment by instalments of the debt in *Foakes* v *Beer*, only constitute part payment because the arrears, like a judgment debt, attract interest, thereby increasing the sum owed. See also *Amos* v *Citibank Ltd* [1996] QCA 129 where *Williams* v *Roffey* was not applied to a creditor's promise to accept less than the capital sum owing.

[77] It was also held that the Inland Revenue officer who spoke to the claimant did not have sufficient authority to grant the concession argued for by the claimant.

[78] *Musumeci* v *Winadell* [1994] 34 NSWLR 723 at 740 and 739 respectively.

[79] This was predicted by Hobhouse J in *The Alev* [1989] 1 Lloyd's Rep 138 at 147: 'Now that there is a properly developed doctrine of ... economic duress, there is no warrant for the Court to fail to recognise the existence of some consideration ...'.

[80] Lanham, 'Duress and Void Contracts' (1966) 29 MLR 615 at 620.

[81] See Bracton, *De Legibus*, fol. 16b–17.

[82] See (1633) Coke on Littleton 253b and (1859) 1 Bl Comm Chitty (ed.) 131.

[83] See Dawson, 'Economic Duress, an Essay in Perspective' (1947) 45 Mich L Rev 253 at 255.

[84] See Dawson, 'Economic Duress and the Fair Exchange in French and German Law' (1937) 11 Tulane L Rev 345 at 347–50 and Whincup (1990) *Contract Law and Practice: The English System and Continental Comparisons*, p. 220.

[85] See *Scott* v *Sebright* (1886) 12 PD 21 at 24.

[86] See Dawson, *op. cit.*, n. 83 above, p. 255.

The first expansion of the principles of duress to cover the field of economic pressure occurred in the so-called 'duress of goods' cases. The pressure exerted resulted from the wrongful seizure or detention of personal property. In 1732 in *Astley v Reynolds*,[87] a pledgee who demanded interest over and above that to which he was entitled before he would return the pledged silver was required to refund the surplus over the legal rate. The doctrine has been affirmed and followed a number of times,[88] and applied to a variety of goods. No distinction is drawn in the cases between actual and threatened seizure.[89] In all of these cases, however, there is still considerable emphasis upon the wrongfulness of the threat made, as opposed to the coercive effect on the 'innocent' party.[90]

A curious distinction was drawn in *Skeate v Beale*:[91] while a payment made under duress of goods was recoverable it was said that a contract entered as a result of such pressure could not be set aside.[92] In *The Siboen and the Sibotre*[93] there was a somewhat overdue judicial recognition in this country[94] of the illogical nature of the distinction introduced by *Skeate v Beale*.

Equity also offered protection against coercion through the doctrine of undue influence.[95] This differed from common law protection[96] in that its early development was not haunted by the spectre of the 'constant man'. Indeed, the relief offered was mainly for the protection of the timid, weak, disadvantaged or submissive. This protection and the allied equitable rules relating to 'catching bargains'[97] are not directly relevant to the problem of modification since the focus is not upon the exploitation of a vulnerability of a contractual partner produced by the very contract that binds the parties in order to secure a modification favourable to the opportunist. Instead it emphasises the psychological reliance induced by a fiduciary relationship which results in the formation of a contract. A sole exception, where the undue influence jurisdiction was extended to a contractual modification,

---

[87] (1731) 2 Str 915. The doctrine may have originated even earlier according to Dalzell, 'Duress by Economic Pressure' I (1942) 20 NCL Rev 237 at 241, n. 8, who refers to *Sumner v Ferryman* (1709) 11 Mod 201, where at pp. 202–3 counsel sought to rely on an even earlier case.

[88] *Hills v Street* (1828) 5 Bing 37; *Ashmole v Wainwright* (1842) 2 QB 837; *Somes v British Empire Shipping Co* (1860) 8 HLC 338.

[89] *Maskell v Horner* [1915] 3 KB 106 at 121, 124, 126.

[90] *Shaw v Woodcock* (1827) 7 B & C 73 at 85 *per* Holroyd J, who declared that there would be recovery whether there was pressing necessity or not.

[91] (1840) 11 Ad & El 983.

[92] The implications of this distinction are not clear but it is obviously illogical to apply different criteria to restitutionary action to recover money paid under pressure and a contractual one to set aside an unperformed promise to pay money which was extracted by the same pressure.

[93] [1976] 1 Lloyd's Rep 293 at 335.

[94] It has been disapproved in the United States, see *Hellenic Lines Ltd v Louis Dreyfus Corp* (1966) 249 F Supp 526 at 529; affd. (1967) 372 F 2d 753 and simply ignored elsewhere, e.g. in Canada.

[95] See Winder, 'The Equitable Doctrine of Pressure' (1962) 82 LQR 165.

[96] See Chunni, 'Duress and Undue Influence: A Comparative Analysis' (1970) 22 Baylor L Rev 572.

[97] Namely, agreements made by expectant heirs in anticipation of their inheritance.

occurred in *Ormes* v *Beadel*.[98] However, the undue influence cases are indirectly relevant in that the persistence of some equitable notions retarded the development of a coherent approach to economic duress.[99]

Historically duress developed in a piecemeal and disjointed way; there were parallel but unharmonised developments in common law and equity. Only the former aimed to control significantly the abuse of economic power. The development of consistent principles of economic duress was hampered, first by the objective standard, and latterly by the case of *Skeate* v *Beale*. With their 'removal' the opportunity offered itself for the formulation of an expanded doctrine. Evidence that the courts were moving towards this was provided in the 1960s by the cases of *Rookes* v *Barnard*[100] and *D & C Builders Ltd* v *Rees*.[101] The former is a leading authority on the tort of intimidation; the latter is an authority on promissory estoppel, which can be regarded as an economic duress case. Whether the courts successfully harnessed this momentum to articulate a unified and consistent doctrine of economic duress[102] will now be considered.

The present approach

Opportunism was defined as the attempt by one party to exploit a vulnerability of his contractual partner created by the contract itself. The oppressed party will agree to such an opportunistic modification where the alternatives, both legal and extra-legal, are less attractive than submission. In other words, he was coerced. So it can be seen that there are two aspects to the opportunistic modification, one focusing upon the origin of the economic power of the oppressor, the other upon the reaction of the victim. The economic power which the oppressor is using must derive from the contractual relation, and it must induce the consent of the victim to the modification.

Similarly, there are two elements to a finding of duress: the application of 'illegitimate' pressure, which then results in 'compulsion'.[103] According to Lord Scarman in *The Universe Sentinel*, there are two elements to a finding of duress: the application of 'illegitimate pressure' and 'compulsion' of the victim.[104] This is a very important statement about the structure and composition of the doctrine of economic duress. It was acted upon in *Pao*

---

[98] (1860) 2 Giff 166; revsd. on other grounds 2 De GF & J 333.

[99] *Infra.*

[100] [1964] AC 1129.

[101] [1966] 2 QB 617.

[102] See generally Muris, *op. cit.*, n. 6 herein above; Aivazian, Trebilcock and Ponny, 'The Law of Contract Modifications: The Uncertain Quest for a Benchmark of Enforceability (1984) 22 Osgoode Hall LJ 173; Halson, 'Opportunism, Economic Duress and Contractual Modifications' (1991) 107 LQR 649. Beatson (1999) *The Use and Abuse of Unjust Enrichment*, ch. 5; Bigwood, 'Coercion in Contract: The Theoretical Constructs of Duress' (1996) 46 Univ Tor LJ 201; Smith, 'Contracting under Pressure: A Theory of Duress' (1997) 56 Camb LJ 343.

[103] *The Universe Sentinel* [1983] 1 AC 366 at 400B, *per* Lord Scarman.

[104] [1983] 1 AC 366 at 400 B.

On v Lau Yiu Long,[105] the only case where the House of Lords or Privy Council have had to examine the operation of the doctrine in the context of a contractual modification. It has also been applied by inferior courts.[106] The rest of this section follows the distinction[107] and examines whether the legal requisites accord with the opportunism analysis.

The legitimacy of the threat

There is a sense in which all contracts may be described as having been entered into under pressure: one party to a bargain may be said to threaten to withhold from the other the contract goods unless the contract price is paid.[108] The liberty to withhold from another goods he desires until he pays the price you demand is usually described as 'freedom of contract'.[109] Therefore, lest every commercial arrangement become impeachable, the question to be asked in suspected cases of duress can never be: was the agreement entered into as a result of pressure? Rather it must be: what are the peculiar characteristics which cause some types of threat to be labelled as 'duress', as opposed to other types which the law regards as 'acceptable'?

---

[105] [1980] AC 614. The transaction involved was in essence simple but in execution complex. The defendant wanted to buy a factory. However, this was to be effected by an exchange of shares. The claimant contracted to sell the defendant all the shares in a privately owned company whose major asset was the factory. The price was to be a large number of shares in a public company in which the defendant was a major shareholder. The defendant refused to perform the main agreement (to which he was not personally a party) unless the claimant 'modified' the protection the defendant had personally promised to him for the period for which he had undertaken to retain a proportion of the shares in the public company. The defendant argued *inter alia* that the modified protection (an indemnity) he had undertaken to provide was obtained by economic duress, i.e. the claimant's threat not to perform the main agreement.

[106] For example, *The Alev* [1989] 1 Lloyd's Rep 138 at 145 and *Atlas Express Ltd v Kafco* [1989] 1 All ER 641 at 644.

[107] A different statement of general structure which differs as to the second element is that of Lord Goff who defines the two elements of the doctrine as first the application of illegitimate pressure which second is a significant cause inducing the claimant to agree to the obligation he now seeks to challenge (*Evia Luck* [1991] 4 All ER 878). Whether in practice there is a difference between the approaches of Lords Scarman and Goff is not clear. (*Huton v Cremer* [1999] 1 Lloyd's Rep 620 at 637–8 appears to apply Lord Goff's approach but also insists that the factors included in Lord Scarman's remain important.) However, it is suggested that there are good reasons of precedent and policy to prefer the approach of Lord Scarman. It is suggested that Lord Goff's formulation apparently reduces the second element to one of causation and thereby prevents it reflecting the policy objectives which the law should pursue. Bigwood appears to share the author's view of Lord Goff's formulation but not of the proper policy to be pursued by the law of duress: 'Coercion in Contract: The Theoretical Constructs of Duress' (1996) 46 Univ Tor Law J 201 at 259.

[108] Hale, 'Coercion and Distribution in a Supposedly Non-Coercive State' (1943) 38 Pol Sci Q 470 at 476–7; Hale, 'Bargaining Duress and Economic Liberty' (1943) 43 Col LR 603 at 612–13.

[109] '…[C]oercion is universal in the exchange of goods and services under the conditions of individualism [and] the "freedom" contemplated by social and economic theory is seen as involving essentially a freedom to coerce': Dawson, 'Duress through Civil litigation' (1947) 45 Mich L Rev 571 at 571.

A threat to refuse future business

When a person enters a contract with another upon terms unfavourable to him, because that other was the only supplier of the goods in question, that fact alone is generally regarded as an insufficient reason to impeach the contract.[110] This reasoning was applied in the context of modification of contract in an Australian case, *Smith* v *William Charlick Ltd*[111] where a miller failed in his claim for reimbursement of 'surcharges' paid to the Wheat Harvest Board as a result of the latter's threats to cut off future supplies to him if they were not paid.

The result accords with the opportunism analysis[112] proposed. The pressure which the Wheat Harvest Board applied in order to obtain the modification derived from the pre-contractual relationship of the parties – Smith was a miller and the Wheat Harvest Board controlled the statutory monopoly in wheat sales. It did not derive from any post-contractual acts of reliance by Smith, so the Board was not preying upon any vulnerability resulting from the contract.[113] The only claim made here is that there are no economic arguments deriving from the modification setting which oppose the result.

In *CTN Cash and Carry* v *Gallagher Ltd*[114] the English Court of Appeal said *obiter dicta*[115] that a threat to perform an otherwise lawful act may exceptionally amount to an illegitimate threat for the purposes of economic duress. The defendants threatened to withdraw credit facilities from the claimant company unless it paid for cigarettes which had been delivered to

---

[110] *Eric Gnapp* v *Petroleum Board* [1949] WN 180 (CA).

[111] (1924) 34 CLR 38. See also, in Canada, *Morton Construction* v *City of Hamilton* (1961) 31 DLR (2d) 323 and *City of Moncton* v *Stephen* (1956) 5 DLR (2d) 722; and in the USA: *US* v *Bethlehem Steel Corp* (1942) 315 US 289; *Carpenter Paper Co* v *Kearney Hub Publishing Co* (1956) 78 NW 2d 80; *Eggleston* v *Humble Pipe Line Co* (1972) 482 SW 2d 905.

[112] Analysing modification problems in terms of opportunism rather than bilateral monopoly avoids confusion between pre and post contractual monopoly. Contra: Posner, 'Gratuitous Promises in Law and Economics' (1977) J Leg Stud 411 and Trebilock in Reiter and Swan (1980) *Studies in Modern Contract Law*.

[113] It is true that economic arguments can be developed for the regulation of such agreements. Such regulation is, however, the province of competition or anti-trust law. The control of monopolies is, however, a matter for Parliament, *per* Steyn LJ in *CTN Cash & Carry* v *Gallagher* [1994] 4 All ER 714 at 717.

[114] [1994] 4 All ER 714. See also *AIS Vaughan & Co Ltd* v *Royscot Trust plc* [1999] 1 All ER (Comm) 856 (goods owner who validly terminated hire purchase contract did not make illegitimate threat when he demanded payment for not exercising right of repossession).

[115] See also *The Universe Sentinel* [1982] 2 All ER 67 at 89 *per* Lord Scarman: 'Duress can, of course, exist even if the threat is one of lawful action.' It is suggested that this statement is not as obvious as Lord Scarman's *obiter dicta* (the threat in that case was a tortious one) suggests. Lord Scarman supports his view by reference to the crime of blackmail which may be constituted by a threat to do what is lawful (see Theft Act 1968, s 21(1)). However, the analogy is not clear. It is unobjectionable if it is meant to suggest that threatening to do something which amounts to the crime of blackmail should be regarded as an illegitimate threat for the purposes of economic duress. If a threat to commit a tort is an illegitimate one, it follows *a fortiori* that a threat to commit a crime is also. However, it is objectionable to use the blackmail analogy if it is meant to suggest that because the criminal law recognises lawful acts as blackmail the civil law of duress should recognise lawful acts (which would not necessarily be sufficient threats to constitute blackmail) as illegitimate ones for the purposes of economic duress. This is because the criminal and civil law serve different, but overlapping, purposes.

the wrong warehouse and stolen. The defendants were not contractually obliged to grant the credit facilities and mistakenly believed that the claimant company was liable to pay for the stolen cigarettes. Steyn LJ with whom the other members of the court agreed said that 'lawful act duress' was 'not necessarily objectionable'.[116] However, he noted the danger that it could introduce 'substantial and undesirable ... uncertainty' in commercial negotiations and that it may enable bona fide settlements of commercial accounts to be re-opened when transactors later fall out. He said:[117]

> The aim of our commercial law ought to be to encourage fair dealing between parties. But it is a mistake for the law to set its sights too highly when the critical enquiry is not whether the conduct is lawful but whether it is morally or socially unacceptable.

On this basis, he thought that the defendants' threat to withdraw credit facilities could not be regarded as an illegitimate one. It seems that two factors persuaded him of this: it was an arm's length dealing between commercial parties and the defendants acted in good faith. English law, therefore, acknowledges the possibility of the concept of legal act duress, but awaits a case in which it is held to operate.[118] For the policy reasons developed above and the reasons given in *CTN* itself, it is suggested that Steyn LJ's caution is fully justified.

It is important not to generalise the policy arguments against regarding a threat to refuse to contract in the future as the exercise of illegitimate pressure. In particular, adopting a formula such as 'It can never be duress to exercise your legal rights'[119] does not accurately represent the law of duress applicable to situations which do not involve contractual modifications.[120] In the United States there are cases not involving contractual modifications where threatening to do what there is otherwise a legal right to do has been said to amount to duress.[121]

A threat to breach a pre-existing contract

The question to be addressed here is whether, when a contractual modification is obtained as a result of a threat to breach a pre-existing contract with the promisee, that threat is considered illegitimate for the purposes of the law of duress.

It may be asserted that whenever you contractually bind yourself to

---

[116] At p. 719.

[117] *Ibid.*

[118] Other cases which are sometimes cited to support the concept of lawful act duress predate the extension of duress to cover economic pressure (e.g. *Thorne* v *Motor Trade Association* [1937] AC 797 at 806–7 and *Mutual Finance Ltd* v *John Wetton & Sons Ltd* [1937] 2 KB 389.

[119] *Contra*: Bigwood, 'Coercion in Contract: The Theoretical Constructs of Duress' (1996) 46 Univ Tor LJ 201 at 235, who argues that the Board's actions were not illegitimate by the standards of 1924 but should be so regarded when judged by contemporary morality.

[120] Hale, 'Bargaining Duress and Economic Liability' (1943) 43 Col LR 603 at 613.

[121] For instance, *Hochman* v *Zigler's Inc* (1946) 50 A 2d 97 (illegitimate refusal of landlord to enter new lease to purchaser of tenant's business); *Lafayette* v *Ferent* (1934) 29 NW 2d 57 (employee's illegitimate threat to strike to induce employer to take on unnecessary labour).

another, you should never be allowed to obtain greater remuneration for the performance you have already promised.[122] It would follow that a threat to breach the pre-existing contract should always be regarded as illegitimate in the law of duress. Alternatively, a contrary argument could be constructed as follows. When a person contracts to do something, all he in effect commits himself to is the alternative of two duties, either to perform or to pay damages, reserving to himself the choice between them.[123] Since the law vests this choice in the promisor, all threats to breach should be considered 'legitimate'.[124]

Each view is too extreme. To regard all threats to breach a contract as illegitimate would certainly protect against opportunism, but would purchase this protection at too great a cost. Contractual flexibility would have to be sacrificed and meritorious, non-opportunistic modifications would be rendered unenforceable. The second argument is also flawed. It would sanction the enforcement of many opportunistic modifications which are economically wasteful. They directly consume resources and discourage future exchanges. Fortunately, neither of these unsatisfactory extreme positions represents English law.

The Privy Council in *Pao On v Lau Yiu Long*[125] endorsed the approach of Mocatta J[126] and Kerr J in earlier cases[127] by admitting to the realm of threats considered capable of founding an action in duress the threat to breach a contract.[128] However, Lord Scarman, delivering the opinion of the Board, stressed that not *all* threats to breach a contract amount to legal duress; they will do so only where the pressure exerted amounts to 'a coercion of the will which vitiates consent'.[129] So it seems that all threats to breach a contract are to be considered illegitimate, and that it is the second stage of the duress test, the effect upon the subject of the pressure, which is used to distinguish cases where the threat to breach amounts to economic duress from those where it does not.

This analysis, fails to take account of a situation where the threat to with-hold performance should be considered legitimate. It is suggested that where parties agree to a contractual modification as a result of the occurrence of circumstances which were not anticipated by the parties at the time of contracting (i.e. the risk was not assigned by the contract to either party),

---

[122] The language of some of the strict applications of the pre-existing duty doctrine would seem to support this view: e.g. *Stilk v Myrick* (1809) 2 Camp 317.

[123] See Holmes, 'The Path of the Law' (1897) 10 Harv L Rev 457 at 462.

[124] There is some old American authority to support this position: *Sistrom v Anderson* (1942) 124 P 2d 372 at 376 *per* Hanson J: 'It is not, however, unlawful to threaten to refuse to proceed under a contract or to pay what is due under it or what is otherwise due.' Modern American authority has retreated somewhat from this extreme position.

[125] [1980] AC 614 at 636 B–C.

[126] *The Atlantic Baron* [1979] 1 QB 705.

[127] *The Siboen and Sibotre* [1976] 1 Lloyd's Rep 293.

[128] See also *Nixon v Murphy* (1925) 25 SR (NSW) 151; *Re Hooper and Grass Contract* [1949] VLR 269; *Sundell & Sons v Emm Yannoulatos (Overseas) Pty Ltd* (1956) 56 SR (NSW) 323.

[129] At p. 636 C; *The Siboen and The Sibotre*, above, at p. 335 *per* Kerr J; *B & S Contracts and Design Ltd v Victor Green Publications Ltd* [1984] ICR 419 at 428 D *per* Kerr LJ.

such a modification should not be impeached for economic duress.[130] Thus a threat to breach under such circumstances should be regarded as a 'legitimate' threat, provided only that the extent of the modification agreed is reasonably related to the cost consequences to the performing party of the unanticipated circumstances.[131] In such circumstances I suggest that any suspicion of duress has been rebutted. There is then no need to consider the second limb of the duress test, the effect upon the victim.

In the United States, modifications agreed under these circumstances are regularly enforced with little or no further consideration of 'duress' once the unanticipated circumstances have been proved.[132] English courts have not directly adopted such an approach. However, the English cases[133] have not as yet included one where unanticipated circumstances have occurred. The closest is perhaps *The Atlantic Baron*,[134] where a Korean shipyard contracted to build a ship for the claimants for a price expressed in US dollars. Following a 10 per cent devaluation in the US dollar, the yard demanded an extra 10 per cent on all outstanding instalments. The claimants agreed to pay the extra monies as they had made a profitable contract to charter the ship when completed. Mocatta J held that this was initially a case of economic duress but that the claimants lost their right to set aside the contract by subsequently affirming it. It could be asserted that the 10 per cent devaluation was analogous to an unanticipated increase in supply costs;[135] each has the effect of reducing the 'profit' made by the promisor. However, the essential inquiry must always be whether the reduced profit was a result of unanticipated circumstances, caused by the materialisation of a risk not assigned by the contract. While it may be possible that sometimes the risk of an increase in supply costs is not to be borne by the supplier,[136] it seems unlikely that a court would regard the currency devaluation as a risk which

---

[130] Such an agreement is now more likely to be supported by consideration as a result of the adoption of a factual rather than legal definition of consideration in *Williams v Roffey Bros & Nicholls (Contractors) Ltd*, considered above.

[131] See below.

[132] *Linz v Schuck* (1907) 67 A 286; *Watkins & Son v Carrig* (1941) 21 A 2d 591; *Angel v Murray* (1974) 322 A 2d 630. It is perhaps true that the earlier cases were not sufficiently alert to the 'duress' problem because they failed to advert to the need for a relationship of proportionality between the unanticipated circumstances and the magnitude of the modification. Such a concern may have been incorporated into the modern view by the requirement that the modification be 'fair and equitable' imported by the Restatement 2d, s 89(a), approved in *Angel v Murray* at pp. 636–47.

[133] To the cases cited, especially at nn. 125–7 above, add also *The Proodos C* [1980] 1 Lloyd's Rep 390; *Alec Lobb (Garages) Ltd v Total Oil (Great Britain) Ltd* [1983] 1 WLR 87, affd. and revsd. in part [1985] 1 WLR 173 without discussion of economic duress; *B & S Contracts and Design Ltd v Victor Green Publications Ltd* [1984] ICR 419; *Hennessy v Craigmyle & Co Ltd* [1986] ICR 461; *The Alev* [1989] 1 Lloyd's Rep 138; *Atlas Express Ltd v Kafco (Importers and Distributors) Ltd* [1989] QB 833; *The Olib* [1991] 2 Lloyd's Rep 108, [1992] 2 AC 152; *Huyton v Cremer* [1999] 1 Lloyd's Rep 629.

[134] [1979] 1 QB 705.

[135] See *Sasso v KK & G Realty Construction Co* (1923) 120 A 158, where such a modification was enforced.

[136] See Rodhe, 'The Adjustment of Contracts on Account of Changed Conditions' (1959) 3 *Scan Stud in Law* 153 at 159.

was not assigned to the yard, for if the yard had wanted to make it clear that it did not bear the risk of such devaluations, there existed the simple expedient of stating the contract price in Korean won. The selection of US dollars as the contract currency does suggest that the risk of currency fluctuation was being assigned to the yard. Similarly, the modifications agreed in *The Siboen and the Sibotre*[137] could not be regarded as a response to unanticipated circumstances. The modification reduced the rate of hire payable in respect of two time charters. The shipowners claimed, *inter alia*, that the modifications were voidable for duress. The tanker market is a very volatile one; rates of freight and hire fluctuated wildly during the periods of the charters.[138] Where a party chooses to charter a ship for a period at a fixed rate, against a fluctuating market, it is a reasonable inference that the risk of fluctuation in the market which may make the bargain less profitable is being assigned to the charterer. A charterer may choose to use a time charter rather than to 'take a chance' on several voyage charters to protect himself from any subsequent increases in world freight rates. The corollary, of course, is that if those rates decrease, the bargain is less beneficial to him.

A threat to commit a tort

A threat to commit a tort like one to breach an existing contract is a threat of an independent legal wrong. As such it will be regarded as an application of illegitimate pressure for the purposes of the doctrine of economic duress. The most obvious example occurs in cases of 'duress of goods' where the actual or threatened seizure of the victim's goods will constitute a trespass against or conversion of the good[139] or amount to the threat of one.

The threat of industrial action by a trade union may well constitute a threat to commit an economic tort[140] against the employer. In the past, trade unions enjoyed wide-ranging statutory immunities from actions for damages in respect of these torts. In *The Universe Sentinel*[141] it was held that the statute conferring these immunities[142] should be interpreted as evidence of Parliament's intention that trade unions should not be liable for the consequences of such torts even where the action by the victim was not one for damages in tort. On this basis, an employer[143] would be unable to recover in a restitutionary action for the return of money paid under duress any sums paid in response to a threat[144] which would not be actionable as a

---

137 [1976] 1 Lloyd's Rep 293: the facts are simplified.

138 See the background discussion of Kerr J at pp. 296 *et seq*.

139 Trespass to goods is the physical act of interfering with another's goods, e.g. kicking someone's football or cat. Conversion is narrower and involves a denial of the owner's rights, e.g. refusing to return a football or kidnapping a cat.

140 Such as inducing a breach of contract with a third party or interfering with a contract with a third party.

141 [1982] 2 All ER 67.

142 Trade Union and Labour Relations Act 1974.

143 The employer was a shipowner operating a ship under a 'flag of convenience'. The trade union organisation, the International Transport Federation, sought to prevent the employment of cheap labour on such ships on terms less generous than the union approved.

144 The threat was to continue 'blocking' the ship, i.e. directing all sympathetic dock labour not to work on the ship and so effectively prevent its leaving port.

tort. However, a sum paid which fell outside the scope of the statutory immunity would be and was recoverable.[145]

The protection afforded to trade unions was greatly reduced during the period of Conservative government in the 1980s and 1990s.[146] In *The Evia Luck*, the House of Lords was again called upon to consider the legitimacy of the International Transport Federation's (ITF) action in this new industrial climate. On this occasion, the House of Lords held that, under English law, the ITF's action could no longer be legitimised by analogy to the reduced statutory immunities extended to trade unions.

The requirement of 'compulsion'

Once a court has satisfied itself that the threat made was an illegitimate one, it must then consider the second limb of the duress test. This focuses upon the effect which the threat has on the victim; did the pressure exerted by the threat amount to what the law recognises as 'compulsion'? The tests adopted by the courts include the following.

Vitiation of consent

The most popular test used by English courts to determine whether an agreement was compelled or not relied on the absence of consent by the victim. His will was said to be coerced in a way which vitiated his consent. In *Pao On v Lau Yiu Long* Lord Scarman, delivering the opinion of the Board, agreed that economic duress rendered a contract voidable provided that the duress amounted to a coercion of the will which vitiated consent.[147] The same test has been used in a number of decisions at first instance[148] and in the Court of Appeal.[149] Such uncritical acceptance is surprising in view of the speciousness of its reasoning.[150] The consent obtained by a threat is in every meaningful sense a real consent. All that has happened is that a party

---

[145] Indeed, the only sum in dispute in the House of Lords was a contribution the ITF required the shipowner to make to its welfare fund. This fell outside the analogy with the statutory immunities and so was recoverable.

[146] Perhaps to the regret of Lord Templeman, the sole dissenting member of the House of Lords in *The Evia Luck* [1991] 4 All ER 871 at 873 who candidly revealed the partisan stance of the law in industrial relations: 'Under the English Common Law an employer has never been guilty of economic duress if, at a time when unemployment is high, workers' wages are low. Under the English common law a trade union is guilty of economic duress if the union forces an employer to increase wages by procuring a boycott of the employer's business.' Contrast Lord Diplock's lack of sympathy in *The Universe Sentinel* [1982] 2 All ER 67 at 70: 'the object ... [of] the blocking policy ... does not always command the support of the crews'.

[147] [1980] AC 614 at 635 B and 636 C–D. See also *The Universe Sentinel* [1983] 1 AC 366 at 383 F *per* Lord Diplock, with whose speech Lord Russell agreed.

[148] *The Proodos C* [1980] 2 Lloyd's Rep 390; *Alec Lobb (Garages) Ltd v Total Oil (Great Britain) Ltd* [1983] 1 WLR 87 affd. and revsd. in part [1985] 1 WLR 173 without discussion of economic duress. See also the Canadian decisions in *Gordon v Roebuck* (1989) 64 DLR (4th) 568 and *Century 21 Campbell Munro Ltd v S & G Estates* (1992) 89 DLR (4th) 413.

[149] *B & S Contracts and Design Ltd v Victor Green Publications Ltd* [1984] ICR 419; *Hennessy v Craigmyle & Co Ltd* [1986] ICR 461 at 468 F. It was at one time popular in the United States where influence of the test may persist.

[150] *Fairbanks v Snow* (1887) 13 NE 2d 596; *Union Pacific Ry Co v Public Service Commission of Missouri* (1918) 248 US 67 at 70.

has been faced with a choice between two evils:[151] submission to a demand or the threatened consequences of resistance. It is true that it is a choice which the law deprecates. However, that should not lead courts to the conclusion that the consent was unreal.[152] Indeed, there is a sense in which one can say that the more extreme the threatened wrong and the concomitant desire of the victim to avoid it, the more 'real' the consent obtained.[153] Therefore, the consent obtained as the result of a threat is a more sincere, more genuine consent than is generally manifested by so-called voluntary agreements.[154]

In view of the wealth of opinion[155] against the vitiation of consent test,[156] it was perhaps surprising to see the test adopted by the English courts so readily and uncritically. It is even more surprising when the analysis of consent in a criminal case, *DPP for Northern Ireland* v *Lynch*,[157] is considered. The House of Lords in that case had rejected the idea that duress in some way overbears the individual's will to deprive him of the ability to give a genuine consent. Indeed, Lord Wilberforce and Lord Scarman even expanded their discussion to take in the civil concept of duress.[158] Lord Morris of Borth-y-Gest, Lord Kilbrandon and Lord Edmund-Davies all appeared to reject the vitiation of consent concept, but without any reference to civil law.[159]

The case against the vitiation of consent test is overwhelming. This has been recognised *obiter dicta* by Lord Goff in *The Evia Luck*.[160] I myself, like McHugh JA,[161] doubt whether it is helpful in this context to speak of the claimant's will having been coerced. It has been suggested that the vitiation

---

[151] As is every potential promise. 'Agreement does not, even today, carry any connotation of real willingness. Acquiescence in the lesser evil is all that need be understood': Llewellyn, 'What Price Contract?' (1931) 40 Yale LJ 704 at 728, n. 49.

[152] See Dalzell's eloquent 'exposure' of the fallacy underlying this test: 'Duress by Economic Pressure' (1942) 20 N Carol L Rev 237 at 238–90. See also Patterson, 'Compulsory Contracts in the Crystal Ball' (1943) 43 Col L Rev 731 at 741 where he says: 'if a man is deemed not to "consent" because he was induced by pressure outside himself, then consent becomes a useless concept in the administration of justice'.

[153] If ever confronted by a disappointed purchaser of this book wielding a big stick and demanding his money back, the author would reluctantly but none the less willingly let him have it.

[154] Dalzell, *op. cit.*, at pp. 239–40; Dawson, 'Economic Duress, An Essay Perspective' (1947) 45 Mich LR 253 at 266–7.

[155] Though there are dissenting voices, see Smith and Tiplady in n. 162 below.

[156] To the articles already cited add: *Williston on Contracts*. 3rd edn, vol. 13, para. 1602; (1977) Calamari and Perillo, *The Law of Contracts* at p. 263; and in England: Coote, 'Duress by Threatened Breach of Contract' (1980) CLJ 40 at 45; Atiyah, 'Economic Duress and the Overborne Will' (1982) 98 LQR 197.

[157] [1975] AC 653; Atiyah, *ibid*. The decision has been overruled in *R* v *Howe* [1987] AC 417 as to the availability of the defence of duress to a secondary party to murder, but the discussion in *Lynch* of the underlying basis of the doctrine of duress is still valuable.

[158] *Ibid.* at pp. 680 and 695 B respectively, endorsing the similar analysis they had preferred in their dissenting judgments in *Barton* v *Armstrong* [1976] AC 104 at 121 D, where they said that 'absence of choice ... does not negate consent in law' (alluding to Holmes J's decision in *Fairbanks* v *Snow* (1887) 13 NE 1d 596).

[159] At pp. 670 F, E and 710 A–B respectively.

[160] *The Evia Luck* [1991] 3 WLR 875 at 883. See also *Huyton* v *Cremer* [1999] 1 Lloyd's Rep 620 at 638.

[161] In *Crescendo Management Pty Ltd* v *Westpac Banking Corp* [1988] 19 NSWLR at 46.

of consent test was never intended to be applied literally, but was just legal shorthand for the judicial finding that a party has been subjected to an improper motive for his action.[162] Indeed, there is some evidence to support this view. Lord Scarman in *The Universe Sentinel* notes that:[163]

> The classic case of duress is however not the lack of will to submit but the victim's intentional submission arising from the fact that there is no other practical choice open to him.

From this statement it would appear that Lord Scarman was aware of the fallacy which Dalzell and others have exposed,[164] but at other points in the same judgment he speaks of 'pressure amounting to compulsion of the will of the victim'.[165] Moreover, in delivering the Board's judgment in *Pao On v Lao Yiu Long*, Lord Scarman did not refer to any logical fallacy in speaking of coercion of the will which vitiates consent, nor does he seem to regard his comments in *The Universe Sentinel* as developing the limb of the duress test which addresses itself to the compulsive effect on the victim.

The evidence that the vitiation of consent formula was never intended to be applied mechanistically is at best equivocal. Even if it were unequivocal, it would be open to all the criticisms that can be levelled at rules which do not directly address the 'policy' issues behind them: the law squanders the opportunity to expand and develop doctrines in a coherent way; it fails to generate debate; the predictive value of the law to counsel and contracting parties is lessened; finally, there is the danger that a subsequent court may try to apply the rule mechanistically, in ignorance of the policy factors to which previous judges have adverted.[166]

Protest

Some early cases appear to regard a protest or reservation of rights at the time of paying as an essential requirement for the later recovery of the money paid.[167] The requisite of a show of protest was probably closely associated with the old objective standard. For the 'constant man' of ordinary firmness could be expected to make manifest his initial resistance to an improper threat, even if later forced to submit.

Perhaps with the abandonment of the objective standard, protest came to be considered good evidence of a coerced payment, but was not considered

---

[162] Tiplady, 'Concepts of Duress' (1983) 99 LQR 188. See also Smith 'Contracting under Pressure: A Theory of Duress' (1997) 56 Camb LJ 343 at 365 who thinks that talk of overborne wills, coercion of the will or vitiated consent is not unintelligible, 'though sometimes overdramatic'.

[163] [1983] 1 AC 366 at 400 C – see Kerr LJ's comment that this quotation contains a typographical error in *B & S Contracts and Design Ltd v Victor Green Publications Ltd* [1984] ICR 419 at 428 F–G.

[164] See also p. 384 B *per* Lord Diplock; and *Hennessy v Craigmyle & Co Ltd* [1986] ICR 461 at 468G.

[165] At p. 400 B; see also p. 385 F *per* Lord Diplock; *Hennessy v Craigmyle & Co Ltd*, above, at p. 468 H.

[166] See Reiter, 'Courts Consideration and Common Sense' (1977) 27 U Toronto LJ 439 at 446.

[167] See e.g. *Valpy v Manley* (1945) 1 CB 594 at 603 and *Pratt v Vizard* (1833) 5 B & Ad 808 at 812.

conclusive.[168] This is surely the better view. A genuine protest or reservation of right, accompanying a payment or the promise of such may be valuable evidence to help substantiate a finding that the payment was compelled. Conversely, a party who accompanies his payment or promise with a protest may actually be paying voluntarily, but merely grudgingly. Here the words of complaint which accompany the payment or promise indicate simply that, like most people, the payer was reluctant to give away his money not that he felt he had to. Moreover a calculating party may make a habit of accompanying non-compelled payments or promises with some kind of verbal reservation with a view to 'duping' a court into thinking that the payment was made involuntarily. Therefore courts must be careful not to attach too much importance to the presence of a protest.

Equally, courts must not attach too much importance to the absence of protest in finding that a payment was not compelled, for the very pressure which compels the payment or extracts the promise of such, may force the victim to withdraw his protest or dissuade him from making one at all. As Lord Scarman eloquently put it in *The Universe Sentinel*:[169]

> The victim's silence will not assist the bully, if the lack of any practicable choice but to submit is proved.

Indeed, the absence of protest may occur merely because the oppressor was deliberately unavailable to receive any complaints.[170] Obviously in such circumstances the absence of protest has no evidential value. The statements of principle in the modern economic duress cases do seem to recognise that protest only has a limited role to play as a determinant of compulsion. In *The Siboen and the Sibotre* Kerr J recognised it as 'one relevant factor'.[171] The Privy Council took a similar view in *Pao On v Lao Yiu Long*.[172]

The existence of an adequate alternative

From the discussion of the 'vitiation of consent' test it emerges that when a promisee is confronted with a promisor who threatens not to perform his obligations unless some demand is met, the promisee is basically faced with a choice between two evils, either submitting to the threat or suffering the consequences of it being carried out. Once it is recognised that it is because

---

168 *Maskell v Horner* [1915] 3 KB 106 at 120 *per* Lord Reading CJ, and *Twyford v Manchester Corp* [1946] Ch 236. Lord Reading's comments were quoted by McTiernan J in his dissenting judgment in *Mason v State of New South Wales* (1959) 102 CLR 108 at 120 and by Windeyer J in the same case at p. 143. In Australia, see also *Donaldson v Gray* [1920] VLR 379 at 382 and *Re Hooper and Grass' Contract* [1949] VLR 269 at 217. A similar position appears to obtain in the USA: see *Williston on Contracts*. 3rd edn, vol. 13, para 1623. For an early statement to similar effect in Canada, see *Doe d Morgan v Boyer* (1854) 9 UCQB 318 at 321; *A-G for Canada v Vancouver* (1943) 1 DLR 510 at 518.
169 [1983] 1 AC 366 at 400 E.
170 As in *Atlas Express Ltd v Kafco (Importers and Distributors) Ltd* [1989] QB 833 at 838 C.
171 [1976] 1 Lloyd's Rep 293 at 336. The only other factor mentioned specifically was whether the settlement was treated as closing the transaction.
172 [1980] AC 614 at 635 C–D. The others were the alternative courses open to the victim and whether he was independently advised. *Cf.* the heavy emphasis of Judson J dissenting in *Eadie v Township of Brantford* (1967) 63 DLR (2d) 561 at 562–3.

of the threat of a more unpleasant alternative that the victim submits, a more rational test for compulsion can be articulated. Courts should examine the choices available to the victim when the threat was made. If the alternatives that faced him were all less attractive, that is, more injurious than submission, then this suggests that the consent to a modifying agreement or payment was obtained under compulsion.

It is necessary to proceed with some caution here because this test of adequacy of an alternative remedy has subtle shades of meaning. There are three main variants of the test. These are that where, as a result of an illegitimate threat, monies or goods are paid or promised, the monies or goods are irrecoverable or the agreement enforceable when:

(i)   the law provides a remedy for the damage which would result if the threat were carried out;

(ii) the law provides a remedy for the damage which would result if the threat were carried out which in all the circumstances of the case is an adequate one; or

(iii) *either* the law provides a remedy for the damage which would result if the threat were carried out which in all circumstances of the case is an adequate one, *or* there exists an extra-legal alternative which in all the circumstances of the case is an adequate one.

The law provides a remedy for the damage which would result if the threat were carried out

This version of the test, which is least favourable to relief, features in some of the older cases.[173] It ignores realities and has little to commend it. It would only be defensible if the legal redress which could be obtained perfectly compensated the victim in every case. As common sense tells us, this is patently not so.[174] The rule was probably bound up with the old objective standard of the constant man, whose granite composition would enable him to resist coercive threats, suffer the consequences and only then seek legal redress. This, even where the later redress failed to fully compensate him. To premise a legal rule on such irrational behaviour is obviously questionable. Therefore, it was to be hoped that this strict rule disappeared at the same time as the constant man.[175] However, one cannot help but think that it still occasionally influences the English courts,[176] as it once did the American courts.[177]

An intermediate category can sometimes be discerned. This is a test which is formulated like (ii) but operates like (i). Such a test[178] enjoyed considerable judicial support in the United States until recently. When the

---

[173] For instance, *Lindon v Hooper* (1776) 1 Cowp 414 at 418.
[174] See (ii) below for an examination of the inadequacy of legal remedies.
[175] That is, in 1886, see *Scott v Sebright* (1886) 12 PD 21 at 24.
[176] See *Twyford v Manchester Corp* [1946] Ch 236 at 242.
[177] See *Silliman v US* (1879) 101 US 465: 'Their [the claimants'] duty, if they expected to rely upon the law for protection, was to disregard the threat of the department, and apply to the courts for redress against its repudiation of a valid contract': *per* Morton J at p. 989.
[178] *Hackley v Headley* (1881) 8 NW 511.

threat was to refuse to pay money due it was *presumed* that the legal action to enforce the debt was an adequate remedy. This plainly may not be true where the creditor is in a particularly parlous financial state.[179] The rule does not enjoy much current support.[180] It does, however, illustrate clearly the necessity that not only should the rule be formulated in 'subjective' terms, namely, the remedy must be adequate for the particular claimant, but also that it be applied in a 'subjective way'; the court must not 'presume' the adequacy of its remedies but must demand that the same be demonstrated.

The law provides a remedy for the damage which would result if the threat were carried out which in all the circumstances of the case is an adequate one

There is old and recent authority in England to support this version of the rule. In the leading case of *Astley* v *Reynolds*[181] it was said that:

> ... this is a payment by compulsion; the claimant may have such an immediate want of his goods, that an action of trover would not do his business.

This quotation recognises that the remedies the law supplies may be inadequate to compensate for the harm done.[182] Where this is so, I suggest that submission to the threat is likely to be compelled. I shall now briefly examine why the legal remedies may be considered inadequate.

In relation to the modification of contracts, the most usual threat is that of breaching the contract which was earlier agreed. The primary remedy which the law provides for such breach would be the award of damages. However, damages sometimes fail to protect fully the victim of breach by ignoring the consumer surplus,[183] that is, the difference between the contract price and the subjective value put upon the performance or goods by the purchasing party.

The law limits the quantum of damages that can be awarded by principles of remoteness, therefore some losses which the victim would incur if he failed to submit to the threat may be irrecoverable. Typically these may include loss of profits on,[184] and possibly damages for breach of, a contract with a third party.

This discussion of the inadequacy of legal remedies is intended to be illustrative rather than exhaustive. However, it emphasises the point that an

---

[179] As he was in *Hackley* v *Headley*, above. For similar fact situations in England being dealt with under the consideration rubric, see *D & C Builders Ltd* v *Rees* [1966] 2 QB 617 and under undue influence doctrines *Ormes* v *Beadel* (1860) 2 Giff 166, revsd. on other grounds (1860) 2 De GF & J 333.

[180] Modern American cases emphasise the need for the remedy to be adequate taking into account the victim's pressing circumstances: *Ross Systems* v *Linden Dari Delite Co* (1961) 173 A 2d 258; *Capps* v *Georgia Pacific Corp* (1969) 453 P 2d 935; and *Pecos Construction Co Inc* v *Mortgage Investment Co of El Paso* (1969) 459 P 2d 842.

[181] (1731) 2 Str 915 at 916.

[182] See most recently *The Alev* [1989] 1 Lloyd's Rep 138 at 146–7.

[183] See generally Ogus, Harris and Phillips, 'Contract Remedies and the Consumer Surplus' (1979) 95 LQR 581.

[184] For example, in *Victoria Laundry (Windsor) Ltd* v *Newman Industries Ltd* [1949] 2 KB 528: profits lost on particularly lucrative dyeing contracts were considered too remote.

alternative means of reducing the opportunism potential in some situations would be to devise a more effective remedial framework.[185]

In *Pau On* v *Lau Yiu Long*[186] the Privy Council recognised that one of the factors to be considered in a determination of duress was whether an adequate legal remedy exists for the wrong threatened. In doing so it alluded to the considerable emphasis laid upon such evidential matters in American decisions. In addition to the use of the adequacy of legal remedies test by the American courts,[187] a similar consideration can be seen in the Canadian 'practical compulsion' cases. These predate the English economic duress cases,[188] but the principles developed have a similar purpose in attempting to expand the traditional categories of duress, and control more subtle economic pressure. In the leading case of *Eadie* v *Township of Brantford* Spence J said,[189] in reply to a submission from counsel that in order to recover money paid the claimant must have been faced with a situation where there was no other alternative open to him:[190]

> I am of the opinion that the bar to the claimant's recovery is not so stringent and that a practical compulsion is alone necessary. In each of the three cases in this court[191] ... there were other courses available to the claimant but those other courses were time-consuming and impractical.

The presence of an adequate legal remedy provides a workable mechanism for distinguishing opportunistic from non-opportunistic modifications, since if a party agrees to a modification of a contract following a threat to breach it, when in all the circumstances of the case the law provides an adequate remedy, it can be inferred that the modification was not compelled. The party must have agreed to it because it in some way benefits him.

This analysis focuses upon the existence or non-existence of an adequate legal remedy rather than on whether the victim was aware of it. If the latter formulation were adopted its effect would be to create an incentive for parties not to appraise themselves of their legal rights when a threat is made. The focus on the existence of the adequate remedy and the rejection of the victim's legal knowledge as relevant helps to motivate the victims of threats

---

[185] See Muris, *op. cit.*, n. 6 above.

[186] At p. 635 G–D. See also *Alec Lobb (Garages) Ltd* v *Total Oil (Great Britain) Ltd* [1983] 1 WLR 87, especially 960 E–F, affd. and revsd. in part without discussion of economic duress [1985] 1 WLR 173; *B & S Contracts & Design Ltd* v *Victor Green Publications Ltd* [1984] ICR 419 at 428 D–F; *The Alev* [1989] 1 Lloyd's Rep 138 at 146–7.

[187] In addition to the cases cited in n. 180 above, see *Thompson Crane and Trucking* v *Eyman* (1954) 267 P 2d 1043 and *Equity Funding Corp* v *Coral Management* (1971) 322 NYS 2d 965.

[188] An early case illustrating the broader basis of recovery was *Pillsworth* v *Cobourg* [1930] 4 DLR 757.

[189] (1967) 63 DLR (2d) 561 at 570.

[190] In effect, my test (i), above.

[191] That is, *Knutson* v *Bourkes Syndicate* (1941) 3 DLR 593; *Municipality of St John* v *Fraser-Brace Overseas Corp* (1958) 13 DLR (2d); *George (Porky) Jacobs Enterprises Ltd* v *City of Regina* (1964) 44 DLR (2d) 179. *Contra*: note (1941) 10 Can Bar Rev 694, which at p. 696 suggests that the adequacy of the legal remedy in *Knutson* was not investigated. In *Re Hooper and Grass' Contract* [1949] VLR 269 Fullagar J at 272 expresses himself to be 'more impressed by the decision than by the criticism'.

to resist them where the law provides an adequate remedy in the event of their being carried out. This reduces the need for litigation because in some instances the threat will be withdrawn.

Either the law provides a remedy for the damage which would result if the threat were carried out which in all the circumstances is an adequate one, or there exists an extra-legal alternative which in all the circumstances of the case is an adequate one

There seems no reason to limit the investigation into the remedies available for the victim to judicial remedies: extra-legal remedies such as substitute performance by another contractor should also be considered. The arguments developed for test (ii) apply *mutatis mutandis* to the addition in test (iii) of extra-legal alternatives; these arguments support the enforcement of any contractual modification agreed at a time when there was either an adequate legal remedy or an extra-legal alternative.

The typical extra-legal alternative is the procurement in the market of a performance equivalent to that which the other party is threatening to withhold. Where such a performance is available at a price equal to, or less than the contract price it should be treated as analogous to an adequate legal remedy. For such a substitute performance to be considered adequate, all the relevant costs of procuring that alternative must be taken into account and it must be available at the right time. It is insufficient simply to compare the two contract prices: the expenses of searching and locating the substitute must also be considered. Only if the sum of the substitute performance and all connected expenses is less than or equal to[192] the contract price should it be considered an adequate remedy. Obviously, the performance offered must be substantially the same although it should be considered so if it differs only in some insignificant way.

Several cases in the United States endorse a test like this, which emphasises the relevance to the question of duress of the existence of adequate alternatives, both legal and extra-legal.[193] In *Pao On* v *Lau Yiu Long* Lord Scarman did appear to recognise that the inquiry into alternatives should not confine itself to those provided by the legal system: his reference to an adequate legal remedy was only illustrative of a larger set of alternatives available to the victim.[194] However, Lord Scarman's approach does differ

---

[192] If the cost is greater then the victim of the threat to breach may be under a 'duty' to mitigate his loss by contracting for the market alternative – see *Payzu Ltd* v *Saunders* [1919] 2 KB 581 and *The Solholt* [1983] 1 Lloyd's Rep 605.

[193] *Tristate Roofing Co* v *Uniontown* (1958) 142 A (2d) 333; *King Construction Co* v *WM Smith Electric Co* (1961) 350 SW (2d) 940; *Austin Instrument Inc* v *Loral Corp* (1971) 272 NE 2d 533; *Rose* v *Vulcan Materials Co* (1973) 194 SE 2d 521.

[194] 'It is material to enquire whether the person alleged to have been coerced ... did ... have an alternative course open to him *such as* an adequate legal remedy' (emphasis added), at p. 635 C–D; and to similar effect, Kerr LJ in *B & S Contracts and Design Ltd* v *Victor Green Publications Ltd* [1984] ICR 419 at 428 D.

from the American approach. He regards adequacy of the alternatives available as merely one factor on his 'checklist' for duress. The American decisions frequently emphasise the necessity for the absence of an adequate alternative course. I submit that the extended alternatives test described in (iii) above should be adopted as the principal test in determining whether a contractual modification was compelled or not.

The arguments developed in relation to the adequacy of legal remedy test, which suggest that the focus should be upon the existence of legal remedies and not the victim's awareness of them apply to the availability of an extra-legal alternative. By ignoring the victim's knowledge the law creates an incentive for the victim to investigate the alternatives open to him. Moreover, an additional advantage is offered by the adoption of such a rule in relation to an extra-legal alternative. The rule when applied to legal remedies will only reduce the extent of litigation where the threat is withdrawn following resistance. Otherwise, its effect is merely to bring forward the time of the litigation, i.e. the suit is one of breach where an adequate legal remedy is discovered and the threat is not withdrawn, rather than a later action to recover money paid. However, if a similar rule is applied to the market alternative it offers the possibility of a further reduction in litigation; for instance, if a cheaper but adequate substitute performance is discovered, the victim may decide not to pursue his action for breach against his first contractual partner.[195]

Independent advice

The presence or absence of independent advice was one of the factors which Lord Scarman considered relevant to the determination of the existence of duress.[196]

As suggested above, the law should concentrate upon the choices reasonably available to the victim of the threat and not merely on those of which he is actually aware. To do otherwise would serve to put a premium on ignorance and to increase litigation. The presence of independent advice does nothing to expand the choices available to the victim[197] of the threat and so should not be considered as a relevant factor in determining whether a contractual modification was compelled or not.[198]

---

[195] Unless his 'search' costs were considerable, in which case he may seek to recover these.

[196] *In Pao On v Lao Yiu Long* [1980] AC 614 at 635 D; see *Alloy Products Corp v US* (1962) 302 F 2d 528 at 530–31; *Oremus v Wynhoff* (1963) 123 NW 2d 441 at 444; *Smith v Lenchner* (1964) 205 A 2d 626 at 628; and in Canada: *Eadie v Township of Brantford* (1967) 63 DLR (2d) 561 at 564 *per* Ritchie J (dissenting).

[197] As was admitted by Rutherford J in *Ronald Elwyn Lister v Dunlop of Canada Ltd* (1978) 19 OR (2d) 380 at 409.

[198] The reason for the belief that the presence or absence of independent advice can be a useful determinant of compulsion probably stems from a confusion between economic duress and undue influence. The presence of independent advice is a good defence to an allegation of undue influence. See generally Chunni, 'Duress and Undue Influence: A Comparative Analysis' (1970) 22 Baylor Law Rev 572; and on the problems caused by the intrusion of equitable defences into common law doctrines see Watkins, 'The Spirit of the Seventies' (1977) 6 Anglo-Am L Rev 119.

Subsequent affirmation

If a party has an opportunity to challenge the payment he has made or the contract he has entered into at a later time when he is free of the coercive pressure, and fails to do so, he may be said to have affirmed the contract.[199] If a party agrees to a contractual modification at a time when he had no adequate legal remedy or extra-legal alternative and did so as a result of an illegitimate threat, but later failed to challenge the modification at a time when he was free of the compulsion, it can be inferred that the modification benefits him in some way. From the point in time when he failed to seek the adequate legal redress or make use of the adequate extra-legal alternative, the modification should be treated in the same way as one which was originally agreed at a time when an adequate remedy or adequate extra-legal alternative existed.

The ability to pass on costs

In a case before the High Court of Australia, *Mason* v *State of New South Wales*,[200] it was submitted by counsel that the ability of the victim of the threats to pass on the cost of a price increase would be relevant to the determination of compulsion. This submission found favour with Menzies J[201] but its relevance was denied by Windeyer J.[202]

The situation envisaged is presumably one where contracts between 'the victim' and third parties are sufficiently flexible for the victim to be able to increase the price clause, or perhaps where the victim could exert extra-legal pressure to renegotiate a new contract at an increased price. However, although a party may be able to pass on these costs in the short term, this practice is likely to affect him adversely in the long term; when present contracts come to an end, the third parties may choose to contract elsewhere with suppliers who have not 'passed on' such costs to their customers. The law should not ignore the long term coercive effect of threats by concentrating on the ability to pass on costs in the short term.[203]

Perhaps one situation where this consideration would be relevant is where the victim himself is a monopoly supplier of some good and is, therefore, able to pass on the increase to his customers. Although the long-term effect of this practice will not be as injurious to the monopolist as to the competitive supplier, it may still be significant; customers will be unable to substitute the goods of alternative suppliers for those of the monopolist, but an increase price will reduce the demand for the goods to some extent.

---

[199] For instance, *The Atlantic Baron, supra; Byle* v *Byle* (1990) 65 DLR (4th) 641 (dealing with contract formulation).
[200] (1959) 102 CLR 108.
[201] At p. 136, although on the facts of the case it was not proved that there was present an 'opportunity and intention' to pass on these costs.
[202] At p. 146.
[203] The law should only 'require' the victim to act reasonably. *Cf.* the doctrine of mitigation examined in ch. 17.

Therefore, I submit that the ability to pass on costs should not alone be considered sufficient evidence to rebut an inference of coercion. In any case where this factor is considered, the long term effects of the practice must not be neglected and the monopoly characteristics of the victim's market must be properly examined.

The non-enforcement rule

It was suggested earlier that an approach which rendered all opportunistic modifications unenforceable was too undiscriminating. It is necessary to subdivide the class of opportunistic modifications, and sometimes allow the innocent victim to offer a credible inducement to the opportunist. The hallmark of such situations is that, in the absence of such a payment, the opportunist will prefer breach to performance. Unfortunately, the statement of facts in the decided cases is usually inadequate to ascertain whether the opportunist would prefer breach to performance if the modification were unenforceable. Therefore, it is difficult to speculate as to how common such cases are. However, perhaps the closest English case is *The Atlantic Baron*, which, being a special case stated by an arbitrator for the opinion of the court on a question of law, was accompanied by a lengthy list of findings of fact.

In this case the threat to breach was opportunistic. It was not a case where the occurrence of unanticipated circumstances rebutted the inference of opportunism. The yard was preying upon a vulnerability of the claimants resulting from their reliance upon the yard. The claimants having concluded lucrative charters with a third party, Shell,[204] had no realistic alternative but to submit. The usual remedy for breach, an action for damages, would probably not fully compensate for the profits lost on the charter and the potential liability to Shell;[205] these were probably too remote.[206] Also, there was no realistic market alternative available at the contract price, or cheaper, at the time the modification was agreed.[207]

Does this case belong to the subset of opportunistic modifications where enforcement is justified in order to protect the victim from further losses (here the lost profits and potential liability resulting from the claimants' breach of the Shell charter)? The distinguishing characteristic of this subset is that if the modification is not enforced the opportunist would still prefer breach to performance. *The Atlantic Baron* does not appear to be such a case. The report reveals no reason why the award of damages in the event of the yard's breach should not be substantial. It would only be where damages were limited, perhaps by a clause of the contract, to less than any loss the

---

[204] See p. 708 F–G.
[205] Which amounted to about $8m: see p. 709 C.
[206] The yard was in fact unaware of the fixture: see p. 709A, so the question of remoteness would turn upon the 'first' limb of the *Hadley* v *Baxendale* test.
[207] If one were available it would have cost about $60m, about twice the contract price.

opportunist yard would incur in performance that the yard would prefer to breach rather than to perform. In this case the damages would prima facie be the difference between the contract price and the cost of obtaining a similar ship at the date of breach. Since this would take account of the currency devaluation, as well as any interim increases in shipbuilding costs, the likely award of damages would be substantial. Moreover, it is not clear that the 10 per cent devaluation would necessarily produce a situation where performance at the original price would result in a loss for the yard; it may simply reduce its profit. Therefore, it appears unlikely that the case was one where the opportunist would prefer breach to performance in the absence of an enforceable modification.

WAIVER

Introduction

Waiver has been famously described as a 'slippery word worn smooth with overuse'. These words, written in 1917, were part of an introduction[208] to a book, *Waiver Distributed*,[209] which advanced the thesis that waiver did not in fact exist![210] So-called cases of waiver were all better explained as involving other legal doctrines or principles. Although today no one would dispute the existence of a doctrine of waiver, there remains considerable confusion about its proper definition.[211]

Waiver seems to be used in three senses which are relevant to the modification setting.[212] These are:

(1) to mean rescission:[213] this usage refers to the dissolution of the contract by agreement;
(2) to mean variation:[214] this usage refers to the binding alteration of a contractual term. To be binding, waiver in the sense of rescission or variation must be supported by consideration and so was discussed earlier;
(3) to mean forbearance:[215] this usage refers to a purported alteration to the contract which is not otherwise binding, perhaps because of lack of consideration or failure to comply with formal requirements.

---

[208] Written by Roscoe Pound.
[209] By Ewart (1917) part of whose analysis is adopted by Rose J in *Danforth Heighty* v *McDormid Bros* (1922) 52 OLR 412, 426–7.
[210] See also *Stackhome* v *Barnston* (1805) 10 Ver 453 at 466 *per* Grant MR.
[211] The editor of Spencer, Bower and Turner at 319–20 thinks that 'waiver ... is not capable of definition in terms of the authorities'.
[212] Following Treitel, p. 97.
[213] For example, *Linz* v *Schuck* (1907) 67 A 286.
[214] For example, *Brikom Investments* v *Carr* [1979] 1 QB 467 *per* Roskill and Cumming-Bruce LJJ.
[215] As described in Blackburn J in *Ogle* v *Earl Vane* (1867) LR 2 QB 275, 282 contrasting 'mere forbearance' with 'binding oneself for a good consideration', i.e. variation.

Waiver as forbearance

The doctrine of waiver as forbearance is a complex one. This is due to two factors: the coexistence of common law and equitable principles and the formal requirements imposed on some modifications.[216]

At common law

At common law the party for whose benefit the forbearance was granted (whom we will inelegantly term the 'waivee') was not permitted to refuse to tender the altered performance, but any damages awarded in the event of the waivee's failure to perform his modified obligation were assessed on the basis that the breach was one of the altered contract. Thus in *Ogle* v *Vane*:[217] the claimant contracted to purchase iron, to be delivered in July. The defendant failed to deliver at that time. The claimant was then asked to wait until February for delivery, which he did. Still no iron was delivered. The claimant then purchased iron from another source.

The claimant sought as damages the difference between the contract price and the market price in February. The Court of Queen's Bench allowed the claimant's action on the basis that this was a mere 'postponement'[218] or 'voluntary waiting'[219] and not an 'alteration in the contract', which would have to be both in writing and supported by consideration to be enforceable.[220] The case was, therefore, distinguished from others which involved attempts to alter contracts which failed.[221] The rule in *Ogle* v *Vane* was extended by the case of *Hickman* v *Haynes*[222] in two ways. It was applied to an action by the seller for non-acceptance following the buyer's request for late delivery. The waivee, in this case the buyer, was not allowed to refuse to accept the altered performance. It was also said to apply where the waiver took place before the breach.[223] In *Ogle* v *Earl Vane* it appears that the waiver took place after the initial breach. The more troublesome case at common law involved the waiver, the party who has granted the forbearance, who refused to perform or to accept the 'new' performance. A number of cases support the view that in such cases the party granting the waiver cannot go

---

[216] Though these are now of reduced importance.

[217] (1867) LR 2 QB 275, (1868) affd LR 3 QB 272 (Ex Ch).

[218] A phrase used by Blackburn J during argument in the Court of Queen's Bench, *ibid.*, pp. 280–81.

[219] *Ibid.*, p. 283.

[220] *Ibid.*, p. 283, see also Lush J at p. 284.

[221] *Stead* v *Dawber* [1839] 10 Ad & E 57 (seller requested and received an extension of time but then refused to make delivery. Seller successfully claimed the oral variation formed part of the parties' bargain which was, therefore, unenforceable because of its failure to comply with the Statute of Frauds 1677). *Marshall* v *Lynn* [1840] 6 M & W 109 (buyer informally requested and received a delay in shipment but subsequently refused to accept the goods. Seller's action failed because he could not prove a complete contract within the Statute of Frauds 1677). See also *Goss* v *Nugent* [1833] 5 B & Ad 58; *Harvey* v *Graham* [1836] 5 Ad & E 61; *Stowell* v *Robinson* [1837] 3 Bing NC 928.

[222] (1875) LR 10 CP 598; see also *Levey and Co* v *Goldberg* [1922] 1 KB 688.

[223] *Ibid.*, p. 606; see also *Hartley* v *Hymans* [1920] 3 KB 475, 491 *per* McCardie J. In *Ogle* v *Earl Vane* (1867) LR 2 QB 275, the waiver took place after the initial breach *per* Lush J at p. 284.

back on it,[224] at least not without giving reasonable notice.[225] So in *Panoutsos v R Hadley*[226] a seller was not allowed, without having given reasonable notice of his desire to return to the original arrangement, to complain that payment was by an unconfirmed letter of credit when he had waived his contractual right to payment by a confirmed letter of credit.

The case of *Plevins v Downing*[227] is, however, in conflict with these authorities. There it was held that a seller could not recover damages for a buyer's refusal to take delivery, when delivery was to be made outside the contract period, but within an extended period requested by the seller.

The common law is clearly deficient and contradictory. Rationalisation of the cases seems to rest upon a difficult distinction between forbearance and variation. This is said to depend upon the intention of the parties.[228] As forbearance allows a waivor to return to the original contractual rights, provided reasonable notice is given and subsequent events do not make such reversion impossible, or perhaps unjust,[229] the following may be deduced: a representation will be said to amount to forbearance where the waivor intends to reserve to himself a power to retract, but to a variation if his intention is *permanently* to abandon rights under the contract. The difficulty of applying this distinction will be apparent from a comparison of *Plevins v Downing*[230] (buyer allowed to reject late delivery – ineffective variation) and *Hartley v Hymans*[231] (buyer not permitted to reject late delivery – effective forbearance). Treitel[232] points out a further deficiency of the common law, which is the utterly illogical result that the more a party tries to bind himself by a subsequent agreement the less successful he will be! Any attempt permanently to alter a contract will be treated as an ineffective variation, in the absence of consideration and possibly writing, while any attempt to merely suspend a right will be given limited effect to as a forbearance.

---

224 *Tyers v Rosedale and Ferryhill Iron Co* (1875) LR 10 Ex 195; *Leather Cloth Co v Hieronimus* (1875) LR 10 QB 140; *Hartley v Hymans* [1920] 3 KB 475.

225 *Dudley, Clarke and Hall v Cooper Ewing and Co* (unreported) per Bailhache J quoted by McCardie J in *Hartley v Hymans* [1920] 3 KB 475, 495–6; *Charles Richards v Oppenheim* [1950] 1 KB 616, 624 *per* Lord Denning (with whom Bucknill and Singleton LJJ agreed) who discusses both common law and equitable principles; *Banning v Wright* [1922] 1 WLR 972, 981 D–E *per* Lord Reid.

226 [1917] 2 KB 473.

227 [1876] 1 CPD 220.

228 *Stead v Dawber* (1839) 10 A & E 57, 64.

229 Although no case at common law appears to have considered the waivor's position if reversion to the original obligation is no longer possible, it should be the same as the position in equity.

230 (1876) 1 CPD 220.

231 [1920] 3 KB 475 a decision of McCardie J described by Lord Denning as 'the most diligent collector of cases that has ever been on the Bench'. It was this case which first alerted Lord Denning to the decision of *Hughes v Metropolitan Railway* [1877] 2 AC 439 which led to the famous decision in *High Trees* considered below. See Denning (1979) *The Discipline of Law*, p. 201.

232 Treitel, pp. 99–100.

Despite these limitations, which have undoubtedly produced unmeritorious decisions,[233] it is submitted that the history of common law waiver reveals – technical requirements notwithstanding – an attempt to enforce unobjectionable modifications.[234]

The modifications frequently given effect to by the doctrine of common law waiver are unobjectionable. The adjustments generally relate to delivery dates[235] but sometimes to other matters.[236] An inference of mutual benefit would more frequently seem to be justified than where the alteration is to a price term. Of course, if the benefit to the waivor amounted to legal consideration then the modification would be enforceable as a contractually binding variation. However, as we have seen, such a modification may still be unenforceable for its failure to comply with formal requirements, or it is possible that benefits might accrue to the waivor which do not amount to consideration. Also the waivor may simply be indifferent to the enforcement of a modification in which case the benefit to the waivee would seem to commend enforcement. This contrasts with an alteration in a price term involving in effect a direct pecuniary transfer[237] from one contracting party to another where the suspicion of opportunism would seem to be greater.

In equity

In response to the inadequacies of the common law approach equity developed a more flexible principle. The classic statement of this principle was by Lord Cairns in *Hughes* v *Metropolitan Railway*:[238]

> it is the first principle upon which all Courts of Equity proceed that if parties who have entered into definite and distinct terms involving certain legal results – certain penalties or legal forfeiture – afterward enter upon a course of negotiations which has the effect of leading one of the parties to suppose that the strict rights arising under the contract will not be enforced, or will be kept in suspense ... the person who otherwise might have enforced those rights will not be allowed to enforce them where it would be inequitable having regard to the dealings which have thus taken place.

---

[233] In *Stead* v *Dawber* (1839) 10 Ad & E 57 Denman CJ came to his conclusion 'reluctantly', p. 65.

[234] The attempt predates the cases cited and may be traced back to *Warren* v *Stagg* [1787] cited in *Littler* v *Holland* [1799] 3 TR 590, 591 but finding fuller expression is *Cuff* v *Penn* [1813] 1 M & S 21. Lord Ellenborough CJ while agreeing that 'parol evidence was not admissible to vary a written contract' (at p. 26) stated that 'here what has been done is only performance of the original contract' (at p. 27) with 'an agreed substitution of other days than those originally specified for its performance' (at p. 27). In such circumstances the action on the effectively modified contract could be maintained.

[235] For example, *Cuff* v *Penn*; *Ogle* v *Earl Vane*; *Hickman* v *Haynes*; *Hartley* v *Hymans*.

[236] For example, *Leather Cloth Co* v *Hieronimus* (1875) LR 10 QB 140.

[237] See Williamson, 'Transaction – Cost Economics: The Governance of Contractual Relations' (1979) 22 J Law & Econ 233, 251. Although the waiver in *Panoutsos* v *R Hadley* related to the pre-term it was not a proposal to reduce it.

[238] (1877) 2 App Cas 439, 448.

It is perhaps interesting to note that no authority at all was cited in support of equity's first principle.[239] It might have been thought that the authority of this decision, notwithstanding the breadth of Lord Cairns' peroration, was limited to relief from forfeiture. However, this was denied by Lord Cairns himself,[240] and this denial was confirmed by the Court of Appeal in *Birmingham and District Land Co* v *London and Northwestern Railway Co.*[241]

The representation may be express or implied but must be unambiguous.[242] In *Hughes* v *Metropolitan Railway*[243] a landlord gave notice to his tenant requiring him to effect repairs within six months. The lease entitled the landlord to forfeit the tenant's interest if such a notice was not complied with. However, during this period the landlord began negotiations with the tenant for the purchase of his lease. When negotiations broke down, after the expiry of the original six month period, the landlord claimed forfeiture of the lease. It was held that the landlord's conduct in negotiating to buy the tenant's interest amounted to an implied but ambiguous representation by the landlord not to insist on his strict contractual rights. This requirement is clearly meant to protect contractual parties from 'losing' contractual rights through an isolated or infrequent failure to insist on strict contractual performance. On this basis a shipowner was not estopped from exercising his power to withdraw a ship for non-payment of hire because in the past he had accepted late tenders of hire.[244] In other words, there must be evidence of a clear intention not to enforce the contract strictly.

The second requirement is that the representation must induce an alteration of the waivee's position. This may be expressed as a requirement of 'detriment' on the part of the waivee. It appears that this condition requires only that there must have been an alteration in the position of the waivee, which was induced by the waivor's representation, such that it would be inequitable, and in this sense detrimental to the waivee, to act inconsistently

---

[239] Nor does there appear to be any. See Wilson (1951) 67 LQR 330, 333, n. 19.

[240] Lord Cairns both insisted that the principle he was articulating had nothing to do with relief from forfeiture and also denied the existence of any blanket discretion in a court of equity to relieve from forfeiture. In a passage immediately preceding that quoted above (1877) 2 App Cas 439, 488 he said: 'it was not argued at your Lordship's Bar, and it could not be argued that there was any right to a Court of Equity or any practice of a Court of Equity to give relief in cases of this kind, by way of mercy or by way merely of saving property from forfeiture'.

[241] (1888) 40 ChD 268, 286 *per* Bowen LJ who after quoting the passage from Lord Cairns' judgment in the *Hughes* case quoted in the text above said: 'it was suggested that proposition only applied to cases where penal rights in the nature of forfeiture, or analogous to those of forfeiture were sought to be enforced. I entirely fail to see any such possible distinction. The principle has nothing to do with forfeiture. It is a principle which lies outside forfeiture and everything connected with forfeiture.' See also *Offredy Development* v *Steinbock* [1972] 221 EG 963 on not interpreting Lord Cairns' speech too restrictively.

[242] *Danforth Heights* v *McDermid Bros* [1922] 52 OLR 412, 416 *per* Sutherland J; *Bremer Handelsgesellschaft MBH* v *Vanden Avenne–Izegem PV BA* [1978] 2 Lloyd's Rep 109, 126 *per* Lord Salmon; *The Post Chaser* [1981] 2 Lloyd's Rep 695, 700. *Drexel Burnham Lambert International NV* v *El Nasr* [1986] 1 Lloyds Rep 356 at 365; *W & R Sack Ltd* v *Fifield* [1996] 2 NZLR 105 at 109.

[243] (1877) 2 App Cas 439 at 448. See also *Whitall* v *Kaur* (1970) 8 DLR 3d 163.

[244] *The Scaptrade* [1983] 2 All ER 894.

with it. It is not necessary for the waivee to have altered his position to his detriment in the sense of having incurred some loss in reliance on the representation.[245]

In *The Post Chaser* Goff J said:[246]

> The fundamental principle is that stated by Lord Cairns, viz. that the representor will not be allowed to enforce his rights 'where it would be inequitable having regard to the dealings which have thus taken place between the parties'. To establish such inequity, it is not necessary to show detriment; indeed the representee may have benefited from the representation and yet it may be inequitable ... for the representor to enforce his legal rights.

The Post Chaser involved a sale of goods on CIF[247] terms where the seller failed to notify the buyer of the carrying vessel as required in the contract of sale. The seller claimed that the buyer had waived his right to timely notification when he requested the seller to send the shipping documents directly to a sub-purchaser. Goff J held that the original buyer's request amounted to a sufficiently unambiguous promise capable of giving rise to a waiver. However, none was established because although the sellers 'did actively rely' on the representation there was nothing 'which would render it inequitable for the buyers thereafter to enforce their legal right ... [particularly] having regard to the very short time [three days][248] which elapsed'.[249]

The effect of a waiver in equity, like that at common law, is suspensory only. It is clear from *Hughes* v *Metropolitan Railway* that the doctrine does not permanently alter the rights of the parties. It was assumed throughout that the landlord could, upon giving reasonable notice, revert to his contractual rights.[250] Of course, the waiver would become permanent if the waivee could no longer effectively perform in the way contemplated by the contract, as in *Birmingham and District Land Co* v *London and Northwestern Railway*.[251]

A further limitation of the doctrine is that it is generally defensive in nature. This would appear to follow from its definition as a representation that the strict rights arising under the contract will not be enforced. However, the principle, though defensive, is not only available to defendants but also to claimants, as illustrated by *Birmingham and District Land Co* v

---

[245] *Alan & Co* v *El Nasr Export* [1972] 2 QB 189, 213 A–B *per* Lord Denning MR; *Finagrain* v *Kruse* [1976] 2 Lloyd's Rep 508, 536 *per* Megaw LJ, 542 *per* Roskill LJ (though in this case the point did not form part of the court's judgment due to a concession by counsel); *The Post Chaser* [1981] 2 Lloyd's Rep 695, 701.

[246] [1981] 2 Lloyd's Rep 695 at 701.

[247] In a CIF contract the purchaser pays a sum of money to represent the *cost* of the goods, their *insurance* and *freight* carriage). Therefore, carriage is the responsibility of the seller.

[248] That is, between the seller's representation and the buyer's objection.

[249] At p. 702.

[250] This is implicit in all the speeches in the House but is stated most clearly by Lord O'Hagan at p. 450 who referred to the lessor's right to inform the lessee that: 'failing to make a new proposal they should understand the negotiations to have been concluded and the parties relegated to their legal rights.'

[251] The tenant was obviously discharged from his obligation to build because the land had been compulsorily acquired and was occupied by the railway company.

London and Northwestern Railway, where the claimant succeeded in his action for a declaration that his building agreement was still subsisting and that he was entitled to have his statutory compensation[252] assessed on that footing.

There is another unnoticed line of authority purporting to follow *Hughes* which supports the use of the *Hughes* principle by a claimant. In *Bruner* v *Moore*[253] it was held that an option could be extended (in the absence of an agreement for consideration) by conduct on the part of the grantor which raised an equity against him. *Bruner* v *Moore* may go beyond the *Birmingham* case in this regard. In *Birmingham* the claimant used the doctrine to substantiate his claim for statutory compensation, whereas in *Bruner* the claimant was able successfully to enforce an extension to a contractual option, in the absence of any consideration to support the extension. So *Bruner* appears to conflict more directly with the common law's insistence on consideration as a requisite for a contractual action. This decision has been adopted and relied on in Canada.[254] A somewhat more equivocal endorsement has been given by an Australian Court.[255] However, in England it appears mainly to be cited with reference to the postal rule.[256] It thus joins a small group of cases including *Hartley* v *Ponsonby*[257] and *Raggow* v *Scougall*,[258] which appear to give legal effect to contractual modifications but which are accommodated within legal orthodoxy only with some difficulty or embarrassment. This may explain their apparent 'lack of publicity'.

PROMISSORY ESTOPPEL

Introduction

We have already met the old common law rule[259] that part payment of a debt can never discharge that debt, which was authoritatively endorsed by the House of Lords in *Foakes* v *Beer*,[260] despite considerable misgivings on the part of Lord Blackburn. This established line of authority would seem to preclude the application of equitable waiver to part payment of debts. However, this bold step was taken by Denning J (as he then was) in the case

---

[252] Under the Land Clauses Consolidation Act 1845.

[253] [1904] 1 Ch 305 and to similar effect *Davidson* v *Norstant* (1921) 61 SCR 493, 513–14 *per* Duff J (dissenting on the decision), 520 *per* Anglin J.

[254] *Pierce* v *Empey* (1939) 4 DLR 672, 674 *per* Duff CJC delivering the court's judgment. See also *Rural Municipality of St James* v *Bailey and Driscoll* (1975) 7 DLR 2d 179, 182 *per* Adamson CJM and 191–2 *per* Schultz JA, Montague JA concurring.

[255] *Ian Hunter Bowman and Another* v *Durham Holdings Pty Ltd* [1973] 47 ALJR 606, 611 col. 1 E–F *per* Stephen J. The comment, it appears, is *obiter*, p. 611 col. 1 F–G.

[256] Treitel p. 20, n. 14.

[257] (1857) 7 E & B 872.

[258] [1915] 31 TLR 564.

[259] And its exceptions.

[260] (1884) 9 App Cas 605.

of *Central London Property Trust Co* v *High Trees House*.[261] This extension was expressed in the language of estoppel.[262] As estoppels had classically to be founded upon a representation of fact,[263] which was absent in this case, a new species[264] of 'promissory' estoppel was born. In the *High Trees* case the claimants let a block of flats to the defendants in 1939 for £2,500 per year. The defendants then sublet the flats. In 1940 the claimants agreed to reduce the rent by half because of the defendants' inability to sublet the flats as a result of the war-time slump in rents. The reduced rent was paid until 1945. The flats were then again full but the claimant company was in the hands of a receiver. The lessor tested the claim for the balance of the rent by suing for the last two quarters of 1945.

Denning J interpreted the modification as only intended to apply while war-time conditions prevailed and so upheld the receiver's claim. However, if the balance of the rent during the war years had been claimed, the action would not have succeeded.[265]

The modification given effect to in *High Trees* may have been agreed in response to an unanticipated and unassigned contractual risk, i.e. the outbreak of World War II. It has been argued that such modifications should be enforced. Enforcement will not have an adverse effect upon the certainty of contract and the parties will be able to realise the mutual benefits which motivated them to agree to the concession in the first place. Benefit to the promisor which is generally difficult to detect is more easily inferred here because the parties were associated companies, the defendant company was in fact a subsidiary of the claimant company. This important fact seems to be ignored in discussions of the case. Forcing the subsidiary company into insolvency by insisting on full payment would clearly be injurious to the parent company. It is perhaps ironic that in such circumstances the parent company should eventually find itself in the hands of a receiver!

The relationship between the doctrine of equitable waiver and that of promissory estoppel is an unclear one. Some judges have treated the two as

---

[261] [1947] KB 130.

[262] *Ibid.*, p. 134.

[263] *Jorden* v *Money* (1854) 5 HL Cas 185.

[264] Although Lord Denning quoted several cases in support of the principle he claimed to have discovered in the *Hughes* and *Birmingham* cases, few are of much precedental value. Three of the cases involved, like *High Trees* itself, were extempore judgments at first instance: *Re Wickham* [1917] 34 TLR 158; *Re William Porter and Co* [1937] 2 All ER 361; *Buttery* v *Pickard* [1946] WN 25. In each case the judgment is either brief or poorly reported or both. The other two authorities cited were *Fenner* v *Blake* [1900] 1 QB 426, a decision of the Divisional Court occupying under four pages of the report, and *Salisbury (Marquess)* v *Gilmore* [1942] 2 KB 38 (a case in which Lord Denning appeared as counsel) and where only Mackinnon LJ based his decision on estoppel and then only after having found that the communication '[i]n substance … stated facts' (p. 52). However, Lord Denning could more convincingly have cited a decision of the High Court of Australia *Barns* v *Queensland National Bank* (1906) 3 CLR 925 or perhaps the poorly reported Canadian case of *Grimsby Steel Furniture Co* v *Columbia Gramophone Records* (1922) 23 OWN 188.

[265] At p. 134–5.

distinct,[266] while others,[267] most notably Lord Denning,[268] have treated them as the same. It is suggested that promissory estoppel should be regarded as an extension of the doctrine of equitable forbearance to cover a creditor's promise to accept part payment of a debt in full settlement. This view is consistent with many judicial statements of the requisites of promissory estoppel which reflect those of equitable waiver.[269] So an unambiguous representation must be made,[270] which leads the representee to believe that strict contractual rights will not be enforced,[271] with the result that the promisee alters his position in reliance, in circumstances where it would be inequitable to allow the representor to act inconsistently with the representation[272] and where the representee has acted equitably.[273]

Unambiguous representations

The requirement that the representation, be it express or implied, must be unambiguous again[274] reflects the law's concern to avoid unintended modifications being given legal force.[275] It has further been suggested that the representation must be part of a 'course of negotiation'[276] but this does not appear to represent English law.[277]

Reliance

The requirement of reliance is one that has aroused much controversy and confusion. Two types of reliance are sometimes contrasted: 'detrimental'

---

266 *Brikom Investments v Carr* [1979] 1 QB 467, 485 E–F *per* Roskill LJ with whose reasoning Cumming-Bruce LJ agreed.

267 *Brickwoods v Butler and Walker* (1970) 21 PCR 256; *Wauchope v Maida* (1972) 22 DLR 142; *Re Tudale Explorations Ltd* (1978) 20 OR 2d 593; *The Scaptrade* [1983] 1 All ER 301 affd [1983] 2 All ER 763 without a discussion of estoppel.

268 The *High Trees* case; *Charles Richard v Oppenheim* [1950] 1 KB 616, 623; *cf. WJ Alan v El Nasr Export* [1972] 2 QB 189, 212 G where the question he poses may be thought to suggest a belief that waiver and promissory estoppel are distinct.

269 For instance, *Combe v Combe* [1950] KB 215, 220; *The Scaptrade* [1983] 1 All ER 301, 304 G–H, affd [1983] 2 All ER 763 without a discussion of estoppel.

270 *Woodhouse AC Israel Cocoa Ltd SA v Nigerian Prod Marketing Co Ltd* [1932] AC 741.

271 The principle may extend beyond representations affecting pre-existing contractual relationships: see Spencer, Bower and Turner, p. 375 *et seq.* and *The Henryk Sif* [1982] 1 Lloyd's Rep 456. Indeed, it has exceptionally been applied to enforce non-contractual promises: *Roberson v Minister of Pensions* [1949] 1 KB 227 (defendant told claimant that his injury would be regarded as attributable to war service for purposes of a disablement pension). *Contra*: Lord Denning, 'Recent Developments in the Doctrine of Consideration' (1952) 15 MLR 1, 4: '... it [the *Hughes* principle] applies ... only to parties who have already entered into a contract ...'.

272 *The Post Chaser* [1981] 2 Lloyd's Rep 695.

273 *D & C Builders v Rees* [1966] 2 QB 617.

274 See above.

275 *Tool Metal Manufacturing v Tungsten Electric* [1955] 1 WLR 561, 564 *per* Viscount Simonds; *James v Heim Galalery* [1980] 256 EG 819; *contra*: *Grimsby Steel Furniture Co v Columbia Gramophone* [1922] 23 OIWN 188, 189 *per* Riddell J: 'silence is sometimes as cogent as speech'.

276 *John Burrows Ltd v Subsurface Surveys Ltd* (1968) 68 DLR 2d 354.

277 *Offredy Developments v Steinbock* (1972) 221 EG 963.

reliance which makes the promisee's position worse (e.g. if the lessees in *High Trees* made an irrecoverable gift such as giving the balance of the rent to charity) and 'mere' reliance which involves any act of reliance, beneficial or detrimental (e.g. investing the balance of the money in readily realisable and very profitable stocks and shares).[278] Judges also seem to be divided over the issue.[279] It is suggested that here and also in relation to estoppel's use as a 'shield' but not a 'sword', much of the confusion and, therefore, the controversy can be avoided by terminological clarity, for as Dixon J stated in *Grundt* v *The Great Boulder Pty Gold Mines Ltd*,[280] an estoppel by representation case, the requirement that the party asserting the estoppel must have been induced to act to his detriment is only a foreshortened way of saying that the promisee must have 'so acted or abstained from acting upon the footing ... that he would suffer a detriment if the [promisor] were afterwards allowed to set up [his] rights'. In other words, detrimental reliance (or 'detriment' improperly so called) is something from which the inequity to the promisee (or 'detriment' properly so called) may be inferred. Unfortunately, the truncated statement of the requirement may be taken to suggest that detrimental reliance must always be necessary to found a promissory estoppel. It is suggested that the view advanced by Dixon J should be preferred as a matter of authority[281] and of principle. By emphasising the equity of the modification, courts may be able to deny

---

[278] See Cheshire, Fifoot and Furmston, p. 107; *Anson's Law of Contract, op. cit.*, p. 114. Treitel uses a slightly different line of cleavage from the other two authors. He tentatively defines (p. 104) the concept I have labelled detrimental reliance as where 'the promisee ... [has] done something *that he was not previously bound to do* and as a result [has] suffered loss' (emphasis mine). The addition of the words shown in italics means that the promisee's reliance in not effecting the repairs in a case like *Hughes*, does not qualify as detrimental reliance. Whereas if detrimental reliance is defined more broadly (see Cheshire, Fifoot and Furmston and *Anson's Law of Contract, op. cit.*), the promisee's action in *Hughes* would qualify as such. These apparently divergent approaches of the leading textbooks reinforce an important point made at various places in this chapter, that the exposition of waiver and estoppel would be considerably assisted by terminological clarity.

[279] Danckwerts LJ seems to assume that detrimental reliance is necessary in *D & C Builders* v *Rees* [1966] 1 QB 617, 627 A, if he is at that point directing his mind to promissory estoppel, and see also Luckhoo JA in *Jamaica Telephone* v *Robinson* [1970] 16 WLR 174; *Morrow* v *Carty* [1975] NI 174, at 181 lines 23–5 *per* McVeigh J; *Augier* v *Secretary of State for Environment* [1978] 38 P & CR 219 at 226; see also *Bank Negara Indonesia* v *Phillip Hoalim* [1973] 2 Malagan LJ 3; *Re Tudale Explorations Ltd and Bruce* (1978) 20 OR 593 and *James* v *Heim Galleries (London) Ltd* (1980) 256 EG 819; *Trustees of the Manchester Homoeopathic Clinic* v *Manchester Corp* [1970] 22 P & CR 241 at 245 (Lands Tribunal). *Contra*: *Alan* v *El Nasr Export and Import Co Ltd* [1972] 2 QB 189, 213 F–214 A *per* Lord Denning; *Brikom Investments* v *Carr* [1979] 1 QB 467 G–M *per* Lord Denning. The inconclusive statement of Viscount Simmons in *Tool Metal Manufacturing* v *Tungsten Electric* [1955] 1 WLR 761, 764 and also that of Lord Hodson in *Emmanuel Ayodej Ajayi* v *RT Briscoe* [1964] 3 All ER 556, 559 G further reinforce the need for terminological clarity. In *Bremer Handelsgesellschaft MBH* v *Vanden Avenne-Izegem PVBA* [1978] 2 Lloyd's Rep 109, 127 Lord Salmon poses the problem but declines to answer it.

[280] (1938) 59 CLR 641, 674. The case involved an estoppel by convention rather than a promissory estoppel. However, the analysis of detrimental reliance is as valid in this context as it is there.

[281] See above.

enforcement to opportunistic modifications, whilst a requirement of detrimental reliance may prevent the enforcement of non-opportunistic modifications when the party has not made his position worse by some act which the law will recognise as detrimental reliance. At best, a requirement of detrimental reliance is superfluous; at worst, it will prevent the enforcement of non-opportunistic modifications.

Promisee must have acted equitably

In *D & C Builders v Rees*[282] the Court of Appeal refused to allow a person who had contracted with a firm of builders for some work to claim that the builders were estopped from recovering the balance of the money owing to them because it would not be inequitable to allow the builders' claim. Lord Denning, with whom Danckwerts LJ agreed, thought that the case was one of an agreement to accept less which was obtained by 'intimidation'[283] and 'undue pressure'[284] because of the builders' difficult financial position of which the defendant was aware.[285]

It appears that the requirement of equitable conduct on the part of the promisee was applied in a way that was consistent with the opportunism analysis developed earlier. The analysis of the legal control of the defendant's opportunism is somewhat cursory, occupying only one paragraph in the judgments of both Lord Denning[286] and Danckwerts LJ.[287] However, it would appear that the defendant was acting opportunistically by preying upon a vulnerability of the claimant, their difficult financial position, which was at least partially caused by their contract with the defendants.[288] The suspicion of opportunism will always be considerable when a zero-sum modification is proposed, whether the proposal is to increase or decrease the contract price.

Indeed, when the contractual modification proposed is a reduction in the contract price the inference of opportunism may be even more compelling than where it is a proposal to increase the contract price. This is because the inference of opportunism in relation to an agreed increase in the contractual price may be rebutted by evidence of the occurrence of an unanticipated and unassigned risk. Many circumstances may have this effect, whereas when a reduction in the contract price is proposed it is perhaps less likely that the risk that circumstances will make the payment of the contract price more

---

[282] [1966] 2 QB 617. The modification aspect of cases like *D & C Builders v Rees* which discuss and qualify the rule in *Pinnel's Case* is partly obscured by the vocabulary adopted. The discussion is often couched in terms of 'discharge' (does a part payment discharge a debt?) as opposed to modification or alteration (has the debt been changed?).

[283] *Ibid.*, p. 625 F.

[284] *Ibid.*, p. 625 D.

[285] *Ibid.*, p. 622 B–C, 626 E–F.

[286] *Ibid.*, p. 625 B–C.

[287] *Ibid.*, pp. 626 F, 627 A.

[288] There was evidence that the claimants had expended over £300 on the job themselves, *ibid.*, p. 621 F–G.

onerous can be regarded as unanticipated and unassigned. Such an inference will, however, be easier to make when the contract involves recurrent payments, as in *High Trees*, as opposed to a single liquidated payment, as in *D & C Builders*. This is because of the longer life of such contracts during which circumstances could change. It is perhaps the greater likelihood of opportunism in relation to contractual modifications which reduce the contract price which has caused the rule in *Pinnel's Case* and *Foakes v Beer* to survive so long.[289] Yet it is perhaps a lesser likelihood of opportunism within the set of 'reducing modifications', when the alteration is to a recurrent obligation, that has caused the major challenge to the rule to occur in *High Trees*, a recurrent payment case.

Is promissory estoppel suspensory or extinctive?

If the three requirements already discussed are satisfied, what is the effect of the estoppel established? Does it operate to extinguish the obligation modified or does it merely suspend rights under it so that they can later be revived?

Lord Denning has asserted that it is extinctive,[290] while the majority of statements, perhaps out of respect for its parentage,[291] treat it as suspensory.[292] If the majority statements were followed this doctrine would no longer be in conflict with the rule in *Pinnel's Case* and *Foakes v Beer* which deal with the *extinction* of debts. However, this approach would fail to give full effect to a non-opportunistic modification which the parties intended to have a permanent (i.e. extinctive) effect. A further complication arises where the obligation is a recurrent one e.g. to pay rent under a lease. Then the question must be addressed whether the estoppel works to suspend obligations in the sense that reversion to the original arrangement for the future is possible, but that the right to the balance of past payments is lost; or in the sense that the right to the balance of past *and* prospective under-payments can be revived. It would seem illogical if a case like *High Trees* were treated differently if the 'rent' was payable as a lump sun than if it were payable monthly. Therefore, to be consistent, if promissory estoppel is suspensory, it must affect recurrent obligations in the second sense. Again, this severely limits the role which estoppel can play in giving full effect to

---

[289] *Re Selectmove* [1995] 1 WLR 474, discussed above, pp. 336–7.

[290] See *High Trees, loc. cit.*, p. 135; *D & C Builders v Rees, loc. cit*, p. 624 D–E; *Brikom Investments v Carr* [1979] 1 QB 467, 485 A–B; *contra* his statements in *Charles Richard v Oppenheim* [1950] 1 KB 616, 624 and *Alan v El Nasr* [1972] 2 QB 189, 213 B–C, though it seems that Lord Denning would only allow reversion to the original agreement where this would not be unjust: *Alan v El Nasr, loc. cit.* at p. 213 C. In support of extinction, see also Mocatta J in *The Ion* [1980] 2 Lloyd's Rep 245, 251 distinguishing recurrent and non-recurrent obligations.

[291] See especially the *Hughes* case – as to the suspensive effect of which, see text accompanying nn. 250–2 above.

[292] *Tool Metal Manufacturing v Tungsten Electric* [1955] 1 WLR 161; *Emmanuel Ayodeji Ajayi v RT Briscoe* [1964] 3 All ER 556; *Wauchope v Maida* (1972) 22 DLR 3d 142; *The Post Chaser* [1981] 2 Lloyd's Rep 695.

non-opportunistic contractual modifications as they will not be 'enforced' in accordance with the parties' wishes where they intend to effect a permanent change in their contract.

Despite what policy and logic might suggest, English law adopts an uneasy compromise on the question whether promissory estoppel is suspensory or extinctive in effect. This emerges from the litigation in *Tool Metal Manufacturing* [TMMC] v *Tungsten Electric* [TECO].

In 1938 TMMC and TECO enter a contract permitting TECO to exploit TMMC's patents in return *inter alia* for the payment of 'compensation'. In 1939 the payment of compensation was suspended. In 1945 TECO sued TMMC alleging fraudulent misrepresentation. TMMC counter-claimed for compensation from 1942. The Court of Appeal[293] affirmed in part the decision of Devlin J that the suspension of compensation extinguished TMMC's rights to claim for compensation until they gave notice of their desire to return to the original arrangement. In 1950 TMMC sued TECO claiming compensation from 1947 on the basis that delivery of a counter-claim in the first action was a sufficient notice to revive their rights. Pearson J agreed and his decision was upheld by the House of Lords.[294]

As a result of these two actions, the legal effect of a promissory estoppel can at least be stated clearly. The first action establishes that promissory estoppel is extinctive as to past obligations[295] and the second that it is suspension as to the future.[296] The implication of this is that *if* the landlord in the *High Trees* case had in 1942 given notice of its intention to revert to the original rent this would have been effective to revive its right to the full rent for the rest of the war (after the expiration of a reasonable period). However, the landlord would be unable to claim the balance of the underpayments from 1939 to 1942. As each underpayment of rent was tendered the landlord's right to claim the balance was extinguished.

In any event, the effect of the estoppel becomes permanent when it is no longer possible in any meaningful sense to restore the promisee to his original position, e.g. where a party is encouraged to allow a limitation period within which an action must be commenced to expire. After the expiration of the period, the potential claimant could not bring an action. Similarly, when shipowners undertook not to object to charterers docking at an unsafe port this could not be reversed after the ship had suffered damage.[297]

---

[293] (1952) 69 RPC 108 at 112.

[294] [1955] 1 WLR 761.

[295] See also *J T Sydenham & Co Ltd* v *Enichem Elastomers* [1989] 1 EGLR 257 (landlord unable to recover balance of rent underpayments tendered after rent review erroneously set too low a rent) and *Je Maintiendra Pty Ltd* v *Quaglia* [1980] 26 SASR 101.

[296] See also *Ajayi* v *Briscoe* [1964] 3 All ER 556 at 558 *per* Lord Hodson; *The Kanchenjunga* [1990] 1 Lloyd's Rep 391 at p. 399 *per* Lord Goff. See also the authorities on equitable forbearance considered above.

[297] See respectively *The Henrik Sif* [1982] 1 Lloyd's Rep 456 and *The Kanchenjunga* [1990] 1 Lloyd's Rep 391.

The offensive limits of promissory estoppel

Introduction

One of the most debated issues in promissory estoppel is whether such an estoppel can itself constitute a cause of action. Cases have undoubtedly foundered when it was realised that one party's cause of action was a 'naked' estoppel.[298] Many commentators and judges[299] have said this cannot be done. So why the debate? Two answers come to mind. First it seems that here, as elsewhere in estoppel,[300] terminological clarity is lacking. The epithet that is most commonly cited to summarise the traditional wisdom on this subject, is the 'vivid' phrase used by counsel,[301] and approved by Birkett LJ[302] in *Combe* v *Combe* which described the doctrine of promissory estoppel as one to be used 'as a shield and not as a sword' which has been described judicially as a 'time-honoured phrase',[303] but it is unhelpfully ambiguous.[304] In truth, the use that can be made of an estoppel can be represented by a spectrum ranging from a defence to the creation of a new cause of action. Courts appear to use the shield/sword dichotomy to refer to some point on this spectrum. Unfortunately, they often seem to be choosing different points. Below we will examine this spectrum and the different points stated by the courts to mark the offensive limits of promissory estoppel. The second answer centres around whether, like proprietary estoppel, promissory estoppel *should*, of itself, be considered a cause of action. This theme is explored in the next section.

(a) Estoppel can only be used as a defence

This is the least ambitious claim that can be made. New legal doctrines often make their first appearance in a truncated and non-threatening guise. Therefore, it should occasion no surprise that in both of the seminal cases, *Hughes* v *Metropolitan Railway*[305] and *Central London Property Trust Co* v *High Trees House*,[306] estoppel was relied upon as a defence. Indeed, as recently as 1960 this circumscribed role for estoppel was apparently contemplated by Buckley J in *Beesley* v *Hallwood Estates Ltd*[307] who said:

---

[298] *Combe* v *Combe* [1951] 2 KB 215; *Sloan* v *Union Oil Co* (1955) 4 DLR 664; *Argy Trading* v *Lapid Developments* [1977] 3 All ER 785; *SS Employment* v *Globe Elastic Thread Co* [1980] AC 506.

[299] See respectively Cheshire, Fifoot and Furmston, p. 103; Spencer Bower and Turner, p. 387 and cases cited in n. 298 above. *Cf. Re Wyvern Developments Ltd* [1974] 1 WLR 1097 at 1104 F–1105 A.

[300] For example, the precise nature of the reliance which is required for any particular estoppel. Another example is provided by the different senses in which a recurrent obligation such as the payment of rent may be said to be suspended.

[301] [1951] 2 KB 215 at 218.

[302] *Ibid.* at p. 224. *Cf. Re Tudale Exploration and Bruce* (1978) 20 OR 2d 593 at 597 *per* Grange J.

[303] *The Proodos C* [1981] 3 All ER 189 at 191.

[304] Lawyers love metaphors. Never more so it seems than when discussing the limits of estoppel. See the metaphor adopted by Spencer, Bower and Turner 'Estoppel by Representation' 1977 at p. 7: 'To use the language of naval warfare, estoppel must always be either a mine layer or a mine sweeper: it can never be a capital unit.'

[305] (1877) 2 App Cas 439.

[306] [1947] KB 130.

[307] [1960] 2 All ER 324 at 324 C–F, affirmed at [1961] Ch 549 without discussion of this point.

As I understand this part of the law, which has been described as promissory estoppel, it is that … the doctrine may afford a defence against the enforcement of otherwise enforceable rights. It cannot, in my judgment, be invoked to render enforceable a right which would otherwise be unenforceable.

(b) Estoppel can be used by a party seeking to enforce a claim based upon a recognised cause of action to defeat the defence or counter-claim of the other party

A simple example of this use of promissory estoppel would be provided by a variation of the facts of *High Trees*.[308]

> The lessor let directly to an occupying tenant. Some time after the representation had been made and reduced rent payments had been accepted, the landlord distrained the tenant's property in order to recover the balance of the rent.
>
> Here the tenant could bring an action for conversion; the landlord would reply that he was rightfully distraining, and the tenant could use estoppel to defeat this defence.

A factually more complex example of this use of estoppel occurred in *The Ion*.[309] In this case the defendant owners chartered their vessel to the claimant charterers. The charter incorporated the Hague Rules, which provide in Art 3, r 6 that the carrier and the ship shall be discharged from all liability unless an action is brought within one year. There were several cargo claims but proceedings were not instituted within the required period. However, the charterers claimed, inter alia, that a letter from the owners' P & I club to the charterers' P & I club should be construed as amounting to a promissory estoppel to the effect that the owners would not rely on the time bar.

The Commercial Court interpreted the letter from the owners' P & I club as containing an implied promise not to insist upon the strict time limit[310] which promise was relied on by the charterers in not making an immediate application under s 27 of the Arbitration Act 1950 for an extension of time.[311] In such circumstances the court held that it would be inequitable to allow the owners to enforce their strict legal rights and so the claimed estoppel was established.

Several judicial statements as to the proper limits of the offensive use of promissory estoppel extend further to one of the following two categories.

(c) Estoppel can be used by a party seeking to enforce a claim to prove one element of a recognised cause of action

This appears to be the effect the promissory estoppel was stated to have in

---

[308] [1947] KB 130.
[309] [1980] 2 Lloyd's Rep 245.
[310] *Cf. The Zhi Jiang Kou* [1991] 1 Lloyd's Rep 491.
[311] The *defendant* is required to plead a defence of limitation.

Robertson v *Minister of Pensions*[312] where the claimant was relieved of the burden of having to prove that his injury was attributable to war service in order to qualify for a disablement pension because the ministry was estopped from denying this causal connection.

The claimant's cause of action was a recognised one; in this case statutory.[313] Yet, it could not be said that the estoppel relieved the claimant colonel of the obligation to prove all the elements of his cause of action, e.g. that he had served long enough and in a sufficient capacity to qualify for a pension, that the injury was serious enough to so qualify, etc. The estoppel related solely to the question of causation; was the injury attributable to military service? This usage may have been what Denning LJ was thinking of when, in *Combe* v *Combe,* commenting upon a number of decisions including the *Robertson* case, he said:[314]

> In none of these cases was the defendant sued on the promise, assurance or assertion as a cause of action in itself: he was sued for some other cause, for example a pension ... and the promise, assurance or assertion only played a supplementary role – an important role, no doubt, but still a supplementary role.

(d) Estoppel can be used by a party seeking to enforce a claim to prove all the elements of a recognised cause of action

This appears to be the way the promissory estoppel was used in *The Henryk Sif.*[315] In this case the first defendants conducted themselves as if they were a party to a contract of carriage, though they were not. This led the claimant to allow the limitation period to run out against the second defendant who was a party to the contract of carriage.

The judge based his finding for the claimant in his action against the first defendants, *inter alia,* upon promissory estoppel.[316] It appears that all the elements (agreement, consideration, etc.) of a recognised cause of action (contract) were proved by the estoppel.

The case of *Bruner* v *Moore,*[317] which, although pre-dating the *High Trees* case, similarly drew upon the *Hughes* principle, may also be explained in this way. The claimant there was allowed to enforce his option out of time, either because the option had been consensually extended[318] or because an equity arose in his favour as a result of the conduct of the grantor. It would appear that the effect of the equity was to prevent the defendant from denying that the claimant had a contractually binding option; the 'equity' provided the

---

[312] [1949] 1 KB 227.
[313] The pension conditions were regulated by Royal Warrant.
[314] [1951] 2 KB 215 at 220.
[315] [1982] 1 Lloyd's Rep 456.
[316] *Ibid.* at pp. 466–7. In *Shearson Lehman Hutton Inc* v *MacLaine Watson & Co Ltd* [1989] 2 Lloyd's Rep 570, Webster J casts doubt on his earlier decision but only in relation to estoppel by convention and estoppel by silence or acquiescence – see pp. 596 and 604.
[317] [1904] 1 Ch 305 and to similar effect *Davidson* v *Norstant* (1921) 61 SCR 493 at 513–14 *per* Duff J (dissenting on the decision) and at 520 *per* Anglin J.
[318] *Ibid.* at pp. 314–15, *per* Farwell J. It is difficult to see what consideration supports a consensual extension.

claimant with all the elements of a recognised cause of action. This decision has been adopted and relied on in Canada.[319] A somewhat more equivocal endorsement has been given by an Australian Court.[320] In England the case seems mainly to be cited in connection with the postal rule of acceptance.[321]

(e) Estoppel has created a new cause of action

This was the effect of the first instance decision in *Combe v Combe*.[322] The judge appeared to have dispensed with the need for consideration in order to enforce a promise, as opposed to giving more limited effect to the promise which the common law and equitable doctrines of waiver and promissory estoppel would allow. This would create a new cause of action and abrogate the requirement of consideration. The Court of Appeal strongly disclaimed this view, Lord Denning saying of promissory estoppel:[323] 'the principle never stands alone as giving a cause of action in itself'.

While no English authority directly supports this use of estoppel and many statements deny it,[324] there is the analogy with cases of proprietary estoppel which can undoubtedly create a cause of action[325] and the opinion of Lord Denning that estoppel by convention can do the same.[326] There have also been attempts to break down technical boundaries which delimit the different types of estoppel. In *Taylor Fashions v Liverpool Victoria Trustees*[327] Oliver J, while analysing the case of *Shaw v Applegate*,[328] said:

> So here once again [we see] the broad test of whether in the circumstances the conduct complained of is unconscionable without the necessity of forcing those incumbrances into a Procrustean bed constructed from some unalterable criteria.

The discovery of this broad test underpinning technically distinct estoppel doctrines led Oliver J to assert that there had been a 'virtual equation of promissory estoppel and proprietary estoppel'.[329] Similarly, in *Crabb v Arun*

---

[319] *Pierce v Empey* (1939) 4 DLR 672 at 674, *per* Duff CJC. See also *Rural Municipality of St James v Bailey and Driscoll* (1978) 7 DLR 2d 179 at 182 *per* Adamson CJM and at 191–2 *per* Schultz JA.

[320] *Ian Hunter Bowman v Durham Holdings Pty Ltd* [1973] 47 AJLR 606 at 611 col. 1 E–F *per* Stephen J. The comment is probably *obiter dicta*, see p. 611 col. 1 F–G.

[321] For example, Treitel, p. 24.

[322] [1951] 2 KB 215.

[323] *Ibid.*, p. 220.

[324] See nn. 298–9 above and *cf.* the position in the USA and Australia considered below.

[325] *Crabb v Arun DC* [1976] 1 Ch 179 at 187 E *per* Lord Denning. This point of contrast is rarely discussed in the proprietary estoppel cases. For a possible explanation, see Treitel, p. 135.

[326] Expressed in *Amalgamated Investments and Property Co Ltd v Texas Commerce International Bank Ltd* [1982] QB 84 at 122 B–C. However, the accepted view seems to be that estoppel by convention cannot create new causes of action that did not exist before, although a claimant might, by relying upon an estoppel, succeed in a cause of action which would fail if it were not for the estoppel. See p. 126 E–F *per* Everleigh LJ and p. 131 E–G *per* Brandon LJ.

[327] [1981] 1 All ER 897 at 918 B–C.

[328] [1978] 1 All ER 123.

[329] *Ibid.* at p. 897 B commenting on *Crabb v Arun DC*. See also *Habib Bank Ltd v Habib Bank AG* [1981] 1 WLR 1265 at 1285 A–B *per* Oliver LJ: 'I detect in myself ... a strong predilection for the view that such distinctions are both archaic and arcane and that ... they have but little significance for anyone but a legal historian.' See also p. 1287 G *per* Stephenson LJ.

DC, a proprietary estoppel case,[330] Scarman LJ said: 'I do not find helpful the distinction between promissory and proprietary estoppel.'[331] This combination of the analogy with proprietary estoppel[332] and the disinclination of certain judges to observe technical distinctions may indicate the way future developments of the doctrine will tend.

However, the greatest impetus towards an expanded role for promissory estoppel has come from overseas. In the United States[333] the *Restatement, Contracts 2d, s 90* summarises the common law in this way:

> (1) a promise which the promisor should reasonably expect to induce action or forbearance on the part of the promisee or a third person and which does induce such action or forbearance is binding if injustice can be avoided only by the enforcement of the promise. The remedy granted may be limited as justice requires.

The above section gives the impression that the doctrine of promissory estoppel in the USA is distinguished by its concern with the protection of reasonable reliance on the part of a promisee. This has certainly appeared as a theme in some of the classic authorities on estoppel, e.g. *Hoffman v Red Owl Stores*[334] where the recovery of lost profits was denied. In contrast, the recovery of such profits is a regular feature of the legal protection afforded to contractors' expectations in an action for breach of contract. However, recent studies in the USA have revealed an increasing use of promissory estoppel as a means for protecting contractual expectations.[335] This produces a tension between traditional contract principles and the doctrine of promissory estoppel which has caused some commentators to speculate about the imminent demise of the latter[336] and others to attempt a synthesis of both types of promissory liability.[337]

---

[330] In *Walton's Stores (Interstate) Ltd v Maher* (1988) 64 CLR 387 *Crabb* was described as 'an instance of promissory estoppel' at 403 *per* Mason CJ and Wilson J. This description is not supported by the judgments in the case.

[331] [1976] 1 Ch 179 at 193 B. *Cf. Re Basham (deceased)* [1987] 1 All ER 405 at 414 B and compare the equivocal comment of the Privy Council in *Maharaj v Chand* [1986] AC 898 at 908 A that '[t]he doctrine of promissory estoppel is now firmly established although its frontiers are still being worked out'.

[332] As to the differences, see Treitel, pp. 134–6.

[333] For a recent comprehensive account of the development of promissory estoppel in the United States, see Holmes, 'Restatement of Promissory Estoppel' (1996) 32 Williamette Law Rev 263; Hillman, 'Questioning the "New Consensus" on Promissory Estoppel: An Empirical and Theoretical Study' (1998) 98 Col Law Rev 580.

[334] (1967) 133 NW 2d 267.

[335] See Metzger and Phillips, 'The Emergence of Promissory Estoppel as an Independent Theory of Recovery' (1983) 35 Rutgers Law Rev 472; Feinman, 'Promissory Estoppel and Judicial Method' (1984) 97 Harv L Rev 678; Farber and Matheson, 'Beyond Promissory Estoppel: Contract Law and the "Invisible Handshake"' (1985) 52 U Chic L Rev 903; Becker, 'Promissory Estoppel Damages' (1987) 16 Hofstra L Rev 131; Yorio and Thel, 'The Promissory Basis of Section 90' (1991) 101 Yale LJ 101; Holmes, 'Restatement of Promissory Estoppel' (1996) 32 Williamette Law Rev 263. *Contra*: Hillman, 'Questioning the "New Consensus" on Promissory Estoppel: An Empirical and Theoretical Study' (1998) 98 Col Law Rev 580. *Cf.* the analysis of the English cases in Cooke, 'Estoppel and the Protection of Expectations' (1997) 17 Legal Studies 258.

[336] See Gilmore's elegant (1974) *The Death of Contract*.

[337] See Farber and Matheson, *op. cit.* (n. 335 herein above).

The most recent developments have taken place in Commonwealth jurisdictions, particularly Australia.[338] Although the doctrine of promissory estoppel was not recognised by the High Court until 1983 in *Legione* v *Hateley*,[339] its subsequent development has been dramatic. A number of Australian cases have demonstrated one of the most fundamental challenges to the basis of orthodox contract law. These recent cases evidence the weakening or removal of a number of the restrictive doctrines or maxims which have traditionally limited the operation of the doctrines of estoppel and thereby avoided an overt challenge to the primacy of the agreement intended to create legal relations and supported by consideration as a means of enforcing promissory obligations.

The first of this line of recent cases was *Walton's Stores (Interstate) Ltd* v *Maher*[340] where the respondent, Maher, a builder, had been negotiating an agreement with the appellant, Walton's, whereby Maher would demolish buildings upon ground which he owned and then construct a building in accordance with Walton's specifications which he would then lease to Walton's. The negotiations proceeded and Maher thought agreement had been reached. Maher demolished the old buildings. Unfortunately, by this time Walton's had repented of the project. Maher sought redress.

In the High Court, Walton's challenged the view, upheld in both courts below, that Maher had acted in reliance upon a mistaken assumption that a binding contract had come into existence. The purpose of this challenge was to preclude Maher from relying upon estoppel by representation or convention which would prevent Walton's from asserting that it had not entered a binding contract. Walton's further argued that no promissory estoppel could arise because that would offend both the rule that such estoppels do not create a cause of action and also the requirement of such estoppels that there be a pre-existing legal relationship between the parties.

The High Court unanimously dismissed the appeal but, unfortunately, its agreement ended there, as the members of the court differed over their view of the facts. Mason CJ, Wilson and Brennan JJ found that Maher had assumed that a contract *would* come into existence,[341] whereas Deane and Gaudron JJ found that the assumption was that a contract *had* come into existence.[342] The finding of the former group prevented Maher from relying upon an estoppel by representation but they found that a promissory estoppel did arise. In reaching this conclusion, they did not feel fettered by the supposed rule that such estoppels do not found a cause of action nor by

---

338 See Carter and Harland (1996) *Contract Law in Australia*. 3rd edn; *Halsbury's Laws of Australia*, Vol. 6, Contract, section 110.

339 (1983) 152 CLR 406. See also the support for a limited doctrine in *Je Maintiendrai* v *Quaglia* (1980) 26 SASR 101 and *Gollin & Co Ltd* v *Consolidated Fertilizer Sales Pty Ltd* [1982] Qd R 435.

340 (1988) 164 CLR 387.

341 *Ibid.*, pp. 398 and 407–8 *per* Mason CJ and Wilson J, and at pp. 428–9 and 430–32 *per* Brennan J.

342 *Ibid.*, p. 443 *per* Deane J, and at pp. 463–4 *per* Gaudron J on the basis that Walton's was bound by the assumption that contracts had been exchanged.

the requirement of a pre-existing legal relationship. They thought that these restrictions simply evidenced a concern that estoppel should not, without more, permit all gratuitous promisees to demand the fulfilment of their expectations. However, only Brennan J tried to fashion the doctrine in a way that would meet this concern. He emphasised that the role of estoppel was to protect a disappointed promisee from the detriment he would suffer in the event of the promisor unconscionably refusing to fulfil his promise; it was not to satisfy the promisee's expectations.[343]

In *Commonwealth of Australia v Verwayen*[344] the High Court of Australia was again called upon to consider the limits of estoppel. The case was not 'contractual',[345] concerning as it did the question whether the Commonwealth was free to dispute its liability to an injured member of the Australian navy and in particular whether it could, at variance with its previous policy, either deny the existence of a duty of care or plead a limitation defence. However, the principles discussed have an obvious application to contractual disputes. Unfortunately, as in *Walton's Stores*, the High Court in *Verwayen* spoke with many different voices. The majority held that the Commonwealth was not able to deny its liability to the claimant, Deane and Dawson JJ on the basis that the Commonwealth was estopped from doing so,[346] Toohey and Gaudron JJ on the basis that it had waived its right to do so.[347]

There is strong support in the case for a rejection of any distinction between common law estoppels based upon representations of existing fact and equitable estoppels[348] which are more flexible both as to the type of statement or the conduct required and the remedy eventually awarded. This approach, which eschews any attempt to distinguish statements or conduct with an element of futurity from those without may spare the court a difficult enquiry. The difficulty presented to a tribunal of fact by the task of ascertaining whether there was a common assumption that an agreement had been, as opposed to, would be, entered is amply evidenced by the divergent views of the facts taken by members of the High Court in *Walton's Stores*.

It appears to be generally assumed by the High Court in *Verwayen* that *Walton's Stores* lays to rest any insistence upon a pre-existing legal relationship. Again, the removal of this requisite seems to free the court from a difficult task. For while it is easy to define the phrase 'legal relationship' in terms of a pre-existing contractual relationship, once that definition is abandoned,[349] the term considerably empties of meaning, for it would surely

---

[343] *Ibid.*, at pp. 423–4.
[344] (1990) 170 CLR 395.
[345] *Cf. Robertson v Minister of Pensions* [1949] 1 KB 227 and *Deane v Attorney-General* [1997] 2 NZLR 180.
[346] *Ibid.*, p. 443 *per* Deane J, and at p. 462 *per* Dawson J.
[347] At p. 475 *per* Toohey J, and at p. 487 *per* Gaudron J.
[348] *Ibid.*, '… it should be accepted that there is but one doctrine of estoppel …' at p. 413 *per* Mason CJ, and at pp. 433–4 *per* Deane J.
[349] *Robertson v Minister of Pensions* [1949] 1 KB 227; *Durham Fancy Goods Ltd v Michael Jackson*

be possible to give some meaning to the term sufficient to encompass the relationship between any two contracting parties to a contractual dispute, since *ex hypothesi* they are at least linked by a common legal system. The approach of Dawson J seems to endorse such a concept of a pre-existing relationship.[350] The rejection of old distinctions and requirements may appear progressive and so desirable. However, there is a price to be paid for such so-called 'progress'; that price is doctrinal uncertainty. It is argued below that the cost is too high.

The rule that promissory estoppel cannot found a cause of action, which is frequently expressed by the unhelpful aphorism that the estoppel may be used as a shield and not as a sword, was given scant attention by the High Court in *Verwayen*. Rather the importance of the decision in *Verwayen* lies in its promotion of a different technique to restrict the over-expansion of estoppel doctrines and thereby reduce conflict between the new estoppel and the doctrine of consideration.[351] In *Verwayen* there was considerable support for the approach developed by Brennan J in *Walton's Stores* which sought to restrict the remedy available to the representee to the consequences of his detrimental reliance. According to Mason CJ (emphasis added):[352]

> ... it should be accepted that a court ... may do what is required, *but no more*, to prevent a person who has relied upon an assumption as to a present, past or future state of affairs ... from suffering detriment in reliance upon the assumption as a result of the denial of its correctness.

According to Brennan J, the application of this reliance based approach meant that the representee's remedy should be restricted to financial compensation in respect of expenses incurred which are directly attributable to his reliance upon the representations made by the Commonwealth.[353] Alternatively, this approach might justify an expectation based remedy, i.e. one which seeks to put the representee in the position he would have been in if the representation, assumption or promise was respectively, true or had been carried out. Indeed in both *Walton's Stores* and *Verwayen* the remedies eventually granted had the effect of fulfilling the representee's expectations. In *Walton's Stores* damages were awarded on the basis that the representor was estopped from retreating from its promise that the contract would be

---

(Fancy Goods) Ltd [1968] 2 QB 839; *The Henryk Sif* [1982] 1 Lloyd's Rep 456 and *Brikom Investments* v *Carr* [1979] 1 QB 467 seem to relax this requirement in this country. See also *James* v *Heim Gallery (London) Ltd* (1980) 256 EG 819 where the Court of Appeal said that whether the pre-existing relationship must be a contractual one was said to be an open question.

[350] 'For the parties here, whilst not in a contractual relationship, were in a legal relationship which began at least with the commencement of the action by the respondent against the appellant': *ibid.*, p. 455.

[351] See Robertson, 'Satisfying the Minimum Equity: Equitable Estoppel Remedies after *Verwayen*' (1996) 20 Melb L Rev 805, especially section 2.

[352] *Ibid.*, p. 413. See also at pp. 429–30 *per* Brennan J, at p. 454 *per* Dawson J, at pp. 475–6 *per* Toohey J, and at p. 501 *per* McHugh J.

[353] *Ibid.* at p. 430. Brennan J thought that there was insufficient evidence before the High Court to specify the extent of recovery.

completed;[354] in *Verwayen* the Commonwealth was prevented from going back on the beliefs they had excited. The point is simply that the proper application of the principles adumbrated in *Verwayen* means that this will not inevitably be so. Yet, despite the clear and careful statements of principle in *Verwayen*, it seems that subsequent Australian experience mirrors that of the United States where the remedy granted seems unreflectively to involve the fulfilment of the expectations of the representee.[355]

A different but related technique exists for restricting the expansion of estoppel doctrines. Rather than restricting the operation of the doctrine by reference to the remedial consequences of its application the range of circumstances in which it may be said to apply may be restricted by reference to the requirement of unconscionability.[356] In *Verwayen* Mason CJ said that 'unconscionable conduct' was the 'driving force' of equitable estoppel.[357] In subsequent cases this concept has been emphasised. For example *The Zhi Jiang Kou*[358] where the Supreme Court of New South Wales applied the *Verwayen* decision. The claimants failed to establish the existence of an estoppel in the case because, *inter alia*, they were unable to prove that a sufficiently clear and unequivocal promise had been made. However, the consideration of *Verwayen* is instructive. For Kirby P applied the test by Deane J in *Verwayen* that:[359]

> The central principle of the doctrine (of estoppel) is that the law will not permit an unconscionable – or, more accurately unconscientious – departure by one party from the subject matter of an assumption which has been adopted by the other party.

In *Austotel Pty Ltd* v *Franklins Selfserve Pty Ltd*[360] the developer of a shopping centre was held not to be estopped from denying that he had entered into a lease in respect of a supermarket that formed part of the development. There was no evidence of the requisite degree of unconscionable conduct on the part of the developer;[361] the parties were of equal bargaining power[362] and the prospective lessee had for commercial reasons deliberately avoided entering a lease.[363] In addition, where a party is not allowed to set up an estoppel as a result of his own conduct, it may be said that the requisite unconscionability is lacking.[364]

---

[354] This may have been a result of the fact that the High Court did not hear argument about the appropriate remedy.

[355] See n. 351 above. *Cf.* Spence (1999) *Protecting Reliance* pp. 68–9.

[356] 'It is the requirement of unconscionable conduct which is now seen as the protection against undue intrusion upon the law of contract, for a voluntary promise will not give rise to an estoppel', *ibid.*, p. 453 *per* Dawson J.

[357] *Ibid.*, p. 407.

[358] [1991] 1 Lloyd's Rep 493.

[359] *Ibid.*, p. 510.

[360] (1989) 16 NSWLR 582.

[361] See also *Gallagher* v *Pioneer Concrete (NSW) Pty Ltd* (1993) 113 ALR 159.

[362] At p. 585 *per* Kirby P.

[363] At p. 620 *per* Rogers A-JA.

[364] *Official Trustee in Bankruptcy* v *Tooheys Ltd* (1993) 29 NSWLR 641.

The development in Australia of a unified basis for estoppel doctrines reflects an earlier trend in the Canadian courts.[365] This is well illustrated by two cases which arose out of a building scheme when this scheme became unattractive to investors as a result of a recession. In both *Revell v Litwin Construction (1973) Ltd* [366] and *Welch v O'Brian Financial Corporation*[367] the investors sought to avoid their obligations by reference to the developer's failure to deliver a prospectus to each investor in accordance with a statutory requirement. In *Revell* the British Columbia Court of Appeal held that the investor was estopped from relying upon the statute even in the absence of detrimental reliance. In *Welch v O'Brian Financial Corporation* the same court held that no estoppel could be raised against the investors by the developers in view of the developer's failure to disclose facts critical to the success of the investments. What is perhaps more significant is the endorsement in both cases of the 'broad principle' laid down in the earlier case of *Litwin v Pan*[368] which rejects the traditional distinctions between 'estoppel, promissory estoppel, waiver'[369] etc. and endorses the 'underlying concept ... of unfairness or injustice' to which 'knowledge, detriment, acquiescence or encouragement' are relevant only in so far as they go to prove the requisite degree of unfairness or injustice.

The development of the doctrine of promissory estoppel in New Zealand[370] has been less radical than that which has occurred in Australia. None the less a number of previous restrictions upon the availability of the doctrine have been relaxed; the requirement of a pre-existing contractual relationship has apparently been dispensed with[371] and there is even equivocal support for the proposition that promissory estoppel may found a cause of action of itself.[372] In addition, cases have demonstrated an enthusiasm for a unified doctrine of estoppel. A typical statement is that of the President of the Court of Appeal in *Gillies v Keogh*:[373]

> The tide is setting or has set, I think, against the view adhered to by Sir Alexander Turner in Spencer, Bower and Turner on *Estoppel by Representation* (3rd ed., 1977) pp. 306–309, that proprietary and promissory estoppel are entirely separate and take their origins from different sources.

---

[365] There are traces of a doctrine 'akin to ... promissory estoppel' as early as 1847 according to *Gilbert Steel Ltd v University Construction Ltd* (1973) 36 DLR (3d) 496 at 506 *per* Pennell J. See *Hurlburt v Thomas* (1847) 3 UCQB 258 and the cases discussed in Waddams (1993) *The Law of Contract*. 3rd edn, p. 131, n. 78.

[366] (1991) 86 DLR (4th) 169.

[367] (1991) 86 DLR (4th) 155.

[368] (1986) 52 DLR (4th) 459. The litigation began as *Litwin (Construction) Ltd v Kiss* (1986) 4 BCLR (2d) 88. See (1991) *The Canadian Abridgement*. 2nd edn, R14D.

[369] *Ibid.*, at p. 468.

[370] See (1997) *The Laws of New Zealand*, Contract, para 85.

[371] *Burberry Mortgage & Savings Ltd v Hindsbank Holdings Ltd* [1989] 1 NZLR 356 and *Secureland Mortgage Investments Nominees Ltd v Harman & Co Solicitor Nominee Co Ltd* [1991] 2 NZLR 399.

[372] *Morton-Jones v RB and JR Knight Ltd* [1992] 3 NZLR 582.

[373] [1989] 2 NZLR 327 at 331.

This approach has been followed in a number of cases which have emphasised a common requirement of unconscionability.[374] However, other cases sound a note of caution. In *National Westminster Finance NZ Ltd* v *National Bank of NZ Ltd*[375] Tipping J spoke of[376] 'a single doctrine of estoppel' through which runs 'the element of unconscionability' but none the less emphasised that 'the broad rationale … is not a test in itself', rather '[f]or ease of analysis it is convenient to examine the particular ingredients of different manifestations … of the doctrine'. This passage has been relied on in the High Court[377] and one judge noted, but did not resolve, the conflict between the 'conventional view' of the requirements of estoppel and the 'somewhat broader view … taken by the Court of Appeal in *Gillies* v *Keogh*'.

Whether the English superior courts will be as bold as their Canadian, New Zealand and particularly their Australian counterparts in bringing together disparate doctrines of estoppel into a unified one and sweeping away some of the time-honoured restrictions upon its availability has yet to be demonstrated. To a certain extent we have seen that the ground has already been laid.[378] The requirement of a pre-existing legal relationship has been interpreted loosely[379] and on occasions ignored.[380] The restriction upon estoppel not founding a cause of action is clearly inapplicable to proprietary estoppel, has been doubted in relation to estoppel by convention, and must be called into question by those English decisions calling for a unified doctrine of estoppel. It will be argued that this momentum should not be permitted to override arguments of policy which support a more restricted role for the doctrine of promissory estoppel.

The estoppel spectrum operationalised

The attempt above to locate different points which have been used to mark the boundaries of estoppel involves some difficult distinctions. The isolation of category (a) necessitates being able clearly to identify the party seeking to enforce a cause of action and the party merely defending his rights. This is often, as we will see, a rather more difficult task than it seems. The distinction between on the one hand category (b) and on the other hand categories (c) and (d) relies upon a clear demarcation between elements which the claimant must prove to substantiate his cause of action and those

---

[374] *Wham-O MFG Co* v *Lincoln Industries* [1984] 1 NZLR 641, *Budget Rent A Car Ltd* v *Goodman* [1991] 2 NZLR 715 at 724 *per* Master J.H. Williams QC and *Butler* v *Countrywide Finance Ltd* [1993] 3 NZLR 623 at 630 *per* Hammond J.

[375] The case was decided in 1993 but not reported until [1996] 1 NZLR 548.

[376] *Ibid.*, pp. 549–50.

[377] This passage was relied on in *Rattrays Wholesale* v *Meredyth-Young & A'Court* [1997] 2 NZLR 363 at 378 *per* Tipping J.

[378] *Contra: Re Goldcorp Exchange Ltd* [1994] 3 WLR 199 at 210 H where the Privy Council derives 'no assistance' from *Walton's Stores* and *Verwayen*.

[379] See *The Henryk Sif* [1982] 1 Lloyd's Rep 456.

[380] For example, by Lord Denning, applying the principles of promissory estoppel in *Brikom Investments* v *Carr* [1979] QB 179 at 187 E.

he must substantiate to negative a defence raised by his opponent; again, this is often a far from simple issue.[381] The distinction between category (c) and (d) is ultimately just a question of degree; what comprises a part and what the whole of a cause of action? In contrast, the line of cleavage between the penultimate category (d) and the creation of a cause of action on estoppel (e) seems to be a clear and workable one. In order to illustrate these difficulties, which only serve to reinforce the imperative need for semantic clarity in this area, we will examine the Canadian case of *Re Tudale Exploration and Bruce*[382] the facts of which were that the respondent (Tudale) had granted the appellant (Teck) an option to develop some mining claims for three years. During this period the claims were held by an escrow agent. If the claims were not taken up by Teck, they were to revert to Tudale. Two extensions of time were granted, but the third one was disputed. Before its expiry, Teck purported to exercise the option.

The litigation arose from a successful application to the Mining and Lands Commissioner, by Tudale, to have the claims vested in it. Grange J, delivering the judgment of the Divisional Court overturned the decision of the Commissioner. He thought the disputed third oral extension sufficient to raise an estoppel against the respondent. While dubious about the value of the shield–sword maxim,[383] Grange J did not feel that he had to investigate that controversy because:[384]

> Not only is Teck the respondent in the proceedings [i.e. before the Commissioner][385] but its claim to the property is based upon the contract. The promise of extension is set up only as a defence to Tudale's assertion that the rights under that contract had expired.

The court therefore clearly thought that Tudale was to be regarded as the party asserting a cause of action, with Teck the 'defendant' using the estoppel by way of defence (that is, category (a) above). However, it is surely more important to ascertain who *in substance* is seeking to enforce a cause of action than merely to have regard to the formal position of the parties (who is the claimant and who is the defendant).[386] To do otherwise would be to encourage any party seeking to rely upon an estoppel wastefully to try and manoeuvre his opponent into bringing the action so that the estoppel is being pleaded defensively. In this case because the shares were held by a third party who received contrary instructions from the parties as to what to do with the shares, it was necessary for one party to commence proceedings.

---

381 See the discussion above of the *The Ion* [1980] 2 Lloyd's Rep 245. The analogy with criminal law is interesting. One might expect to find prosecution and defence elements more clearly defined in the criminal law but often this is not so; see *R v Smith* [1974] QB 358.

382 (1978) 20 QR 2d 593.

383 *Ibid.*, p. 597.

384 *Ibid.*, p. 597.

385 Tudale was the applicant before the Commissioner, with Teck the defendant. On appeal, Teck was the appellant and Tudale the respondent.

386 'It strikes me that although estoppel is here said to be raised as a defence only; it is *functionally* raised in the character of a counterclaim.' (emphasis added) *Prudential Building Investment Society v Hankins* [1997] 1 NZLR 114 at 122 *per* Hammond J.

It was really little more than a matter of chance that Tudale did so.[387] Moreover, since the original option had expired, the usual result of which would be that the shares would revert to Tudale, it was in substance Teck who were asserting a new cause of action. Thus, the case would seem to lie within my category (d) or (e) and not (a) as the judge asserted. The court should have explored rather than sidestepped the shield–sword maxim. It would seem that in order to keep the case within an orthodox interpretation of that maxim (that is, (d)) the court would have to be satisfied that Tudale was estopped from denying Teck had an enforceable, recognised cause of action, here a valid contractual option.

In the similar case of *Conwest Exploration v Letain*,[388] which was relied upon by the court in *Tudale*, an option was again enforced. The majority found that the option had been exercised within time but in the alternative considered Letain estopped[389] from denying there was a 'subsisting'[390] option contract with Conwest. Cartwright J, a member of the majority, pointed out that Letain was the 'claimant in substance as well as in form'.[391] This finding presumably relieved the majority of any obligation to discuss the shield–sword maxim and the limits of estoppel. However, considering only the court's second ground of decision (i.e. estoppel), it would seem that Conwest was attempting to enforce an option out of time and so, in substance, was trying to enforce a cause of action. Moreover, the only reason that Letain had formally to bring the proceedings was because the claims were transferred to Conwest pending the exercise of the option. It would be harsh if this fact were held to preclude Letain's reliance upon an estoppel. So clearly some discussion of the proper limits of promissory estoppel should have formed part of the majority judgment. It is, therefore, surprising that only one judge, and he dissenting, considered such an issue to be raised on the facts.[392] The court, if it had considered the matter, may have viewed the case as falling within category (d) as *Bruner v Moore* and *Re Tudale* seem to.

The analysis of *Re Tudale* and *Conwest v Letain* has revealed three things. Firstly, the need to articulate clearly the proper limits of promissory estoppel. This must take the form of a test which is clearer and more helpful than the familiar shield–sword maxim[393] which may decide one of a number of lines of demarcation all of which find some support in the cases. Secondly, whichever test is adopted it must inquire into the substance and not just the form of the parties' arrangements. Thirdly, it would seem that the least

---

[387] See *Watson v Canada Permanent Trust Co* (1972) 27 DLR (3d) 735.

[388] (1964) 41 DLR 2d 198.

[389] *Ibid.*, pp. 206–7.

[390] *Ibid.*, p. 207.

[391] *Ibid.*, p. 200.

[392] *Ibid.*, p. 202.

[393] In *Prudential Building Investment Society v Hankins* [1997] 1 NZLR 114 at 122, Hammond J, immediately after recognising the importance of examining who in substance is bringing the action, resorted to the familiar maxim: 'To put this another way, if estoppel is to be wielded in the manner of a sword, should it not attract all the incidents appropriate to an offensive weapon?'

arbitrary line which can readily be accommodated within the legal orthodoxy would be (d). Whether the courts should go further and adopt the most ambitious claim made for promissory estoppel (i.e. category (e) that it has created a new cause of action) will be examined in the next section.

Should promissory estoppel create a new cause of action?

As stated earlier it still remains to be seen if the approach of the Australian, Canadian and New Zealand Courts will be endorsed by our own appellate courts. In addition to the support of prominent members of the judiciary,[394] there has been considerable academic enthusiasm for a unified principle of estoppel.[395] However, the contrary arguments have not been examined so exhaustively.[396]

The most frequently articulated criticism of an expanded doctrine of promissory estoppel is that it would create uncertainty. This is usually taken to refer to the unpredictability of outcome of any dispute to counsel and contractors.[397] This general unpredictability can itself be ascribed to several specific uncertainties in the doctrines. These include the use of vague concepts.

In order to establish a promissory estoppel, it is necessary that the following be present: an unequivocal promise by one party to another that he will not insist upon his strict rights, reliance by the promisee to the extent that it would be inequitable to allow the promisor to renege on his promise and equitable conduct on the part of the promisee.

The first requisite should not occasion the courts undue difficulty as it is really the analogue of rules as to certainty and the effect of silence in relation to promises supported by consideration. However, the second and third requirements, reflecting the dimension of unconscientious conduct which some believe to be the common thread running through estoppel doctrines, may lack definition. The application of these broad standards which introduces uncertainty. However, close attention to the policy considerations which inform the doctrine of promissory estoppel can help give greater definition to these concepts. The opposite effect would result from any attempt to construct a single unified doctrine of estoppel.

---

[394] See text accompanying nn. 326–32 above.

[395] For instance, Spence (1999) *Protecting Reliance*, especially ch. 2; Cooke (2000) *The Modern Law of Estoppel*, especially chs. 4 and 8; Thompson, 'From Representation to Expectation: Estoppel as a Cause of Action' [1983] Camb Law Rev 257; Duthie, 'Equitable Estoppel, Unconscionability and the Enforcement of Promises' (1988) 104 LQR 362; Kirk, 'Confronting the Forms of Action: The Emergence of Substantive Estoppel' (1991) 13 Adelaide Law Rev 225; Lunney, 'Towards a Unified Estoppel – The Long and Winding Road' [1992] Conv. 239; and the limited enthusiasm of Halliwell, 'Estoppel: Unconscionability as a Cause of Action' (1994) 14 Leg Stud 15.

[396] For an exception, see Parkinson, 'Equitable Estoppel: Developments after *Walton's Stores v Maher*' (1990) 3 JCL 50.

[397] The predictive value of the law in this regard must not be limited to legal personnel since most disputes are settled out of court. The parties are more likely to arrive at a settlement, and therefore expend less resources in doing so if their legal entitlements are subject to little doubt. See Harris and Veljanovski (1983) 5 Law and Policy Qu 97.

Under orthodox contract law the identification of the precise moment when the promisor assumes obligations towards the promisee is reasonably clear; it is as soon as agreement (supported by consideration and an intention to create legal relations) has been reached. Doubt may arise as to the precise identification of the instant when an obligation is assumed under the new estoppel doctrines; is it when the act of reliance begins, when the act is complete or at some other time?[398] The answer is presumably that it is when the cumulative weight of the promisee's conduct and reliance is such that we can say that it would be inequitable to allow the promisor to go back on his promise. However, the existing case law does not suggest that this temporal uncertainty has given rise to any particular problems.

The plea for a unified concept of estoppel seems to be based upon an unarticulated premise: that the disparate doctrines share a common purpose. Perhaps at a general level this is so; each doctrine expresses the courts' disapproval of the unconscientious departure from beliefs excited in another. However, such an expression of purpose is over-inclusive; it would encompass much of the law of contract and trusts. Rather the question posed here is whether the expression of common purpose at such a level of generality serves only to obscure the location of the objectionable conduct. The danger is that the pursuit of a universal panacea might squander such expertise as the law has acquired in dealing with specific problems. A major thesis of this book is that different policy considerations are relevant to different episodes in the life of a contract. In this Part we have seen that the different doctrines which collectively comprise the law of contractual modifications can be analysed in terms of the tension between the policy objectives of encouraging contractual flexibility and restraining opportunism. In Part I we examined the very different rationale which inform the legal control of pre-contractual negotiations.

Further dangers attend such an enterprise.[399] The law fails to accumulate expertise in dealing with particular problems. Lawyers and judges thus robbed of the accumulated expertise of the courts may apply the general doctrine in a way that is in conflict with policy considerations specific to a particular context. For the future such inappropriate cataloguing of legal disputes fails to generate sensible debate. Not only do the parties to the particular dispute have their conflict resolved by reference to inappropriate considerations, but their misfortune is not a stimulus to further discussion of the subject.

It is important not to over-emphasise the point being made in this section. It is not claimed that the promotion of contractual flexibility and the attenuation of opportunism is the only purpose of the doctrine of promissory estoppel. Rather what is claimed is that these policies are significant enough to merit protection from a dedicated doctrine the jurisprudence of which

---

[398] See Collins (1997) *The Law of Contract*. 3rd edn, pp. 80–81.
[399] See Reiter, 'Courts, Consideration and Common Sense' (1977) 27 Univ Tor LJ 439 at 445–7.

should not be confused by forced mating with inappropriate bedfellows where different policies are pursued or where policies are hard to identify.

The House of Lords has recently gone some way towards recognising the force of these arguments. In *The Indian Grace*[400] Lord Steyn, with whom the other members of the House agreed, had to consider the requirements and province of the doctrines of estoppel by convention and estoppel by acquiescence (a type of proprietory estoppel). While declining to embark on a full scale review of these doctrines he said:

> The question was debated whether estoppel by convention and estoppel by acquiescence are but aspects of one overarching principle. I do not underestimate the importance in the continuing development of the law of the search for simplicity. I also accept that at a high level of abstraction such an overarching principle could be formulated. But Mr Rokison QC, for the owners, persuaded me that to restate the law in terms of an overarching principle might tend to blur the necessarily separate requirements, and distinct terrain of application, of the two kinds of estoppel.

FRUSTRATION

Introduction

In English law, frustration[401] of a contract is said to occur when events after its formation render its performance impossible or illegal or in certain analogous situations. The effect of frustration is automatically to discharge the contract[402] so that any 'modification' of the contract agreed by the parties after the frustrating event will be prima facie enforceable as a new contract. It cannot fall foul of the pre-existing duty rule (of consideration) as the pre-existing duty has been discharged. Here we will examine the role that frustration can play in the modification setting. It is the 'analogous situations' limb of the aforementioned definition which is most pertinent. Any so-called 'modification' agreed in response to the impossibility or illegality of the original contract will bear little resemblance to that contract if it is to avoid the same fate of discharge under the doctrine of frustration. If the original contract is impossible to perform, typically because of the physical destruction of the contract subject matter,[403] the 'modification' must relate to a different subject matter. Similarly, if performance of the original contract is illegal, the powerful policy reasons which operated to

---

[400] *The Indian Endurance (No. 2) Republic of India and Others* v *India Steamship Co Ltd* [1997] 4 All ER 380 at 392e.

[401] The term frustration derives from the case of *Jackson* v *Union Marine Insurance* (1874) LR 10 CP 125 from the judgment of Bramwell B at pp.145 and 148.

[402] *Hirji Muliji* v *Cheong Yue Steamship Co* [1926] AC 497, 505: 'frustration brings the contract to an end forthwith, without more and automatically', *per* Lord Sumner delivering the judgment of the Privy Council. This is now subject to the statutory adjustment of the parties' rights under the Law Reform (Frustrated Contracts) Act 1943, considered later.

[403] For example, *Taylor* v *Caldwell* (1863) 3 B&S 826. This may not be as clear a case of impossibility as previously assumed: the contract was for the use of the gardens as well, which were still usable after the fire, see below.

discharge it under the doctrine of frustration will infect any 'modification' which does not avoid the taint of illegality. Such 'modifications' may properly be considered to be new contracts. However, a question frequently discussed under the analogous situations limb is whether an unanticipated rise in costs may operate to frustrate the contract. Any modification agreed as part of a new contract, assuming the original contract to be discharged, will be enforceable. This supposed 'new' contract may well be identical to the original, with a new, increased, price term added. As such, it genuinely seems better described as a modification than as a new contract, and this is how contractors would probably regard it. If the rise in costs in such a case is an unanticipated one, the risk of which is unassigned by the contract, the approach developed earlier has labelled it a non-opportunistic modification and recommended enforcement.

Frustration is a doctrine that has provoked considerable judicial debate and confusion. Much of the debate has been directed to discovering the true juristic basis of frustration, whether it makes any difference what it is, and whether the doctrine should be expanded or kept within strict confines.[404] The confusion seems to arise from categoric and over-general statements which when investigated serve only to reveal exceptions and subterfuge. Two such statements will be investigated in this section. Firstly, that the courts have no power to vary the parties' contract but rather, must slavishly give effect to their intention. This principle is perhaps most clearly articulated by Lord Atkin[405] in the mistake[406] case of *Bell* v *Lever Bros*:

> Nothing is more dangerous than to allow oneself liberty to contract for the parties contracts which they have not in terms made by importing implications which would appear to make the contract more business like or more just.

The second definitive generalisation sometimes proffered by the courts is that a 'mere' increase in costs cannot alone operate to frustrate a contract. As Viscount Simon said in *National Carriers* v *Panalpina*:[407]

> The appellants were undoubtedly put to considerable expense and inconvenience. But that is not enough.

Here as elsewhere[408] confusion is caused when a clear general rule is stated but courts depart from it in order to achieve an instinctive sense of justice.

---

[404] These more general issues together with the circumstances when the impossibility or illegality of performance will amount to frustration and the statutory scheme for loss sharing under the Law Reform (Frustrated Contracts) Act 1943 are discussed in ch. 14.

[405] [1932] AC 161 at 226 – see to similar effect Viscount Simon's comments upon Denning LJ's judgment in the Court of Appeal in *British Movietonews* v *London and District Cinemas* (reported at [1951] 1 KB 190, 197 *et seq.*) where he vehemently denies that the court possesses the 'qualifying power' which Denning LJ claimed [1952] AC 167, 181–4.

[406] The doctrines of common mistake and frustration are functionally similar but doctrinally distinct. The former deals with the impact upon a contract of events occurring *before* the contract was entered; the latter with events occurring after contract formation. For this reason common mistake is sometimes called initial impossibility and frustration subsequent impossibility. Common mistake is considered below.

[407] [1981] AC 675, 707 B.

[408] See above, and the discussion of the pre-existing duty rule.

Frustration and the allocation of risk[409]

When a court is called upon to determine whether or not a particular contract has been frustrated, it is basically being asked how the risk of a certain event should be allocated.[410] Unfortunately, the manner in which the courts have addressed this question has at times been very unclear.

The starting point must be the express terms of the contract. Contracts themselves are devices for the allocation of risks,[411] and the principle of sanctity of contract[412] demands that the parties' allocation of risks be respected.[413] By enforcing a bargain according to its terms, mutual benefits from trade are guaranteed and productive behaviour is encouraged.[414] Courts will sometimes explicitly interfere with the sanctity of contract on the basis of procedural concerns.[415] Earlier in this chapter, a further justification for not enforcing the parties' initial allocation of risks was proposed, to give the victim of duress the ability to offer a credible bribe to his oppressor, in order to avert the greater loss which the victim would suffer from breach whenever changed circumstances cause the oppressor to prefer breach to performance. Otherwise, generally when the express terms of the contract unequivocally allocate to one party the risk of an event occurring, then *prima facie* it should be borne by that party.

Some statements of the doctrine seem to suggest that the court has a power to hold a contract to be frustrated even when the parties have expressly allocated the risk of a certain contingency. In *Tatem* v *Gamboa*, a decision at first instance, Goddard J said *obiter*:[416]

---

[409] See generally Hall, (1984) 4 Legal Studies 300.

[410] For an English judicial discussion of a 'frustration type' of problem in terms of risk allocation, see *Hurst* v *Ustorre* (1856) 18 CB 144, 155. But the question is, who takes the risk quoted by Cleasby B in his dissent in *Jackson* v *Union Marine Insurance* (1874) LR 10 CP 125, 136. See the more equivocal statement of Lord Sumner in *Bank Line* v *Arthur Capel* [1919] AC 435, at pp. 455–6. Elsewhere: frustration problems have long been perceived in terms of risk allocation: in Scotland: Cooper, 'Frustration of Contract in Scot's Law' [1946] *Journal of Comparative Legislation*, Part III; in Germany: Zweigert and Kötz (1992), Weir translation, *Introduction to Comparative Law*, ch. 44, especially p. 574, and the USA: Patterson, 'The Apportionment of Business Risks through Legal Devices' (1924) 24 Col L Rev 335, 348.

[411] See Holmes' famous example in (1881) *The Common* Law, p. 300: 'In the Case of a binding promise that it shall rain tomorrow. The immediate legal effect of what the promisor does is, that he takes the risk of the event within certain defined limits, between himself and the promisee.' See, to similar effect, Holmes J speaking in his judicial capacity in *Day* v *United States* (1917) 245 US 159, 161. In England, see Lord Sumner in *Larrinaga* v *Société Franco-Américaine* (1923) 92 LJ KB 455, 465: 'contracts are made for the purpose of fixing the incidence of … risks in advance'.

[412] The ultimate expression of which must be the theory of absolute contracts (i.e. that a promisor assumes an unconditional obligation to perform); see *Paradine* v *Jane* (1647) Aleyn 26 and its American equivalent of *Stees* v *Leonard* (1874) 20 Minn 448.

[413] See Pollock writing in the *Encyclopaedia Britannica* (1929) 14th edn, Contract, vol. 6, p. 342: 'the business of the law therefore, is to give effect, so far as possible to the intentions of the parties …'.

[414] See generally Cooter and Ulen (1997) *Law and Economics*. 2nd edn, ch. 6.

[415] That is, where there is some defect in the 'procedure' of agreement. See the doctrines of mistake and undue influence, for example.

[416] [1939] 1 KB 132 at 138. The statement is *obiter* because Goddard J had earlier found that

If the foundation of the contract goes, it goes whether or not the parties have made a provision for it ... the contract is at an end, that result follows whether or not the event causing it was contemplated by the parties.

However, this is immediately followed by the following conflicting passage:[417]

It seems to me ... that when one uses the expression 'unforeseen circumstances' in relation to the frustration of a contract one is really dealing with circumstances for which ... the contract makes no provision.

So it seems that Goddard J meant only to suggest that where a contract provides literally for a certain event, but properly construed the terms do not cover it, then frustration can still operate. This interpretation is supported by the judge's quotation from,[418] and comment upon,[419] Viscount Haldane's judgment in *Tamplin Steamship Co v Anglo Mexican Petroleum Products.*[420]

The view that frustration can override the parties' own allocation of risk may also be supported by an *obiter dictum* of Lord Findley LC in *Bank Line v Arthur Capel Ltd.*[421] He said,[422] when analysing the speeches of the House in the *Tamplin* case:

The concurrence of Lord Parker and of Lord Buckmaster LC with Lord Loreburn was to some extent rested on the ground that a clause in the charter party providing for the case of restraint of princes would exclude the doctrine of frustration of the adventure. This proposition should not, in my opinion, be regarded as forming part of the judgment of the House.

However, a close reading of the Lord Chancellor's judgment reveals that he probably only meant to suggest, like Goddard J, that whether the doctrine of frustration can operate when there is a contractual clause dealing with the materialised circumstance is, at base, a question of the proper construction of that clause.[423] If the clause, properly construed, allocates the risk then, prima facie, the courts should respect that allocation; however, if the clause only literally covers the situation but was not intended by the parties so to

---

there was insufficent evidence to find that the risk of a seizure of the type that took place was contemplated by the parties, *ibid.* at p. 135.

[417] *Ibid.*, p. 138.

[418] *Ibid.*, p. 139: 'Although the words of the stipulation may be such that the mere letter would describe what has occurred, the occurrence itself may yet be of a character and extent so sweeping that the foundation of what the parties are deemed to have had in contemplation has disappeared, and the contract itself has vanished with that foundation.'

[419] *Ibid.*, p. 139: 'I regard the learned Lord as saying there that, unless the contrary intention is made *plain*, the law imposes this doctrine of frustration ...' (emphasis added).

[420] [1918] The quotation from Viscount Haldane above was followed in *Countess of Warwick SS Co v Le Nickel SA* [1918] 1 KB 372.

[421] [1919] AC 435, the statement is *obiter* because he found that upon their proper construction neither of the clauses covered the event which occurred, *ibid.*, pp. 442–3.

[422] *Ibid.*, p. 443.

[423] This is reasonably clear from the Lord Chancellor's comments at *ibid.*, pp. 441 and 443.

do, then the court is not compelled to adopt the literal meaning of the clause.[424]

Difficult problems are presented to a court when the express terms of a contract either completely fail to provide for the allocation of a particular risk, or deal with it in an ambiguous or incomprehensible way. As Lord Atkin noted:[425]

> Business men habitually adventure large sums of money on contracts which, for the purpose of defining legal obligations, are a mere jumble of words.

This is no more than a judicial acknowledgement[426] of the limited ability of contractors to provide for all future events the general implications of which we have already considered.

When faced with such a silent or ambiguous contract, the court must not 'turn a blind eye', and leave the loss where it lies, without first considering whether or not there is any evidence beyond the express provisions of the parties which may indicate that they have understood the risk to have been allocated to one of them. To refuse relief to the party whose position has been made worse by the event is as much an allocation of the risk of that event occurring, as a decision that that party should be relieved of those damaging consequences.

It is possible that the court, when faced with a contract whose express terms fail to deal with a contingency which has arisen, may not 'turn a blind eye' and refuse to address the question of who bears the risk but actually address that question and merely assert that the risk has been allocated to the promisor. To do this without adducing any evidence from the surrounding circumstances to show that the risk has been positively allocated is to show scant regard for the 'intention' of the parties which Lord Atkin suggested was paramount.[427] One form such an assertion may take is that if a contract is silent as to a particular risk then the promisor must be assumed to have taken that risk upon himself.[428] Rarely is the assertion made in so bold a form as it is surely recognised to be the vestigial remains

---

[424] An interpretation like that advanced above of the comments of Goddard J and Lord Findley LC may resolve the apparent disagreement between Denning LJ in the Court of Appeal in *British Movietonews* v *London and District Cinemas* (1951) 1 KB 190, 197 and that of Viscount Simon in the House of Lords [1952] AC 166, 181–4. Denning LJ may have only intended to advance the more modest proposition outlined in the text above but was interpreted by Viscount Simon as claiming a more sweeping power to revise the parties' contract.

[425] *Phoenix Insurance Co of Hartford* v *De Monchy* [1929] 141 LTR 439, 445, and to similar effect Lord Wright's extra-judicial statement in *Legal Essays and Addresses* (1939) p. 258: '[I]t is ... the incurable habit of commercial men in their contracts not to anticipate expressly or provide for all that may happen.'

[426] See also Denning LJ in *British Movietonews* v *London and District Cinemas* [1951] 1 KB 190, 202: 'We no longer credit a party with the foresight of a prophet or his lawyer with the draftsmanship of a Chalmers'. Chalmers was responsible for drafting the Sale of Goods Act 1893, which is widely regarded as a model statute for its economic and clear expression.

[427] *Bell* v *Lever Bros* [1932] AC 161, 226 quoted above.

[428] See Cleasby B's dissent in *Jackson* v *Union Marine Insurance* (1874) LR 10 CP 125, 139.

of the doctrine of absolute contracts.[429] However, a modern variant of it merely imports a requirement of foresight (it was foreseen) or foreseeability (it was capable of being foreseen). A risk is assumed to be allocated if it is considered to have been either foreseen or foreseeable when the contract does not, by its express terms, allocate the risk. Although this proposition does not form the *ratio decidendi* of any English case it is supported by *dicta*,[430] a leading textbook,[431] and by some American authorities.[432] It is suggested that these authorities should not be followed. However, first we must be clear how the courts use the term foreseeability.

Foreseeability is a slippery concept! All events are foreseeable if by that we mean capable of being foreseen. However, the probability of some things occurring is high while that of others is low. Foreseeability only becomes a meaningful concept when the range of probability is conjoined with an acknowledgement of the limited ability of contractors to provide for all future events. Contractors' limited computational capacities cannot assimilate and evaluate all possible contingencies that may materialise.[433] Courts seem to use the concept of foreseeability to distinguish those remote contingencies which the limited capacity of the reasonable contractor would not comprehend, from these more probable consequences which the reasonable contractor would consider. Only the latter type of consequence seems to be considered foreseeable on the part of contractors, by the courts.[434]

---

[429] See introduction to Chapter 14.

[430] With the possible exception of *Walton Harvey* v *Walker Homfrays* [1931] 1 Ch 274 (CA). The only House of Lords' *dictum* is *Fareham* v *Davis Contractors* [1956] AC 696, 731 *per* Lord Radcliffe, but see also *Denmark Productions* v *Boscobel Productions Ltd* [1969] 1 QB 699, 725 B *per* Salmon LJ only tersely discussing frustration; and at first instance *Bailey* v *De Crespigny* (1869) LR 4 QB 180, 185 *per* Hannen J and *Re Basische Co Ltd* [1921] 2 Ch 331, 379 *per* Russel J. These *dicta* support the proposition that if a risk should have been foreseen, it may be considered as allocated to the promisor. *A fortiori* if it was actually foreseen it can be considered to be so allocated. Treitel also cites at p. 840 n. 55 House of Lords' *dicta* in *Tamplin Steamship* Co v *Anglo-Mexican Petroleum Co* [1916] 2 AC 397, 426; *Bank Line* v *Arthur Capel and Co* [1919] AC 435, 455, 462; and *Cricklewood Property and Investment Trust* v *Leightons Trust* [1945] AC 221, 228. It is submitted that the *dicta* in these latter three cases only support the more modest proposition that when risk is not merely foreseeable but rather has actually been foreseen and provided for in the contract then the court should respect the parties' allocation of risk.

[431] Treitel, p. 679; see criticisms of authorities cited in the previous footnote. Cheshire, Fifoot and Furmston at p. 591 only discuss events expressly provided for and not those merely foreseen or foreseeable, while *Anson's Law of Contract, op. cit.* pp. 519–20 discusses both those expressly provided for and foreseen events but not foreseeable events.

[432] *Glidden Co* v *Hellenic Lines* (1960) 275 F 2d 253 (risk foreseen) promisor assumed risk of carriage by a longer route because he had actually foreseen the possibility that the Suez Canal might close though no express term provided for it; *Savage* v *Peter Kiewit Sons Co* (1967) 432 P 2d 519 (risk foreseeable) no frustration when open sand blasting prior to painting was prevented because the promisor 'should have anticipated that he might have to take out-of-the ordinary precautions to avoid damages to businesses near the work area'.

[433] Which economists economically refer to as 'bounded rationality'. For its general relevance to the law of contract, see Eisenberg, 'The Limits of Cognition and the Limits of Contract' (1995) 47 Stan L Rev 211.

[434] '[Frustration] was ... evolved by the courts to meet the case in which a contract became impossible of performance through some supervening event, not reasonably foreseeable': Salmon LJ in *Denmark Productions Ltd* v *Boscobel Productions Ltd* [1969] 1 QB 699, 725 B.

The objection to this approach is substantive, not semantic. It is that the approach which treats silence in the face of a foreseeable risk as an allocation of it, ignores the *equivocality* of contractual silence.[435] The fact that a contract fails to make provision for a foreseeable risk (i.e. one which a reasonable man would have foreseen) *may* be evidence from which a court can infer that the risk was allocated to the promisor; but it is not necessarily such evidence. Likewise, that the parties actually foresaw a particular risk may be, but is not necessarily, evidence from which the allocation of that risk can be inferred. The promisor may fail to provide in the agreement for a risk because he thinks that discussion of non-performance at the time of contracting would be injurious to the contractual relation,[436] because the promisor does not consider the risk sufficiently serious to be worth discussing,[437] or because the promisor considers his bargaining position to be weak.[438]

So while there will clearly be cases 'when the contingency in question is sufficiently foreshadowed at the time of contracting to be included among the business risks which are fairly to be regarded as part of the dickered terms'[439] this is not necessarily so in every case. In an admirably clear passage Judge Wright expressed this idea thus:[440]

> Foreseeability ... of a risk does not necessarily prove its allocation ... Moreover, that some abnormal risk was contemplated is probative but does not necessarily establish an allocation of the risk of the contingency ...

An approach to frustration which, without more, assigns foreseen or foreseeable risks to the promisor is clearly inadequate. The question then arises what other evidence may the court draw upon to ascertain whether the risk was allocated? The answer is that the court must thoroughly investigate the circumstances leading up to and surrounding the parties' bargain.

---

[435] *Cf.* the court's approach to silence as evidence of acceptance, examined in ch. 3, where the equivocality of silence is arguably over-emphasised.

[436] See Trakman, 'Interpreting Contracts: A Common Law Dilemma' (1981) 59 Can Bar Rev 241, n. 93 and accompanying text.

[437] *Ibid.*

[438] Whether the courts should try to control the abuse of dominant bargaining positions by setting aside agreements reached by parties when there is an inequality of bargaining power is a much debated question. Here we are dealing with the limited question whether silence in the face of a foreseeable risk must necessarily be evidence of an unequivocal assumption of that risk. Some commentators have further suggested that even where it is clear that the weaker party unequivocally assumed a risk, the courts should be free to grant discharge by frustration. See: Hillman, 'Debunking Some Myths About Unconscionability: A New Framework for UCC Section 2-302' (1981) 67 Cornell Law Review 1, 31–32; Hillman, 'An Analysis of the Cessation of Contractual Relations' (1983) 68 Cornell Law Review 617, 621; Trakman, 'Frustrated Contracts and Legal Fictions' (1983) 46 MLR 39, 53. It does, however, seem to be a cumbersome and indirect way of dealing with the problem of bargaining power to control it by manipulating the frustration doctrine.

[439] UCC, s 2-615, comment 8.

[440] *Transatlantic Financing Corp v US* (1966) 363 F 2d 312, 318. This statement was approved in *Aluminum Co of America v Essex Group* (1980) 499 F Supp 53, 76. Such approval was *obiter* because the latter case involved a risk which the court found to be unforeseeable, *ibid.*, p. 76. *Contra: Savage v Peter Kiewit and Sons* (1967) 432 P 2d 519.

Courts may derive considerable assistance from the parties' course of dealing, including pre-contractual statements and actions. In the case of *Austin Co v United States*,[441] the voluntary preparation by the promisor of specifications for information gathering systems led the court to conclude that the promisor bore the risk of failure to comply with those specifications.

The price term of a contract may be examined by the courts in order to ascertain the parties' desired allocation of risks. Where a service or good is provided at a price which exceeds that which is usual, the court may infer from this that a particular risk is being borne by the promisor. In effect, the promisor is being paid 'an insurance premium' for taking upon himself that risk. Such an analysis supports the result, if not the reasoning, in *Krell v Henry*,[442] where a very high price[443] was paid for the hire of a flat for a day from which to view Edward VII's coronation procession; the court 'relieved' the promisee of his obligation to pay for the flat by holding that the cancellation of the procession had frustrated the contract. The very similar case of *Chandler v Webster*[444] is more equivocal because although a higher rent[445] was to be paid, it was to be paid in advance. The requirement of advance payment may be considered to be slight evidence that the risk of events causing the cancellation of the procession would not affect the owner's right to retain the money. Of course, there may be other more convincing explanations of the requirement for advance payment, most obviously as a way of assuring the owner that the renter was neither a cheat nor a time waster. In any case, the owner was able to retain the money paid and, indeed, to recover the balance owing, because the effect of frustration is not to discharge obligations *ab initio* but only from the time the frustrating event occurred; obligations accruing before that time were still enforceable. Since the obligation to pay hire for the room had arisen before the 'frustrating' event occurred, it continued afterwards.[446] The case of *Tatem v Gamboa*[447] is similar to *Krell v Henry* in that a high price[448] was paid for the hire of a ship and the hire contract was held to be discharged when that ship was seized by nationalists during the Spanish Civil War. Again, perhaps the high cost of hire included an 'insurance premium' being paid to compensate the shipowner for bearing the risk of the boat being seized. If this analysis is correct, then the result which, like that in *Krell v Henry*, relieved the defendant of his obligation to pay[449] is clearly right.

The agreement may provide other clues which will be of assistance to a

---

[441] (1963) 314 F 2d 518 cert den'd (1963) 375 US 830.

[442] [1903] 2 KB 740.

[443] £75.

[444] [1904] 1 KB 493.

[445] £141 15s. Obviously, a proper comparison of the cases would also need to investigate the size of the accommodation offered, the quality of the view, etc.

[446] The case predated the loss sharing provisions of the Law Reform (Frustrated Contracts) Act 1943, considered further in Chapter 14.

[447] [1939] 1 KB 132.

[448] *Ibid.*, p. 140.

[449] All monies in *Krell v Henry* but only further hire in *Tatem v Gamboa*.

court in ascertaining the parties' allocation of risks. If the contract provides for the modification or discharge of a party's obligation in certain specified circumstances, that may be considered to be evidence from which the court can infer that the party assumed certain other risks. This can be illustrated by two American cases. In *Missouri Public Service Co v Peabody Coal Co*[450] a vendor's obligation was not discharged by increased costs when the contract contained an escalator clause which provided for other cost increases. That this is only slight evidence, which *may* be outweighed by stronger, contrary evidence, is apparent from a comparison between this case and *Alcoa Co of America v Essex Group Inc*[451] where, despite the presence of a well researched escalator clause,[452] the contract was still held to be discharged as a result of increased performance costs.

The approach of inferring the possible assumption of a risk from a negative, the failure to provide for that particular risk when other similar risks are provided for, may be adapted to the analysis of 'insurance' already discussed; the fact that a party declines to insure himself against some risk when he could easily do so may be evidence to bolster a conclusion that the party meant to assume that risk. It is important when considering this question not to restrict the search for insurance possibilities to the archetypal insurance arrangement; a contract with a third party insurer who in return for a premium takes upon itself certain risks. To do so would be to ignore the possibility of self-insurance by an increased price clause which has already been discussed. However, self insurance may take other forms, a promisor may diversify his commitments in order to pool different risks in much the same way that an insurance company does. Alternatively, if the promisor has bound himself to supply some good or service, then he may enter into a contract with a third party in order to 'guarantee' to the promisor the supply of that good or service at a reasonable cost.[453]

This principle is illustrated by another American case, *Canadian Industrial Alcohol Co v Dunbar Molasses*,[454] where an intermediary, who contracted to

---

[450] (1979) 583 SW 2d 655 cert den'd (1979) 444 US 865. The same principle could have been applied to the escalator clause used by Westinghouse Electric Corp in its uranium supply contracts, discussed in the text accompanying nn. 455–7 below. It apparently only provided for changes in certain labour and materials cost indices and was not geared to the uranium market itself, see Joscow, 'Commercial Impossibility, the Uranium Market and the Westinghouse Case' (1977) 6 J Leg Stud 119, 144.

[451] (1980) 499 F Supp 53 where at p. 68 it is summarised by the Latin maxim *expressio unius est exclusio alterius*.

[452] Prepared by an eminent economist Alan Greenspan, now President of the US Federal Reserve, *ibid.*, pp. 58 and 69.

[453] That forward contracts are basically contracts of insurance has been recognised judicially in the UK by Lord Sumner in *Larringa v Société Franco-Américaine des Phosphates de Medulla* (1923) 92 LJ KB 455, 464: 'In effect most forward contracts can be regarded as a form of commercial insurance.' Of course, such contracts do not, in fact, guarantee supply unless they are specifically enforceable. But in any case they will, in the event of a failure by the third party to supply, allow the promisor of the first agreement to claim damages from the third party. The measure of damages will prima facie be the difference between the contract price and the market price at the time of breach.

[454] (1932) 179 NE 383.

supply molasses from a particular source, was not relieved of his obligation to supply when the source cut back production, because a sufficient supply could have been ensured by a contract with the source. Another case whose facts would appear to invite the application of this principle is that of *Re Westinghouse Electric*:[455] Westinghouse Electric contracted to build and supply uranium for 49 nuclear power stations, the uranium to be supplied at a fixed price. When, later, the market price of uranium began to rise steeply, Westinghouse refused to honour its contracts. The actions brought by 13 power companies were consolidated.

It seems staggering that when Westinghouse committed itself to fixed price supply contracts it did not 'self-insure' by buying forward suitable quantities of uranium to meet its commitments. It appears that by not doing so Westinghouse was assuming the risk of any increase in the price of uranium. The motive behind this decision may have been an ill-conceived conviction that the price of uranium would fall rather than rise, allowing Westinghouse to make a considerable profit on its supply contracts.[456] Unfortunately for Westinghouse, 'it gambled ... and lost'.[457] The court's conclusion that Westinghouse had no sufficient excuse and was liable in full for expectation damages would seem to be in accord with the analysis proposed here. As a reasoned opinion was not filed, and the litigation subsequently compromised, we will never know on what basis the court reached its conclusion.

Trade usage may also be of considerable assistance to the court. It may be easy for the courts to infer that the parties intended a particular allocation of risk when they use terms which convey particular allocations of risk to businessmen conversant with them (like CIF or FOB contracts). Also, where the contract does not include such terms, the surrounding circumstances may warrant one of two possible inferences: that the parties intended to depart from the usual terms, or that they felt the terms to be so obvious as not to need expression. Which inference, if any, is most appropriate will obviously have to be gleaned from the individual circumstances of each case.

Therefore, it can be seen that the investigation of the allocation of risks contemplated by a contract 'requires a scrupulous examination of the thing expressed, the thing not expressed and the context of the expression'.[458] The requirement that the court examine carefully the context of the agreement is of paramount importance. Courts must reject any approach based upon

---

[455] The case has not been fully reported. The actions were consolidated in *Re Westinghouse Electric Corporation Uranium-Contracts Litigation* (1975) 405 F Supp 316. A very full account of the economic and legal background to the dispute is to be found in Joskow, *op. cit.* (n. 450 above); see also Eagan, 'The Westinghouse Uranium Contracts. Commercial Impracticability and Related Matters' (1980) 18 Am Bus LJ 281.

[456] See Joskow, *ibid.*, pp. 145–6.

[457] *Ibid.*, p. 174.

[458] *Per* Judge Teitelbaum in *Aluminum Co of America v Essex Group Inc* (1980) 499 F Supp 53, 68. However, some commentators have questioned whether Judge Teitelbaum lived up to his own demand for a thorough investigation of the context of the agreement. See generally Joscow, *ibid.* For further criticism, see Dawson, 'Judicial Revision of Frustrated Contracts: The United States' (1984) 64 BULR 1.

vague and inflexible generalisations. To do otherwise would be to ignore the vastly differing motives which cause parties to enter into contracts. Some are entered only in order to purchase protection from a particular risk, while in others many risks are truly uncontemplated and unallocated.

If at the end of its inquiry the court still considers the risk to be unallocated, the contract may be held to be frustrated without threatening the hallowed principle of the sanctity of contract. The approach developed in this chapter has commended the enforcement in such circumstances of any modification agreed by the parties. If the original contract is frustrated then the 'modification' is enforceable as a new contract. There are no consideration problems because the pre-existing duty has disappeared.

Increases in performance costs

Courts have often articulated the view that a mere increase in costs will not operate to frustrate a contract.[459] It seems that for a contract to be held to be frustrated where there has been an increase in performance costs, the increase must be accompanied by *some other factor* which renders performance 'radically different' from that contemplated under the original contract.[460] In *Davis Contractors v Fareham UDC* builders contracted to erect 78 houses for a local authority within eight months at a contract price of £94,000. Due mainly to labour shortages, construction took 22 months and cost the contractors £115,000. The builders' plea of frustration was rejected, the delay and the increase in cost of 22 per cent more than the contract price did not involve a sufficiently 'radical' or 'fundamental' change in the promisor's obligation.

Similarly, in an analogous case *Exportelisa SA v Rocco Giuseppe & Figli Soc Coll*,[461] involving the interpretation of an express excuse clause, the Court of Appeal held that when the cost of supplying wheat rose by over 26 per cent this should not be considered sufficient to render performance 'impossible' and thus allow discharge within the clause. These cases are supported by the results of litigation consequent upon the closing of the Suez Canal in 1956 and 1967. Both sellers of goods,[462] and shipowners[463] who shipped goods

---

459 *British Movietonews v London and District Cinemas* [1952] AC 166, 185 *per* Viscount Simon and *Davis Contractors v Fareham UDC* [1956] AC 696, 729 *per* Lord Radcliffe; *National Carriers v Panalpina Ltd* [1981] AC 675, 707 B. A similar approach seems to be taken in Scotland, see *The Hong Kong and Whampoa Dock Co v The Netherton Shipping Co* 1909 SC 34; *Blacklock and Macarthur v George G Kirk* 1919 SC 57. *Contra*: see *Wilkie v Belhame* (1848) 11 D 132: employer contracted to pay servant in potatoes. Crop failure caused a rise in potato prices. Servant only held to be entitled to monetary equivalent of potatoes promised. In this case not only was the master's obligation under the old contract discharged, but the court created a new one.

460 *Davis Contractors v Fareham UDC* [1956] AC 696, 729.

461 [1978] 1 Lloyd's Rep 433.

462 *Tsakiroglou and Co v Noblee Thorl QtbH* [1962] AC 93 overruling *Carapanayoti and Co Ltd v ET Green Ltd* [1959] 1 QB 131 which had allowed a claim of frustration.

463 *The Eugenia* [1964] 2 QB 226 overruling *The Massalia* [1961] 2 QB 278 which had allowed a claim of frustration; see also *Palmco Shipping Co v Continental Ore Corp* [1970] 2 Lloyd's Rep 21.

round the Cape of Good Hope, were held bound to do so; the extra distance and expense involved did not discharge the contract. It seems that this view that a 'mere' increase in costs cannot operate to frustrate a contract is so firmly entrenched that frustration will not even be called in aid by a party when the cost increases it is facing are 'quite devastating'.[464]

However, there are other lines of authority, dicta, and overseas decisions which suggest a more lenient approach. In *Metropolitan Water Board* v *Dick Kerr and Co Ltd*[465] the facts were: a contractor in 1914 agreed to build a reservoir within six years. There was a provision in the contract for an extension of time in the case of delay for any 'just cause'. In 1916 the government ordered the contractor to stop work. The court held that notwithstanding the express provision the contract was discharged; the proviso could not have been meant to apply to as substantial an interference with performance as occurred.

Treitel suggested[466] that the above case can be distinguished from cases like *Davis Contractors* v *Fareham UDC*, because in the former performance was for a period impossible rather than just impracticable. There is no express support for this view in *Davis Contractors* v *Fareham UDC* where, despite *Metropolitan Water Board* v *Dick Kerr* being cited in argument, it is not considered in any of the judgments. The consideration of analogous cases seems to have been largely centred on the poorly reported and severely criticised case of *Bush* v *Whitehaven Port and Town Trustees*.[467] There is also little support in *Dick Kerr* for the view that performance was and would remain impossible. However, at the time of appeal performance was still illegal. Yet, although the four members of the House discussed the illegality aspect,[468] three of them also explained the case in a broader way, as being based on the principle that conditions had so altered that any performance would be that of a different contract.[469] So the four judgments do not provide support for the view that a qualitative distinction should be drawn between the *Fareham* case and the *Dick Kerr* case, either, as Treitel suggests, based on the impossibility of performance in the latter case or the illegality of performance as the judgments equivocally suggest. The better distinction may be quantitative, the *Dick Kerr* case involving a longer interruption to normal working conditions. If this is so, it appears to lend support to the view that a 'mere' increase in costs can operate to frustrate a contract, even if *unaccompanied* by other factors, if the increase is large enough.

This view finds further support from a dictum of Lord Denning in *Staffordshire Area Health Authority* v *South Staffordshire Waterworks Co*.[470] In 1919 a hospital ceded to a water company its right to draw water from a

---

[464] *Finland Steamship Co* v *The Felixstowe Dock and Railway Co* [1980] 2 Lloyd's Rep 287, 288.
[465] [1918] AC 119.
[466] Treitel, p. 821.
[467] *Hudson's Building Contracts*. 4th edn, vol. 2.
[468] [1918] AC 119, 126 *per* Lord Finlay LC, 128 *per* Lord Dunedin, 135 *per* Lord Atkinson, 139–40 *per* Lord Parmoor.
[469] *Ibid.*, 126–7 *per* Lord Finlay, 128–9 *per* Lord Dunedin, 135–6 *per* Lord Atkinson.
[470] [1978] 3 All ER 769.

well. In return the company agreed to supply the hospital with water at a fixed price 'at all times hereafter'. At the time when the water company claimed to be able to terminate the old agreement at six months' notice the company was supplying water to the hospital at one-twentieth of its normal charge.[471] Lord Denning took the view that inflation had so radically changed the value of money that the contract should be regarded as frustrated.[472]

The other judges in the Court of Appeal provided a different explanation for the result in the case. Properly construed, the agreement was to be considered to be terminable by reasonable notice. With respect, this interpretation does seem a little strained when the agreement was silent on the issue.[473] It involved interpreting (rewriting?) the phrase 'at all times hereafter' as 'at all times hereafter during the subsistence of the agreement',[474] a very different matter.

Lord Denning's *dictum* in the *Staffordshire* case was presaged 27 years earlier in *Brauer & Co v (James) Clark*,[475] where he considers a hypothetical situation posed by the trial judge involving a hundred fold increase in the cost of performance due to the imposition of export regulations requiring the purchase of a licence. Lord Denning, quoting *British Movietonews Ltd v London and District Cinemas*, the House of Lords' decision and not that of his own court,[476] said:

[it] depends on how much was the price they had to pay to get the licence. If it was, to take the judge's illustration, one hundred times as much as the contract price, that would be 'a fundamentally different situation'.

In the United States there are general statements about the effect of an

---

[471] *Ibid.*, p. 773 E.

[472] *Ibid.*, p. 777 E–F. Lord Denning states that the old agreement is to end after a period of reasonable notice has expired. This is unusual as frustration operates automatically and immediately the frustrating event or circumstance occurs, see *Hirji Muliji v Cheong Yue Steamship Co Ltd* [1926] AC 497, 505 *per* Lord Sumner delivering the Privy Council's judgment. The only explanation seems to be that termination by six months' notice was all that the Water Co requested: [1978] 3 All ER 769, 770 H–J.

[473] Treitel at p. 822 approves of the grounds of decision put forward by Goff and Cumming Bruce LJJ. He also disapproves of Lord Denning's approach to the case, partly because he says Lord Denning relies upon passages of his own judgment in *British Movietonews v London and District Cinemas Ltd* which were disapproved in the House of Lords. However, it appears to be reasonably clear that the House of Lords was in that case only disapproving of a particular interpretation of Lord Denning's words when perhaps a less contentious one is available (see n. 424 above).

[474] [1978] 3 All ER 769, 778 C–E and 781 B–C *per* Goff LJ and 783 J–784 A *per* Cumming-Bruce LJ.

[475] [1952] 2 All ER 497; the case seems to be almost forgotten. It is not quoted in *Anson's Law of Contract* (1998) 27th edn, or in Cheshire, Fifoot and Furmston who discuss Lord Denning's statements in the *Staffordshire* case. Treitel does note the case but seems to regard it as confined to the principle discussed by Singleton LJ. This despite Lord Denning's discussion of frustration, evidenced by his reference to the *British Movietonews* case.

[476] *Ibid.*, p. 501 G–H, Singleton LJ concluded that such an increase would mean the sellers were not liable apparently because they can only be regarded as having assumed a duty to take reasonable steps to obtain an export licence and it was not reasonable to pay such an increase, *ibid.*, p. 500 D.

increase in performance costs similar to those quoted above. For instance, in *Neal Cooper Grain Co* v *Texas Gulf Sulphur Co*[477] it was said that:[478]

> the fact that performance has become economically burdensome or unattractive is not sufficient for performance to be excused.

Indeed, the Suez cases in the United States[479] reached conclusions broadly in accord with the English cases. However, there are cases where a mere increase in the cost of performance has operated to frustrate a contract. In *Mineral Park Land Co* v *Howard*[480] the defendants contracted to remove sufficient sand and gravel from the claimant's land to build a bridge. However, the defendants only fulfilled part of their requirements from the claimant's land and acquired the balance elsewhere because the cost of removing the sand and gravel left on the claimant's land was ten to 12 times the price at which its equivalent could be bought elsewhere.

The further performance of the contract was impracticable and, therefore, discharged by frustration. These apparently conflicting cases are reconciled in the Uniform Commercial Code[481] in the following way:

> Increased cost alone does not excuse performance unless the rise in cost is due to some unforeseen contingency which alters the essential nature of the performance. Neither is a rise or a collapse in the market in itself a justification for that is exactly the type of business risk which business contracts made at fixed prices are intended to cover. But a severe shortage of raw materials, or of supplies due to a contingency such as war, embargo, local-crop failure, unforeseen shutdown of major sources of supply or the like, which ... causes a marked increase in cost is within the contemplation of this section.

Although at first glance the comment gives the impression that the increase in performance costs must be accompanied by some other factor (e.g. 'a severe shortage of raw materials, etc') the list of factors given is not complete ('or the like'). The purpose of enumerating some of the possible factors seems to be to reinforce the idea that the rise in performance cost must be of a considerable degree; otherwise it will be considered to be the materialisation of an assigned risk ('for that is exactly the type'). So, despite the generality of the opening sentence, it appears that 'unforeseen' increases in cost will be held to discharge a seller's obligation. This interpretation is supported by the Restatement 2d.[482]

It is submitted that the interpretation of s 2-615, comment 4 proposed above should be followed in England. A contract should be considered discharged by a mere increase in performance costs if that increase is of an extent which was not within the risks assigned by the contract. Statements of the principle should avoid over-generality, lest they be taken to suggest a

---

[477] (1974) 508 F 2d 283.

[478] *Ibid.*, p. 293; see to similar effect *Transatlantic Financing Corp* v *US* (1966) 363 F 2d 312, 319.

[479] *Ibid.* and *American Trading & Prod Corp* v *Shell International Marine* (1972) 453 F 2d 139.

[480] [1916] 156 P 458.

[481] Section 2-615, Comment 4.

[482] Paragraph 265, especially Comment D.

requirement of some extra factor. Courts must, however, properly address the issue of what risks are assigned by the contract, or else for no good reason parties will be relieved of risks which they assumed.[483] It is partly the courts' concern to avoid this undesirable and wasteful risk shifting, which has provoked some of the misleading generalisations about mere increases in costs not discharging contracts. However, just because the risk of some price movements are allocated by contracts does not necessarily mean that all are.

Re Westinghouse Electric, referred to earlier,[484] has the superficial appearance of involving increases in performance costs the very magnitude of which suggests that they may not have been assigned by the contract. Whereas previous American cases, where performance of the contract had been held not to be impracticable had involved more modest cost increases,[485] Westinghouse was faced with large increases in performance costs and enormous losses. Against an average contract price of $10 a pound, by 1975 the market price had risen to some $40 a pound and then rose higher. Projected losses on the contracts if performed were around $2 billion.[486] Despite the first impression that the risk of losses of such a magnitude cannot have been implicitly assumed by Westinghouse, strong evidence exists to the effect that they were. Perhaps the most cogent of this evidence was their refusal to buy forward uranium at similar prices to those in their supply contracts. The motive for their disastrous policy must have been a naive hope that uranium prices would fall!

The *Westinghouse* litigation[487] was eventually compromised. The enforcement of such compromises is supported by powerful public policy arguments based on the desire to minimise litigation. However, an interesting problem may have arisen if the parties had instead simply modified their original agreement to increase the contract price. The analysis I have developed would have suggested that since the modification was an attempt to reallocate a risk assigned by the original contract, such a modification should not generally be enforced, nor is it clear that such a modification would 'qualify' for enforcement on the grounds that otherwise Westinghouse would prefer breach to performance, since it appeared that Westinghouse would have to pay full expectancy damages. However, if it can be said that the promisor is truly indifferent between breach and performance, then the modification should be enforced in order to induce the promisor to tender

---

483 Good reasons would be the receipt of valuable consideration or the fact that if the risk is not shifted the promisor would still prefer breach to performance (see earlier in this chapter).
484 See note 455 above.
485 See e.g. *International Paper Co* v *Rockefeller Corp* (1914) 146 NYS 371 (cost of delivering timber would have been $20 unit compared with contract price of $5.50 unit); *Maple Farms* v *City Schools District* (1974) 352 NYS 2d 784 (a 23% rise in the price of milk caused the cost of delivered milk to exceed the contract price by 10.4%); *Eastern Air Lines* v *Gulf Oil* (1975) 415 F Supp 429 (agreement to supply jet fuel followed by a doubling in the domestic price of such); *Publicator Industries* v *Union Carbide* (1975) 17 UCC Rep 989 (agreement to supply ethanol, one ingredient of which doubled in price to produce a loss of $5.8m).
486 See Joscow (1977) 6 J Leg Stud 119.
487 See also the very similar case of *Iowa Electric Light and Power Co* v *Atlas Corp* (1978) 467 F Supp 129 where the claimant was awarded specific performance.

performance when the original promisee prefers actual performance to his remedy for breach. Such a preference in the *Westinghouse* case may perhaps be inferred from the apparently lenient settlements that were reached.[488] It should hardly be surprising that the companies with whom Westinghouse contracted to supply uranium should want to ensure its continued trading; the supply contracts were only adjuncts to contracts to build nuclear power stations, so obviously the companies had an interest in Westinghouse's continued availability to service and repair those stations.[489]

A problem analogous to that of an increased cost of performance confronted an English court in *Anderson* v *Equitable Life Assurance Society*.[490] In this case, as in *Staffordshire Area Health Authority* v *Staffordshire Waterworks Co*,[491] inflation had had a dramatic effect upon the parties' obligations. However, instead of making performance more burdensome, the effect was to make it valueless. The contract was a life assurance policy with benefits payable in German marks. When the policy came to be paid, due to German hyperinflation it was worth less than an old English penny, despite the sterling value of the premiums paid amounting to some £2,377. This very harsh rule,[492] which allocates the risk of inflation to the promisee whether the contract did so or not, is at variance with the approach of the courts in Germany.[493] It is not clear that in the instant case, even if the particular insurance contract had been held to be frustrated, the result would have been any different.[494] However, if the general rule that inflation cannot frustrate a contract is applied to all cases where, in real terms, inflation reduces the value of the benefit a party receives under a contract, this is inconsistent with the approach developed because it treats a risk which may or may not be assigned by the contract as if it were always so assigned.

Imposed modifications

Judges frequently state what they take to be a pre-eminently obvious proposition that courts have no power to alter contracts made by the

---

[488] [1981] New York Times, 15 March.

[489] See generally the Joscow study, *op. cit.* (n. 450 herein above).

[490] [1926] 42 TLR 302.

[491] [1978] 3 All ER 769.

[492] See also *British Movietonews* v *London and District Cinemas Ltd* [1952] AC 166, 185 *per* Viscount Simon who says that 'a sudden depreciation of currency … does not … affect the bargain'. *Contra*: *National Carriers* v *Panalpina Northern Ltd* [1981] AC 675, 712 D–E where Lord Roskill refers to 'inflation', *inter alia*, as a circumstance 'in which the doctrine has been invoked, sometimes with success sometimes without'.

[493] As to which, see Dawson, 'Judicial Revision of Frustrated Contracts. Germany' (1983) 63 BULR 1039. For the approach of other countries, see the interesting appendix to *Alcoa Co of America* v *Essex Group Inc* (1980) 499 F Supp 53, 93–4.

[494] Insurance contracts are not within the Law Reform (Frustrated Contracts) Act 1943 according to s 2(5)b, therefore, the policy holder or his estate could not recover the premium under s 1(2).

parties.[495] When they think that the contrary has been suggested by one of their number the vehemence of their censure is perhaps a measure of what they consider to be the obviousness of the proposition.[496]

However, this attitude is inconsistent with those expressions of the juristic principle underpinning the doctrine of frustration which appear, to some degree, to reserve to the court a power to 'rewrite' the parties' bargain. This is especially true of the 'just and reasonable solution' theory, but also appears to be true, to a lesser extent, of the objective implied term explanation, and perhaps, of the frustration of the adventure approach. These approaches are described in Chapter 14.

The most startling and clear example of a court-imposed contractual modification occurred in the United States. While both the Restatement (2d) of Contracts,[497] and the Uniform Commercial Code,[498] equivocally hint at some limited power of adjustment, the case of *Alcoa Co of America* v *Essex Group Inc*[499] is surely unprecedented in the common law.[500] Alcoa contracted with Essex to melt alumina provided by Essex and to redeliver it as aluminium. A price was set subject to a complex escalation clause.

The contract initially was for 16 years. During the first nine years it operated well and Alcoa made $25m profit.[501] In the next two years they lost about $12m.[502] Alcoa estimated, and the judge apparently accepted, that they would lose about $60m during the remainder of the contract.[503] This was disputed by Essex though the judge does not appear to have examined properly the basis of this projection.[504] The court held that Alcoa was

---

[495] See *FA Tamplin Steamship Co* v *Anglo-Mexican Petroleum Co Ltd* [1916] 2 AC 397, 403 *per* Earl Loreburn: 'a court can and ought to examine the contract and the circumstances in which it was made, *not of course to vary*, but only to explain it …' (emphasis mine), quoted by Lord Radcliffe in *Davis Contractors* v *Fareham UDC* [1956] AC 696, 727. See also *Joseph Constantine Ltd* v *Imperial Smelting* [1942] AC 154, 185 *per* Lord Wright: 'It is thus seen that the court is not claiming to exercise a dispensing power or to modify or alter contracts …'.

[496] See the House of Lords' comments upon Denning LJ's judgment in the Court of Appeal in *British Movietonews* v *London and District Cinemas* (reported at [1951] 1 KB 190, 197 *et seq.*). Denning LJ was strongly censured by Lord Simmonds [1952] AC 166, 188 and especially by Viscount Simon, pp. 181–4, 185. The criticism was concurred in by Lord Tucker, p. 188; see n. 424 above for a different interpretation of Denning LJ's words.

[497] The Restatement (2d) 1981 para 272(2) provides: 'In any cases governed by the rules stated in this chapter, if those rules together with the rules stated in [the chapter on remedies] will not avoid injustice, the court may grant relief on such terms as justice requires including protection of the parties' reliance interests.'

[498] The official comment on UCC, s 1-615 states (comment 6): 'In situations in which neither sense nor justice is served by either answer when the issue is posed in flat terms of excuse "or no excuse" adjustment under the various provisions of this Article is necessary …'.

[499] [1980] 497 F Supp 53.

[500] Though it seems a frequent occurrence in German law, Dawson, *op. cit.* (n. 493 herein above) and Zweigort and Kötz (1992) *An Introduction to Comparative Law*. 2nd edn, Weir (trans.) at pp. 361–2; and elsewhere see appendix to *Alcoa* decision at pp. 93–4. Perhaps the closest common law equivalent is *National Presto* v *United States* (1964) 338 F 2d 99, cert den'd (1965) 380 US 962.

[501] (1980) 499 F Supp 53 – computed by adding the non-cumulative profit figures in the chart on p. 59.

[502] *Ibid.*

[503] *Ibid.*, p. 66.

[504] See Dawson, 'Judicial Revision of Frustrated Contracts. The United States' [1984] 64 BULR 1, 26–7. Dawson apparently was consulted prior to the litigation, *ibid.*, n. 7.

entitled to relief, *inter alia*, under the doctrine of impracticability.[505] The relief took the form of reformulating the parties' contract;[506] the court rejected as a 'hoary maxim' the idea 'that the courts will not make a contract for the parties'.[507] It is submitted that such an example should not be followed. It is wrong for the courts to assume that they can remould the parties' contract any better than the parties can themselves. This much was even conceded by the judge:[508]

> Judges are seldom able businessmen the court willingly concedes that the management of Alcoa and Essex are better able to conduct their business than is the Court.

The basic objection must surely be that the whole system of contract invests contractors with the ability to realise mutual gains from trade. There is simply no reason to assume that the court is better able to do this than the parties. Indeed there is often good reason to suspect the contrary. Perhaps the most cogent evidence of this is that, following the court's reconstruction of the parties' bargain, the judge's decree was appealed, and after argument was heard in the Court of Appeals for the Third Circuit, a settlement was reached. Alcoa's action was, therefore, voluntarily dismissed and Alcoa gave up any rights it acquired under the court's decree.[509] These are hardly the actions of parties satisfied with the court's modification of their contract.

MITIGATION

In the preceding pages the question of when will the law enforce a contractual modification has been examined. However, there is another way in which the law may encourage reasonable contractual adjustments. This is through the principle of mitigation of loss. That principle imposes upon a claimant a duty to take all reasonable steps necessary to mitigate any loss consequent upon the breach of a contract, and prevents recovery in respect of any loss which is due to his failure to take such steps.[510] The rule[511] is of interest here only insofar as the duty referred to may apply to the offer of a party to a contract to modify that contract. In so far as the offeree is under a 'duty'[512] to accept that modification, the law may be said to be encouraging parties to modify these contracts.

---

[505] (1980) 499 F Supp 53, 76. In the USA contract is frustrated when its underlying purpose can no longer be actioned. Frustration is supplemented by two similar doctrines of discharge; impossibility where further performance is physically impossible and impracticability where continued performance would be impracticable.

[506] *Ibid.*, p. 78, *et seq.*

[507] *Ibid.*, p. 91.

[508] *Ibid.*, p. 91.

[509] Apparent from Dawson's private communication with Essex's counsel (1984) 64 BULR 1, n. 71.

[510] *British Westinghouse Electric and Manufacturing Co Ltd v Underground Electric Railway Co of London Ltd* [1912] AC 673, 689.

[511] There are also two subsidiary rules. See (1980) *McGregor on Damages.* 14th edn, para 209.

[512] Breach of a duty usually implies that the victim of that breach has some affirmative action he can take to gain redress, as in the breach of a tortious duty of care. In this context breach of the 'duty' to mitigate simply operates to limit the claimant's recovery. However, the duty terminology is widely used and so will be followed here.

The duty to mitigate will arise only after a breach has occurred and the innocent party has elected to treat it as such.[513] If the breach was sufficiently serious to justify termination by the innocent party and that party elected to so terminate, thereafter any proposal to perform upon slightly altered conditions would technically be considered to be the offer of a new contract. This is because the outstanding primary obligations under the old one are discharged by the promisee's acceptance of the promisor's repudiation.[514] However, where the proposal of a new contract is just a copy of the old, with a single or small number of terms altered, the proposal is perhaps better described as a modification. Again, this is probably how the contractors would describe it.

In *Payzu v Saunders*[515] cloth was sold, to be delivered in monthly instalments. When the claimant failed to pay punctually for the first instalment the defendant refused to make further deliveries other than on terms of cash on delivery. The defendant refused the new terms. It was held that, although the defendant was liable to pay damages, these should be limited to the value of the month's credit, as the claimant was under a duty to mitigate his loss and accept the defendant's offer. However, the Court of Appeal emphasised that the claimant must only take such steps as are reasonable to mitigate his loss;[516] he is not bound to accept every offer made by his contractual partner. This reasoning was endorsed in the Court of Appeal in *The Solholt* case.[517] Indeed, in *The Solholt* the court went one step further, since it said that the claimant will not only be unable to claim damages for a loss that could have been avoided by accepting a reasonable offer from the party in breach, but also that the claimant will not be allowed to recover for loss that could have been avoided by a timely offer from the claimant himself, where it would be reasonable to expect him to make one.[518] In *The Solholt* it was held that the buyers who wished to claim damages were under a duty to offer the contract price for the ship after they had justifiably repudiated the contract on the grounds of late delivery.

It is difficult to ascertain the limits of the application of this principle. There appears to be a paucity of case law[519] and contrary trends are found in the cases that have come before the courts. Some judicial statements appear to display disapproval of any defendant who, when in breach of contract,

---

[513] *Harries v Edmonds* (1845) 1 Car & K 686, 687; *Shindle v Northern Raincoat Co Ltd* [1960] 1 WLR 1038, 1048.

[514] *Photo Production Ltd* v *Securicor Transport Ltd* [1980] AC 827, 849 D–G *per* Lord Diplock.

[515] [1919] 2 KB 581.

[516] *Ibid.* at p. 588 *per* Bankes LJ and p. 589 *per* Scrutton LJ. See also at first instance p. 586 *per* McCardie J.

[517] [1983] 1 Lloyd's Rep 605.

[518] *Ibid.*, pp. 609–10.

[519] The account of mitigation in *Halsbury's Laws of England.* 4th edn, vol. 12 covers less than five pages. This paucity of case law may be due to two factors: the late development of the doctrine in its modern form, see Schmitthoff, 'The Duty to Mitigate' [1961] JBL 361, and the fact that what it is reasonable to expect a party to do in mitigation of his loss is treated as a question of fact; thus the findings of trial judges are rarely interfered with on appeal, see e.g. *Payzu v Saunders* [1919] 2 KB 581, 589.

attempts to argue that the damages he is liable for should be reduced as the result of a new offer made by him.[520] In contrast, other judges appear to address the issue more dispassionately, absent any punitive overtones and demand the same detachment from transactors.[521] Despite this uncertainty, some generalisations may be proffered as to the limits of the duty to mitigate in this situation. It would appear that it cannot apply if it would effectively require the claimant to give up completely the remedy of damages to which he is entitled.[522] Further, the courts seem to single out employment contracts for special treatment. They are less ready to view acceptance of any subsequent offer as reasonable and, therefore, 'required' by the duty to mitigate than they are with other types of contract.[523] This may be an acknowledgement of, and concession to, the weak bargaining position of an employee *vis-à-vis* his employer.

The concern on the part of the courts with harsh terms which might require a potential claimant to give up his right to litigate and with the unequal bargaining position of the parties may be evidence of any attempt by the courts to distinguish extortionary modifications from non-extortionary ones. This would enable the courts only to encourage the latter category of modification by the imposition of a duty to mitigate.

CONCLUSION

It is apparent from this analysis of the judicial approach to contractual modifications that the results of the decided cases are consistent with certain policy objectives. Indeed, these policy objectives have occasionally been made explicit. This is perhaps most evident in the early consideration cases and the recent cases developing of economic duress. These 'policy' factors are a desire to enforce freely negotiated contractual modifications but to deny legal sanction to extorted modifications. However, analysis of judicial policy in this area is difficult for a number of reasons.

First, the legal response to a contractual modification may involve an analysis of several disparate doctrines; there is no single doctrine of modification. It is obviously difficult to discern a common policy when similar problems are addressed with different language through different doctrines. Moreover, the problem extends beyond difficulties of exposition as it hampers sensible legal development. The courts, when developing new doctrines, may fail to draw upon the valuable experience of addressing similar questions in the past, when that experience is disguised under other rubrics. It is possible that the development of economic duress in English law was retarded by the courts' failure to recognise and consider its past experience of addressing similar questions under different doctrines.

---

[520] *Harlow & Jones Ltd* v *Panex (International) Ltd* [1967] 2 Lloyd's Rep. 509, 530 *per* Roskill J; *Coppola* v *The Maiden Orth & Hastings Co* (1917) 18 NE 499.
[521] See *Payzu* v *Saunders* [1919] 2 KB 581, 586 *per* McCardie J at first instance.
[522] *Strutt* v *Whitnell* [1975] 1 WLR 870.
[523] *Clayton Greene* v *De Courville* (1920) 36 TLR 790; *Basnett* v *Jackson* [1976] ICR 63.

Secondly, analysis is hindered by doctrines whose primary orientation is not modification; frustration and mitigation are good examples. Here there are other policy objectives which might outweigh the modification issues but the tension between these competing objectives is rarely addressed. This means there is a risk that even the subsidiary role which these doctrines play in modification problems may be overlooked. This danger is often reflected in the language of the doctrine. Frustration is inevitably expressed in terms of termination though it may play an important role in determining the enforceability of a contractual modification. In contrast, in other jurisdictions frustration may have been relied upon too heavily as a panacea for modification problems.[524]

Thirdly, the policy objectives being pursued by the courts often lay hidden beneath the black letter law. An analysis of the early history of the pre-existing duty rule reveals a transition from openly articulated policy goals to a rule stated in general terms. The promulgation of a general rule of wide application may be said to increase contractual certainty; parties can more easily comprehend such a rule and be more confident in planning their dealings as a result. However, such a rule must be dispositive of all the factual situations which come within its ambit. The pre-existing duty doctrine had the appearance of such a rule but this appearance was illusory. Its mechanistic application was frequently resisted by the courts who embraced theories like rescission to justify its evasion. A simpler route now exists; a finding of factual consideration. Even if the result reached by the courts is defensible, the tendency to disguise the vital enquiry into the existence of extortion can only create waste and uncertainty. Three particular consequences may be emphasised.[525] The predictive value of the law to lawyers and contractors[526] is reduced when cases with similar facts are dealt with under different heads perhaps absent of any recognition of the overlapping nature of the rules. The failure to address the policy questions directly results in the law failing to generate sensible debate. The law is deprived of the direct stimulus to academics, practising lawyers and judges which might inform future developments. However, perhaps the most serious consequence is that a subsequent judge may be ignorant of the policy considerations operating in an area and as a result may apply the general rule mechanistically, resulting in the non-enforcement of a non-extorted modification. Corbin was perhaps the first to recognise these dangers:[527]

> ... a better brand of justice may be delivered by a court that is clearly conscious of its own processes than by one that states hard-bitten traditional rules and doctrines and then attains an instinctively felt justice by an avoidance of them that is only

---

[524] See particularly the discussion of the *Alcoa* case above.

[525] See generally Reiter, 'Courts Consideration and Common Sense' (1977) U Tor LJ 439.

[526] The predictive role of the law must not just be limited to legal personnel since most disputes are settled out of court. The parties are most likely to arrive at a settlement and expend less resources in doing so if their legal entitlements are free from doubt. See Harris and Veljanovski, 'Remedies Under Contract Law; Designing Rules to Facilitate Out of Court Settlements' (1983) 5 Law and Pol Q 97.

[527] (1950) *Corbin on Contracts*, Vol. 3, para 561.

half conscious, accompanied by an extended exegesis worthy of a medieval theologian.

The law relating to contractual modifications can best be understood in terms of a tension between the objectives of encouraging contractual flexibility by enforcing freely negotiated modifications and of discouraging extortive behaviour by denying legal force to coerced modifications. These policy factors must be addressed directly and coherently. There is some evidence that this is being done via the doctrine of economic duress. However, it is clear that a properly orchestrated legal response to issues of modification must await a recognition of the issue of modification as a separate one, raising issues distinct from those of contractual formation and termination.

13

PERFORMANCE

When parties enter a bilateral contract each assumes an obligation towards the other. In this chapter we will consider a number of issues relating to the performance of those obligations, including the circumstances when one party is considered to be justified in withholding his performance, the remedies available to a party who tenders incomplete performance and the situation where a party commits an illegal act in the course of discharging his contractual duties.

WITHHOLDING PERFORMANCE

Withholding performance refers to the situation where one party refuses to perform until some condition is satisfied, usually the tender of the agreed counter-performance. In two important respects withholding performance should, therefore, be distinguished from termination for breach. First, withholding performance is conditional and so a temporary refusal to perform; termination for breach is unconditional and so a permanent refusal to perform. Second, withholding performance is a so-called 'self-help' remedy because it may be exercised without the assistance of the court. Because the court is not involved, it is a cheap and quick remedy. Termination for breach is in part a self-help remedy. The party terminating can, unaided by the court, refuse to perform further. However, if he also wants to claim damages, the court would become involved.

Whether one party is entitled to withhold his contractual performance depends upon the nature of the obligations he assumed. For present purposes these may be of three kinds: conditions precedent, concurrent obligations and independent promises. If you observe two children in a playground swapping toys, an impasse is sometimes reached where each holds his own toy with one hand and the object of his trade with the other. Often the transaction founders there with each refusing to give up his toy until the other leaves go of his. Such children are precocious lawyers. Each is insisting that the full performance of the other's agreed obligations is a condition precedent to the performance of his own.

In *Cutter* v *Powell*[1] a sailor agreed to work a voyage from Jamaica to

---

[1] (1795) 6 Term Rep 320.

Liverpool for which he was to be paid 30 guineas after landing 'provided he … does his duty as second mate'. The sailor died before the ship reached Liverpool and his widow unsuccessfully sued[2] to recover a proportionate part of the sum promised for his work. The contract entered by the deceased looks like a unilateral one in which the sum of money was promised in exchange for an act, i.e. working the ship home. In a unilateral contract the promisee cannot enforce the promise until he has completed the act stipulated. However, it is reasonably clear that this was a bilateral, rather than a unilateral, contract. It is of the essence of a unilateral contract that the promisee does not assume any obligation. Here the deceased agreed to do his '*duty*' as second mate. This is the language of obligation and so the contract must be a bilateral one. The action failed because the full performance of the voyage was a condition precedent to the right to be paid. In other words, the contract allocated to the sailor the risk of events preventing him from completing his performance. There was some evidence to support this apparently harsh conclusion. The fee agreed was a very high one; the prevailing rate of pay for a second mate on such a voyage was £8. It is a reasonable inference that the extra money was being offered as compensation for assuming the risks described.[3]

Cutter v *Powell* is often described as illustrating the so-called entire contracts rule. Professor Treitel correctly points out that it is more accurate to speak of entire obligations rather than entire contracts;[4] one obligation will not arise until a counter obligation has been entirely performed. Another illustration of the entire obligations rule is the case of *Sumpter* v *Hedges*.[5] A builder failed to recover anything for the work he did in building two houses when because of financial difficulties he abandoned the job only two-thirds complete. The builder undertook an obligation to build two houses, which was quantitatively entire. The completion of the two houses was a condition precedent to his right to be paid.

The second possibility is that the parties have undertaken concurrent liabilities. Where this is so each party is obliged to perform simultaneously. In practice this means that each party is entitled to the performance of the other if he himself is ready and willing to perform. In a contract for the sale of goods, delivery and payment are concurrent conditions,[6] i.e. the seller is only entitled to payment if he is prepared to deliver and the buyer is only entitled to delivery if he is prepared to pay.

The third category of independent promises can be illustrated with an example relevant to many students. A landlord's covenant to repair and a

---

[2] Causes of action subsisting in someone at the time of his/her death survive for the benefit of that person's estate. The deceased died intestate, i.e. without leaving a will and so his estate was represented by his administratrix, his widow.
[3] Lord Kenyon CJ described it as 'a kind of insurance'.
[4] At pp. 730–1.
[5] [1898] 1 QB 673.
[6] Sale of Goods Act 1979, s 28.

tenant's covenant to pay rent are independent promises.[7] A tenant is not entitled to withhold rent if the landlord refuses to repair the premises; a landlord is not entitled to refuse to effect repairs if the tenant declines to pay rent. However, in a contract between a commercial seller of goods or provider of services and a consumer, any clause which makes the consumer's obligation to pay an independent promise is regarded as presumptively unfair.[8]

INCOMPLETE PERFORMANCE

In a number of situations a party who has failed to tender his full contractual performance is none the less entitled to some payment. First, the promisor may be able to rely on the Apportionment Act 1870, s 2, which provides that 'All rents, annuities, dividends and other periodical payments in the nature of income ... shall ... be considered as accruing from day to day and shall be apportionable in respect of time accordingly'. Section 5 defines annuities to include 'salaries and pensions'. If this Act was in force in 1795, Cutter's action for a due proportion of the promised fee might have succeeded unless the contract 'expressly stated that no apportionment shall take place'.[9]

Second, the promisor may be able to recover on the basis of a new contract if one can be implied from the promisee's conduct. In *Sumpter* v *Hedges* the defendant completed the houses himself using some materials left behind by the builder. The defendant had to pay for these materials because he voluntarily accepted them.

Third, the promisor may be able to recover stage payments if the contract is severable. It may be severable if the contract expressly provides for stage payments or because that is the custom of the trade. Contracts for the construction of ships generally include stage payments to be made at key times, e.g. the laying of the keel. In *Cutter* the undertaking to sail to Liverpool might have been regarded as severable if the consideration was expressed to be 15 guineas from Jamaica to the Azores and the same from the Azores to Liverpool. On these facts if the claimant had died after leaving the Azores, his widow could have claimed payment for the first half of the voyage.

Fourth, if the reason for non-completion is the wrongful act of the promisee, the promisor may bring an action for a *quantum meruit* (so much as he deserved) at the contract rate. If in *Cutter* the captain had forcibly alighted his second mate at the Azores, he could have brought a *quantum meruit* action. Such an action was successfully brought by an author against a publisher who stopped publishing the periodical in which the author's book was to be serialised.[10]

---

[7] *Tito* v *Waddell* (*No. 2*) [1977] Ch 106 at 290 and *Yorbrook Investments Ltd* v *Aylesford* (1986) P & CR 51.

[8] Unfair Terms in Consumer Contracts Regulations 1999, No. 2083, reg 5(5) and Sch 2(o).

[9] Section 7.

[10] *Planché* v *Colburn* (1831) 8 Bing 14.

Fifth, the courts will disregard any trivial shortfall in performance under the *de minimis* principle. This is a pervasive principle which states that the law will not concern itself with little things (*de minimis non curat lex*).[11] The principle was applied in one case where there was an excess delivery of 55 lbs of wheat pursuant to a contract to deliver 4,950 tons.[12] A statutory application of the general principle prevents a non-consumer buyer of goods from rejecting the whole quantity delivered on the basis of an excess or shortfall, which is 'so slight that it would be unreasonable ... to do so'.[13]

The final and most significant exception is the doctrine of substantial performance. In *Hoenig v Isaacs*[14] the defendant employed the claimant to refurbish his flat for £750. The defendant claimed that the workmanship was sub-standard and that he was not liable to pay the contract price until the claimant had entirely fulfilled his contractual obligations; at most he was liable to pay a reasonable sum for the work done. The Court of Appeal rejected this argument and held that the claimant was entitled to payment at the full contract rate subject to a small deduction of £55 for the cost of making good the defects. This may be contrasted with *Bolton v Mahadeva*[15] where a similar action was denied. The contractor had agreed to install a central heating system for £560 but had done so incompetently with the result that it emitted fumes and would cost £174 to make good. The Court of Appeal rejected the county court judge's finding that there had been substantial performance.

The doctrine of substantial performance tries to strike a balance between the interests of the parties in a way, which reduces the 'hold' each has over the other. The promisee may not refuse to pay until every last detail is sorted and the promisor is not allowed to claim the price subject to a set off for the defective element of the work unless he has substantially completed the job. Professor Treitel denies the need for any such doctrine. If it is remembered that obligations rather than contracts are entire the cases can be explained without reference to substantial performance. In *Hoenig* he says that the builder's obligations were quantitatively but not qualitatively entire. The builder had finished all the work but not to the required standard. Therefore, the deficiency was not in relation to an entire obligation and so the claimant was entitled to recover the price subject to the counter-claim without recourse to the doubtful doctrine of substantial performance. Professor Treitel's suggestion that building contracts should be regarded as entire in

---

[11] The following limerick might help to commit this principle to memory:
> There was a law student name of Rex,
> Who had incredibly small organs of sex,
> When charged with exposure,
> He replied with composure,
> *De minimis non curat lex.*

[12] *Shipton Anderson & Co v Weil Bros* [1912] 1 KB 574.
[13] Sale of Goods Act 1979, s 30(2A).
[14] [1952] 1 TLR 1360.
[15] [1972] 1 WLR 1009.

relation to the obligation to complete all work has been contradicted by at least one recent case.[16]

The law on this topic is undoubtedly fragmented. The Law Commission had proposed to clarify it by introducing a new restitutionary remedy for the promisor to recover a sum representing the value to the recipient of what the promisor has done.[17] Unusually, a dissenting note accompanied the report by one of the Law Commissioners. He made a persuasive case for the retention of the entire obligations rule on the basis that it gives valuable security to householders in their dealings with small builders.

ILLEGALITY IN PERFORMANCE

In Chapter 6 we examined a number of different circumstances where the law regards the formation of a contract as illegal. Now we will examine the situation where it is the performance, rather than the formation, of the contract, which is illegal. This distinction is drawn in a number of cases[18] and is justified by the different effects of contracts illegal as formed and those illegal as performed. It is a major theme of this book that different episodes (such as birth and death)[19] in the life of a contract require separate treatment because considerations relevant to one are not necessarily important in another. This may help to explain why the law distinguishes so clearly between the legal effects of contracts illegal as formed and those illegal as performed.[20]

Another reason for the occasional criticism of the distinction is that it is sometimes difficult to make. As with many legal distinctions, clear cases are easy to identify but intermediate ones less so. In order to illustrate this difficulty, we will consider statutory illegality.[21] Consider the following examples.

---

16 *Williams v Roffey Bros & Nicholls* (Contractors) Ltd [1991] 1 QB 1 (sub-contractor recovered instalments subject to a deduction for defective and *incomplete* items.

17 Law Commission (1983) *Pecuniary Restitution on Breach of Contract*, No. 121. See Burrows (1984) 46 MLR 76.

18 *Re Mahmoud and Ispahani* [1921] 2 KB 716, 725 *per* Bankes LJ and 729 *per* Scrutton LJ; *Anderson v Daniel* [1924] 1 KB 138 at 149 *per* Pearce LJ.

19 See discussion in Chapter 1.

20 The distinction is criticised by some commentators, for example, Furmston (ed.) (1999) *The Law of Contract*, para 5.30.

21 Illegality in performance is discussed here in relation to statutory illegality. Of course, it can apply to the common law heads of illegality as well, e.g. a man accused of a crime pays someone to bribe a witness (contract illegal as formed because it is a contract to commit a crime or a contract prejudiced to the administration of justice). However, if the accused employs a lawyer to act for him and the lawyer of his own initiative bribes a witness, the contract between the lawyer and his client is illegal as performed.

> The (hypothetical) Lorries Act 2000, s 1 states: It is forbidden to contract for the carriage of goods in unlicensed lorries.[22]
>
> Example 1: A contracts to carry B's goods in his lorries, all of which are unlicensed.

The contract made is expressly prohibited. It is also illegal as formed.

> The (hypothetical) Transport Act 2000, s 1 states: It is an offence to carry goods for profit in unlicensed lorries.
>
> Example 2: C, who runs a lorry haulage business, contracts with D to carry his goods. C's lorries are not licensed.

There are two possibilities. First, the contract made is not expressly prohibited. Is it impliedly prohibited? The section must be interpreted in a way which gives effect to Parliament's intention. If that intention was to promote public safety by licensing vehicles only after a safety inspection, the contract is impliedly prohibited. It is illegal as formed. Second, if Parliament had some other purpose, such as that it intended to raise revenue by selling licences, the contract is not impliedly prohibited; it is not illegal as formed.

> Example 3: As 2(a) above, except that C has some lorries which are licensed and some which are not. C uses an unlicensed lorry to perform the contract.

Here it is the choice of C to use an unlicensed lorry, which offends the implied prohibition of the statute. The contract is illegal as performed.

A flow chart can summarise the questions to be asked (see Fig. 13.1).

Archbolds v *Spanglett*[23] is an example of a contract, which is illegal as performed. The defendants contracted to transport whisky from Leeds to London. The vehicle used by the defendants was properly licensed. The defendants were aware of this but the claimant goods' owners were not. When the goods were stolen en route as a result of the driver's negligence, the claimants' action succeeded notwithstanding the illegal performance. The claimants were ignorant of the illegality and so were allowed to enforce the contract.

A similar result was achieved in *Marles* v *Philip Trent & Son Ltd*[24] where a farmer purchased wheat from the defendant seed merchants. The defendants, who also failed to deliver an invoice as required by statute, misdescribed the goods. The claimant recovered damages despite the fact that the contract was performed in an illegal way. In short, it seems that the usual prohibition upon the enforcement of an illegal contract will not apply when the contract is illegal as performed and the innocent party brings the action.

---

[22] *Cf. St John Shipping Co* v *Spanglett Joseph Bank Ltd* [1957] 1 QB 267 (overloading of ship did not prevent carrier from suing for freight (price of carrying goods).
[23] [1961] 1 All ER 47.
[24] [1954] 1 QB 29.

Fig. 13.1 Is the contract illegal?

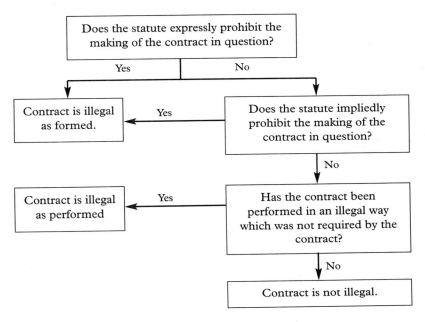

PART IV

THE DEATH OF THE CONTRACT

14

FRUSTRATION[1]

INTRODUCTION

In the past most contractual obligations were considered to be absolute. In *Paradine* v *Jane*[2] a tenant was not excused from paying rent for land overseas 'merely' because enemy forces had forcibly ejected him from it! Gradually the law recognised the injustice of this strict approach and developed a doctrine of frustration which, exceptionally, operates to relieve the non-performing party from the usual consequences of a failure to perform. Frustration[3] of a contract is said to occur when events subsequent to the formation of the contract render its performance impossible or illegal in certain analogous circumstances. The timing of the event should be emphasised. The doctrine of frustration only applies to events which take place after contracting. Where parties enter a contract on the basis of a mistaken assumption that its performance is possible, legal or in other analogous circumstances the legal effect of their misapprehension is determined by the doctrine of common mistake. When we are called upon to assess the legal effect upon the parties' contract of some event, we need to know when the event occurred and when the contract was made. If the event precedes the contract, the relevant doctrine is common mistake; when the event post-dates it, the relevant doctrine is frustration. Where there is doubt about the timing it may be necessary to consider both doctrines. In *Amalgamated Investment & Property Co Ltd* v *John Walker & Sons Ltd*[4] on 25 September the claimant property developer contracted to purchase property from the defendants for £1.71m. Unknown to either party on 14 August the building had been included in a list of buildings to be considered for historic building status. On 22 August government officials decided that the building would be accorded that status and on 26 September wrote to inform the defendants. The status was actually effective from the following day when ministerial approval was given. The effect of this was to remove the

---

[1] See also Chapter 12 where the doctrine of consideration is considered in relation to contractual modifications.
[2] (1847) Aleyn 26. See Ibbetson, ch. 1 in Rose (ed.), (1996) *Consensus ad Idem*.
[3] The term frustration derives from the case of *Jackson* v *Union Marine Insurance* (1874) LR 10 CP 125 from the judgment of Bramwell B at 145 and 148. For general overviews, see Treitel (1994) *Frustration and Force Majeure*; McKendrick (ed.) (1995) *Force Majeure and Frustration of Contract*, 2nd edn.
[4] [1977] 1 WLR 164.

development potential of the site and so reduce its value to £0.2m. The date of the contract was clear but what was the relevant event? If it was the officials' decision to list the building as of historic interest, the facts raised an issue of common mistake. If it was the ministerial approval, the facts raised an issue of frustration. The Court of Appeal held that all events prior to the minister's approval were mere preparatory administrative steps and so it was frustration which had to be considered.

Lord Sumner delivering the opinion of the Privy Council in *Hirji Muliji* v *Cheong Yue Steamship Co* described the operation of the doctrine in this way: 'frustration brings the contract to an end forthwith, without more and automatically'.[5] Its effect is, therefore, to be distinguished from that of a breach of condition, which gives rise to an election for the innocent party, which, *if exercised*, will bring an end to the contract. The boundary between cases of breach and frustration is raised by cases of so-called 'self-induced frustration'.[6] This refers to the situation where the allegedly frustrating event is attributable to the party pleading frustration. Self-induced frustration is an inexact label, which covers a number of different circumstances. Most obviously it refers to the situation where the supposed frustrating event results from one party's deliberate act. If a singer agrees to perform a concert, he should not be able to plead frustration if he is unable to perform because of a heavy drinking session the night before.[7] Second, there is the situation where the supposed frustrating event results from the negligent, rather than the deliberate, act of a contracting party. If the singer had foolishly tried to clear his head by going for a walk in the rain and as a consequence lost his voice, should he be able to rely upon frustration? Despite a contrary suggestion,[8] it is now settled that if the negligence of a contracting party caused the event, it cannot constitute frustration. On this basis the Court of Appeal held that a shipowner would not be entitled to plead frustration of a contract to carry cargo if the carrying vessel was lost as a result of the shipowner's negligence.[9] The third situation considered under the heading of self-induced frustration is when subsequent events prevent a contractor from meeting all his commitments and so he has to choose which to honour. In *Maritime National Fish Ltd* v *Ocean Trawlers Ltd*[10] the defendants used five trawlers, three of which they owned and two of which they chartered from others. The defendants were only granted three out of

---

[5] [1926] AC 497 at 505. See also *Maritime National Fish Ltd* v *Ocean Trawlers Ltd* [1935] AC 524 at 527 and *Joseph Constantine Steamship Line Ltd* v *Imperial Smelting Corporation Ltd* [1942] AC 154 at 163, 170, 171, 187 and 200.

[6] See generally Treitel, ch. 15 in Beatson and Friedmann (eds.) (1995) *Good Faith and Fault in Contract Law*.

[7] *Sumnall* v *Statt* (1984) 49 P & CR 367 (tenant who had contracted to continuously reside in premises could not rely upon the doctrine of frustration when he was sent to prison).

[8] *Joseph Constantine SS Co* v *Imperial Smelting Corp Ltd* [1942] AC 154 at 166–7 *per* Lord Simon and *Cheall* v *Association of Professional Executive, Clerical and Computer Staff* [1983] 2 AC 180 at 188–9 *per* Lord Diplock.

[9] *Super Servant Two* [1990] 1 Lloyd's Rep 1 at 10 and 13–14.

[10] [1935] AC 524.

the five fishing licences they had requested and applied them to two of the ships they owned and one they chartered. The Privy Council rejected the defendant's argument that the remaining charter was frustrated. The inability to fish was caused by the defendants' allocation of licences for which they were accountable. In a subsequent case *The Super Servant Two*[11] the principle was taken further and used to reject a plea of frustration where the defendant was faced with a situation where however he allocated his resources he would be unable to meet his commitments.[12] The defendants had contracted to carry a drilling rig in one of two ships they owned. Unfortunately, the ship they allocated to the contract sunk at a time when the other vessel was already committed elsewhere. The Court of Appeal rejected the defendants' argument that the sinking frustrated the contract of carriage because the defendants had taken the prior decision to apply their other vessel to different contracts. If a defence of frustration is rejected on the basis that the so-called frustrating event was self-induced,[13] in the absence of any other relevant excuse,[14] the defendant will be liable to the claimant for breach of contract.

Further limitations on the application of the doctrine of frustration have been considered elsewhere in this book.[15] These include the desirable principle, which is imperfectly followed by the common law, that the doctrine of frustration should not upset any allocation of risk agreed by the parties. Where the parties' contract expressly or impliedly, but none the less clearly, allocates to one party the risk of a certain event occurring, that party should not be able to escape that responsibility by relying on the doctrine of frustration. However, when applying this principle it is important that the allocation of risk under the contract be carefully investigated. It is sometimes said that foreseeable events cannot ground a plea of frustration. This proposition must be handled with care or its application may usurp the parties' own contractual allocation of risk.

By now it will be appreciated that the doctrine of frustration operates within narrow limits. It may well be more generous than the doctrine of common mistake but it is indisputably limited. This may be attributable to two factors one of which is perhaps more obvious than the other. The more obvious reason is that a broader doctrine of 'excuse' would be injurious to the certainty of commercial undertakings. Lord Roskill articulated this concern when he said that the doctrine of frustration was '... not lightly to be invoked to relieve contracting parties of the normal consequences of

---

[11] [1990] 1 Lloyd's Rep 1.

[12] See Goode (1995) *Commercial Law.* 2nd edn, p. 143 for an argument that this situation should not be regarded as 'self-induced'.

[13] The burden of proving that the frustrating event was self-induced is cast on the party who asserts that it was so. *Joseph Constantine SS Line* v *Imperial Smelting Corp Ltd* [1942] AC 154 (ship owner not required to disprove his fault for on board explosion which prevented him from meeting his obligations under a charter).

[14] For instance, a valid exemption clause.

[15] See Chapter 12.

imprudent bargains ...'.[16] This concern is most clearly expressed in the principle that 'mere' increases in costs cannot alone operate to frustrate a contract.[17]

The less obvious reason is the extent to which commercial contractors themselves make provision in their contracts for circumstances which might disrupt contractual performance. Professor McKendrick has written:[18]

> Textbooks on English contract law devote a considerable amount of space to the doctrine of frustration but little, if any, to a discussion of *force majeure* clauses. This approach fails to reflect the experience of the vast majority of legal practitioners: for them a frustrated contract is a novelty rarely, if ever, encountered. *Force majeure* clauses are, on the other hand, an everyday occurrence.

Force majeure clauses[19] are contractual terms that seek to relieve the parties of their obligations under the contract when events occur which are beyond their control. Such clauses are usually drafted in broad terms. For example, the Refined Sugar Association's contract provides that the delivery period is to be extended and the contract thereafter void if supply or delivery is prevented by:

> EEC legislation, Government Intervention, ice, war, strikes, rebellion, political or labour-disturbances, civil commotion, fire, stress of weather, act of God or any cause of *force majeure* (whether or not of like kind to these before mentioned) beyond the Seller's control ...

Parties may insert into their contracts two other types of clause, which are designed to deal with unforeseeable events, which make performance more onerous. Hardship clauses are intended to make the contract responsive to commercial problems, which might impede one party's performance. Such a clause might oblige the parties to re-negotiate the contract price if certain specified events occur. Of course, it might be difficult for the parties to reach agreement on such a question. For this reason the parties may include an intervener clause empowering a named third party to resolve any outstanding difference between them.[20]

We can conclude that the narrow ambit of the doctrine of frustration is attributable to the need to promote certainty in commercial transactions and is balanced by the considerable liberty enjoyed and exploited by commercial parties to make provision for events which might affect their ability to perform the contract.

---

[16] *The Nema* [1982] AC 724 at 752.
[17] See generally *Davis Contractors* v *Fareham UDC* [1956] AC 724 and the full discussion in Chapter 12.
[18] In Beatson and Friedmann, *op. cit.*, ch. 12, p. 323.
[19] Such clauses should not be confused with the French legal doctrine of the same name which has the effect of relieving a party from a particular obligation when its performance has become impossible.
[20] Schmitthoff, 'Hardship and Intervener Clauses' [1980] JBL 82 and McKendrick in Beatson and Friedmann, *op.cit.*, ch. 12, pp. 323–31.

THE JURISTIC BASIS OF FRUSTRATION

As many as five theories[21] have been canvassed as providing the juristic basis and the appropriate test for frustration. As well as not agreeing upon the appropriate juristic basis which underlies the doctrine of frustration, judges seem undecided as to whether it makes any difference at all which juristic basis they adopt[22] and whether the doctrine should be expanded or kept within strict confines.[23] We will now briefly examine and evaluate the different theories.

The implied term theory

This has its origin in the classic judgment of Blackburn J in *Taylor* v *Caldwell*,[24] which is regarded as the beginning of the modern law of frustration. In a somewhat more concise statement Earl Loreburn described it thus in *FA Tamplin Steamship Co Ltd* v *Anglo-Mexican Petroleum Products Co Ltd*:[25]

> a court can and ought to examine the contract and the circumstances in which it was made, not of course to vary, but only to explain it, in order to see whether or not from the nature of it the parties must have made their bargain on the footing that a particular thing or state of things would continue to exist. And if they must have done so, then a term to that effect will be implied ...

This theory is superficially attractive. It appears to have the considerable merit of furthering that 'great object' of making the legal construction such as to fulfil the intention of those who entered into the contract.[26] A term providing for discharge will be implied only when the parties so wished it. The law in implying a term 'is only doing what the parties really (though subconsciously) meant to do themselves'.[27] However, if this is taken literally

---

21 *National Carriers* v *Panalpina Ltd* [1981] AC 675, 687 B *per* Lord Hailsham, *cf. Davis Contractors* v *Fareham UDC* [1956] AC 696, 719 *per* Lord Reid, who suggests there are only three.

22 *Davis Contractors* v *Fareham UDC* [1956] AC 696 at 719 (it does make a difference). *Cf. National Carriers* v *Panalpina* [1981] AC 675 at 693 (it makes no difference).

23 *Compare Bank Line* v *Arthur Capel* [1919] AC 435, 459 per Lord Sumner (there should be no expansion) with *National Carriers* v *Panalpina* [1981] AC 675, 707 G *per* Viscount Simon (frustration should be more flexible).

24 (1863) 3 B & S 826, 833–4, Blackburn J giving the judgment of the Court of Exchequer Chamber said: 'Where, from the nature of the contract it appears that the parties must from the beginning have known that it could not be fulfilled unless when the time for the fulfilment of the contract arrived some particular specified thing continued to exist so that, when entering into the contract they must have contemplated such continuing existence as the foundation of what was to be done; there in the absence of any express or implied warranty that the thing shall exist, the contract is not to be construed as a positive contract, but as subject to an implied condition that the parties shall be excused in case, before breach, performance becomes impossible from the perishing of the thing without default of the contractor.'

25 [1916] 2 AC 397, 403.

26 *Per* Blackburn J in *Taylor* v *Caldwell* (1863) 3 B & S 826, 834.

27 *Per* Lord Sumner in *Hirji Muliji* v *Cheong Yue Steamship Co* [1926] AC 497, 504.

several difficulties become apparent. As Lord Sands said in *James Scott and Sons v Del Sol*:[28]

> It does seen to me somewhat far-fetched to hold that the non-occurrence of some event, which was not within the contemplation or even the imagination of the parties was an implied term of the contract.

There is a further problem in that even if the parties would have provided for the event, they would not necessarily have provided for the discharge of the contract; they may well have preferred to adjust their bargain.[29]

In order to meet these objections, the implied term approach is often couched in objective rather than subjective terms: in terms of what a reasonable contractor would have agreed to.[30] This shift of emphasis really involves an intellectual sleight of hand; it allows the courts to maintain the vitality of their power to discharge contracts in certain circumstances, while at the same time protecting that power from charges of judicial invention by resting it on the presumed intention of the parties. In an eloquent passage Lord Radcliffe[31] exposed the speciousness of this approach.

> By this time it might seem that the parties themselves have become so far disembodied spirits that their actual persons should be allowed to rest in peace. In their place there rises the figure of the fair and reasonable man. And the spokesman of the fair and reasonable man, who represents after all no more than the anthropomorphic conception of justice, is and must be the court itself.

The same point was made with equal seriousness but more humour by Lord Sands:[32]

> A tiger has escaped from a travelling menagerie. The milkgirl fails to deliver the milk. Possibly the milkman may be exonerated from any breach of contract; but, even so, it would hardly seem reasonable to base that exoneration on the ground that 'tiger days excepted' must be . . . written into the milk contract.

---

[28] 1922 SC 592 at 596–7. Aff'd 1923 SC 37. See his example on p. 597. See to similar effect Lord Radcliffe in *Davis Contractors v Fareham UDC* [1956] AC 696, 728; Corbin, 'Recent Developments in Contracts' [1937] 50 Harv L Rev 449, 465.

[29] *Denny, Mott and Dickson v James B Fraser and Co* [1944] AC 265, 275 *per* Lord Wright; *The Eugenia* [1964] 2 QB 222, 238 *per* Lord Denning.

[30] *Dahl v Nelson* (1881) 6 App Cas 38, 59 *per* Lord Watson: 'the meaning of the contract must be taken to be not what the parties did intend ... but that which the parties as fair and reasonable men, would presumably have agreed upon ...'. See also *Hirji Muliji v Cheong Yue Steamship Co Ltd* [1926] AC 497, 509 *per* Lord Sumner delivering the judgment of the Privy Council.

[31] *Davis Contractors v Fareham UDC* [1956] AC 696, 728 and an equally incisive passage by Corbin, *op.cit.* (n. 28 herein above), pp. 449, 465 discussing *Taylor v Caldwell* (1863) 3 B & S 826:

> How easy it was to make the decision turn upon the presumed intention of the parties! By a process of interpretation, the promise was found to be conditional on the continued existence of the building a result reached without introducing evidence as to the exact words of the parties and in spite of a high probability that the possibility of fire never entered their minds.

[32] *James Scott & Sons Ltd v Del Sol* 1922 SC 592 at 597. See also *FC Shepherd & Co Ltd v Jerrom* [1987] 1 QB 301 at 322 *per* Mustill LJ.

Perhaps as an acknowledgement of the judicial fiction involved in the appeal to the presumed intention of the parties, there began a tendency to quote the classic statement of Earl Loreburn and then either: to state a test which was at variance with it, absent any acknowledgement of the conflict;[33] or to claim that the juristic foundation of the doctrine made no difference;[34] or perhaps more honestly, consciously to frame a new approach.[35] However, despite the general trend, the implied term approach still has its adherents.[36]

Total failure of consideration

In *National Carriers* v *Panalpina*,[37] counsel for the respondent (claimant) submitted that frustration can only apply to obligations that are wholly executory, i.e. where there has been a total failure of consideration.[38] This submission is not only inconsistent with the result of several cases,[39] but probably could not even provide an alternative rationalisation of *Taylor* v *Caldwell*[40] as counsel submitted. The Lord Chancellor accordingly tersely rejected it.[41]

The just and reasonable solution

A small number of judicial statements support a broader foundation for the doctrine of frustration. Thus Lord Sumner, delivering the Privy Council's judgment, said in *Hirji Muliji* v *Cheung Yue Steamship Co*:[42] 'It is really a device by which the rules as to absolute contracts are reconciled with a special exception which justice demands.'

However, Lord Wright was probably the most consistent proponent of the view that the frustration doctrine really represented no more than the qualification of contract by standards of justice. Speaking extra judicially he once said:[43] 'It would be truer to say that the court in the absence of express intention of the parties determines what is just.'

---

33 See Lord Sumner delivering the Privy Council's judgment in *Hirji Muliji* v *Cheong Yue Steamship Co* [1926] AC 497, 506. The test he propounds at p. 510 is discussed below. See text accompanying nn. 42–4 in this chapter.

34 See Lord Porter in *Denny, Mott and Dickson* v *James B Fraser & Co* [1944] AC 265, 281.

35 See Lord Radcliffe in *Davis Contractors* v *Fareham UDC* [1956] AC 696, 727–9.

36 See Lord Simon in *British Movietonews* v *London and District Cinemas Ltd* [1952] AC 166, 183 and Diplock J in *Port Line* v *Ben Line Steamers* [1958] 2 QB 146, 162. See also Smith, 'Contracts – Mistake, Frustration and Implied Terms' (1994) 110 LQR 400.

37 [1981] AC 675.

38 *Ibid.*, p. 681.

39 For instance, *Tatem* v *Gamboa* [1939] 1 KB 132; *Denny, Mott and Dickson* v *James B Fraser & Co* [1944] AC 265.

40 (1863) 3 B & S 826: it appears that the gardens were still usable after the fire – see Treitel, p. 808, n. 31 quoting contemporary newspaper reports.

41 [1981] AC 675, 687 E–F.

42 [1926] AC 497, 510.

43 (1939) *Legal Essays and Addresses*, p. 258; see also *Joseph Constantine Steamship Line* v *Imperial Smelting Corporation* [1942] AC 154, 184; *Denny Mott and Dickson* v *James B Fraser & Co* [1944] AC 265, 275; also Denning LJ in the Court of Appeal in *British Movietonews Ltd* v *London and District Cinemas Ltd* [1951] 1 KB 190, whose comments were disapproved on appeal [1952] AC 167, 181–4 and 185 *per* Viscount Simon.

Despite this approach having the considerable merit of candour, judges not being required to 'disguise' their motives for holding a contract to be frustrated, it does seem to be stated in terms which reserve to the court a restrained discretion to upset the allocation of risks agreed to by the parties, whenever the court considers it just to do so. Such an approach would threaten all the values and benefits promoted by the principle of sanctity of contract. While there appears to be little evidence that the advocates of this approach intended an expansion of the doctrine beyond its accepted limits, the breadth of these statements when read out of context has perhaps resulted in the approach's failure to gain popularity.[44]

Frustration of the adventure

The comments of Lord Sumner in *Hirji Muliji* v *Cheong Yue Steamship Co* quoted above were really, according to Lord Hailsham,[45] expressing a 'more sophisticated theory' of 'frustration of the adventure' or the 'foundation of the contract', which he says originated in the judgment of the majority in *Jackson* v *Union Marine Insurance*.[46] However, it is perhaps most concisely stated by Goddard J in *Tatem* v *Gamboa*:[47] 'if the foundation of the contract goes ... the performance of the contract is to be regarded as frustrated'.

The 'radical difference' approach

This approach finds its clearest expression in Lord Radcliffe's words:[48]

> ... frustration occurs whenever the law recognises that without default of either party a contractual obligation has become incapable of being performed because the circumstances in which performance is called for would render it a thing *radically different* from that which was undertaken by the contract. *Non haec in foedera veni*.[49] It was not this that I promised to do. [my emphasis]

---

[44] See *Notcutt* v *Universal Equipment Co (London) Ltd* [1986] 1 WLR 641 at 646–7 (Court of Appeal rejecting 'just and reasonable' approach).

[45] *National Carriers* v *Panalpina Ltd* [1981] AC 675, 687 H.

[46] (1874) LR 10 CP 125. However, although Baron Bramwell appears to refer to frustration of the adventure, on p. 141 his words may also lend support to the 'radical difference' or 'construction theory' examined below and perhaps the 'implied term theory' at p.154.

[47] [1939] 1 KB 132, 139 endorsing a similar statement of Viscount Haldane (dissenting) in *FA Tamplin* v *Anglo Mexican Petroleum Products Ltd* [1916] 2 AC 397, 406–7; also supported by Lord Sumner in *Larringa and Co* v *Société Franco-Américaine des Phosphates de Medulla, Paris* [1922–3] 39 TLR 316, 321; Pickford LJ in *Countess of Warwick Steamship Co* v *Le Nickel SA* [1918] 1 KB 372, 376–7.

[48] *Davis Contractors Ltd* v *Fareham UDC* [1956] AC 696, 729.

[49] The Latin phrase appears to have first been used by Lord Finlay LC in *Bank Line Ltd* v *Arthur Capel and Co* [1919] AC 435, 442. It has its origin in Virgil's Aeneid, Book IV, lines 338–9, according to a letter to *The Times* from Sir John Megaw, 20 December 1980.

The approach is sometimes also known as the construction theory,[50] as its application first requires the court to construe the parties' actual bargain in the light of the surrounding circumstances. In this way the parties' original obligations can be ascertained. The court then considers whether performance in the changed circumstances can be said to be radically different from that contemplated. If so the contract is discharged.

The obvious merit of this approach is that it incorporates a clear instruction to courts to construe the contract and, implicitly, to respect the contractors' own assignment of risk. It would appear also to represent the most popular approach to frustration at the present time.[51] It is this test which is applied in many of the more recent cases examined in the next section.

THE MAIN APPLICATIONS

Impossibility

Where the performance of the contract has become impossible, the contract is frustrated. In *Taylor* v *Caldwell*[52] the claimant agreed to hire the 'Surrey Gardens and Music Hall' in order to stage four music concerts. Almost a week before the first concert the music hall burnt down. Blackburn J held that the defendants were not liable to the disappointed concert organiser because it was 'impossible'[53] to hold the concerts.[54] In this case Blackburn J drew upon older authorities[55] which hold that the death or incapacity of a person who was required by a contract to tender a personal performance could discharge that contract.

The unavailability of the contractual subject matter may justify holding the contract to be frustrated. On this basis charters have been held to be frustrated when ships have run aground[56] or been requisitioned.[57] In each case it is necessary to take account of the length of the period of unavailability compared to duration of the contract.

[50] See *Davis Contractors* v *Fareham UDC* [1956] AC 696, 729 *per* Lord Radcliffe. *National Carriers* v *Panalpina* [1981] AC 675, 688A–C per Lord Hailsham, 702C *per* Lord Simon of Glaisdale; *contra* p. 717C–D *per* Lord Roskill who seems to treat the radical difference and construction approaches as distinct. *The Nema* [1982] AC 724, *Wates* v *GLC* [1983] 25 BLR 1 at 26–7. On the construction theory, see also Viscount Simon in *British Movietonews Ltd* v *London and District Cinemas Ltd* [1952] AC 166, 186; *Davis Contractors* v *Fareham UDC* [1956] AC 696, 720–1 *per* Lord Reid, with whom Lord Somervell agreed.

[51] *National Carriers* v *Panalpina* [1981] AC 675, 702C *per* Lord Simon. See also *The Nema* [1982] AC 724.

[52] (1863) 3 B & S 826.

[53] *Ibid.* at p. 830.

[54] Even *Taylor* v *Caldwell* may not be as clear cut a case as it first seems because, as Treitel points out at p. 808, contemporary newspaper reports suggest that the gardens were still open and usable; see *The Times*, 3 June and 19 December 1861.

[55] *Brewster* v *Kitchell* (1691) 1 Salk 198 and *Atkinson* v *Ritchie* (1809) 10 East 530 at 534–5.

[56] *Jackson* v *Union Marine Insurance* (1874) LR 10 CP 125 (ship ran aground in January but not repaired until August).

[57] *Countess of Warwick Steamship Co* v *Le Nickel SA* [1918] 1 KB 372 (six months left to run of one year charter at time of requisition). Compare *Tamplin SS Co Ltd* v *Anglo-Mexican Petroleum Co* [1916] 2 AC 397 (requisition in early 1915 did not frustrate five-year charter due to expire at end 1917).

Illegality

A contract will be frustrated where its performance has become illegal. Such supervening illegality may occur after the outbreak of war when trading with the enemy is illegal. In the *Fibrosa*[58] case the appellants ordered machinery from the respondents to be delivered to a particular Polish port. Following the outbreak of war, the port in question was occupied by the German army. Despite the fact that performance of the contract was not impossible, the overwhelming public interest in prohibiting trade that might benefit the enemy meant that the contract was frustrated. This public interest is so compelling that it overrides even an express term to the contrary in the contract.[59] A different example of supervening illegality during wartime is provided by the *Denny, Mott* case[60] where a contract for the sale of timber was frustrated by a ban on trade in timber. A non-wartime example is provided by *Gamerco SA v ICM/Fair Warning (Agency) Ltd*[61] where a contract was entered to promote a pop concert to be held at a venue in Madrid. Subsequently the venue was examined by engineers who concluded that it must be considered unsafe until further testing was done. The contract was held to be frustrated because the authorities had banned the use of the contemplated premises.

Frustration of objective

Supervening circumstances sometimes operate to frustrate the common objective or purpose of the contract. Courts will not easily be persuaded that this has occurred because this would encourage people to seek to escape from transactions simply because they do not turn out as planned. The court's reluctance to develop this head of frustration is linked with their refusal to admit that 'mere' increases in costs can result in frustration. Frustration of purpose will be invoked by promisees when the promisor's performance proves less valuable than originally anticipated; the effect of cost increases is considered when the promisor's performance becomes more burdensome than originally anticipated. The approach of the law is to make it difficult for either party to invoke the doctrine of frustration.

In *Krell v Henry*[62] a room was hired for two days for the purpose of viewing Edward VII's coronation procession. The procession had to be postponed because of the King's illness. The Court of Appeal held that the contract was frustrated. This may be contrasted with *Herne Bay Steamboat Co v Hutton*[63] where a boat was hired for the purpose of viewing the naval review and inspecting the fleet at Spithead. In this case it was held that the

---

[58] *Fibrosa Spolka Akcyjna v Fairbairn Lawson Combe Barbour Ltd* [1943] AC 32.
[59] *Ertel Beiber & Co v Rio Tinto Co Ltd* [1918] AC 260.
[60] *Denny, Mott & Dickson v James B Fraser & Co* [1944] AC 265.
[61] [1995] 1 WLR 1226.
[62] [1903] 2 KB 740.
[63] [1903] 2 KB 683.

cancellation of the naval review did not amount to frustration. The fleet was still assembled and could be looked at and so it could not be said that the purpose of the contract was lost. In this respect *Herne Bay* is similar to an example used in *Krell* by Vaughan Williams LJ of someone who booked a 'taxi', perhaps at an enhanced rate, to take him to Epsom on Derby Day.[64] If the race were cancelled, this would not operate to frustrate the contract because the objective of the contract could not be considered to be the viewing of a single race. The difficulty of successfully making out frustration of objective is clear from the *Amalgamated Investment* case considered earlier where it was held that the objective or purpose of the sale of property for development was not frustrated when the building was listed as of historic interest thereby reducing its redevelopment potential so much that its value fell from over £1.7m to £0.2m.

THE EFFECTS OF FRUSTRATION[65]

At common law frustration automatically brings the contract to an end. This discharges the parties from the performance of any obligations which, at the time of frustration, had not yet arisen. Obligations which accrued before frustration remain enforceable. The injustice of these common law rules is apparent from the case of *Chandler* v *Webster*.[66] This was another 'coronation' case where a room was hired overlooking the route of the coronation procession. The contract of hire provided for £141 15s to be paid in advance of which £100 had in fact been paid when the procession was cancelled. The contract was frustrated but the hirer was required to pay the balance of the advance payment, i.e. £41 15s because this had fallen due prior to the occurrence of the frustrating event. The hirer's claim for the return of the £100 was rejected. It was said that this could only be ordered where there has been a total failure of consideration. It was thought that the failure was not total where a valid agreement and enforceable agreement existed up to the time of frustration. In other words, a total failure of consideration only occurred when the contract was void from the outset.

The latter aspect of *Chandler* v *Webster* was overruled in the *Fibrosa* case. The contract was one to sell machinery for £4,800 of which £1,600 was payable in advance. In fact, only £1,000 had been paid when the contract was frustrated. The House of Lords held that the £1,000 was recoverable on the basis of a total failure of consideration. In an important passage[67] for the law of restitution Viscount Simon explained that there was an important difference between the contractual and the restitutionary concepts of consideration. In the law of contract a promise can and often does constitute

---

[64] The 'Derby' is a famous horse race held annually.
[65] See Stewart and Carter, [1992] CLJ 66.
[66] [1904] 1 KB 493.
[67] [1943] AC 32 at 48.

consideration. In the law of restitution, where one of the major grounds for restitution is the total failure of consideration, consideration has a different meaning. In this context it refers not to the promise *per se* but to the performance of that promise. As the Polish company had not received any machinery, the consideration to support the company's advance payment had totally failed and so the £1,000 had be returned.[68]

Unfortunately the *Fibrosa* case remedied one injustice but created two others. First, it only applied where there was a total failure of consideration. It would not apply to a case where a father paid £25 for his son to be apprenticed to a watchmaker, and after the first year the watchmaker died. The father in this case was unable to reclaim any part of the £25 because the failure of consideration was partial rather than total.[69] Second, it failed to provide any compensation for the party who was forced to return the advance payment despite the fact that he incurred expenses himself.[70]

The Law Reform (Frustrated Contracts) Act 1943[71] was passed to try to achieve a more equitable adjustment of the parties' rights following frustration of their contract. Section 1(2) has three effects. First, all sums payable before the time of frustration cease to be payable, e.g. the £41 15s in *Chandler* v *Webster*. Second, any sums actually paid must be returned, e.g. the £100 in *Chandler* v *Webster*. Third, the court may permit the party to whom sums were paid or payable to retain or recover money to cover his own expenses, e.g. the preparatory expenses of the seller in *Fibrosa*. However, the amount of the prepayment is the upper limit upon the recovery of expenses.

The discretion under s 1(2) to permit the retention or recovery of expenses was recently considered and applied in *Gamerco SA* v *ICM/Fair Warning (Agency) Ltd*.[72] The promoters of a pop concert advanced $412,000 to the performers before the performance contract was frustrated. The performers had incurred expenses of about $50,000. These facts alone would suggest that the promoters should have been able to recover their advance, perhaps subject to the performers' retention of $50,000 to cover their expenses. However, Garland J said that '[I]t is self-evident that any rigid rule is liable to produce injustice'.[73] In this case the promoters had themselves incurred expenses of $450,000.[74] Garland J concluded that he was entitled to exercise a 'broad discretion' with regard to the retention of expenses. He permitted the promoter to recover the advance payment in full, i.e. without deduction of any expenses because the promoter had himself

---

[68] It is implicit that the outstanding £600 ceased to be payable.
[69] *Whincup* v *Hughes* (1871) LR 6 CP 78.
[70] In the *Fibrosa* case the manufacturer had used the advance payment to cover pre-production expenses.
[71] Certain contracts are excluded from the Act, including voyage charters and contracts of insurance; see s 2(5)(a)–(b).
[72] [1995] 1 WLR 1226.
[73] *Ibid.*, p. 1237.
[74] Which must not have benefited the performers at all because it gave rise to no claim under s 1(3). See *ibid.*, p. 1234.

incurred expenses in excess of the prepayment which were nine times greater than those which the performers sought to retain.[75]

Where, before the contract is frustrated, one party has obtained a valuable benefit from the other, the first party can recover from the other a 'just sum' not exceeding the value of the benefit to the recipient.[76] The leading case on s 1(3) is *BP Exploration (Libya) Ltd* v *Hunt* where Goff J's judgment was upheld[77] by the Court of Appeal and the House of Lords. Goff J held that there were two stages to quantifying a claim under s 1(3). First, it is necessary to identify and value the benefit. The section provides little guidance here but the choice is essentially between the cost of performance incurred by the claimant and the 'end product' received by the other party. In *BP* v *Hunt* the benefit was quantified by reference to the end product.[78] It might be necessary to take a different approach if there is no end product, e.g. where the contract was one to survey or transport something or perhaps also if the service produces an end product with no objective value, such as where eccentric works of redecoration are commenced which reduce, rather than increase, the value of the property. However, where the value of the benefit (namely, the end product) is destroyed by the frustrating event, the provider of it has no claim under s 1(3) because there is no benefit. This means that if a decorator is half way to completing a redecoration of a house when the property burns down, he can recover nothing for the work he has done.[79]

The second stage involves the assessment of a just sum. The just sum awarded cannot exceed the value of the benefit arrived at under the first stage. Subject to this restriction Goff J suggests that the guiding principle should be the award of such sum as is necessary to prevent the unjust enrichment of the defendant at the claimant's expense. The terms of the frustrated contract may be useful in quantifying the just sum because the contract consideration might provide evidence from which a just sum might be calculated or provide a ceiling upon recovery.[80]

The Law Reform (Frustrated Contracts) Act 1943 is not a model for law reform. It certainly addresses some of the fundamental failings of the common law. However, its provisions are difficult to interpret and fail to provide for some needy cases. The failure to clearly identify the benefit conferred with the cost of the services provided may be a source of injustice to parties in the position of the decorator. Further, the Act fails to release a party from an obligation other than one to pay money which accrues before frustration. If in *Whincup* v *Hughes*[81] the father had agreed to 'pay' the

---

[75] Legislation in Canada and Australia provides for the equal distribution of losses between the parties.

[76] Section 1(3) as interpreted in *BP Exploration (Libya) Ltd* v *Hunt* [1979] 1 WLR 783.

[77] With minor amendment.

[78] See also *Parsons Bros Ltd* v *Shea* (1966) 53 DLR (2d) 86.

[79] Compare *Appleby* v *Myers* (1867) LR 2 CP 651.

[80] The Court of Appeal appears to endorse a less principled approach, which gives greater discretion to the trial judge.

[81] See n. 69 above in this chapter.

apprentice master by supplying 25 cases of wine but at the time of his death had only delivered one. Nothing in the Act would prevent the apprentice master's personal representatives from suing for the missing bottles. If the payment had been one in cash, s 1(2) would render the unperformed part unenforceable. However s 1(3) which deals with benefits in kind only extends to benefits conferred prior to frustration and not to those which the father was obliged, but had failed, to supply.

15

TERMINATION FOR BREACH

The terms of a contract, like the parties to it, come in all shapes and sizes. Terms can be classified in two different ways: according to their source and according to their remedial effect. The former classification was described in Chapter 10; the latter is examined here. Any breach of contract will give rise to a right to damages but some will also give the innocent party the right to terminate the contract.

At the outset two points about the right to terminate need to be emphasised. First, termination, unlike frustration,[1] does not operate automatically. The breach of certain terms in a contract called conditions or certain breaches of another type of term called innominate terms, both of which are discussed in detail below, give rise to an election which the innocent party may or may not exercise. To exercise this election, the innocent party must unequivocally communicate his desire to do so.[2] Exceptionally, this test might be satisfied by the innocent party's failure to perform.[3] Second, termination operates prospectively. It relieves both parties of their primary obligation to perform the contract and substitutes for the party in breach an obligation to pay damages.[4] It is this prospective effect which distinguishes termination for breach from rescission for misrepresentation which, if available (i.e. no bars to rescission have arisen), avoids the contract *ab initio* (i.e. from the outset).[5] In this book[6] to avoid confusion between the remedies, they are described respectively as termination and rescission. Lord Millett has recently observed that the failure to make this distinction '... has led many courts astray and continues to do so'.[7]

---

[1] See Chapter 14.

[2] *Vitol SA v Norelf Ltd* [1996] AC 800.

[3] *Ibid.* at p. 811 Lord Steyn gives the example of a contractor who is told by his employer not to turn up for work tomorrow. The contractor's absence in the morning may itself amount to an exercise of his election to terminate.

[4] The analysis of termination in terms of primary and secondary obligations derives from Lord Diplock's judgment in *Photo Production Ltd v Securicor Transport Ltd* [1980] AC 827.

[5] That is, no so-called 'bars' to rescission have arisen.

[6] Elsewhere, e.g. Treitel, both remedies may be described as rescission and distinguished only by the following words, i.e. rescission for misrepresentation and rescission for breach.

[7] *Hurst v Bryk* [2000] 2 All ER 193 at 199–200.

ANTICIPATORY BREACH

A breach of contract can be either anticipatory or actual. An anticipatory breach occurs when before the time for performance the promisor either announces that he will not perform his obligation as required by the contract or disables himself from doing so. In *Hochster v De La Tour*[8] on 12 April a courier was employed by the defendant to perform duties beginning on 1 June. On 11 May the defendant told the courier that he had changed his mind. On 22 May the courier brought an action for damages and was successful. To recover damages before the time for performance had arisen, there must have been a breach of contract by the defendant, and to justify the courier in not performing the contract, the term breached must have been a condition. Lord Campbell CJ described it as a 'promise that ... neither will do anything to the prejudice of the other inconsistent with that relation'. The right of the innocent party to bring an action for damages before the time for performance has arisen benefits both parties. The innocent party is able to recover damages at an earlier point in time than if he was required to wait for an 'actual' breach. The party in breach is also advantaged because, as soon as he has exercised his election, the innocent party comes under an obligation to mitigate his loss. The principle of *Hochester* was again applied in a case where the defendant promised to marry the claimant on the death of the defendant's father.[9] The defendant broke off his engagement while his father was still alive. The claimant's action for damages was successful. The defendant argued that he should not be liable because he might never be required to perform anything under the contract, e.g. if the claimant predeceased the defendant's father. This objection was dismissed because the action was not one for actual breach. It was an action for anticipatory breach. The term breached was an implied term that prior to the time of performance the claimant had 'a right to have the contract kept open as a subsisting and effective contract'. Again, the term breached must have been must be a condition because it justified the claimant's termination.

In most cases when the promisor announces his future intention not to perform this is a clear breach of the implied term not to do anything inconsistent with keeping the contract alive. A more difficult situation arises where the party who before the time for performance has arisen tells the other that he will not be able to perform erroneously thinks he is justified in doing so. In *Woodar Investment Development Ltd v Wimpey Construction UK Ltd*[10] Wimpey contracted to buy land from Woodar. It was a term of the contract that Wimpey could withdraw if prior to completion a statutory authority 'shall have commenced' compulsory purchase proceedings. As both parties knew, such proceedings had been commenced in respect of just over two of

---

[8] (1853) 2 E & B 678.

[9] *Frost v Knight* (1872) LR 7 Ex 111. The action for breach of a promise to marry was actionable (though not specifically enforceable!) until it was abolished by Law Reform (Miscellaneous Provisions) Act 1970, s 1(1).

[10] [1980] 1 WLR 277. Nicol and Rawlings (1980) 43 MLR 696.

the 14 acres being sold. Wimpey purported to exercise its power of withdrawal. The House of Lords held that Wimpey was not actually entitled to withdraw under the clause. The compulsory purchase proceedings were well under way when the contract was made. Indeed, the parties' contract acknowledged this by providing for a reduction in price if Woodar was unable to convey the whole site.[11] Wimpey's real reason for trying to withdraw was that there had been a catastrophic fall in land prices and so the contract was an unattractive one. Wimpey successfully argued that even if it had no such right, the company's honest belief[12] that it had should prevent its actions from amounting to an anticipatory breach of contract.[13] Lord Wilberforce said that:

> ... it would be a regrettable development of the law of contract to hold that a party who bona fide relies on an express stipulation in a contract in order to rescind or terminate a contract should, by that fact alone, be treated as having repudiated his contractual obligations if he turns out to be mistaken as to his rights.

In *Vaswani* v *Italian Motors Ltd*[14] a father decided to buy a car for his son. The car was a Ferrari Testarossa and was to cost £179,500. In the contract of sale the seller reserved the right to increase the sale price in certain circumstances. The seller claimed that he was entitled under this clause to increase the price to £218,800. In the circumstances of the case the clause did not justify the price increase. The Privy Council held that the seller had acted in good faith when asserting his honest but erroneous belief that he was entitled to the increase. Like the buyer in *Woodar*, this had the effect of preventing the party's actions from constituting an anticipatory breach of contract.[15] This principle of good faith protection was applied for the benefit of a payee, rather than a payer as in *Woodar*, a party whose actions would otherwise amount to an anticipatory breach.

This principle of good faith protection could work a considerable injustice. Woodar actually sold the land to a third party because if, as Woodar asserted, Wimpey was in breach of contract, Woodar would be subject to a duty to mitigate its losses. Against a falling property market (the land was sold for £330 against a contract price of £850), this would require Woodar to sell the land as soon as it was reasonable to expect it to do so. If after the decision of the House of Lords but before the date of completion, the value of land had risen to more than the contract price, Wimpey would have been able to sue Woodar for its failure to complete. The fact that Woodar had acted in good

---

11 Nicol and Rawlings, *op. cit.*, p. 697.
12 This was not challenged by Woodar.
13 The majority of the House of Lords (Wilberforce, Scarman and Keith) and a dissenting member of the Court of Appeal (Buckley) found for Wimpey. The two dissenting members of the House of Lords (Salmon, Russell), a majority of the Court of Appeal (Lawton, Goff) and the trial judge (Fox) found for Woodar. This is, therefore, one of those strange cases where the party who had more judicial support (five to four) nevertheless lost because 'his' judges were not in a majority in the highest court to consider the case.
14 [1996] 1 WLR 270.
15 The sellers were held to be entitled to retain the buyer's deposit.

faith would not have protected it from an action for breach of contract. The failure to convey the property at the time set for completion would be an actual, rather than an anticipatory, breach of contract and the doctrine of good faith protection applies only to anticipatory rather than actual breaches of contract. That this is so was confirmed in *Bliss* v *South East Thames Regional Health Authority*[16] where an employee wrote a number of angry and offensive letters to work colleagues. The employer eventually suspended the employee when he refused to submit to a psychiatric assessment. It was held that the employer's demand was a breach of a term of the contract of employment, which required the employer to do nothing to damage the relationship of trust and confidence with its employees. The fact that the employer had acted in good faith on medical advice did not protect it from an action for actual breach.

Where there has been an anticipatory breach of contract, the innocent party might decide not to exercise his election to terminate for breach. Rather, subject to certain limitations, he may continue with the contract, tender his own performance and sue in debt for the contract price.[17] This course of action is not without risk because by keeping the contract 'alive' the innocent party runs the risk that the contract could be frustrated.[18]

CONDITIONS AND WARRANTIES

A condition is a term every breach of which gives rise to a right in the innocent party to terminate the contract. A warranty is a term every breach of which gives rise to a right to damages only.[19] The classification of terms into conditions and warranties promotes certainty because parties know in advance what rights the innocent party will acquire if a particular term is broken. We will now examine the different grounds on which terms are classified as either conditions or warranties.

By statute

The terms implied into contracts for the sale of goods by the Sale of Goods Act 1979 will usually state that the term is to operate as either a condition or a warranty. These implied terms are classified as follows: *title* s 12(1) condition, *no encumbrances* s 12(4) warranty, *quiet possession* s 12(5) warranty, *description* s 13(1) condition, *satisfactory quality* s 14(2) condition, *fitness for a particular purpose* s 14(3) condition, *sample* s 15(2) condition. However, this is subject to an important caveat in respect of the conditions implied by ss 13–15. According to s 15A, if a term would otherwise have operated as a condition

---

[16] [1987] ICR 700.

[17] See Chapter 16 for an account of the action and its limitations.

[18] *Avery* v *Bowden* (1855) 5 E & B 714: defendant agreed to supply a cargo for a vessel within 45 days. Ship was told to go away but declined. Before 45 days elapsed, war broke out rendering further performance illegal – contract frustrated.

[19] Sale of Goods Act 1979, s 61(2)(b).

under these sections if the breach is so slight that it would be unreasonable for the buyer to reject the goods, then, if the buyer does not deal as a consumer the breach will be treated as a breach of warranty only.

By the parties' own classification

The parties to a contract can themselves classify the term as a condition or a warranty in one of three ways. First, the contract may describe the term as either a 'condition' or a 'warranty'. Such a description will be very strong evidence from which the court can infer the parties' choice, but it is not conclusive. The court looks to the substance rather than the form. So in *Schuler* v *Wickman*[20] clause 7(b) of a four-year distributorship said it was a condition that W send named representatives to visit six UK manufacturers at least once a week. On some occasions W failed to do this and S claimed to be entitled to terminate for breach of condition. The House of Lords concluded that the parties could not possibly have intended that missing a single visit would justify termination, particularly when the contract did not deal with the situation of when one of the named representatives was ill, had retired or died.

Second, parties might make their intention clear by using other words than condition sufficient to make clear their intention that the term is to operate as one. In *Lombard North Central plc* v *Butterworth*[21] a contract for the hire of computers said that it was of the essence of the contract for the hire to be paid promptly. The hirer failed to pay promptly and so the owners repossessed the machines. Such a clause will entitle the hirer to terminate the contract for the failure to pay a single instalment.[22]

Third, it might be possible to infer the parties' intention from the importance of the thing required. In one case[23] the court classified a statement in a charter party that the ship was 'now sailed or about to sail' as a condition. It was obviously very important for the charterer to know when the ship sailed so that he would be able to make arrangements, which were dependent on its arrival. The condition was held to be breached when the ship did not sail until nearly four weeks later. In *The Naxos*,[24] where sugar was sold on FOB terms,[25] the majority of the House of Lords held that the seller's obligation to have the goods ready was a condition because it was crucial to the buyer's ability to meet commitments to sub-purchasers.

---

[20] [1974] AC 239.
[21] [1987] QB 527.
[22] The breach by the hirer entitle the claimant to recover unliquidated damages in respect of arrears and all future payments, this enabled the claimant to recover a similar sum to that which was specified in another clause that was unenforceable for being a penalty.
[23] *Bentsen* v *Taylor* [1883] 2 QB 274.
[24] [1990] 1 WLR 1337.
[25] That is, the seller undertook to deliver the goods free (of duties, etc.) on board the vessel. The buyer had to arrange carriage.

The courts' classification

A court might itself classify the term as a condition if there is an established commercial usage to that effect. In *The Mihalis Angelos* a ship was chartered to go to Haiphong to load ore. The ship was said to be 'now trading and expected ready to load about July 1'. On 23 June the ship arrived at Hong Kong and was still there on 17 July when the charterers terminated the contract. The Court of Appeal followed the trade custom that 'expected ready to load' clauses were conditions.

The approach to established trade usage was generalised in *Bunge Corp* v *Tradax Export SA*[26] where the House of Lords had to consider the status of a clause in an FOB sale which required the buyer to name the vessel which was to transport the goods by a certain date. This was classified as a condition because the performance of the innocent party's obligation to deliver was dependent upon the buyer's nomination and the contract was likely to be one of a string of sales and sub-sales where delay would adversely affect many parties. However, the House of Lords went further and laid down a general presumption that stipulations as to time in commercial or mercantile contracts will be conditions. This general principle was applied in a case where a voyage charter required the ship owners to nominate the performing vessel by a certain date. Staughton J held that being a time stipulation in a commercial contract the term would, in the interests of commercial certainty, be classified as a condition.[27]

INNOMINATE TERMS

The certainty and predictability of classifying terms as conditions and warranties is purchased at the cost of a lack of remedial flexibility. It is possible to conceive of many terms where one can say that some or most breaches will be serious ones. However, some breaches will be trivial and if one party is able to terminate a contract for a trivial breach he will choose to do so whenever the bargain turns out to be unprofitable for him. To remedy this situation the courts have developed a category of innominate terms where it is the effect of breach which may, or may not, justify termination.

In *Hong Kong Fir Shipping Ltd* v *Kawasaki Kisen Kaisha*[28] a ship was time chartered for two years. However, the ship's engines were prone to over-heating as were the crew members, particularly the ship's engineer who was an alcoholic. A delay of over two weeks resulted. This was undoubtedly a breach of the shipowner's express 'seaworthiness' clause under which the owner contracted to provide a ship 'in every way fitted for ordinary cargo service'. The Court of Appeal thought that this was an innominate or intermediate term, where the remedy to which its breach gives rise depends upon the effects of that breach. Diplock LJ proposed the following test. The

[26] [1981] 1 WLR 711.
[27] *The Mavro Vetranic* [1985] 1 Lloyd's Rep 586.
[28] [1962] 2 QB 26.

breach will justify termination if it is such that the innocent party is deprived[29] 'of substantially the whole benefit which it was intended that he should obtain from the charter'.

A different and maybe less generous test was proposed by Sellers LJ:[30]

> If what is done or not done in breach of the contractual obligation does not make the performance a totally different performance of the contract from that intended by the parties it is not so fundamental as to undermine the whole contract.

In *The Hansa Nord* a contract was entered for the sale of citrus pulp pellets to be shipped in good condition. Due to overheating, the goods deteriorated and were rejected by the buyer on arrival. The goods were sold by the court and were purchased by the buyer who used them as he had originally intended. The Court of Appeal held that the buyers were not justified in rejecting the cargo because the term breached was an innominate one and the breach insufficiently serious.

Terms may be classified as innominate terms when they do not fall within the categories of conditions considered above. Further, it seems that one of the statutory implied conditions that are imposed by the Supply of Goods and Services Act 1982 (s 13) into contracts for the provision of a service may also be an innominate term because the statute does not specify otherwise. Before leaving the topic of innominate terms, we will look at one case which illustrates the uncertainty which this approach causes.

In *The Hermosa*[31] the need to effect repairs to a ship arose from two causes: the ship was not seaworthy at the commencement of the charter and it was subsequently involved in a collision. The charterers claimed that they were entitled to terminate the charter for breach of the seaworthiness term. However, applying Lord Diplock's test from the *Hong Kong Fir* case, it was held that it was not possible to say that the charterers had thereby lost substantially the whole benefit of the charter. Therefore, not only were the charterers not entitled to treat their obligations at an end, but their unjustified act of doing so itself amounted to a breach of contract, which justified the other party in terminating it. It is clear that whenever a party must weigh up the seriousness of the other party's breach in order to ascertain his own rights, like all judgments of degree, it is a hard call with expensive consequences if you get it wrong.

---

[29] At pp. 70–1.
[30] At p. 57, Upjohn LJ agreeing.
[31] [1982] 1 Lloyd's Rep 570.

PART V

THE AFTERMATH

16

LITERAL PERFORMANCE

INTRODUCTION

Literal performance describes the group of remedies whereby a court orders a party to a contract to do the very thing he has undertaken to do. Where a positive obligation, other than one to pay a sum of money, is enforced, the appropriate remedy is specific performance; where a negative obligation is enforced, the appropriate remedy is an injunction. Where the obligation enforced is a primary[1] one to pay a sum of money, the action is one in debt.

SPECIFIC PERFORMANCE

Civil and common law jurisdictions are said respectively to award specific performance and damages as the primary remedy for breach of contract. There is some justification for the contrast but like any caricature it exaggerates the features of its subject. The account of the common law[2] fails accurately to represent the historical development of specific performance[3] and has not proved to be an accurate prediction of the more generous availability of specific performance in recent times. In German law it is 'of the very essence of an obligation'[4] that a promisee may demand a court order compelling the promisor to perform; it is regarded as so fundamental that it is not stated in any legislative text, although some provisions clearly assume it.[5] However, the principle is subject to a number of exceptions which 'in practice ... are far more important than the general rule'[6] and, even where available, promisees will bring such an action 'only when their

---

[1] Where the obligation to pay a sum of money is a contingent one which arises upon a breach of contract by the payer, the action is one for liquidated damages, considered in chapter 17.

[2] Often summarised by Holmes' famous statement that 'the only universal consequence of a legally binding promise is that the law makes the promisor pay damages if the promised act does not come to pass': (1881) *The Common Law*, p. 301. See also the views of Coke who inveighed against any incursion by the equitable remedy. See *Bromage* v *Genning* (1616) 1 Roll Rep 368.

[3] Certainly until the establishment in the late eighteenth century of the requirement that damages be inadequate.

[4] Zweigert and Kötz (1992) *An Introduction to Comparative Law* (translated by Weir), 2nd edn, p. 505.

[5] For example, the Civil Code, para 249.

[6] Treitel (1988) *Remedies for Breach of Contract: a Comparative Account*, p. 53.

interest in performance cannot easily be reckoned in money'.[7] In contrast, French law *explicitly* recognises the claim for performance of a contract[8] but in common with German law, a focus on the general rule can be misleading because courts enforce them 'in a very grudging way'.[9] Lord Hoffmann's prediction that civil and common law judges 'take much the same matters into account in deciding whether specific performance would be appropriate in a particular case'[10] would seem to be true.

Should specific performance be more widely available?

Restrictions upon the availability of specific performance are sometimes justified by reference to economic efficiency. Kronman argues that contractors would prefer to reserve their freedom of action to buy or sell elsewhere the contractual subject matter unless it is unique. In this way the common law merely provides a set of 'default rules' which the parties would otherwise have provided for themselves. Many economic arguments in favour of the common law position build upon the concept of efficient breach,[11] that the law should encourage breach of contract when this facilitates the movement of resources to more highly valued uses.[12] Some economists dispute these conclusions[13] on the basis that it is when a good has a unique quality that a rational transactor will be least prepared to accept a regime of enforced performance[14] or because the theory of efficient breach disadvantages the promisee by concluding that a breach is efficient upon the basis of a comparison between the value put on the performance of the original promisee at the time of *contracting* with that put upon it by the new promisee at the time of *breach*.[15]

The severe nature of the sanction available to enforce specific performance is often emphasised in non-economic arguments opposing any expansion in its availability. Disobedience of a court order is punishable by the imposition

---

[7] Zweigert and Kötz, *op. cit.*, p. 507.

[8] Code Civil, Art 1184, para 2 (general provision) and Art 1610 (sales contracts).

[9] Zweigert and Kötz *op. cit.*, p. 511.

[10] *Co-operative Insurance Society Ltd* v *Argyll Stores (Holdings) Ltd* [1997] 2 WLR 898 at 903 B–C.

[11] See also Birmingham (1970) 24 Rutgers LR 273; Goetz and Scott (1977) 77 Col LR 554; Shavell (1984) QJ Econ 121; Bishop (1985) 14 J Leg Stud 229; Posner (1992) *Economic Analysis of Law*. 4th edn, pp. 117–26 and 130–2.

[12] A contracts to supply 100 widgets to B for £200. C offers A £300 for the same widgets. A is unable to supply both buyers. If A breaches his contract with B in order to supply C, this may be called an 'efficient breach' because it moves resources to more highly valued uses, i.e. to C who is prepared to pay more for them.

[13] In *Butler* v *Countrywide Finance Co Ltd* [1993] 3 NZLR 623 Hammond J noted that the economic debate was far from conclusive but none the less thought that the relative efficiencies of possible remedies were a relevant factors for a court to consider.

[14] Because of the exaggerated effect of a change in demand upon the price of a unique good. See Schwartz (1979) 89 Yale LJ 271.

[15] MacNeil (1982) 68 Virg L Rev 947 and Harris (1983) 3 Inter Rev of Law and Econ 69.

of fines and ultimately imprisonment,[16] a power which is no longer available in respect of the failure to satisfy an award of damages.[17] In *Co-operative Insurance* v *Argyll Stores Ltd*,[18] Lord Hoffman said: 'The heavy-handed nature of the enforcement mechanism is a consideration, which may go to the exercise of the court's discretion ...'.

A party who is entitled to an order of specific performance is not subject to the general duty to mitigate loss.[19] If the avoidance of waste is a valid policy goal, this is a further argument against an expansion of the scope of specific performance.[20] A promisee who obtains a decree of specific performance, or is able to convince the promisor as to his entitlement to one, is in a very strong position and may be able to force an out-of-court settlement approaching the value to the promisor of being released from his obligation. Such compensation will be in excess of actual loss and therefore wasteful.[21]

Insolvency principles provide another argument against the wider availability of specific performance. Whenever the effect of an order for specific performance is to give to the claimant an equitable interest in the contractual subject matter,[22] he will thereby gain unjustified priority over other creditors.

Those who favour an expansion of the jurisdiction to grant specific performance often emphasise the sanctity of promise and the role of contract law in protecting the expectation interest.[23] Some also stress the historical accident that caused the equitable jurisdiction to grow up as a supplement to that of the common law.[24]

The recent impetus[25] in this country to expand the ambit of the remedy of specific performance does not derive from any philosophical premise. Rather it reflects a lack of any coherent justification for some of the older

---

16 *Bromage* v *Genning* (1616) 1 Roll Rep 268. If the decree was disobeyed, 'there is no other remedy than imprisoning his body'.

17 See Debtor's Act 1869, ss 4–5 and the Administration of Justice Act 1970, s 11.

18 [1997] 2 WLR 898 at 904 A.

19 *Buxton* v *Lister* (1746) 3 Atk 383 at 384 and *Re Schwabacher* (1908) 98 LT 127.

20 Or any other type of literal enforcement, such as the action in debt. See *White & Carter (Councils)* v *McGregor* [1961] 3 All ER 1178 *per* Lords Morton and Keith dissenting at pp. 1184 C–E and 1188 H–1189 C respectively.

21 See Lord Hoffmann in *Co-operative Insurance Society Ltd* v *Argyll Stores (Holdings) Ltd* [1997] 2 WLR 898 at 906c–d.

22 This will not always be the case according to *Tailby* v *Official Receiver* (1888) 13 App Cas 523 at 548 and *Re London Wine Co (Shippers)* [1986] PCC 121 at 149.

23 This approach is conveniently summarised by Waddams (1993) *The Law of Contracts*. 3rd edn, pp. 459–60: 'From the point of view of protecting the expectation of the promisee, the form of remedy that springs first to mind, where a promise has been broken, is an order directed to the promisor to perform what was promised ...'
  Cf. Charles Fried (1981) *Contract as Promise* who finds the moral obligation to perform a promise in a respect for the autonomy and trust of individual but who does not think that this principle requires the promotion of specific performance as the primary remedy available for breach of contract.

24 *Van Camp Chocolates Ltd* v *Auslebrooks Ltd* [1984] 1 NZLR 354; *Day* v *Mead* [1987] 2 NZLR 443; *Newmans Tours Ltd* v *Ranier Investments Ltd* [1992] 2 NZLR 68 at 96. See generally Burrows, Finn and Todd (1997) *Law of Contract in New Zealand*, pp. 772–3.

25 To which the decision in *Co-operative Insurance Society Ltd* v *Argyll Stores (Holdings) Ltd* [1997] 2 WLR 898 may have called a (temporary?) halt.

restrictions on its availability and a desire to correct iniquities caused by other restrictive contract doctrines such as privity.[26]

What the parties want

It is open to the parties to include a contractual clause providing that specific performance or an injunction should be available to the innocent party in the event of a breach of the agreement. Courts are usually hostile to any attempt to limit their remedial discretion[27] and it has been said that '... parties cannot contract themselves out of the law...'.[28] However, it has been argued[29] that the reasons supporting this approach elsewhere do not apply with the same force in this context and the issue awaits authoritative judicial discussion.

History

Specific performance grew out of petitions to the Chancellor in his Court in Chancery to require someone to do the very thing he had promised. The remedy is an equitable one which is available at the discretion of the court.[30] This discretion is exercised to deny the remedy when certain 'bars' arise, most importantly when damages are an adequate remedy.

Restrictions

A party who seeks specific performance is asking the court to enforce a contract. It follows that the remedy cannot be granted if no contract comes into existence (often, but misleadingly, described as a 'void' contract) or if the contract was liable to be set aside (i.e. 'voidable') and has been set aside.

There are several restrictions or 'bars' upon the availability of specific performance. The most important of these is the principle that specific performance will not be granted if an award of damages would be an adequate remedy.

Damages are an adequate remedy

Running through the cases is the question whether an award of money would permit the recipient to purchase a satisfactory substitute, which is in turn often expressed in terms of the 'uniqueness' of the contractual subject matter.

---

[26] See *Beswick* v *Beswick* [1968] AC 58.
[27] See later in this chapter.
[28] *Warner Bros Pictures Inc* v *Nelson* [1937] 1 KB 209 at 221 *per* Branson J. See also *Quadrant Visual Communications Ltd* v *Hutchinson Telephone (UK) Ltd* [1993] BCLC 442.
[29] Burrows (*Remedies*), at p. 381 points out that unlike a penalty clause it cannot be regarded as unconscionable or unfair to stipulate for actual performance. *Cf.* Sharpe (1992) *Injunctions and Specific Performance*. 2nd edn, paras 7.710–7.810.
[30] *Lamare* v *Dixon* (1873) LR 6 HL 414 at 423 *per* Lord Chelmsford.

Land

Historically, most petitioners sought specific performance of contracts to sell land. The courts will not, on the ground that damages would be an adequate remedy, refuse to grant specific performance of a contract to sell or grant an interest in land. Over time this became a proposition of law, justified by reference to the particular value to a purchaser of a unique plot of land.[31] The grant of specific performance of contracts for the sale of land is now commonplace, absent any reference to the circumstances of the individual case to demonstrate the inadequacy of a monetary remedy (e.g. that the purchaser's lover lives next door).[32] In this country the routine award of specific performance for contracts for the sale of land is now so dissociated from the requirement that damages are inadequate that it will be granted in respect of a modest flat in a block of identical properties many of which are for sale[33] and will ignore the fact that the property is purchased for immediate resale.[34]

The vendor of land has a reciprocal[35] claim to specific performance[36] despite the only obligation owed to him being payment of money. Again, the law rests on a generalised presumption that damages are not an adequate remedy, absent any need to justify the presumption by reference to the facts of the case. One effect of the entitlement to specific performance is that he is not subject to any obligation to mitigate his loss by finding a substitute purchaser.

Goods

In a number of old cases[37] the Court of Chancery was willing to order the delivery[38] of a chattel[39] where the item possessed special qualities[40] and

---

[31] *Sudbrook Trading Estate Ltd* v *Eggleton* [1983] 1 AC 448 at 478 *per* Lord Diplock.

[32] The excess value a particular party would place on a property above the market price is sometimes termed the 'consumer surplus' by economists. See Harris, Ogus and Phillips (1979) 95 LQR 581.

[33] *Cf. Centrex Homes Corp* v *Boag* (1974) 320 A 2d 194 (refusal of specific performance to a *developer* offering many identical flats for sale).

[34] *Cf.* the approach of some Canadian courts discussed by Sharpe, *op. cit.* (n. 29 above), paras 8.4–8.5.

[35] This symmetry of remedies is called 'affirmative' mutuality by Sharpe, *ibid.*, paras 7.820–7.880. See below for an examination of mutuality as an independent bar to rescission.

[36] *Adderley* v *Dixon* (1824) 1 Sim & St 607; *Eastern Counties Railway Co* v *Hawkes* (1855) 5 HLC 331.

[37] Collected by Burrows, *op. cit.* at p. 454 and Jones and Goodheart (1996) *Specific Performance.* 2nd edn, pp. 143–4.

[38] Not strictly actions for specific performance of a contract but actions for the 'delivery up' of goods where the defendant is committing a tort (conversion or trespass to goods) by interfering with them.

[39] For example, *Pusey* v *Pusey* (1684) 1 Vern 273 (an old horn); *Somerset* v *Cookson* (1735) 3 P Wms 390 (a religious artefact); *Lowther* v *Lowther* (1806) 13 Ves 95 (a Titian painting); *Earl of Macclesfield* v *Davies* (1814) 3 Ves & B 16 (conditional order if an old chest contained certain heirlooms); *Thorn* v *Public Works Commissioners* (1863) 32 Beav 490 (stonework from the old Westminster bridge).

[40] *Falcke* v *Gray* (1859) 4 Drew 651 at 658 *per* Kindersley VC (specific performance refused on other grounds).

therefore financial compensation was inadequate.[41] It might have been expected that s 52 of the Sale of Goods Act 1893 would increase the availability of specific performance in relation to contracts for the sale of goods. The current provision is contained in s 52, Sale of Goods Act 1979, which gives the court a discretion to award specific performance in favour of the buyer of 'specific or ascertained goods', but the old requirement of uniqueness continues to apply. In *Behnke* v *Bede*[42] specific performance was granted of a contract to sell a ship which was 'of peculiar and practically unique value to the [claimant]'[43] because being built in the nineteenth century the ship was inexpensive but none the less fitted with engines satisfying German regulations and so enabling the claimant to register the vessel in his home country. The requirement of damages being an adequate remedy has been applied strictly in a number of cases where specific enforcement has been refused, most notably *Société des Industries Métallurgiques SA* v *The Bronx Engineering Co Ltd*[44] in respect of the sale of a 'Bronx combined driver and pull through slitting machine, a Bronx stop/start cut to line' complete with 'flying shear' which in total weighed 220 tons and took 9–12 months to manufacture. In *The Stena Nautica (No. 2)*,[45] Parker J refused specific performance of a contract to sell a ship on the ground that the ship was insufficiently distinctive. To obtain the remedy it would be necessary to show that the design was specifically suited to the claimant's needs.

Certain analogies with the specific enforcement of contracts concerned solely with the sale of goods would seem to support a more generous exercise of the discretion than is suggested in the cases considered above. Apart from the cases already considered ordering delivery up following the wrongful detention of a chattel, contracts for the sale of goods which are associated with the sale of land will be enforced by specific performance of the obligation to deliver the house contents.[46] In addition, in contracts for the sale of shares specific performance is the rule unless the shares are freely available on the market.[47] There are cases where specific performance has been ordered of obligations pertaining to, but not for the sale of, goods.[48]

---

[41] A man should not be 'liable to the estimate of people, who have not his feelings': *Fells* v *Read* (1796) 3 Ves 70 at 71–2 *per* Lord Loughborough LC and *Nutbrown* v *Thornton* (1804) 10 Ves 159 at 163 *per* Lord Eldon LC.

[42] [1927] 1 KB 649.

[43] *Ibid.* at p. 661 *per* Wright J. There was evidence that there was only one comparable ship which might have been sold.

[44] [1975] 1 Lloyd's Rep 464.

[45] *CN Marine Inc* v *Stena Line A/B and Reige voor Maritem Transport* [1982] 2 Lloyd's Rep 336.

[46] *Phillips* v *Lamdin* [1949] 2 KB 33 and *Record* v *Bell* [1991] 1 WLR 863. *Cf. Butler* v *Countrywide Finance Ltd* [1993] 3 NZLR 623 (sale of contents of commercial premises where specific performance was refused on the ground that it was impractical to require the defendant to replace the large number of damaged and missing items).

[47] *J Sainsbury plc* v *O'Connor (Inspector of Taxes)* [1991] 1 WLR 963 at 971–2 *per* Lloyd LJ.

[48] *Lingen* v *Simpson* (1824) 1 Sim & St 600 (contract ending a partnership required a former partner to make available for copying a book of patterns) and *Bristol Airport plc* v *Powdrill* [1990] Ch 744 at 759 *per* Browne-Wilkinson VC (lease of an aircraft can be specifically enforced).

An expansion of the jurisdiction occurred in *Sky Petroleum v VIP Petrol Ltd*[49] where specific performance was effectively[50] granted to oblige the defendants to continue to supply fuel to the claimants' petrol stations. At the time the market for petrol was in turmoil and there was evidence that the claimants would 'have no great prospect of finding any alternative source of supply'.[51] This case supports a broader view of uniqueness[52] which takes account of commercial reality by emphasising *practical* unavailability rather than the non-existence of substitutes.[53] This approach is supported by an old authority[54] and subsequent *dicta* discussing the availability of specific performance[55] and the analogous remedy of 'delivery up'.[56] It is also supported by the Uniform Commercial Code[57] and Australian[58] and Canadian[59] case law, although in his short judgment in *Sky Petroleum* Goulding J did not refer in to any such authorities. The case is also good authority for the proposition that specific performance is available for goods falling outside the Sale of Goods Act, s 52,[60] since the goods were not 'specific or ascertained'.

Building contracts[61]
It is often said that there is a general rule that specific performance is not

---

[49] [1974] 1 WLR 576.

[50] In fact, the action was for an interlocutory injunction to prevent the defendants from ceasing to supply fuel but Goulding J said at p. 578: 'The matter is one of substance and not of form ... it is ... quite plain that I am, for the time being, specifically enforcing the contract if I grant an injunction.'

[51] *Ibid.*, p. 578 H and C respectively.

[52] Treitel (10th edn) at p. 952 uses the phrase 'commercial uniqueness'.

[53] *Cf.* economic duress where compulsion may be established by proving that the victim of the pressure had no other practical choice. *Astley* v *Reynolds* (1731) 2 Str 915 at 916 (nothing else 'would ... do his business') and *Eadie* v *Township of Brantford* (1967) 63 DLR (2d) 561 at 570 *per* Spence J, who, in reply to a submission from counsel that in order to recover money paid the claimant must have been faced with a situation where no other choice was open to him, said that 'a practical compulsion alone is necessary'.

[54] *Taylor* v *Neville*, cited in *Buxton* v *Lister* (1746) 3 Ark 383.

[55] *The Oro Chief* [1983] 2 Lloyd's Rep 509 at 521 *per* Staughton J, who said that a presumptive case for the award of specific performance would be made out if the goods were not 'readily' available elsewhere.

[56] *Howard E Perry & Co* v *British Railways Board* [1980] 1 WLR 1375 at 1383 *per* Megarry VC (delivery up ordered of a strike bound quantity of steel to avert the owner having to lay off staff and lose custom and risk possible insolvency).

[57] The comment to para 2-716(1) states that 'The test of uniqueness must be made in terms of the total situation, which characterises the contract.' This section was applied to a fuel supply contract in *Eastern Airlines Inc* v *Gulf Oil Corp* (1975) 19 UCC Rep 721.

[58] *Dougan* v *Ley* (1946) 71 CLR 142 (specific performance of sale of licensed taxi cab where there were restrictions on the number of licences and their transfer). See also *Aristoc Industries Pty Ltd* v *R A Wenham (Builders) Pty Ltd* [1965] NSWR 581.

[59] *Fuller* v *Richmond* (1850) 2 Gr 24 and 4 Gr 657 and *Stevenson* v *Clarke* (1853) 4 Gr 540.

[60] *Cf.* Atkin LJ's comments in *Re Wait* [1927] 1 Ch 606, *Leigh and Sillivan Ltd* v *Aliakmon Shipping Co Ltd* (1986) 2 WLR 902 and *Re London Wine Co (Shippers)* [1986] PCC 121.

[61] *Cf.* covenants contained in leases to build or repair the premises. A landlord's covenant to repair may be specifically enforceable at common law, *Jeune* v *Queens Cross Properties Ltd* [1974] Ch 97 or under Landlord and Tenant Act 1985, s 17 'notwithstanding any equitable rule restricting the scope of the remedy'. A lessee's covenant to build or rebuild premises has been held capable of specific performance: *City of London* v *Nash* (1747) 3 Atk 512, but not a covenant to repair, see *Hill* v *Barclays* (1810) 16 Ves 402.

available to enforce a building contract.[62] This is justified by reference to the adequacy of damages,[63] the difficulty of formulating the order if the contract is too vague[64] and the objections that the courts will be unable to properly supervise the order[65] or that building contracts are analogous to contracts for personal services.[66] The courts have now departed from the general principle so many times that it is inappropriate to rely on it.[67] However, in *Co-operative Insurance v Argyll Stores Ltd*[68] Lord Hoffman drew a distinction between 'orders to carry on activities and to achieve results'. It is still meaningful to speak of a general prohibition on specific performance in the former category but not the latter.

The Court of Appeal[69] has held that specific performance is available if three conditions are satisfied. First, the building work must be sufficiently defined by the contract to enable a workable order to be formulated.[70] Second, damages must be an inadequate remedy.[71] Third, the defendant must be in possession of the land upon which the work is to take place. Where specific performance is sought by the contractor to enable him to complete the contract work, the courts have frequently refused to grant specific performance or an equivalent injunction requiring the employer not to interfere with the work of the contractor.[72] In *Hounslow London Borough Council v Twickenham Garden Developments Ltd*[73] Megarry J controversially[74] suggested that specific performance might be available to a contractor.[75]

Contracts to carry on a business

In *Co-operative Insurance v Argyll Stores Ltd*[76] the House of Lords reversed the Court of Appeal's decision, which had departed from previous authorities in granting specific performance of a covenant contained in a

---

[62] *Flint v Brandon* (1808) 3 Ves 159; *Merchant's Trading Co v Banner* (1871) LR 12 Eq 18; *Cubitt v Smith* (1864) 11 LT 298; *Wilkinson v Clements* (1872) 8 Ch App 96.

[63] *Ryan v Mutual Tontine Westminster Chambers Association* [1893] 1 Ch 116 at 128 *per* Kay LJ.

[64] *Wolverhampton Corporation v Emmons* [1901] 1 QB 515 at 524 *per* Collins LJ.

[65] *Blackett v Bates* (1865) 1 Ch App 117.

[66] *Johnson v Shrewsbury and Birmingham Rly Co* (1853) 22 LJ Ch 921 at 924 *per* Knight Bruce LJ and 925–6 *per* Kay LJ.

[67] Jones and Goodhart, *op. cit.* (n. 37 herein above), p. 184.

[68] [1997] 2 WLR 898 at 904.

[69] *Wolverhampton Corporation v Emmons* [1901] 1 QB 515 and *Carpenters Estates Ltd v Emmons* [1940] Ch 160.

[70] *Tito v Waddell (No. 2)* [1977] Ch 106 at 322 *per* Megarry VC.

[71] *Molyneux v Richard* [1906] 1 Ch at 43–6. It is perhaps significant that the claimant was a local authority seeking to improve living conditions in its area. However, the inadequacy of damages might also be caused by the defendant's possession of the land, which may prevent the claimant from retaining another builder.

[72] *Munro v Wivenhoe and Brightlingsea Rly Co* (1864) 12 LT 654 and *Cork Corp v Rooney* (1881) 7 LR Ir 191.

[73] [1971] Ch. 233.

[74] It has not been followed elsewhere. See *Mayfield Holdings Ltd v Moana Reef Ltd* [1973] 1 NZLR 309 and *Graham H Roberts Pty Ltd v Maurbeth Investments Pty Ltd* [1974] 1 NSWLR 93.

[75] *Ibid.*, p. 251.

[76] [1997] 2 WLR 898. *Cf. Highland and Universal Properties Ltd v Safeway Properties Ltd* [2000] SLT 414 (the 'keep open' covenant was specifically enforced under Scottish law).

35-year lease of a supermarket requiring the store (the largest in a shopping centre and so a 'draw' for other shops) to remain open during local business hours. The House of Lords refused to grant specific performance on several grounds, namely that damages would be adequate to compensate for the breach of such a covenant,[77] the need for constant supervision[78] and the danger that an order for specific performance might allow the defendant to enrich himself at the claimant's expense.[79]

This decision gives insufficient weight to commercial realities and established principle. The nature of a shopping centre development is that certain 'lead' businesses are able to negotiate very favourable terms because of their value to the lessor in attracting custom to other smaller units. When considering an application for specific performance the courts have often been persuaded to grant the remedy in cases where a defendant has already derived a benefit from the partial performance of a contract.[80] It is possible that this line of cases may be applied to the 'benefit' derived by a business such as the supermarket in the *Argyll* case, to support a claim to specific performance.

Constant supervision

Specific performance is inapplicable when the continued supervision of the court is necessary to ensure the fulfilment of the contract. In a number of cases specific performance has been refused on this basis[81] sometimes operating singly and sometimes in combination with other reasons for denying an order. In a series of cases a number of judges, particularly Megarry J, questioned the force of this bar to specific performance.[82]

In *Co-operative Insurance v Argyll Stores Ltd*[83] Lord Hoffman[84] disagreed as a matter of principle and authority with the approach taken by Megarry J and declared that properly understood 'arguments based upon difficulty of supervision remain powerful'. Lord Hoffmann stated that the rationale behind the constant supervision bar has frequently been misunderstood.

---

[77] *Ibid.*, p. 903.
[78] Understood as the risk that recourse would be had to the court on several occasions to ensure compliance with the order.
[79] By permitting the claimant to 'extract' from a defendant as the cost of not enforcing the injunction an amount up to the value to the defendant of being released from the continuing obligation. If the claimant is an effective bargainer, this may exceed the claimant's loss.
[80] *Sanderson v Cockermouth and Workington Rly Co* (1842) 2 Y & C Ch Cas 48 and *Hart v Hart* (1881) 18 Ch D 670 at 685.
[81] *Pollard v Clayton* (1855) 1 K & J 462 (contract to mine) and *De Mattos v Gibson* (1858) 4 D & J 276 (voyage charter). *Cf. The Scaptrade* [1983] 2 AC 694 at 700–1 (time charter); *Blackett v Bates* (1865) 1 Ch App 117 (building contract); *Dominion Coal Co Ltd v Dominion Iron and Steel Co Ltd* [1909] AC 293 (coal requirements contract); *Dowty Boulton Paul Ltd v Wolverhampton Corp* [1971] 1 WLR 204 (contract to keep an airfield open).
[82] *CH Giles & Co v Morris* [1972] 1 WLR 307 at 318. *Tito v Waddell (No. 2)* [1977] Ch 106 at 321–3 and *Posner v Scott-Lewis* [1987] Ch 25.
[83] [1997] 2 WLR 898 at 907.
[84] With whose judgment the other members of the House agreed.

Properly construed it refers to 'the possibility of the court having to give an indefinite series of ... rulings in order to ensure execution of the order',[85] which is more likely where the obligation sought to be enforced is, as in the instant case of a covenant to operate a supermarket, one to carry on an activity rather than to produce a result. It is this latter distinction which is said to justify the exceptional specific performance of building contracts and repairing covenants.

Contracts of personal service

It has frequently been held that specific performance,[86] or other equivalent relief,[87] will not be granted to enforce contracts involving personal service; to hold otherwise would be to create 'contracts of slavery'.[88] Other arguments are that employers should not have an unwelcome employee thrust upon them;[89] that once trust and confidence is lost between the parties, it is useless to continue the relationship;[90] and that in many such contracts it will be difficult to draft an effective order,[91] which might in turn necessitate frequent reference to the court.[92]

This bar will only apply when the service is one of a personal nature. This means that some contracts involving the provision of a service may be specifically enforced.[93] In addition, a distinction is drawn between an order to specifically enforce a contract for services and an order to execute one, although the former will not be granted the latter may be.[94]

For employees, the refusal of the common law to grant specific performance is now enshrined in statute. The Trade Union and Labour Relations (Consolidation) Act 1992, s 236 provides:

No court shall, whether by way of –

(a)   an order for specific performance ... of a contract of employment, or

---

85   *Ibid.*, p. 903.
86   *Clark v Price* (1819) 2 Wils Ch 157; *Brett v East India Shipping Co* (1864) 2 H & C 404; *Byrne v Australian Airlines Ltd* (1995) 131 ALR 422 at 432.
87   *Taylor v NUS* [1967] 1 WLR 532 (declaration); *Page One Records v Britton* [1968] 1 WLR 157 (injunction).
88   *De Francesco v Barnum* (1890) 45 Ch D 430 at 438 *per* Fry LJ and *Emerald Resources Ltd v Sterling Oil Properties Management Ltd* (1969) 3 DLR (3d) 630 at 647 *per* Allen JA.
89   *Johnson v Shrewsbury and Birmingham Rly Co* (1853) 22 LJ Ch 921 at 926 *per* Knight Bruce LJ and *Alexander v Standard Telephones and Cables plc* [1990] IRLR 55.
90   *Warren v Mendy* [1989] IRLR 210.
91   *CH Giles & Co v Morris* [1972] 1 WLR 307 at 318 *per* Megarry J.
92   *Blackett v Bates* (1865) 1 Ch App 117 at 125 *per* Lord Cranworth LC and *Ryan v Mutual Tontine Westminster Chambers Association* [1893] 1 Ch 116. *Cf.* '... the prospects of repetition, although an important consideration, ought not to be allowed to negative a right' *per* Megarry J in *CH Giles & Co v Morris* [1972] 1 WLR 307.
93   For example, *Barrow v Cappell & Co* [1976] RPC 355 (decided in 1951!) (contract to publish music).
94   In *C H Giles & Co v Morris* [1972] 1 WLR 307 at 316, Megarry J said: 'The distinction between an order to perform a contract for services and an order to procure the execution of such a contract seems to me to be sound both in principle and authority.'

(b) an injunction ... restraining a breach or threatened breach of contract, compel an employee to do any work or attend at any place for the doing of any work.

In contrast, the employer's ability to resist an order of specific performance is subject to a number of exceptions and qualifications deriving from the common law and statute as well as the incursion of public law principles.[95] Modern industrial conditions do not always reflect explanations of the bar to specific performance. The relationship of a large employer and his employee may not be as intimate as that which some of the objections to specific performance assume. Indeed, modern unfair dismissal legislation[96] provides for a remedy of reinstatement and re-engagement.[97] Industrial relations often extend beyond a bi-partite relation and so the law must take account of the actions of third parties such as trade unions. Where an employee is dismissed as a result of pressure applied by a trade union,[98] the traditional objection to specific performance based upon the breakdown of trust and confidence between employer and employee may be irrelevant where an employee seeks only a technical continuance of the employment relationship in order to allow him to utilise a contractual disciplinary procedure rather than to permit him to resume work.[99] In view of these developments, it is perhaps more accurate to speak in terms of a 'strong reluctance' rather than a 'rule' against specific performance.[100]

Severe hardship

Specific performance may be refused when it would cause severe hardship to the defendant, such as effectively requiring him to bring legal proceedings against a third party which might prove unsuccessful or be disruptive to family relations.[101] Severe hardship to third parties will sometimes be taken into account.[102] An analogous principle is used to justify the refusal of specific

---

[95] For example, relief amounting to specific performance was granted in *Hill v CA Parsons Ltd* [1972] Ch 305 (employee dismissed for refusing to join trade union when employer entered closed shop agreement) and *Irani v SW Hamps AHA* [1985] IRLR 203 (employee dismissed because of irreconcilable differences with senior colleague).

[96] See now Employment Rights Act 1996, ss 113–17, replacing the Employment Protection (Consolidation) Act 1978.

[97] Though ultimately non-compliance with such an order will only result in a financial penalty.

[98] For example, because he refused to join a trade union as in *Hill v CA Parsons Ltd* [1972] Ch 305. Such an employee has had the benefit of statutory protection since 1971.

[99] *Robb v London Borough of Hammersmith and Fulham* [1991] IRLR 72. See also the *Hill* and *Irani* cases considered above (n. 95) where it was a condition of the court's order that the claimant should not actually attend for work.

[100] *Ibid.*

[101] *Wroth v Tyler* [1974] Ch 30 (defendant contracted to sell property but could only give vacant possession if he took legal proceedings against his wife which would not necessarily succeed). *Cf. Walters v Roberts* (1980) 41 P & CR 210 (specific performance granted against a seller who could easily obtain possession from the occupier).

[102] *Thomas v Dering* (1837) 1 Keen 729 at 747–8; *Hartlepool Gas and Water Co v West Hartlepool Harbour and Rly Co* (1865) 12 LT 366 (an injunction case); *Bugler v McManaway* [1963] NZLR 427; *Jacob v Bills* [1967] NZLR 249; *Butler v Countrywide Finance Ltd* [1993] 3 NZLR 623.

performance when the cost of performance is of a different magnitude to the benefit to be derived from that performance by the claimant.[103] However, the courts have reiterated many times that this bar provides no escape for a defendant who has merely made a bad bargain,[104] such as agreeing to sell property at a time when the market is rising.[105] The court is prepared to take account of severe hardship which arises after the contract was entered[106] and for which the claimant bears no responsibility.[107]

Conduct and inaction of the claimant

There is an equitable maxim[108] that *he who comes to equity must come with clean hands*. This has been held to justify the refusal of specific performance where the purchase price of a business was dictated by the number of customers on completion and the vendor failed to fully disclose that he had inflated the number of customers by giving away free goods.[109]

The doctrine of 'laches' affords a defence where it would be unjust to grant the claimant a remedy because of delay in asserting his rights. Delay is not enough of itself, rather the delay must have the effect of making it unjust to award the remedy sought.

Absence of mutuality

A distinction may be drawn between positive and negative mutuality.[110] Positive mutuality refers to a claimant's entitlement to specific performance on the basis that it could have been ordered against him.[111] Negative

---

[103] *Tito v Waddell (No. 2)* [1977] Ch 106 at 326 (cost of reinstating land after the completion of mining out of all proportion to the benefit to the former inhabitants of the mined land) and *Markholm Construction Co Ltd v Wellington City Council* [1985] 2 NZLR 520 (specific enforcement of ballot arrangements with over 240 applicants involved huge cost compared to the benefit accruing to the claimant).

[104] 'A [claimant] should not, of course, be deprived of relief to which he is justly entitled merely because it will be disadvantageous to the defendant', *per* Buckley J at p. 730 in *Charrington v Simons & Co Ltd* [1970] 1 WLR 725 (mandatory injunction case). See also *Francis v Cowcliffe* (1976) 33 P & CR 368 (impecunious claimant) and *O'Neil v Arnew* (1976) 78 DLR (3d) 671 *per* Krever J.

[105] *Mountford v Scott* [1975] Ch 258. *Cf. Mok v Mao* [1995] DCR 845 (time given to find alternative accommodation).

[106] See also *Hewett v Court* (1983) 149 CLR 639 at 664. In *Jaggard v Sawyer* [1995] 1 WLR 269 (an injunction case) Sir Thomas Bingham MR said at p. 283 B that 'the test is one of oppression … [which] must be judged as at the date the court is asked to grant an injunction …'.

[107] *Patel v Ali* [1984] Ch 283 (specific performance refused of contract to sell house after long delay for which neither party was responsible during which vendor became disabled and so dependent upon local help).

[108] There is another which states that *he who seeks equity must do equity*.

[109] *Quadrant Visual Communications Ltd v Hutchinson Telephone (UK) Ltd* [1993] BCLC 442.

[110] See *Corbin on Contracts*, vol. 5A, para 1178.

[111] So-called positive mutuality is said to justify the award of specific performance to a *vendor* of land in respect of the buyer's promise to pay the purchase price. The principle based upon an intuitively appealing remedial symmetry appearance is to be specious and no convincing argument of substance has been put to support it. See generally Corbin (*ibid.*) who typically points out the logical incompatibility of the two aspects of the rule.

mutuality is more frequently referred to by the courts and refers to the refusal of specific performance on the basis that it would not be available to the defendant.

Negative mutuality was considered by the Court of Appeal in *Price* v *Strange*.[112] The case concerned an agreement whereby a tenant promised to effect repairs in exchange for the lessor's promise to grant a new under-lease. The tenant did half the repairs but was prevented from completing them by the head lessor who finished the works. The Court of Appeal granted the tenant specific performance of the lessor's promise to grant a new lease and thereby dismissed the lessor's objection that the remedy should not be available because she could not have obtained specific performance of the tenant's promise to effect repairs.

Expectation longstop

Specific performance will not be granted in such a way as to put the claimant in a better position than he would have been in had there been no breach of contract. On this basis specific performance has been granted to a purchaser of shares subject to the condition that the seller receive interest from the date when the shares should have been transferred until payment is received.[113] In this way the claimant is not placed in a better position, by taking any increase in the value of the shares at the same time as enjoying the use of the purchase monies, than he would have been in if the defendant had performed his obligation promptly.

INJUNCTION

The appropriate remedy to compel the performance of a contract, or a clause within a contract, which imposes an obligation *not* to do or permit something, is by means of an injunction. The negative obligation in respect of which the claimant seeks injunctive relief will usually be express. The courts will seek to ensure that injunctive relief will not amount to indirect specific performance, in circumstances where one of the limits upon the availability of that remedy would apply. Contracts for the provision of services often contain an express negative promise by an employee not to work elsewhere. One of the major limits upon the availability of specific performance is that it will be refused in respect of a contract for personal services. The court must satisfy itself that the remedy sought will not indirectly 'force' the employee to perform the positive obligation assumed under the remainder of the contract, since otherwise it will offend against the general principle that specific performance is not available for contracts for personal services.

An injunction may be sought to enforce only part of the negative

---

[112] [1978] Ch 337.
[113] *Harvela Investments Ltd* v *Royal Trust Co of Canada Ltd* [1985] 2 All ER 966.

obligation undertaken. Severance may permit the claimant to avoid the objection that he is seeking indirect specific performance of an obligation which is unsuited to the grant of that remedy. In *Warner Bros v Nelson*[114] the defendant undertook not to act for third parties or 'to engage in any other occupation'. The claimant would have failed if it had sought an injunction to restrain her from any remunerative employment,[115] but was able to succeed in injuncting her from acting for third parties.

It might be objected that there is an air of unreality to the court's statement that the injunction would not force her to perform her contract with the claimant because she could undertake other work in a different capacity.[116] More recent cases have emphasised the reasonableness of the alternatives available to the defendant if the injunction is granted. In two cases concerning long-term management contracts entered by a musician[117] and a sportsman[118] injunctions were refused,[119] where the practical effect of the remedy would be to force the client to make use of the original manager.[120] It is suggested that the move away from the 'starvation test' whereby an injunction will be refused only if its grant would confront the defendant with a choice between the performance of his contract with the claimant or starvation[121] is to be welcomed. In determining the reasonableness of the other options open to the defendant it seems likely that regard should be taken of the duration of the injunction[122] and the preparedness of the claimant to continue to pay salary throughout the period of restraint.[123] The nature of the professions where such contractual restraints are often used is that current reputation is very important.[124] Therefore, an employer's offer to continue paying the defendant's salary will be insufficient if during the period of restraint his reputation and long-term prospects would be seriously harmed.

---

[114] [1937] 1 KB 209.

[115] See also *William Robinson & Co Ltd v Heuer* [1898] 2 Ch 217.

[116] *Warner Bros Pictures v Nelson* [1937] 1 KB 209 at 217.

[117] *Page One Records Ltd v Britton* [1968] 1 WLR 157.

[118] *Warren v Mendy* [1989] 1 WLR 853.

[119] In the latter case directed at a third party with whom the defendant had subsequently entered a management contract.

[120] See also *Heine Bros (Aust) Pty Ltd v Forrest* [1963] VR 383. Older authority concerning so-called 'output' contracts whereby the total output of a specified source is purchased seem to apply a test which looks to the practical consequences of granting an injunction. See *Fothergill v Rowland* (1873) LR 17 Eq 132 (contract to sell all coal mined from a particular seam).

[121] *Warner Bros Pictures Inc v Nelson* [1937] 1 KB 209 at 216.

[122] Compare *Lumley v Wagner* (1852) 1 De GF & J 604 (three months' duration, two unexpired at the time the injunction was sought) with *Ehrman v Bartholomew* [1898] 1 Ch 671 (salesman promised firm not to be involved in any other business for ten years – injunction refused) and the long-term management contracts in *Page One Records* and *Warren v Mendy*.

[123] *Evening Standard v Henderson* [1987] ICR 588 (reporter gave two rather than 12 months' notice – employer agreed to pay full salary and to let him work if he desired).

[124] *Cf. Thomas Borthwick & Sons (Australasia) Ltd v South Otago Freezing Co Ltd* [1978] 1 NZLR 538 (injunction granted in respect of promise not to process frozen food for third parties because the machinery for the enforcement of the obligation was routine and the personnel involved would not be affected by the litigation).

ACTION IN DEBT

An action in debt is an action to recover an agreed sum. Like an action for damages, it is an action to recover a financial sum.[125] However, it is considered in this chapter because, like an action for specific performance, it is the court's direction that a party to a contract should do the very thing he has undertaken to do. Despite this relationship with specific performance, the action in debt is more widely available. It is available as of right rather than at the discretion of the court. Therefore, it is not subject to the various bars that limit the availability of specific performance. A further important difference is that a simpler and expedited process can be used to recover a debt. If a defendant fails to answer a claim for a debt judgment may be entered immediately without the need for further enquiry.

In essence, an action in debt will become available as soon as the debt has 'accrued', i.e. arisen. In a contract for the sale of goods where the price becomes payable 'on a day certain irrespective of delivery', the seller may thereafter bring an action to recover the price of the goods.[126] A party will usually bring an action for the price when he has tendered his own contractual performance and received nothing in return. This is reflected in the Sale of Goods Act 1979 s 49(1) which allows the seller to sue for the price of goods when property in the goods has passed to a buyer who then refuses to pay for them.

In the usual case the seller of goods would not become aware of the buyer's intention to default upon payment until it happened. A more difficult problem arises when, before the time for performance comes about, the promisor indicates that he intends to default.[127] Should the innocent party be allowed to continue with the contract, tender his own performance and then sue for the price? Or should the innocent party be 'compelled' to 'accept' the breach by being limited to an action for damages? The facts of *The Puerto Buitrago*[128] illustrate the importance to the parties of the answer to these questions. The case involved a time charter under which the charterer undertook to redeliver the ship in the same condition in which it was received 'wear and tear excepted'. During the currency of the charter the vessel developed engine problems which would cost $2 million to rectify. However, when repaired the ship would only be worth $1m. Should the shipowner be entitled to hold the ship available for the charterter and insist on payment of hire and the repair costs? Or should the shipowner be

---

125 On the relationship between debt and damages see *Jervis* v *Harris* [1996] 1 All ER 303 (action by landlord to recover cost of repairs undertaken, which tenant, in breach of covenant, failed to effect, is action in debt not damages).
126 Sale of Goods Act 1979, s. 49(2).
127 Either by saying so or otherwise disabling himself from tendering the contract performance, e.g. disposing of the contract goods elsewhere.
128 [1976] 1 Lloyd's Rep 250.

relegated to an action for damages, which would reflect the value of the repaired ship?[129]

The possibility of the innocent party tendering an unwanted performance and suing in debt for the contract price follows from the decision of the House of Lords in *White & Carter (Councils) Ltd* v *McGregor*.[130] The pursuer and the defender[131] entered a contract under which the former was to advertise the latter's business for three years on litter bins supplied to local authorities. Later the same day the defender tried to cancel the contract. The pursuers refused to accept the cancellation and proceeded to perform the contract. The pursuers successfully claimed the full sum payable under the contract.[132] The majority reasoned from first principles. Lord Reid said:[133]

> The general rule cannot be in doubt ... If one party to a contract repudiates it in the sense of making it clear to the other party that he refuses or will refuse to carry out his part of the contract, the other party, the innocent party, has an option. He may accept that repudiation and sue for damages for breach of contract whether or not the time for performance has come; *or he may if he chooses disregard or refuse to accept it and then the contract remains in full effect* [emphasis added].

In this passage Lord Reid was stating the accepted principle that a breach of a condition[134] does not operate automatically to terminate a contract, rather it gives rise to an election to terminate which the innocent party may or may not choose to exercise. If he declines to exercise it, he may continue with his own contractual performance and thereafter sue in debt to recover the price. However, this election is not unfettered. Lord Reid stated that it was subject to two preconditions. First, it is only available where the innocent party is able to complete his performance without the assistance of the other party. Where this is not so the other party may, by refusing to co-operate, effectively restrict the innocent party to a claim for damages. Second, Lord Reid said:[135]

> It may well be that, if it can be shown that a person has no legitimate interest, financial or otherwise, in performing the contract rather than claiming damages, he ought not to be allowed to saddle the other party with an additional burden with no benefit to himself.

---

[129] Damages would be calculated by reference to the diminution in value of the ship as a result of the failure to repair rather than the cost of curing those defects. In addition, the shipowner would be subject to a duty to mitigate his loss. This would require him not to increase his losses by undertaking uneconomic repairs.

[130] [1962] AC 413 and [1961] 3 All ER 1178.

[131] Respectively the equivalent of the claimant and the defendant. The case was a Scottish appeal.

[132] The pursuer claimed the full three years' advertising fee before the expiry of that period relying upon a term of the agreement which 'accelerated' all sums due under the contract if the advertiser fails to make prompt payment of any instalment. Lord Reid said that such acceleration clauses did not fall within the penalty jurisdiction.

[133] At p. 1181.

[134] The expression of a desire to 'cancel' the contract obviously goes to the root of it and so constitutes a breach of condition. See further Chapter 15.

[135] At p. 1183.

These limitations were only clearly articulated in Lord Reid's speech. However, they still necessarily form part of the *ratio decidendi* of the case.[136] As Megarry J explained in another case:[137]

> ... the ratio of the *White* case involves acceptance of Lord Reid's limitations, even though Lord Tucker and Lord Hodson [the other majority judges] said nothing of them:[138] for without Lord Reid there was no majority for the decision of the House. Under the doctrine of precedent, I do not think that it can be said that a majority of a bare majority is itself a majority.

The decision in *White & Carter* is a controversial one. One commentator has said of the majority decision that the 'reasoning is logical; but the result might be grotesque'.[139] Criticism of the majority decision is of two kinds: procedural and substantive. Both types of concern are reflected in the minority judgments of Lords Keith and Morton. Procedural criticism emphasises the comparison with specific performance.[140] We have already seen that specific performance will not be awarded when damages would be an adequate remedy. The action for debt is effectively one for specific performance of the promise to pay[141] and, so the argument against *White & Carter* goes, should not be available where specific performance would not be granted. This argument is not totally convincing and in any case probably not raised by the facts of *White & Carter*. The argument builds upon the premise that the availability of the action in debt should mirror that of specific performance. Acceptance of this argument would have consequences beyond anticipatory breach. For instance, the expedited procedures available to obtain judgment in default of defence would be called into question. Indeed, the argument might not be raised by the actual facts of *White & Carter* where none of the 'bars' to the availability of specific performance would seem to be made out.[142]

Substantive criticism of *White & Carter* often suggests that the decision

---

136 *Contra* the view expressed in Burrows, Finn and Todd (1997) *Law of Contract in New Zealand*, p. 608, n. 114.
137 *Hounslow London Borough Council* v *Twickenham Garden Developments Ltd* [1971] Ch 233.
138 It could possibly be argued that the language of Lord Hodson's judgment (with which Lord Tucker agreed) may impliedly though not expressly support the first of Lord Reid's limitations. At p. 1192 he refers to the appellants 'being always ready to perform the contract and having performed it'. If the reference to actual performance can be regarded as stating a requirement, this supports Lord Reid's view.
139 Cheshire, Fifoot and Furmston, p. 631.
140 'Here the appellants are saying that they will do something which the courts will not enforce ...', *per* Lord Keith at p. 1187.
141 *Per* Lord Morton at p. 1184: '... the appellants are claiming a kind of inverted specific implement of the contract.'
142 Possible bars might be that the contract was one of personal service. Whether this service would for these purposes be considered personal is open to doubt. Further bars might be that the lack of mutuality and that the enforcement of the promise to pay would require the 'constant supervision' of the court. However, neither bar applies where the contract has been fully performed by one party (as this one, by operation of the acceleration clause, is assumed to have been) and the other's only outstanding liability is one to pay money. See generally Treitel at pp. 948–9. *Contra* the view of Lord Morton dissenting in *White & Carter* at p. 1184: 'The present case is one in which specific implement could not be decreed ...'.

encourages waste.[143] Why should a party be entitled to continue with a performance when he has been told that it is no longer wanted? The policy behind the doctrine of mitigation is often thought to be the avoidance of waste. It is the inapplicability of that doctrine to an action in debt, as opposed to an action for damages, which creates the incentive for such wasteful behaviour. In his dissenting judgment Lord Morton illustrated his concern with the example of an expert engaged by a company to travel abroad and prepare an elaborate report. What is the position if, before the expert had done any work, the company said that it no longer needed the report. In Lord Morton's view the majority decision in *White & Carter* would mean that the expert was entitled to compile the unwanted report and sue in debt for his fee and travel expenses – a result he considered indefensible.

The argument against waste has been followed in the United States where the law is ostensibly the opposite to that in the United Kingdom. When, prior to the time for performance, one party either announces that he will not perform or disables himself from being able to perform, this 'repudiation' unilaterally operates to terminate the contract. The innocent party is not, therefore, entitled to continue to perform and claim the contract price. In *Richardson v Davis*[144] the claimants continued to perform a contract involving film advertisements containing images of the defendants' premises even though the defendants had repudiated the contract when they began to trade elsewhere.[145] However, the difference between the two regimes is not as stark as the above might suggest. In the UK the election available to the innocent party is subject to limitation; in the USA the doctrine of unilateral waiver is also subject to limitation. Indeed, one limitation upon the American doctrine seems to echo the 'legitimate' interest qualification formulated by Lord Reid in *White & Carter*. Under American law, repudiation will not preclude the innocent party from performing and claiming the price when it would be unreasonable to relegate the innocent party to a claim in damages, e.g. because it would be difficult to compute the innocent party's losses if performance was incomplete.[146]

It is suggested that the substantive criticism of *White & Carter* that it encourages waste has considerable force. However, it is at least partly met by the two limitations upon the innocent party's election described by Lord Reid. A further substantive criticism of the decision is that these very qualifications make the principle a difficult one to apply to concrete circumstances. Lord Hodson emphasises the undesirable effects of such uncertainty upon commercial dealings[147] and this helps explain why he did not qualify the

---

[143] For example, Nienaber [1962] CLJ 213 at 233.

[144] (1931) 2 P 2d 860.

[145] See also *Clark v Marsiglia* [1845] 1 Denio 317 and *Western Advertising Co v Mid-West Laundries* (1933) 61 SW 2d 251. See also Restatement 2d, s 253 for an authoritative statement of the American rule that repudiation alone (i.e. without any election by the innocent party) gives rise to a claim for damages.

[146] *Drowling v White's Lumber & Supply Co* 170 Mis 267 (1934).

[147] At p. 1193.

innocent party's rights in the same way as Lord Reid. We will now examine how those limitations have been developed in subsequent case law.

The first limitation is that the innocent party must be able to complete his performance without the co-operation of the other party. In *Hounslow London Borough Council* v *Twickenham Garden Developments*[148] co-operation was defined broadly, reducing the occasions when the innocent party could continue with his performance and claim the price. Megarry J explained:

> Suppose that A, who owns a large and valuable painting contracts with B, a picture restorer, to restore it over a period of three months. Before the work is begun, A receives a handsome offer from C to purchase the picture, subject to immediate delivery in its unrestored state, C having grave suspicions of B's competence. If the work of restoration is to be done in A's house, he can effectually exclude B by refusing to admit him to the house: without A's [active] 'cooperation' to this extent B cannot perform his contract. But what if the picture stands in A's locked barn, the key to which he has lent to B so that he may come and go freely, or if the picture has been removed to B's premises? In these cases can B insist on performing his contract, even though this makes it impossible for A to accept C's offer?

Megarry J answers this question negatively explaining that the requirement of co-operation extends beyond active co-operation to include the passive co-operation of A which would be necessary if B were to complete the restoration when the painting was in the barn or at B's studio.

Application of this limitation requires the court to carefully define what the contract requires of the performing party. When a time charter is concluded what precisely has the shipowner undertaken? Has he promised to hold his vessel available for a particular period of time?[149] Or has he promised to perform services which will be notified to him by the charterer?[150] If it is the former, the charterer's repudiation cannot prevent the shipowner from performing the contract by holding the ship available to the charterer's order. If it is the latter, the charterer can, by refusing to give any orders, relegate the shipowner to an action for damages and thereby subject him to a duty to mitigate, i.e. to re-charter the vessel. The question is an open one, but at least serves to show the importance of defining the contractual undertaking of the performing party.

The second of Lord Reid's two proposed limitations, the requirement of a legitimate interest in continuing with performance, has also resulted in case law that is difficult to reconcile. In *White & Carter* itself Lord Reid gave a clue as to its operation. He said that it might apply to his example of the expert's report discussed in Lord Morton's dissenting judgment. The principle is also stated to be subject to a *de minimis* principle where the law will disregard any genuine but trifling interest the expert might have in continuing with performance. Lord Reid does not give any examples of what might constitute a substantial and legitimate interest in continuing to press

---

[148] [1971] Ch 233.
[149] *The Odenfeld* [1978] 2 Lloyd's Rep 357.
[150] *The Alaskan Trader* [1984] 1 All ER 129. See also *The Puerto Buitrago* [1976] 1 Lloyd's Rep 250.

for performance. However, it is suggested that such might be disclosed by a variation of the expert example if the failure to complete the report would damage the reputation of the expert in a way that was not easily quantifiable and so which might not result in an award of damages for breach of contract.

In *The Puerto Buitrago*,[151] the facts of which we considered above, the charterer was held to have no legitimate interest in continuing with performance because of the substantial disproportion between the cost of performance and the value of it to the shipowner. In contrast, in *The Odenfeld*[152] it was said that it was not 'wholly unreasonable' for the shipowner to keep a charter alive when, if he accepted the charterer's repudiation, third parties would be affected, i.e. the party to whom the shipowner had assigned payments of hire. After a careful review of the authorities, Lloyd J, in the *Alaskan Trader*,[153] concluded that the court is required to find that 'point at which the court will cease, on general equitable principles, to allow the innocent party to enforce his contract according to its strict legal terms'. The difficulty is that this involves a judgment of degree to distinguish between the situation where the innocent party's continuance is 'wholly unreasonable' and so impermissible and where it is merely 'unreasonable' which even Lord Reid agrees is permissible:[154]

> It might be, but it never has been, the law that a person is only entitled to enforce his contractual rights in a reasonable way and that a court will not support an attempt to enforce them in an unreasonable way.

---

[151] [1976] 1 Lloyd's Rep 250.
[152] [1978] 2 Lloyd's Rep 257.
[153] [1984] 1 All ER 129 at 136–7.
[154] *White & Carter* at p. 1182.

17

DAMAGES FOR BREACH
OF CONTRACT

INTRODUCTION

The principal judicial remedy for breach of contract is an award of unliquidated damages.[1] Unliquidated damages are damages which are assessed by the court as appropriate to be paid to the victim of a breach of contract in respect of his, or exceptionally another's, losses caused by that breach. Damages for breach of contract generally seek to compensate the victim for his loss rather than to punish the wrongdoer for his conduct. In the absence of provable loss, only nominal damages will be awarded. The assessment of compensatory damages is a two-stage process: first, the prima facie measure is ascertained; second, a number of limiting factors are considered. The different measures of damage are outlined below and thereafter the various limiting factors are examined.

Liquidated damages clauses are terms of a contract, which require a contracting party to pay a specific sum in the event of a payer's breach. Such clauses are unenforceable if they are 'penalties', whereby the sum to be paid exceeds a genuine pre-estimate of loss.

An action in debt to recover the contract price is literally an action to enforce a contract. However, it is not the only type of literal performance. Where a party has made a negative promise in a contract, he may be restrained by injunction from departing from it. When a party has made a positive promise other than one to pay a sum of money, this may be literally enforced by the grant of an order of specific performance. The availability of injunctions and specific performance and the action in debt were examined in Chapter 16.

THE GENERAL COMPENSATORY AIM

In *Johnson* v *Agnew* Lord Wilberforce said that 'the general principle for the assessment of damages is compensatory'.[2]

---

[1] Perhaps most famously summarised by Holmes as 'The duty to keep a contract at common law means a prediction that you must pay damages if you do not keep it – and nothing else.' 'The Path of the Law' (1897) Harv LR 457, 462.

[2] [1980] AC 367 at 400. See also *British Westinghouse Electric and Manufacturing Co Ltd* v *Underground Electric Railways Co of London Ltd* [1912] AC 673 at 689.

More recently, the compensatory aim has been said to be 'beyond dispute'.[3] The compensatory aim of an award of damages for breach of contract is sometimes not addressed. Rather a number of 'rules of thumb' have evolved which are applied in different circumstances. These rules and sub-rules are examined in detail in the sections that follow. However, as the House of Lords emphasised in the case of *South Australia Asset Management Corp* v *York Montague Ltd*,[4] these rules and sub-rules are only applications of the general compensatory principle. In *Ruxley Electronics* v *Forsyth*[5] the claimant failed to build a swimming pool to a specified depth. Despite the 6–9 inch shortfall, the trial judge held that the pool was safe for diving as the defendant had requested. Argument centred around whether the appropriate way to quantify the defendant's loss was by an award based upon the cost of cure (the cost of rebuilding the pool to the contract depth) or diminution in value (the difference in value between the pool with the promised quality and its value without it). Lord Mustill said: 'there are not two alternative measures of damage ... But only one: namely, the loss truly suffered by the promisee'.[6]

In *Ruxley*, the application of the compensatory principle did not require damages to be assessed by reference to either the cost of cure or the difference in value. The House of Lords therefore left in place a modest[7] award of damages in respect of loss of amenity without assessing damages on either of the above two bases.

The three types of award

There are in fact three different bases of awarding damages, all applying the general compensationary aim. The first seeks to place the victim of the breach, so far as an award of damages can, in the position he would have been in if the contract had been performed. In the classic judgment[8] of Parke B in *Robinson* v *Harman*:[9]

> the rule of the common law is that where a party sustains a loss by reason of a breach of contract he is so far as money can do it to be placed in the same situation as if the contract had been performed.

---

[3] *Attorney General* v *Blake* [1988] 1 All ER 833 at 844 *per* Lord Woolf MR; *The Heron II* [1969] 1 AC 350 at 414; *Tito* v *Waddell (No. 2)* [1977] Ch 106 at 328–334; *Surrey County Council* v *Bredero Homes Ltd* [1933] 3 All ER 705 at 710; *Ruxley Electronics* v *Forsyth* [1995] 3 All ER 268 at 270, 277, 282; *Freeman* v *Niroomand* (1997) 52 Con LR 116 at 120 *per* Millett LJ; *Total Liban SA* v *Vitol Energy SA* [2000] 3 WLR 1142 at 1160.

[4] [1996] 3 All ER 365.

[5] [1995] 3 All ER 268.

[6] *Ibid.*, p. 277 E.

[7] Namely, £2,500.

[8] For example in *Ruxley Electronics* v *Forsyth* [1995] 3 All ER 268 at 272.

[9] (1848) 1 Exch 850. See to similar effect Viscount Haldane LC in *British Westinghouse Electric and Manufacturing Co Ltd* v *Underground Electric Railways Co of London Ltd* [1912] AC 673 at 689: 'The first is that, as far as possible, he who has proved a breach of a bargain to supply what he contracted to get is to be placed, as far as money can do it, in as good a situation as if the contract had been performed. The fundamental basis is thus compensation for pecuniary loss naturally flowing from the breach.'

This award of damages is referred to as *the* 'contractual' measure of damages[10] or damages for 'loss of a bargain'.[11] However, there is no doubt that in some cases damages for breach of contract are assessed on a different basis.

The second type of award seeks to restore the victim of the breach to the position he was in before the breach occurred. In *Anglia TV* v *Reed* Lord Denning MR said: '... He can claim ... The expenditure, which has been thrown away, that is, wasted by reason of the breach.'[12]

The award of damages for wasted expenditure is sometimes referred to as the tortious measure of damages. The classic expression of this measure in a tort case is Lord Blackburn's statement in *Livingstone* v *Raywards*[13] where he described it as:

> ... That sum of money which will put the party who has been injured, or who has suffered, in the same position as he would have been in if he had not sustained the wrong for which he is now getting his compensation or reparation.

The third type of award arises where the party in breach of contract has been unjustly enriched by the breach and is therefore required to pay a sum of money to the victim of the breach in respect of that gain. Such a claim may be of two distinct kinds. The first is where there has been a total failure of consideration: the victim of a breach of contract has conferred a benefit on the contract breaker but has received nothing in return. The second is where the party in breach has in some way profited from that breach; this is classified as enrichment by wrongdoing.

Total failure of consideration and enrichment by wrongdoing may be considered to be part of the law of restitution[14] rather than the law of contract. The unifying principle of restitution is the reversal of unjust enrichment. However, although the remedy may be described as a restitutionary one, i.e. it seeks to reverse an unjust enrichment, the setting is contractual. In most instances[15] the first type of restitutionary claim (e.g. a claim for the

---

10 *Nykredit plc* v *Edward Erdman Ltd* [1977] 1 WLR 1627 at 1634 *per* Lord Nicholls of Birkenhead.

11 Although there is considerable controversy as to the relative frequency of each type of award. See Adams and Brownsword (1995) *Key Issues in Contract*, ch. 4; Atiyah (1990) *Essays on Contract*, ch. 2; Atiyah (1995) *An Introduction to the Law of Contract*. 5th edn, ch. 1 and 22; Collins (1997) *The Law of Contract*. 3rd edn, chs. 4 and 5. *Contra*: Burrows (*Remedies*), pp. 20–1; Harris (1988) *Remedies in Contract and Tort*, pp. 39–40; Treitel (10th edn), p. 873, n. 83.

12 [1972] 1 QB 60 at 64 A.

13 (1880) 5 App Cas 25 at 39. Applied in *Hayes* v *Charles Dodd* [1990] 2 All ER 815 at 818.

14 Though in different senses. Total failure of consideration is an example of autonomous unjust enrichment, i.e. the restitutionary response is independent of any other civil wrong. Enrichment by wrongdoing involves an independent legal wrong for which restitution is merely one possible remedial response. Although both are generally discussed in texts on restitution, the distinction between them is a 'major divide' in the subject. See generally Birks (1989) *An Introduction to the Law of Restitution*, pp. 6–7, 23–4 and 313–14. The distinction between autonomous unjust enrichment and unjust enrichment by wrongdoing was recognised in *Halifax Building Society* v *Thomas* [1996] 2 WLR 63.

15 The exceptional situation when the first type of claim is not compensatory is where a claim is brought for the repayment of money or the conferral of a non-monetary benefit pursuant to a loss-making contract.

return of a deposit paid to the seller of a car who now refuses to deliver it) may also be regarded as compensatory. The same cannot easily be said of the second type of action (e.g. the claim by the disappointed car purchaser to be entitled to a share of the extra profit made by selling the car to a third party).[16]

For this reason, the first type of claim will be examined under the heading below dealing with awards of Unliquidated damages and the second under that dealing with Extra compensatory damages.

In an important article by Fuller and Perdue[17] the three measures of damages outlined above were characterised by reference to the 'interest' of the claimant which they are said to protect. The first measure of damages seeks to put the claimant in the position he would have been in if the contract had been performed. It looks forward to performance; hence, it is said to protect his 'expectation' interest. The second measure of damages looks at the money expended by the claimant which is wasted as a result of the defendant's breach of contract. This looks backwards and seeks to restore the claimant to the position he was in prior to these acts of reliance, hence it is said to protect his reliance interest. In the third measure of damages, the focus is upon the gain to the defendant rather than the loss of the claimant. The claimant's suit is that the defendant should pay him a sum of money by way of restitution, hence it is said to protect the claimant's restitution interest. The terminology introduced by the article is widely used and will be adopted in this chapter to describe the three measures of damage.

Loss, proof and opportunity

In contract, damage (loss) must generally[18] be demonstrated before substantial damages can be awarded. The burden of proof is borne by the claimant who must prove the breach of contract and consequent recoverable loss according to the normal civil burden (i.e. upon the balance of probabilities). Claims for wasted expenditure will fall within this category.[19] However, where the loss being claimed requires an investigation of future events, a different approach is taken.[20] Then damages are only recoverable if

---

[16] However, see *Wrotham Park Estate Co* v *Parkside Homes Ltd* [1974] 1 WLR 798 and *Jaggard* v *Sawyer* [1995] 1 WLR 269. *Cf. Surrey County Council* v *Bredero Homes Ltd* [1993] 3 All ER 705 at 714e *per* Steyn LJ and *Attorney-General* v *Blake* [1998] 1 All ER 833 at 844 *per* Lord Woolf MR.

[17] 'The Reliance Interest in Contract Damages' (1936) 46 Yale LJ 52, 373. See *C & P Haulage (a Firm)* v *Middleton* [1983] 3 All ER 94 at 98g–h *per* Ackner LJ and the terminology used by Steyn LJ in *Surrey County Council* v *Bredero Homes Ltd* [1993] 3 All ER 705 at 714. See also *Bowlay Logging Ltd* v *Domtar Ltd* (1978) 87 DLR (3d) 325.

[18] An exception is an action against a bank for loss of reputation by their failure to honour a cheque. *Wilson* v *United Counties Bank Ltd* [1920] AC 102 and *Kpohraror* v *Woolwich Building Society* [1996] 4 All ER 119.

[19] For example, *Lloyd* v *Stanbury* [1971] 1 WLR 1461; *McRae* v *Commonwealth Disposals Commission* (1951) 84 CLR 377; *Anglia TV* v *Reed* [1972] 1 QB 60; *C & P Haulage* v *Middleton* [1983] 1 WLR 1461.

[20] *Davies* v *Taylor* [1974] AC 207, 212, 219; *Mallet* v *McMonagle* [1970] AC 166, 177.

the item of loss claimed for can be proved with reasonable certainty.[21] The policy behind the application of different burdens of proof in respect of past facts and future events is unclear. It is possible that the imposition of a higher standard of proof in relation to future events derives from the greater ease by which such claims may be exaggerated or falsified.

Nevertheless, even when a claimant is unable with reasonable certainty to prove an item of future profit, he may still recover damages for being deprived of chance of making that profit. Damages for loss of a chance are arrived at by starting with the profit, which the claimant could make, and discounting it to reflect the likelihood that he would be able to do so. In *Chaplin* v *Hicks*,[22] the defendant's breach of contract deprived the claimant of the opportunity of competing in a beauty contest. There were 50 contestants and a total prize fund of £7,488,[23] which would suggest an award of approximately £150 (£7,488/50). In fact, a sum of £100 was awarded. Such awards for loss of a chance are not quantified with arithmetic precision but rather reflect the court's robust and practical sense of justice. None the less, there appears to be a *de minimis* principle operating whereby nothing will be awarded when there is less than 'a substantial chance' of loss.[24]

There are many differing scenarios in which damages for loss of a chance have been awarded to a claimant who has been deprived of the opportunity to, for example, earn gratuities,[25] race a horse,[26] bring a legal action within time,[27] have effective indemnity insurance,[28] tender for a flight concession,[29] enhance pension rights,[30] and for loss of the chance of negotiating more advantageous terms in a takeover.[31]

Where the occurrence of the chance may be prevented by the defendant then damages for loss of a chance will not be awarded, for example, if the hairdresser in *Manubens* v *Leon*[32] had been claiming a discretionary bonus paid by his employer rather than tips offered by customers.[33] This derives

---

21 *Ratcliffe* v *Evans* [1892] 2 QB 524, 532–3. In *McRae* v *Commonwealth Disposals Commission* (1951) 84 CLR 377 it was 'impossible to say that *any* assessable [expectation] loss had resulted' (emphasis added) *per* Dixon and Fullagar JJ at p. 412. However, reliance and restitution damages were recovered. A recent Australian case may cast doubt on this principle: see *Commonwealth of Australia* v *Amman Aviation Pty Ltd* (1992) 66 ALJR 123; Treitel (1992) 108 LQR 226.
22 [1911] 2 KB 786.
23 $(4 \times 5 \times 156) + (4 \times 4 \times 156) + (4 \times 3 \times 156) = £7,488$.
24 *Allied Marples* v *Simmons & Simmons* [1994] 4 All ER 907 at 919c *per* Stuart-Smith LJ. See also *Otter* v *Church, Adams, Tatham & Co* [1953] 1 WLR 156.
25 *Manubens* v *Leon* [1919] 1 KB 208.
26 *Howe* v *Teefy* (1927) 27 SR (NSW) 301.
27 *Kitchen* v *Royal Air Forces Association* [1958] 1 WLR 563, *Prior* v *McNab* (1976) 78 DLR (3d) 319.
28 *Dunbar* v *A & B Painters Ltd* [1986] 2 Lloyd's Rep 38.
29 *Blackpool and Fylde Aero Club Ltd* v *Blackpool Borough Council* [1990] 1 WLR 1195. (Only issues of liability were discussed.)
30 *Scally* v *Southern Health and Social Services Board* [1992] 1 AC 294.
31 *Allied Maples* v *Simmons & Simmons* [1995] 4 All ER 907, though on the facts the Court of Appeal thought recovery was unlikely.
32 [1919] 1 KB 208.

from the broader principle that damages are assessed upon the assumption that the defendant tendered the minimum performance permitted by the terms of his contract with the claimant.

The net loss principle

Damages for breach of contract are awarded on a 'net loss' basis.[34] Therefore, the compensation which the claimant receives will be adjusted to take account of any 'betterment' he enjoys following the breach of contract. The defendant's defective performance may in itself create a situation of betterment. For example, if the goods delivered were more valuable than the contracted goods then the buyer would be precluded from claiming damages.[35]

Alternatively, the betterment may derive from market movements. If the seller of goods is sued for non-delivery in respect of a sale agreed at the then prevailing market price, then a buyer who has not yet paid for the goods will be unable to prove any loss, if the price has in fact fallen by the due delivery date.[36]

The claimant's own actions may create betterment. In *C & P Haulage (a firm) v Middleton*[37] the licensee of a yard used to run a car repair business, in breach of contract, was forced to leave the premises. He failed to recover damages for breach of contract, *inter alia*, because, with the local authority's permission, he had continued to run his business from home. As the claimant did not pay any extra rent to do so and no other loss attributable to the licensor's breach of contract was proved,[38] the claimant's overall position was better as a result of the breach; the claimant recovered only nominal damages.

A loss of the claimant is not reduced by his own subsequent action unless that action forms part of a continuous transaction beginning with the original contract. On this basis, the Court of Appeal declined to reduce the damages awarded against a surveyor whose pre-purchase survey of leasehold property failed to reveal defects which were subsequently remedied by the landlord.[39] In the past the question as to whether recovery is reduced by betterment caused by the claimant's own actions was said to depend upon an elusive distinction between direct and collateral benefits.[40]

---

[34] *McAlpine v Property and Land Contractors* [1995] 76 BLR 59; *Dimond v Lovell* [2000] 2 WLR 1121.

[35] *Taylor v Bank of Athens* (1922) 27 Com Cas 142.

[36] The position may be different if the market price has not fallen below the contract price but the claimant is able to purchase the goods at less than the market price. See Goode (1995) *Commercial Law*. 2nd edn, p. 395.

[37] [1983] 1 All ER 94.

[38] The claimant 'lost' certain equipment, which he had put into the yard. However, this loss was said to follow from the terms of the licence which said that fixtures put into the premises could not be removed; it was not a consequence of the licensor's breach of contract.

[39] *Gardner v Marsh & Parsons* [1997] 1 WLR 489 (Peter Gibson LJ dissenting on this point) following *Hussey v Eels* [1990] 2 QB 227 (action by purchaser of house in respect of vendor's tortious negligent misrepresentation not affected by subsequent profitable resale).

[40] [1967] 1 QB 278.

The net loss principle can extend beyond the varieties of betterment discussed above and may exceptionally take account of a potential right of recoupment which the victim may have from a third party. In *St Albans City and District Council v International Computers Ltd*[41] a local authority purchased a computer system to assist with the collection of the Community Charge. The system was defective and overstated the number of charge payers in the area. The local authority claimed damages under two heads. First it claimed the extent to which, in reliance upon the erroneous estimate, it had overpaid its contribution to the county council. These overpayments were not refundable and so were properly recoverable by the local authority in a claim for damages against the defendants. However, the shortfall in revenue as a result of setting too low a community charge was not recoverable from the defendants. The local authority did not suffer any loss thereby because it could recoup the shortfall in revenue by levying an increased charge in the following year. Nor would the charge payers suffer any prejudice because they were only being asked to pay at a later date what otherwise they would have been required to pay earlier.

Certain sources of compensating advantage are singled out for special treatment by common law or statute. A general principle operates that a claimant should not be deprived of the fruits of his own thrift and forethought; to hold otherwise would discourage potential victims from making provision for future misfortune.[42] Therefore, the proceeds of insurance are not deducted. Damages recovered by a building society from solicitors acting for it in relation to a mortgage were not affected by the society's entitlement to the proceeds of a mortgage indemnity guarantee.[43] Charitable donations are also disregarded otherwise it is feared that donors would not be prepared to give to good causes.[44] A similar principle has been applied to payments made by Lloyd's out of a central fund to meet the liabilities of its 'Names' in an action by the Names against their managing and underwriting agents.[45] On occasion, the policy underlying these refusals to deduct these monies seems to be punitive; a belief that the wrongdoer deserves to pay for the consequences of his action without relief.[46]

Where the defendant is entitled to perform a contract in different ways, damages are assessed on an assumption of self-interest, i.e. that the defendant would choose to perform in the way least onerous to him. In *Cockburn v Alexander* Maule J said:[47]

---

[41] [1996] 4 All ER 481.
[42] *Shearman v Polland* [1950] 2 KB 43 at 46 *per* Asquith LJ.
[43] *Bristol & West BS v May, May and Merrimans (No. 2)* [1998] 1 WLR 336.
[44] *Ibid.* at p. 16 *per* Lord Pearson; *Redpath v Belfast Railway* [1947] NI 167; *Hunt v Severs* [1994] 2 AC 350 at 357–8 *per* Lord Bridge.
[45] *Deeny and Others v Gooda Walker (in liq) and Others* [1995] 4 All ER 289 at 293–4.
[46] 'If the claimant cannot recover, the wrongdoer pays nothing and takes all the benefit of a policy of insurance without paying the premium': *Yates v Whyte* (claimant's damages following a collision between ships should not be reduced to take account of an insurance payment) (1838) 4 Bing (NC) 272 at 283 *per* Tindal CJ.
[47] (1818) 6 CB 791 at 814.

... Where there are several ways in which the contract might be performed, that mode is adopted which is the least profitable to the claimant and the least burdensome to the defendant.

This was reiterated by Diplock LJ in *Lavarack* v *Woods of Colchester* (emphasis added):[48]

the first task ... is to estimate ... what the claimant would have gained ... if the defendant had fulfilled his legal obligation and *had done no more*.[49]

Although this appears a simple principle, it is helpful to use a distinction introduced by Lord Diplock between primary and secondary obligations.[50] Initially both parties to a bilateral contract assume a primary obligation to tender the performance they promise under the terms of that contract. Where one party is in breach of his primary obligation to perform, then a secondary obligation to pay damages arises.[51]

The first stage in applying the principle is to construe the contract to determine the primary obligations of the defendant. In an action for wrongful dismissal an actor's claim that he had been deprived of the opportunity of improving his reputation by appearing at a famous theatre was not permitted when the employer had an unqualified option to select the venues.[52] Bonuses[53] and fees[54] which are payable at the discretion of the party in breach will be irrecoverable.[55] The rule in contracts of employment that claims for loss of earnings are limited to any applicable notice period is a straightforward application of the minimum performance rule.[56]

Where the contract expressly or impliedly qualifies the choice between different modes of performance, the minimum performance due must be similarly qualified. A dress manufacturer sued a distributor for the breach of an obligation to order a minimum number of dresses each year. The distributor claimed he had an unrestrained choice as to which dresses to order and so damages should be calculated by reference to the claimant's cheapest dresses. Mustill J construed the contract to require the defendant to make a *reasonable* selection from the claimant's range with a variety of styles and sizes and so damages must be assessed on that basis.[57] A publisher who in breach of contract failed to publish an author's work had damages

---

[48] [1967] 1 QB 278 at 294.

[49] See also *Abrahams* v *Herbert Reiach* [1922] 1 KB 477; *Gomez* v *Olds Discount (TCC) Ltd* (1964) 7 WIR 98; *The Rijn* [1981] 2 Lloyd's Rep 267; *Biotechnology Australia Pty Ltd* v *Pace* (1988) 15 NSWLR 130; *The World Navigator* [1991] 2 Lloyd's Rep 23; *The Commonwealth of Australia* v *Amman Aviation Pty Ltd* (1991) 174 CLR 64.

[50] For instance, *Photo Production Ltd* v *Securicor Transport Ltd* [1980] AC 827 at 848–9.

[51] The effect of such a breach will depend upon the nature of the term breached and the election of the innocent party.

[52] *Withers* v *General Theatre Corp Ltd* [1933] 2 KB 536.

[53] *Lavarack* v *Woods of Colchester* [1967] 1 QB 278.

[54] *Beach* v *Reed Corrugated Cases* [1956] 2 All ER 652.

[55] *Cf.* above the position when they are payable at the discretion of a third party *Manubens* v *Leon* [1919] 1 KB 208.

[56] *British Guiana Credit Corporation* v *Da Silva* [1965] 1 WLR 248.

[57] *Paula Lee Ltd* v *Robert Zehil & Co Ltd* [1983] 2 All ER 390.

assessed on the basis that it was obliged to publish the minimum reasonable number of copies rather than the minimum required to amount to publication (presumably one).[58]

When the defendant has an option under the contract to terminate, the minimum performance principle must be accepted. The minimum performance principle would require that the damages payable by the defendant must not exceed the sum which the defendant would be required to pay if he exercised his option to cancel. In *The Mihalis Angelos* Megaw LJ said that the victim of a breach of contract could recover the value of the rights under the contract he had been deprived of as a result of the breach but that:[59]

> if they were capable by the terms of the contract of being rendered either less valuable or valueless in certain events, and if it can be shown that those events were ... predestined to happen ... the damages which he can recover are not more than the true value, if any, of the rights he has lost, having regard to those predestined events.[60]

The facts of the case demonstrate the application of this. A ship was chartered to go to Haiphong, Vietnam to load ore. The vessel was stated to be 'now trading and expected ready to load about July 1st'. The charter also contained a cancellation clause 'should the vessel not be ready to load ... on or before July 20th', but the charterers sought to exercise their right to cancel on 17 July. The Court of Appeal held that this premature cancellation was capable[61] of amounting to an anticipatory breach of the charter which was accepted by the shipowners and in respect of which they were entitled to damages. However, since the ship was still unloading at Hong Kong on 17 July, it was inevitable that it would not be ready to load at Haiphong by 20 July, at which point the charterers could have lawfully cancelled. Nominal damages only were, therefore, awarded.

The minimum performance rule operates harshly against claimants who prior to breach enjoyed a reasonable expectation of receiving some discretionary benefit from the defendant, particularly evident in an employment situation. Although the strict application of the rule has been avoided by a number of techniques,[62] the principle may still require further modification. For an employee in today's enterprise culture, performance-related pay forms an increasingly large part of his or her remuneration, whereas in a claim for wrongful dismissal damages will be limited to the notice period. The application of the minimum performance rule contradicts the primary

---

[58] See also *Abrahams* v *Herbert Reiach* [1922] 1 KB 477.
[59] [1971] 1 QB 164 at 210.
[60] 'Where the obligations under a contract are ... qualified ... damages must be assessed with the qualification in mind ... [the] measure should be adopted which is the least burdensome to the defendant': *Gomez* v *Olds Discount Co (TCC) Ltd* (1964) 7 WIR 98 at 111 *per* Hyatali JA.
[61] In fact, the shipowners were in breach of condition because at the time of entering the charter party they could not reasonably expect the vessel to be ready to load at Haiphong by 20 July.
[62] For instance, interpreting the contract so that the discretion must be exercised reasonably or taking account of the defendant's broader commercial or social interests.

aim of compensatory damages of placing the victim of the breach, so far as an award of money can do so, in the position he would have been in if the contract had been performed. There may well be a challenge to the application of the minimum performance rule in cases of wrongful dismissal or at least an expansion of the evasion techniques.[63]

By analogy, the Commercial Agents (Council Directive) Regulations 1993 provide for the payment of compensation to commercial agents upon the termination of their agency and the basis of such compensation has been considered by The Court of Appeal, which held[64] that it is arguable that such compensation 'should not be based upon the minimum performance required by the principal, but rather should be based upon what the agent would have earned if the principal had performed his contractual obligations in the normal manner'.

EXTRA COMPENSATORY DAMAGES

We have seen that there are many statements and illustrations of the principle that the damages awarded for breach of contract are compensatory. The most obvious departure from that principle would be an award of exemplary damages or an award based upon the restitutionary measure of damages, both of which are considered below. However, the compensatory principle also demands a close attention to the definition of loss itself.

Exemplary and aggravated damages

Exemplary damages are damages whose purpose extends beyond compensation to punitive or admonitory functions. In contrast to the position elsewhere,[65] such damages are not available in a purely contractual action.[66] The Law Commission recently described the law relating to exemplary damages as 'unprincipled and illogical';[67] however, its recommendations did not involve any reform of the law in relation to the availability of exemplary damages for pure breach of contract.[68] The maintenance of the status quo was justified[69] by the difficulties of expressing the limits of any expansion and any associated uncertainty, the fact that commercial rather than personal

---

[63] See *Commonwealth of Australia* v *Amman Aviation Pty Ltd* (1991) 66 ALJR 123 where the majority of the court considered the possible renewal of the contract as relevant to determine whether in a claim for reliance measure damages the claimant was seeking to escape the consequences of his own bad bargain.

[64] *Page* v *Combined Shipping and Trading Co Ltd* [1997] 3 All ER 656.

[65] For example, *Vorvis* v *Insurance Corp of British Columbia* (1989) 58 DLR (4th) 193 (Canada).

[66] *Reed* v *Madon* [1989] Ch 408 and *Ruxley Electronics* v *Forsyth* [1995] 3 All ER 268 at 270e *per* Lord Bridge and at 282b–c *per* Lord Lloyd.

[67] Consultation Paper No. 132 (1993) at p. 6 and Report No. 247 (1997) at p.101.

[68] *Ibid.*, p. 139.

[69] *Ibid.*, pp. 138–9.

interests are involved, economic theory[70] and the protection already offered by awards of damages for disappointment and mental distress.

If a claimant is able to bring his action in contract or in tort, he may, by adopting the latter course, recover exemplary damages. An example is provided by the case of a defendant who fraudulently substituted inferior animals when he contracted to supply pedigree ones[71] and a tenant who was wrongfully evicted:[72] the supplier and the landlord may have committed a breach of contract as well as a tort (respectively, trespass and deceit.) Although the stated purpose of awards of damages for disappointment and mental distress is always compensation, the availability of such damages does at least operate to mitigate the non-availability of exemplary damages.[73]

Aggravated damages are considered to be compensatory awards where the circumstances of the infliction of the wrong, including the motive of the defendant, are taken into account when assessing the appropriate level of compensation.[74] Aggravated damages, like exemplary damages, are not available in a purely contractual action.[75] Again, the situation may be said to be ameliorated by the availability in certain cases of damages for disappointment and mental distress.[76]

The requirement of a property interest

When a claimant brings an action for breach of contract in respect of lost or damaged goods he must be able to demonstrate a property interest in the goods at the time of damage or loss. In the absence of such an interest the claimant cannot show loss. In *The Albazero*[77] the claimant shipped goods on board the defendant's vessel in the course of which voyage the ship and cargo were lost. The claimant's action against the defendants failed as at the time of the assumed breach of the contract of carriage the goods had become the property of a third party. The House of Lords declined to extend any exception[78] to the general requirement of a proprietary interest to cover the

---

70 The so-called theory of efficient breach maintains that efficiency is encouraged when resources gravitate to their most highly valued uses, even if this inevitably involves a breach of contract by the promisor and the re-sale of the performance to a second promisee.

71 *Tak & Co Inc* v *AEL Corp Ltd* (1995) 5 NZBLC 99 and 357.

72 *Drane* v *Evangelou* [1978] 1 WLR 455.

73 The case of *Chelini* v *Nieri* 196 P 2d 915 (1948) cited by Treitel, p. 921 appears to go further. Damages of $10,000 were awarded for injured feelings in respect of a breach of contract by an undertaker.

74 *Rookes* v *Barnard* [1964] AC 1129 at 1221. The continuing difficulty of distinguishing exemplary from aggravated damages is demonstrated by the tort case of *Ketley* v *Gooden* (1997) 73 PCR 305 where a modest award of £6,650 included an element for exemplary damages but was upheld by the Court of Appeal on a compensatory basis.

75 *Addis* v *Gramophone Co Ltd* [1909] AC 488; *Kralj* v *McGrath* [1986] 1 All ER 54 at 61 E–G *per* Woolf J; *Levi* v *Gordon*, 12 November 1992 (unreported).

76 See below in this chapter.

77 [1977] AC 774.

78 Argument centred around the exception established in *Dunlop* v *Lambert* (1839) 6 Cl & F 600 considered below.

claimant's claim.[79] This may be contrasted with the case of *The Sanix Ace*[80] where the claimant was again an FOB buyer who sued a shipowner in respect of damage to goods. The claimant succeeded in his action as at the relevant time the claimant had property in the goods and their recovery was not affected by the contracts for onward sale entered into by the claimant, the terms of which allowed the claimant to demand the price of the goods.

An exception established in the *Dunlop* v *Lambert* case was summarised by Lord Diplock in *The Albazero* in the following way:[81]

> the consignor may recover substantial damages against the shipowner if there is privity of contract between him and the carrier ... although, if the goods are not his property or at his risk, he will be accountable to the true owner for the proceeds of his judgment.

The exception favours the consignor in seeking to solve the problem where the right of action (possessed by the consignor) and the property interest (possessed by the consignee) are separated. The rule fell into disuse after the Bills of Lading Act 1855 solved the problem in favour of the consignee who by the 'statutory assignment' introduced by s 1 had transferred to him 'all rights of suit' contained in the contract of carriage when property in the goods passed to him by endorsement of the bill of lading.[82]

The House of Lords declined to apply the *Dunlop* exception in *The Albazero*, but it was not overruled and was applied in *Linden Gardens Trust Co Ltd* v *Lenesta Sludge Disposals Ltd*.[83] In this case a company was in breach of a contract it entered with the owner of a building for the removal of asbestos. The building had already been sold by the time the company breached its contract. The House of Lords held that the original owner of the building was entitled to substantial damages even though he was no longer the owner of the property and the cost of remedial work had been borne by the subsequent owner.[84] The majority[85] adopted the explanation given by Lord

---

[79] In these circumstances it would be usual for the third-party purchaser to bring an action in respect of the goods, even though he is not a party to the contract of carriage under the provisions of Carriage of Goods by Sea Act 1992 repealing the 'statutory assignment' introduced by the Bills of Lading Act 1855, s 1. Despite the fact that the claimant and the consignee were associated companies, the action was not brought by the third-party consignee apparently because of a mistake in issuing the writ in the wrong name. See Ormrod LJ in the Court of Appeal at p. 824 F.

[80] [1987] 1 Lloyd's Rep 465.

[81] At p. 844. This summary is disputed by Lord Clyde in *Alfred McAlpine Construction Ltd* v *Panatown Ltd* [2000] 3 WLR 946.

[82] See now Carriage of Goods By Sea Act 1992 which repealed the Bills of Lading Act 1855, s 1 and was introduced to remove technical anomalies in the operation of the statutory assignment and specifically to deal with problems posed by cargoes shipped in bulk. See generally Wilson (1993) *The Carriage of Goods by Sea*. 2nd edn, pp. 148–58.

[83] [1994] 1 AC 185. See the discussion in Law Commission Report, No. 242 (1996) at pp. 26–9.

[84] To whom the original owner had made an invalid assignment of the contract with the company.

[85] Lord Browne-Wilkinson, Lords Ackner, Bridge and Keith agreeing.

Diplock in *The Albazero* which stated the *Dunlop* v *Lambert* exception[86] as follows:

> ... in a commercial contract concerning goods where it is in the contemplation of the parties that the proprietary interests in the goods may be transferred from one owner to another after the contract has been entered into and before the breach which causes loss or damage to the goods, an original party to the contract, if such be the intention of them both, is to be treated in law as having entered into the contract for the benefit of all persons who have or may acquire an interest in the goods before they are lost or damaged, and is entitled to recover by way of damages for breach of contract the actual loss sustained by those for whose benefit the contract is entered into.

Lord Browne-Wilkinson concluded that the company and the original building owner entered the contract in the knowledge that the building would be occupied and possibly purchased by third parties.[87] In addition, the prohibition on assignment (which prevented the subsequent owner from obtaining rights of action against the company) convinced him that it must have been the parties' intention that the original building owner should 'be entitled to enforce contractual rights for the benefit of those who suffered from defective performance'.[88] The only extension of the *Dunlop* exception that was required to apply it to the facts of *Linden Gardens* was to cover the transfer of rights in real property. However, it was suggested that it would not apply if 'the ultimate purchaser is given a direct cause of action against the contractor'.[89] This restriction was confirmed by the majority decision of the House of Lords in *Alfred McAlpine Construction Ltd* v *Panatown Ltd*,[90] where a company which employed a contractor to do building work on the land of a third party was denied substantial damages when the work proved deficient. Damages were denied because the third party enjoyed a direct right of action against the contractor under a separate 'duty of care deed'.

Lord Griffiths[91] took a different approach. In his opinion the promisee 'has suffered loss because he did not receive the bargain for which he contracted'[92] and so is entitled to 'the cost of securing the performance of that bargain'.[93] Lord Griffiths recognised that his approach was a denial of the supposed requirement of a proprietary interest in the claimant. However,

---

[86] At p. 847 E–F.

[87] Interestingly at p. 437e–f Lord Browne-Wilkinson suggests that the possibility that a large development might need to be sold before completion was something which was more likely, and so more foreseeable, at times of recession in the property market than in a more buoyant economic climate.

[88] At p. 437b–c.

[89] At p. 437g *per* Lord Browne-Wilkinson.

[90] [2000] 3 WLR 946.

[91] Lords Ackner and Bridge appeared to have some sympathy with his approach. In *Darlington Borough Council* v *Wiltshier Northern Ltd* [1995] 3 All ER 895 at p. 908a Steyn LJ said that he was in agreement with the wider principle propounded by Lord Griffiths subject to a qualification considered below. See also the dissenting judgments of Lords Goff and Millett in *Panatown*.

[92] At p. 422a.

[93] *Ibid.*

he limited the principle in two ways. First, it was stated only to apply to contracts for 'work, labour and the supply of materials'.[94] Second, it was dependent on the court being satisfied 'that the repairs have been or are likely to be carried out'.[95]

In *Darlington Borough Council* v *Wiltshier Northern Ltd*[96] a local authority wanted to build a recreation centre on land it owned, but a bank contracted with a builder for the work in order to circumvent government restrictions on local authority borrowing. A separate agreement was entered into between the bank and the local authority under which the bank agreed to pay the builder sums due under the building contract which the local authority would reimburse to the bank. In addition, this agreement provided that the bank was not liable for the building works but would upon request assign to the local authority any rights against the builder. The local authority alleged that the building work was defective and the Court of Appeal had to consider whether it could recover substantial damages which in turn depended upon whether the bank, which had assigned to the local authority its rights under the building contract, was entitled to such damages.

The difficulty presented by the case was that the bank had *never* had a proprietary interest in the land; it was not a case like *Dunlop* or *Linden Gardens* where the claimant had transferred ownership before breach. The Court of Appeal was prepared to extend the exception to cover the facts of *Darlington* and so the exception must be stated in terms which provide for continuity of ownership. A proposed reformulation is:[97]

> wherever there is a breach of a contract for work on property causing loss to a third party who is an owner of that property, and it was known or contemplated by the parties that a third party *was*, or would become, owner of the property and that owner has no direct right to sue for breach of contract [emphasis added].

Restitution measure damages: enrichment by wrongdoing

General statements may be found in a number of cases to the effect that damages for breach of contract are always based upon the loss of the victim rather than the gain, if any, made by the party in breach.[98] In *Tito* v *Waddell*

[94] At p. 421h.
[95] At p. 422g. In *Darlington Borough Council* v *Wiltshier Northern Ltd* [1995] 3 All ER 895 Steyn LJ disagreed with this restriction. See also the dissenting judgments of Lords Goff and Millett in *Panatown*.
[96] [1995] 3 All ER 895.
[97] Law Commission Report, No. 242 (1996) p. 28.
[98] A non-compensatory award may be provided for by statute, e.g. the Housing Act 1988, s 27 provides for the award of damages for the unlawful deprivation of occupation, which according to s 28, are to be assessed as the difference between value of the landlord's interest if the occupier continued in occupation and if the occupier ceased to occupy the property. See *Regalgrand Ltd* v *Dickerson and Wade* (1997) 74 P & CR 312.

(No. 2)[99] Megarry VC said: 'The question is not one of making the defendant disgorge what he has saved by committing the wrong, but one of compensating the claimant.' If, in breach of the terms of a charter party, a shipowner withdraws his vessel, the profit the shipowner derives from a more lucrative deployment elsewhere will be disregarded in assessing damages.[100] In *Surrey County Council* v *Bredero Homes Ltd*[101] the Court of Appeal restated this general refusal to award restitutionary damages. A property developer built a greater number of houses than was allowed under the contract to purchase the site from the local authority. Damages for that breach did not take account of the developer's increased profit.

However, a small number of cases hold that restitutionary damages may in exceptional circumstances be available in respect of a breach of contract. The issue in these cases is whether the defendant's wrongdoing[102] (i.e. breach of contract) justifies an award of damages based upon the defendant's gain rather that the claimant's loss.

In *Wrotham Park Estate Co Ltd* v *Parkside Homes Ltd*[103] the defendant purchased land subject to a restrictive covenant in favour of an adjoining estate. In breach of the covenant, the defendant built houses and the estate owners unsuccessfully sought an injunction. Brightman J awarded the claimants substantial damages assessed as 5 per cent of the profit the developer made from the breach of covenant, justified as equating to the sum which the claimants might reasonably have demanded to relax the covenant.

In *Bredero Homes*, Steyn LJ said the *Wrotham Park* case was 'only defensible on the basis of the ... restitutionary principle' but none the less was 'rightly decided and represents a useful development in our law'.[104] However, for a variety of reasons, the Court of Appeal did not feel able to extend the recovery of restitutionary damages further.[105]

In *Attorney-General* v *Blake*[106] the majority of the House of Lords approved the interpretation of *Wrotham* advanced by Steyn LJ.[107] Lord Nicholls said the case stood:[108]

---

[99] [1977] Ch 106, 332.
[100] *The Siboen and The Sibotre* [1976] 1 Lloyd's Rep 293, 337.
[101] [1993] 3 All ER 705.
[102] A distinction may be drawn between two types of restitutionory claim where the defendant's unjust enrichment results from his wrongdoing (here a breach of contract) and where it is 'autonomous', i.e. independent of that wrongdoing (e.g. because a benefit was received and nothing given in return). In the latter case the defendant's punishment is said to occur by 'subtraction' from the claimant's wealth.
[103] [1974] 1 WLR 798.
[104] [1993] 3 All ER 705 at 714.
[105] Dillon and Rose LJJ said that *Wrotham* involved an award of equitable damages in lieu of an injunction. Steyn LJ distinguished the *Wrotham Park* case on the basis that it involved the invasion of property rights. Rose LJ added a further ground of distinction, that in *Wrotham* the claimants continuously objected to the defendant's breach of contract.
[106] [2000] 3 WLR 625, Lord Hobhouse dissenting.
[107] Which was previously rejected in *Jaggard* v *Sawyer* [1995] 1 WLR 269. *Jaggard* is treated in *Blake* as limited to the award of damages in lieu of an injunction.
[108] At p. 637.

As a solitary beacon, showing that in contract ... damages are not always narrowly confined to recoupment of financial loss. In a suitable case damages for breach of contract may be measured by the benefit gained by the wrongdoer from the breach.

Suitable cases were 'exceptional'[109] and could perhaps be identified as those where the [claimant] had a legitimate interest in preventing the defendant's profit-making activity.[110] *Blake* was itself such a case where the defendant, a former member of the Intelligence Services and a convicted and escaped 'spy', was deprived of the profits he derived from publishing his memoirs in breach of a continuing obligation of secrecy imposed by his contract of employment.[111]

The approach of the House of Lords in *Blake* goes beyond the proposals of the Law Commission,[112] which recommended no legislative expansion of the court's power to award restitutionary damages for breach of contract.[113]

The rule in *Cory* v *Thames Ironworks Co*[114]

A claimant cannot recover anything in respect of a loss which he has not suffered. However, in this case the compensatory principle was relaxed in the interests of justice. The claimant coal merchants contracted to purchase a floating boom derrick, which was delivered six months late. The defendant has reasonably assumed that it was to be used for the storage of coal; in fact, the claimants planned to put it to more profitable work transferring in a previously unpractised way cargoes from ships to barges. The defendants were held liable for the value of the hull as a coal store even though the claimants did not intend to use it in that way. There is said to be no injustice to the defendant to hold him accountable for a smaller loss which the claimant did not suffer when the defendant's breach of contract has in fact caused the claimant to suffer a larger loss. However, before any award can be made, the court must have before it evidence from which it can calculate 'usual' losses.[115] This principle must be distinguished from cases where recovery for unusual losses is refused but there is an award of damages for ordinary losses, which were in fact incurred.[116]

---

[109] At p. 639. Lords Browne-Wilkinson and Goff agreed with Lord Nicholls. The basis of Lord Steyn's judgment might be even narrower. He would support such damages only when necessary to achieve 'practical justice' (at p. 646).

[110] At p. 639.

[111] A public law claim for an injunction restraining the defendant from receiving royalties was dismissed by the House of Lords.

[112] Law Com No. 347, 1997.

[113] Following Consultation Paper No. 132 (1993).

[114] (1868) LR 3 QB 181.

[115] *North Sea Energy Holdings NV* v *Petroleum Authority of Thailand* [1997] 2 Lloyd's Rep 418 at 439 *per* Thomas J.

[116] For instance, *Foaminol Laboratories* v *British Artid Plastics* [1941] 2 All ER 393 (breach of contract to provide perfume bottles – recovery for usual wasted advertising expenditure but not for an extraordinary promotion scheme). It is not absolutely clear whether in the *Victoria Laundries* case the award of damages for loss of normal laundering business is an application of the *Cory* principle.

UNLIQUIDATED DAMAGES

The time of assessment

The prima facie rule applied is that damages are assessed by reference to the date upon which the breach of contract occurred.[117] The so-called 'breach date' rule has been 'recognised and embodied'[118] in the Sale of Goods Act 1979. When a buyer brings an action for non-delivery, s 51 provides that if there is an available market in the goods 'the measure of damages is prima facie to be ascertained by the difference between the contract price and the market or current price of the goods at the time ... when they ought to have been delivered ...'. This provision illustrates the close relationship between the breach date rule and the principle of mitigation of loss[119] which requires the victim of a breach of contract to do all that is reasonable to minimise his losses and to refrain from unreasonably increasing them. Where there is an available market, the breach date rule is premised on the assumption that the disappointed buyer will on the date of breach mitigate his loss by going out into the market and purchase substitute goods.

Similarly, if the buyer of goods is in breach of contract according to s 50(3), the measure of damages is again the difference between the contract and the market or current price at the date of breach, i.e. when the goods ought to have been accepted. Again, the rule is premised upon the assumption that the innocent party will go out into the market and mitigate his loss; in this case the assumption is that the seller will dispose of the contract goods.

At common law, in equity and under the Sale of Goods Act the breach date rule is only a prima facie one. In *Johnson* v *Agnew*[120] the House of Lords held that when equitable damages are awarded in lieu of specific performance under Lord Cairn's Act,[121] they are to be assessed on the same basis as damages at common law.[122] Lord Wilberforce said of the breach date rule[123] 'this is not an absolute rule; if to follow it would lead to injustice, the court has power to fix such other date as may be appropriate in the circumstances'.[124] Three such circumstances merit special treatment.

---

[117] *Johnson and Another* v *Agnew* [1980] AC 367 and *The Texaco Melbourne* [1994] 1 Lloyd's Rep 473 at 476 *per* Lord Goff.

[118] *Johnson and Another* v *Agnew* [1980] AC 367. The case pre-dates the 1979 Act.

[119] 'No doubt the measure of damages and the claimant's duty and ability to mitigate are logically distinct concepts ... But to some extent, at least, they are mirror images, particularly in cases of damages for breach of contract ...', *per* Oliver J in *Radford* v *De Froberville* [1978] 1 All ER 33 at 44b.

[120] [1980] AC 367.

[121] Chancery Amendment Act 1858, s 2. See now Supreme Court Act 1981, s 50.

[122] The common law has always admitted some exceptions to the rule, e.g. *Ogle* v *Earl Vane* (1867) LR 2 QB 275 aff'd (1868) LR 3 QB 272 (the time when the innocent party went into the market) and *Hickmam* v *Haynes* (1875) LR 10 CP 598 (a reasonable time after the defendant buyer's final request to stall delivery).

[123] 'It is sometimes said that the ordinary rule is that damages fall to be assessed at the date of breach. That, however, is not a universal principle ...', *per* Oliver J in *Radford* v *De Froberville* [1978] 1 All ER 33 at 55h–j.

[124] See *contra* the arguments of Waddams (1981) 97 LQR 445.

The first is where the breach of contract was not discoverable with reasonable diligence.[125] In an action for breach of contract and misrepresentation in respect of a racehorse warranted to have a certain pedigree, damages were awarded on the basis of the difference between the contract price and its value at the time of discovery of its true pedigree.[126]

The second situation is where the victim of the breach is unable to mitigate his own loss. In *Wroth v Tyler*[127] the claimant sought specific performance, or damages in lieu, of a contract to purchase a bungalow for £6,000. Specific performance was refused[128] but damages were assessed by reference to the difference between the contract price and the value of the house at the date of judgment (£11,500) rather than at the date of completion (£7,500). Megarry J justified the selection of the later date by reference to the claimant's inability to mitigate his loss; he was unable to go into the market and purchase a substitute house at any earlier time as he could not raise a mortgage sufficient to purchase a house in excess of £6,000.[129]

The third situation is when the victim of breach continues to reasonably demand performance.

The expectation measure: pecuniary loss

This measure of damages seeks, so far as an award of money can, to place the claimant in the position he would have been in if the contract had been performed. The cases which consider the quantification of such an award may broadly be divided into those with a commercial flavour where damages for loss of profit may be awarded and consumer cases where damages for disappointment are appropriate.

Cost of cure and diminution in value

Baron Parke defined the contractual measure of damages as that sum of money which;[130] 'so far as money can do it [puts the claimant] ... in the same situation as if the contract had been performed'. However, this deceptively simple definition conceals an ambiguity. Should the claimant's lost expectation under the contract be quantified by reference to the 'cost of cure' (i.e. the cost of remedying the breach of contract), or by reference to 'diminution in value' (i.e. the amount by which something has become less valuable as a result of the breach)? Both methods of quantification may in fact produce the same award. In one case[131] damages awarded for breach of

---

[125] *Saunt v Belcher* (1920) 26 Com Cas 115; *Van den Hurk v Martens & Co Ltd* [1920] 1 KB 850.

[126] *Naughton v O'Callaghan* [1990] 3 All ER 191.

[127] [1974] Ch 30.

[128] The defendant could only convey title to the property if he brought an action against his wife.

[129] See also *East Ham BC v Bernard Sunley & Sons* [1966] AC 406.

[130] *Robinson v Harman* (1848) 1 Exch 850, 855.

[131] *Dean v Ainley* [1987] 1 WLR 1729. See also *Keeley v Guy MacDonald* (1984) 134 New LJ 522 and perhaps *Drummond v SU Stores* (1980) 258 EG 1293, quoted by Treitel, p. 880.

a promise to undertake building work prior to conveyance to prevent water from seeping into a cellar from a patio were described as the 'cost of the works' and the degree to which the property was rendered 'less valuable'. In other cases the two methods of assessment may produce very different awards and some guidance is needed to determine the appropriate method. It has been suggested that the common law[132] approach this choice on the basis of a number of presumptions.[133]

Where the breach of contract consists of defective building work, the claimant is prima facie entitled to damages assessed on the basis of the cost of cure.[134] However, the presumption was a weak one which was departed from when the cost of cure was out of proportion to the good to be obtained[135] or, more controversially, if the claimant had no intention of effecting the cure.[136]

In a contract between surveyor and purchaser, where the surveyor fails to advise about a defect in the property, the damages recoverable are the amount by which the client was caused to pay more for the property. The facts of each case will none the less affect the way in which this formula is applied.[137]

The surveyor has not warranted that the property has a particular feature; he has simply undertaken to use reasonable care in the compilation of his report. If damages were awarded on the basis of the work undertaken, this would be tantamount to enforcing a warranty by the surveyor that the house was as described in the survey. That would be to impose on surveyors a more extensive duty than they have assumed, a consequence which the House of Lords has recently rejected in *South Australia Asset Management Corp* v *York Montague*,[138] in the related context of an action by a mortgagee against a surveyor who negligently undervalued property at a time when property values began to fall.

The decision of the House of Lords in *Ruxley Electronics & Construction* v *Forsyth*[139] is a crucial development in the law of damages. The speeches

---

132 The common law presumptions are exceptionally reversed by statute. See Landlord and Tenant Act 1927, s 18 (damages for tenant's failure to leave premises in good repair – diminution of value method to be used).

133 Treitel, p. 880.

134 *Hoenig* v *Isaacs* [1952] 1 TLR 1360; *Bellgrove* v *Eldridge* (1954) 90 CLR 613; *East Ham BC* v *Bernard Sunley & Sons Ltd* [1966] AC 406; *Radford* v *De Froberville* [1978] 1 All ER 33; *Darlington Borough Council* v *Wiltshier Northern Ltd* [1995] 3 All ER 895 at 906 *per* Lord Steyn.

135 *Jacob & Youngs Inc* v *Kent* (1921) 230 NY 239 (particular plumbing specified and not installed, correction would require considerable demolition of completed work); *James* v *Hutton* [1950] 1 KB 9 (restoration of a shop window of no economic value).

136 *Wigsell* v *School for the Indigent Blind* (1882) 8 QBD 357; *Tito* v *Waddell (No. 2)* [1977] 1 Ch 106; *Maori Trustee* v *Rogross Farm Ltd* [1991] 3 NZLR 369. See now *Ruxley Electronics and Construction* v *Forsyth* [1995] 3 All ER 268, considered below.

137 *Watts* v *Morrow* [1991] 4 All ER 302. See also *Oswald* v *Countryside Surveyors Ltd* [1996] 2 EGLR 104 and *Derry* v *Sidney Phillips & Son* [1982] 1 WLR 1297.

138 [1996] 3 All ER 365. Perhaps surprisingly *Watts* v *Morrow* was not referred to in the opinions.

139 [1995] 3 All ER 268.

addressed[140] a number of matters of first principle. The case concerned a swimming pool that was constructed 9 inches shallower than the contractual specification. The House of Lords held that the defendant was not entitled to damages assessed on the basis of the cost of cure because it would be unreasonable for the claimant to insist on the cost of cure when that cost would be out of all proportion to the benefit to be obtained.[141] Cure involved a complete replacement since it was not technically possible to make the existing pool deeper. Further, the claimant's intention, or lack of such intention, to effect a cure was relevant to the issue of reasonableness but was certainly not conclusive.[142] Here the courts must be sensitive not to attach too much weight to the undertaking of the defendant to effect the cure if damages are awarded on that basis lest 'he be allowed to create a loss which does not exist in order to punish the defendants'.[143]

There was an emphasis on the need to respect the subjective wants of the victim of the breach when applying the test of reasonableness.[144] Lord Mustill referred to the economic concept of the 'consumer surplus' (the excess value placed upon a contractual performance by a promisee over the market value of that performance).[145] In *Ruxley* it was considered that the value placed by the defendant[146] upon a 7 foot 6 inch deep pool over the pool he in fact received was adequately recognised by leaving in place the award of £2,500 damages for loss of amenity made by the trial judge.[147] This was the only sum the defendant was entitled to as there was no diminution in the value of his property as a result of the shortfall in depth.[148]

It is suggested that the common law presumptions, which were already weak, as to whether cost of cure or diminution in value damages should be awarded in relation to particular types of contract, may not have survived intact the House of Lords' decision in *Ruxley*.

Non-delivery and the market-price rule

Where the seller, in breach of contract, fails to deliver[149] the contract goods

---

[140] *Ruxley* v *Forsyth*.

[141] *Per* Lord Bridge at p. 270h–j, *per* Lord Jauncey at p. 274f–h, *per* Lord Mustill at p. 277j, *per* Lord Lloyd at p. 285g, Lord Keith concurring.

[142] *Per* Lord Jauncey at p. 276a–d, *per* Lord Lloyd at p. 287h–j, Lords Keith, Bridge and Mustill concurring.

[143] *Per* Lord Lloyd at p. 288h.

[144] *Per* Lord Jauncey at p. 275e and j, *per* Lord Mustill at p. 277f–g, *per* Lord Lloyd at p. 286f, Lords Bridge and Keith concurring.

[145] Referring at p. 277f–g to Harris, Ogus and Phillips, 'Contract Remedies and the Consumer Surplus' (1979) 95 LQR 581.

[146] Mr Forsyth was the defendant to an action by the builder to recover the final instalment due under the building contract.

[147] This was not the subject of argument before the House of Lords.

[148] More than this sum was still owing for the construction of the pool.

[149] Where there is a delay rather than a failure in delivery the Sale of Goods Act 1979 does not provide any prima facie rule. Where the goods are merely defective the buyer can sue for breach of warranty. Section 53(3) provides a prima facie rule that damages are given by the difference in the time of delivery between the goods as they are and the goods as they should have been.

to the buyer, the buyer may bring an action for non-delivery.[150] Where there is an available market[151] for the contract goods the measure of damage is prima facie given by the difference between the contract price and the market price of the goods at the time they should have been delivered.[152]

This rule is intertwined with the principle of mitigation of loss and causation.[153] It is assumed that the buyer will go out into the market and purchase equivalent goods after the seller has failed to deliver. If the buyer fails to do so and the market is rising, further losses are assumed to be caused by his failure to mitigate and not by the seller's breach of contract.

This prima facie measure of damage may be said to represent both the cost of cure and also the diminution in value. This is another example where the two methods of quantification yield the same result.[154] The measure of damages may be expressed as the cost of curing the breach by purchasing a substitute or the difference in value between the performance that was promised and the one (i.e. nothing at all) that was tendered.

A number of factors determine whether there is an 'available market'[155] for goods: when a precise substitute[156] for the contract goods is available, within a reasonable time[157] and geographical distance,[158] in sufficient quantities[159] and possibly at a price which fluctuates with supply and demand.[160]

The prima facie rule laid down in the Sale of Goods Act, s 51(3) is not easily displaced. Even if the buyer in fact goes into the market at a later date and purchases substitute goods at a different price,[161] the rule will still apply. Further, any sub-contract entered by the buyer to resell goods of the same description will be ignored whether the sub-contract is at a higher[162] or lower[163] price than the main contract. The justification for the former rule is

---

[150] Sale of Goods Act 1979, s 51(1).

[151] Where there is no available market, the damages awarded will depend upon the use the buy intended for the goods, e.g. were they purchased for immediate resale or for the buyer's other commercial use.

[152] Sale of Goods Act 1979, s 53(3) or if no time for delivery was fixed at the time of the refusal to deliver.

[153] *Contra*: Goode (1995) *Commercial Law*. 2nd edn, pp. 415–18.

[154] See the discussion above.

[155] See generally Goode, *op. cit.*, pp. 410–12.

[156] *Lazenby Garages v Wright* [1976] 1 WLR 459. So stated the rule is surely too strict. See the excellent discussion in Ogus (1973) *The Law of Damages* at pp. 327–8, which pre-dates *Lazenby Garages v Wright*.

[157] *Lesters Leather and Skin Co Ltd v Home and Overseas Brokers Ltd* (1948) 64 TLR 569.

[158] No-one is expected 'to go hunting the globe' according to *Lesters Leather and Skin Co Ltd v Home and Overseas Brokers Ltd, ibid.*

[159] That is, there is an excess of supply over demand. If the action is by the seller it is necessary for demand to exceed supply: *WL Thompson v Robinson (Gunmakers) Ltd* [1955] Ch 177.

[160] *Charter v Sullivan* [1957] 2 QB 117. This requirement may well be otiose. See Ogus, *op. cit.* (n. 156 above), pp. 326–7.

[161] *R Pagnan & Fratelli v Corbisa Industrial Agropacuaria Lda* [1970] 2 Lloyd's Rep 14.

[162] *Williams v Reynolds* (1865) 6 B & S 495; *Mohammad Habib Ullah (Sheikh) v Bird & Co* (1921) 37 TLR 405.

[163] *Rodocanachi, Sons & Co v Milburn Bros* (1886) 18 QBD 67; *Williams Bros Ltd v Edward T Agius Ltd* [1914] AC 510.

that the buyer can perform his sub-contract by purchasing goods at the market price and that for the latter rule is said to rest upon the liberty of the buyer to choose to purchase goods at the prevailing market price to satisfy his sub-purchaser.

The situation is different if the sub-sale relates to the actual goods, rather than goods of the same description, forming the subject of the main sale. If it was within the reasonable contemplation of the seller that the buyer would enter a sub-sale to sell the same goods the seller is precluded from relying upon s 51(3) as there is then said to be no available market for the buyer; the tender of any other good by the buyer would simply not fulfil his obligation under the sub-sale.[164] The practical result is that the buyer will be able to recover the difference between the contract price and the sub-sale price so long as this loss is not too remote.

It is possible in very limited circumstances to depart from the market-price rule, even when there is an available market. Such an exceptional case occurred where buyers properly rejected goods and subsequently bought the same goods from the seller at a reduced price and sold them on at a profit.[165] If the market price rule had been applied, the buyers would have been compensated for a non-existent loss when they in fact made a profit.

A seller of goods may sue a buyer who in breach of contract refuses to take delivery

The action for damages for non-acceptance by the buyer,[166] is the seller's equivalent of the buyer's claim to damages for non-delivery. In both cases, the Sale of Goods Act 1979 provides a prima facie rule of assessment, which is to apply where there is an available market[167] in the goods. The buyer's claim is assessed as the difference between the contract price and the market or current price at the time the goods should have been delivered;[168] the seller's action is based on the difference between the contract price and the market or current price at the time the goods ought to have been accepted.[169]

The action for non-acceptance is also bound up with the principles of mitigation of loss and causation. It is effectively assumed that the seller will go out into the market and secure an equivalent sale after the buyer has failed to accept. If the seller fails to do so and the market is rising further losses are assumed to be caused by his failure to mitigate and not by the buyer's breach of contract.

---

[164] *Re R & H Hall and WH Pim Jr* (1928) 139 LT 50.

[165] *Pagnan and Fratelli* v *Corbisa Industrial Agropacuaria Limitada* [1970] 2 Lloyd's Rep 14.

[166] A disappointed seller could also sue for the price of the goods if the property in them has passed. See s 49, Sale of Goods Act 1979.

[167] See above n. 151 for a definition of an available market. See also on the definition of an available market for the seller, *Shearson Lehman Hutton Inc* v *Maclaine Watson & Co Ltd (No. 2)* [1990] 3 All ER 723.

[168] See above, Sale of Goods Act 1979, s 51(3).

[169] Sale of Goods Act 1979, s 50(3).

Both the cost of cure and the diminution in value are represented by this measure of loss.[170] The measure of damages may be expressed as the cost of curing the breach by securing a substitute sale or the difference in value between the performance that was promised and the one (i.e. nothing at all) that was tendered.

The expectation measure: non-pecuniary loss

In actions for breach of contract[171] the recovery of damages for non-pecuniary loss has been considered exceptional so that the decisions about to be examined are often categorised as a limit upon the recovery of damages for breach of contract.

In *Malik v Bank of Credit and Commerce International SA (in liquidation)*[172] the appellants were senior employees who were made redundant after the collapse of the bank because of its involvement in a massive international fraud of which they were not aware. The appellants sought damages from their former employer for breach of contract for 'stigma compensation' as, following their redundancy, they were unable to secure alternative employment because of their association with the bank. The appellants were successful before the House of Lords which held that the bank had breached an implied term of the contract of employment by conducting business in a way likely to seriously damage the relationship of confidence and trust with its employees. If it was a reasonably foreseeable consequence of breach that employee's future employment prospects would be adversely affected,[173] then damages would be recoverable. There was nothing contrary to principle in the recovery of damages for loss of reputation caused by breach of contract.

The *Malik* case was not strictly a case about the recovery of non-pecuniary damages for breach of contract. The appellants sought compensation for continuing financial losses.[174] However, a number of restrictions upon the availability of damages for non-pecuniary loss were considered, particularly the troublesome old case of *Addis v Gramophone Co Ltd*[175] which, though not overruled, was interpreted narrowly.[176] The most distinctive feature of the approach of the House of Lords in *Malik* is that the recovery of so-called 'stigma compensation' 'should be assessed in accordance with ordinary

---

170 See above the discussion of *Dean v Ainley* [1987] 1 WLR 1729.
171 Tort where damages for loss of reputation are recoverable in several torts, e.g. defamation. Further, in actions for personal injury damages for pain and suffering and loss of amenity are routinely awarded. Actions for personal injury are usually but not necessarily brought in tort.
172 [1997] 3 All ER 1.
173 The case proceeded upon the basis of an agreed set of facts; however, the liquidators did not admit the accuracy of these facts, *ibid. per* Lord Nicholls at p. 4g.
174 *Per* Lord Nicholls at p. 7d and *per* Lord Steyn at p. 19d, Lords Goff, Mackay and Mustill agreeing.
175 [1909] AC 488, applied in *Johnson v Unisys* [1999] 1 All ER 854.
176 *Per* Lord Nicholls at p. 9b–f and *per* Lord Steyn at pp. 19f–20g, Lords Goff, Mackay and Mustill agreeing.

contractual principles'.[177] This may signal a greater willingness to base the recovery of damages for non-pecuniary losses upon general principle, and may modify the detailed and overlapping divisions that exist in the present case law. The pre-existing categories are therefore presented within the general framework of the expectation and reliance measures of damage.

Contracts for the provision of pleasure

Damages for disappointment and mental distress were awarded in the case of *Jarvis* v *Swans Tours*,[178] upon a breach of contract relating to a package holiday. The Court of appeal departed from earlier authority[179] by awarding a modest sum, on the basis that this was a 'contract to provide entertainment and enjoyment'.[180] The availability of such damages in relation to contracts to provide holidays is now well settled.[181] Similar damages have been awarded against those who have contracted to provide services[182] for weddings.

In *Ruxley Electronics* v *Forsyth*[183] the first instance judge made an award of £2,500 for loss of amenity when a swimming pool was 9 inches short of its contracted depth. The House of Lords did not hear argument on this award but Lord Lloyd[184] said that '(t)his was a view which the judge was entitled to take'.[185] Therefore, non-commercial building contracts may be classified as contracts for the provision of enjoyment.

The equivalent of damages for disappointment or mental distress in a consumer contract is the claim for loss of profits in a commercial dealing. In the consumer case the provision of pleasure or happiness is anticipated,[186] in the commercial one a profit was envisaged; in both cases the expectation measure of damages must seek to put the claimant, so far as an award of

---

[177] *Per* Lord Nicholls at p. 9f and *per* Lord Steyn at pp. 21e and 22c–d, Lords Goff, Mackay and Mustill agreeing.

[178] [1978] RTR 474.

[179] *Hamlin* v *Great Northern Railway Co* (1856) 1 H & N 408 and *Hobbs* v *London & South Western Railway Co* (1875) LR 10 QB 111. Damages were said to be 'at large' in the old action for breach of promise to marry and so may have included compensation for loss of enjoyment. *Finlay* v *Chirney* (1988) 20 QBD 494. The action was abolished by the Law Reform (Miscellaneous Provisions) Act 1970, s 1(1).

[180] Lord Denning: [1973] 1 QB 233 at 238A.

[181] *Jackson* v *Horizon Holidays* [1975] 1 WLR 1468; *Kemp* v *Intasun Holidays Ltd* [1987] 2 FTLR 234; *The Mikhail Lermontov* [1991] 2 Lloyd's Rep 155 (Supreme Court of New South Wales). See also *Newell* v *Canadian Pacific Airlines Ltd* (1976) 74 DLR (3d) 574.

[182] *Dunn* v *Disc Jockey Unlimited Co Ltd* (1978) 87 DLR (3d) 408, *Chandle* v *East African Airways Corp* [1964] EA 78, *Cole* v *Rana* [1993] CLJ 392 (transport); *Diesen* v *Sampson* 1971 SLT 49, *Wilson* v *Sooter Studios* (1989) 55 DLR (4th) (photography), (entertainment); *Hardy* v *Losner Formals* [1997] Current Law Digest 60, September (clothing); *Morris* v *Britannia Hotels Ltd* [1997] Current Law Digest 63, June (accommodation). The latter suggested that disrupted wedding arrangements justified higher awards.

[183] [1995] 3 All ER 268.

[184] The other members of the court did not express a view.

[185] At p. 289e.

[186] In a small number of cases damages for disappointment or mental distress have been awarded where it would be hard to conclude that the contract was exclusively one for the provision of pleasure, e.g. *Jackson* v *Chrysler Acceptance* [1978] RTR 474 and *Bernstein* v *Pamson Motors (Golders Green) Ltd* [1987] 2 All ER 220 (sabotage of cars).

money can, in the position he would have been in if the contract had been performed. This results in an award of damages for disappointment or mental distress *or* one for loss of profit depending upon the type of contract broken. The two claims appear to be mutually exclusive. Staughters LJ trenchantly expressed this view in *Hayes v James & Charles Dodd* when he said:[187]

> I would not view with enthusiasm the prospect that every shipowner in the Commercial Court, having successfully claimed for unpaid freight or demurrage, would be able to add a claim for distress suffered while he was waiting for his money.

Contracts to provide peace of mind or freedom from distress

Contracts for the provision of enjoyment are clearly related to contracts for peace of mind or freedom from distress; the former is concerned with the provision of pleasure the latter is concerned with the avoidance of displeasure. However, they are none the less distinct. In *Bliss v South East Thames Regional Health Authority*[188] Dillon LJ said that damages for mental distress are available 'where the contract which has been broken was itself a contract to provide peace of mind or freedom from distress'. Although this *dictum* has been acted on many times,[189] its exact ambit is unclear. Contracts which fall within this category include the employment of a solicitor in *Heywood v Wellers*[190] to obtain a non-molestation order, a contract to provide disability insurance[191] and contracts to provide burial services.[192]

Failure to enhance reputation

Are damages for loss of reputation claims for pecuniary or non-pecuniary loss?[193] To the extent that the loss for which compensation is sought is the financial consequences of a damaged reputation the suit is a pecuniary one; to the extent that damages are claimed for the loss of reputation *per se* the claim is for non-pecuniary loss. Damage to reputation may consist of a failure to enhance the reputation of the claimant. This will form part of the claimant's suit to be put, so far as an award of money can, in the position he would have been in if the contract had been performed, i.e. as part of the

---

187 [1990] 2 All ER 815 at 823.

188 [1987] ICR 701 at 718B.

189 For example, *Hayes v James and Charles Dodd* [1990] 2 All ER 815 at 824a–b and *Watts v Morrow* [1991] 1 WLR 1421 at 1441 B–C.

190 [1976] QB 446. See also *McLeish v Amoo-Gottfried & Co* (1993) 137 Sol Jo LB 204. *Contra: Cook v S* [1967] 1 All ER 299 (claimant's illness too remote a consequence of solicitor's negligence to be recoverable).

191 *Warrington v Great-West Life Assurance Co* (1996) 139 DLR (4th) 18.

192 *Lamm v Shingleton* (1949) 55 SE 2d 810 and *Mason v Westside Cemeteries* (1996) 135 DLR (4th) 361.

193 'Sometimes, in practice, the distinction between damage to reputation and financial loss can become blurred': *Malik v BCCI* [1997] 3 All ER 1 *per* Lord Nicholls at p. 10j.

expectation measure of damages. Actors[194] and authors[195] may recover damages from a defendant whose breach of contract has resulted in a failure to enhance their reputation. The damages are often described as being for 'loss of publicity'.[196] Further analogies are a claim brought by an apprentice in respect of the premature termination of his training where damages are recoverable for the consequent disadvantage in future employment prospects[197] and damages for loss of business awarded following the defendant's failure to publish an advertisement in a newspaper.[198] Although such claims are often described as being for financial loss,[199] the difficulty of computation must leave a suspicion that an element of the award comprised compensation for non-pecuniary losses.

Loss of amenity

Loss of amenity is one of the heads of recovery of non-pecuniary loss in personal injury actions. It now seems that damages for loss of amenity may be awarded in actions for breach of contract. Such an award has been made in respect of the defective tiling work by a builder[200] and was proffered by Lord Lloyd as a possible alternative explanation of the award made by the trial judge and left in place by the House of Lords in *Ruxley Electronics* v *Forsyth*.[201] Such awards are likely to be routinely made in proceedings brought in a county court and before deputy judges acting as arbitrators. The approach of the higher appellate courts appears to be at odds with the robust common sense practised by inferior courts.

The reliance measure: pecuniary loss

The reliance measure of damages seeks to restore the claimant to the position he was in before he entered the contract.[202] For this reason, it is sometimes said to protect the *status quo ante*.

The reliance measure[203] of damages may be awarded when the expectation measure is unavailable because the assessment of such damages would be too speculative. This seems to be a characteristic of many 'entertainment'

---

[194] *Marbe* v *George Edwardes (Daley's Theatre) Ltd* [1928] 1 KB 269 and *Herbert Clayton* v *Oliver* [1930] AC 209.
[195] *Tolnay* v *Criterion Film Productions Ltd* [1936] 2 All ER 1625, *Joseph* v *National Magazine Co* [1959] Ch 14.
[196] *Herbert Clayton & Jack Waller Ltd* v *Oliver* [1930] AC 209 *per* Lord Buckmaster at 419.
[197] *Dunk* v *George Waller & Sons Ltd* [1970] 2 QB 163.
[198] *Marcus* v *Myers and Davis* (1895) 11 TLR 327. *Cf. Aerial Advertising* v *Bachelor's Peas Ltd* [1938] 2 All ER 788.
[199] Perhaps, strategically, to circumvent the restrictions on recovery laid down in *Addis* v *Gramophone Co Ltd* [1909] AC 488. The distinction was observed in *Aerial Advertising Co* v *Batchelor's Peas Ltd* [1938] 2 All ER 788 (unusual promotion contract).
[200] *G W Atkins Ltd* v *Scott* (1980) 7 Const LJ 215.
[201] [1995] 3 All ER 268 at 289h–290a.
[202] This is of course the 'tortious' measure of damages and is sometimes so called even in a contractual setting, e.g. in the law of misrepresentation.
[203] And the restitution measure.

contracts.[204] The issue was explored in *McRae* v *Commonwealth Disposals Commission*[205] which involved the sale of a wrecked oil tanker. When assessing expectation measure damages Dixon and Fullagar JJ said that 'the claimants have no starting point'. This comment needs explanation. In a normal action for non-delivery the buyer's damages are given by the difference between the market price and the contract price of the goods.[206] In *McRae* the claimant was, unsurprisingly, unable to prove the former, the value of a non-existent ship. However, if the claim is cast as one for reliance measure damages, the claimant is seeking compensation for the extent to which his resources have been depleted in reliance upon the promise of performance; he has a starting point.

Post-contractual reliance

Post-contractual reliance refers to any expenditure of the claimant which is wasted as a result of the defendant's breach of contract. Such expenses are recoverable and will depend upon the nature of the contract breached. In a contract to manufacture one part of a machine, recoverable expenses included the cost of making and painting other parts,[207] in a boxer's contract to fight – the promoter's expenses,[208] in a contract to purchase the right to salvage a wreck – the cost of preparing an abortive salvage operation,[209] in a contract to sell land for poultry farming – the cost of moving a caravan onto the land, installing toilet facilities, purchasing and constructing chicken pens and transporting personal furniture,[210] and in a contract to employ an actor in a television play – fees paid to designers, directors, other actors and staff.[211]

Pre-contractual reliance[212]

In *Hodges* v *Earl of Lichfield* Tindal CJ said:[213]

> The expenses preliminary to the contract ought not to be allowed. The party enters into them for his own benefit at a time when it is uncertain whether there will be any contract or not.[214]

---

[204] *Chicago Coliseum Club* v *Dempsey* (1932) 265 Ill App. 542 (boxer's contract with his promoter); *Anglia TV* v *Reed* [1972] 1 QB 60 (actor's contract with TV company); *CCC Films (London) Ltd* v *Impact Quadrant Films Ltd* [1985] QB 16 (licence to reproduce certain videotapes).

[205] (1951) 84 CLR 377.

[206] Sale of Goods Act 1979, s 53(3).

[207] *Hydraulic Engineering Co* v *McHaffie* 12 (1878) 4 QBD 670.

[208] *Chicago Coliseum Club* v *Dempsey* (1932) 265 Ill App 542.

[209] *McRae* v *Commonwealth Disposals Commission* (1951) 84 CLR 377.

[210] *Lloyd* v *Stanbury* [1971] 2 All ER 267.

[211] *Anglia TV* v *Reed* [1972] 1 QB 60.

[212] See Ogus (1972) 35 MLR 43.

[213] (1835) 1 Bing NC 492, 498. This is supported by some American case authority: *Gruber* v *S-M News Co Inc* (1954) 126 F Supp 442. *Cf. Security Stove and Manufacturing Co* v *American Railway Express Co* (1932) 51 SW 2d 572. See Treitel (1988) *Remedies for Breach of Contract*, pp. 85–6.

[214] Applied by Thesiger J in *Perestrello & Compania Limitada* v *United Paint Co Ltd* [1969] *The Times*, 16 April.

Lord Denning MR[215] did not accept this proposition in *Anglia TV* v *Reed*, and awarded damages which included 'expenditure incurred *before* the contract was entered, provided that it was such as would reasonably be in the contemplation of the parties as likely to be wasted if the contract was broken'. The reliance measure of damages seeks to restore a claimant to the position he was in before he entered the contract, whereas the award in *Anglia* restored the claimant to the position it was in *many months before* it entered into the contract with Reed. How can the expenses be incurred in *reliance* upon the contract? They were clearly incurred *in anticipation* of the contract. The cause of the wasted expenditure was not the breach of contract by Reed but the act of incurring considerable expenses well before the services of Reed had been secured. The recovery of such losses undermines the role of a contract as a device for the allocation of risk and so is inconsistent with decisions in other areas.[216] Any proposal[217] to permit the recovery of pre-contractual expenditure is open to this objection, since it both offends the rules of causation and is contrary to general principle.

The reliance measure: non-pecuniary loss

There is little evidence that the courts are prepared to recognise as reliance measure damages an award in favour of a claimant seeking damages for loss of existing reputation or physical inconvenience and consequent mental distress. Yet, in effect, the claimant is asking to be compensated for the deterioration in his position caused by the defendant's breach of contract.

Physical inconvenience

This is the type of non-pecuniary loss most readily accepted by the courts, as reflected in the wide variety of circumstances in which such awards have been made. These include actions by a sailor[218] and a railway passenger[219] who as a consequence of a breach of contract respectively left and alighted from the appropriate conveyance. Damages for physical inconvenience were awarded in an action against a solicitor who failed to recover posses-sion of his client's home[220] as well as numerous claims against surveyors

---

215 [1972] 1 QB 60 at 63H–64B. The phrase 'not unlikely' should now be substituted for the phrase 'likely' as denoting the degree of probability appropriate in the test of remoteness.

216 *Attorney General of Hong Kong* v *Humphrey's Estate (Queen's Gardens)* [1987] AC 114 (estoppel should respect a 'contractual' allocation of risk) and *Regalian Properties plc* v *London Dockland Development Corp* [1995] 1 WLR 212 (a restitution claim should not subvert a contractual allocation of risk).

217 For instance, the suggestion in Ogus (1973) *The Law of Damages* that the 'best solution' is that there should be recovery for any expense incurred after 'substantial agreement' had been reached: *op. cit.*, p. 350 and Burrows (*Remedies*), p. 255.

218 *Burton* v *Pinkerton* (1867) LR 2 Exch 340.

219 *Hobbs* v *London and South Western Rly Co* (1875) LR 10 QB 111.

220 *Bailey* v *Bullock* [1950] 66 TLR (Pt 2) 791.

whose negligence has resulted in the inconvenience of repairs being carried out.[221]

Physical inconvenience causing mental distress

This is more difficult to establish. In *Watts* v *Morrow*[222] the claimants purchased a holiday home in reliance upon the defendant's negligent survey. As a result they suffered considerable inconvenience while repairs were effected. In the Court of Appeal, the judge's award of £4,000 to each claimant for 'distress and inconvenience' was reduced to £750 'for distress caused by physical consequences of the breach of contract'.[223] Similar awards have been made in a number of cases.[224]

Damage to existing reputation

The difficulty of classifying claims brought in respect of damage to reputation has already been noted. Damage to existing reputation has traditionally been regarded as recoverable in a number of cases. A 'trader' has long been entitled to recover substantial damages for loss of business reputation without proof of actual damage.[225] The restriction to 'traders' resulted in some strange distinctions[226] and has now been abandoned.[227] In *Malik* v *BCCI*[228] an attempt[229] to confine recovery to the failure to enhance reputation and thereby deny recovery for damage to existing reputation was overruled. Similar damages have been recovered in other disparate circumstances, where advertising caused offence by disrupting remembrance services[230] and when defective goods were supplied and incorporated into another product, which was sold on.[231]

Following the decision by the House of Lords in *Malik*,[232] pecuniary damages for loss of reputation will be determined by general principles of contract law; it will no longer be necessary to come within a pre-existing

---

[221] *Perry* v *Sidney Phillips & Son* [1982] 1 WLR 1297; *Cross* v *David Martin & Mortimer* [1989] 1 EGLR 154; *Biss* v *Howard Son & Gooch* [1990] 1 EGLR 173; *Oswald* v *Countryside Surveyors* (1994) 47 Con LR 50, upheld by CA (1996) 50 Con LR 1.

[222] [1991] 1 WLR 1421.

[223] *Ibid. per* Ralph Gibson LJ at p. 1442 C and *per* Bingham LJ at p. 1445 G–H, Sir Stephen Brown agreeing.

[224] For example, *Cross* v *David Martin & Mortimer* [1989] 1 EGLR 154; *Biss* v *Howard Son & Gooch* [1990] 1 EGLR 173; *Ezekiel and Another* v *McDade and Others* [1995] 2 EGLR 107 (a tort case).

[225] *Rolin* v *Stewart* (1854) 14 CB 595; *Wilson* v *United Counties Bank Ltd* [1920] AC 102; *Davidson* v *Barclays Bank Ltd* [1940] 1 All ER 316.

[226] *Bank of New South Wales* v *Milvain* (1884) 10 VLR 3 (farmer not a trader); *Davidson* v *Barclays Bank Ltd* [1940] 1 All ER 316 (bookmaker is a trader).

[227] *Kpohraror* v *Woolwich Building Society* [1996] 4 All ER 119 departing from *Gibbons* v *Westminster Bank* [1939] 2 KB 882 and *McRae* v *Yorkshire Bank Ltd* [1988] BTLC 35.

[228] [1997] 3 All ER 1.

[229] *Withas* v *General Theatre Corp Ltd* [1933] 2 KB 536.

[230] *Aerial Advertising* v *Batchelor's Peas Ltd* [1938] 2 All ER 788.

[231] *GKN Centrax Gears* v *Matbro Ltd* [1976] 2 Lloyd's Rep 555.

[232] [1997] 3 All ER 1.

category of recovery.[233] However, what is unclear is the extent to which claims may be directly[234] made in respect of non-pecuniary losses. The case of *Addis v Gramophone Co Ltd*[235] has often been treated as authority to the contrary. Identifying the precise *ratio decidendi* of *Addis* was always a matter of some controversy; after *Malik* the task is even more difficult. Although *Addis* was not overruled in *Malik*, and has been applied by the Court of Appeal in *Johnson v Unisys*,[236] and the *ratio* of *Malik* cannot strictly extend beyond the recovery of financial losses. None the less, the logic which compelled the House of Lords to regard a claim for financial damage to reputation as unexceptional and subject only to the usual limiting factors would seem as applicable to a claim for non-pecuniary loss. It is submitted that both such claims should be recognised for the following reasons. First, the admitted difficulty of separating pecuniary and non-pecuniary loss. Second, the suspicion that many awards of pecuniary loss may contain an element of compensation for non-pecuniary loss. Third, such awards are likely to be modest. Fourth, the concerns expressed in *Addis* that such a claim is in effect an action for defamation have been examined and dismissed.[237] Fifth, as with the award of damages for pecuniary loss this would bring the courts into line with awards made by employment tribunals in cases of unfair dismissal. Sixth, *Addis* has been criticised and not followed overseas.[238]

The restitution measure

The restitution measure of damages seeks to restore to the victim of a breach of contract any benefit he has conferred on the perpetrator. Such an award falls to be considered in two circumstances. The first is where a party has performed some or all of his obligations under a contract but has not received any counter performance. In such circumstances, the consideration to be provided by the party in breach may be said to have failed. This situation is considered below. The second is where the party has profited from the breach of contract other than by the transfer of goods or money from the innocent party; the defendant has been enriched by his wrongdoing otherwise than by subtraction from the claimant's wealth.[239] This situation has already been examined above under the heading of Extra Compensatory Damages.

---

[233] 'I regard these cases not as exceptions but as the application of ordinary principles of contract law': *ibid. per* Lord Steyn at p. 21e.

[234] It has already been suggested that claims for pecuniary loss may conceal an element of recovery for non-pecuniary loss.

[235] [1909] AC 488.

[236] [1999] 1 All ER 854.

[237] For example, *per* Lord Atkinson at p. 496. See *per* Lord Nicholls at p. 10c–j, *per* Lord Steyn at p. 21 f–g citing *Spring* v *Guardian Assurance plc* [1995] AC 296 where a similar argument was dismissed in relation to the tort of negligence.

[238] *Rowlands* v *Collow* [1992] 1 NZLR 178 (New Zealand High Court); *contra: Bloxham* v *Robinson* [1996] 2 NZLR 664; *Anderson* v *Davies* [1996] NZLR; *Peso Silver Mines Ltd (NPL)* v *Cropper* (1966) 58 DLR (2d) 1 (Supreme Court of Canada).

[239] The terminology was developed by Birks, *op. cit.* (n. 14 herein above).

A claimant may recover money paid to a defendant if the consideration provided by the defendant may be said to have totally failed. In this context, consideration bears an unfamiliar meaning; here it will usually refer to the bargained-for performance rather than the promise of such.[240]

Recovery in respect of non-monetary benefits

A claimant who has terminated a contract[241] for breach may bring a *quantum meruit* action in respect of goods[242] delivered or services rendered.[243] Such an action may be maintained even though the party seeking the remedy has received part of the performance, i.e. 'partial' failure of consideration is sufficient.[244]

The question then arises, how do you quantify the extent to which the recipient of goods or services has been unjustly enriched? Where the claim is in relation to money transferred (e.g. an advance payment for goods that were never supplied), the defendant may be said to have incontrovertibly benefited. Money is of value to us all. Where the defendant receives a benefit in kind, such as goods or services, the answer is more difficult. The extent to which the recipient who refuses to pay for such may be said to be unjustly enriched should reflect the value to him of the goods or services.[245] However, where the goods or services were tendered under a contract, the defendant should not usually[246] be allowed to deny that they were of any value to him. After all, he got all or part of what he had bargained for.[247]

It has been argued that the contract should operate as an upper limit upon recovery to avoid the situation where the claimant in a restitutionary action can recover more for partial performance than he would be able to in a contractual action following complete performance.[248] However, this approach

---

240 Two difficult questions are omitted here. First, has there been a total lack of consideration when the defendant's performance has not conferred a benefit on the claimant, but the defendant has incurred a detriment. Second, will the use of contractual subject matter necessarily preclude a finding that there has been a total failure of consideration? These issues are discussed in Furmston (1999) *The Law of Contract*, pp. 1268–9.

241 *De Bernardy v Harding* (1853) 8 Exch 822; *Chandler Bros Ltd v Boswell* [1936] 3 All ER 179.

242 The action in respect of goods is sometimes termed *quantum valebat*. Here the more modern usage of *quantum meruit* to cover actions in respect of goods and services is adopted.

243 A *quantum meruit* will also lie where there is no express provision for payment in respect of goods (Sale of Goods Act 1979, s 8(2)) or services (Supply of Goods and Services Act 1982, s 15(1)) and where there is no concluded contract: *William Lacey (Hounslow) Ltd v Davis* [1954] 1 QB 428 and *BSC v Cleveland Bridge & Engineering Co Ltd* [1984] 1 All ER 504; *contra: Regalian Properties plc v London Dockland Development Corp* [1995] 1 WLR 212 (it was clear that the risk of a breakdown in negotiations was assumed by the party undertaking preparatory work). See Treitel, pp. 915–19.

244 The language of 'failure' of consideration is simply absent from cases where restitution is sought in respect of services or goods. An exception is *Pearce v Brain* [1929] 2 KB 310.

245 The defendant is said to be allowed to 'subjectively devalue' the benefit received. See Birks, *op. cit.* pp. 109–14.

246 This reasoning may not always apply, e.g. where the cost of completion is for some reason greater than the total contract price.

247 Burrows (*Restitution*), pp.14–15.

248 Treitel, p. 989, n. 71, where he describes such a conclusion as 'absurd'.

is not supported by the case law. In *Boomer* v *Muir*,[249] an American case, the claimant recovered $257,000 for the work of completing a dam when only $20,000 remained unpaid under the contract. In any event, it should be emphasised than any such ceiling on recovery derives from the manner of valuing the defendant's benefit and not from the contract *per se* limiting the restitutionary remedy. In other words, actions in restitution in respect of benefits in kind may, like the same action to recover money paid,[250] permit the claimant to escape from a bad bargain.

The relationship between the measures of damage

The principles governing the relationship between the three measures of damage for breach of contract are easy to state but can be difficult to apply. There are three principles, which are outlined below.

Combining claims and overlap

A claimant may combine claims under the different measures of damage, so long as there is no overlap between the items of loss claimed. For example, in breach of contract a singer fails to turn up for a concert. The promoter seeks as damages:

1. the £100,000 fee paid to the singer;
2. £500,000 for the cost of hiring a venue to stage the concert;
3. £2m gross ticket receipts which have to be returned.

The promoter will not be able to claim items 1 (restitution) and 2 (reliance) as well as item 3, his gross profit (expectation). An award of damages based upon gross profits would effectively include compensation for the fee and cost of hire as these were costs the promoter intended to discharge from the gross receipts.

In *Naughton* v *O'Callaghan*[251] a race horse was sold with a warranted pedigree; damages for breach of that warranty were based upon the difference between its value with the warranted quality (which was taken to be the contract price), and its value when its true pedigree was discovered,[252] (expectation) as well as the cost of training and stabling fees (reliance). Indeed, it may be possible in an appropriate case to recover all three measures of damage. In a case involving the sale of machinery,[253] the purchaser recovered the price paid (restitution), the cost of installation (reliance) as well as his net loss of profit (expectation).

---

[249] (1933) 24 P 2d 570. See also *Lodder* v *Slowey* [1904] AC 442.
[250] See below the example under heading of: Escaping from bad bargaining expectation and restitution.
[251] [1990] 3 All ER 191.
[252] Some two seasons later by which time it had failed as a racehorse. Justice required departure from the breach date rule laid down in Sale of Goods Act 1979, s 53(3) and the adoption of a later date for the assessment of damages within the discretion permitted by *Johnson* v *Agnew* [1980] AC 367.
[253] *Millar's Machinery Co Ltd* v *David Way & Son* (1935) 40 Com Cas 204.

Escaping from bad bargains – expectation and reliance

The second principle is that a claimant is not entitled to his claim as one for wasted expenditure (reliance) in order to escape the consequence of a bad bargain.[254] Whether the bargain is a bad one or not can only be ascertained by considering the claimant's expectation. The principle is that the expectation interest controls the reliance interest.

In *C & P Haulage (a firm)* v *Middleton*[255] a licensee was wrongfully ejected from commercial premises. In an action by the licensor to recover unpaid rent the licensee counter-claimed reimbursement for works of improvement he had undertaken. The Court of Appeal declined to award substantial damages on the counterclaim because it was a term of the licence that the works of improvement became the property of the licensor and it was not possible for the licensee to recoup his outlay in the period the licence had lawfully to run. In any case, the licensee had obtained permission from the local authority to run his business from home for which privilege he paid no extra rent. In these circumstances the breach of contract did not cause him any loss; the licensee was better off as a result of the breach of contract. In so far as he did suffer a loss, it was caused by the impropriety of entering the original contract; he was trying to escape from a bad bargain.

A claimant who is unable to prove his expectation claim with the requisite degree of certainty therefore may seek to recover his reliance loss, e.g. in *McRae* v *Commonwealth Disposals Commission*[256] the claimant could not prove the amount of salvageable metal, etc. which would be recovered from a non-existent tanker. If to recover his reliance losses the claimant must prove that the bargain was a good one (namely, that it was profitable), he would be unable to do so. The very thing which relegated him to a reliance claim would then seem to bar that claim. Therefore, it has been held[257] that a claimant seeking to recover reliance measure damages does not have to prove that the bargain was a good one, rather the defendant bears the burden of defeating the claim by proving that the bargain was a bad one.

Escaping from bad bargains – expectation and restitution

The third principle is that a claimant may bring an action for the restitution

---

[254] *L Albert and Son* v *Armstrong Rubber Co* (1949) 178 F 2d. 182; *Bowlay Logging Ltd* v *Domtar* [1978] 4 WWR 105; *C & P Haulage (a Firm)* v *Middleton* [1983] 3 All ER 94; *CCC Films (London) Ltd* v *Impact Quadrant Films Ltd* [1984] 3 All ER 298; *Milburn Services Ltd* v *United Trading Group* (1997) 52 Con LR 130. *Contra* the approach of the Australian High Court in *Commonwealth of Australia* v *Amman Aviation Pty Ltd* (1991) 66 ALJR 123 where Mason CJ and Dawson, Brennan and Deane JJ seek to express the recovery of reliance losses as a part of an expectation claim thereby relegating the principle of English law which defines the relationship between the measures to an assumption or inference of profitability. While the substantive result accords with the English rule, the approach does seem overly elaborate and is at least resisted by Toohey and MacHugh JJ.

[255] [1983] 3 All ER 94.

[256] (1951) 84 CLR 377.

[257] *L Albert and Son* v *Armstrong Rubber Co* (1949) 178 F 2d 182; *Bowlay Logging Ltd* v *Domtar* [1978] 4 WWR 105; *CCC Films (London) Ltd* v *Impact Quadrant Films Ltd* [1984] 3 All ER 298.

measure of damages and thereby escape the consequence of a bad bargain.[258] Unlike the reliance measure, the restitution measure of damages is not controlled by the expectation claim. An example will illustrate this.

A agrees to purchase a second-hand Ford Motor car from B for £10,000 (the market price) and pays a £500 deposit. Before the date set for delivery, Ford reduces the price of all its new cars. As a consequence, the second-hand value of all cars is reduced by 10 per cent. If for some reason the defendant refuses to deliver the car, the claimant is entitled to recover his deposit even though the bargain turned out to be a bad one (i.e. he could not recover anything by way of expectation damages).

Such claims will not be common as the defendant is unlikely to breach a contract of sale on a falling market. In addition, the action is subject to a precondition that the failure of consideration must be total. The inability of a claimant to show that there had been the required failure of consideration may have the effect of relegating a claimant to an action for reliance measure damages in order to recover sums paid to the defendant.[259] Then, of course, the claimant's action will fail if the defendant is able to prove that the bargain was a bad one.

LIMITS UPON RECOVERY

Causation

Issues of causation are only infrequently raised in contract, as opposed to tort, cases. However, when causation is discussed,[260] the courts take a robust and pragmatic approach to questions of causation preferring 'common sense'[261] to philosophical niceties.

A claimant is able to recover damages when the defendant's breach of contract is not the only cause of his loss.[262] However, recovery will be refused unless the loss would not have occurred *but for* the breach of contract. In *Monarch SS Co v Karlshamns Oljefabriker (A/B)*[263] it was said that though a shipowner may be in breach of the seaworthiness term in a charter if the ship does not carry the proper complement of medical supplies this will not assist cargo owners whose goods are lost if the ship subsequently founders in a storm. However, the so-called 'but for' test establishes a necessary rather than a sufficient causal link. So there was no liability where the claimant

---

258 *Bush v Canfield* (1818) 2 Conn 485 (US case – buyer of a quantity of flour for $14,000 terminated the contract and recovered a $5,000 part payment when the market price had dropped by some $4,000); *Wilkinson v Lloyd* (1845) 7 QB 27 (sale of shares – purchase price recovered when shares had fallen in value).
259 For example, *CCC Films (London) Ltd v Impact Quadrant Films Ltd* [1984] 3 All ER 298.
260 *Monarch SS Co v Karlshamns Oljefabriker (A/B)* [1949] AC 196; *Quinn v Burch Bros (Builders) Ltd* [1966] 2 QB 370; *Galoo v Bright Grahame Murray* [1995] 1 All ER 16.
261 *Galoo Ltd v Bright Grahame Murray* [1994] 1 WLR 1360 at 1375 A *per* Glidewell LJ.
262 A defendant will be liable even if his 'breach of contract is one of two causes, both ... of equal efficacy': *Heskell v Continental Express* [1950] 1 All ER 1033 at 1048 *per* Devlin J.
263 [1949] AC 196 at 226.

suffered a personal injury which would have been avoided if the defendant had fulfilled its duty and provided a step ladder.[264] In addition, it is said that the breach of contract must be a substantial cause; it will not be a substantial cause of loss where there is an unforeseeable intervention by a third party.

Where such intervention is foreseeable, it will generally be held not to have broken the chain of causation.[265] In this way a newspaper was held responsible for losses incurred following its recommendation of a dishonest stockbroker.[266] A decision that a railway was not to be held liable to a passenger who was robbed while travelling on an overcrowded train may be explained on the basis that the act of the thief was not foreseeable.[267]

Where the intervening act is that of the claimant himself, a court may hold that the claimant has failed to mitigate his loss or that his own negligence has contributed to the damage. However, it is possible that the act of the claimant may be considered so unreasonable that it operates to break the chain of causation with the consequence that the claimant recovers nothing because he is considered to be the author of his own losses.

Contributory negligence

In the tort of negligence the Law Reform (Contributory Negligence) Act 1945 will apply where the claimant suffers loss partly as a result of his 'fault' and partly as a result of the defendant's 'fault'. If the Act applies, the claimant's suit will not fail, as happened prior to the Act, but rather his recovery will be 'reduced to such extent as the court thinks just and equitable having regard to the claimant's share in the responsibility for the damage.[268] Whether the 1945 Act applies to actions for breach of contract[269] is not an easy question to answer. Hobhouse J in *Forsikringsaktieselskapet Vesta* v *Butcher*[270] distinguishes three situations:

1. where the defendant's liability arises from some contractual provision which does not depend on negligence on his part;
2. where the defendant's liability arises from a contractual obligation which is expressed in terms of taking care (or its equivalent) but does not correspond to a common law duty to take care which would exist in the given case independently of contract;

---

[264] *Quinn* v *Burch Bros (Builders) Ltd* [1966] 2 QB 370.

[265] *The Silver Sky* [1981] 2 Lloyd's Rep 95.

[266] *De la Bere* v *Pearson* [1908] 1 KB 280.

[267] *Cobb* v *GW Ry* [1894] AC 499. An alternative explanation of these cases is that the chain of causation will not be broken where the defendant's contractual duty to the claimant was to prevent the intervening act of the third party. Cf. *Weld-Blundell* v *Stephens* [1920] AC 956 (no recovery even though intervening act was foreseeable and exactly what defendants should guard against).

[268] Section 1(1).

[269] See the discussions in Burrows (*Remedies*) at pp. 83–5 and Treitel, pp. 886–8.

[270] [1988] 2 All ER 43 affirmed without reference to contributory negligence at [1989] AC 880.

3. where the defendant's liability in the law of contract is the same as his liability in the tort of negligence independently of the existence of any contract.

These may be summarised and exemplified as:

1. strict liability in contract, e.g. seller's obligation under Sale of Goods Act 1979, s 14(2) to provide goods of satisfactory quality;
2. liability for breach of a contractual duty of care, e.g. a service provider's liability under Supply of Goods and Services Act 1982, s 13 to perform the service with reasonable care and skill;
3. concurrent duties of care owed in contract and tort eg. those owed by many professionals, such as solicitors.[271]

The court's approach to contributory negligence is outlined in the *Vesta* case which involved an action by the insurers of a fish farm against brokers who arranged reinsurance of the risk. The allegation of contributory negligence arose from the claimants' failure to confirm that their initial request for the deletion of a requirement of a 24-hour watch on the premises had been complied with. As the claimants succeeded in their action against the reinsurer, the comments upon the broker's position were *obiter dicta*. None the less, Hobhouse J and the Court of Appeal (the House of Lords did not discuss this point) analysed the facts as falling within category 3 and said that if the claimants had recovered substantial damages against the brokers, these would fall to be reduced to reflect the claimant's contributory negligence.

The decision in the *Vesta* case has been followed and applied in a number of subsequent cases and so the availability of contributory negligence to reduce damages in category 3 cases would now seem to be settled. The position in relation to category 1 cases has also been recently considered by the Court of Appeal in *Barclays Bank v Fairclough Building Ltd and Others*[272] where a contractor employed to clean an asbestos roof[273] who was in breach of contract for failing to take adequate safety precautions alleged that his employer was contributorily negligent because it had assumed architectural responsibilities for the work. The Court of Appeal held that the defendant was in breach of a strict contractual duty[274] and that as a matter of construction the 1945 Act had no application.

---

[271] *Midland Bank Trust Co Ltd v Hett, Stubbs and Kemp* [1979] Ch 384.
[272] [1995] 1 All ER 289.
[273] In fact, the defendant sub-contracted the work to C who in turn employed T to do it. *Barclays Bank v Fairclough Building Ltd* [1995] 1 All ER 289 was concerned with the contract between *BB and F and Barclays Bank v Fairclough (No.2)* [1998] IRLR 605 with the contract between C and T. The former was a category 1 situation and the latter category 3 situation.
[274] Namely, the requirement to execute the work in an expeditious, efficient and workmanlike manner and to comply with any statutory provisions applicable to the work. The trial judge had considered the case to fall within category 3. In *Barclays Bank plc v Fairclough Building Ltd (No. 2)* [1998] IRLR 605 it was held that concurrent duties of care in contract and tort were owed by the party who actually cleaned the roof to the sub-contractor who employed him (i.e. their relationship fell within category 3).

The Law Commission has recommended that the Act should be amended to cover category 2 cases, resiling from its original proposal that it should be applied to category 1 cases as well.[275] Although originally moved by the injustice that the present law can perpetrate,[276] the Commission became more impressed by the countervailing argument to the effect that too radical a reform would create uncertainty which might prolong and complicate litigation with its attendant consequences. A significant development in this regard is the recent expansion in the scope of concurrent liability in contract and tort.[277] The result will be an increase in the number of cases falling within category 3 and a concomitant decrease in the number falling within category 2.

Remoteness

The general aim of an award of damages is compensation. However, 'this purpose, if relentlessly pursued, would provide him with a complete indemnity for all loss *de facto* resulting from a particular breach, however improbable, however unpredictable'. Therefore, a consistent feature of the common law is that a person is not held liable for the infinite consequences of their wrongful act. The intuitive appeal of a limit upon a person's responsibility for damage he/she causes is more easily illustrated in tort than in contract. Consider the following newspaper extract:[278]

> Nigel McNaughton 30, hit a 'socket shot' as he attempted to reach the 12th green at the High Peak Golf Club in Buxton, Derbyshire. The ball whizzed on to the A6, where it whacked motorcyclist, Tony Evans, and knocked him off his £15,000 Ducati. Bouncing off Evans' crash helmet, the ball shattered the windscreen of a BMW behind him while the bike smashed into a caravan being towed by a Range Rover behind the BMW. Moments later, Tony hit the caravan. No one, fortunately, was badly hurt, but the damage was expected to cost thousands.

Should Mr McNaughton be liable in the tort of negligence to the full extent of the losses he has caused? Most, including the author who is a Ducati rider, would think not.

The following example was offered in a nineteenth-century case.[279] Where a man going to be married to an heiress, his horse having cast a shoe on the journey, employed a blacksmith to replace it, who did the job so unskilfully that the horse was lamed, and, the rider not arriving in time, the lady married another; and the blacksmith was held liable for the loss of the marriage.

---

275 Law Com No 219 (1993) and No. 114 (1990). This proposal is contrary to recent authority. See *Raflatac v Eade* [1999] 1 Lloyd's Rep 506.

276 For an example, see *Schering Agrochemicals Ltd v Resibel NV SA*, 26 Nov 1992, unreported, but noted at (1993) 109 LQR 175.

277 *Henderson v Merrett Syndicates* [1995] 2 AC 145.

278 *The Independent* [1994] 31 December.

279 Referred to as *British Columbia Saw Mill Co Ltd v Nettleship* (1868) LR 3 CP 499 at 508.

This result was described in the case as 'absurd'. The instinctive appeal of the court's criticism of the result in this case is premised upon a lack of moral culpability on the part of the blacksmith. Where some moral opprobrium may be said to attach to the 'wrongdoer' the instinct to limit liability will be felt less strongly.[280]

In the present day this intuitive justification for principles which bar recovery on the basis that a loss is 'too remote' has been replaced by economic arguments.[281] The principle or principles of remoteness derived from *Hadley* v *Baxendale*[282] are thought to promote economic efficiency and facilitate the optimal allocation of risk. Efficiency is said to be advanced by the facilitation of mutually beneficial exchanges through the avoidance of overly extensive liabilities. Optimal risk allocation is said to be promoted by the imposition of liability for loss arising 'in the ordinary course of things'; this provides the promisor with an incentive to take precautions to avoid loss to the promisee which may be effected at low cost to himself. In addition, the imposition of liability on the promisor in respect of unusual losses of which he was aware is said to encourage both parties to address the risks associated with non-performance. The promisee is encouraged to communicate the possibility of such losses to the promisor; the promisor may then 'price' (through an increased contract price) the insurance he is in effect being asked to provide. This in turn gives the opportunity to the promisee to procure this insurance at less cost elsewhere perhaps by traditional third-party insurance.

In *Hadley* v *Baxendale*[283] Baron Alderson stated the test, which determines the recovery of damages for breach of contract as follows First, the victim of a breach of contract may recover damages in respect of losses which 'may fairly and reasonably be considered [as] arising naturally, i.e. in the ordinary course of things'.[284] Second, the victim may also recover damages in respect of losses 'which may reasonably be supposed to have been in the contemplation of the parties as the probable result of the breach'.[285] Both limbs are applied at the time of entering the contract.

In *Hadley* the owner of a mill was unable to recover anything for loss of profit because his mill stood idle when, in breach of contract, a carrier delayed delivery to the original makers of the broken mill shaft which was needed as a pattern for a replacement. The loss of profit claimed was not thought to arise 'in the ordinary course of things' as the carrier was entitled

---

[280] See Hart and Honore (1985) *Causation in the Law.* 2nd edn, p. 304.
[281] Perloff, 'Breach of Contract and the Foreseeability Doctrine of *Hadley* v *Baxendale*' (1981) J Leg Stud 39; Landa, '*Hadley* v *Baxendale* and the Expansion of the Middleman Economy' (1987) 16 J Leg Stud 455; Eisenberg, 'The Principle of *Hadley* v *Baxendale* (1992) 80 Cal Law Rev 563.
[282] (1854) 9 Exch 341.
[283] See Simpson (1975) 91 LQR 272–7; Danzig (1975) 4 J Legal Studies 249; Danzig (1978) *The Capability Problem in Contract Law*, p. 76.
[284] At p. 354.
[285] *Ibid.*

to reasonably suppose that the mill owner possessed a spare mill shaft which could be utilised while the original was removed. Also, it must have been the case there was no evidence that the carriers had been informed that the mill was lying idle.[286]

In *Victoria Laundries* v *Newman*[287] the defendant engineers contracted to sell a boiler to the claimant launderers. The boiler was delivered some months late as a result of which the claimants suffered a loss of profit deriving from two sources: they lost some normal laundering business but, in addition, they did not obtain some particularly lucrative dying and laundering contracts from the Ministry of Supply. It was held that the claimants were able to recover the first, but not the second, item of loss. The Court of Appeal preferred the view that there was only one rule of remoteness applicable in the law of contract that recovery be made in respect of 'loss actually resulting as was at the time of the contract reasonably foreseeable as liable to result from the breach'.[288]

However, when considering this rule two types of knowledge are relevant: imputed knowledge, which everyone is presumed to possess, and actual knowledge of unusual circumstances, which must be proved. It is important to realise that whether one refers to two rules deriving from *Hadley* or one rule deriving from *Victoria Laundries* to which two types of knowledge are relevant, it is a semantic rather than a substantive distinction.[289] However, in order to make the contract breaker liable under either formulation, it is never necessary to show that he actually asked himself what loss was liable to result from breach, rather the test is whether, *if* he had considered the matter, he would have concluded that the loss was liable to result from his breach.[290]

The next major case, *The Heron II*[291] involved a charter to carry a cargo of sugar to Basrah where the charterer intended to sell it immediately after un-loading. In breach of contract the shipowner deviated from the contract route with the result that the cargo arrived in Basrah late when the market price for sugar had dropped. The charterer recovered damages in respect of this fall.

The House of Lords rejected the interpretation of *Victoria Laundries* that the test of remoteness to be applied in contract was the same as the one applied in the tort of negligence. Rather their Lordships were of the view that the general test of remoteness to be applied in contract was less generous to

---

[286] *Hydraulic Engineering* v *McHaffie* (1878) 4 QBD 670 at 676 *per* Brett J. A statement to the contrary in the headnote must be wrong. See *Victoria Laundries (Windsor)* v *Newman Industries Ltd* [1949] 2 KB 538 at 537.

[287] [1949] 2 KB 528.

[288] *Ibid.*

[289] The major change effected by the case was the formulation adopted to express the likelihood of occurrence which must be foreseen in order to ground recovery; in *Hadley* the word probable was used, in *Victoria* liable and several other supposed synonyms, considered below.

[290] *Ibid.*, p. 540. See also *Monarch Steamship Co Ltd* v *A/B Karlshamns Oljefabreker* [1949] AC 196.

[291] *Koufos* v *C Czarnikow Ltd (The Heron II)* [1969] 1 AC 350.

claimants than the one in tort[292] and this feature was not captured by the phrase 'on the cards'. Unfortunately, unanimity ended there and a variety of formulae were used to express the requisite degree of probability. The most popular formulation (probably!) was that the loss must be reasonably contemplated as a 'not unlikely' consequence of breach.[293] As Lord Reid explained, there is good reason for this apparent lack of generosity towards the victim of a breach of contract; a prospective party to a contract may expand the liability of his contractual partner by communicating to him with sufficient particularity the details of the potential loss.

H Parsons (Livestock) Ltd v *Uttley Ingham & Co Ltd*[294] concerned the sale and installation of a hopper for storing animal foodstuff. The hopper was defective as the ventilator, which had been sealed for carriage to the claimant's premises, was not unsealed upon installation by the defendants. This caused the pig food to become mouldy and a large number of pigs died of a rare intestinal infection. The Court of Appeal unanimously rejected the defendant's argument that he was not liable[295] for the death of the pigs and consequent losses[296] because these were too remote.[297] However, there are two different justifications for this result offered by the judgments in the case.

Lord Denning held that there are two different tests for remoteness which may be applied when the claimant's cause of action is breach of contract. The first test is the *Wagon Mound* 'tort' test where the defendant is liable for any possible consequence of breach which he should have foreseen, even if it was only foreseeable as a possibility.[298] The second test is the less generous (i.e. to claimants) contract test laid down in *The Heron II*, where the defendant is liable for any consequence of breach which was reasonably contemplated as 'not unlikely'. According to Lord Denning, the former test was applicable where physical damage was concerned and the latter where economic loss was suffered. In *Parsons* the loss was physical and so Lord Denning permitted recovery under the *Wagon Mound* test.

Lord Denning's approach raises a number of questions, is it coherent? And if so, is it based upon sound policy? The distinction between physical and economic loss is an elusive one which is stated rather than explored by Lord Denning. How would one characterise the claim if the effect of the illness was to cause the pigs to put on weight at a lesser rate? Is this a claim for the

---

292 According to the *Wagon Mound (No. 1)* [1961] AC 388, an item of loss is not too remote even if it is only reasonably foreseeable as a remote possibility.

293 See also the judgment of Lord Shaw in *R & H Hall Ltd* v *WH Pim & Co Ltd* (1928) 30 Lloyd's Rep 585 referred to by Lord Reid. For modern applications, see *Balfour Beatty Construction Ltd* v *Scottish Power plc* (1994) SLT 807 and *The Kriti Rex* [1996] 2 Lloyd's Rep 171 at 202–3.

294 [1978] QB 791.

295 Under Sale of Goods Act 1893, s 14(1). See now Sale of Goods Act 1979, s 14(3).

296 That is, lost sales and turnover.

297 The defendant claimed his liability was limited to the extra cost of bagged food (just over £18) used while the nuts were taken away for scientific examination.

298 [1978] 1 All ER 525 at 523.

physical damage to their metabolism or is it a claim for an economic loss, the profit on the sale of rashers of bacon which are not produced? Further, should all economic losses be treated equally?[299]

If a meaningful distinction can be drawn between the two kinds of loss, does such a distinction have a sound basis in policy? There is certainly an intuitive appeal to achieving consistency within the law of obligations which eschews artificial distinctions between different causes of action. This appeal is felt more strongly where facts give rise to concurrent liability in contract and tort. Why in such circumstances should the ultimate recoverability of an item of loss turn upon whether the claimant writes 'contract' or 'tort' at the head of his statement of claim? However in *Henderson v Merrett Syndicates*[300] the House of Lords expanded considerably the area of overlap between contract and tort but nonetheless rejected 'the temptation of elegance'[301] as an argument of policy and accepted that there may be strategic advantage in framing an action as one in either contract or tort.[302] Indeed, it was expressly acknowledged that 'the rules as to remoteness of damage ... are less restricted in tort than they are in contract'.[303]

An alternative argument of policy which might support the distinction drawn by Lord Denning builds upon the explanation offered by Lord Reid in *The Heron II* for the ungenerous nature of the 'contractual' test. Perhaps it is the case that economic loss is less easy to anticipate and so by the imposition of a more stringent test of remoteness the law provides a valuable incentive to those who may suffer such losses to disclose the danger to their contractual partners.

The majority[304] of the Court of Appeal permitted recovery on the more conservative basis that it is the *type* of loss but not its *extent* that must be reasonably contemplated. The defendants were in breach of contract by supplying a hopper unfit for the purpose of storing animal food and it was within the reasonable contemplation of the parties that such a breach would result in illness for the pigs. That the illness was more serious (extensive) than would have been reasonably contemplated did not matter as the loss that did occur (the death of the pigs) was of the same type as the loss which was reasonably contemplated (illness to the pigs).[305]

How narrowly must the type of damage be defined? In the *Victoria Laundries* case some economic loss was reasonably foreseeable (the loss of normal laundering business) but recovery in respect of the full extent of the claimant's economic loss (profit on lucrative dying contracts was disallowed)

---

[299] See *Spartan Steel and Alloys v Martin & Co Ltd*.

[300] [1994] 3 WLR 761.

[301] *Ibid.* at p. 781 D *per* Lord Goff with whose judgment the other members of the house agreed.

[302] In *Henderson* any contractual actions were out of time.

[303] *Ibid.* at p. 781 B *per* Lord Goff with whose judgment the other members of the house agreed.

[304] Scarman LJ with whom Orr LJ agreed.

[305] The tort of negligence distinguishes between (recoverable) economic loss, which is consequent on physical damage, and (irrecoverable) 'pure' economic loss, which is not.

was not permitted. If these were losses of the same type, the case must be wrongly decided. As this has not been suggested, it must be assumed that the definition of type imports more than a broad distinction between physical losses and economic ones.[306] Another difficulty is in reconciling certain comments of Scarman LJ. At one point he says that it would be 'absurd that the test of remoteness of damage should, in principle, differ according to the legal classification of the cause of action', but at another that 'the formulation of the remoteness test is not the same in tort and contract'.

Recovery for ordinary losses

A claimant may recover for an item of loss when it may be said to arise naturally, i.e. in the ordinary course of things within the first limb of *Hadley* v *Baxendale* or, using the language of *Victoria Laundries* (which amounts to the same thing) when knowledge of that item of loss may be imputed to the contract breaker. The latter formulation emphasises that the test is primarily an *objective* one. Imputed knowledge is 'knowledge, which a contract breaker is assumed to possess whether he actually possesses it or not'.[307] However, although the standard to be applied is the objective one of a reasonable businessman,[308] it is a reasonable businessman, in the position of the defendant. Therefore, the status of the defendant might be important.[309] Knowledge that the goods were bought for resale and liability for consequential loss of profit will more readily be imputed to a merchant[310] than to a carrier.[311] However, if the carrier is a specialist in a particular trade he may have imputed to him more extensive knowledge than that reasonably possessed by a general carrier.[312] Whenever the claimant's activity involves 'complicated construction or manufacturing techniques' the mere supply of a commodity does not 'fix' the supplier with knowledge of details of those techniques and the effect upon them of any deficiency in the commodity supplied.

Knowledge may also be imputed to the party in breach on the basis of the contractual subject matter. Where the contract involves an obvious profit-earning chattel, such as a ship[313] or some essential part of one,[314] a claim for

---

[306] *Homsy* v *Murphy* (1997) 73 P & CR 26 at 45 *per* Hobhouse LJ. See also *Brown* v *KMR Services Ltd* [1995] 4 All ER 598 at 621 *per* Stuart Smith LJ: 'loss of ordinary business profits is different in kind from that flowing from a particular contract which gives rise to very high profits ...' and *North Sea* v *PTT* [1997] 2 Lloyd's Rep 418 at 437–8: 'loss of profits claimed by reference to an extravagant or unusual bargain are not of the same type as damages referable to bargains that are usual'.

[307] *Victoria Laundry (Windsor) Ltd* v *Newman Industries Ltd* [1949] 2 KB 528 at 540.

[308] *The Heron II* [1969] 1 AC 350 at 400 *per* Lord Morris. See also *Monarch Steamship Co Ltd* v *A/B Karlhamns Oljefabriker* [1949] AC 196 at 222 *per* Lord Wright.

[309] *Victoria Laundry (Windsor) Ltd* v *Newman Industries Ltd* [1949] 2 KB 528 at 537.

[310] *R & H Hall Ltd* v *WH Pim (Junior) & Co Ltd* (1928) 33 Com Cas 324.

[311] *The Arpad* [1934] P 189.

[312] *The Baleares* [1993] 1 Lloyd's Rep 215 at 217.

[313] *Fletcher* v *Tayleur* (1855) 17 CB 21 and *Re Trent and Humber Co, ex parte Cambrian Steam Packet Co* (1868) LR 6 Eq 396.

[314] *Wilson* v *General Ironscrew Company* (1878) 47 LJQB 23 (propeller) and *Saint Line* v *Richardson* [1940] 2 KB 99 (engine).

loss of profit will usually succeed on the basis of knowledge imputed to the contract breaker[315] and the cost of works of improvement.[316] Similarly, a purchaser who bought a house with a defective title was unable to recover damages from his solicitor in respect of interest on his overdraft and hotel and other expenses incurred when he changed employment and was unable to purchase a closer residence.[317] The former loss was said to be attributable to the claimant's own impecuniosity, knowledge of which was no more to be imputed to the defendant than an awareness of his client's proposed career change.

Recovery for unusual losses

An unusual loss, which is nevertheless with the reasonable contemplation of the parties is recoverable under the second limb of *Hadley* v *Baxendale*. In the language of *Victoria Laundries* (which amounts to the same thing) the claimant will recover when the knowledge of that item of loss was actually possessed by the contract breaker.

Something more than mere communication is necessary. The communication must be in circumstances such that the party in breach would, if he had bothered to think about it, have become aware of the loss which in fact occurred[318] irrespective of whether such communication would be sufficient to support a contractual term to that effect.[319] This implies that communication should be complete[320] and not be made in informal circumstances.[321]

A defendant could escape liability by showing that because of some personal deficiency he would not have contemplated the loss of the claimants although a reasonable person in his position would have. Baron Alderson's famous statement refers to the *reasonable* contemplation of the parties. The true test becomes: the communication must be in circumstances such that a reasonable person in the position of the party in breach would, if he had bothered to think about it, have become aware of the loss which in fact occurred irrespective of whether such communication would be sufficient to support a contractual term to that effect. This emphasis upon the reasonable man *in the position of the defendant* enables the court to take account of the

---

315 *Diamond* v *Campbell-Jones* [1961] Ch 22; *Cottrill* v *Steyning and Littlehampton Building Society* [1966] 1 WLR 543; *Cochrane (Decorators) Ltd* v *Sarabandi* [1983] 133 NLJ 558.

316 *Lloyd* v *Stanbury* [1971] 1 WLR 535.

317 *Pilkington* v *Wood* [1953] Ch 770: the claimant did recover the difference at the date of breach between the value of the property with a good title and its value with a defective title.

318 *Horne* v *Midland Ry* (1873) LR 8 CP (carrier was aware of the need to deliver consignment by a particular date) – no recovery; *Kemp* v *Intasun Holidays Ltd* [1987] 2 FTLR 234 (travel agent was told of claimant's asthma when holiday booked).

319 *Hydraulic Engineering Co Ltd* v *McHaffie* (1878) 4 QBD 670, *The Heron II* [1969] 1 AC 350 at 422 *per* Lord Upjohn and *GKN Centrax Gears Ltd* v *Matbro Ltd* [1976] 2 Lloyd's Rep 555 and *The Pegase* [1981] 1 Lloyd's Rep 175 rejecting the contrary rule in *British Columbia Saw Mill* v *Nettleship* (1868) LR 3 CP 499.

320 The communication in *Horne* v *Midland Ry* [1873] LR 3 CP 131 may have been incomplete.

321 *Kemp* v *Intasun Holidays* [1987] 2 FTLR 234; *Patrick* v *Russo-British Grain Exports* [1927] 2 KB 535.

status of the defendant. Again,[322] the courts have been reluctant to impose liability on carriers for loss of profit unless the carrier could reasonably be supposed to be aware that the goods were for resale[323] or further manufacture.[324]

A claimant may possibly recover more extensive damages than he would otherwise be entitled to if the extra losses were attributable to the claimant's impecuniosity which was communicated to the defendant in the required manner.[325] This position contrasts starkly with the tortious rule.[326]

Mitigation

Mitigation refers to the rule that a claimant may not recover damages for breach of contract in respect of losses which he might reasonably have been expected to avoid. It is often expressed in terms of a *duty* on the claimant to mitigate his loss.[327]

It has been pointed out that, though commonplace, talk of a duty to mitigate is strictly inappropriate.[328] This is because the breach of a legal duty usually gives rise to a liability to pay damages rather than, as here, operating to reduce the damages payable.

Mitigation has been said to involve a question of fact rather than one of law, with the important consequence that appellate courts will rarely interfere with the judgment of the trial judge on this issue.[329] This helps to explain the lack of reported decisions discussing the doctrine.[330]

The principle of mitigation of loss is closely connected to a number of central features of the law of damages. Damages are to be assessed at the time of breach[331] upon the assumption that a purchaser of goods who has not received the contract performance will go into the market and purchase a

---

[322] For example, *Kemp v Intasun Holidays* [1987] 2 FTLR 234.

[323] *Simpson v L & NW Ry* (1876) 1 QBD 274 (animal food samples to be transported between agricultural shows).

[324] *Montevideo Gas v Clan Line Steamers* (1921) 37 TLR 544 at 545 *per* Roche J, upheld in the Court of Appeal (1921) 37 TLR 866.

[325] *Muhammad Issa El Sheikh Ahmed v Ali* [1947] AC 414; *Trans Trust SPRL v Danubian Trading Co Ltd* [1952] 2 QB 297; *Wroth v Tyler* [1974] Ch 30; *Perry v Sidney Phillips* [1982] 3 All ER 705. *Cf. Bacon v Cooper Metals* where the issue of impecuniosity was not discussed in terms of remoteness.

[326] *Owners of the Dredger Liesbosch v Owners of Steamship Edison, The Liesbosch* [1933] AC 449. See the discussion in Cane (1995) *Tort Law and Economic Interests.* 2nd edn, pp. 96–8.

[327] [1912] AC 673 at 689 *per* Viscount Haldane LC.

[328] *Rock v Vandive* (1920) 189 P 157; *Wallems Rederij v Muller* [1927] 2 KB 99 at 104–5 *per* Mackinnon J; *The Solholt* [1983] 1 Lloyd's Rep 605 at 608 *per* Sir John Donaldson MR.

[329] See *Payzu v Saunders* [1919] 2 KB 581 at 589 *per* Scrutton LJ and *The Solholt* [1983] 1 Lloyd's Rep 605 at 608 *per* Sir John Donaldson MR. *Cf.* 'Now a serious question of *law* arises on the question of damages' (emphasis added) *per* McCardie J in *Payzu v Saunders* [1919] 2 KB 581.

[330] Another reason is the late development of the doctrine in its present form. See Schmitthof, 'The Duty to Mitigate' [1961] JBL 361.

[331] *Johnson and Another v Agnew* [1980] AC 367. See above under: The time of assessment.

substitute.[332] If he fails to do so and the market for the contractual subject matter is rising, the loss he suffers is said to be attributable to his own failure to mitigate his loss.[333] Where the claimant is not reasonably able to do so, justice may require damages to be assessed at a different point in time.[334] This connection between the date at which damages are assessed and the principle of mitigation is so close that the latter is effectively incorporated into the statutory formulae for the calculation of damages for non-delivery[335] and non-acceptance.[336]

A claimant is not entitled to recover damages for breach of contract in respect of losses which he might reasonably have been expected to avoid. This rule has two consequences. The first is that he must not take unreasonable steps which would increase his loss; the second is that the claimant is required to take reasonable steps to reduce his loss.

The crux of the issue is the reasonableness of the extra expense incurred. In the above two examples, the expenditure was unreasonable and so irrecoverable. Where expenditure in fact increases the loss of the claimant, this is recoverable so long as it was reasonably incurred.[337] On this basis, hire purchase charges incurred to obtain replacement machinery have been considered reasonable and so recoverable.[338] Indeed, the courts have explicitly approved a statement that there may be recovery in respect of reasonable but unsuccessful attempts to mitigate loss.[339]

Many of the report cases applying the second aspect of the rule involve the rejection by the victim of the contract breacher's offer to perform on the breacher's amended terms. These cases have already been considered as part of the law relating to contractual modifications. As with the first aspect of the doctrine, the determining factor is the standard of reasonableness. The reported cases provide considerable guidance as to what this standard requires of the claimant in different situations.

A claimant will not be required to act in a way which will ruin his business reputation or injure innocent third parties, for example by suggesting to the owner of a Rolls-Royce that he should drive a less prestigious marque[340] or,

---

[332] The same principle applies *mutatis mutandis* to the case of a disappointed seller where the market is falling.

[333] *Radford* v *De Froberville* [1978] 1 All ER 33 at 44b *per* Oliver J.

[334] For example, *Wroth* v *Tyler* [1974] Ch 30.

[335] Sale of Goods Act 1979, s 51(3).

[336] Sale of Goods Act 1979, s 50(3).

[337] *Lloyds and Scottish Finance Ltd* v *Modern Cars and Caravans (Kingston) Ltd* [1966] 1 QB 764 (claimants incurred cost disputing the seizure by the sheriff of a caravan sold to them by the defendants which was not in fact the property of the defendants). The statement was in *Mayne and McGregor on Damages* (12th edn). See now (1997) *McGregor on Damages*. 16th edn., p. 216.

[338] *Bacon* v *Cooper (Metals) Ltd* [1982] 1 All ER 397.

[339] See also *Esso Petroleum Co* v *Mardon* [1976] QB 801 (defendant renewed lease for a petrol station to try to recoup losses caused by the claimant's breach of the first lease) and a statement in *The World Beauty* [1970] P 144 at 156 *per* Winn LJ. See also *Hoffberger* v *Ascot International Bloodstock Bureau Ltd* [1976] *The Times*, 29 January.

[340] *HL Motorworks* v *Alwatibi* [1977] RTR 276 (a tort case).

where the claimant was a building society, by enforcing against a mortgagor his personal covenant to pay when, due to the negligence of the defendant surveyors, the property proves to be inadequate security for the sum advanced.[341]

When a claimant is seeking a substitute performance, a balance must be struck between the interests of the parties. Whilst a claimant who has been wrongfully dismissed must not be too ambitious in his quest for alternative employment, a buyer of goods will not be expected 'to go hunting the globe' for replacement goods.[342]

The financial position of the claimant is also relevant; he will not be required to do something which his means do not allow.[343] So when the vendor of a house failed to convey the property, the purchaser's damages were not assessed on the assumption that he should purchase another house at that time because the market was rising and he could not raise a larger mortgage.[344]

It can be seen that the standard of reasonableness is applied in a robust and common sense way with a certain sympathy for the position of the victim. As Lord Macmillan commented, the actions of the victim of a breach of contract should not be minutely examined because:[345]

> It is often easy after an emergency has passed to criticise the steps which have been taken to meet it, but such criticism does not come well from those who have themselves created the emergency.

LIQUIDATED DAMAGES AND PENALTIES

Contractors are usually optimists. When they enter contracts, they think of performance rather than breach.[346] None the less, commercial contractors will sometimes seek to plan for breach by including a clause in the contract, which stipulates for the payment of a sum of money upon breach. Such clauses seek to liquidate the losses of the innocent party and so when enforceable are known as liquidated damages clauses; when unenforceable, they are described as penalties.

---

[341] *London & South of England Building Society* v *Stone* [1983] 1 WLR 1242.

[342] *Lesters Leather & Skin Co* v *Home and Overseas Brokers* (1948) 64 TLR 569 at 569 *per* Lord Goddard CJ.

[343] '... if the position of the [victim] is aggravated because he is without the means of mitigating it, so much the worse for the wrongdoer ...': *Clippens Oil Co* v *Edinburgh and District Water Trustees* [1907] AC 291 at 303 *per* Lord Collins (a tort case) applied in *Robbins of Putney* v *Meek* [1971] RTR 345 (a sale of goods case).

[344] *Wroth* v *Tyler* [1974] Ch 30. *Quaere* whether this principle would extend to a commercial buyer. See *Aronson* v *Mologa* (1927) 32 Com Cas 276 at 289–91 *per* Atkin LJ who seems to suggest that it might.

[345] *Banco de Portugal* v *Waterlow* [1932] AC 452 at 506.

[346] *Victoria Laundry (Windsor) Ltd* v *Newman Industries Ltd* [1949] 2 KB 528 at 540 *per* Asquith LJ delivering the judgment of the court. This observation is supported by an empirical study by Beale and Dugdale (1975) 2 BJLS 45.

Policy

There are clearly advantages in seeking to quantify in advance the amount of money which the victim of a breach of contract should receive. Prior to breach the promisor is able to calculate the amount of damages he would have to pay in the event of his breach[347] which in turn enables him to decide if it would be profitable to sell his performance elsewhere.[348] A promisor may be able to convince a promisee of his reliability by offering this type of clause. From the perspective of the promisee, such a clause makes him aware of his likely recovery in the event of breach.[349] If the sum stipulated is insufficient to compensate him, he is thereby encouraged to insure against that risk.[350] Post-breach the clauses should save legal costs because the court will not be required to assess as unliquidated damages the losses of the promisee.[351]

A number of these advantages are overstated. To the extent that the law draws a distinction between valid liquidated damages clauses and invalid penalty clauses several of these advantages are reduced. Any indeterminacy in the rule[352] will mean that a promisor cannot act with assurance when considering whether to breach and the promisee may take out unnecessary insurance. The saving in legal and court time is particularly unconvincing. It ignores the cost of negotiating the clause and any 'counter measures'. When a promisor is confronted with a liquidated damages clause, he will often only agree to it if a *force majeure* clause is inserted for his own protection.[353] Again, the resolution of any doubt as to whether such a clause is enforceable will be a very costly process.

Since the traditional policy arguments are somewhat unconvincing and contradictory, many commentators have examined the penalty jurisdiction from an economic perspective. Unfortunately, their attempts to find a convincing policy basis for the law also are far from conclusive. The present regime is explained as an attempt to ensure that recovery is limited to loss actually suffered either because compensation is the sole legitimate aim of an award of damages[354] for breach of contract or because if recovery exceeds loss so-called 'efficient breach'[355] will not occur.[356] Elsewhere it has been

---

[347] *Philips Hong Kong* v *A-G of Hong Kong* [1961] BLR 41 at 55 *per* Lord Woolf.
[348] *Infra.*
[349] *Philips Hong Kong* v *A-G of Hong Kong* [1961] BLR 41 at 54 *per* Lord Woolf.
[350] See below for the argument that the promisee is the party who can provide that insurance at least cost.
[351] *Diestal* v *Stevenson* [1906] 2 KB 345 at 350 *per* Kennedy J.
[352] And there is a great deal.
[353] For example, *The Suisse Atlantique* [1967] 1 AC 361 (demurrage clause in time charter and *force majeure* clause). See *infra* for the classification of demurrage clauses as liquidated damages clauses.
[354] MacNeil, 'Power of Contract and Agreed Remedies' (1962) 47 Cornell LQ 495.
[355] Efficient breach refers to a breach of contract which enables the contract breaker to tender his contractual performance to a third party who is prepared to pay more for it than the original contractor. This relocation is said to be efficient because it places the resource in the hands of the person who values it most highly. See generally Posner (1992) *Economic Analysis of Law.* 4th edn, pp. 117–26 and 130–2.
[356] Fenton (1975) 51 Ind. LJ 189. See also generally Birmingham (1970) 24 Rutgers Law Rev 273.

pointed out that 'efficient breach' may occur by private bargaining between the parties irrespective of the legal rule.[357] It has also been convincingly argued that a rule such as the present one which denies enforceability to penalties is necessary to deter contractors from trying to obtain the stipulated sum by inducing their contractual partner to breach the contract. Such 'breach inducement' is wasteful in itself and might cause the other party to waste further resources in his attempt to avoid it.[358]

It has been argued that both liquidated damages clauses and penalties should be enforced either on the basis that such clauses allow the promisee to insure effectively against otherwise irrecoverable idiosyncratic loss with the person able to provide such insurance at least cost, i.e. the potential contract breaker[359] or because to do otherwise would be to deprive the recipient of a benefit he has in fact paid for.[360]

The resolution of these differences of opinion is in part an empirical question.[361] Until that work is done, no single policy prescription emerges from the economic literature.[362] Rather the area remains 'a major unexplained puzzle in the economic theory of the common law'.[363]

Lord Dunedin's guidelines

In the Privy Council decision of *Philips Hong Kong Ltd* v *A-G of Hong Kong* Lord Woolf said that the clear summary of principle (expressed as a number of rules) in Lord Dunedin's judgment in *Dunlop Pneumatic Tyre Co* v *New Garage and Motor Co*[364] 'authoritatively set out'[365] the law relating to liquidated damages and penalties. However, he also emphasised that Lord Dunedin's rules should be applied in a pragmatic way and the court should not be over-zealous in declaring a clause to be a penalty when to do so would defeat the pre-contractual intentions of commercial contractors. In an important passage Lord Woolf said:[366]

---

[357] For example, Goetz and Scott (1977) 77 Col LR 554 at 568. This is a simple application of Coase's famous theorem that in the absence of transaction costs the imposition of legal liability is irrelevant to the attainment of efficiency. See Coase (1960) 3 Journal of Law and Econ 1.

[358] Clarkson, Miller and Muris (1978) Wisconsin Law Rev 351.

[359] Goetz and Scott (1977) 77 Col LR 554.

[360] Rea (1984) 13 Journal Leg Stud 147.

[361] For example, do the benefits of a penalty rule by reducing breach inducement identified by Clarkson, Miller and Muris exceed the costs imposed by more costly third party insurance against idiosyncratic loss described by Goetz and Scott?

[362] See also Talley (1994) 46 Stanford Law Rev 1195.

[363] Posner (1979) 46 U Ch LR 281 at 290. Richard Posner is regarded as one of the founders of modern law and economics scholarship.

[364] [1915] AC 79. Although the modern jurisdiction can be traced back to earlier decisions. In *Wallis* v *Smith* (1882) 21 Ch D 243 at 261 Jessel MR described *Astley* v *Weldon* (1801) 2 B & P 346 as 'the foundation of the ... subject'.

[365] *Philips Hong Kong Ltd* v *A-G of Hong Kong* [1993] 61 BLR 41 at 56 *per* Lord Woolf.

[366] *Ibid.*, p. 59. See also *Robophone Facilities* v *Blank* [1966] 1 WLR 1428 at 1477 *per* Diplock LJ.

... the court has to be careful not to set too high a standard and bear in mind that what the parties have agreed should normally be upheld. Any other approach will lead to undesirable uncertainty especially in commercial contracts.

The basic test
Lord Dunedin said:[367]

> The essence of a penalty is a payment of money stipulated as *in terrorem* of the offending part; the essence of liquidated damages is a genuine covenanted pre-estimate of damage.

This statement ostensibly contains two definitions: a penalty and a liquidated damages clause. Each derives from a different source.[368] However, the definition of a penalty does not provide a test sufficient to identify one. Taken literally it appears to state a test of intention. Cases applying the definition do not turn on whether the beneficiary of the clause intended it to operate in a coercive way. Rather they focus upon the definition of a liquidated damages clause and a penalty is simply defined as its negative counterpart, i.e. a clause that provides for something *in excess of* a 'genuine ... pre-estimate of loss'. On this view 'a payment of money stipulated *in terrorem* of the offending part' describes a conclusion of law arrived at by the application of the 'genuine pre-estimate' of loss test, to which it adds nothing. This was apparently the view of Lord Radcliffe in his important but much neglected[369] statement that:

> I do not myself think that it helps to identify a penalty, to describe it as in the nature of a threat 'to be enforced *in terrorem* ...'. I do not find that that description adds anything of substance to the idea conveyed by the word 'penalty' itself, and it obscures the fact that penalties may quite readily be undertaken by parties who are not in the least terrorised by the prospect of having to pay them and yet are, as I understand it, entitled to claim the protection of the court when they are called upon to make good their promises.

There must be a breach
The contractual provision which the House of Lords was called upon to consider in *Dunlop* was one that required payments to be made to Dunlop if New Garage did certain acts 'in breach of the agreement'. Therefore, the House of Lords did not consider the question of whether the penalty jurisdiction extended to payments conditional on events other than a breach of contract by the payor. However, their Lordships assumed that it did not.

---

[367] At p. 86 referring to *Clydebank Engineering and Shipbuilding Co v Don Jose Ramos Yzquierdo y Castenada* [1905] AC 6. See also his earlier judgment in *Public Works Commissioner v Hills* [1906] AC 368 at 375–6.

[368] Penalty – *Elphinstone v Monkland* (1886) 11 App Cas 332 at 348 *per* Lord Halsbury, repeated in *Clydebank Engineering Co v Don Jose Ramos Yzquierdo y Castenada* [1905] AC 6 at 10. Liquidated Damages – *Wallis v Smith* (1882) 21 Ch D 243 at 267 *per* Cotton LJ.

[369] For example, it is not mentioned in McGregor, *op. cit.* (n. 339 herein above) or Treitel, p. 898. *Cf.* Cheshire, Fifoot and Furmston (13th end), p. 635, n. 5.

Alder v *Moore*[370] illustrates the distinction. An injured football player received a sum of money from his insurers which was paid in consideration of his giving up professional football and was to be repayable in the event that he did resume his career. The defendant began to play again and the insurers claimed the return of their payment. The defendant argued that the insurers were trying to enforce a penalty against him. The Court of Appeal held that the term requiring repayment could not be reviewed as a penalty because there was 'no contractual ban upon the defendant from playing professional football again';[371] the payment was not conditional upon any breach of contract by the payor, and therefore the defendant had to return the money.[372] Making the payment of money conditional upon a non-promissory condition is the basis of one of the techniques used by draftsmen seeking to avoid the penalty rule.

This limit upon the ambit of the penalty jurisdiction has caused particular problems in cases involving the termination of contracts. In *Bridge* v *Campbell Discount Co Ltd*[373] the appellant entered an agreement[374] with the respondents for the hire purchase of a car. After he made the first monthly payment, the appellant returned the car to the dealers. A clause of the agreement provided that 'if the hiring be terminated for any reason ... the hirer shall pay ... by way of agreed compensation for depreciation ... such further sum as may be necessary to make the rentals paid and payable hereunder equal to two-thirds of the hire purchase price'. The Court of Appeal held that the appellant had to pay the amount owing under the clause as this was not a sum payable on breach of contract and so according to the orthodox approach the penalty doctrine was irrelevant.[375] However, this decision was reversed by the House of Lords which by a majority[376] held that the hirer was in breach of contract and so the clause fell to reviewed as a penalty. Further, the amount to be paid under the clause was not a genuine pre-estimate of loss as the amount payable under the clause would *decrease* as the car became older whereas depreciation of a wasting asset *increases* with the passage of time.[377] The clause was, therefore, unenforceable. Lords

---

[370] [1961] 2 QB 57.

[371] *Ibid.* at p. 76 *per* Slade J in the Court of Appeal.

[372] If the penalty jurisdiction had been applicable the result would have been the same. The sum to be repaid was a genuine pre-estimate of the insurer's loss and so would be enforceable as a valid liquidated damages clause.

[373] [1962] AC 600 approved and applied by the High Court of Australia in *O'Dea* v *Allstates Leasing System (WA) Pty Ltd* (1983) 152 CLR 359.

[374] The agreement would now be subject to the Consumer Credit Act 1974. Any agreement to provide credit of less than £15,000 (a 'regulated' agreement within s 8) if it is a conditional sale or hire-purchase agreement is subject to a statutory right of termination under s 99 which may be exercised at any time by the debtor so long as arrears owing are paid. However, the debtor comes under a liability to pay one half of the total price, though this can be reduced if the creditor's loss is less (ss 100–3).

[375] *Associated Distributors Ltd* v *Hall* [1938] 2 KB 83.

[376] Lords Morton, Radcliffe, Devlin and in the alternative Lord Denning.

[377] 'It produces [a] result, absurd in its own terms ... a sliding scale of compensation, but a scale that slides in the wrong direction ...' *ibid.* at p. 623 *per* Lord Radcliffe.

Denning[378] and Devlin[379] considered that the result would have been the same even if the appellant was not in fact in breach of contract.[380] Lord Denning pointed out[381] the 'absurd paradox' of any other conclusion; the court 'will grant relief to a man who breaks his contract but will penalise the man who by exercising a contractual option to return the car keeps it'.[382]

In a working paper[383] the Law Commission referred to Lord Denning's comments and suggested an expansion of the penalty doctrine whereby the court should have the power to deal with such clauses in the same way whether or not they come into operation by breach.[384] The Law Commission identifies the problem as how to define the scope of this power of review in a way that does not subject to review every contractual term requiring the payment of money.[385] Its conclusion[386] was that 'the rules as to penalties should be applied wherever the object of the disputed contractual obligation is to secure the act or result which is the true purpose of the contract'.[387]

Despite attempts to argue for an expanded penalty doctrine, the House of Lords nevertheless authoritatively restated the orthodox view in *Export Credits Guarantee Dept* v *Universal Oil Products Co*.[388] The case arose out of a

---

378 This was his preferred view of events. However, in a characteristically bold attempt to reason from rather than to a conclusion he said, 'If I am wrong about all this, however, and there is no jurisdiction to grant relief unless the hirer is in breach, then I would be prepared to hold in this case Bridge was in breach' *ibid*. at p. 630.

379 On the narrow ground if Bridge was in breach of contract the compensation clause would be classified as an unenforceable penalty because it did not genuinely quantify what it purported to quantify, compensation for depreciation, then it could not properly be construed as intended to quantify the same when it operates in conjunction with the exercise of a contractual option. 'I do not see how an agreement can be genuine for one purpose and a sham for another. If it is a sham, it means that it was never made and does not exist; if it does not exist, it must be ignored altogether' *ibid*. at p. 634.

380 Viscount Simmonds and Lord Morton disagreed and Lord Radcliffe expressly declined to decide the question.

381 *Ibid*. at p. 629. See also *AMEV-UDC Finance Ltd* v *Austin* (1986) 162 CLR 170 at 197–201 *per* Deane J dissenting.

382 See also *Lombank Ltd* v *Kennedy* and *Lombank Ltd* v *Crossan* (1961) 19 January, Court of Appeal in Northern Ireland (unreported) referred to in *Bridge* v *Campbell Discount Co Ltd*, *ibid*.

383 No. 61, *Penalty Clauses and Forfeiture of Monies Paid*.

384 *Ibid*., para. 22.

385 *Ibid*. Following *Jobson* v *Johnson* [1989] 1 All ER 621 considered supra it would be realised that the task is even more difficult as it must encompass clauses stipulating for the transfer of property as well.

386 The Law Commission rejected the approach embodied in the South African Conventional Penalties Act 1962 which extends the power to review penalties to provisions which state that a party is to remain liable to the performance of some obligation upon withdrawal from the agreement. This formulation would appear to cover 'minimum payment' clauses like that in *Bridge* v *Campbell Discount Co Ltd*. See Hepple (1961) 78 SALJ 445.

387 *Ibid*. at para 26 giving the following example: 'If ... a building contract were to provide for completion of the building by a certain date unless delayed by bad weather there would be no breach of contract if completion were delayed by bad weather. If the contract were also to provide that the builder should pay £50 for every day's delay caused by bad weather, the recoverability of the specified sum would depend on its being a genuine pre-estimate of the loss caused by the delay.'

388 [1983] 1 WLR 399. See also *United Dominion Trust (Commercial) Ltd* v *Ennis* [1968] QB 54 at 67 *per* Haman LJ and *Granor Finance* v *Liquidator of Eastor* (1974) SLT 296.

complicated scheme to finance the building of an oil refinery. The clause in question required: a payment to be made by the defendant builder to the claimant if, at any time when the defendant is in breach of a contract entered into with a consortium of Newfoundland companies, the consortium fails to honour promissory notes which it issued. The House of Lords held that the penalty jurisdiction was inapplicable to the clause because the sum to be paid under it by the defendant was not payable upon the breach of any contractual obligation owed by the contemplated payer (the defendant) to the contemplated payee (the claimant); rather the sum was payable upon the breach of a contractual obligation owed by the defendant to the consortium. It follows *a fortiori* that the penalty rule does not apply if the sum is payable upon an event or events which do not include the breach by the defendant of a contractual obligation owed to *anyone*.

This limit upon the common law jurisdiction is apparently repeated[389] in the Unfair Terms in Consumer Contracts Regulations 1999.[390] These regulations control unfair terms in certain classes of contract where a consumer who fails to 'fulfil his obligation' has to pay a disproportionately high sum in compensation.[391] However, it is possible that a consumer may be considered to have failed to fulfil his obligation when he has a lawful excuse for non-performance in which case the regulations could be said to extend further than the common law regime.[392]

Not only payments

The *Dunlop* case concerned payments of money to be made by the party in breach. A provision, which purportedly entitles the victim of the breach to withhold, rather than make a payment which is otherwise due will also be subject to review.[393] Consistency would also seem to require that the penalty doctrine should extend to terms requiring the transfer of something other than money in the event of the transferor's breach of contract. However, this had not been definitively stated[394] before the decision of the Court of Appeal in *Jobson v Johnson*[395] when it was held that a clause requiring a purchaser of shares to re-transfer them in the event of his default on paying any instalment was a penalty.

---

[389] *Cf.* Treitel, pp. 905–6.
[390] SI 1999 No. 2083, reg 4(4).
[391] Sections 2(1), 3(1) and 5(1) and Sch 3.
[392] At common law such a person would not be considered to be in breach of contract.
[393] *Gilbert-Ash (Northern) Ltd v Modern Engineering (Bristol) Ltd* [1974] AC 689.
[394] The only instances where the court has refused to enforce contractual provisions on the basis of the penalty jurisdiction which involved something other than a payment of money are *Re Dagenham (Thames) Dock Co, ex parte Hulse* (1873) LR 8 Ch App 1022 (right of re-entry reserved by vendor of land) and *Public Works Comr v Hills* [1906] AC 368 (forfeiture of security deposit and retention monies in building contract).
[395] [1989] 1 All ER 621 where the transfer was at undervalue. *A fortiori* if the transfer was a gratuitous one. See DR Harris [1990] LMCLQ 158. Now see also *PC Developments Pty v Revell* (1991) 22 NSWLR 615 and *Wollondilly Shire Council v Picton Power Lines Pty Ltd* (1994) 33 NSWLR 551 at 555. *Cf. CRA Ltd v NZ Goldfields Investments* [1989] VR 870.

The disproportion principle
Lord Dunedin stated:[396]

> It will be held to be a penalty if the sum stipulated for is extravagant and uncon-scionable in amount in comparison with the greatest loss that could conceivably be proved to have followed from the breach.

It is difficult to generalise because of the varying circumstances in which the disproportion principle has been applied. However, it seems that the greater the attempt to gradate the loss, the more likely it is that the clause will be upheld. If the sum payable is proportional to the degree of non-performance, e.g. if you find that it is so much per acre for ground which has been spoilt by mining operations,[397] it will prima facie be categorised as liquidated damages. In the words of Lord Radcliffe,[398] this would be a scale which slides the right way.

Whether or not a term is a genuine pre-estimate of loss is judged at the time of contracting. In the *Public Works Commissioner* v *Hills*[399] Lord Dunedin stated: 'the circumstances must be taken as a whole, and must be viewed as at the time the bargain was made'.

Therefore, when applying the disproportion principle the 'greatest loss that could conceivably be proved to have followed from the breach' is to be judged by reference to this time. The actual loss which is incurred might provide 'valuable evidence' as to what was conceived at the time of con-tracting to be the consequence of breach.[400]

In *Dunlop* Lord Dunedin stated a further test which was said to be an application of the disproportion principle. This states that a clause will be construed as a penalty where the breach is a failure to pay a sum of money and the sum stipulated is greater than the one which should have been paid[401] though it seems that a small increase will be disregarded.[402]

Clauses which provide that a sum or sums of money payable in the future, usually in instalments, shall become immediately payable in full, are known as 'acceleration' clauses. In *White & Carter (Councils) Ltd* v *McGregor* Lord Reid said that:[403]

> A question was debated whether this clause provides a penalty or liquidated damages but ... it need not be pursued. The clause merely provides for acceleration of payment of the stipulated price ...

---

[396] [1915] AC 79 at 87.
[397] *Clydebank Engineering and Shipbuilding Co Ltd* v *Don Jose Ramos Yzquierdo y Castenada* [1905] AC 6 at 10.
[398] In *Bridge* v *Campbell Discount Co Ltd*.
[399] [1906] AC 368 at 376. Repeated in *Dunlop* at pp. 86–7. See also *Webster* v *Bosanquet* [1912] AC 394 and *Lombank Ltd* v *Excell* [1963] 3 All ER 486.
[400] *Philips Hong Kong Ltd* v *A-G of Hong Kong* [1993] 61 BLR 41 at 59 *per* Lord Woolf.
[401] *Ibid.* at p. 87, where it is described as 'one of the most ancient instances'.
[402] *Lordsvale Finance plc* v *Bank of Zambia* [1996] QB 752 (1% increase in rate of interest payable on a loan in the event of borrower's default).
[403] [1961] 3 All ER 1178 at 1180 I–1181 A.

Such statements[404] to the effect that acceleration clauses are subject to the penalty jurisdiction[405] but will be held to constitute valid liquidated damages clauses would seem to be a straightforward application of Lord Dunedin's test. However, the payment is to be made earlier than otherwise, and so assuming positive inflation the payor is effectively being asked to pay more than he originally contracted to do. None the less it is suggested that this further test should not be applied to 'automatically' render such clauses ineffective. Rather their validity should be determined by the general disproportion principle.

What loss?

There is authority to suggest that a liquidated damages clause may enable a party to recover for items of loss that would be too remote to form part of an unliquidated damages award.[406]

The wording of the clause

In *Dunlop* Lord Dunedin said:[407]

> Though the parties to a contract who use the words 'penalty' or 'liquidated damages' may prima facie be supposed to mean what they say, yet the expression is not conclusive.

The wording has sometimes been given excessive emphasis and it is suggested that it is now of no importance.[408] Clauses described as 'penalty'[409] have been

---

[404] See also *The Angelic Star* [1988] 1 Lloyd's Rep 122 at 125 *per* Sir John Donaldson MR (if the clause had been construed as requiring the repayment of capital and interest it would have been penal) and *Wadham Stringer Finance Ltd* v *Meany* [1981] 1 WLR 39 at 48C–E *per* Woolf J.

[405] The penalty jurisdiction will not apply if the clause does not condition the payment upon a breach of contract. See *supra* and *O'Dea* v *Allstates Leasing Systems (WA) Pty Ltd* (1983) 152 CLR 359 *per* Gibbs CJ at 366–8.

[406] *Robophone Facilities* v *Blank* [1966] 1 WLR 1428 at 1448 *per* Diplock LJ. *Cf.* the Law Commission's Working Paper No. 61, para 44, which suggests that it is the amount that could be recovered as unliquidated damages which should be considered. A *via media* has been proposed where limitations imposed by the doctrine of remoteness should be ignored but, in the interests of avoiding waste, those imposed by the doctrine of mitigation should be considered relevant. See Beale, *op. cit.*, p. 57. However, mitigation is not relevant to the action in debt so why should it be relevant to the recovery of liquidated damages which it closely resembles.

[407] *Ibid.* at p. 86.

[408] In some of the older cases, too much weight was placed on the parties' choice of words: '... clause 15 should be regarded as a penalty. One excellent reason is that it is so called, a reason which I am aware is not conclusive, but is certainly weighty', *Wall's Case* [1915] 3 KB 66 at 74 *per* Bailache J. Also '... I have no doubt that clause 13 is a penalty clause ... To read it otherwise is to ignore the first word "penalty" ', *Watts, Watts and Co Ltd* v *Mitsui and Co Ltd* [1917] AC 227 at 246 *per* Lord Sumner. This overemphasis may be a relic of the court's reference in several older cases to the intention of the parties as a justification for the penalty jurisdiction, e.g. *Smith* v *Dickinson* [1804] 3 B & P 630. This justification was soon discredited; see *Kemble* v *Farren* [1829] 6 Bing 141.

[409] *Diestal* v *Stevenson* [1906] 2 KB 345 and *Alder* v *Moore* [1961] 2 QB 57 (*obiter dicta* as the penalty jurisdiction did not apply).

enforced and those said to provide 'agreed compensation'[410] or 'liquidated damages'[411] have not. The courts will enquire into the substance rather than the form of the clause[412] and to suggest that the wording is even of 'prima facie' relevance probably overstates the case. At most reference to the parties' own description may bolster a conclusion reached on other grounds.[413] Baron Bramwell's statement[414] that 'the names ... are immaterial' is probably a more accurate reflection of the modern approach.[415]

Sum payable on one of several events

Where a single sum is payable on the occurrence of 'one or more or all of several events, some ... serious and others but trifling'[416] a presumption[417] is said to operate that the sum is a penalty.

When the loss likely to result from breach will be difficult to assess it seems that the presumption operates with some latitude. There is a separate rule that a sum is not prevented from being liquidated damages simply because 'precise pre-estimation [is] almost an impossibility'.[418] In the *Dunlop* case the respondents undertook 29 separate obligations in respect of each breach of which they undertook to pay £5. The presumption was rebutted because the damage caused by each breach would be 'of such an uncertain nature that it cannot be accurately ascertained'.[419] Lord Woolf has recently said that particularly with regard to commercial contracts the court 'has to be careful not to set too stringent a standard' and should discourage argument based on 'unlikely illustrations'.[420]

Lord Parker said that it was acceptable to stipulate for the recovery of a sum which represents the average damage which would be incurred in the event of breach.[421] However, what is not acceptable is to stipulate for the payment of a sum which might be a proper reflection of loss if the obligation were breached

---

410 *Cooden Engineering Co Ltd* v *Stanford* [1953] 1 QB 86; *Bridge* v *Campbell Discount Co Ltd* [1962] AC 600.

411 *Kemble* v *Farren* (1829) 6 Bing 141 and *Bradley* v *Walsh* (1903) 88 LT 737.

412 *Clydebank Engineering and Shipbuilding Co Ltd* v *Don Jose Ramos Yzquierdo y Castenada* [1905] AC 6 at 9 *per* the Earl of Halsbury LC: 'the court must proceed according to what is the real nature of the transaction'.

413 For example, *Ariston SRL* v *Charly Records Ltd* [1990] *Financial Times*, 21 May.

414 *Sparrow* v *Paris* (1862) 7 H & N 594 at 599.

415 *Cf.* Cheshire, Fifoot and Furmston, p. 635.

416 *Dunlop ibid.* at p. 342 referring to *Elphinstone* v *Monkland* (1886) 11 App Cas 332 at 342 *per* Lord Watson.

417 *Ibid.* Previously this principle had operated as a rule of law, see *Astley* v *Weldon* (1801) 2 Bos & P 346.

418 *Dunlop ibid.* at p. 87 *per* Lord Dunedin. See also *Webster* v *Bosanquet* [1912] AC 394 at 398 *per* Lord Mersey.

419 *Ibid.*, p. 96.

420 *Philips Hong Kong* v *A-G of Hong Kong* [1993] 61 BLR 41 at 58–9.

421 *Ibid.* at pp. 98–9: 'Supposing it was recited in the agreement that the parties had estimated the probable damage from a breach of one stipulation at from 5l. [i.e. £5] to 15l. and the probable damage from breach of another stipulation at from 2l. to 12l., and had agreed on a sum of 8l. as a reasonable sum to be paid on the breach of either stipulation, I cannot think that the Court would refuse to give effect to the bargain between the parties.' However, the maths are slightly suspect as $(19 + 7) \div 2 = 8.5$.

in its most serious way but where it could also be breached in less injurious ways as well.[422] If a sum is stipulated which can be regarded as a genuine pre-estimate of the loss that could and in fact did occur the clause will nonetheless be a penalty if in respect of other contemplated breaches it would be.

THE EFFECT OF LIQUIDATED DAMAGES CLAUSES AND PENALTIES

Liquidated damages clause

A claimant may recover the amount stipulated in a valid liquidated damages clause. Even if his actual loss is less than the recovery provided in the clause. In *Clydebank Engineering and Shipbuilding Co Ltd* v *Don Jose Ramos Yzquierdo y Castenada*[423] the House of Lords rejected the argument of the seller that they were not liable for damages in respect of the non-delivery of certain torpedo boats because, if delivered on time, they would have been lost in a disastrous naval engagement which subsequently took place. The argument was to the effect that the actual losses of the purchaser were limited to the value of the ships to them for the short period in time they would have had them.

Where the amount stipulated in the liquidated damages clause overstates the actual loss incurred the amount recovered will be the amount stipulated. In *Diestal* v *Stevenson*[424] a contract for the sale and delivery of coal provided for damages to be paid at a fixed rate per ton plus some freight charges. The purchasers recovered £90 under this clause when it was agreed that their actual losses amounted to £320. When, as here, the stipulated sum is less than actual loss the clause will be challenged by the payee; when, as above, the stipulated sum exceeds actual loss it is the payer who will dispute its validity.

If a party to a contract sues to recover a sum owed under a liquidated damages clause he is under no obligation to minimise his losses; the doctrine of mitigation does not apply.[425]

Penalty clauses

In the usual case, if a clause is considered to be a penalty, an action will lie for unliquidated damages[426] to be assessed in the usual way.[427] However, particular problems are raised in the following two unusual situations.

---

[422] *Ariston SRL* v *Charly Records* [1990] *Financial Times*, 21 May.
[423] [1905] AC 6 at 10.
[424] [1906] 2 KB 345.
[425] *Abrahams* v *Performing Rights Society* [1995] ICR 1028.
[426] In *Jobson* v *Johnson* [1989] 1 All ER 621 it was suggested that an action may be maintained to enforce the penalty up to the limit of his actual loss. In most cases the practical result is the same and so the action to enforce the penalty has been described as a 'dead letter' *per* Nicholl LJ at 632d.
[427] *Supra.*

Actual loss exceeds sum stipulated

The mechanical application of Lord Dunedin's guidelines might result in a contractual clause being categorised as a penalty even though the claimant suffers a greater loss than the sum stipulated, e.g. where the clause provides for the same sum to be payable on the occurrence of different breaches of contract and the breach that occurs is an especially serious one.

The question then arises whether the penalty operates as a limit upon recovery of unliquidated damages. According to *Wall's* case[428] this is not so; the claimant is entitled to recover to the full extent of his actual loss. It is suggested that this decision should not be followed for a number of reasons.[429] Rather Lord Ellenborough's view that 'beyond the penalty you shall not go; within it, you are to give the party any compensation which he can prove himself entitled to'[430] is to be preferred. In other words, the penalty clause should be regarded as setting an upper limit upon recovery.[431] In this way the law avoids committing itself to the absurdity, whenever the payee's actual loss exceeds the sum stipulated, of placing the person who deliberately stipulates for a penalty in a better position than someone who inserts a genuine pre-estimate of loss.[432] In *Elsey* v *JG Collins Insurance Agencies Ltd*[433] the Supreme Court of Canada adopted the solution proposed here.

Liquidated damages set at less than anticipated loss

A clause may stipulate for a sum of money, which is calculated to be less than a genuine pre-estimate of loss. Such a clause is a hybrid and has some of the features of a liquidated damages clause and some of a limitation clause. Like liquidated damages it does not stipulate for payment in excess of a genuine pre-estimate of loss but like a limitation clause it will only permit the recovery of an amount which is less than the full loss.

It might be argued that if a clause stipulating for the recovery of a genuine pre-estimate of loss is to be upheld it should follow *a fortiori* that a clause stipulating for less than that amount should be enforceable. In two cases the House of Lords have upheld this. It seems that such a clause will not be subject to the legal controls imposed upon limitation clauses as the cases draw a clear distinction between the two. The hybrid clause is 'one agreeing a

---

428 [1915] 3 KB 66 approved by the House of Lords in *Watts, Watts and Co Ltd* v *Mitsui and Co Ltd* [1917] AC 227. See also the older cases of *Winter* v *Trimmer* (1762) 1 Wm Bl 395 and *Harrison* v *Wright* (1811) 13 East 343.

429 Including the excessive weight attached to the parties' own description of the clause and a possible error of logic. Bailache J at p. 74 states that because the clause is not a limitation clause it must be a penalty when it could be a valid liquidated damages clause.

430 *Wilbeam* v *Ashton* (1807) 1 Camp 78. See also *Elphinstone* v *Monkland* (1886) 11 App Cas 332 at 346 *per* Lord Fitzgerald.

431 *Cf.* McGregor, *op. cit.* (n. 339 above), pp. 326–7, who does not refer to *Elsey* v *JG Collins Insurance Agencies Ltd* (1978) 83 DLR (3d) 1, considered below.

432 Hudson (1974) 90 LQR 31, (1975) 91 LQR 25 and (1985) 101 LQR 480.

433 (1978) 83 DLR (3d) 1 at 15 *per* Dickson J; *Cellulose Acetate Silk Co* v *Widnes Foundry Ltd* [1933] AC 20; *Suisse Atlantique Société d'Armement Maritime SA* v *Rotterdamsche Kolen Centrale NV* [1967] 1 AC 361; *AMEV-UDC Finance Ltd* v *Austin* (1986) 162 CLR 170 at 192–3, 201–3 and 212, which have left the question open.

figure and not ... imposing a limit',[434] it permits the recovery of a fixed sum *'no less* and no more';[435] whereas a limitation clause simply places an upper limit upon the recovery of proven loss. As a result, the clause is not subject to the usual[436] common law[437] and statutory control of exemption clauses.[438]

The Unfair Terms in Consumer Contracts Regulations 1999[439] provide that in contracts for goods or services between sellers or suppliers of goods and consumers terms which have not been 'individually negotiated' are unenforceable if they are unfair.[440] A 'grey list' of terms is included which are to be regarded as presumptively unfair including a contractual provision which demands that 'any customer who fails to fulfil his obligation to pay a disproportionately high sum in compensation'.[441] There is obviously a considerable area of overlap between the common law control of penalties and the regulations but generally the common law control is more extensive than that under the regulations. For example, the regulations do not apply to contracts between two (commercial) suppliers or sellers and, in any case, do not apply to contracts of employment.[442]

EVASION OF THE JURISDICTION

Several of the techniques already used by draftsmen to avoid the penalty jurisdiction have been examined indirectly. However, they are gathered together here for comparison particularly with one technique which has not yet been encountered.

Sum made payable on an event other than breach of contract by the payer[443]

The penalty jurisdiction does not apply when the event which 'triggers' the payment is an event other than a breach of contract by the payer. This enables a penalty clause to be disguised, for instance, a car hire company

---

[434] *Suisse Atlantique Société d'Armement Maritime SA* v *Rotterdamsche Kolen Centrale NV* [1967] 1 AC 361 at 436 *per* Lord Wilberforce.

[435] *Cellulose Acetate Silk Co* v *Widnes Foundry Ltd* [1933] AC 20 at 25 *per* Lord Atkin (emphasis added).

[436] It may be unenforceable if it is contained in an unsigned document or notice which is not incorporated into the parties' contract: *Interfoto Picture Library Ltd* v *Stiletto Visual Programmes Ltd* [1989] QB 433.

[437] The various rules of construction designed to control such clauses have in any event been relaxed in the case of limitation clauses in commercial contracts: *Ailsa Craig Fishing Co Ltd* v *Malvern Fishing Co* [1983] WLR 964 and *George Mitchell (Chesterhall) Ltd* v *Finney Lock Seeds Ltd* [1983] 2 AC 803 at 814.

[438] Unfair Contract Terms Act 1977, though it may be caught by the Unfair Terms in Consumer Contracts Regulations 1999, considered below.

[439] SI 1999 No. 2083, reg 4(4).

[440] Sections 2(1), 3(1) and 5(1).

[441] Paragraph 1(e).

[442] Schedule 1.

[443] *Supra.*

concerned to ensure the prompt payment of its usual rate of hire of £100 per day might use the following techniques. First, by using the alternative considerations technique, the rate of hire of the car might be expressed to be £100 per day paid in advance or £200 per day if paid in arrears. Second, by using the discount technique, the rate of hire might be expressed to be £200 with a 50 per cent discount for payment in advance. The key to either technique is that the contract must be drafted to ensure that the hirer's failure to pay £100 in advance is not a breach of contract.

Creation of a present debt and an acceleration clause

Clauses which simply accelerate liability are currently (but wrongly I suggest) not considered to be penalties. If a payee wants to ensure the timely tender of payments, the contract might state that the failure to pay an instalment makes the outstanding instalments due.

Termination clause in *Lombard North Central* v *Butterworth*

A clause which in the event of a breach of contract gives the victim the right to terminate the contract in circumstances which would otherwise not entitle him to do so[444] will not be considered as a penalty. However where unliquidated damages may be claimed for loss of bargain[445] the payee may rely on the clause to recover unliquidated damages, even though liquidated damages would be irrecoverable. Such a clause will have a considerable coercive effect in dissuading the party subject to it from breaching the contract. However, it should be noted that the decision in *Lombard* has attracted considerable criticism[446] and, although the Court of Appeal regarded the result as inevitable on the law as it stands, Nicholls LJ expressed 'considerable dissatisfaction' with the conclusion 'a skilled draftsman can easily side-step the effect of [*Financings Ltd* v *Baldock*]' and Mustill LJ '[did] not … view with much satisfaction [the fact that] the claimants have achieved by one means a result which the law of penalties might have prevented them from achieving by another'.

THE FORFEITURE OF DEPOSITS AND ADVANCE PAYMENTS

Deposits and advance payments can be distinguished from liquidated damages and penalties by reference to the time at which they are paid or

---

444 That is, because the conduct of the party in breach does not of itself amount to repudiation of the agreement.
445 In *Financings Ltd* v *Baldock* [1963] 2 QB 104 it was held that an owner of goods who exercises an express power to terminate a hire agreement may only recover damages in respect of instalments which were unpaid at the time of termination. In *Lombard* this principle was said to be inapplicable where the contract itself makes the breach a breach of condition.
446 See Treitel [1987] LMCLQ 143 and Beale (1988) 104 LQR 355.

payable. Liquidated damages and penalties become payable after breach; deposits and advance payments before it. Considerable doubt surrounded the question whether deposits are subject to the penalty jurisdiction.[447] The decision of the Privy Council in *Workers Trust and Merchant Bank Ltd v Dojap Investments Ltd*[448] brought the two areas of law into closer alignment.[449]

Nevertheless, it is not possible to say that deposits are subsumed within the penalty jurisdiction.[450] The tests are different: a penalty is a sum in excess of a 'genuine pre-estimate of loss', whereas the enforceability of a deposit is said to turn on its reasonableness. Lord Woolf has asserted that the test for a penalty is an objective one[451] but there still remains the doubt that the subjective formulation of the penalty test may produce a different result to one based upon reasonableness. Second, a sum may, at least in the case of sale of land, be forfeit as a deposit even though it is in excess of a genuine pre-estimate of loss.[452]

If a deposit or advance payment has been made and there is a subsequent breach of contract by the *payee* the sum paid is recoverable as part of the restitutionary measure of damages.[453] The following paragraphs address the question whether the *payer* may recover all or part of the deposit or advance payment when he is *himself* in breach of contract.

Deposits

A deposit is 'an earnest to bind the bargain'.[454] Here[455] the courts attach considerable weight to the parties' description of a payment as a deposit as evidence of the parties' intention that the sum be forfeit in the event of the payer's breach.[456] This is justified by a common understanding as to what a deposit is in law.[457] Where a deposit is paid the payer will not, subject to the exceptions considered below, be entitled to recover any of it in the event that

---

[447] *Public Works Commissioners v Hills* [1906] AC 368 and *Pye v British Automobile Commercial Syndicate Ltd* [1906] 1 KB 425. *Cf. Lock v Bell* [1931] 1 Ch 35 and *Galbraith v Mitchenhall Estates* [1965] 2 QB 473 (deposits are *not* subject to the penalty rule).

[448] [1993] 2 All ER 370.

[449] The Law Commission proposed that all deposits become subject to the penalty jurisdiction with a saving in respect of sales of land for deposits below a conventional threshold. Working Paper No. 61, Part V.

[450] *Cf.* Treitel, p. 937.

[451] *Philips Hong Kong Ltd v A-G of Hong Kong* [1993] 61 BLR 41 at 59–60.

[452] *Workers Trust* case at p. 373b *per* Lord Browne-Wilkinson. If such a sum can be termed 'reasonable' the second point of difference simply becomes an illustration of the first.

[453] *Cole v Rose* [1978] 3 All ER 1121. See above.

[454] *Howe v Smith* (1887) 27 Ch D 89 at 101. *Workers Trust* case at p. 373d *per* Lord Browne-Wilkinson.

[455] See above the use of the word condition and liquidated damages or penalty. There does not appear to be any empirical evidence (e.g. that penalty conveys the idea of an irrecoverable sum, and deposit that of a forfeitable sum) to support these differing emphases.

[456] *Howe v Smith* (1884) 27 Ch D 89. However, a payment to be as an earnest for a future performance will not be deprived of its character as a deposit by being described as 'liquidated damages' according to the Privy Council in *Union Eagle Ltd v Golden Achievements Ltd* [1997] 2 All ER 215 at 218e.

[457] 'Everyone knows what a deposit is – it is a guarantee that the purchaser means business': *per* Lord MacNaughton in *Soper v Arnold* (1889) 14 App Cas 429 at 435.

he is in breach of contract.[458] Further, if at the time of breach any part of the deposit was due but not paid the payee may recover the amount outstanding without having to prove any loss.[459]

The Workers Trust case[460]

A deposit must be reasonable before it can be forfeit. In the *Workers Trust* case the Privy Council held that on the sale of land a deposit of 25 per cent was not reasonable, despite evidence that it was usual for financial institutions in Jamaica selling property at auction to demand deposits of between 15 and 50 per cent.[461] It would be wrong to 'allow the test of reasonableness to depend upon the practice of one class of vendor, which exercises considerable financial muscle'.[462] The starting point for determining a reasonable deposit would be the ancient custom in the United Kingdom and formerly in Jamaica of a 10 per cent deposit. Only special circumstances could justify a departure from this norm.[463] As none existed, the deposit could not be retained.[464] Where as here the deposit is unenforceable, there is no power in the court to rewrite the parties' contract[465] the retention of a lesser reasonable deposit. The deposit must be repaid in full subject only to a retention of a sum representing the actual loss of the payee.

Law of Property Act 1925, s 49(2)[466]

This provides that '... in any action for the return of a deposit, the court may if it thinks fit, order the repayment of any deposit'. This confers a broad discretion on the court to order repayment if justice requires it.[467] However, the evidence suggests a reluctance to invoke the discretion.[468] Where it is

---

458 'The payer cannot insist on abandoning the contract and yet recover the deposit, because that would be to enable him to take advantage of his own wrong', *Howe* v *Smith per* Bowen LJ at p. 98. See also *Union Eagle Ltd* v *Golden Achievements Ltd* [1997] 2 All ER 215.

459 *Hinton* v *Sparkes* (1868) LR 3 CP 161 at 161 *per* Willes J.

460 *Workers Trust and Merchant Bank Ltd* v *Dojap* [1993] 2 All ER 370: approving *Lingii Plantations Ltd* v *Jagatheesan* [1972] 1 MLJ 89.

461 *Workers Trust*, p. 374c.

462 *Ibid.* p. 374c–d *per* Lord Browne-Wilkinson.

463 *Ibid.* at p. 374e–f *per* Lord Browne-Wilkinson.

464 An argument was rejected that the 25 per cent deposit was justified by particular features of the Jamaican fiscal system.

465 As with penalty clauses '... the courts have always avoided claiming that they have any general jurisdiction to rewrite the contracts that the parties have made ...': *Philips Hong Kong Ltd* v *A-G of Hong Kong* [1993] 61 BLR 41 at 55.

466 The section is not relevant where the vendor not the purchaser is in default: *Dimsdale Developments (South East)* v *De Haan* (1983) 47 P & CR at 11 *per* Godfrey QC and they will not be affected by any clause 'excluding' s 49(2): *County and Metropolitan Homes Surrey Ltd* v *Topelcim Ltd* [1997] 1 All ER 254.

467 *Universal Corporation* v *Five Ways Properties Ltd* [1979] 1 All ER 552 at 555 *per* Buckley LJ. Prior to these decisions it was thought that the jurisdiction was intended to apply to cases where the vendor was not able to complete or the purchaser was for some reason otherwise entitled to rescind. For a careful application of the modern approach see *Safeheaven Investments Inc* v *Springbok Ltd* (1996) 71 P & CR 59 at 70–72.

468 See Megarry J's observations in *Schindler* v *Pigault* (1975) 30 P & CR 328.

invoked, there is a failure to articulate the general grounds which are thought to justify its exercise.[469]

Consumer Credit Act 1974

Under this Act the court has extensive powers[470] to review 'extortionate'[471] credit bargains and these extend to ordering the repayment of part or all of any sum paid by the debtor.[472]

Unfair Terms in Consumer Contract Regulations 1999[473]

These regulations provide that terms in contracts for the sale or supply of goods or services to consumers which have not been 'individually negotiated' are unenforceable if they are unfair.[474] Schedule 3 contains a 'grey list' of terms that are regarded as presumptively unfair including a contractual provision 'permitting the seller or supplier to retain sums paid by the consumer where the latter decides not to conclude or perform the contract, without providing for the consumer to receive compensation of an equivalent amount from the seller or supplier where the latter is the party cancelling the contract'.[475] This provision is apparently based upon civil law[476] but may nonetheless, where the regulations apply, render undertakings by consumers to make such payments unenforceable[477] and perhaps also require such payments to be returned.[478]

Advance payments

If there is express provision that an advance payment shall be forfeit in the event of the payer's breach, the courts have developed a principle of relief against forfeiture. This relief is available to a purchaser who despite his breach of contract is ready and willing to perform,[479] but it is difficult to state clearly any further limits.

Stockloser v *Johnson*[480]

In the case the majority of the Court of Appeal held that the court had an equitable jurisdiction to relieve against a provision, in a contract to buy

---

[469] For instance, *Dimsdale Developments (South East)* v *De Haan* (1983) 47 P & CR 1.
[470] Sections 137–40. This jurisdiction extends to agreements providing credit in excess of the usual limit of £25,000 and even to exempt agreements within s 16.
[471] Under s 138 a bargain is extortionate if it requires the debtor to make payments which are grossly exorbitant or otherwise grossly contravene ordinary principles of fair dealing.
[472] Section 139(2).
[473] SI 1999 No. 2083, reg 4(4).
[474] Sections 2(1), 3(1) and 5(1).
[475] Paragraph 1(d).
[476] Treitel, p. 912.
[477] Paragraph 5(1).
[478] This seems to be assumed but not spelt out by Sch 3, para 1(e).
[479] *Re Dagenham (Thames) Dock Co, ex parte Hulse* (1873) 8 Ch App 1022 and *Kilmer* v *British Columbia Orchard Lands Ltd* [1913] AC 319.
[480] [1954] 1 QB 476.

machinery by instalments, that upon the purchaser's default the seller could terminate the contract and retain any instalments paid.[481] Denning and Somervell LJJ said[482] that the jurisdiction was dependent upon the sum retained being out of all proportion to the damage and, further, that it must be unconscionable for the seller to retain the monies. Romer LJ denied the existence of any general 'equity ... in favour of a purchaser who has failed to complete his contract through no fault of the vendor'.[483] He saw nothing wrong in the retention of 'instalments of purchase money which the vendor is contractually entitled to retain'.[484]

Subsequent cases do not provide any clear statement as to when the power to relieve from forfeiture may be invoked; either they state negative propositions or *Stockloser* v *Johnson* is distinguished on the facts.[485] The jurisdiction did not apply to a contract such as a time charter[486] or a contractual licence[487] which did not create or transfer proprietary rights.[488] Decisions demonstrate that in the *Workers Trust* case[489] *Stockloser* was distinguished on the ground that it was concerned with relief against forfeiture where the purchaser had taken possession of the property.

The *Dies* principle

Where there is no express forfeiture provision in the contract the payment is recoverable by the party in breach of contract subject to a counter-claim for damages. So in *Dies* v *British and International Mining and Finance Corporation Ltd*[490] a buyer who, in breach of contract, refused to accept delivery of a consignment of ammunition was entitled to recover an advance payment of £100,000, subject only to the seller's right to damages for breach of contract.[491]

---

[481] Although in the circumstances of the case it was not unconscionable for the seller to retain the instalments paid amounting to some 40 per cent of the purchase price because the buyer had received substantial benefits.

[482] *Ibid*, pp. 490 and 484 respectively.

[483] Quoting Farwell J in *Mussen* v *Van Diemen's Land Co* [1938] 1 All ER 210.

[484] *Ibid* at p. 501 adopted by Sachs J in *Galbraith* v *Mitchenhall Estates Ltd* [1954] 1 QB 476 at 501.

[485] A typical example is: 'The boundaries of the equitable jurisdiction to relieve against contractual penalties and forfeiture are in some places imprecise. But their Lordships do not think that it is necessary in this case to draw them more exactly because ... the facts lie well beyond the reach of the doctrine.' *Union Eagle Ltd* v *Golden Achievements Ltd* [1997] 2 All ER 215 at 218f *per* Lord Aweigh.

[486] *The Scaptrade, Scandinavian Trading Tanker Co AB* v *Flota Petrolera Ecuatoriana* [1983] 2 AC 694. A time charter is a contract for the provision of services. In contrast, a demise or bareboat charter does create a proprietary interest by virtue of the control exercised by the charterer. See *Sea & Land Securities* v *Dickinson* [1942] 2 KB 65 at 69 *per* Mackinnon LJ.

[487] *Sport International Bussum BV* v *Inter-Footwear Ltd* [1984] 1 WLR 776.

[488] *Cf. BICC plc* v *Burndy Corp* [1965] Ch 232 (Court of Appeal granted an extension of time in respect of a failure to pay monies which otherwise entitled the payee to an assignment of patent rights).

[489] [1993] AC 573 at 581–2.

[490] [1939] 1 KB 724.

[491] See also *Fitt* v *Cassenet* (1842) 4 Man & G (payment misdescribed in head note as a 'deposit') and *Mayson* v *Clouet* [1924] AC 980.

Dies was not followed in two cases[492] involving contracts to build ships where the House of Lords held that advance payments could not be reclaimed by defaulting customers. This conclusion was justified by the nature of the contract. The obligations assumed by the shipyards extended beyond the duty to deliver the finished product to include the design and construction of the vessel, which was well advanced at the time of the purchaser's repudiation. Therefore, unlike in *Dies*, there was no failure of consideration sufficient to justify the return of the instalments.

---

[492] *Hyundai Heavy Industries Co Ltd* v *Papadoulos* [1980] 2 All ER 29 and *Stoczia Gdanska SA* v *Latvian Shipping* [1998] 1 All ER 883.

INDEX

Acceleration clauses, 519
Acceptance
  meaning, 140
  bilateral contract, in, 146–55
  communication of, 146–8
  conduct, by, 147–8
  counter-offer, 142, 144, 146
  'cross-offer', 156–7
  e-mail, by, 146–7, 151
  fax, by, 146–7
  methods of, 48
  post, by
    application of rule as to, 150–1
    consequences of rule as to, 151–2
    third parties and, 256
    when complete, 148
  revocation of, 152
  reward cases, 155–6
  silence as, 152–5
  telegram, by, 151
  telephone, by, 146
  telex, by, 146
  time for, 144–5
  traditional view of, 145–6
  unilateral contract, where, 155–7
Accountant's duty of care, 69
Advance payment
  forfeiture of, relief against, 522–4
  recovery of, where breach by payee, 520
Advertisement
  auction, for, 128
  invitation to treat or offer, 123–5, 128
  package holiday, for, 259
Affirmation of contract
  express, 47
  implied, 47–9
  rescission, loss of right to, 47–9
Agency
  fiduciary relationship of principal and agent, 101
  intervention of agent, effect of, in deceit cases, 60
  privity of contract rule and, 264–5
  termination of, payment of compensation, 471
Aggravated damages, role of, 471
Agreement
  acceptance *see* Acceptance
  compromise agreement, 135, 166
  elements of, 20, 119
  formation of contract, requisite for, 20
  lock-out agreement, 90–2, 190
  objective test of *see* Objective test
  offer *see* Offer
  subjective test of, 5, 20–1
Annuity, action for due proportion of, 409
Anson, Sir William, 1
Anti-competitive practices
  contracts in restraint of trade *see* Restraint of

trade, contracts in
  statutory control of, 214–16
Anticipatory breach of contract
  see Breach of contract
Apportionment Act, remedy under, 409
Aquinas, Thomas, 4
Arbitration clauses, 205
Assignment
  meaning, 268
  availability of, 268
  effect of, 268–9
  privity of contract doctrine and, 268–9
  statutory, 472
Atiyah, views of, 3–7, 9
Auction
  advertisement for, 128
  invitation to treat or offer, 127–8, 161
Auditor's liabilities, 69, 73
Australia, estoppel in 74, 175

Bailment, 163, 281–2
Bank
  cheque, failure to honour, 465
  duty of care, 69
  irrevocable banker's credit, 139
  manager and client, undue influence, 99
Barrister's duty of care, 69
Barter, 296
Bilateral contract
  acceptance of offer in, 146–55
  form of, 119
  primary obligations, 468
  revocation of, 134–6
  secondary obligations, 468
  unilateral distinguished, 136
Bills of lading, 180, 260–1, 265, 276, 472
  See also Contract of carriage
Bingo, 217
Bona fide *see* Good faith
Breach of contract
  acceptance of, by innocent party, 41
  advance payment, forfeiture of, 522–4
  affirmation of contract, effect of, 47–9
  anticipatory breach
    meaning, 432
    examples, 432–4
    remedies available, 434
    good faith protection, 433
  condition, breach of *see* Condition
  damages *see* Damages
  deposit, recovery of *see* Deposit
  economic duress *see* Economic duress
  fundamental breach, 306–7
  injunction, availability of *see* Injunction
  limitation of action, 120, 173
  mitigation of loss, duty *see* Mitigation of loss

Breach of contract (*continued*)
  quantum meruit claims, 85, 409–10
  remedies generally, 2, 30
  repudiation *see* Repudiation of contract
  rescission for *see* Rescission
  restitutionary damages for, 474–6
  specific performance as remedy, 272
  termination of contract for *see* Termination of
    contract
  trivial, 436
  waiver *see* Waiver
  warranty, breach of, 285–6, 434
Breach of promise of marriage, 207–8
Building contract
  deed, use of, 119
  specific performance, 447–8, 450
  tenders, use of, 131–2
Business
  contract to carry on, 448–9
  goodwill, sale of, 211–12
  loss of reputation, damages for, 491
  partners, fiduciary relationship, 101

Cancellation of contract
  third party rights and, 255
Capacity to contract
  addict, 245
  company, 242, 246
  drunkenness, effect of, 245
  mentally incapacitated person, 242, 245–6
  minors *see* Minors
  reform of law, 246
Carriage of goods by sea
  bills of lading, 180, 260–1, 265, 276, 472
  charterparty, 260
  CIF terms, 260, 394
  damages and requirement of proprietary interest,
    471
  exemption clauses, 259
  FOB terms, 260, 394
Cartels, control of, 214
Caveat emptor rule, 95
Certainty
  business contracts and, 200
  need for, 144, 187–8
  vagueness, removal of, 188
Champerty, 205–6
Charitable donations, damages and, 467
Charterparties, 260
CIF contracts, 260, 394
Circular
  invitation to treat or offer, 125
Civil law
  damages, as to, 441
  heads of liability, 81
  jurisdictions, 3, 15–16
  specific performance, 441–2
Classical contract law, 3–5, 298–9
Collateral contract
  case law, 88–93
  duty to disclose and, 112
  express terms, 87, 94
  implied, 88–90, 94
  omitted term taking effect as, 178
  parol evidence as to, 289–90

role of, 16, 87, 221
  third party, enforcement by, 265–8
  unfair terms, 308
Commission on European Contract Law, 11, 115
Commodity futures, sale of, 218
Common law
  breach date rule, 477
  civil law and, 3, 15–16
  equitable jurisdiction and, 443
Company, capacity to contract, 242, 246
Competition law, 214–16
Compromise agreement
  meaning, 135
  consideration, 166
Condition
  meaning, 285, 434
  breach of, effect of, 285, 431
  classification as
    courts, by 436
    parties, by 435
  commercial contracts, presumption in 436
  condition precedent, 407–9
  insurance contract, 98
  service contracts, 437
  statutory, 434–5
Conditional fee agreements, 206
Conditional gift, contract distinguished, 161–2
Conduct as representation, 104
Confidential information, protection of, 210
Consideration
  adequacy of, 162–3, 165
  cautionary function, 168, 169
  channelling function, 168
  compromise agreement, 166–8
  deed as substitute for, 119, 173–4
  definitions of, 119, 159–61, 169
  economic consideration, 165–6
  estoppel as substitute for, 2, 174–5
  evidentiary function, 168
  executed consideration, 164
  modification of contract *see* Modification of
    contract
  moral consideration, 165
  need for, 119
  past consideration, 164
  pre-existing duty, performance of
    law, from, generally, 168, 171–3
    subsequent promisor, contract with, 168, 171
    third party contract with, 168–71
  promise principle and, 6
  restitution purposes, for, 83–4, 428
  salvage agreement, 163
  substitutes for, 173–5
  total failure of
    damages, 462
    frustration of contract, 423
    restitution, action for, 41, 244
Construction of exclusion clause *see* Exclusion
    clause
Consumer contracts
  generally, 120
  judicial control, decline in, 301
  unfair terms *see* Unfair terms
Consumer credit
  cancellation rights, 194

Consumer credit (*continued*)
  cooling off period, 158
  'extortionate' credit bargain, review of, 522
  regulated agreements, formal requirements as to, 179
  scope of statutory provisions, 97
Continental law
  good faith, negotiation in, 110–11, 114, 116
Contra proferentem rule, 304, 307
Contract
  gift distinguished, 161–2
  use of term, 119–20
Contract of carriage (*see* Bill of lading), 372
Contractors
  attitudes of, in real world, 10
  tenders and, 131–2
Contractual terms *see* Terms of contract
Contributory negligence
  damages, effect on
    deceit cases, in, 60, 65–6
    generally, 495–7
    negligent misrepresentation cases, 65–8
    Hedley Byrne action, effect in, 71–3
    Misrepresentation Act, action under, effect in, 72
Convention, estoppel by *see* Estoppel by convention
Conversion, tort of, 23
'Cooling off' periods, 97, 158
Corporation, capacity to contract, 246
Costs
  importance of, 8
  litigation, in, generally, 115
  passing on, 355–6
  rise in, frustration and, 386–7, 395–400
Counter-claim, 523
Counter-offer
  acceptance of, 142, 144, 146
  effect of, 139–144
Court
  classification of terms by, 436
  order of, disobedience to, 442–3
  ouster of jurisdiction of, 204–5
Crime
  access to proceeds of, 201
  contract to commit, 120
Criminal law, tort of deceit and, 54
'Cross-offers', 156–7
Custom, terms implied by, 285, 290, 296
Customer lists, protection of, 210

Damages
  action in debt compared, 455
  aggravated damages, 471
  amenity, loss of, for, 486
  assessment of
    stages of, 461
    time of, 64, 477–8, 505
  assignment of right to, 269
  award of
    net loss principle, 466–70
    three types of, 462–4
  breach of
    condition, for, 285
    contract, for, 431, 441, 461–524
    innominate term, for, 285, 286
    warranty, for, 285, 286

building contract, in respect of, 448
causation, issues of, 494–5
commercial agents, 470
compensatory aim, 461–2
contractual measure of, 463, 464
contributory negligence, role of, *see* Contributory negligence
Cory v Thames Ironworks Co, rule in, 476
counter-claim for, 523
damage *see* loss, *below*
deceit, for *see* Deceit, tort of
defective building work, for, 479–81
disappointment, for, 471, 478, 484–5
discrimination for non-compliance with regulations, for, 132
economic loss, for 68–73, 269–71, 501–2
exemplary, 54, 194, 195, 470–1
expectation measure of
  meaning, 464
  cost of cure and diminuition of value, 478–80
  non-acceptance of goods by buyer, for, 482
  non-delivery and market-price rule, 480–1
  non-pecuniary loss, for, 483–6
  pecuniary loss, for, 478–82
  reliance measure and, 493–4
  restitution measure and, 493–4
extra compensatory, 472–8
freedom from distress, contracts to provide, 485
indemnity distinguished, 52–3
insurance proceeds and, 467
interests of justice, 476
limitation of action, 120
limits on recovery of, 494–502, 517–18
liquidated damages
  deposit and advance payments distinguished, 521
  hybrid clause, 517–18
  penalties and, 506–20
  sum stated in clause overstating loss, 515–17
loss
  meaning, 470
  amenity, of, 486
  burden of proof, 464–5
  chance of, 465–6
  economic, 68–73, 269–71, 501–2
  mitigation of, *see* Mitigation of loss
  net loss principle, 466–70
  profit, of, 478
  publicity, of, 485–6
  wasted expenditure, 465
measure of
  contract, in, 56, 72
  expectation measure *see* expectation measure, *above*
  reliance measure *see* reliance measure, *below*
  relationship between difficult types of, 492–4
  restitutionary measure *see* restitutionary measures *below*
  tort, in, 56–60, 72, 463–4
mental distress, for, 471, 484–5, 489–90
minimum performance rule, 468–71
mitigation of loss *see* Mitigation of loss
negligent misrepresentation, for *see* Negligent misrepresentation
nominal damages, award of, 461

Damages (*continued*)
  peace of mind, contracts to provide, 485
  physical inconvenience for, 488
  pleasure, contracts for provision of, 484–5
  proprietary interest, requirement as to, 471–2
  punitive damages, 54, 194
  recovery
    ordinary losses, for 502–3
    unusual losses, for, 503–4
  reliance measure of
    meaning, 464
    expectation measure and, 492–4
    non-pecuniary loss, 488–90
    pecuniary loss, 486–88
    pre-contractual reliance, 487–88
    post-contractual reliance, 488
    role of, 486
  remoteness test, 58–60, 66, 72, 351, 470,
    497–502
  reputation, damage to, for, 485–6, 488–90
  rescission in lieu of *see* Rescission
  restitutionary measure of
    meaning, 464
    aim of, 491
    deposits or advance payments, 520
    enrichment by wrongdoing, 475–7
    expectation measure and, 493–4
    generally, 470
    non-monetary benefit, recovery as to, 491
  specific performance and, 444–9
  third party loss, for, 257, 275–8
  time of assessment, 478–80, 504
  tortious remedy, as, 9, 23, 26, 54, 72
  trade unions, 345–6
  unjust enrichment, as to, 463–4
  unliquidated damages
    meaning, 461
    examples of, 464
    penalty clauses and, 516–17
  use of, as contract remedy, 6, 7
  work, labour and materials contracts, 474
De minimis principle, 410
Death
  offeree, of, effect of, 145
  offeror, of effect of, 145
Debt
  action in
    meaning, 455
    accrual of cause of action, 455
    availability of, 455–60
    generally, 434
    mitigation of loss, 458
    specific performance and, 457
  clause creating, and accelerating liability, 519–20
  part payment of
    common law rule, 335–7, 363
    equitable waiver, application of, 363–4
Deceit, tort of
  criminal law and, 54
  damages
    contributory negligence no defence, 60, 65
    intervention of agent, effect of, 60
    measure of, 56–60, 71–3
    mitigation of loss, 59–60
    remoteness test, 58–60, 66, 72

distinguishing feature of, 54–6
  generally, 23, 40
  proof of commission of, 55–6, 68, 72, 80
Deed
  limitation period, 120
  requirements for, 119, 173
  'simple' contract distinguished, 119–20
  use of, 119–20, 173–4
Defamation, action for, 490
Delay as a defence, 452
Deposit
  meaning, 520
  penalties and, 519–20
  recovery of
    consumer credit legislation and, 522
    discretion of court, 521
    payee in breach of contract, where, 521
    payer in breach of contract, where, 521–2
  retention of, 317
Director-General of Fair Trading
  consumer contracts, powers as to, 314
Disappointment, damages, for, 471, 479, 484–5
Disclosure
  contract terms, of
    common law principle, 96–7
    statutory measures, 96–7
  duty to negotiate in good faith and, 94, 109
  information, of
    encouragement of, 105, 106
    statutory requirements, 104, 178–80
  material facts, of, 96–9, 104–5
  sale of goods legislation and, 104, 105
  uberimmae fidei contracts, 98–9
  wider duty to, arguments as to, 106–9
  see also Non-disclosure
Doctor and patient
  undue influence, presumption of, 99
Domestic arrangements, enforceability of, 119
Drunkenness, effect of, 245
Duress,
  allocation of risk and, 387
  economic duress *see* Economic duress
  elements of, 339
  protection from, 7
  history of law as to, 337–9
  restitution, justifying, 225
  undue influence, comparison with, 338

Economic analysis of law, 7–8
Economic duress
  'compulsion'
    ability of victim to pass on costs, 455–6
    as element of, 339
    existence of adequate alternative, 349–54
    independent advice, relevance of, 354
    protest, presence of, 348–9
    subsequent affirmation of contract and, 355
    vitiation of consent test, 346–8
  development of doctrine, 339, 404, 406
  'duress of goods' cases, 346
  elements of, 339
  non-enforcement rule, 356–7
  threat
    breach of pre-existing contract, 342–5, 351
    commission of tort, 345–6

Economic duress (*continued*)
    'illegitimate pressure', 339
    refusal of future business, 341–2
Economic loss
  contract, claim in, 270
  damages for, 9, 68–73, 269–71, 501–2
  tort action by third party for, 269–71
Economic torts, 279, 345
E-mail
  acceptance of offer by, 146–7, 151
Electronic commerce, 12, 149, 158
Employment
  contract
    damages for loss of earnings, 468
    implied terms, 299
    injunction to restrain breach etc. of, 451
    minor, for, 243
    mitigation of loss, rule as to, 404
    restraint of trade, 209–11
    specific performance, 450–1
    written statement of terms, 97
  employee, third party rights and, 258–9
  law as to, development of, 8, 157
  trade unions, role of, 212
  unfair dismissal, 451, 490
Enforcement
  modification of contract, 320–1, 323–5, 329
  privity of contract doctrine *see* Privity of contract
  specific performance *see* Specific performance
Engineering contracts, 119, 131–2, 143
Equity
  breach date rule, 477
  common law, fusion with, 45
  jurisdiction, 239–40, 443
  negligent misstatements, liability for, 68
  specific performance *see* Specific performance
  maxims, 452
Estoppel
  meaning, 73
  acquiesence, by *see under* Proprietary estoppel
  cause of action for, 78
  consideration and, 2, 174–5
  convention, by *see* Estoppel by convention
  encouragement, by *see under* Propietary estoppel
  metaphors as to, 18
  promissory estoppel *see* Promissory estoppel
  proprietary estoppel *see* Proprietary estoppel
  role of, 6
  unified doctrine, 380–5
  US, in, 175
Estoppel by convention
  cause of action, creation of, 373
  definition of, 16–17
  duty to disclose and, 112
  objective test of agreement and, 18–20
  origins of, 74
  paucity of case law, 17–18
  requisites for, 17
  role of law as to, 16–20, 26, 80, 174
European Contract Law, 11, 115, 144, 150, 248
European Convention on Human Rights, 11, 200,
    201, 202
European Union
  acceptance of offer by post, 149–50
  competition law, 215

consumer contracts, 301, 314
  consumer credit law, 97
  Directives, role of, 11
  electronic commerce, 12, 158
  employment legislation, 97
  membership of, effect of, 11, 114, 215
  model codes, use of 11
  public works contracts, 132
  third party rights, 248
Evidence
  bill of lading as, 260
  condition or warranty, as to 435
  consideration as, 168
  contract, as to, 96–7
  parol evidence rule, 289–90
  posting, of, 149
  written, 176–7
Ex turpi causa oritur non actio, 181, 191, 194, 220
Exclusion clause
  construction
    contra preferentem rule, 304, 307
    fundamental breach, 306–7
    negligence alleged, where, 305
    sale of goods legislation and, 305
    supply of goods and services legislation and,
      305–6
    unfair terms legislation, effect of, 304–6
  death or personal injury, 308, 313
  misrepresentation, 313, 314
  privity of contract legislation, effect of, 253, 257
  tortious duty of care, 308
  unfair terms *see* Unfair terms
  see also Exemption clause
Executed consideration, 164
Execution of contract, order to procure, 450
Executory contracts, 6, 243
Exemplary damages, 54, 194, 195, 470–1
Exemption clause
  meaning, 300, 301, 308
  carriage of goods by sea, 259
  categories of, 307–8
  construction *see under* Exclusion clause
  consumer contract, 302
  forms of control, 301–2
  'Himalaya clause', 266, 267
  incorporation
    previous course of dealing, 304
    signed document, in, 302
    unsigned document, in case, of, 303–4
  judicial intervention, role of, 300–1
  legislative controls, sources of, 301
  negligence claim by third party, 271
  role of, 204
  unfair terms *see* Unfair terms
  see also Exclusion clause, limitation clause
Express terms
  allocation of risk, as to, 387–9
  breach of, choice of remedy for, 285–6
  custom and, 296
  source of, 285

Family arrangements
  disclosure, duty of, 99
  intention to create legal relations, 182–4
Fax, acceptance of offer by, 146–7

Fiduciary relationships, 101, 355
Flexibility
    contract, of, encouragement of, 320–1, 343
    modification of contract, as to, 406
    remedial, 431, 436
FOB contracts, 260, 394, 472
Football club
    retain and transfer system, 210
Football pool, submission of, 217
Force majeure clauses, 420
Form
    cautionary formal requirements, 178–9
    informational formal requirements, 179–80
    standard form *see* Standard form contracts
    transferable obligations, where, 180
    writing, requirements as to, 176–80
Formation of contract
    agreement *see* Agreement
    capacity of parties *see* Capacity to contract
    certainty *see* Certainty
    consideration and its substitutes *see*
        Consideration
    form *see* Form
    illegality in *see* Illegality
    intention *see* Intention
    modification distinct from, 406
    non-agreement mistakes *see* Mistake
    parties to, 2
    principles as to, 9
    third parties *see* Third party
France
    good faith, negotiation in, 111
    specific performance as remedy, 442
Fraudulent misrepresentation, *see* Deceit, tort of;
        Misrepresentation
Freedom of contract
    definition, 340
    generally, 205
    judicial intervention, justification for, 300–1
Fried, theories of, 6, 8, 106–8, 159
Fundamental breach, doctrine of, 306–7
Frustration
    meaning, 385, 417
    breach of condition and, 418
    common mistake and, 241, 417–19
    destruction of subject-matter, 385
    development of doctrine of, 417
    effects of
        Act of 1943, under 428–30
        common law, at 385, 427, 429
    factors to be considered
        allocation of risk, 387–95
        context of agreement, 394–5
        course of dealing, 392
        trade usage, 394
    force majeure clause 420
    foreseeability, 391–2
    hardship clauses, 420
    illegality and, 385–6, 426
    impossiblity of performance, for, 425
    intervener clauses, 420
    juristic basis
        frustration of the adventure, 424
        generally, 386
        implied term theory, 421–3

just and reasonable solution, 423–4
    'radical difference' approach, 424–5
    total failure of consideration, 423
    limitations on, 419
    'modification' of contract due to
        court imposed modifications, 400–2
        enforcement of, 385, 395, 405
        generally, 319
        illegality, on account of, 385–6
        impossibility of performance, where , 385–6
        new contract, formation of, 386
    objective, of, 426–7
    performance costs, increase in, 386–7, 395–400
    self-induced, 418–19
    termination of contract distinguished, 431

Gambling contracts, 316–20
Gazumping, 92
Germany
    good faith, negotiation in, 111
    specific performance in, 441–2
Gift
    contract distinguished, 161–2
    law as to, 119
Good faith
    consumer contracts and, 315
    definitions of, 109–11
    express references to, 112–13
    need to introduce doctrine of, 109, 113–16
    pre-contractual negotiations, in, 15, 31, 89–90,
        109–16
    US law, 113
Goodwill of business,
    protection of, 211–12
Gordley, views of, 4–5, 108
Guarantees, 176–9

Half-truths, 104–5
Hardship clauses, 420
Hedley Byrne action
    meaning, 61
    negligent misrepresentation, for *see* Negligent
        misrepresentation
    'Himalaya' clause, 266, 267
Hire, contract of, 296
Hire purchase
    implied terms, 296
    unfair terms, 308–9
History of contract law
    classical contract law, 3–5
    modern law, 5–9
    philosophical tradition, 4–5
Human rights legislation, effect of, 11

Illegality
    administration of justice, contract prejudicial to,
        203–6
    common law, at
        court's attitude to, 192
        examples of, 199–214
        statutory illegality contrasted, 200
    consequences of, 220–8
    crime
        access to proceeds of, 120
        contract to commit, 201

Illegality (*continued*)
deterrence principle, application of, 193
dignity of courts and, 196
discrimination, 200–1
enforcement of contract, 220–1
ex turpi causa oritur non actio, 181, 191, 194, 220
family life, contracts injurious to, 199, 206–8
formation of contract, as to
  performance of contract distinguished, 192–3, 197, 411–12
  scope of, 191, 232
frustration and, 385–6, 426
gambling contracts, 216–20
good government, contract inconsistent with, 209
good morals, contracts contrary to, 199
locus poenitentiae, role of, 194
lottery, 192
maintenance and champerty, 205–6
marriage, contracts injurious to, 206–8
moneylending contract, 200
ouster of jurisdiction of court, 204–5
performance of contract, in
  meaning, 193n
  examples of, 411–13
  frustration of contract, 426
  generally, 407
  illegality as formed contrasted, 192–3, 197, 411–12
policy objectives, 193–6
profit from wrongdoing, 195–6
public policy and, 199
punishment, policy of, 194–5
recovery of money and property
  court's attitude to, 193
  exceptions to general rule, 222–30
  general rule, 222
  restitution, law of, and, 222–3
  trust law and, 228–30
  where parties not equally guilty, 224–6
  withdrawal from illegal enterprise, where, 223–4
  without reliance on illegal contract, 226–8
reform of law, 231–2
restraint of trade, contracts in
  employment, in case of, 209–11
  sale of business, as to, 209, 211–12
  solus agreement, 192, 209–10, 213
severance of illegal part, 230–1
sexual indecency, contracts involving, 196, 202–3
social morality and, 196
solus agreements, 192, 209–10, 213
state's relations with other states, affecting 209
statutory prohibition, for
  common law role contrasted, 200
  court's attitude to, 192
  examples, of 197–9
  performance of contract, 411–12
surrogacy agreement, 208
tort, contract to commit, 201–2
trading with enemy, 209
wagering contract, 217–20
Implied terms
business efficacy test, 297–8
common law, at
  generally, 285, 290

implication in fact, 297–8
implication in law, 296–7, 298–9
custom, by, 285–290, 296
discharge of contract, as to, 421–3
employment, contract of, 299
hire, contract of, 296
hire purchase contract, 296
landlord and tenant, 299
officious bystander test, 298
parol evidence as to, 289
services contracts, 290, 296
sources of, 285, 290, 296, 296–7
statute, by
  exclusion of, 312–14
  generally, 285, 290
  identification of, 296
  miscellaneous legislation, under 296
  sale of goods etc. legislation, *see* Sale of goods
  services, as to, 437
  unfair terms legislation and, 291
Impossibility of performance
frustration, due to *see* Frustration
Incompleteness, 188–90
Indemnity
rescission and, 52–3, 72
unfair terms, 308
Indeterminacy of legal rules, 5–6
Inequality of bargaining power
employee and employer, 212, 404
setting aside contract for, 101–3
US provision as to, 101
Information, disclosure of
encouragement of, 105, 106
statutory requirements, 104, 179–80
Injunction
availability of, 444, 451, 453–5, 462
clauses in contract as to, 444
Director-General of Fair Trading, for, 314
part of negative obligation, enforcement of, 454
third party and, 257
Innocent misrepresentation, use of term, 61
Innominate term
meaning, 285
breach of, effect of, 285, 286, 431
development of category of, 436–7
service contract, 437
Insolvency principles, 443
Insurance
allocation of risk, 393
CIF contracts, 260
contract
  gambling contract distinguished, 218
  unfair terms, 308
insurance law, 8
managing agents' duty of care, 69
proceeds, damages and, 467
third party rights, 259
uberrimae fidei, 98–100, 112
Intention
business arrangements between strangers, 184–7
condition or warranty, 435
family arrangements, 182–4
formation of contract, for, 119, 180–2
objective test, 122–3
presumption as to, 182–7

Intention (*continued*)
  statement of
    misrepresentation and, 61
    statement of fact contrasted, 27–9
  term or mere representation, 286–90
Interest in land
  proprietary estoppel and, 74
  sale of, 177, 445
  transfer of, unfair terms, 308, 317
Interest-rate swap transactions, 218–19
Interference with contractual rights, 279–80
Intermediate term *see* Innominate term
International Commercial Contracts,
  Principles for, 11
International Sale of Goods, UN Convention on
  Contracts for, 12, 113
International supply contracts, 308
International trade contracts, 12
International Trade Law, UN Commission on, 12
Intervener clauses, 420
Intimidation, tort of, 339
Investment agreement
  disclosure of information, 104
Invitation to treat
  auction, 127–8
  advertisement, 13–15, 128
  definition of 120–1
  display of goods as 125–7
  examples of, 121–2
  offer distinguished, 119–21
Irrevocable banker's credits, 139

Laches as a defence, 452
Land
  interest in *see* Interest in land
  proprietary estoppel and, 76–80
  restrictive covenant, 213–14
  title to, 226
Landlord and tenant law
  development of, 157
Law of obligations
  Atiyah's views on, 6–7
  good faith, role of, 15–16
  restitution and, 85, 142
  three branches of, 9–10
Letters of comfort, 186–7
Letters of credit, 120
Letters of intent, 187
Liability insurance claims, 259
Life insurance claims, 259
Limitation clause
  liquidation damage clause and, 517–18
  misrepresentation, 313, 314
  reasonableness, 309–10
  role of, 204–5
  unfair terms *see* Unfair terms
  see also Exemption clause
Limitation of action
  contracts, period for, 120, 173
  deed, in respect of, 120, 173–4
  personal injuries, as to, 120
Litigation
  cost of, 115, 144
  maintenance and champerty, 205–6
  out of court settlements, 115–16, 144

Lock-out agreements, 91–3, 190
Locus poenitentiae, role of, 194, 223
Lottery, 192, 217

Maintenance and champerty, 205–6
Marriage
  contracts injurious, to, 206–8
  promise in consideration of, 184
Materials, contracts for
  implied terms, 296
Maxims
  ex turpi cause oritur non actio, 181, 191, 194, 220
  he who comes to equity must come with cleans
    hands, 452
  in pari delicto potior est conditio defendentis, 193,
    220, 222, 224–5
Mental distress, damages for, 471, 478, 484–5,
  489–90
Mentally incapacitated person
  capacity to contract, 242, 245–6
  necessaries for, 246
  protection of court, 246
Minor
  meaning, 242
  beneficial employment, contract for, 243
  capacity to contract, 242
  necessaries sold to, 242–3
  ratification of contract by, 244
  restitution by, 244–5
  services, provision of, for, 243
  voidable contracts, 244
Misrepresentation
  conduct as, 104
  continuing representation as, 105
  contract voidable for, 24, 26, 41, 42
  damages, 26–7, 42, 49–53, 61–8, 72, 73
  deceit, action for *see* Deceit, tort of
  estoppel by encouragement and, 75
  exclusion clause, 313, 314
  fraudulent misrepresentation
    generally *see* Deceit, tort of
    lapse of time, effect of, 49
    statutory bars to remedy and, 49
    victims of, remedy for, 23
  general principles as to, 27–40
  half-truths as, 33–4, 104–5
  inducement to act
    awareness by representee of untruth, 35–6
    materiality of representation, 39–40
    need to show, 34–5
    reliance by representee on some other
      inducement, 36–7
    representee unaware of misrepresentation,
      where, 38
    representee would have entered transaction
      even if aware of untruth, 38–9
  innocent, use of term, 61
  intention, statements of, and 27–9, 61
  limitation clause, 313, 314
  mistake, doctrine of, and 41–2
  negligent misrepresentation *see* Negligent
    misrepresentation
  opinion, statements of, and 29–30, 61
  remedies
    comparison of, 72, 73

Misrepresentation (*continued*)
 remedies (*continued*)
  range of, 26–7
  'third party situations', in, 55
 requisites to prove, 34, 42
 rescission for, *see* Rescission
 responsibility for, 6
 representations of fact, 27–31
 role of law as to, 16
 sale of goods contract, 47–9
 silence as, exceptions to general rule, 31–4
'Missing term', formulation of, 189
Mistake
 common mistake
  effect of, on agreement, 233–4
  existence of subject matter, as to, 234–7
  frustration and, 241, 417–19
  mutual mistake distinguished, 233
  ownership of property, as to, 240–1
  quality, as to, 237–40
 contract terms, as to, 96
 equity jurisdiction, 239–40
 misrepresentation, doctrine of, and, 41–2
 identity, as to
  contract void for, 24–6
  mistake as to attributes distinguished, 24
  pre-contractual negotiations, in, 22–6
  role of law as to, 16
 quality, as to, 96, 237–40
 mutual mistake
  common mistake distinguished, 233
  use of term, 233
 snap-up cases, 157
 unilateral mistake: meaning, 233
Mitigation of loss
 meaning, 477, 504
 action in debt, 458
 breach date rule and, 477
 causation and, 495
 damages, action for, 458
 financial position of claimant,
  relevance of, 506
 generally, 64
 modification of contract, 319, 402–4, 405,
  505
 reasonableness, 59–60, 504–7
 sale of goods cases, 482–3
 specific performance, cases of, 443
Modification of contract
 consideration
  factual definition, 325–6, 332–7
  function of, 168, 318
  legal definition, 326, 332, 336–7
  new, finding of, 330–7
  overseas judicial views as to, 327–8
  US law, 331
 economic duress and *see* Economic duress
 enforcement of, 320–1, 323–5, 329
 flexibility of contract,
  encouragement of, 320–1, 343
 frustration, role of *see* Frustration
 issues raised by, 2–3
 lack of orchestration of law as to, 318, 320, 404,
  406
 mitigation of loss and, 319, 402–4, 505

multi-layered legal response to, diagram of, 319
opportunism, restraint of, 321–5, 339–41, 343,
 352, 357, 367
performance *see* Performance
policy objectives, 319, 324–5, 404–6
pre-existing duty doctrine, 325–37, 385, 405
promissory estoppel, role of *see* Promissory
 estoppel
rescission and new contract device, 328–30
separate and distinct episode, as, 318
termination distinct from, 406
undue influence jurisdiction and, 338–9
waiver, role of *see* Waiver
Morals, illegality and, 199–200
Mortgages, law as to, 8
Motor insurance claims, 259

Negligence
 contributory *see* Contributory negligence
 economic loss, recovery for *see* Economic loss
 exclusion of liability, 307, 310–11, 313
 standard of care, 30–1
 unfair contract terms, 307, 310–11, 313
Negligent misrepresentation
 meaning, 61
 breach of contract, action for, 72, 73
 damages
  common law, at *see Hedley Byrne* action,
   below
  MRA, s 2(1), under *see* statutory action,
   below
  prior to 1965, 61
 Hedley Byrne action
  auditor's liability, 69, 73
  availability of, 73
  contributory negligence, effect of, 66, 71–3
  imposition of liability, approaches to, 68–70
  measure of damages, 72, 73
  role of, 81
  solicitor's liability, 69, 71
  statutory action compared, 70–3
  valuer's liability, 69, 71
 statutory action
  burden of proof, 62–3, 70, 72
  contributory negligence, effect of, 65–8
  damages in lieu of rescission, 50–1
  date of assessment of damages, 64–5
  deceit action compared, 72, 73
  Hedley Byrne action compared, 70–3
  measure of damages, 63–4
  scope of statutory provision, 61–2
 tort of, history of, 68
 see also Misrepresentation
Negotiation, pre-contractual *see* Pre-contractual
 negotiations
Neo-classical law and economics, 7–8
Nominal damages, award of, 461
Non-disclosure
 arguments for and against wider disclosure,
  106–9
 exceptions to general rule, 96–101, 112
 general rule, 95–6, 112
 misrepresentation, law of, and, 31–4
 pre-contractual negotiations, during, 95–6
 see also Disclosure

Non est factum, doctrine, 302
Objective test
  agreement, of
    departure from, 21–2
    estoppel by convention and, 18–20
    operation of, 21
  intention to create legal relations, 122–3
  penalty clause, as to, 522
  use of, 5, 16, 26
Offer
  meaning, 120
  advertisement as, 123–5, 128
  counter offer, 139–44, 146
  'cross-offer', 156–7
  death, effect of, 145
  display of goods as, 126–7
  inquiry, effect of, 140–1
  invitation to treat distinguished, 119–20
  lapse of time, 144–5
  rejection of, 139–44
  revocation of
    bilateral contract, in case of, 134–6
    unilateral contract, in case of, 136–9
  'snapping up' cases, 20–1, 157
  standing offer, 133
  tender as, 128–33
  termination of
    death of offeror or offeree, on, 145
    lapse of time, by, 144–5
    modes of, 134–45
    rejection, by, 139–44
    revocation, by, 134–9
    ticket cases, 133–4
  use of word, inconclusiveness of, 122
Omission to act
  legal consequences of, 94–5
  non-disclosure *see* Non-disclosure
Opinion, statement of
  negligent misrepresentation, action for, 61, 73
  statement of fact contrasted, 29–30
Options, contractual, 145
Out of court settlements, 115–16, 144
Ownership of property
  disputes as to, 226
  mistake as to, 240–1
  see also Title

Package holidays
  disclosure of information, 104
  statutory requirements, 179–80
Parol evidence rule, 289–90
Part performance, doctrine of, 177, 178
Past consideration, 164
Parties
  intention *see* Intention
  skill and knowledge of, relative, 287–9
Part payment of debt
  common law rule, 335–7, 363
  equitable waiver, application of, 363–4
Penalty clause
  deposits and advance
    payments and, 519–20
  disguising, 519–20
  effect of, where sum payable on one of several
    events, 515–16

liquidated damages and, 506–20
  time for payment, 519–520
  unenforceable, when, 461
  unfair terms legislation and, 308, 317
Performance of contract
  frustration, effect of *see* Frustration
  generally, 2
  illegality in performance, 409
    examples of, 411–13
    formation of contract distinguished, 411
    frustration and, 426
    generally, 407
    impossibility of, 425
  incomplete performance, 409
    Apportionment Act, remedy under, 409
    de minimis principle, 410
    new contract, recovery on basis of, 409
    quantum meruit, action for, 409–10
    stage payment, recovery of, 409
    substantial performance, 410–11
  literal performance
    meaning, 441
    action in debt, role of *see* Debt, action in
    injunction, role of *see* Injunction
    remedies for, 441–60
  minimum performance rule,
    damages and, 468–71
  substitute performance, 353
  withholding of
    meaning, 407
    concurrent liabilities, where, 407–9
    condition precedent, where, 407–8
    entitlement to, factors to be considered, 407–9
    independent promises, where, 407, 409
    termination distinguished, 407
Personal injuries
  limitation of action, 120
Personal services contract
  injunction, bar as to, 454–5
  specific performance, 450–1
Post, acceptance of offer by, 148–52
Pre-contractual negotiations
  allocation of risk and, 392
  disclosure *see* Disclosure; Non-disclosure
  estoppel by convention and *see* Estoppel by
    convention
  fair dealing, standard of, 20–1, 87
  failed contracts, range of remedies for, 80 *et seq*
  generally, 1
  good faith *see* Good faith
  inequality of bargaining power, 101–3
  misrepresentations *see* Misrepresentation
  mistake as to identity, effect of, 22–6
  objective test of agreement, role of *see* Objective
    test of
  proprietary estoppel *see* Proprietary estoppel
  restitution, role of *see* Restitution
  separate and distinct problems as to, 318
Pre-nuptial contract, 208
Presumption
  intention to create legal relations, 182–7
  undue influence, of, 99–100
Price
  allocation of risk and, 386–7, 392
  price list, invitation to treat or offer, 125

Price (*continued*)
  unanticipated rise in, effect of, 386–7, 395–400
Principal and agent
  fiduciary relationship, 101
Privity of contract
  meaning, 247
  burdens on third party
    exception to rule, 278–82
    rule as to, scope of, 278
  common law exceptions
    agency, 264–6
    assignment, 268–9
    damages for third party's loss, 275–8
    specific performance, use of, 271–2
    tort, claims in, 269–71
  construction industry and, 248–9
  criticism of doctrine, 247
  damages and, 472–5
  judicial dissatisfaction with, 247
  Law Commission Report, 248, 251–3, 256–7, 269, 278
  rule as to
    common law exceptions *see* common law exceptions, above
    scope of, 249–51
    statutory exceptions *see* statutory exceptions, *below*
  statutory exceptions
    Act of 1999, under, 249, 252–61, 301n
    bills of lading, 260–1
    first general statutory exception, 249
    insurance claims, as to, 259
    package holidays, as to, 259
    trusts exception, 261–4
Promise
  promisee, actions by, 271–8
  representation distinguished, 27
Promissory estoppel
  cause of action, 373–85
  defence, as, 370–1
  detrimental reliance test and, 256
  equitable conduct on part of promisee, 367–8
  equitable waiver and, 363–5
  High Trees doctrine, 332, 363–5, 368
  leading cases, 339
  modification of contract and, 318
  offensive limits of, 370–3
  overseas jurisdictions, in, 374–80, 383
  proprietary estoppel and, 370, 373
  reliance, 365–7
  requisites of, 365, 383
  rise of, 2
  shield not sword, 366, 370, 377, 382
  suspensory or extinctive, 368–9
  unambiguous representation, 365
  use of doctrine of, 5
Promissory notes, 180
Proprietary estoppel
  cause of action, 18, 78, 178, 370, 373
  defence, as, 78
  discretion to grant relief, 77
  duty to disclose, 112
  estoppel by acquiescence, 75
  estoppel by encouragement, 75
  land, promises as to, 76–80

origins of, 74
orders available, 77–8
promissory estoppel and, 370, 373–4
requisites for, 74–5
role of law as to, 16, 74, 80, 174–5
two kinds of, 75
when it arises, 75
Prostitution, contracts and, 192, 202
Public law, role of, 216
Public works contracts, 132–3
Punitive damages, 54, 194

Quantum meruit, action for, 85, 409–10

Ratification of contract
  minor, by, on attaining full age, 244
Real property, proprietary estoppel and, 76–80
Rectification of contract
  term omitted from original contract, where, 178
Rejection of offer, 139–44
Remoteness of damage
  deceit, tort of, 58–60, 66, 72
Repairing covenants
  specific performance, 450
Representation
  mere representation or term
    distinction, 286
    pointers as to which, 286–90
  misrepresentation *see* Misrepresentation
Repudiation of contract
  American law, 458–9
  election by innocent party, 456–8
Reputation, damage to
  bank's failure to honour cheque, 464n
  damages for, 485–7, 488–90
  defamation action, 490
Rescission
  affirmation as bar to, 47–9
  bars to, 41, 43–52
  breach of
    innominate term, for, 286
    warranty, for, 286
  damages in lieu of
    breach of contract, for, 52
    discretion of court, 49–51, 72
  date from which effective, 42–3
  inability to make restitution as bar to, 45–7
  indemnity, role of, 52–3, 72
  intervention of third-party rights, effect of, 44–5
  lapse of time as bar to, 48–9
  misrepresentation, for
    effect of, 72, 73, 431
    other remedies compared, 72, 73
    modification of contract and, 328–30
  notice by representee to representator, need for, 42–3
  retrospective nature of right to, 40
  sale of goods, contract for, 44
  termination of contract disringuished, 40–1, 432
  use of, as a remedy, 3, 23, 41–2
  use of term, 40
  variation distinguished, 177
  waiver in the sense of, 357
Restitution
  consideration: *meaning*, 83–4

Restitution (*continued*)
contractual principles and, interplay of, 85–7
definition, 10
duress and, 225
essential elements of claim, 81–5
head of civil liability, as, 10, 81, 87, 143
illegal contracts and, 222–3
inability to make, as bar to rescission, 45–7
locus poenitentiae, where, 223
role of, 10, 16, 80–1, 94, 112, 220
unjust enrichment, 81–5, 143, 463–4, 491
when contractual negotiations fail, 10, 16, 112
Restraint of trade
anti-competitive practices within, 212–14
contracts in employment, as to, 209–11
sale of business, as to, 209, 211–12
severance, application of, 230
solus agreement, 209, 213
statutory controls, 214–16
Restrictive covenants affecting land, 213–14, 279
Revocation
acceptance, of, 152
offer, of
before time expired, 145
bilateral contract, where, 134–6
standing offer, 133
unilateral contract, where, 136–9

Sale of business, contracts for, 209, 211–12
Sale of goods
auction, by, 127–8
breach date rule, 477–9
damages
non-acceptance by buyer, for, 482
non-delivery, action for, 477, 480–3
disclosure, duty as to, 106
exclusion clause, interpretation of, 305
implied terms
conditions, 434–5
description, as to, 290, 292–3, 313, 314, 434
exclusion of, 312–14
fitness for purpose, 290, 295–6, 312–14, 434
practical importance of, 290–1
quiet possession, as to, 434
sale by sample, 290, 296, 313, 314, 434
satisfactory quality, 290, 293–5, 305, 312–14, 495
title, as to, 290–2, 434
unfair terms legislation, effect of, 291
warranties, 434–5
international, 12
performance of contract
concurrent liabilities, where, 407, 408–9
specific performance, 445–7
perishable goods, 235–7
price of goods, 189, 455–6
rescission of contract for, 44, 47–9
secondhand goods, 295
specific performance, 445–7
Vienna Convention, 12, 144
warnings and instructions, 295
Sale of land
caveat emptor rule, 95, 106
deeds, use of, 119
deposit *see* Deposit

interest in land, 177
lock-out agreements, 91–3
'subject to contract', 92, 185
written contract, need for, 176, 177
Sale of shares, 446, 453
Salvage agreements, 101, 112, 163
Sample, sale by, 290, 296, 313, 314, 434
Sanctity of contract
allocation of risk and, 387, 395
contractual modifications and, 404
Secondhand goods, sale of, 295
Services, contract for
conditions, 437
innominate terms, 437
personal services
injunction, bar as to, 454–5
specific performance, 450–1
Services, supply of
charge for, 189
contractual duty of care, 495
exclusion clause, interpretation of, 305
implied terms, 290, 296
reasonable care and skill in provision of, 293
Set-off, third party's right of, 258
Setting aside contract
inequality of bargaining power, for, 101
undue influence, for *see* Undue influence
Severance, doctrine of
application of, 230–1
incomplete performance, where, 409
Shares, sale of, 446, 453
Silence
acceptance, as, 152, 337
allocation of risk, as to, 389, 391
misrepresentation, as, 31–4
'Simple' contract
use of term, 119
Skill and knowledge of parties, 287–9
Social arrangements
enforceability of, 119
intention to create legal relations, 182–4
Social morality and illegality, 196, 202–3
Solicitor
conditional fee arrangement, 206
duty of care, 69, 71
Practice Rules, breach of, 220
Solus agreements, 192, 209–10, 213
Specific performance
absence of mutuality as to, 452–3
action in debt and, 455, 457
availability of, as a remedy, 441–50, 455, 461
building contract, 447–8, 450
business, contract to carry on, 448–9
clause in contract as to, 444
conduct of claimant and, 452
constant supervision as bar to, 449–50
execution of contract, for, 450
expectation longstop as bar to, 453
goods, sale of, 445–7
history of, 444
indirect, 453–4
laches as a defence, 452
land, sale of, 445, 446
mitigation of loss and, 443
personal service, contract as to, 450–1

Specific performance (*continued*)
  public law principles, 451
  repairing covenant, 450
  restrictions on, 444–9
  severe hardship cases, 451–2
  severe nature of, as sanction, 442–3
  third party and, 257
  use of, 6, 271–2
Standard form contract
  exemption clause *see* Exemption clause
  use of, 4, 141, 300
Standing offers, 133
Stay of action, 272–5
Stock Exchange listing
  disclosure, duty of, 104
Stocks and shares, sale of, 218
Sub-bailment, 281–2
Sub-contractors
  extra-legal pressure on, 10
  tenders by, 131–2
Subjective test of agreement
  use of, 5, 20–1
Supply of goods, implied terms, 296
Supply, services of *see* Services, supply of
Surrogacy agreement, 208

Telegram
  acceptance of offer by, 151
Telephone
  acceptance of offer by, 146
Telex
  acceptance of offer by, 146
Tenders
  building and engineering projects, 131–2
  invitation to treat or offer, 128–33
  sub-contractors, by, 131–2
Termination of contract
  breach of contract, for *see* Breach of contract
  clause in *Lombard North Central* v *Butterworth*, 519
  commercial agent's agency, of, 470
  election as to
    anticipatory breach, where, 434
    communication of, 431, 469
  frustration distinguished, 431
  modification of contract and, 406
  prospective nature of right to, 40–1, 431
  rescission distinguished, 40–1, 431
  use of term, 40–1, 45
  withholding performance distinguished, 407
Terms of contract
  acceleration clauses, 519–20
  arbitration clauses, 205
  CIF terms, 260
  classification of, 285, 431, 434
  conditions *see* Conditions
  exclusion clause *see* Exclusion clause
  exemption clauses *see* Exemption clause
  FOB terms, 260
  force majeure clauses, 420
  hardship clauses, 420
  incorporation
    exemption clause, 317
    previous course of dealing, 304
    signed document, in, 302
    unsigned document, in, 303–4

injunction, as to, 444
innominate *see* Innominate terms
intermediate *see* Innominate terms
intervener clauses, 420
limitation clause *see* Limitation clause
liquidated damages clauses, 506–18
mere representation
  distinguished, 286
  pointers as to whether terms or, 286–90
penalty clauses *see* Penalty clause
source of, 285–99
termination clause, 519
unfair terms *see* Unfair terms
warranty *see* Warranty
Theseiger LJ, correspondence with, 1
Third party
  bailment on terms, 281–2
  company, contract with, 246
  contract with, misrepresentation and, 55
  contractual duty to,
    performance as consideration, 168–71
  enforcement of contract by or for benefit of
    Act of 1999, under, 252–61, 301n
    action by promisee, 271–8
    agency situation, where, 264–5
    beneficiary of trust, as, 261–4
    collateral contract, 265–8
    damages, 275–8
    European Union, in, 248
    insurance contracts, as to, 259
    manufacturer, against, 254
    married women's property legislation, 249n
    package travel etc, as to, 259
    privity of contract rule and, *see* Privity of
      contract
    specific performance, use of, 271–2
    stay of action, use of, 272–5
    sub-contractor, against, 254–5
    tort, claims in, 269–71
  interference with contractual rights by, 279–80
  intervener clause, 420
  intervention of, to bar rescission, 44–5, 51
  postal rule of acceptance and, 256
  privity of contract rules scope of *see* Privity of
    contract
  restrictive covenant as to land, 279
  severe hardship to, specific performance and, 452
  transfer of child to, by parent, 208
Ticket cases, 133–4
Time
  action in debt, 455
  assessment of damages, 504–5
  limitation of action *see* Limitation of action
  locus poenitentiae, 194, 223
  offer, lapse of, 144–5
  status of statement, to determine, 287
  stipulation as to commercial contract, 436
Title
  bill of lading as document of, 260
  implied term as to, 290–2, 313, 314
  land, to, dispute as to, 226
Tort
  meaning, 9, 54
  causation, issues of, 494
  compensation for harm, 6

Tort (*continued*)
  contract to commit, 201–2
  deceit *see* Deceit, tort of
  economic tort, 279, 345
  exemplary damages, 470–1
  measure of damages in, 56–60, 72
  negligence *see* Negligence
  privity of contract and, 269–71
Trade custom, reference to, 188
Trade secrets, protection of, 210
Trade union
  economic torts, liability for, 279
  immunities of, 345–6
  role of, 211, 214
Trade usage, 394, 436
Trust
  privity of contract rule and, 261–4
  trust law, 228–30

Uberirrimae fidei contracts, 98–9, 112
Uncertainty
  commercial contracts and, 200
  compensation, effect on, 144
  settlement of dispute, effect on, 144
Undertaking, enforcement of, 272–3
Undue influence
  actual, 99–100
  duress, comparison with, 338
  fiduciary relationships and, 101
Unfair dismissal, 451, 490
Unfair terms
  meaning, 112–14, 315, 317
  Act of 1977
    business liabilities, 308, 310
    clauses outside, 308, 317
    collateral contract, 308
    Consumer Contract Regulations and, 308,
      313–15
    contractual liability, 311–12, 313
    definitions, 307–9
    exclusion clauses, effect on, 304–5
    exemption clauses and, 302, 307–8
    indemnity clauses, 308
    misrepresentations, 313, 314
    negligence liability, 307, 310–11, 313
    reasonableness, concept of, 307–9, 314, 317
    scope of, 307–9, 316–17
    statutory implied terms, exclusion of, 312–14
    tortious duty of care, 307
  categories of, 307–8
  consumer contract
    Act of 1977 and, 308, 313–15
    definitions, 315, 317
    Director-General of Fair Trading, powers of,
      314
    EC Directive, 302, 314
    exemption clauses and, 302
    'grey list' of terms, 316, 518, 522
    regulations as to, 313–17
    penalties, common law control of, 518–19
  overview of controls, 316–17
  US law, 101
Unidroit, 11, 115, 144, 150
Uniform Commercial Code, 101, 114, 144, 331,
  398, 401, 447

Unilateral contract
  acceptance of offer, 155–7
  bilateral distinguished, 136
  form of, 119
  revocation of, 136–9
United States
  anti-trust law, 214
  contractors' attitudes in, 10
  estoppel in, 175
  frustration of contract in, 401–2
  good faith, negotiation in, 110, 113
  inequality of bargaining power, 101
  offer and acceptance, 126–7
  Uniform Commercial Code, 101, 113, 144, 331,
    398, 401, 447
Unjust enrichment
  restitution in case of *see* Restitution

Vagueness, removal of, 188
Variation of contract
  consideration, 357
  rescission distinguished, 177
  third party rights and, 255
  waiver meaning, 357, 359–60
Vienna Convention, 12, 113, 144
Void contract
  meaning, 444
  gambling contract, 217
  illegality, for *see* Illegality
  mistake, for *see* Mistake
  money paid under, recovery of, 220
Voidable contract
  meaning, 444
  minor, in case of, 244
  misrepresentation, for *see* Misrepresentation

Wagering contracts, 217–20
Waiver
  existence of doctrine, 357
  forbearance, as
    common law, 358–60
    equitable principle, 360–6
    promissory estoppel and, 363–5
    rescission, meaning, 357
    USA doctrine, 458
    variation, meaning, 357, 359–60
Warranty
  meaning, 285, 434
  breach of, effect of, 285, 286
  classification as
    court, by, 436
    parties, by, 435
  implied
    free of incumbrances, 291
    quiet possession of goods, 291–2
    statutory, sale of goods, 434–5
Waste, avoidance of, 458–9
Written document
  cautionary role, performance of, 178
  deed *see* Deed
  evidence of contract, as, 176–7
  Statute of Frauds, requirements of, 176–8
  transferable obligations, where, 180